Armenia
with Nagorno Karabagh

the Bradt Travel Guide

Nicholas Holding
with Deirdre Holding

edition
3

www.bradtguides.com

Bradt Travel Guides Ltd, UK
The Globe Pequot Press Inc, USA

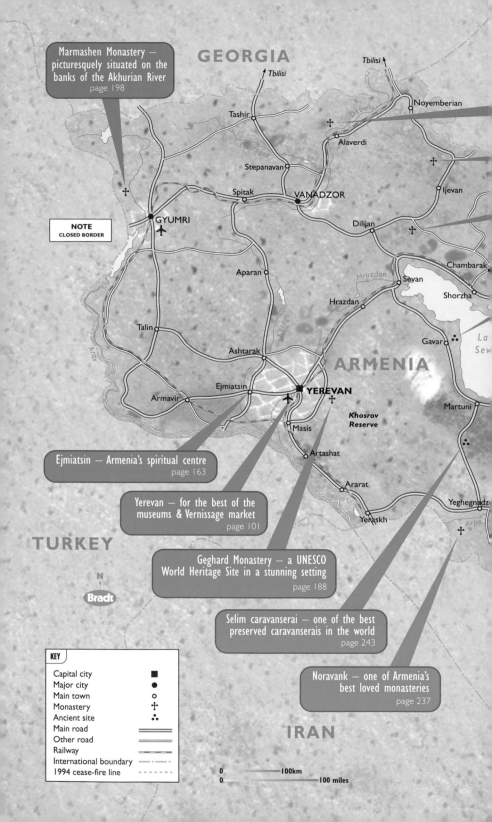

GEORGIA

Marmashen Monastery — picturesquely situated on the banks of the Akhurian River
page 198

Tbilisi

Tbilisi

Noyemberian

Tashir

Alaverdi

Debed

Stepanavan

Spitak

VANADZOR

Ijevan

GYUMRI

Dilijan

NOTE
CLOSED BORDER

Chambarak

Aparan

Hrazdan

Sevan

Shorzha

Hrazdan

Talin

ARMENIA

Gavar

La
Sev

Ashtarak

Arax

Ejmiatsin

YEREVAN

Martuni

Armavir

Masis

Khosrov
Reserve

Ejmiatsin — Armenia's spiritual centre
page 163

Artashat

Yerevan — for the best of the museums & Vernissage market
page 101

Ararat

Yeghegnadz

TURKEY

Yeraskh

Arpa

N

Bradt

Geghard Monastery — a UNESCO World Heritage Site in a stunning setting
page 188

Selim caravanserai — one of the best preserved caravanserais in the world
page 243

Noravank — one of Armenia's best loved monasteries
page 237

IRAN

Monasteries of Debed gorge — Sanahin, Haghpat, Akhtala, Kobayr & Odzun
page 202

Makaravank — for its many exquisite carvings
page 225

AZERBAIJAN

Goshavank — home to one of Armenia's most famous khachkars
page 230

Field of khachkars, Noratus — site of Armenia's largest collection of khachkars
page 177

Dadivank — the final resting place of 1st-century apostle & martyr St Thaddeus
page 277

NOTE
CLOSED BORDER

NOTE
1994 CEASE-FIRE LINE
CLOSED BORDER

Vardenis

Tartar

Martakert

Gandzasar Monastery for an insight into a restored working monastery & seminary
page 277

NAGORNO KARABAGH (Self-declared Republic)

NOTE
1994 CEASE-FIRE LINE
CLOSED BORDER

Jermuk

Aghavnavaget

Stepanakert

Shushi

Petroglyphs of Mount Mets Ishkhanasar — hundreds of ancient carvings are scattered on this extinct volcano
page 251

Sisian

Goris

NOTE
OSED BORDER

Vorotan

Hadrut

Kapan

AKHIJEVAN (Azerbaijan)

Voghji

Kajaran

Shikahogh Reserve

Tatev Monastery — one of Armenia's most famous sites, now served by the world's longest cable car
page 255

Meghri

Teheran

Arax

Armenia
Don't
miss...

Exquisite stone carvings
Khachkars, carved memorial stones such as this one at Ejmiatsin, are an important, conspicuous, and beautiful feature of Armenian decorative art (IMPLIP/A) page 38

Mountains
Armenia's mountains provide a stunning backdrop to the town of Kajaran (A/D) page 260

Monasteries
Tatev Monastery is just one of Armenia's many fascinating monasteries in beautiful settings
(JS) page 255

People
Armenians are generous to a fault and have a strong pride in the country's history and language
(SS) page 28

Apricots
Armenians claim, with some justification, that their apricots are the best in the world
(F/D) page 4

above left The cathedral in Yerevan is dedicated to St Gregory the Illuminator (DH) page 121

above right Yerevan's covered market is a good place to buy both fresh produce and the superb Armenian dried fruits (AB) page 129

below Yerevan's Republic Square is certainly one of the finest central squares created anywhere in the world during the 20th century (NH) page 117

bottom The Spendiarian Armenian Theatre of Opera and Ballet in Yerevan is one of the most attractive buildings designed by Alexander Tamanian (G/D) page 128

top   The statue of Alexander Tamanian below the
Cascade in Yerevan is carved from a single
block of basalt (DH) page 128

above left   One of Yerevan's many delightful statues
(DH)

right   The statue of Mother Armenia in Yerevan was
constructed in 1950 as the Victory Memorial
in memory of the Great Patriotic War
(RN/A) page 120

top   The field of 900 *khachkars* at Noratus is
          one of Armenia's most amazing sights
          (H/D) page 177

above   Garni Temple, as it is called, is Armenia's
          only Graeco-Roman-style building
          (MGC/A) page 186

right   This famous statue in Stepanakert,
          Nagorno Karabagh, is universally
          referred to as *Mamik yel Babik* (*Granny
          and Grandad*) (S/D) page 276

Born in Wigan (then in Lancashire, but now part of Greater Manchester), **Nicholas Holding** moved to Scotland in 1965 and graduated from the University of St Andrews with a degree in electrical engineering. **Deirdre Holding** moved to Scotland from Liverpool in 1963 and graduated with a degree in medicine, also from St Andrews University. They married in 1970. Both always had an interest in the communist world, and made their first visit to the Soviet Union in 1973. The downfall of communism enabled them to travel more freely around the former Soviet bloc, and sparked their interest in Armenia. After a career in the Scottish electricity supply industry, Nicholas took early retirement in 2000. Deirdre also retired early, in 2003, after a career in the Scottish National Health Service as a consultant eye surgeon. Nicholas wrote the first two editions of the Bradt guide to Armenia. He became ill not long after the second edition was published and he died in 2008. Having always been closely involved with the guide, Deirdre has updated the book for this third edition. She still lives in Scotland.

AUTHORS' STORY

We first went to Armenia in 2001, on holiday. We were enthralled by the country: its landscapes, wild flowers, medieval monasteries and churches all over the place, its unique alphabet, the welcome given to us, its complex history at so many crossroads – geological, historical, political and religious. But there were frustrations. There was virtually no information in Armenia itself. Even road signs were in short supply. Yes, there was internet information but how many printouts can be packed before a suitcase is overweight? Many times we bewailed the absence of a practical and informative guidebook, such as the Bradt guides we had used elsewhere.

So when, after our return, Nick was asked to write the first Bradt guide to Armenia he accepted willingly. We enjoyed getting to know the country better and feeling that we were making some contribution. It was also hard work! It wasn't just the journeys on dreadfully pot-holed roads but also the research involved. I remember Nick once spent the whole day researching an apparently authoritative statement that a certain cave held a colony of fruit bats. Fruit bats? In Armenia? It turned out that the species of bat referred to wasn't fruit-eating at all and it was quite another species which actually inhabited the cave! Nick always hoped to write the third edition but his death prevented that. It is a tribute to Bradt and the freedom they allow their authors that, for those who knew Nick, his personality can so often be glimpsed in his text.

From the start our hope was that the Bradt guide to Armenia would inform and make a visit there even more enjoyable than it is bound to be. That continues to be my hope for this edition.

PUBLISHER'S FOREWORD   *Hilary Bradt*

When we published the first edition of this groundbreaking guide I noted that Armenia seemed to have everything: a fascinating history, vibrant culture and rewarding natural history. And in Nicholas Holding we had an author who could do justice to this marvellous yet little-known country. Sadly, Nicholas has passed away since the last edition was published. For this edition, Deirdre Holding – who travelled with Nicholas, her husband, during his journeys around the country – picks up the reins. Armenia remains well off the beaten track, and adventurous travellers have the benefit of Deirdre's latest discoveries in this fascinating land.

Third edition published May 2011 First published 2003
Bradt Travel Guides Ltd, IDC House, The Vale, Chalfont St Peter, Bucks SL9 9RZ, England
www.bradtguides.com
Published in the USA by The Globe Pequot Press Inc, PO Box 480, Guilford, Connecticut 06437-0480

Text copyright © 2011 Deirdre Holding
Maps copyright © 2011 Bradt Travel Guides Ltd
Photographs copyright © 2011 Individual photographers (see below)
Project Manager: Elspeth Beidas

ISBN: 978 1 84162 345 0

British Library Cataloguing in Publication Data

A catalogue record for this book is available from the British Library

Photographs Alamy: dbimages (d/A), Imagebroker (I/A), Imagestate Media Partners Limited – Impact Photos (IMPLIP/A), Maria Grazia Casella (MGC/A), Paul Carstairs (PC/A), RIA Novosti (RN/A), Wolfgang Kaehler (WK/A); Adam Balogh (AB); Neil Bowman/FLPA (NB/FLPA); Vanick Der Bedrossian (VDB); Dreamstime: Avatavat (A/D), Fortish (F/D), Galstyan (G/D), Haikik (H/D), Lookingfor12 (L/D), Marianna Meliksetyan (MM/D), Salajean (S/D), Shapenko (Sh/D); Deirdre Holding (DH); Nicholas Holding (NH); shalunts/Shutterstock (s/S); Jon Smith (JS); Superstock (SS)
Front cover Amberd Church (MM/D)
Back cover Carving (AB), Countryside near Makaravank (SS)
Title page Apricots (F/D), Monument symbolising mothers' grief, Stepanakert, Nagorno Karabagh (NH), Hrevank (d/A)

Maps David McCutcheon (regional maps in this guide based on ITM map *Armenia*)

Typeset from the authors' disc by Wakewing
Production managed by Jellyfish Print Solutions; printed in India

Acknowledgements

Special thanks are due to Anahit Shahverdyan who has continued to be my advisor, interpreter and guide to all things Armenian. Secondly, great thanks are due to Saro Boick who drove me cheerfully and safely the length and breadth of Armenia, on roads both good and bad.

Thanks are also due to the staff at Armenia Travel + M in Yerevan, particularly Kristina Gharibyan and Nina Dadayan, for their willing efficiency when making arrangements; to Hasmik Shahverdyan for giving me so much of her time and company in Yerevan and for finding the answers to innumerable questions; to Syuzanna Azoyan of Armenia Information for her help; to David Sayers (author of the Bradt guide to the Azores) for guidance on botanical matters; to Carl Meadows of Regent Holidays for his help; and to Neil Taylor who, as author of Bradt guides to Estonia and the Baltic cities, provided encouragement and advice. I would also like to thank the many other people in Armenia, and in Nagorno Karabagh, who gave freely of their time and knowledge, so contributing much to this guidebook.

In their dealings with me the staff at Bradt, in particular Anna Moores, Adrian Phillips and Elspeth Beidas, have encouraged and helped, shown patience and understanding, all laced with cheerfulness and humour.

DEDICATION

In memory of Nick.

UPDATES WEBSITE AND FEEDBACK

For the latest travel news about Armenia, please visit the update page on Bradt's website: updates.bradtguides.com. This page supplements the printed information in the Bradt guidebook and provides an online space where both author updates and reader feedback can be shared.

If you have any comments, queries, grumbles, insights, news or other feedback please contact us on: 01753 893444; info@bradtguides.com. The best and most useful comments will be posted on our website.

Contents

NOTE ABOUT MAPS

Several maps use grid lines to allow easy location of sites. Map grid references are listed in square brackets after listings in the text, with page number followed by grid number, eg: [104 C3].

LIST OF MAPS

Introduction

Second edition, Nicholas Holding, 2006

This is a guidebook to the present-day Republic of Armenia together with the territory of Nagorno Karabagh. In the English-speaking world, an individual's knowledge of Armenia generally falls into one of two categories. Most people know nothing about it at all, not even where it is. The others, a small minority, not only speak the Armenian language, although neither they nor their parents were born in Armenia, but also have some knowledge of Armenian culture and Armenia's often tragic history. When it comes to who actually visits Armenia nowadays the numbers in the two categories are more evenly balanced. The explanation is that Armenia has one of the most successful and supportive diasporas in the world and that present-day Armenia is very dependent on them. So far as Nagorno Karabagh is concerned, the contrast is even more stark with the diaspora being wholly familiar with its recent past while few others would claim even to have heard of it, apart from those who are well informed politically and might recall its name as the scene of some half-remembered conflict around the time that the Soviet Union disintegrated.

This book is aimed primarily at the general tourist who is interested in seeing the country and understanding something of its long and complex history. The author is not a member of the diaspora and does not speak Armenian. Nevertheless, even fairly knowledgeable members of the diaspora should find it useful as they, like virtually all other visitors to Armenia, unfortunately confine themselves at present to only half a dozen places which are not always the most interesting ones. It appears that few visitors know anything about many of the other sights in Armenia which warrant a visit. As a consequence, only a handful of visitors to Armenia spend more than a week in the country and the average visit lasts a mere four or five days. This book seeks to rectify that regrettable situation and demonstrate that Armenia has a huge potential for visitors. Not just for general sightseeing, although its spectacular gorges and medieval buildings certainly provide plenty of excellent opportunities for that, but also for activities such as hiking, birdwatching, architectural tours, historical visits, botanical trips, angling, horseriding and caving. Although many visitors will probably continue to combine a visit to Armenia with one to neighbouring Georgia or Iran, there is quite enough in Armenia alone to occupy several holidays without ever going to the same place twice. Indeed, the most commonly heard complaint from visitors is that they had insufficient time. Sometimes the visitors are in a tourist coach lamenting that they are faced with long journeys and few stops as the tour operator decided that they must see the prescribed sights with the minimum possible number of nights in the country. At other times, fitter people gaze longingly out of the bus window at the fantastic potential for hiking which they have no opportunity to explore.

Armenia is actually a very easy country to visit for three reasons. Firstly, its people are overwhelmingly friendly, helpful and welcoming: I have only ever once encountered an unhelpful and unwelcoming attitude in my travels around the country. Secondly, Armenia is unique in that any tourist from any country can get a 21-day visa over the internet and pay for it by credit card. Thirdly, there is relatively little crime and the risk of theft or being short-changed is much less than in most other European countries.

Is Armenia in Europe? It certainly feels far more like a southern European country than an Asian one and it is a member of the Council of Europe and the Organisation for Security and Co-operation in Europe. In addition, the Armenian people have been Christian for 1,700 years and from 1828 to 1991 they were ruled by another country whose culture, the Bolshevik Revolution notwithstanding, was fundamentally Christian. On a more practical level, Armenia has an international telephone dialling code (374) in the European sequence and the British post office charges the European rate for letters sent to Armenia from Britain.

By contrast to these factors making it easy to visit Armenia the drawbacks are the language barrier, the lack of good maps and the sometimes poor infrastructure. Fortunately the last two are improving but very, very few people outside the large hotels and travel agents in Yerevan speak English or any other western European language. The main second language is, and is likely to remain, Russian so visitors travelling on their own may well find it convenient to consider employing an English-speaking guide or else arranging accommodation in advance. Either can be done through one of the Yerevan travel agents or an overseas agent who specialises in the country. When hiring a car, it is generally cheaper to hire one with driver than to drive oneself although the car is then likely to be older. Depending on the expected destinations a 4x4 vehicle can be requested, essential for getting to some places and quite helpful for many others.

Things are changing fast in Armenia. Six years ago (2000) Western airlines operated only six flights a week to Armenia. There are currently (2005) 22, indication enough of the increasing number of visitors. Some sights, notably Goshavank and Selim caravanserai have become much more accessible because the roads have been improved. Diaspora support has enabled some of the museums to be refurbished and better displays to be introduced though this generous support has rarely been invested in better labelling in English or other Western languages. Unfortunately, members of the diaspora do not seem to see the need for this – being Armenian-speaking themselves they do not always put themselves into the position of a non-speaker. Where material in English is available, the standard of translation varies considerably. It seems ridiculous that a potentially invaluable series of guides in English to particular sights which is being introduced, should have been so wretchedly translated: see page 239 for an example. On the practical front, the standard of restaurants is increasing as, slowly, is the number of hotels outside Yerevan. There are, however, still areas of the country where homestays are much the best option.

There is no doubt that many comments made in this book will quickly be superseded. Armenia has so much to offer visitors. It will never become a mainstream tourist destination like Mallorca or Florida but few visitors to Armenia leave disappointed apart from wishing that they had had more time in the country. The author very much hopes that this guide will encourage others to go to such off-the-beaten-track places as Makaravank and Dashtadem. They will be rewarded by seeing enthralling sights in a country in transition. After centuries of foreign domination Armenia is now once again an independent nation preserving for future generations its unique heritage.

INTRODUCTION TO THIRD EDITION *Deirdre Holding, 2010*

The introduction to the second edition still describes Armenia very well even though there have been rapid changes in the last five years. The first thing to strike the returning visitor is the amount of building work, particularly in the capital. An important but less immediately visible change is the vast improvement in the reliability of water supply. Accommodation has expanded and not just in Yerevan. There are new small hotels and well-renovated large Soviet-era hotels in many places. However, there are still parts of the country where homestays remain the best option, providing an insight into Armenian family life. Significant advances on the technological side have resulted in better internet access, a much improved telephone system and an explosion in mobile-phone use.

Many roads have been upgraded, allowing better access to worthwhile sights such as Makaravank and Anipemza but there are still some extremely poor roads and the transition from one to the other can be abrupt. Russian seems to be disappearing from road signs while English increases. At many historic sites welcome information boards, in several languages, have sprung up. A significant amount of restoration of historic sites has been carried out, some of it good, some of it questionable.

Political problems remain for Armenia. Perhaps the most obvious to visitors is the unresolved question of the status of Nagorno Karabagh, resulting in the continued closure by Azerbaijan and Turkey of their respective borders with Armenia. The refusal of Turkey to recognise as genocide the 1915 massacre of Armenians in the Ottoman Empire continues to influence Armenia's relations with Turkey.

Many of the best things in Armenia have not changed: the hospitality of the people, the wonderful quality of seasonal fruit and vegetables, the scenery, and the abundant ancient sites, both prehistoric and medieval. It remains a country well worth visiting.

AN IMPORTANT WORD OF WARNING Do not try to take a copy of this book into Azerbaijan. It will be confiscated at the border.

NOTE ON TRANSLITERATION There is no standard transliteration from the Armenian alphabet into English. For example the principal city of northwest Armenia can appear in English as Gyumri, Gyumry, Giumri, G'umri or even Kyumrï while the province of which it is the capital is Shirak in English, Schirak in German or Chirak in French. Some transliteration schemes even resort to letters borrowed from Czech and Slovak such as č, š and ž which few English speakers know how to pronounce anyway.

For place names in this guide the authors have usually followed those used by Brady Kiesling and Raffi Kojian in *Rediscovering Armenia* (see page 295). Occasionally this does result in combinations of consonants appearing such as those in Smbataberd, Aghjkaghala and Ptghni but these are actually quite close to the Armenian pronunciation. So far as surnames are concerned, the ending '...ian' has been preferred to '...yan' for the many which end this way (eg: Abovian rather than Abovyan) except where this would result in the ending '...aian' or something similar and there '...ayan' has been used (eg: Babayan rather than Babaian). In this guide the transliteration Karabagh has usually been preferred to Karabakh, except where an organisation itself uses the latter form.

Part One

GENERAL INFORMATION

Location A landlocked country in the southern Caucasus between the Black Sea and the Caspian Sea bordered by Georgia, Azerbaijan, Iran and Turkey. The border with the self-declared Republic of Nagorno Karabagh is not recognised internationally. Yerevan, the capital, is on the same latitude as Naples, Madrid and New York. It is on the same longitude as Volgograd, Russia, Baghdad and Sana'a, Yemen. It is five hours' flying time from London.

Area 29,800km^2 – similar to Belgium and the US state of Maryland. Note, however, that following the 1994 cease-fire the territory administered is 31,200km^2.

Status Presidential parliamentary republic with universal adult suffrage

Population 3.2 million resident in the country at the date of census (Oct 2001) with a 2008 estimate at 3.24 million; 97.9% are ethnic Armenians, 1.3% Yezidis, 0.5% Russians, 0.05% Kurds. The balance comprises a wide range of nationalities.

Major cities Yerevan (the capital, population 1.1 million); Gyumri (149,500); Vanadzor (106,100). Note that the Yerevan population figure covers only those living within the city. Urban sprawl into the surrounding provinces results in a much larger figure for the Yerevan conurbation.

Administrative divisions The country is divided into the capital (Yerevan) and ten provinces (*marz*): Shirak, Lori, Tavush, Aragatsotn, Gegharkunik, Kotayk, Armavir, Ararat, Vayots Dzor, Syunik.

Language Armenian, an Indo-European language. Russian is also widely understood but western European languages are not, although English is becoming a little better known, mainly in the capital.

Alphabet The unique Armenian alphabet, currently with 39 letters, was devised around AD400.

Religion Very predominantly Armenian Apostolic. There are a few Roman Catholics, mostly in Shirak province, and there are several sects seeking converts. The Yezidis are Zoroastrian and the Kurds are Muslim.

Currency Dram (AMD) divided theoretically into 100 luma.

Exchange rate £1 = AMD586, US$1 = AMD365, €1 = AMD498 (Feb 2011)

International telephone code +374

Time GMT + 4 hours

Electricity 220V AC; European two-pin plug

Weights and measures Metric system

National flag Three horizontal stripes: red, blue, orange

National anthem 'Land of Our Fathers, Free, Independent' (Mer Hayreniq, azat, ankakh); words adapted from a poem by Mikayel Nalbandian (1829–66); music by Barsegh Kanachian (1885–1967).

Symbols of Armenia The classical symbol is the khachkar ('cross stone'). The grape and pomegranate are also used as symbols as is the eagle which appears on the country's coat of arms.

Public holidays See pages 87–8.

I

Background Information

GEOGRAPHY AND CLIMATE

GEOLOGICAL FEATURES Visitors to Armenia can hardly fail to be aware of two key geological features of the country: the **Lesser Caucasus** mountain range that projects into the country, with the **dormant volcano of Mount Aragats** being the highest peak at 4,090m; and the frequency of earthquakes. The two are both accounted for by the theory of plate tectonics. Under this theory, which has been generally accepted internationally since the 1960s, the outermost shell of the earth or lithosphere is formed of a dozen or so large, rigid slabs of rock together with many smaller ones. These slabs, called tectonic plates, are around 75km thick and comprise the thin outer crust plus the solid part of the mantle. The plates float on the liquid part of the mantle or asthenosphere, which is several hundred kilometres thick, and the slow movement of the plates is due to convection currents in the asthenosphere caused by heat escaping from the earth's core. As the enormous plates move, they grind against each other and stress builds up until there is a sudden movement of one plate against another resulting in an earthquake when rocks break along fault lines. Armenia is on the line where the Arabian plate, moving at about 2.5cm per annum, is colliding with the larger Eurasian plate and it is consequently very prone to earthquakes. About 25 million years ago the Caucasus Mountains themselves were formed as a consequence of this collision. Quite young as mountain ranges go, they are largely volcanic rocks such as basalt, andesite and tuff, all three of which have been used as building materials in Armenia. **Basalt and andesite** are magma (liquid material from the asthenosphere) which escaped to the surface during the collision of the plates and then solidified. The difference between the two is in the relative proportions of silica, iron and magnesium. **Tuff** by contrast is formed when small rock fragments (less than 2mm across) which have spewed out from a volcano become fused together on the ground. Tuff has long been the building material of choice in Armenia when it is available and it is highly characteristic of the country. Today the biggest working tuff quarry is close to the town of Artik in Shirak province. Another consequence of the volcanic past is that the semi-precious stone obsidian can be found here. **Obsidian**, which occurs in a range of colours and is used to make jewellery, is a glassy rock formed through the very rapid solidification of lava. In Armenia it occurs most commonly in the Hrazdan region. Apart from these volcanic rocks, Armenia also has substantial deposits of the sedimentary rock **limestone** and in some of these are extensive though little-known cave systems. The most important mineral deposits are of copper (7.4 million tonnes, of which 4.5 million tonnes are at Kajaran), molybdenum (711,000 tonnes, of which 600,000 tonnes are at Kajaran) and gold (268 tonnes, of which 97 tonnes are at Zod).

GEOGRAPHICAL FEATURES Armenia is a very high country. The lowest part, the Debed Valley at the Georgian border in the northeast, lies at 400m above sea level while the average altitude is 1,370m and only 10% of the land is under 1,000m. Although mountainous in parts, much of Armenia is more a high plateau fissured by deep gorges. The volcanic soil in the valleys means that the ground is highly fertile but irrigation is essential because of the low rainfall and about 10% of the entire land is irrigated. Even so, Armenia is a net importer of food. The growing of food crops is obviously unfeasible in the mountainous areas but is equally unfeasible on much of the plateau because of the lack of water although some of the alpine meadows are used for the production of hay. The mountains do support a surprisingly large population of cattle as well as sheep and goats, and livestock can often be encountered at unexpected elevations in fairly inaccessible places. About 20% of the land is arable, while 24% is pasture and about 15% is forest. **Fruit growing** is important. Fruits as diverse as pomegranates, grapes, strawberries, peaches, persimmons and apples are grown but two fruits native to Armenia and which were consequently first eaten here remain important although they have now spread to the rest of the world. One is the **apricot** – its scientific name reflects this – *Armeniaca vulgaris* – and Armenians claim with some justification that their apricots are the best in the world. Apricot stones 6,000 years old have been found at archaeological sites and today there are about 50 varieties in the country. The other is the **sweet cherry** or mazzard, *Prunus avium*, from which all the world's 900 varieties of sweet cherry have been cultivated. It spread to the West very early and was known in Greece by 300BC. Walnuts, pistachios, almonds and hazelnuts grow wild in Armenia and they too are now extensively cultivated. Also of great importance is that Armenia is possibly the country where wheat was first cultivated, perhaps about 10,000 years ago. Two native species of wheat *Triticum urartu* and *T. araraticum* still grow in protected fields in the Arax Valley. The importance of both culinary and medicinal herbs, collected from the hillsides, can be seen in any Armenian market.

A major feature of the country is **Lake Sevan** whose surface area was formerly 1,416km² but this has been reduced by abstracting water for hydro-electric and irrigation purposes. It is one of the world's largest high-altitude lakes with its surface originally 1,915m above sea level. By 2001, it had fallen to 1,896m but it has now started to rise again. There is commercial exploitation of fish stocks although the introduction of alien species has led to the virtual extinction of the endemic trout.

Armenia has a number of **significant rivers** which all flow east into the Caspian Sea. **Hydro-electric schemes** on these rivers are important as the only indigenous energy resource within the country which has been developed apart from a small wind farm on the top of the Pushkin Pass in Lori province. Hydro-electric schemes provide around one third of electricity requirements and small hydro-electric schemes are under construction throughout the country. Another third of electricity is generated using **nuclear power** and the balance is **thermal generation** mostly using imported gas. Electricity is exported to Georgia and there are seasonal exchanges with Iran. Gas is mostly imported from Russia by pipeline through Georgia although the Armenian and Iranian gas networks are also linked. Armenia itself has no known reserves of coal, oil or gas but geological and seismic surveys for oil and gas have started.

CLIMATE Armenia has a highland continental climate with hot, dry summers (June to September) and cold winters (December, January and February being the coldest months). However, this simple statement masks the fact that the weather can vary greatly within short distances because of differences in altitude and other factors affecting local micro-climates. Variation in altitude often has more influence on the weather than north–south distances. For example, Gyumri can be much cooler than Yerevan even although the distance between them is only 122km, and Amberd, about an hour's drive from Yerevan, can be snowbound until late May (see also *Chapter 2, When to visit,* page 51 and *Chapter 3,* page 101 for Yerevan's weather). April and May are the wettest months: although this usually means heavy showers the rain can be continuous for long spells. Spring can be very short, the weather changing from wintery to summery in just a few days. During the hottest months of June, July and August low humidity mitigates the high temperatures. Autumn is relatively long and often very pleasant.

ARMENIA'S BORDERS Prior to the war with Azerbaijan, landlocked Armenia was bordered to the north by Georgia, to the east by Azerbaijan, to the south by Iran and to the west by Turkey and by the detached part of Azerbaijan known as Nakhichevan. The borders totalled 1,254km: 164km with Georgia; 566km with Azerbaijan; 35km with Iran; 268km with Turkey; and 221km with Nakhichevan. The area of the country was 29,800km^2, slightly smaller than Belgium or slightly larger than the American state of Maryland. An additional complication was that five small detached enclaves within Armenia were actually part of Azerbaijan while Azerbaijan had a small Armenian enclave within its borders. The ceasefire in 1994 has led to a considerable change. Firstly, all these small enclaves were occupied by the surrounding power. Secondly, Nagorno Karabagh, which had been an autonomous region within Azerbaijan, declared itself an independent republic; the present-day republic of Nagorno Karabagh does not incorporate all the territory of the former autonomous region since Azerbaijan holds the northern part. Thirdly, Armenia was left in control of a considerable area of the territory of Azerbaijan and much of this is now administered by the self-declared Republic of Nagorno Karabagh. A noticeable change in 2002 was that for the first time maps were starting to show the occupied territories either as a part of Armenia or as a part of the Republic of Nagorno Karabagh. Relatively few people live in them since the Azeri population has fled and Armenian refugees have not chosen these territories in which to settle. The international community still recognises the pre-1991 boundaries with the apparent exception that foreign diplomats driving from Yerevan to southern Armenia do not bother to avoid the former Azeri enclave through which the main road passes.

NATURAL HISTORY AND CONSERVATION

The number of species of animals and plants in Armenia is very high for a country of its size which lies wholly outside the tropics. This is largely accounted for by the great altitudinal variation and the diversity of vegetation zones. Armenia is normally described as having **six distinct zones**: semi-deserts, dry steppes, steppes, forest, subalpine and alpine. **Semi-deserts** account for about 10% of the country and occur in the Ararat Valley and adjacent mountain slopes up to altitudes of 1,200–1,300m, as well as in the Arpa Valley around Vaik, and in the Meghri region. The land has generally been cultivated for millennia except for a few patches where sand has accumulated and a semi-desert landscape has resulted. Cultivation has required extensive irrigation and these irrigated areas now account for most of the fruit, vegetable, and wine production. **Dry mountainous steppes** are found at higher altitudes than semi-deserts (above 1,500m) in the Ararat Valley and some other areas, but are also found at lower altitudes (above 800m) in the northeast in areas which were originally forested. A range of soils is found and in the Ararat Valley these are mostly stony. Irrigation of dry steppes has allowed some cultivation of crops and fruit. Mountain steppes are the dominant landscape for most of the country, particularly at altitudes above 1,500m. In the northeast of the country and also in the south, ridges among these highland meadow steppes often contain patches of forest. Elsewhere **forests** are usually found on the mid-zone of mountains though in some regions the forests were much affected by the cutting of trees for fuel during the energy shortage years in the early 1990s. The most extensive forested areas are now in the northeast. **Subalpine meadows** occur at higher altitudes than steppes and forests, including highland mountain ranges. **Alpine meadows** occur higher still and are important pasture lands even though climatic conditions are severe with long cold winters and snow cover lasting up to nine months. So-called **azonal landscapes** (meaning that the soil type is determined by factors other than the local climate and vegetation) cover the remaining 10% of the territory of the country and include wetlands, as well as saline and alkaline areas in the Ararat Valley where the underground waters are close to the earth's surface, resulting in water vaporisation and salt precipitation.

MAMMALS Armenia's mammal list was recently increased from 76 to 83 when seven additional species of bat were identified. However, one of the mammals on the list, striped hyena (*Hyaena hyaena*) is probably extinct in the country and the status of Caucasian birch mouse (*Sicista caucasica*) is unknown. Another six are officially classified as endangered: the distinctive Armenian subspecies of mouflon (*Ovis orientalis gmelini*), Persian ibex or wild goat (*Capra aegagrus*), marbled polecat (*Vormela peregusna*), otter (*Lutra lutra*), Pallas's cat (or manul) (*Felis manul*) and brown bear (*Ursus arctos*) (or grizzly bear as the same species is known in North America). Despite bears being classified as endangered, their droppings can often be encountered while walking in the mountains, sometimes surprisingly close to habitation. Other interesting mammals include leopard (*Panthera pardus*), now the subject of a WWF protection programme in Armenia, lynx (*Felis lynx*), wild cat (*Felis sylvestris*), wolf (*Canis lupus*), Bezoar ibex (*Capra aegagrus*), porcupine (*Hystrix indica*), roe deer (*Capreolus capreolus*) and wild boar (*Sus scrofa*). However, no mammals in Armenia can be described as easy to see and, apart from a wolf disturbed from its daytime retreat and a few unidentified bats, I have only ever observed red fox (*Vulpes vulpes*), brown hare (*Lepus capensis*), European souslik (*Citellus citellus*) and Vinogradov's jird (*Meriones vinogradovi*), the jird being one of five species of gerbil found in Armenia.

BIRDS The standard field guide, *A Field Guide to the Birds of Armenia* (see page 294), lists 346 species of bird as having been recorded in Armenia up to 1997. However, as there are only a few observers many vagrants and casuals must go unrecorded. Armenia is at the boundary of two faunal zones and the north sees northern species at the southern limit of their range while the south sees southern species and those from the eastern Mediterranean at their northern limit. Raptors are surprisingly common and easy to see. Five species of eagle breed in Armenia: lesser spotted, golden, booted, steppe, and short-toed snake-eagle. This is in addition to osprey, four vultures, two harriers and a good selection of buzzards and falcons. Other large and conspicuous birds include white and black storks, the former mainly in the Arax Valley where their nests are conspicuous in some places on top of electricity poles. The Dalmatian pelican breeds in the country and great white pelicans are year-round visitors. Specialities of the Caucasus include

Caucasian grouse and Caspian snowcock, both of which are endangered and difficult to see without a knowledgeable local guide in their subalpine and alpine meadows. Smaller birds of note include both eastern and western rock nuthatches, white-tailed lapwing, Persian wheatear, Armenian gull, white-throated robin and Finsch's wheatear. Raptor migration in autumn is very rewarding as Armenia is on a major flightway between the Black and Caspian seas with the most numerous species being steppe buzzard, steppe and lesser spotted eagles, and Montagu's and pallid harriers, honey buzzard, Levant sparrowhawk, lesser kestrel and black kite. September sees migrating demoiselle cranes at Lake Sevan with daily totals of up to 4,500 being recorded.

Anyone interested in Armenia's birds is strongly recommended to join the **Ornithological Society of the Middle East, Caucasus and Central Asia** (*c/o The Lodge, Sandy, Bedfordshire, SG19 2DL, UK;* e *secretary@osme.org; www.osme.org*) who can assist with birdwatching trips to the country as well as funding small projects such as the survey of Armash fish ponds currently under way.

AMPHIBIANS AND REPTILES Armenia's dry climate is reflected in the paucity of **amphibian species** and lack of specialities. All eight species in the country have a wide distribution even though only one is also native to the UK. Widespread European species are marsh frog (*Rana ridibunda*), green toad (*Bufo viridis*), eastern spadefoot toad (*Pelobates syriacus*), European tree frog (*Hyla arborea*), and smooth newt (*Triturus vulgaris*). The others, not included in most field guides, are banded frog (*Rana camerani*), lemon-yellow tree frog (*Hyla savignyi*) and banded newt (*Triturus vittatus*).

By contrast, Armenia is very rich in **reptile species** with a total of 50 although some are now threatened by denudation of the habitat as a result of overgrazing. The Mediterranean tortoise (*Testudo graeca*) may occasionally be encountered as one crosses a track. Ponds may contain one of two species of terrapin, European pond terrapin (*Emys orbicularis*) and stripe-necked terrapin (*Mauremys caspica*).

The **geckos** which can frequently be seen on the outside walls of buildings in the countryside are Caspian rock geckos (*Tenuidactylus caspius*). The Caucasian agama (*Laudakia caucasia*) is a lizard with a decidedly prehistoric dragon-like appearance. Like all agamas, it has a plump short body with a long thin tail, a triangular head and long legs. Agamas are capable of some colour change to match their background. Two **legless lizards** which might be mistaken for snakes (though being lizards rather than snakes they have eyelids and they can shed their tails to escape a predator, a practice known as autotony) are the slow worm (*Anguis fragilis*) and the European glass lizard (*Ophisaurus apodus*). **Skinks** are lizards which, while not usually completely legless, generally in Europe only have vestigial legs of little or no apparent value for locomotion. The Armenian fauna includes several skinks: two-streaked lidless skink (*Ablepharus bivittatus*); Chernov's lidless skink (*Ablepharus chernovi*); golden grass skink (*Mabuya aurata*); and the Berber skink (*Eumeces schneideri*). The other lizard species are typical lizards belonging to the large family Lacertidae. Ones of particular interest are those with a limited range outside Armenia such as stepperunner (*Eremias arguta*), Balkan green lizard (*Lacerta trilineata*) and Caucasian green lizard (*Lacerta strigata*). Even more unusual is the Armenian lizard (*Lacerta armeniaca*) in which a proportion of the females practise parthenogenesis – in other words without fertilisation by a male they lay eggs which hatch and produce a daughter that is an exact genetic copy of the mother.

Snakes are very well represented with 23 species and they are more commonly seen than in many countries. Interesting snakes include the sand boa (*Eryx jaculus*), one of Europe's few snakes which kill their prey by constriction, mostly small lizards and rodents in this case. Largely nocturnal it rests by day in rodent burrows or under large stones. Unusually the snake is viviparous, the female giving birth to about 20 live young which feed on small lizards. The Montpellier snake (*Malpolon monspessulanus*) belongs to the family Colubridae, snakes whose fangs are at the back of the mouth. Such snakes find it difficult to inject their venom into large objects. Unusually for a snake this diurnal species possesses good vision and, when hunting, it sometimes rises up and looks around rather resembling a cobra. The Montpellier snake reaches 2m in length. A much smaller colubrid is the Asia Minor dwarf snake (*Eirenis modestus*) which grows to only 15cm and feeds on insects. Dahl's whip snake (*Coluber najadum*) is another diurnal snake. Very slender, it is extremely fast moving but rarely exceeds 1m in length. Another whip snake is the secretive and weakly venomed mountain racer (*C. ravergieri*). Caucasian rat snake (*Elaphe hohenackeri*) is one of Europe's smaller snakes, growing up to about only 80cm. Very unusually for a snake it is often found in the vicinity of human habitations where it frequents piles of stones and holes in old stone walls.

Vipers are among the snakes which, unlike the colubrids, have fangs at the front of their mouth. They are consequently much more dangerous because they do not need to get their mouth round the victim in order to inject poison. There are several interesting species in Armenia which have a very limited distribution. Armenian viper (*Vipera raddei*) is now seriously threatened in the country through pasturing and overgrazing while Darevsky's viper (*V. darevskii*), described as recently as 1986, also has a very limited range and is similarly threatened. Bites from these species can be fatal as can those from Armenia's more widely distributed vipers. Perhaps the most dangerous of all is the blunt-nosed viper (*V. lebetina*), at 2.5m one of the largest of its genus. An able climber of trees, the danger from this snake lies mainly in the extreme speed of its attack and the method of biting: rather than bite and withdraw, it keeps its teeth lodged in its target and works its jaws to pump more venom in. It is not a snake to be approached lightly, although it generally makes a loud hissing before attacking, thus giving some warning. (See *Chapter 2, Snakebite* page 65.)

FISH Of the 31 species of fish found in Armenia, six have been introduced. Common whitefish (*Coregonus lavaretus*) was introduced into Lake Sevan from Lake Ladoga in Russia with a view to increasing commercial fish production and this was followed by goldfish (*Carassius auratus*) from eastern Asia. Fish farms are responsible for introducing silver carp (*Hypophthalmichthys molitrix*) from China and Pacific salmon (*Salmo gairdneri*). Presumably Pacific salmon was preferred to the native Caspian salmon (*S. caspius*) because of the ease of obtaining stock. Grass carp (*Ctenopharyngodon idella*) came from China with the hope of improving water quality in irrigation systems and marshy lakes as it is herbivorous and so helps to control aquatic vegetation. By contrast mosquito fish (*Gambusia affinis*) was brought from the southeast part of the USA because, as its name implies, it eats mosquito larvae and hence assists in the control of malaria.

Apart from these exotics there has been some stocking of waters with common carp (*Cyprinus carpio*) which has been introduced to lakes in Lori province as well as Dilijan and Ijevan reservoirs. On the other hand, overfishing of rivers has led to a decline in the abundance of trout (*Salmo trutta*) and European catfish or wels (*Silurus glanis*). However, chub (*Leusciscus cephalus*) remains common in lakes. Drastic reduction in the water level of Lake Sevan has led to the virtual extinction in Armenia of the endemic Sevan trout (*Salmo ischchan*) (see page 173). Paradoxically its successful translocation into Lake Issyk-kul in Kyrgyzstan, although having negative consequences for the indigenous Issyk-kul fish fauna, has probably saved this fish from extinction. Stocks in Lake Sevan of Sevan khramulya (*Varicorhinus capoeta*) have also seriously declined but it survives in some of the lake's tributaries.

OTHER FAUNA About 17,000 species of **invertebrate** have been identified in Armenia but this must only represent a small fraction of the total. Two groups may be of particular interest to visitors but for very different reasons. Armenia has three species of **scorpion** which fortunately are rarely encountered. That said, they occur on the rocky and stony ground such as that which surrounds many monasteries and form an additional reason to wear robust footwear as well as taking care when scrambling up slopes. Far more conspicuous is the abundance of **butterflies**. About 570 species of lepidoptera (moths and butterflies) have been identified in Armenia but that is clearly only a small percentage of the total since it compares with a figure of 2,600 for the UK which, although larger, has a much less suitable climate. A well-illustrated guide to the butterflies of the whole of the former Soviet Union including Armenia (*Guide to the Butterflies of Russia and Adjacent Territories*) is available – it was published in Sofia, Bulgaria, and is obtainable from specialist booksellers worldwide – but unfortunately its two enormous heavy volumes make it difficult even to take to Armenia let alone carry around. More portable is *A Field Guide to the Butterflies of Turkey* published in 2007. Obviously it does not cover Armenia specifically but there is enough overlap to make it more useful than no guide at all. For details of these books see *Appendix 2, Natural history*, page 294. The American University of Armenia, which published *A Field Guide to the Birds of Armenia*, promises a field guide to the butterflies of Armenia – planned publication date 2012.

FLORA Identified so far in Armenia have been 388 species of algae, 4,166 fungi, 2,600 lichens and 430 mosses in addition to the very large total of 3,200 species of vascular plants, including some endemics – plants found only in Armenia. Since Armenia's flora is very large it is perhaps surprising that gymnosperms (basically conifers) should be poorly represented by a mere nine species: five junipers, one pine, one yew and two shrubby members of the family Ephedraceae whose American relatives include Nevada joint fir and desert tea.

One third of the forests are oak forests and they are widely distributed across the country. Of the four oak species found in Armenia, two (Caucasian oak (*Quercus macranthera*) and Georgian oak (*Q. iberica*) are typical of these forests. Caucasian oak is the more frost-tolerant species and is found throughout the country at altitudes as high as 2,600m. By contrast, Georgian oak is typically restricted to altitudes between 500 and 1,400m, and is mostly found in the north and the extreme south. Other species found in oak forests are ash (*Fraxinus excelsior*), hornbeam (*Carpinus betulus*), Georgian maple (*Acer ibericum*), cork elm (*Ulmus suberosus*) and field maple (*Acer campestre*). A third oak species – Arax oak (*Q. araxina*) – is now declining, probably because of agricultural development.

Another third of the forest is the beech forest of northern Armenia. They are dominated by Oriental beech (*Fagus orientalis*). They are mostly on north-facing slopes at an altitude of 1,000–2,000m. Other species in beech forests include small-leaved lime (*Tilia cordata*), Litvinov beech (*Betula litwinow*) and spindle-tree (*Euonymus europaeus*). Hornbeam forests occur at altitudes of 800–1,800m. Other trees found in these forests include the various oaks, field maple, ash, Caucasian pear (*Pyrus caucasicum*) and Oriental apple (*Malus orientalis*). Scrub forests are found in both the north and south of the country occurring at altitudes of 900–1,000m in the north, but at much higher altitude in the south (1,800–2,000m).

These forests support around 80 species of xeric trees and shrubs, all of which are drought tolerant and light-loving. As well as thorn forest dominated by juniper, broad-leaved forests also occur, characterised by species such as Georgian maple, various cherries, pistachio (*Pistacia mutica*), almond (*Prunus dulcis*), buckthorn (*Rhamnus catharticus*) and wild jasmine (*Jasminum fruticans*). There are groves of virgin yew (*Taxus baccata*) in Dilijan National Park and a relict plane (*Platanus orientalis*) grove in Shikahogh Reserve in the south of the country.

A number of Armenia's plants will be familiar to visitors because they have become popular cultivated plants of temperate gardens such as the florist's scabious, the oriental poppy which is flamboyant in so many herbaceous borders, the ubiquitous catmint, burning bush and grape hyacinth. Different types of vegetation can be seen within relatively limited areas, often accessed easily from the principal roads. Many flowers are to be found in the dry mountain habitats typical of central Armenia; apparently unpromising, thinly grassed areas or patches of low spiny shrubbery can yield a surprising number of species. It is here, for example, that the almost impossible to cultivate, but striking and often bizarre Oncocyclus iris, can be found. The extensive grasslands surrounding the high passes crossed by the main highways, the river gorges and the broadleaved deciduous forests are all worth exploring for interesting and attractive plants. One of the great joys of Armenia is that botanical excursions and visits to ancient churches and monasteries so often happily coincide.

CONSERVATION ISSUES Conservation has not been a priority in Armenia, a country still coping with the aftermath of the severe earthquake in 1988, the war over Nagorno Karabagh and the associated closure of borders by Azerbaijan and Turkey, and the loss of most of its industrial base following the collapse of the Soviet Union. The loss of heavy industry did at least have the beneficial result of a reduction in atmospheric pollution. The economic crisis resulted in over-exploitation of natural resources and it is probably fair to say that awareness of environmental issues is not generally high, although it is increasing. Even where awareness exists, the priority for those who are poor is, understandably, simply to survive. There are many active environmental NGOs and international foundations which support conservation activities, large investments are made to support environmental education programmes and action for particular species but there is little positive result to be seen on the ground, in spite of considerable relevant expertise in Armenia. The reasons for this include bureaucracy, corruption and political manoeuvring.

There is a **Ministry of Nature Protection** responsible for protecting the environment but it also sells mining and logging concessions. Powerful businesses seem to be able to operate even in protected areas and the status of a protected area may be downgraded to allow such activity. There are four main **protected areas** in Armenia: Shikahogh State Reserve (see page 259), Khosrov Forest State Reserve (page 158), Dilijan National Park (page 228), which was reduced to park status from reserve in 2002, and Sevan National Park (page 173), as well as a number of smaller sites. Until now Shikahogh has been the best protected, mainly because of its isolation. The fear is that the new road to the south of the country, built through the reserve, will alter this. The problems of Lake Sevan are being addressed (see pages 173–5).

Voluntary organisations exist; for example, the **Armenia Tree Project** (*www.armeniatree.org*) aims to repair the damage done to forests during the years of power shortages in the early 1990s (see *Chapter 5, Gyumri*, page 194). The

American University of Armenia has a research centre for the environment, the Acopian Centre for the Environment (ACE) (*www.ecrc.am*).

In rural areas there is no governmental waste-disposal management and people have to dispose of waste as best they can. There is no recycling industry in Armenia. Visitors will unfortunately see examples of a lack of concern for the environment such as litter, vehicles with high exhaust emissions (although Armenia also leads the world in the use of clean natural/bottled gas to run cars) and the loss of much of Yerevan's green space.

HISTORY

Visitors to Armenia are confronted by the country's history everywhere they look and not just in the prehistoric sites or splendid medieval monasteries that are a major attraction of Armenia for most visitors. Other aspects of Armenia's history are reflected in the legacy of Soviet-era apartment blocks identical to those in Kaliningrad or Omsk, and in the huge investment in modern Armenia funded by the country's large, important and successful diaspora. Further observations soon strike the visitor: that the oldest surviving building in the country, at Garni, looks Greek rather than Armenian and quite different from any other; that there are no Roman remains; that the old churches and monasteries were built within certain very restricted time periods interspersed with long periods from which nothing seems to have survived; that different foreign influences seem to have been significant at different epochs. Visitors will also see everywhere signs written in a distinctive and unique alphabet, the use of which is a large factor in determining what it means to be Armenian. Beginning to make sense of all this jumble of impressions necessitates gaining some understanding of Armenia's long and varied history.

During this history there were periods of independence as an Armenian nation, though often with the nation divided into separate kingdoms because of internal struggles for supremacy by individual families. These periods were separated by much longer spells of foreign rule, by a whole host of different peoples at different times. The 20th-century regaining of independence after centuries of foreign rule, briefly at first from 1918 to 1920 but then lastingly since 1991, owes little to the nations, notably Britain, which repeatedly let down the Armenian people between 1878 and 1923. However, perhaps the west can take some of the responsibility for the Soviet Union's bankruptcy and collapse.

THE LEGENDARY ORIGINS OF THE ARMENIAN PEOPLE Although all foreigners call the country Armenia, Armenians themselves call it Hayastan: literally the 'Land of Haik'. Chapter 8 of Genesis states that Noah's ark grounded on Mount Ararat. Chapter 10 records that Togarmah was a son of Gomer who was a son of Japheth who had accompanied his father Noah on the Ark. According to Armenian legend the Armenian people are the descendants of Haik who was the son of Togarmah and therefore the great-great-grandson of Noah. Their name for their country records this.

According to the legend, of the three sons of Noah, Japheth and Ham settled with their families in the Ararat region while Shem subsequently moved away to the northwest. Ham's and Japheth's sons gradually spread out to the various regions of the Armenian Plateau. When Japheth's great-grandson Haik was 130 years old, he travelled south to the city of Shinar (probably what we know as present-day Babylon in Iraq) and worked on the building of the Tower of Babel (Genesis: Chapter 11). After the Tower eventually collapsed, Haik, a handsome man and a strong warrior (despite his age) with curly hair and good eyesight was able to defy even Nimrod (or Bel as he is known in the legend), the tyrannical ruler of Assyria. Nimrod had ordered that he should be worshipped by his people but Haik refused and moved back north with his family (including his 300 sons) to the lands around Ararat. Nimrod resented Haik's departure, and ordered him back, even seeking to lure him by reminding him that Armenia had a less favourable climate than Assyria. When Haik refused, Nimrod marched north with his army (which outnumbered Haik's) and battle was joined on the shores of Lake Van. Nimrod, according to the legend, wore iron armour but Haik drew his bow, and shot him with a three-feathered arrow which pierced the armour killing the king. Seeing this happen, the Assyrian army turned and fled. Haik returned to Ararat and died at the age of 400. The discovery of boundary stones and of Babylonian writings dating from Nimrod's reign confirm the battle and the manner of Nimrod's death as described in the legend.

The name Armenia by which everybody else knows the country was first used by Greek historians about 3,000 years ago although in legend the name commemorates the great leader of the country Aram who was sixth in line of descent from Haik.

ANCIENT HISTORY Crudely worked stone tools found on the slopes of Mount Aragats have been dated to around 600,000 to 800,000 years ago and more sophisticated ones such as spear points and knives to the period between 40,000 and 100,000 years ago. The transition from hunting and gathering to a more settled way of life sustained by agriculture began in Armenia in the Arax Valley about 10000BC. However, the first people to leave significant traces on the Armenian landscape did so in the form of **petroglyphs**, or images carved on rock, which can be found in various regions of Armenia. Those in the Gueghamian Mountains west of Lake Sevan have been studied in detail but the carvings in other regions are similar. They are believed to date from around the period 5000–3000BC. The oldest show both wild animals such as deer, wild boar, wolves, foxes, snakes, rabbits, storks and game birds as well as the earliest domestic animals such as dogs and goats. Pictures of hunters using bows, clubs or slings are common and the hunters are often accompanied by their dogs. However, the carvings also show many animals tethered or bound indicating that some of the game may have been kept alive either for future consumption or even for breeding.

In the later carvings the portrayal of human figures had developed considerably from the original vertical line with a circle for the head. As well as outstretched or raised arms some figures began to have waving arms as one of the first representations of movement. There are also many carvings of celestial bodies: the sun, moon, stars, and also lightning. Some of the later carvings show a multitude of carts and chariots drawn by oxen or bulls with stellar symbols on their fronts and these are likely to be connected with a cult of the sun.

Little is known about these hunters but during the period when the later carvings were created a series of villages and fortified settlements developed in the Arax Valley based on **metalworking**. Local high-quality supplies of ore led to the forging of copper and bronze and then the smelting of iron by around 3000BC. Artefacts found in these settlements include black-varnished red and grey pottery in geometric patterns, similar to those of contemporary Minoan culture. Burial goods suggest a religious belief centred on the sun and planets. Armenia has two monuments from this period believed to be astral observatories. At Metsamor (Armavir province) there is a series of stone platforms dated to 2800BC oriented towards Sirius, the brightest star visible, and there are also numerous carvings showing the position of stars in the night sky together with a compass pointing east.

At Karahunj (near Sisian in Syunik province) there is an elaborate arrangement of stones in which holes are bored strongly suggesting an astronomical purpose and possibly enabling the tracking of solar and lunar phases. It has even been suggested that it was in Armenia at this period that the signs of the zodiac were named: certainly the animal signs are all of creatures which would have been familiar in Armenia with no obvious omissions apart possibly from the leopard.

URARTU These early peoples spoke a variety of languages but, probably around 1165BC, another people migrated into Armenia and they spoke the language from which present-day Armenian is descended. Their close affinity to the Phrygians (who lived in the north of present-day Turkey) is attested by classical writers such as Herodotus and Eudoxus and this suggests that they came into Armenia from the west.

During the 9th century BC the empire of Urartu developed eventually to incorporate much of Anatolia and most of present-day Armenia. Why the local rulers should have decided to co-operate under central leadership is not clear but it may have been the result of increasing Assyrian aggression. By the reign of the Urartian king Sarduri I (reigned c840–c825BC) the capital had been established at Tushpa, present-day Van in Turkey. Expansion was achieved through a series of military campaigns with Argishti I (reigned c785–c763BC) extending Urartian territory as far as present-day Gyumri and his successors taking the land west and south of Lake Sevan. Urartian expansion provoked Assyrian concern and in 735BC the Assyrian king Tiglath Pileser III invaded as far as Van. It was not, however, until 715BC that Urartu began to suffer a series of catastrophic defeats, not just against the Assyrians but also against other neighbours, and in 714BC King Rusa I committed suicide on hearing news of the sack of the temple at Musasir. The 7th century BC was to become a period of irreversible decline with Urartu finally disappearing around 590BC: it did, however, outlive Assyria which had fallen to Babylon in 612BC and its name survives to this day in the form of Mount Ararat.

This first state on Armenian territory, Urartu was briefly an important regional power able to rival powerful neighbours. An inscription reveals that it had 79 gods of whom 16 were female. Clearly the most important was Tushpa, god of war: he had over three times the volume of sacrifices offered to his nearest rival. Seventeen bulls and 34 sheep were specified, presumably on some regular basis. The accumulation of animal remains in temples must have been a problem: a room at one site yielded to archaeologists 4,000 headless sheep and calves sacrificed over a 35-year period. Armenia's metalworking skills were important in sustaining Urartu and irrigation works supplied water to vineyards, orchards and crops. The empire was more or less self-sufficient in most goods with the exception of tin (needed to make bronze) which was probably imported from Afghanistan. However, fragments of Chinese silk have been found, providing evidence of foreign trade.

Urartu's cities, linked by a network of good roads, were well developed with high walls, moats, and towers at their entrance gates. One Assyrian opponent claimed that the walls reached to 240 cubits – around 120m – but this looks suspiciously like exaggeration to prove his own valour. Van probably had a population of around 50,000 while Armavir had around 30,000. Numerous forts were built throughout the country for defence and as bases for future attacks. They were built in defensible sites and surrounded by walls whose height may have reached 20m and whose walls were from 2m to 3m thick. They were constructed of massive stone blocks up to a height of 2m. Above this level construction was in mud brick.

FOREIGN RULE AFTER URARTU The Medes dealt the final blow to Urartu in 590BC. What happened to the Armenians subsequently is not clear but during the 6th century BC the Persian Achaemenids under Darius extended their empire to include the country. Political autonomy vanished, a situation that prevailed until the Persians were defeated by Alexander the Great in 331BC. However, the Persians did not seek to impose their culture or religion on their subject peoples though there was in practice probably some influence on Armenian religion – it is thought that the Persians followed an early form of Zoroastrianism which involved belief in a supreme creator God opposed by an uncreated evil spirit. The Armenians did not follow Zoroastrianism absolutely: whereas Zoroastrianism disapproved of animal sacrifice the Armenians continued to practise it, notably by sacrificing horses to the sun god. The defeat of the Persians in 331BC did not lead to Greek rule over Armenia. Armenia in fact achieved a greater degree of independence. Alexander's policy in the captured Persian Empire was to continue the existing administrative system under Iranian satraps. For Armenia he appointed Mithrenes who was probably the son of the deposed Persian king Orontes. Mithrenes took the title of King of Armenia. The Greek Empire did not long outlive Alexander's death in 323BC as there was a period of rivalry and war between his erstwhile successors. By 301BC, Seleucus had become satrap of Armenia but his dynasty was to control Armenia only nominally and sporadically with real power in the hands of the Orontid kings, the successors of Mithrenes. The impact of Greek civilisation was, however, increasingly felt and there was a partial revival of urban life which had largely disappeared under the Persians. In around 200BC the satrap Antiochus III was probably involved in the removal of the last Orontid king, Orontes IV, but ten years later he provoked the wrath of Rome through his invasion of Greece. Defeated at the Battle of Magnesia, his own generals then switched sides to Rome and for this they were rewarded by Rome in 189BC with the title of kings of independent Armenia.

EMPIRE The settlement with Rome compromised the territorial integrity of Orontid Armenia but also marked the start of a period of territorial expansion which saw the reacquisition, for the first time since defeat by the Medes in 590BC, of much of present-day Armenia. In particular the area south of Lake Sevan as far as the present-day Iranian border was taken back from the Medes. The acquisition of empire reached its apogee under Tigranes the Great who came to power in c95BC but Tigranes's success clearly created a hindrance to further Roman expansion in the east. Tigranes's father-in-law was Mithridates VI, King of Pontus, and Tigranes unwillingly got dragged into the (third) war between Rome and Pontus when he refused to surrender his father-in-law to the brusque and offensive Roman envoy. Tigranes's new capital Tigranocerta, which he had modestly named after himself, consequently fell to a Roman siege in 69BC and, although Tigranes subsequently made good some of the losses, his son deserted him for Rome and formed an alliance with Pompey. Tigranes was forced to make peace and Pompey rearranged the political geography. Armenia suffered considerable territorial losses and Antiochus I, a distant descendant of Darius the Great, became king. For the next 80 years Armenia, although independent, had kings appointed by Rome and it became increasingly dependent on Rome for keeping them in power. In due course Roman authority weakened and by the 50s AD Rome was unable to prevent the Parthians imposing their choice of king, Trdat I, on Armenia. After a period of instability reflected in further fighting it was agreed by Parthians and Romans in AD63 that Trdat would be king of Armenia but crowned by the Roman emperor Nero.

There then began a fairly stable period for the Armenian kingdom with the kings holding the throne with Roman approval. This was punctuated by the Roman emperor Trajan's policy of expansion which saw Armenia conquered in AD114 only for the Romans to suffer defeat and withdraw after a rebellion in AD116. In AD253, Armenia was captured by the Persian Sasanians and it remained under Persian rule until a Roman victory over Persia in AD298. There were Christians elsewhere in the region from around AD100 and by AD300 there were Christians in Armenia, albeit in small numbers and with few in the elite. Zoroastrianism remained the main religion and animal sacrifice continued to be practised.

CONVERSION TO CHRISTIANITY The adoption of Christianity as the state religion of Armenia, the first country in which this happened, is perhaps the single most important event in Armenian history. Although traditionally said to have happened in 301 there is debate over the precise date but it had certainly happened by 314. King Trdat IV held power, like his predecessors, with the support of Rome against the continuing threat from Persia. The precise date of Armenia's conversion is interesting as it reflects differently on Trdat's motives depending on when it was: AD301 was before the persecution of the Christians by the Roman emperor Diocletian in 303 and it was also before the Roman edict of toleration of Christianity in 311 and the conversion of the Emperor Constantine in 312. A later date for Armenia's conversion suggests a much closer alignment with imperial thinking, as adopting Christianity in 314 would have been more than likely to please an emperor who had himself just become a Christian. There is an account of Armenia's conversion which claims to have been written by a contemporary but in reality it was written c460, a century-and-a-half after the events. In this account, well known and much quoted in Armenia, Trdat had Gregory the Illuminator, who was in his service, tortured to persuade him to give up Christianity. Gregory refused and Trdat additionally realised that Gregory's father had murdered his, Trdat's, father. As a consequence Trdat then had Gregory imprisoned in a snake-infested pit for 12 years at a place now occupied by the monastery of Khor Virap, and he also persecuted other Christians including the nuns Hripsime (whom Trdat tried to rape) and Gayane who were refugees fleeing from Rome. Divine punishment was sent: Trdat is said to have behaved like a wild boar (though in what respect he imitated these rather engaging animals is not clear), while torments fell on his household and demons possessed the people of the city. Eventually Trdat's sister had a vision after which Gregory was released, the martyrs were buried and the afflicted were cured. Trdat himself proclaimed Christianity the state religion, and Gregory became Bishop of Caesarea.

Conversion required much change in social customs and this change did not happen quickly. In particular Zoroastrianism permitted polygamy and it promoted consanguineous marriages between the closest of relatives as being particularly virtuous. A Church council in 444 needed to condemn the apparently continuing practice of consanguineous marriage while as late as 768 another needed to emphasise that a *third* marriage is detestable adultery and an inexpiable sin. The Church also found it difficult to suppress mourning customs including wailing, pulling of hair, rending of garments, slashing of arms and faces, dancing and the playing of trumpets.

PARTITIONED ARMENIA By c387 Rome and Persia had decided to abolish Armenia as an independent state and to divide the country between them, a move which was finally accomplished with the removal of the last Armenian king in 428. The intervening 40 years were ones of weakness, decline and foreign domination though with a strengthening Christian presence. Present-day Armenia lies in the part which came under Persian rule after 428. A major hindrance to the acceptance of Christianity was removed through the creation in c400 of the Armenian alphabet by Mesrop Mashtots. This permitted the Scriptures to be made available in Armenian for the first time and for other religious works to be published. Although this important education programme was centred in Persian-controlled Armenia, permission was obtained from the Roman Empire (whose capital had by this time been moved to Constantinople) to set up schools there as well. However, the Persian monarchy's increasing dependence on the Zoroastrian religious establishment led to pressure on Armenian Christians under Persian rule to convert to Zoroastrianism. The first crisis occurred in 450 when taxes were imposed on the Church and the nobility was ordered to convert. The Armenians, in alliance with some Huns, inflicted heavy casualties on a much larger Persian force at the Battle of Avarayr in 451. Although the Armenians were ultimately defeated and their leader Vardan Mamikonian killed, Armenians see it as a moral victory because continuing resistance subsequently resulted in the taxes being removed and freedom of religion granted, although the patriarch and some clergy were executed and many nobles were imprisoned. Persia continued to discriminate in favour of Zoroastrians in making important appointments, a situation which prevailed until the death of the Persian king in 484.

Roman expansion finally restarted in the 6th century but it was to make little headway despite several campaigns against Persia until 591 after which the frontier was redrawn to place some of the western parts of present-day Armenia under Roman rule: the new border ran just west of Garni. However, neither Rome nor Persia was prepared for a new wave of invaders – Arabs who, from the 630s, invaded, fighting in the name of Islam. The Persians were soon defeated and the Romans lost major provinces. By 661, Armenia was under Arab rule though there were promises of religious freedom. Armenian revolts in the early 8th century gave rise to some temporary Arab repression but it was only from the rule of Caliph Umar I (717–20) onwards that Armenian Christianity was seriously threatened. Orders were given that Christian images should be torn down, financial levies were increased and pressure was applied to convert to Islam. This stimulated the creation of a cycle of rebellion, harsher treatment, another rebellion, even harsher treatment, until by c800 annual taxation on Armenia amounted to 13 million dirhams, 20,000 pounds of fish, 20 carpets, 200 mules, 30 falcons and 580 pieces of cloth. Under these conditions many Armenians chose to leave the country for Roman areas.

RESTORATION OF MONARCHY Conditions eased in the 9th century to the extent that the caliph agreed in 884 to the restoration of Armenian monarchy for the first time in 456 years and Ashot I was crowned King of Armenia, the first ruler of the Bagratid dynasty. For the next 40 years, however, Armenia went through a period of continued unrest as different leaders struggled with each other for power and territory. In addition, a prolonged rebellion against the caliph led by his governor in Azerbaijan, who was responsible for collecting Armenian taxes, led to both caliph and governor presenting their own separate tax bills. Armenia was not a united nation but this time was one of a great flourishing of Armenian scholarship, literature and church building. This was particularly the case during the reign of King Abas (928–52) who succeeded in establishing a degree of security, but during the 960s and 970s after his death, the renewed struggle for succession led to increasing fragmentation of the country and by the end of the

10th century there were five separate Armenian kingdoms – three Bagratid (based at Kars, Ani and Lori); one Artsruni based in Vaspurakan east of Lake Van, and one Syunian in the south of present-day Armenia. Armenia's political fragmentation, however, inevitably left it unable to cope with renewed expansion by the Roman Empire's successors in Byzantium during the 11th century, though Byzantine rule was to be benign in comparison with the new invaders from the south, the Seljuk Turks, who ravaged cities and brought political and economic disruption even to the Byzantium-controlled areas after 1045. The victory of the Seljuk Turks over the Romans in 1071 led to the latter's demise as a significant power and to the establishment of Seljuk rule over Armenia. The immediate consequence of the Seljuk conquest was another period of migration: this time to areas such as Georgia, Ukraine and Syria. A new separate Armenian kingdom arose in Cilicia (on the Aegean coast of Turkey) which was to last until it was overrun in 1375 by the Mamluks, the Turkish military dynasty which then ruled Egypt. Although important in Armenian history, Cilicia lies wholly outside present-day Armenia and is therefore not relevant to this guidebook.

Seljuk power in turn waned and in a series of campaigns culminating in 1204, a Georgian army which included many Armenians defeated the sultan's forces. Georgian influence increased, reflected in the style of a number of Armenia's finest churches in present-day Lori province, only for Armenia to be conquered yet again, this time by the Mongols in a series of campaigns culminating in 1244. High taxation created the usual resentment and rebellion. In 1304 matters worsened for Armenians when Islam became the official religion of the Mongol Empire and religious persecution became a matter of policy. In turn Mongol power declined and between 1357 and 1403, following a series of invasions by the Mamluks, tens of thousands of Armenians were transported as slaves. By 1400, most of Armenia had passed to a Turkmen dynasty called the Black Sheep. A second Turkmen dynasty, called the White Sheep, became established further west.

RUSSIA VERSUS TURKEY The end of the Byzantine Empire came in 1453 when the Ottomans took Constantinople (Istanbul). Further Ottoman aggression saw Armenia itself conquered and taken from the White Sheep, who were now ruling it, by the 1530s. Yet again Armenia became a battleground as hostility grew between the Ottomans and Persia, until in 1639 the two powers agreed that western Armenia would be controlled by Turkey and eastern Armenia by Persia. A further wave of emigration from the Persian territories began around 1700 because of taxation and persecution; this time many went to India. A local rebellion in southern Armenia led by David Bek, together with invasion in 1722 by Russian forces under Peter the Great, saw Persian rule largely end and in 1724 most Persian territory was divided between the Ottomans and Russia although Persia retained Nagorno Karabagh. David Bek died in 1728 and in 1730 his successor Mkhitar Sparapet was betrayed by Armenian villagers as a result of Turkish threats. That same year David Bek's territory, centred at Tatev, fell to Turkey. Russian expansionism in the area restarted under Catherine the Great. In the conquered lands, largely Muslim, Russian policy was to encourage Christians to settle and Muslims to leave. Starting in 1796 the Russians began a further series of campaigns conquering the west Caucasian khanates. These khanates were effectively autonomous Turkish principalities (although nominally vassals of the Persians under the 1724 treaty) and they occupied an area roughly equivalent to present-day Armenia and Azerbaijan.

At that time Armenians, having been subject to so many varieties of foreign rule, and often persecution, for so long, were scattered throughout the Caucasus and eastern Anatolia rather than concentrated in the Armenian heartland. However, in 1826 Russia began a forced exchange of population which resulted ultimately in the creation of an Armenian-dominated state in the khanate of Yerevan. Russia gained dominance in the south Caucasus by defeating Persia in the war of 1826–28 and the Ottomans in the war of 1828–29 and these victories further encouraged Armenians to migrate into Russian-controlled areas of Armenia while they simultaneously continued to encourage Turks to leave. Conditions in Ottoman-controlled regions were certainly difficult for Christians. Muslim courts did not even allow testimony from them until 1854 and even after that it was usually discounted. Christians paid higher taxes than Muslims, and they were not allowed to bear arms to defend themselves whereas Muslims were. The conditions within Ottoman-controlled Armenia became known in the West through exiles, travellers' publications and official reports, and started to cause wide concern.

BRITAIN AND ARMENIA Britain and Turkey were on the opposite side to Russia in the Crimean War. The treaty which ended the war in 1856 required Russia to evacuate some Armenian areas which it had occupied during the war. Although this was put into effect, British officers on the spot, especially in the 1870s, were still stressing the risk to the trade routes across the Ottoman Empire which they believed were threatened by Russia's renewed interest in southerly expansion. In 1877, the British ambassador in Constantinople went so far as to write (considerably exaggerating) that in the event of a Russian conquest of Armenia: 'The consequence would be the greatest blow ever struck at the British Empire.' Britain therefore supported Turkey against Russia though there was a simultaneous British realisation that Turkey's chance of retaining Armenia would be greater if it treated the native Armenian population better. The British government's concern, however, was with who controlled Armenia and hence the trade routes. It was not with the Armenian people except insofar as their support for Russia would weaken Turkey's hold on the region.

Russia again defeated the Ottomans in 1877–78, thereby gaining control of eastern Anatolia. The three treaties of 1878 are crucial to understanding subsequent British concern over Armenia. The first was signed between Russia and Turkey in March. In it Turkey ceded large areas to Russia and this, of course, increased British concern about the threat to trade routes. In the second, signed in June, Britain promised to defend Turkey against further Russian aggression in exchange for two commitments by Turkey: one was to hand Cyprus over to Britain; and the other was to agree with Britain reforms which would improve the lot of Christians in the Ottoman territories – principally Armenia. The third treaty, signed in July, restored to Turkey large areas which had been ceded in March. In it Turkey also promised to introduce reforms to improve the lot of the Armenians. Crucially those reforms no longer had to be agreed with Britain, and Russia was to evacuate the specified areas even before the reforms had been introduced. What had been in June 1878 Britain's responsibility to enforce became in July nobody's. Moreover in July the sultan lost any real threat of action being taken if he did not comply, as the power best able to make him do so, Russia, was the last which Britain wished to see involved. It was this crucial abandonment of British influence on the plight of the Armenians, together with the increasingly harsh and cruel treatment of the Christian Armenians by the Muslim Turks and Kurds, which led the devoutly Christian and humane Gladstone to make the Armenians' plight the subject of the last major speech of his career in 1896. His speech to an audience of 6,000 in his home city of Liverpool led to the resignation of the leader of his party, Lord Rosebery, a fortnight later. There is no doubt that the removal of pressure on the sultan by Britain between June and July 1878 led to the disastrous consequences culminating in the genocide of 1915.

The Muslim Ottoman government saw Christian Armenians as likely supporters of the Christian Russian conquerors: other Christian parts of the Ottoman Empire such as Greece and Bulgaria had already experienced revolution with foreign support. The Armenians meanwhile saw the Ottomans as oppressors of their increasingly nationalistic feelings just as the Greeks and Bulgarians already had. Consequently the migration of both Christian Armenians and Muslim Turks increased after the Russian victory in 1878. Demonstrations by Armenians for greater autonomy and against the imposition of tribute demanded by local Kurds were violently suppressed (over 1,000 demonstrators were massacred on one occasion) and a refusal to pay the tribute demanded by the Kurds in addition to government taxes led to weeks of slaughter. Western ambassadors protested about the excessive violence used against the demonstrators but took no other action, not even when 300,000 Armenians died in the pogroms of 1894–96. Conditions grew even worse when the Young Turk movement, which had previously promulgated a programme of reform and courted the Armenian population, changed tack and adopted in 1909 a policy of Turkisation of all Ottoman subjects. This was strengthened by a growing pro-Islam movement. Twenty thousand were massacred among the Armenian community in Cilicia that year, ostensibly to prevent an Armenian uprising.

Meanwhile in the Russian-controlled areas, the climate of liberalism was in recession. The Russian government was no more enthusiastic about Armenian nationalism than the Ottoman, and a policy of Russification, similar to that adopted at the time in other parts of the Russian Empire such as Finland, came into being. Armenian schools, societies and libraries were closed. References in print to the Armenian nation or people were banned and Armenian Church property was taken over by the Tsar. Not surprisingly many Armenians emigrated, principally to the USA.

WORLD WAR I AND GENOCIDE The Ottoman Empire entered World War I on the German side but it was already in a state of rapid decline: between 1908 and 1912 it had lost 33% of its territory and the Armenians were the only significant Christian people to remain under Ottoman rule. In 1915, Russia, which had joined the Allied side, inflicted a disastrous defeat on the Ottomans. The Ottomans saw Russian and diaspora Armenians fighting against them and this inflamed their existing suspicions concerning the loyalty of their Armenian subjects: their knowledge of how they had treated the Armenians would in any case hardly have reassured them concerning their likely loyalty. The 60,000 Armenians serving in the Ottoman forces were quickly demobilised and organised into labour groups in February 1915, only to be massacred by April. It was also ordered that Armenians living in regions near the war front should be moved to the Syrian Desert and the Mesopotamian Valley with the clear expectation that, even if they survived the forced marches under difficult conditions, they would not survive the inhospitable terrain and hostile tribesmen of these regions for long. In reality, not only those Armenians in the frontier regions but also those living nowhere near the frontier regions were deported and then either massacred or left to starve in the desert. Large-scale massacres of Armenians developed, including the Armenian intelligentsia in Constantinople and other cities who were arrested on 24 April and then murdered. There is some dispute as to the authenticity of evidence, which suggests that it was the central Ottoman government which ordered the massacres, though they were evidently carefully planned as they were carried out simultaneously in all regions of the Ottoman Empire, but there is no doubt at all that around 1.5 million Armenians died in the first genocide of the 20th century. It was recognised as such by the European Parliament in 1987 and by Western governments including Germany, Switzerland, Italy, the Vatican, Sweden, Belgium and Canada (but not the UK or USA). However, no Turkish government has ever accepted that these very well-attested events happened. The message of the genocide was not lost on Adolf Hitler, a keen student of history, who, on the eve of his invasion of Poland in 1939 rallied his generals with the words: 'Who still talks nowadays of the extermination of the Armenians?'

THE FIRST ARMENIAN REPUBLIC Following the Russian Revolution in November 1917, Russian forces began withdrawing from the areas of Ottoman Armenia which they had occupied: Lenin was well aware that disillusion with the war was rampant in the Russian army and that withdrawal was necessary to ensure the soldiers' loyalty. Consequently in Anatolia, Armenians were fighting the Ottomans virtually alone. There was a short respite from fighting following the formation in Moscow of a Caucasian federation on 24 April 1918 uniting Armenia, Georgia and Azerbaijan but ethnic and religious differences quickly led to its demise. Turkey then started a new offensive attacking Armenia from the west while Russian Menshevik and Turkish forces based in Azerbaijan attacked from the north and east. The Turks advancing from the west were initially successful, retaking the territory west of the Arax River and capturing Alexandropol (Gyumri) on 15 May. They invaded the Arax Valley, occupying the village and railway station of Sardarapat on 21 May from which they launched an offensive towards Yerevan the following day. It was to be a decisive defeat for Turkey. For three days the Turks attacked the Armenian forces under Daniel-Bek Pirumian but were repelled and on 24 May the Armenians went over to the offensive and routed the Turks. The victory at Sardarapat followed by others at Bash-Aparan and Gharakilisa between 24 and 28 May led to a declaration of independence on 28 May 1918 when the first Republic of Armenia was established under the Dashnak Party. The territories of Nakhichevan and Nagorno Karabagh were incorporated into the Armenian republic but were excluded from Armenia only a week later when Armenia and Turkey signed a peace treaty at Batum on 4 June. However, Turkey's involvement in World War I ended with its capitulation on 30 October and the question of Nakhichevan and Nagorno Karabagh was automatically reopened.

The Armenians hoped that the victorious Allies would keep their promises and enlarge the borders of the new Armenian state after the armistice in November. Eventually the Treaty of Sèvres in August 1920 granted Armenia borders which were adjudicated by President Woodrow Wilson of the USA in November of that year. Meanwhile, Turkey had invaded Armenia in September and seized part of the country. In parallel to these events the Bolsheviks had invaded Armenia in April 1920 and the combined pressure of Turks and Bolsheviks caused the collapse of the Armenian government, notwithstanding the deliberations about its borders taking place far away in France. In reality, acceptance of Bolshevik rule was for the Armenians the only real defence against the Turks. Armenia was formally incorporated into the Transcaucasian Soviet Federated Socialist Republic on 29 November 1920.

The Bolsheviks made large territorial concessions to Turkey, notably by handing over areas which had been under Russian rule even prior to 1914 including the historic Bagratid capital of Ani and the city of Kars. Soviet historians have claimed that the Bolsheviks wanted a quick agreement with Turkey because they believed that a Turkish delegation was in London where David Lloyd George, much more in favour of newly secularised Turkey under Ataturk than Bolshevik Russia under Lenin, was offering Turkey rule over the Caucasus as a protectorate. This protectorate, the Bolsheviks believed, would include Armenia but, much more important from both Russian and Western perspectives, the Baku oilfields in Azerbaijan. It is, however, more likely that Lenin's real motive was to encourage Ataturk whom he (mistakenly) believed would be an ardent supporter of the communist cause. He probably also believed that Turkey was militarily too strong for Russia to be able to win a campaign in Armenia and these two factors led to Russia's concurrence with Turkey's proposals for the border. Had any Armenians been involved in the Moscow discussions between Russia and Turkey it is inconceivable that Ani would have been relinquished. The Treaty of Sèvres was formally replaced in 1923 by the Treaty of Lausanne, effectively abandoning any pretence of Western support for an independent Armenia and reconfirming the message of 1878 that the Western powers, whatever their feelings about the sufferings of the Armenian people, would relegate action to the 'too difficult' pile.

SOVIET ARMENIA From 1921 Lenin made overtures to the new Turkish government, led by Ataturk, which was under attack by Greek forces, Turkey having reneged on its promise to return historic Greek lands in Asia Minor in return for Greek support during the war. By 1921, Greek troops were approaching Ankara. Soviet Russia initially helped Turkey, Lenin still believing that Ataturk was intent on building a socialist state on the Soviet model. Lenin also agreed with Turkey that Nagorno Karabagh, Nakhichevan, Syunik and Zangezur would be incorporated into Azerbaijan. However, Lenin eventually came to realise that Ataturk had no intention of building a socialist state and withdrew support. Meanwhile, led by Garegin Nzhdeh, an Armenian who had fought successful guerrilla campaigns against the Turks during Bulgaria's struggle for independence, Armenian forces fought a successful campaign in Syunik and Zangezur (southern Armenia) against the Red Army and the Turks simultaneously. Stalemate developed and Nzhdeh forced Lenin to compromise and accept his terms that Syunik and Zangezur would be incorporated into the Republic of Armenia rather than into Azerbaijan. He can thus be seen as the person who saved the south of Armenia for the country. Subsequently he went into exile and, after Hitler's coming to power, pursued fruitless negotiations with Nazi Germany in an attempt to regain for Armenia the lands occupied by Turkey. He died in a Soviet prison in 1955 but his remains were secretly returned to Armenia in 1983. He is buried at beautiful (but little-visited) Spitakavor Monastery in Vayots Dzor province.

Between 1921 and 1924 Armenia witnessed a resurgence of intellectual and cultural life and Armenian intellectuals, believing that they at last had a homeland, came from abroad, notably the architect Alexander Tamanian who had drawn up ambitious plans for the creation of a fine capital for the First Republic and who returned to complete his plans. These resulted in the creation of the buildings around Republic Square, possibly the finest of all Soviet architectural ensembles, admittedly not a field in which the competition is stiff. He also planned green belts, gardens and residential areas for a city capable of housing a then unimaginable population of 150,000. Yerevan State University was also constructed and professors were recruited from the West. This was also the era of Lenin's New Economic Policy, forced on him by the failure of communist orthodoxy to deliver material benefit, and limited private enterprise was consequently tolerated.

In 1923, Stalin, who was then Commissar for Nationalities, adopted a divide and rule policy which led to Nagorno Karabagh (whose population was largely

Armenian, according to most sources, although this is disputed by Azerbaijan) and Nakhichevan (which had a substantial Armenian minority) being placed in Azerbaijan. Additionally the new Soviet republics were created in such a way that they did not have continuous boundaries: for example, isolated villages deep inside Armenia were designated part of Azerbaijan. This was a deliberate, conscious attempt by Stalin to encourage ethnic tensions between Armenians and Azeris so as to discourage them from uniting together against Soviet rule. The Transcaucasian Federation was abolished in 1936 and Armenia became a Soviet republic in its own right though still with the artificial 1923 boundaries.

Economic growth was impressive but the abolition of the New Economic Policy caused considerable resentment, especially among farmers. Although Armenia did not suffer deliberate mass starvation during the forced collectivisation of agriculture in the same way as Ukraine did in 1932–33, it did suffer along with other parts of the Soviet Union during Stalin's purges between 1934 and 1939. At least 100,000 Armenians were victims. Persecution of Christians also reached a height in the mid to late 1930s and all churches except Ejmiatsin were closed by 1935. The head of the Church was murdered in 1938 and the entire Armenian political leadership along with most intellectuals was condemned to death for the crime of bourgeois nationalism (ie: being perceived by Stalin as a threat to himself).

Stalin's pact with Hitler in August 1939 did not save the Soviet Union from attack for long and Germany invaded on 22 June 1941. German troops never reached Armenia: they approached no closer than the north Caucasus where the oilfields around Grozny were a principal objective as Hitler simultaneously wanted to secure their output for Germany and to deprive the Soviet Union. About 630,000 Armenians out of a then population of two million fought during World War II (or the Great Patriotic War as it is called throughout the former Soviet Union) of whom about half died.

Armenia experienced rapid growth after 1945 with Yerevan's population increasing from 50,000 to 1.3 million. Huge chemical plants were established in Yerevan, Leninakan (Gyumri) and Kirovakan (Vanadzor) and Armenia became one of the most highly educated and most industrialised of the Soviet republics. By contrast, a new wave of repression began in 1947 with the deportees being exiled to the infamous gulag camps of Siberia. After Stalin's death, probably by poisoning at the instigation of the secret police chief Lavrentii Beria, conditions relaxed and during the Brezhnev era (1964–82) dissenters were merely certified insane and kept among the genuinely mentally ill in mental hospitals.

The coming to power of Gorbachev in 1985 saw an upsurge in Armenian nationalism, especially over the question of the enclave of Nagorno Karabagh. Gorbachev refused to allow its transfer from Azerbaijan to Armenia. There were demonstrations in both republics and, especially following Soviet government inaction after the killing of 30 (or some estimates claim up to 120) Armenians by their Azeri neighbours at Sumgait, an industrial city north of Baku, in February 1988 many Armenians fled from Azerbaijan to Armenia while at the same time many Azeris fled in the opposite direction. This unprecedented killing shocked the Soviet Union; the perpetrators were tried and sentenced in Moscow. Thereafter ethnic tensions continued to rise and during the fighting over Nagorno Karabagh there were civilian deaths on both sides. Perhaps the incident which gained most international notice and condemnation was the deaths of 161–613 (numbers are disputed) Azeri civilians, fired on by Armenian forces in February 1992, as they tried to leave Khojaly, near Aghdam, as it was about to be occupied by Armenian forces. (Khojaly was used as a military base by the Azeris to shell Stepanakert.) In July

THE CHANGED POLITICAL SITUATION
FOLLOWING THE 1994 CEASE-FIRE

KEY

- International boundary
- Pre 1991 Autonomous Region of Nagorno Karabagh
- Post 1994 Self-declared Republic of Nagorno Karabagh

KEY

- Territory lost by Armenia to Azerbaijan
- Territory lost by Azerbaijan to Armenia

GEORGIA

AZERBAIJAN

NAGORNO KARABAGH

STEPANAKERT

Caucasus

Lesser

Lake Sevan

ARMENIA

Closed border

Closed border

Closed border

Mo Mountains

Kapan

Tatev

Sisian

Goris

Vardenis

Jermuk

Martuni

Gavar

Noravank

Meghri

NAKHICHEVAN
(Azerbaijan)

IRAN

Geghard

Garni

Tigranashen

Ararat

YEREVAN

ABOVIAN

HRAZDAN

Serap

Dilijan

Gosavank

Haghartsin

Sanahin

Haghpat

ALAVERDI

Stepanavan

Spitak

VANADZOR

Ijevan

Mt Ararat
5165m

4090m
Aragats

Ashtarak

EJMIATSIN

Armavir

GYUMRI

Ani

Tashir

Mameuli,
Tbilisi

Mameuli,
Tbilisi

Akhalkalaki,
Batumi

TURKEY

Closed border

0 — 50km
0 — 30 miles

N
Bradt

23

1988, Nagorno Karabagh declared its secession from Azerbaijan and in December the pressure group known as the Karabagh Committee, which had meanwhile broadened its objectives to include democratic change within Armenia itself, was arrested and held in Moscow without trial for six months. In early 1989, Moscow imposed direct rule on Nagorno Karabagh and rebellion broke out. In November that year Armenia declared that Nagorno Karabagh was a part of Armenia (a claim it no longer makes) as a result of which Turkey and Azerbaijan closed their borders with Armenia and imposed an economic blockade: the problems this caused were greatly exacerbated because of the closure, as a precautionary measure, of Metsamor nuclear power station following the major earthquake in December 1988.

THE THIRD REPUBLIC In July 1990, elections were won by the Armenian National Movement which had developed from the Karabagh Committee. Its leader, Levon Ter-Petrossian, became president of the Armenian Supreme Soviet which declared independence from the Soviet Union in August. (This was quite legal as, under the Soviet constitution, all republics were nominally free to secede.) The new government took a moderate line over the Nagorno Karabagh dispute and tried to distance itself from the fighting. The collapse of the Soviet Union in August 1991, following the failed putsch against Gorbachev, was followed by a referendum on 21 September in which the population of Armenia overwhelmingly voted in favour of independence. Meanwhile Azerbaijan likewise declared itself independent. However, after Armenia signed a mutual assistance treaty with Russia and certain other members of the Confederation of Independent States (CIS) in May 1992, Russia started supplying arms to Armenia which was able to drive Azerbaijan out of most of Nagorno Karabagh, the area between Armenia and Nagorno Karabagh, as well as border areas with Iran. After the death of around 25,000 combatants a ceasefire was declared in 1994 and largely holds firm at the time of writing. During the conflict the closure of the Turkish and Azerbaijan borders together with frequent sabotage of the gas pipelines in southern Georgia (used to supply gas to Armenia) resulted in Armenia becoming heavily dependent on Iran for supplies. It might now be possible to resolve the dispute if Armenia were willing to give up the southernmost part of its territory bordering Iran in exchange for Nagorno Karabagh, but the Armenian government's understandable wish to retain this direct link with Iran makes any short-term settlement of the dispute unlikely. Meanwhile Azerbaijan apparently hopes that Russia will lose interest in the area and cease supporting Armenia.

Armenia adopted a new presidential constitution in 1995 and in September 1996 Ter-Petrossian was re-elected president. Ter-Petrossian appointed Robert Kocharian, a former leader of Nagorno Karabagh, as prime minister and he was elected president in turn when Ter-Petrossian resigned in 1998. Parliamentary elections in May 1999 brought the opposition Unity Alliance to power with Vagen Sarkisian of the nationalist Republican Party (HHK) as prime minister and Karen Demirchian (loser of the presidential election) as speaker but on 27 October 1999 both of them, along with six others, were assassinated when gunmen stormed into parliament. The trial of the killers in late 2001 has not clarified the motives behind the attack. On 22 March 2000, Arkady Gukasian, the president of the self-declared Republic of Nagorno Karabagh, narrowly escaped an assassination attempt for which the former defence minister Samuel Babayan was jailed for 14 years.

A bitter struggle for power within the Armenian government led to some senior ministers being ousted and by mid 2001 the People's Party of Armenia (HZhK, led by Stepan Demirchian, son of the assassinated speaker) was becoming unhappy with its role as junior partner in the ruling coalition. Some of its members joined communists and the Hanrapetutian (Republic) party of former prime minister Aram Sarkisian (the assassinated prime minister's brother) in blocking an important bill on civil service reform. In August 2001, Kocharian proposed controversial changes to the constitution while the opposition predictably called on him to resign. In September 2001, HZhK left the coalition and joined the opposition in calling for Kocharian's impeachment on charges of violating the constitution, condoning terrorism, and causing a political and economic crisis. A further scandal blew up that month when an Armenian resident of Georgia, a member of the pro-Kocharian Dashnak Party, was beaten to death in the gentlemen's toilet of Yerevan's Aragast jazz club by members of Kocharian's bodyguard. The president had just left the club and the bodyguard apparently objected to anti-Kocharian remarks which they had heard him making. The following month around 25,000 joined anti-Kocharian demonstrations and 400,000 signed a petition demanding his resignation. A conspicuous feature of the subsequent trial of one of the bodyguards on the fairly minor charge of involuntary manslaughter was the unwillingness of any of the several dozen people who had witnessed the events to come forward and testify, apparently because of fear of what might happen to them at the hands of the police.

THE PRESENT In the first round of the presidential election held on 19 February 2003, there were nine candidates, all male, including the incumbent Robert Kocharian. The official result was that Kocharian had received 49.48% compared with 28.22% for Stepan Demirchian and 17% for Artashes Geghamian in third place. Since a candidate must achieve 51% of the vote for an outright victory a second round of voting was required. The entire campaign had been conducted with a great deal of mudslinging, little discussion of important issues such as education, taxation and welfare, and little in the way of specific proposals for constitutional or legislative change. Neither Demirchian, son of the parliamentary speaker assassinated in 1999, nor Geghamian even mentioned Nagorno Karabagh with all its implications for the country. However, both advocated closer ties with Russia and, though Demirchian was non-specific, Geghamian advocated joining the rouble zone, and changing Armenia's legislation in the fields of customs and taxation to match Russia's. One of Demirchian's few concrete proposals was to abandon the 1996 local government reforms and revert to the Soviet-era divisions.

Two invited teams of international observers spent six weeks in the country prior to the election. The reports of those from the Organisation for Security and Co-operation in Europe (OSCE) differ markedly from those of the CIS observers. Among the shortcomings, the OSCE observers noted that there had been pre-election intimidation and incidents of disruption of campaign events, including one instance of violence, pre-election manipulations including schemes to impersonate voters, and the heavy use of public resources in support of the incumbent. The international observers on polling day assessed the voting process positively in 90% of polling stations but noted that there were unauthorised people including government officials in 23% of polling stations who often acted in an intimidatory manner. Irregularities noted at some stations included cases of ballot-box stuffing, individuals voting more than once, a policeman carrying a box of at least 50 passports (used in the election as evidence of identity) out of a polling station and intimidation of candidates' proxies, two of whom were seen being assaulted. (In Armenian elections a proxy is the appointed representative of a candidate in a polling station, who acts as an observer on the candidate's behalf; if he notices any irregularity his report must be attached to the result of the count submitted by the returning officer.) The count itself was negatively assessed by the international observers in 20% of polling stations, some of whose results showed a striking disparity both in voter turnout and outcome from the otherwise consistent pattern of results.

The second round with two candidates was held on 5 March and resulted in a win for Kocharian with 67.44% of the vote as opposed to 32.56% for Demirchian. The OSCE observers were even more condemnatory of the process. Indeed, this time some polling stations recorded more votes than there were registered voters. Between the rounds the police arrested 142 of Demirchian's supporters on charges of hooliganism of whom 77 were given short prison sentences and the others fined. Publicly funded television and radio made no attempt to fulfil their legal obligation to report even-handedly and the state-funded newspaper *Hayastani Hanrapetutian* also gave overwhelming support to the incumbent. The extent of all this election fraud led the observers to conclude that the election 'fell short of international standards for democratic elections'. All this was in complete contrast to the CIS observers who considered the elections to be 'democratic and legitimate' with 'no mass violations of the Electoral Code'. As one local newspaper commented it was rather a 'dialogue of civilisations' with the (mostly western) European observers having different expectations from those from former Soviet republics.

The parliamentary election held on 25 May 2003 resulted in a similar clash of views although, as on previous occasions, there was less actual malpractice than in the presidential election. The Western observers referred to 'serious incidents and shortcomings' and hoped that 'there will be no return to the sense of impunity evident in the recent presidential election'. The CIS observers thought the election 'transparent and democratic' and praised the Armenian authorities for 'ensuring fair elections'. Turnout in the poll was 52% with six of the 21 parties and blocs breaking the 5% threshold required to gain seats in the new parliament. The largest share of the vote, 24.5% of the votes cast, went to the Republican Party which is supportive of the president. The next largest share of the vote, 14.2%, went to the Justice bloc led by Stepan Demirchian who had been runner-up in the presidential election in March. The Communist Party gained a mere 1.6% of the votes and bottom of the poll with 0.3% was the Fist of Armenian Braves Party.

As a result of the May 2007 parliamentary elections, in which the Republican Party led by Serge Sarkisian swept to power, and with the decision in February 2008 of the Country of Law Party to join the governing coalition, 113 seats in the National Assembly, out of a total of 131, are held by pro-government parties. The only opposition faction in parliament, the Heritage Party, holds seven seats while the remaining 11 seats are held by independents who are mostly aligned with pro-government parties.

Presidential elections were held in February 2008. Serge Sarkisian (previously Defence Minister) was declared the winner with 52.9% of votes in the first round. The election was followed by ten days of street protests by thousands of opposition supporters claiming that voting was rigged. Clashes between demonstrators and security personnel left ten dead and hundreds injured. Dozens of opposition supporters, and some innocent bystanders, were imprisoned. A 20-day state of emergency was declared. International groups criticised the detentions as being politically motivated. OSCE observers reported that the vote had mostly met international standards, although later it was found to be marred by similar problems as previous elections such as ballot stuffing, intimidation and vote buying. Sarkisian eventually took office as president in April 2008.

The next parliamentary elections are due in 2011 and presidential elections in 2013.

In Transparency International's annual surveys of corruption worldwide Armenia's relative position has declined steadily, from 88th place in 2005 to 120th in 2009. It is still rated as better than two of its neighbours, Azerbaijan (137th in 2005, 143rd in 2009) and Iran (joint 88th with Armenia in 2005, 168th in 2009). Turkey continues to beat Armenia, its position having improved to 61st place (65th in 2005). Armenia has been overtaken by Georgia which has risen from 130th place in 2005 to 66th place in 2009.

In October 2010, after what has been termed 'football diplomacy' (their presidents meeting during football matches between the two countries), Armenia and Turkey signed an accord agreeing to establish diplomatic ties and to reopen the border between the two countries. At the time of writing this agreement still has to be ratified by both parliaments. There are obstacles in both countries to the agreement although it is generally perceived that both would benefit from a reopening of the border. The main Armenian objection to the accord is the continuing refusal of Turkey to recognise as genocide the massacres of 1915. The agreement calls for a joint commission of independent historians to study the genocide issue but Armenians say that ratifying the accord would hinder international recognition of the Armenian genocide. Difficulties for Turkey include an undertaking to its ally Azerbaijan that it will not open the border with Armenia until the Nagorno Karabagh dispute is resolved and Armenia has withdrawn its forces from what Azerbaijan considers occupied territory, a move unacceptable to Armenians. However, this has not been included as a condition in the protocol for establishing diplomatic ties between Turkey and Armenia, Turkey viewing it as a parallel process which is under the auspices of the Organisation for Security and Co-operation in Europe (OSCE). Meanwhile the border remains closed.

ECONOMY

Between 1960 and 1988 Soviet Armenia achieved growth of 30% in GNP (during the same period, growth of GNP in the USA was 135%) but the following years were catastrophic for the economy. Firstly the devastating earthquake in northwest Armenia in December 1988 resulted in 25,000 deaths, 20,000 injured and 500,000 made homeless and caused huge damage to infrastructure. This was to be followed by the break-up of the Soviet Union and war with Azerbaijan so that between 1989 and 1994 GNP fell from US$4,500m to US$652m. By 1994, however, the Armenian government had launched an ambitious IMF-sponsored economic programme which has resulted in positive growth rates of about 6% or more since then. This is partly because the well-educated Armenian population has a much stronger work ethic than in some other states of the region, partly because the country has enjoyed relative political stability and partly because the support of the diaspora has been considerable. Even so, in 1998 average monthly income was as low as US$16 and about 60–70% of the population was estimated to be living below the poverty line.

By 2009 Armenia had made a full switch to a market economy and is rated the 31st most economically free nation in the world. Inflation too has been brought under control, falling from a horrific 4,964% in 1994 to as low as 2% in 2002 although there has since been an increase. Since 2005 there has been steady economic growth which has brought increasing support from international organisations such as the International Monetary Fund (IMF), World Bank and European Bank for Reconstruction and Development.

Prior to the Soviet collapse in 1991, Armenia had developed a large industrial sector, supplying machine tools, textiles and other manufactured goods to the other

Soviet republics in exchange for raw materials and energy. By 1994, most of this had closed. Given the state of the plants, the privatisation of industry has inevitably been slow but there has been renewed emphasis by the Kocharian administration and a few plants have partially reopened. There has been a reversion to small-scale **agriculture** away from the large agro-industrial complexes of the Soviet era, but the sector has considerable need for investment and updated technology. Armenia remains a net food importer, and its mineral deposits are small. This, combined with the lack of energy resources, ensures that Armenia runs a current account deficit.

Agriculture employs around 46% of the working population while 15% work in industry and 38% in services – this last figure has increased considerably as the economy has restructured. Unemployment is estimated at 15%. Another source cites 7% of the working population as unemployed although both of these figures are somewhat misleading as perhaps 70% of the population isn't actually paid wages: the many subsistence farmers, tradesmen and owners of small businesses receive no salary as such.

The main **exports** are cut diamonds (which are imported uncut – Armenia has no sources of diamonds of its own), brandy and minerals: copper and molybdenum. By value the main export trading partner is Russia at 19.7%, then Germany at 17.4%, Netherlands at 12.4%, Belgium at 8.5% (to which the diamonds go), Georgia at 7.7% and the US at 5%. The principal **imports** are natural gas, petroleum, tobacco products, foodstuffs and diamonds and the source of imports is Russia at 19%, China at 8.6%, the UK at 7%, Turkey at 6%, Germany at 5.7%, the US at 5% and Iran at 4.6%.

PEOPLE

The long periods of foreign rule, often accompanied by religious persecution, led to the Armenian people becoming widely scattered and not comprising a majority in any territory. What distinguished them as Armenians was their Church and their language. During the 19th century this changed as a result of the Russian conquest of eastern Armenia. There was a deliberate Russian policy of encouraging Christian immigration and Muslim emigration. Although the Tsarist regime was initially tolerant of Christians who were not Orthodox believers this changed as a consequence of increasing Armenian nationalism as well as more general concern about national feelings and socialism in the Russian Empire. By the end of the century a policy of deliberate Russification of subject people was being applied. The movement of population resulted, at the start of the Bolshevik regime, in the new Armenian Soviet Socialist Republic having an Armenian majority but with a significant Azeri minority. Similarly Azerbaijan had many Armenians within its boundaries, a number increased through the boundaries being deliberately gerrymandered. There was little Russian immigration to Armenia in either Tsarist or Soviet periods but the large population movements during the conflict with Azerbaijan between 1988 and 1994 resulted in massive emigration of Azeris and immigration of ethnic Armenians from Azerbaijan.

The population at the 1979 census was 3.8 million of whom 91% were ethnic Armenians. The census in February 1989 gave a population of 3.3 million but is regarded as unreliable since it took place only two months after the devastating earthquake in northwest Armenia which made obtaining data within the region almost impossible. The most recent census in October 2001 gave a figure of 3.2 million which suggested that a net 600,000 people had left the country since independence. Population estimates since 2004 indicate a steady increase, the 2008 estimate putting the population at 3.238 million. Emigration from Armenia has fallen from 9.2 to 6.7 per thousand and there has also been a small increase in the birth rate. At present about 98% of the population is ethnically Armenian, 1.3% Yezidi and 0.5% Russian.

LIFE IN ARMENIA Life for many ordinary Armenians is still far from easy. Many, perhaps even most, people in what was in Soviet times a fairly heavily industrialised country have either reverted to subsistence agriculture if they live in rural areas or else have sought to become small-scale vendors of some kind of goods or other if they live in towns. For parents it is their hope that education will help their children to escape the widespread poverty. The population has fallen by about 20% since the 1980s as a result of emigration in search of work, and the low birth rate. Yet it cannot really be said that Armenians look either despairing or unhappy. They cope with the problems and family members help each other out. It has to be said that the vast majority of those old enough to have worked in the Soviet era look back on it as a golden age – they are generally too young of course to remember Stalin's terror and overlook the failure of the Soviet Union to deal with the civil war which broke out between Armenia and Azerbaijan in 1989. Younger people see things differently and to an observer their preoccupations appear much the same as their contemporaries in the West, their mobile phones in constant use. However, they are also to be seen lighting candles in churches and on Genocide Memorial Day it was striking to see the large number of young people joining the commemoration in Yerevan.

One of the big changes has been the improvement in the water supply. Five years ago it was a significant problem. Leaking mains meant that the water supply in most towns and cities had to be restricted to a few hours a day to prevent large quantities running away to waste. Sometimes it could even be cut off for days and in both urban and rural areas water had to be stored in quantity for use when needed. Now in the towns, at least, there is usually running water 24 hours a day, although in summer there can still be supply problems, even in Yerevan. The situation in villages has also improved but in rural areas water still has either to be obtained from the village spring and carried in buckets, or else there might be a well in the garden (or even in the kitchen).

Virtually every family except for those living in flats grows as much food as it can with all the family members, children included, working hard planting and harvesting potatoes and other vegetables by hand. In late summer, women can be encountered in the villages winnowing grain, preserving fruit for the winter by drying it in the sun, and making fruit juices and homemade vodkas to last through the winter. Throughout the year they also join their neighbours in the baking of *lavash*, Armenia's classic flatbread (see box, page 83). Keeping the home clean is difficult for women as few have domestic appliances. The level of dirt is increased by the wood-burning stoves which are very common and the seas of mud which almost engulf villages particularly in late winter at the time of snow melt and which are aggravated by the numbers of livestock kept in the villages.

Very many families keep their own livestock and even in towns cattle and sheep can often be seen being tended by a family member. (Unlike western Europe even sheep have to be taken back to the house at night because of the danger from wolves.) In some areas free-range pigs wander through the village foraging for food. Armenians are very hard working, even more important now when so much work has to be done by hand because machinery, fertilisers, weedkillers and pesticides are all unaffordable. (This has the incidental benefit of making much Armenian food organic, albeit unofficially.) Even so, lack of suitable land results in Armenia being a net importer of food, which results in a permanently adverse trade balance.

For well-educated Armenians, life is not necessarily much easier. Salaries are low, there is serious underfunding of education and health, and career prospects are limited. Many such people seek work abroad, mostly in Russia, although the global economic recession of recent years has made even this option less available.

The Christian faith is important to very many Armenians, their Church binding them together as a community as it has for 1,700 years while simultaneously uniting them internationally with Christians elsewhere. It is the Armenian Christians of the diaspora who pay for most of the very necessary infrastructure investment in Armenia. Few countries are so heavily dependent on help from abroad. Yet despite all these difficulties, Armenians are generous to a fault. Desperately poor people welcome you into their homes and provide refreshments, often unintentionally embarrassing Western visitors who feel awkward about accepting from those who obviously have so much less. Especially in rural areas, people are fascinated by the few Westerners who appear and are genuinely touched that people from so far away could even have heard of Armenia let alone be interested enough to come. Having said that, pride in the country's history and language is intense, with Armenians well aware of the artistic and spiritual achievement of their great monasteries and of the contributions made by many distinguished Armenians in history.

LANGUAGE

Armenian is an Indo-European language with its own branch, thus not closely related to any other language. It has its own unique alphabet created in AD405, originally with 36 letters, three more being added later. It is a synthetic language – the construction of one word with declensions and various endings gives as much information as a whole phrase in English. There are two forms of Armenian, eastern Armenian (as spoken in Armenia) and western Armenian (as formerly spoken in Anatolia and still spoken by the diaspora). Although different the two are mutually intelligible. For further information see *Appendix 1, page 283.*

The second language is **Russian**, which is spoken virtually everywhere. **English** is becoming more common but can only be relied upon in places popular with tourists such as the hotels in Yerevan and some shops. Outside Yerevan it is common to find that no English is spoken. Other European languages are even less well known although of course interpreters can be employed. Independent travellers can hire an English-speaking guide and an increasing number of drivers of hired cars also speak some English. Learning the Armenian alphabet and a few common words certainly enhances a visit to Armenia and Armenians are delighted if a foreigner makes even a small effort with their language.

RELIGION

Ethnic Armenians are overwhelmingly members of the Armenian Apostolic Church, whose head, the Katholikos, has his seat at Ejmiatsin. The Katholikos is elected, following the death of his predecessor, by an electoral college of around 400 delegates comprising members of the senior clergy and representatives of all branches of the Armenian Church worldwide. The present Katholikos, Karekin II, was elected in 1999. The Church is called Apostolic because Christianity is believed to have been brought to Armenia by Jesus' disciples Bartholomew and Thaddeus (or Lebbaeus as he is called in St Matthew's gospel). It is also sometimes called the Gregorian Church because it was founded in Armenia by St Gregory the Illuminator. Most visitors to Armenia will visit several of the churches. The layout

CHURCH NAMES

The great majority of Armenian churches are dedicated to a small number of people or events. Although this guidebook uses English names throughout, visitors will often see an English transliteration of the Armenian name used on the spot. Apart from a few dedicated to Armenian saints, the common ones are:

Sourb Amenaprkich	Holy Redeemer
Sourb Astvatsatsin	Holy Mother of God
Sourb Asvatsnkal	Holy Wisdom of God
Sourb Arakelots	Holy Apostles
Sourb Grigor	St Gregory the Illuminator
Sourb Hakob	St Jacob
Sourb Haratyun	Holy Resurrection
Sourb Karapet	Holy Forerunner (ie: St John the Baptist)
Sourb Nshan	Holy Sign (of the Cross)

and form of worship are quite different from that in the West. They are more similar to the Orthodox Church but there are even here some major differences in that Armenian churches do not have an iconostasis with its royal doors and, doctrinally, the Armenian Church has not adopted the views of the Council of Chalcedon (AD451) concerning the duality of Christ's nature. (The Council of Chalcedon affirmed that Christ was both fully human and fully divine, having two natures in one being. The Armenian Church did not participate in the Council nor accept its formulation. It holds that the nature of Christ is beyond human understanding.)

At one end of the church will be a raised altar dais called a *bema*. In active churches a curtain can be drawn across it during parts of the service (see page 32). A legacy of the Soviet period is that there is still a shortage of priests, but numbers are increasing as are seminaries to train priests. (Training for the priesthood lasts seven years.) New churches are being built and old ones renovated although in many places there is a shortage of money to pay priests and repair churches. Accordingly, many churches do not have regular worship and an individual priest might have to look after several churches.

When visiting any Armenian church it is normal to buy candles on entry and then to light them (matches are provided), placing them upright in the trays of sand. The only exception to this rule is the new cathedral in Yerevan where candles are forbidden (there is a special chapel for them to the southeast of the cathedral). Women do not need to wear headscarves unless taking communion. It is correct to leave a church walking backwards so as not to turn one's back on God. It is still common for an animal (and, more particularly the salt with which the animal will be seasoned), always male and usually a ram or a cock, to be presented by a family for sacrifice. Sacrifice is usually carried out by the priest outside the church after the Sunday service. Firstly the priest blesses the animal and salt at a special stone called the *orhnakar* ('blessing stone') and then he sacrifices the animal at the *mataghatun* ('sacrifice house'). The animal will have been given in thanksgiving for some event, such as recovery from a serious illness, or as a particular request to God. It is partly a form of charity since some of the meat from the slaughtered animal will be given to the poor although the donor's family and friends will eat the rest, always boiled and never roasted or barbecued. The animals destined for slaughter are beautifully groomed before being offered to God in this way. Families will sometimes slaughter a cock themselves and evidence of such sacrifice is not uncommon at small shrines and churches. Another frequent sight outside churches is a tree or shrub to which numerous scraps of cloth are tied. Each scrap is attached by a person making a private prayer.

WORSHIP Worship usually lasts for about 2½ hours, the service having been extended by additional prayers at various times over the centuries. Despite its length there were traditionally no seats but pews are now becoming more common. Worship is quite different from that in Western churches. Visitors need not attend the whole service (which usually starts at 10.30) and can come just for part except that at some churches (notably Sevan) the building is so crowded that it is difficult either to enter or to leave. (Geghard is a good option on a Sunday morning for those staying in Yerevan with access to transport.) Even for those with no knowledge of the Armenian language the beauty of the singing is deeply impressive.

The devout fast on Sunday mornings before going to church. For the celebrant priest the liturgy begins in the vestry. He acknowledges his sinfulness and how privileged he is to be able to lead the people in worship. The deacon then hands him in turn the various items of the vestments and he puts each of them on with a brief prayer. The priest and deacon now enter the nave but do not go immediately up to the *bema*. At first they remain among the congregation where the priest symbolically washes his hands and then asks the congregation to pray for his forgiveness. Once they are up on the *bema*, the curtain is drawn across it to avoid distracting the congregation with the preparations. After the elements have been prepared the curtain opens and the deacons lead the priest in a procession round the altar and down into the nave, walking round the whole church offering incense and inviting the faithful to kiss the cross which the priest carries.

After two hymns, one of which is sung every Sunday and the other of which varies, the deacon symbolically holds the Gospel book over the priest's head and there is a further procession around the altar accompanied by another hymn. This is followed by readings from the Bible and more prayers. The main part of the service, the liturgy of the Eucharist, starts with the priest removing his crown and slippers in obedience to God's command to Moses at the burning bush. The deacon processes around the altar holding the veiled chalice above his head. At the end of the procession the deacon hands the elements to the celebrant. The so-called kiss of peace which follows is a ritualised greeting everyone makes to their neighbours. A long sequence of prayers and hymns concludes with the curtain being again closed, this time for the priest to receive communion while hidden from view – it is traditional in all Eastern Churches for the celebrant to receive communion out of sight of the congregation. Communion is now distributed: as communicants stand before the priest they make the sign of the Cross and say 'I have sinned against God.' Thereupon the priest places a small part of the bread which has been dipped into the wine directly into the mouth of the communicant who again makes the sign of the Cross. (The sign is made in the same way as in the Orthodox Church – right breast before left – but the opposite way from the Roman Catholic practice which is left breast before right.) This is followed by more prayers and hymns during part of which the curtain is closed while the priest and deacons reorganise the altar. The priest then raises his right hand to bless the congregation in Armenian style – with the thumb and ring finger forming a circle to represent the world and the other fingers pointing upward to represent the persons of the Trinity. The service ends with the congregation kissing the Gospel book.

MARRIAGE IN ARMENIA Traditional marriage in Armenia differs somewhat from that in many other European countries and in North America. Tourists are almost bound to see weddings unless visiting during either Lent, when weddings cannot be held in church, or during May, Armenians having adopted the old Russian custom of considering that weddings in May will lead to an unhappy marriage. Weddings are particularly common on Saturdays, and readers might be interested to know more about what is happening.

The first point to note is that fewer young people than formerly are getting married, but not because they are simply living together as in many Western countries. In general Armenian couples do not do this. Young Armenian couples marry and then expect to have their first child a year or so after the wedding and the wife will stay at home to look after it. A young Armenian man will often not make a proposal of marriage unless he feels confident that he will be able to support his wife and child. In the uncertain economic climate (after decades of Soviet predictability) many young men felt unsure that they would be able to support a family and hence stayed single. Armenia's marriage rate fell by 50% after the Soviet collapse. However, 2007 and 2008 saw small increases in the number of marriages, and also in the birth rate, perhaps reflecting the improved economic situation. The problem of housing also arises. Economic uncertainty means that young people are reluctant to borrow money to buy a house or flat and the alternative of living with the husband's parents may or may not be feasible. Rising house prices also have to be taken into account.

A second point to note is that Armenians tend to have quite small families. A couple will generally only have further children if they believe that they can support them. This is similar to the view of many Western couples but economic uncertainty, or at least the perception of it, is greater in Armenia than in the West and this impacts on family size.

As traditionally happened in the West, if a man wishes to marry a woman he will go to her father to ask for her hand in marriage. A difference in Armenia is that he will usually be accompanied by his parents and possibly by other very close relatives such as his brother or sister. Unlike the West, wedding ceremonies are not planned long in advance: rarely more than a month ahead and sometimes only a few days, although this is changing as churches and reception venues become busier; it can now be as long as two or three months. On the wedding day the bride will be helped to get ready by her maid of honour (the equivalent of chief bridesmaid): this is always one of her unmarried sisters if she has any and only a close friend if she has no unmarried sister. It is never a married woman: the concept of a matron of honour doesn't exist in Armenia. The bridegroom's family provides and pays for the bride's dress, the bridegroom and the brother of the cross (the equivalent of best man) bringing it to her family's house on the day of the wedding. The bridegroom will normally also be accompanied by members of his family and friends (though not by his mother) and they, together with the bride's relatives and friends, eat and drink at the house while the bride is putting on her dress and being helped to get ready. Traditionally the bride would have worn a gown of red silk with a headpiece, often made of cardboard, shaped into wings and decorated with feathers. Nowadays she usually wears a long white dress similar in style to those worn throughout the West and probably imported from France, the Netherlands, Russia or the US. The bridegroom often wears a suit, though in a rather more interesting colour than one bought for sober office wear. Relatives and friends, including the maid of honour, tend to dress much as in the West although pale suits for all the prominent younger men are common.

Eventually the bride and bridegroom set off for the church together (no bridegroom waiting for the bride at the altar!) accompanied by their relatives and friends. Traditionally the bride's mother stays at home and does not attend her daughter's wedding: for her to do so is considered to bring bad luck upon the couple. However, this tradition is changing and nowadays the bride's mother often does attend the wedding. The bridegroom's mother has always attended. The couple may have either a church service, a civil ceremony or both. If they opt to have a church service but no civil ceremony their marriage is valid in the eyes of God although it is not recognised in Armenian law and the couple are, in theory at least, both free to remarry. Nevertheless many couples do in fact have only a church service: the subsequent rate of separation is in practice low. The wedding party enters the church with a large decorated basket containing wedding favours to be distributed to the guests: in the past these might have been small ceramic containers with almonds in them but many modern brides choose something much less traditional and there is a demand for such exotica as glass containers decorated with sea shells. During the service the officiating priest puts a ring on the finger of the bridegroom and then of the bride before joining their hands. The bridegroom then makes his vows followed in turn by the bride.

After the ceremony, all present, though still without the bride's mother (if she has stayed at home), traditionally go to the bridegroom's family house for the reception although nowadays a room in a hotel or restaurant is sometimes hired for the occasion. *En route* there is likely to be a motorcade with blaring horns and in Yerevan driving three times round Republic Square is an essential and audible part of the proceedings. On arrival at the reception the groomsmen and bridesmaids, holding their flowers aloft, form arches through which the young couple walk and two white doves are traditionally released to symbolise their love and happiness. There is more eating and drinking, this time at the expense of the bridegroom's family (although this too is changing with costs being shared), accompanied by dancing in an amalgam of traditional Armenian and more modern styles. The food will almost certainly be the menu invariably eaten on all Armenian celebratory occasions: *khorovats* – barbecued meat, most commonly pork but sometimes lamb or chicken, accompanied by salads and vegetables together with *lavash*. There will be the inevitable toasts. Friends, neighbours, and indeed almost anyone passing, drop in to wish the newlyweds well. The party goes on until everyone has had enough.

That isn't quite the end of marriage customs. Trndaz (Purification) day, 13 February, commemorates the purification of Mary 40 days after the birth of Jesus, as laid down in the rules given in Leviticus, chapter 12. After a church service during the evening, the priest blesses a fire. Candles lit in this fire are then taken to the homes of couples who have been married in the previous year and also to the homes of young women who have become engaged. A fire is kindled at the house using the candles lit from the fire at the church which the priest blessed. Then the couples jump over it to get rid of the small devils hanging from the edge of their clothes. The ceremony is the pretext for a large family celebration.

In some years Trndaz coincides with St Sargis's Day whose date is variable and fixed by the Church calendar. As with so many Armenian customs the actual details vary from family to family but traditionally young people fast on the eve of St Sargis's Day. They then eat unleavened salt bread which has been baked either by their grandmother or by a happily married middle-aged woman, and retire to bed without either drinking or speaking. Their inevitable thirst will supposedly make them dream of the person whom they will marry. If a footprint appears in the bowl of flour left outside the house overnight then the young man of the house will marry in the coming year. On St Sargis's Day itself there is a service of blessing for young people at the church.

EDUCATION

The Soviet education system was successful in producing a well-educated population, and a literacy rate of 100% was reported as early as 1960. In the Soviet period, Armenian education followed the standard Soviet programme with control from Moscow of curricula and teaching methods. After independence Armenia made changes. Curricula were altered to emphasise Armenian history and culture while Armenian became the dominant language of instruction. Russian is still widely taught now as a second language but the former compulsory clutter – subjects such as History of the Communist Party of the Soviet Union, Dialectical Materialism, Historical Materialism, Foundations of Marxist-Leninist Aesthetics, and Foundations of Scientific Communism – was rapidly jettisoned.

Children formerly started ten years of compulsory education at the age of seven, but after independence the starting age was changed to six and is now five, giving 12 years of compulsory education. The school year normally begins on 1 September – as in most parts of the former Soviet Union children in all classes can be seen making their way to school immaculately dressed and clutching bunches of flowers for their class teacher. University courses last five years or more, four years for a basic Bachelor's degree and typically another two years for a Master's. Education has suffered from lack of funding since independence and the low salaries paid to teachers have discouraged young people from entering the profession. A particular difficulty at present is the gap which has developed between what children have learned during their ten or 11 years, on which they are examined on leaving school, and what they are required to know to pass the universities' entrance exams. The only way to bridge this gap is to pay for extra tuition and so important is their children's education to parents that almost all are willing to pay for it. It is hoped that the extension of schooling to 12 years will remove the gap in knowledge. So highly is education regarded that Yerevan's 12 state universities have, despite the falling population, been augmented by 25 private ones since independence. Armenians who do not seek a university education are very much in a minority despite recent figures showing that only 20% of university graduates find jobs after graduation. The ministry is keen to reduce the number of graduates and to increase the extent of vocational training as there are significant shortages of trained specialists such as hairdressers and construction workers. The most highly regarded degrees and diplomas are those from the state institutions, and especially those from students who scored so well in the entrance examination that they gained a free place.

CULTURE

ARCHITECTURE

Church building For some members of the diaspora, to experience Armenia's culture and language on its home territory will be their overriding memory of a visit to Armenia, but for the majority of visitors it is the historic buildings which will make the greatest impression, above all the monasteries but also to a lesser degree the secular medieval buildings such as fortresses and caravanserais. Only a very few buildings survive from the pre-Christian era: little more than the foundations can be observed of the cities of the Kingdom of Urartu such as Erebuni. By far the best-known pre-Christian building is the sole-surviving example of Graeco-Roman architecture in Armenia, built at Garni some time in the first two centuries AD at a time when the country was an ally of Rome. (See pages 186–7.) The Greek style was widely employed in contemporary Roman buildings throughout the

Sundials can be seen on the walls of many Armenian monasteries and churches. The details of some are easily seen, such as that on the eastern façade of the small St Stephen's Church at Haghartsin Monastery. By contrast, the elaborately carved sundial at Harichavank is positioned so high up on the eastern wall of the Mother of God Church that binoculars are almost needed to appreciate the detail. Sundials were sometimes placed high up on a wall to avoid them being shaded from the sun by surrounding trees but, if this was originally the case at Harichavank, it is certainly not a problem now. The sundials themselves are not dated and it is not always possible to ascertain if they are contemporaneous with the building they adorn or if they were added later.

Armenian sundials are of the vertical type, with a horizontal gnomon at right angles to the wall. The dials are a semicircle which is usually divided into 12 (occasionally 11) equal petal-like divisions, each division representing an hour. Such dials show unequal hours, the hours of daylight being divided into 12 periods regardless of the length of daylight so an 'hour' in winter will occupy less time than an 'hour' in summer. The hours are counted from one at sunrise on the horizontal line at the left, to 12 at sunset on the horizontal line at the right. Visitors may be more familiar with sundials showing equal hours, with their divisions of variable width and gnomons at an angle to the vertical, the angle determined by the sundial's latitude.

The divisions of some Armenian sundials carry letters of the Armenian alphabet. Armenian letters were (and sometimes still are) used to represent numbers. The first nine letters of the Armenian alphabet represent the units one to nine, the next nine letters represent the tens (ten, 20 ... 90), the next nine letters the hundreds (100, 200 ... 900), etc. The first ten divisions on a sundial bear the first ten letters of the alphabet, 11 and 12 usually being represented by a repeat of the first two letters. Very occasionally, as seen on a more recently carved sundial at Zvartnots, 11 is shown, correctly, as a combination of the tenth letter (representing ten) and the first letter (representing one). Similarly 12 is shown as the tenth letter plus the second letter of the alphabet.

empire and the survival of no other buildings in Armenia from this era is largely the consequence of Christians destroying pagan temples after the conversion of the country. Almost certainly others would have been constructed.

The early churches were often built on the site of pagan shrines employing the same foundations, and hence they had the same dimensions as the temple which they replaced; moreover the Christian altar was usually placed directly over the previous pagan one as can be seen at Ejmiatsin. From the earliest times the churches were built in stone, most commonly the volcanic tuff which is easily carved and tends gradually to harden when exposed to the atmosphere. The need to build in stone was dictated by the unavailability of suitable timber, even for roofing, and the weight of the heavy vaulted stone roof in turn dictated the need for thick walls to support it with few windows. Where tuff was unavailable, most commonly in border areas, other volcanic rocks such as basalt or andesite were used.

From fairly early days almost all churches were built with a cupola supported by a cylindrical structure called a tambour. Tambours are usually circular in cross-section when viewed from the interior of the church but are often polygonal on the outside.

The preference for churches to have a cupola supported by a tambour is one of Armenian architecture's most abiding features and makes its churches very distinctive. The style rapidly developed after the conversion to Christianity and continued until the Arab invasion and conquest in the mid 7th century. Thereafter no churches were built for over 200 years until the establishment of the Bagratid dynasty in the late 9th century. Under this re-established regime new churches began to be built, initially copying the old style but gradually starting to develop this style to provide greater height and space. Once again church building ceased after foreign invasion, this time by the Seljuk Turks after the middle of the 11th century.

The establishment of Georgian independence together with the Armenian Zakarid dynasty in the late 12th century led to a renewal of church building and, in particular, to the development of the large monastic complexes with their multiple churches and ancillary buildings which are probably nowadays the most visited tourist sights in the country. Again the traditional style was used but the quest for greater space was now satisfied by building several churches on the same site rather than by increasing the size of each structure. Inevitably, construction ceased at the end of the 13th century after the Mongol invasions and the Armenian kingdom of Cilicia also ceased to exist in 1375 following the Mamluk invasions. No more churches were built until the 17th century when construction, still in the traditional style, restarted at a time when Armenia was ruled by the Safavid Shahs of Iran. Church building increased in the 19th century as Armenian national consciousness grew, only to come to a complete stop with the genocide of 1915 in western Armenia and the Bolshevik Revolution in the east. Independence has led to a resurgence in church building, largely with funds provided by the diaspora, with the traditional style generally retained but with extensive use of modern materials. Some new churches are also being built in the hallmark tuff and, from a distance, it can be difficult for the visitor to know what is new and what is renovated old.

Church construction Two overriding practical constraints influenced early church architects: the need to use stone for roofs because of the lack of suitable timber, and the need to withstand fairly frequent earthquakes. The necessary strength was provided by the use of an early type of concrete in a method probably copied from Roman architects. The earliest churches were built of massive stone blocks, with mortar separating them, forming the outer and inner surfaces of the walls; between them was a thin layer of concrete. This concrete was compounded of broken tuff and other stones, lime mortar and eggs. During the 5th and 6th centuries the technique evolved, the slabs of the stone shell becoming thinner and the cement core thicker. The method of construction was then to erect finely cut slabs of tuff or other stone a few rows at a time and without mortar to form the surfaces of the outer and inner walls after which concrete was poured into the cavity between them. This concrete adhered to the facing slabs and formed a solid strong core and it is this core, rather than the thin slabs of tuff which forms the building's major support. The slabs were varied in size and height to break up the vertical and horizontal rows and thus provide protection against parts of the concrete core falling out during earthquakes. Great thought was given to enhancing the artistic appearance of churches, and different churches had the tuff slabs erected in different ways. In some churches the slabs were carved and either different colours of slab might be employed to provide a contrast or else a uniform colour might be used, sometimes with mortar applied between the slabs to give a completely uniform appearance. As the technique evolved the largest stone blocks gradually came to be reserved for the lowest courses of stonework as well as for corners and smaller

Khachkars, carved memorial stones, are an important, conspicuous, and beautiful feature of Armenian decorative art. The word 'khachkar' literally means 'cross stone'. In quiet streets in central Yerevan it is possible to see even today the stone carvers at work, using traditional methods to create these endlessly varied monuments in a revival of this ancient tradition. The earliest khachkars date from the 9th and 10th centuries, a period when Armenia had gained effective independence from the Arab caliphate and separate Armenian kings each ruled their individual states. This flowering of Armenian craftsmanship under independence was paralleled in architecture: some of Armenia's finest monasteries date from this period.

The earliest datable khachkar is one erected at Garni by Queen Katranide, wife of King Ashot Bagratuni I, in 879 in mediation for her person. Securing the salvation of the soul was the most common reason for erecting khachkars but some were put up to commemorate military victories or the completion of churches, bridges, fountains and other constructions. Even unrequited love might be commemorated this way. The dominant feature of the design is generally a cross, occasionally a crucifix, resting on a rosette or sun disc design. The remainder is covered with complex patterns of leaves, bunches of grapes or abstract geometrical patterns. Occasionally the whole was surmounted by a cornice showing biblical characters or saints. The absolute peak of khachkar design was probably between the 12th and 14th centuries. Amazingly elaborate and delicate patterns were created using the same elements of design. Depiction of the Crucifixion and Resurrection become more common and at this time some khachkars came to be erected as a spiritual protection against natural disasters. The supreme masterpieces are probably those by Timot and Mkhitar in the porch of Geghard Monastery which dates from 1213, the Holy Redeemer khachkar at Haghpat Monastery which was created by Vahram in 1273, and that at Goshavank created by Poghos in 1291. Some good examples have been transported to the Historical Museum in Yerevan and the cathedral at Ejmiatsin. There can, however, be no substitute for seeing them where they were originally erected.

The Mongol invasion at the end of the 14th century led to a decline of the tradition and although there was a revival in the 16th and 17th centuries, the artistic heights of the 14th were never regained.

Some khachkars, often recording donations, are embedded in the walls of monasteries but the majority are free-standing. Armenia has over 40,000 surviving khachkars. An amazing sight is the so-called field of khachkars at Noratus, the largest of several groupings of khachkars in Armenia. This is an old graveyard with 900 khachkars marking graves and the endless variations of design make a visit there particularly rewarding. Noratus is especially interesting because examples there span the whole period from the 10th to the 17th century. Note that at Noratus, as at all places where khachkars are still in their original location, they face west. This means that they are best photographed in the afternoon.

ones were used elsewhere. Although windows were, from structural considerations, never a significant feature of Armenian church architecture, their size and number did tend to increase over time.

Styles of church All the earliest-known churches were either of basilica construction (ie: rectangular with an apse at the east end and with three aisles) or else a simpler version of this with a single aisle. Variations included having a covered porch, one or more rooms adjoining the apse, or corner rooms at both ends. A single roof covered all three aisles. Cupolas started to make their appearance in the 5th or 6th century and both single and three-aisle churches were then built incorporating them. In single-aisle churches the cupola rested on massive piers which jutted out from the north and south walls but in three-aisle basilica churches four free-standing pillars were usual.

The incorporation of a cupola as a central feature caused changes to church layout and the basilica style gave way to a more centrally planned church built around the cupola, sometimes with four apses or else with four arms of equal length, or sometimes with three apses and one extended arm. This resulted in what was essentially a cross-shaped church but the addition of corner rooms between the arms of the cross resulted in many church buildings being more or less rectangular in plan when seen from the outside but with the church itself cross-shaped in plan when on the inside. Churches with a cupola and four arms are often referred to as cross-dome churches although cross-cupola would perhaps be less misleading as most English speakers think of domes as being hemispherical. The ultimate exemplar of this centrally planned style, the Church of St Hripsime at Ejmiatsin, is still further developed. Four semicircular apses are separated from each other by four circular niches each of which leads to a square corner room, all this being incorporated within the basic rectangular shape. Another variant of the centrally planned church was to make the entire building circular although relatively few of this type were constructed and the best known, the ruined 7th-century church at Zvartnots, isn't strictly circular but has 32 sides.

The basic style of Armenian church architecture has remained to this day the centrally planned church, built around its cupola and with two or more corner rooms. However, two later developments were the additions of a narthex or *gavit* as it is usually referred to in Armenia, and the building of a bell tower. Both *gavit* and bell tower came into being during the great upsurge in monastery building from the 10th century onwards. A *gavit* is a square room usually attached to the west end of the church and serving as a vestibule, a room for meetings, and a burial place for notables. Apart from the relatively few free-standing ones *gavits* could also house the overflow when the congregation was too large for the main church. They were sometimes very large with massive walls and, like the other parts of the church, were frequently elaborately carved. Bell towers appeared at monastery complexes from the 13th century onwards and were often detached from the church building itself. The walls of later churches, both the exterior and the interior ones, sometimes incorporate *khachkars* (cross stones, see box text opposite). There are also occasionally carvings of the donors, often holding a model of the church.

Inside Armenian churches there may or may not be carving but the most conspicuous feature is the altar dais or *bema* at the eastern end with steps leading up to it. The entire dais forms the altar and in an active church it can be shut off by a curtain though the curtain is never closed except during parts of services. Unlike the Orthodox Church there is never an iconostasis. A few churches have a decorated wooden or stone altar screen, as at Sevanavank or Mughni, but this never obscures the holy table as does the iconostasis in the Orthodox Church.

A word which visitors might hear when any small church is being referred to is *zham*, as opposed to *vank* for a monastery. *Zham* is the Armenian word for hour or time. Using it to mean a church dates from when the church was the (only) means of telling the time, either by bell or sundial. *Zham* is also often used to refer to simple hall-like village churches without a dome and often with wooden rather than stone pillars supporting the roof. They are rarely thought worthy of being pointed out to tourists but they are quite widespread and often have interesting older khachkars incorporated into their walls.

Secular medieval architecture Two types of secular medieval building will attract the attention of visitors: castles and caravanserais. Unlike the churches, neither is distinctively Armenian. Essentially Armenia's **castles** were sited and built according to the general thinking in castle design of the day and followed the same principles as applied throughout Europe. **Caravanserais** were built along the main east–west trade routes to provide secure lodging for merchants and their pack animals. They are generally rectangular and sometimes surprisingly large, reflecting just how important this trade was. Only a single, fairly small, door was provided so that the caravanserai would be easily defensible against robbers. Inside there were rows of stalls with feeding troughs for animals and booths for the merchants.

THE ARTS
Illuminated manuscripts If khachkars are the symbol of Armenia, the painting of illuminated manuscripts is undoubtedly Armenia's other great contribution to the world of art. The beauty and skill represented in the many surviving examples are rarely equalled and seldom surpassed in other cultures. Extensive sets of pictures were used to illustrate manuscripts of the books of the Bible and obviously books such as Genesis or Exodus, where there is plenty of physical action, lent themselves particularly to this art form, with some manuscripts having up to 750 illustrations. The most elaborate manuscripts tended to be those of the four Gospels which were frequently bound with sumptuous covers of ivory or metalwork. A characteristic feature of these copies of the Gospels is the set of canon tables which were designed to show which passages of the individual Gospels were in agreement with any of the other three. They were arranged with columns of figures under decorative arches, often highly elaborated and usually accompanied by scenes or symbols of the evangelists. Before the Gospel itself there is a picture of the evangelists, again within an architectural structure and also with writing desk, lectern and writing implements.

The purpose of these books was to aid worship. They were made to be displayed on the altar as well as to be used by the priest reading to the congregation. A very few examples survive which pre-date the Arab conquest in 640. The subsequent repression of Christianity by the Muslims led to the suspension of artistic activity until after the end of Arab occupation in the 9th century. From then the art flourished. The importance of manuscripts to the Armenian Church is comparable to that afforded to icons by the Orthodox Church. The large number that has survived testifies to how valuable they were considered to be and how closely they were guarded in times of war. Manuscripts, particularly those believed to be endowed with miraculous powers, were given special names such as Saviour of All or Resurrector of the Dead. The manuscripts were also thought of as pledges for the salvation of the donors, as treasures in heaven, and they are therefore rarely anonymous productions. The names of the sponsor and the creators are carefully recorded so that they might be recalled by those who used the manuscripts. Given the importance of manuscripts and their beauty, it is unfortunate that the only place in Armenia where manuscripts can readily be seen is the Matenadaran ('Manuscript library') in Yerevan where a handful are on display in the two exhibition rooms.

Music Both traditional folk music and classical music have fallen on hard times since 1991 with the reductions in state funding. **Folk music** can now most often be heard on national holidays but a more convenient option is to go to one of the Yerevan restaurants where a folk ensemble plays each evening. The *oud* is a 12-stringed (two strings for each note) ancestor of the lute and guitar with a distinctive bent neck. The *tarr* is another lute-like instrument but smaller than the *oud*. The *kemenche* is a three-stringed violin played with the instrument held vertically resting on the lap. The *duduk* makes the sound most often associated with Armenian music. It is a low-pitched woodwind instrument, with a large double reed, made from apricot wood. The *shvi* ('whistle') by contrast is a high-pitched woodwind instrument without a reed and with eight holes, seven for playing and a thumb hole. The *dhol* is a cylindrical drum with one membrane being thicker to give a low pitch and the other thinner to give a higher pitch. Other distinctive instruments which may be encountered include the *zurna*, a higher-pitched wind instrument than the *duduk* but also with a double reed and made from apricot wood; the *kanun*, a plucked box zither, trapezoid in shape, which is played resting on the player's knee or on a table, the strings being plucked by plectra attached to the fingers; and the *dumbeg* which is an hourglass-shaped drum with a membrane made of lamb skin at only one end, the other end being open.

It was the Russian conquest in the 19th century which brought Western **classical music** to Armenia and the fusion of the folk-inspired Russian nationalistic composers such as Rimsky-Korsakov and Borodin with the existing Armenian traditional music was to result in distinctively Armenian style. Full of bright colours and rhythms it is vigorous rather than cerebral, music of the heart rather than the head. The best-known Armenian composer outside the country is undoubtedly **Aram Khachaturian** (1903–78), though broadcasters frequently and incorrectly refer to him as Russian. In particular his violin and piano concerti are regularly encountered in concert and the ballets *Spartacus* and *Gayaneh* have often been staged outside Armenia. Most people would probably recognise the Sabre Dance from *Gayaneh*. Armenian **opera** has made little impact abroad but in recent years there have been American stagings of *Arshak II* by **Tigran Chukhadjian**, first heard (incomplete) in Italian at Constantinople in 1868, and *Anoush* by **Armen Tigranian** which was first performed at Alexandropol (present-day Gyumri) in 1912. To make these acceptable to Stalinist censors both had to have their plots changed during Soviet times: the alterations required to *Arshak II* in 1945 at the end of the Great Patriotic War included changing the character of Arshak from that of a tyrannical leader to that of a virtuous and unselfish one, and changing the composer's tragic ending into a hymn of rejoicing. Presumably this was in the hope that the audience would identify Stalin with the now virtuous, unselfish and victorious Arshak. *Arshak II* is considerably influenced by Verdi but *Anoush* aims at a fusion of classical Western music with distinctive Armenian melody and harmony. In Yerevan the **Armenian Philharmonic Orchestra** gives regular concerts and opera and ballet are staged in the Opera and Ballet Theatre except during the summer break.

Another distinctive Armenian form is that of **liturgical music**. It is sung without instrumental accompaniment and is based on a so-called Phrygian scale rather than the major and minor scales familiar in Western music. The number of surviving compositions is considerable: more than 1,000 from the Middle Ages survive on parchment and the range is diverse, sometimes quick and sprightly, sometimes solemn, sometimes dramatic. Only later did composers start to write polyphonically. The best-known more recent composer is Komitas (1869–1935) who wrote many wonderful chants as well as other compositions in traditional

Armenian style. To listen to this beautiful music in any of Armenia's churches on a Sunday morning is an experience which every visitor should seek out.

Dance Dance in Armenia can broadly be divided into traditional dance and classical ballet, the latter considerably influenced by the Russian school. The **traditional dances** which are encountered in Armenia today are those of eastern Armenia and as such differ in some respects from the dances of Armenian groups abroad which usually represent the western Armenian tradition. The energetic men's dance *Jo Jon* (also called *Zhora Bar*) comes from Spitak province. *Mom Bar*, meaning 'Candle Dance', was originally from the Lake Sevan region and is now traditionally the last dance at wedding parties. The candles are blown out at the end of the dance signalling that it is time for guests to leave. Women's solo dances called *Naz Bar*, meaning 'Grace Dance', are improvisatory with intricate hand gestures used to tell stories of love, betrayal, conflict and triumph. In Yerevan in particular choreographic schools and song and dance ensembles preserve the tradition in a form suitable for stage presentation, although funding is more difficult than in the Soviet era.

The musical accompaniment can be played on traditional instruments or sung (or both). **Costumes** for women are invariably sumptuous, whether based on medieval court dress or on simpler peasant dress. Brightly coloured shimmering dresses are decorated with gold embroidery and pearls. A light lace veil surmounts the embroidered hat. For men costume is simpler. Full trousers and embroidered tunics or else the *cherkessa*, traditional Caucasian dress similar to Cossack style, with red, white or black silk trousers, leather boots, woollen or fur hat, and a dagger in the belt. Men's dances are martial and vigorous; women's are graceful with elaborate gestures.

Funding is also more difficult for **classical ballet**, performed at the Spendiarian Opera and Ballet Theatre. The standard of dance remains high but numbers of Armenian dancers are making successful careers in western Europe and North America and the pool of talent remaining in Yerevan has diminished.

Drama In ancient times **Greek drama** was popular in Armenia and several amphitheatres were built during the Hellenistic age including one at Tigranakert, the new capital which Tigran II built. When the Romans sacked the city in 69BC the actors were killed during the celebration games which followed. After the conversion of Armenia to Christianity in the 4th century drama was suppressed by the Church and there is no record of any Armenian theatre until the 18th century when plays were put on by the Armenian community in Venice. The first recorded performance of a play in Armenia proper since the 4th century is often said to have been of **Alexander Griboyedov**'s *Woe from Wit* in 1827 at the palace of the Yerevan Fortress with members of the Imperial Russian Army as the cast. That seems highly unlikely as this scathing satire on corruption, ignorance and bribery in Tsarist society was banned during the author's lifetime and not staged until 1831.

The **first regular theatre** in Yerevan opened in 1865 and in that year **Gabriel Sundukian** (1825–1912) published *Khatabala* which may be said to represent the foundation of a realistic Armenian drama. Theatres were established in several Armenian communities both in Armenia and among the diaspora in cities such as Teheran and Tbilisi but those in Ottoman-controlled areas were repressed after anti-Armenian action started in earnest in 1894. During the Soviet period drama blossomed with a healthy diet of Armenian and Russian works as well as Armenian translations of foreign classics, particularly Shakespeare, who translates very well into Armenian. Since 1991, as with all the arts, the curtailment of government subsidies has led to considerable retrenchment although several theatres survive at Yerevan and Gyumri.

Literature Written Armenian literature could clearly not develop until the creation of the alphabet by Mesrop Mashtots in the early 5th century and any early pagan oral tradition would almost certainly have been suppressed after the conversion to Christianity. Apart from the Bible, other theological works were soon translated from both Greek and Syriac after the creation of the alphabet. Some of Mesrop Mashtots's pupils also wrote original works: **Eznik** wrote a treatise on the origins of evil and the subject of free will called *Refutation of the Sects* while **Koriun** wrote a biography of Mashtots in about AD443. The *Epic Histories* were written in the 470s by an anonymous cleric and give an account of Armenian history between about 330 and 387 bringing together traditional stories about kings from Khosrov III to Arsaces II and patriarchs. The author sought to draw parallels between historic and contemporary events, and, when he wrote about a dying ruler urging his son to die bravely for their Christian country since by doing so he would be dying in the service of God and the Church, it was undoubtedly meant to apply to his readers.

This tradition of martial resistance and martyrdom was continued in the *History* written by **Lazarus of Parp**, abbot of the monastery of Vagharshapat (modern Ejmiatsin), which continues the story after 387, when the *Epic Histories* break off, as far as 485. In describing the events of 451, the author describes the Armenians finding the Persians unprepared at Avarayr and then holding off since they wanted martyrdom more than victory. He wrote that the face of one martyr was illuminated before his death as a sign of his imminent transformation into an angel. Widows of martyrs and women whose husbands were imprisoned by the enemy were considered to be living martyrs.

From the late 5th century onwards, **translations from the Greek** were made of secular works including the writings of philosophers such as Aristotle and Plato and of the medical writers Hippocrates and Galen. Meanwhile the writers of histories continued to stress martyrdom. In the *History* by **Yeghishe**, probably written in the late 6th century, the account of the revolt in 451 goes even further than had Lazarus of Parp in emphasising martyrdom and justifying armed resistance as well as giving the clergy a leading role. The Armenians are depicted as treating Persian promises of religious freedom as deceitful.

The period after the Arab conquest was a low point for Armenia generally and it was the 10th century before a literary revival took place. Competition between monasteries for endowments led to an interesting forgery. The *History of Taron* (Taron is the area north of Lake Van) was written sometime between 966 and 988 but claims to have been started in the 4th century by Zenob of Glak, the first Bishop of Taron, and then continued by John Mamikonyan, the 35th Bishop of Taron, in the 7th century. The book states that Glak was Gregory the Enlightener's first foundation, earlier even than Ejmiatsin, while the truth was that Glak was a new foundation in the 10th century. The supposed history includes a completely bogus story of Glak's possession of miracle-working relics of John the Baptist which had produced divine intervention in war. The purpose of all this monastic skulduggery was twofold. Firstly it was an attempt to show that Glak, being Armenia's oldest monastery, was worthiest of endowment, more so even than Ejmiatsin and Dvin. Secondly, and even more explicitly, in the book some ascetics pray that anyone who makes generous gifts to the monastery from their 'sinful' wealth should be delivered from tribulation; they are answered by a voice from heaven which assents. Rather more prosaic is the description of the cutting off of enemy noses: 24,000 on one occasion.

The 10th century produced several rather more **reliable histories** while the *Book of Lamentations* by **Gregory of Narek** (c950–1010), a long poem comprising prayers about the wretchedness of the soul, the sinfulness of mankind and the certainty of salvation, remains a classic of Armenian literature. It is the earliest written work still to be widely read and was completed in 1002. Its author is usually considered to be Armenia's greatest poet and has been translated into 30 languages. Armenia's national epic, *David of Sassoun*, also dates from the 10th century although it was not committed to print until 1873. It recounts the story of David's family over four generations with Sassoun, its setting, symbolising Armenia. David in particular incarnated a symbol of the Armenians who fought foreign oppression in the 7th and 8th centuries.

Nerses Shnorhali ('Nerses the Gracious') (1100–73) was a great **lyrical poet**, musician, theologian and philosopher who became Katholikos Nerses IV in 1166. His greatest poem *Lament on the Fall of Edessa* (present-day Urfa in Turkey) records the capture of that city in 1144 by the Turks who slaughtered most of its inhabitants together with the archbishop. Nerses is also the author of several hymns still used in the Armenian communion service. By the late 13th century, poems on love and other secular themes began to appear and grow as an important force in Armenian literature. The greatest of these poets, **Constantine of Erznka**, wrote poetry of springtime, love, beauty and light, allegorically exalting the Christian mysteries. Constantine broadened the scope of Armenian poetry, moving away from religious terminology towards the imagery of the natural world. This was taken even further until in the 15th and 16th centuries pure love poetry came to Armenia. Its first great exponent was **Nahapet Kuchak**, who is thought to have lived near Lake Van in the 16th century but may have lived earlier and elsewhere. His poems have deep, often erotic, emotional passion, stunning imagery and wit, and are as vividly alive today as when they were written. **Sayat Nova** (1712–95) was perhaps the culmination of this tradition. Poet and composer in Georgian and Persian as well as Armenian, he wrote of courtly love and the beauty of his unattainable beloved.

The development of the **novel** throughout the Western world in the late 18th century inevitably impacted upon Armenia. The first great Armenian novelist was **Khatchatur Abovian** (1805–48). He was the first author to abandon the classical Armenian language and use modern spoken Armenian for his works. His most famous novel is *Armenia's Wounds*, set during the Russian conquest of Armenia from Persia in 1826–28 and dealing with the Armenian people's suffering under foreign domination. Abovian was also a noted translator of Homer and Schiller. Further impetus to the quest for Armenian identity was given in the novels of the other great 19th-century Armenian novelist, **Raffi** (pen name of Hakop Melik-Hakopian) (1835–88). The grandeur of Armenia's historic past was recalled in novels such as *The Madman* (1881), *Samvel* (1886) and *The Spark* (1887).

The writings of **Hovhannes Tumanian** (1869–1923) encompass **fables and epic poetry**. An admirer of Shakespeare and translator of Byron, Goethe and Pushkin it is regrettable that his work is not better known outside Armenia. He wrote patriotic verse with titles such as *In the Armenian Mountains*, *Armenian Grief* and *With My Fatherland* but also legends such as *A Drop of Honey* in which the eponymous drop is the cause of a war. The work, based on a medieval legend, concludes with the few terrified survivors asking themselves what caused the worldwide conflagration. Tumanian moralised without preaching, notably in works such as *My Friend Nesso*, a story about how the most handsome boy in the village turns into an evil, dishonest man and ends up dragging out a deprived life at the bottom of society. Similarly, *The Capture of Fort Temuk* traces the criminal path which leads from simple ambition to treason. Most Armenians consider that Tumanian's masterpiece is *Anoush*, a tragic story of village life in which Anoush's brother kills her lover for breaking a village taboo. The work is much more than a simple story, the author expressing his philosophy of life, his ideas about the existence of man and the world of human passions. His ardently expressed love for Armenia led to his being tried in 1908 for anti-Tsarist activities and he was later very active in seeking to help victims of the genocide.

Tumanian appears on the AMD5,000 banknote while the figure on the AMD1,000 note is the poet **Eghishe Charents** (1897–1937). Born in Van, then under Turkish rule, Charents was involved in anti-Turkish activity as part of the Armenian self-defence corps as early as 1912. His early work reflects this in pieces such as *Three Songs to a Pale Girl* (1914) and *Blue-Eyed Homeland* (1915). In 1915, he moved to Moscow to continue his education at the university thereby witnessing the Bolshevik Revolution and becoming greatly influenced by its ideology. In 1918, he joined the Red Army. Returning to Yerevan an enthusiastic supporter of communism in 1919, at this stage of his life his writings covered topics such as civil war in Russia and Armenia, world communism, famine, poverty, World War I and the Bolshevik Revolution. From the mid 1920s there is a gradual change in his work as he became disillusioned with communist rule and increasingly nationalistic. His satirical novel *Land of Nairi* (1925) starts to reflect this but his last published collection of poems, *Book of the Road*, published in 1933 was to make him notorious. One poem called 'The Message', ostensibly in fulsome praise of the genius of Stalin, contains a second message hidden in the second letter of each line: *Oh! Armenian people, your salvation lies only in your collective power.* Inevitably deemed nationalistic by the Soviet authorities he was arrested shortly afterwards by the NKVD (forerunner of the KGB). He died in prison, an early victim among the tens of millions killed at Stalin's behest, although it was claimed by the Soviet authorities that he had committed suicide while on hunger strike. All his works were banned until his rehabilitation in 1954, the year after Stalin's death.

Later Armenian writers could inevitably have no personal experience of a pre-Soviet world or even of the genocide. **Hovhannes Garabedian** (1915–84), however, came much closer than most since his mother was widowed by the genocide shortly before his birth. Growing up in considerable poverty, he attracted attention when his first work *Beginning of Spring* was published in 1935. He acquired the name Hovhannes Shiraz because one writer commented that his 'poems have the fragrance of roses, fresh and covered with dew, like the roses of Shiraz'. (Shiraz is a town in Iran.) His work includes parables and translations as well as a great deal of poetry and is immortalised for Armenians by such lines as: 'Let all nations reach the moon, but Armenians reach Ararat.' A critic of Armenia's corrupt Soviet government, his protests included publicly urinating one evening on the statue of Lenin in Yerevan.

Gevorg Emin was born in 1919, slightly later than Shiraz. Qualifying as a hydraulic engineer in 1940, his knowledge of the technological world of dams, pipelines and power stations is reflected in the concrete images and complex relationships between people and technology which he employs metaphorically. Subtle and witty, his work was translated into Russian by Boris Pasternak. A more establishment figure than Shiraz, his book *Land, Love, Era* was awarded the Soviet State Prize for Literature in 1976.

Paruyr Sevak (1924–71) was another staunch critic of the corrupt Soviet government to the extent that most Armenians believed that his death was murder at the hands of the KGB rather than the result of a road accident – and certainly the spot where the alleged accident took place is a straight unobstructed section of road with little traffic. The tenor of his writings is conveyed in titles such as *The Unsilenceable Belfry* (1959) and *Let There be Light* (1971).

Not all Armenian writers spoke Armenian as their native language. The novelist **Gosdan Zarian** (1885–1969) was the son of a staunchly Armenian father who was a general in the Tsarist army and he was brought up speaking Russian and French but not Armenian. His youth was spent in various Western countries where he frequently ate with Lenin in Geneva and knew Picasso in Paris. He started to learn Armenian only in 1910, studying with the Mekhitarists on the island of San Lazarro in Venice. He moved to Constantinople in 1913 and two years later was one of the few Armenian intellectuals who managed to escape the genocide, in his case by fleeing via Bulgaria to Rome. He returned to Istanbul in 1920 and in 1922 moved to Yerevan. Thoroughly disappointed with the Soviet regime, he left in 1925 and spent a nomadic existence including spells in the USA and Lebanon before returning to Armenia in 1961. His poem *The Bride of Tetrachoma*, first published in Boston in 1930, was republished in Yerevan in 1965 while a bowdlerised edition of his novel *The Ship on the Mountain*, first published in Boston in 1943, appeared in Yerevan in 1963.

Probably the best-known Armenian writer outside Armenia is **William Saroyan** (1908–81). Born to Armenian parents at Fresno, California, he sprang to fame in 1934 with his first book *The Daring Young Man on the Flying Trapeze*. His first successful Broadway play *My Heart's in the Highlands* was first performed in 1939. He was awarded both the Drama Critic's Circle Award and the Pulitzer Prize for *The Time of Your Life* (1939) but he refused to accept the latter since he believed that 'Commerce should not patronise art.' A prolific writer, Saroyan acknowledged Armenian culture as an important source of his literary inspiration and his work gave international recognition to Armenia. A year after his death, half of his cremated remains were interred in the Pantheon of Greats in Yerevan, while the other half remained in Fresno.

Painting Russian expansionism into Armenia and subsequent greater contact with western European painting greatly influenced the development of Armenian realistic painting in the 19th century. The first notable painter to break away from the medieval manuscript tradition was **Hakop Hovnatanian** (1806–81) whose family had been painters for nearly 200 years. (His grandfather's grandfather had contributed to the decoration of Ejmiatsin Cathedral in the late 17th century.) He painted portraits of his contemporaries in an original manner which fused elements of the painting of illuminated manuscripts with European traditions of portraiture: everything in these portraits is expressed through the face, above all the eyes, and the hands of the conventionally posed sitter.

By contrast **Hovhannes Aivasovsky** (1817–1900), often referred to as Ivan Aivasovsky – its Russian equivalent – shows little Armenian influence. He was born to an Armenian father at Feodosia in the Crimea and painted wonderful seascapes, calm seas with beautiful lighting effects, violent storms sometimes with men struggling to survive (over half his seascapes) or surprisingly vivid pictures of the historic sea battles of the Russian navy. Though with few equals to his ability to capture the many moods and colours of the sea, his non-marine pictures are decidedly more pedestrian. His achievements were probably more recognised internationally than is the case with any other 19th-century Armenian painter and he was even awarded the Légion d'Honneur in 1857.

Another recipient of the Légion d'Honneur was **Zakar Zakarian** (1849–1923) who left his home in Constantinople to train as a doctor in Paris but he later turned to painting. His still lifes with their careful composition and interplay of light and dark frequently incorporate a glass of water, interpreted by his contemporaries as expressing his feeling from his Paris home of the tragic events in his homeland. **Gevork Bashinjaghian** (1857–1920) developed the painting of landscapes with his calm, serene views, mostly of Armenia although he also travelled. **Vardghez Sureniants** (1860–1921) was a much more versatile artist. Like Bashinjaghian a painter of landscapes, he also painted many Armenian subjects and his 1895 painting *Desecrated Shrine* was a response to the massacres of the Armenians by the Turks. He additionally painted historical subjects; he was a gifted book illustrator and in 1899 was chosen to illustrate Pushkin's *Fountain of Bakhchisarai* as part of the centenary celebrations; and as a stage designer he was chosen by Konstantin Stanislavsky in 1904 to design his Moscow production of Maurice Maeterlinck's symbolist drama *Les Aveugles* (*The Blind*).

The landscapes of **Eghishe Tatevosian** (1870–1936) reflect the strong influence of French painters as well as of his teachers in Moscow, and the French influence is even stronger in the works of **Edgar Shaheen** (1874–1947) who studied in Paris. **Vano Khodjabekian** (1875–1922) was a complete contrast: a primitivist who on his arrival in Yerevan in 1919 created some moving scenes of the plight of the refugees who had escaped the Turkish massacres. **Hovsep Pooshman** (1877–1966) was another painter of still lifes, mostly incorporating oriental statuettes with titles such as *The Golden Decline of Life* and *The Murmur of Leaves*.

Probably the most brilliant and certainly the most influential Armenian artist of the early 20th century was **Martiros Sarian** (1880–1972) whose works mirror the creative intellectual ferment in the artistic world of the day and show an amazing feel for colour and form. He was born near Rostov-on-Don in Russia and studied in Moscow. His first visit to Armenia in 1901 resulted in the cycle *Stories and Dreams* which shows much symbolist influence. From 1909 he turned towards a more representational style using large areas of single colour with great attention to shapes and contrasts and the qualities of light. Another artist working through the revolutionary period was **Hakop Kojoyan** (1883–1959). He produced haunting landscapes as well as works which take a stylised medieval approach and book illustrations for authors such as Gorki. His *Execution of Communists at Tatev*, however, seems likely to have been painted for political reasons.

The Soviet period saw those Armenian painters who remained in the country and were approved by the regime supported, while others were harassed regardless of their talent. **Gyorgy Yakulov** (1884–1928) worked as a stage designer in Tiflis and Yerevan before being invited to Paris by Diaghilev where his work had immense success. He travelled in both China and Italy and his paintings reflect an attempt to combine traditional orientalism with the Italian high Renaissance. **Sedrak Arakelian** (1884–1942) was a follower of Sarian whose own lyrical landscapes successfully capture ephemeral moments in the Armenian countryside. Another follower, **Arutiun Galents** (1908–1967), was one of the children who escaped the genocide of 1915. His parents both died and he was brought up in an orphanage in Beirut. Not surprisingly his work reflects the tragic circumstances of his childhood. **Minas Avetissian** (1928–75) is regarded particularly highly in Armenia. Again a follower of Sarian, much of his work was destroyed either in a fire at his studio in 1972 (widely believed in Armenia to have been deliberately started by the Soviet security forces) or in the 1988 earthquake which destroyed both his frescoes at Leninakan (present-day Gyumri) and the museum dedicated to his work at Dzhadzur, his native village. He himself was tragically killed when he was knocked down by a car which had mounted the pavement. A complete contrast to these followers of Sarian is **Alexander Bazhbeuk-Melikian** (1891–1966) who can be regarded more as a follower of Degas. He painted women. In warm clear colours, whether exercising on a swing or combing their hair, they are elegant and at ease.

Ervand Kochar (1899–1979) was a sculptor and designer as much as a painter and his best-known work in Armenia is perhaps the striking statue of David of Sassoun on horseback which stands outside Yerevan railway station, while the work most noticed by visitors may be the statue of Haik Bzhshkian, also on horseback, which stands by the road to Garni (see page 138). The three-dimensional quality of his paintings tends to express his interest in sculpture and he created some amazing three-dimensional paintings, examples of which are in the Kochar Museum, Yerevan, and the Pompidou Centre, Paris. An immensely gifted artist, he had lived and worked in Paris from 1923 until 1936 but then, although highly successful there, he returned to Soviet Armenia. After his return he was accused of the Soviet crime of formalism and suffered periods of imprisonment. While in Paris in 1930 he married Melineh Ohanian and the couple had a son. Although Melineh was of Armenian descent, she had been born in France and the Soviet government would allow neither her nor Kochar's son to enter the Soviet Union. Neither was Kochar ever allowed to leave, not even during the period of the Khrushchev thaw, so he never saw his wife or son after his return.

Petros Konturajian (1905–56) was another child who was orphaned by the genocide of 1915. He went to Paris and became a successful painter of the city under the influence of Cézanne and the Cubists. In 1947, he returned to Armenia but he failed to come to terms with Soviet conditions and committed suicide. **Hakop Hakopian** (1928–75) also moved to live in Armenia at a similar age to Konturajian but was able to adapt, perhaps because life under Brezhnev was less intolerable than under Stalin. His still lifes and landscapes have a dramatic quality expressing deep anxiety. **Girair Orakian** (1901–63), is another painter who was driven from his home city of Constantinople. He spent most of the rest of his life in Rome. His paintings expressing the struggles between life and death for the poor can again be understood against his childhood background.

If Ivan Aivazovsky is Armenia's best-known 19th-century painter outside the country, the best-known 20th-century one is probably **Garnik Zulumian**, also known as Carzou (1907–2000). He worked as a stage designer as well as a painter and engraver and his paintings do often reflect a decorative and theatrical quality. Claiming that Picasso was no painter at all, he claimed the only truly great painters were Claude Lorrain, Watteau and Dalí. Carzou's response to the Armenian earthquake of 1988 was the painting *Armenia: Earthquake. Hope*, in which a naked woman is shown standing over ruins against a background of Armenian buildings and mountains.

Foremost among artists born after the establishment of Soviet power is **Sergei Parajanov** (1924–90). Although better known as a film director, he also created a wide range of extraordinary works of art including collages and mosaics which were frequently made using everyday materials – perhaps he developed this technique during his involuntary periods in Siberian labour camps. Many of his works display strong egocentricity. Of the artists alive today, the one whose work visitors are most likely to notice is **Ara Shiraz** (born 1941) as his 9m-high sculpture of Andranik Ozanian riding two horses is at the foot of the slope leading up to Yerevan Cathedral.

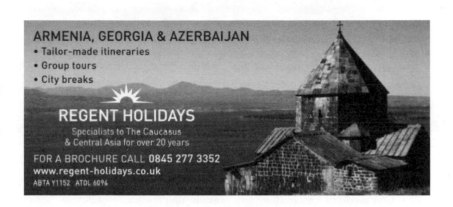

A JOURNEY THROUGH ARMENIA & GEORGIA

3 MAY & 13 SEPTEMBER 2011

with Tour Lecturer - Keith Miller

Our escorted tour to these two contrasting countries makes for a splendid introduction to a little known but richly historic region. Both countries boast breathtaking mountainous scenery and proudly maintain their separate cultural identities through a strong link with their past. Visits include Zvartnots Cathedral and Geghard Monastery in Armenia and Tblisi and Gori in Georgia where we will visit the Josef Stalin museum.

Our tours are carefully created to appeal to like-minded travellers who share an interest in the destination and subject of the tour and typically consist of between 12 and 22 participants.

Price from £2,346 per person for 11 nights
Price includes flights, accommodation with breakfast, ten lunches & ten dinners, all entrance fees & gratuities and the services of the Kirker Tour Lecturer.

To make a booking or request a brochure please call us on

020 7593 2283

Please quote source code SBO

Kirker

FOR DISCERNING TRAVELLERS

ABTA AITO | HOLIDAYS WITH 100% FINANCIAL PROTECTION

www.kirkerholidays.com

2

Practical Information

WHEN TO VISIT

Winter in Armenia can be bitterly cold and should be avoided by visitors if at all possible. Also, many of the sights outside the Arax Valley are inaccessible because of snow. That apart, the timing of any visit has to be a compromise because of the altitudinal variation in the weather. The best times to go are generally **late May and June** or else **late September and October**. The former sees the flowers at their very considerable best and is the nesting season for birds. The latter is drier but of course there are few flowers and much of the country is parched and brown. These periods of late spring and late summer are also when visibility is better with frequent views of Mount Ararat. It is usually invisible in **summer** because of heat haze.

HIGHLIGHTS

I am particularly fond of medieval buildings such as monasteries or fortresses in spectacular scenic settings and having a pleasant walk to get there adds to the enjoyment. Despite its accessibility by a good road and despite the number of tourists who go there, **Noravank** with its splendid setting and wonderful carvings is a must-see. **Khor Virap** is worthwhile if the visibility is good for giving the best views of Ararat. Other fine sites accessible to tourist buses are the monasteries of **Haghpat**, **Goshavank**, **Amberd** (together with its adjacent castle), **Selim caravanserai**, the field of khachkars at **Noratus** and the prehistoric stones at **Karahunj**. The final stretch of road to the monastery of **Marmashen** is in such poor condition that it is not really suitable for large buses, but this may change once construction of a small hydro-electric scheme is finished. **Tatev** in its dramatic setting gives a good idea of the layout of monasteries and can now be reached by the world's longest cable car ride.

However, my favourites are the wonderful **carvings at Makaravank**, the fortress of **Smbataberd** on its ridge (which makes a fine walk combining it with **Tsakhatskar Monastery**), **Khuchap and Khorakert monasteries** (reached by 4x4; see also page 218), **Spitakavor Monastery** (best to walk up the gorge), **Akhtala Monastery** (with its wonderful frescoes), **Kobayr Monastery** (short uphill walk), **Hnevank** (especially in early summer when the flowers are in bloom – short walk), the **petroglyphs** on Mount Mets Ishkhanasar (4x4) and the monastery of **Gndevank** approached along the old road from the north (walk or 4x4 if there haven't been recent rockfalls).

SUGGESTED ITINERARIES

A minimum of two or three days should be devoted to **Yerevan's museums** though check carefully the opening hours and days they are closed when planning your trip. Try to be in Yerevan at the weekend so as to get to **Vernissage market**. (An extra two or three days in Yerevan would allow visits to some of the worthwhile sites which can be reached as day trips from the capital.) In planning a trip round the rest of the country, there are three major factors to consider: whether or not to hire a car and, if so, whether or not to hire one with a 4x4; whether or not one wishes to do any walking; and whether some of the chosen places to visit will be inaccessible because of snow. The following would show a great deal of the country and could be tailored to suit individual requirements:

DAYS 1–3 Yerevan (or split time in Yerevan between start and end of tour).

DAY 4 Drive to Gyumri (see pages 194–7) visiting Talin (see pages 156–7), Mastara (see pages 157–8) and Harichavank (see pages 201–2) *en route*. Visit Marmashen (see pages 198–9) from Gyumri. Overnight Gyumri.

DAY 5 Drive via Spitak (see page 206) and the Pushkin Pass tunnel (see page 207) to Stepanavan (see pages 207–8). Visit Lori Berd (see page 208). Then drive via Kurtan (visit Hnevank, see page 220) to the Dzoraget/Alaverdi area for overnight (see pages 202 and 204).

DAY 6 Visit the monasteries of the Debed Gorge: Akhtala (see pages 217–18), Haghpat (see pages 215–17), Sanahin (see pages 212–15) and Kobayr (see pages 210–11). Overnight in the Dzoraget/Alaverdi area (see pages 202 and 204).

DAY 7 Drive via Noyemberian (see page 227) to Dilijan (see pages 227–8) visiting Makaravank (see page 225) *en route* and also Haghartsin (see pages 228–30). Visit Goshavank (see page 230) if not going to Makaravank. Alternatively, drive via Vanadzor (see pages 205–6) visiting Goshavank and Haghartsin. Overnight in Dilijan or Ijevan (see pages 223–4).

DAY 8 Visit Sevanavank (see pages 175–6), the field of khachkars at Noratus (see page 177) and Selim caravanserai (see page 243) before descending into Vayots Dzor (see page 233). Overnight in Vayots Dzor.

DAY 9 Walk to Tsakhatskar (see pages 240–1) and Smbataberd (see page 241). Overnight in Vayots Dzor.

DAY 10 Walk to Spitakavor (see pages 244–5). Overnight in Vayots Dzor.

DAY 11 Visit Tatev (see pages 255–6). Then return to Sisian for overnight (see page 253).

DAY 12 Visit Karahunj (see pages 252–3). Then drive via Gndevank (see pages 247–8) to Vayots Dzor for overnight.

DAY 13 Drive via Noravank (see pages 237–9) and Khor Virap (see pages 160–1) to Garni or Yerevan for overnight.

DAY 14 Visit Garni temple (see pages 186–7) and Geghard (see pages 188–91) before travelling via Yerevan to Ejmiatsin (see pages 163–7). Return to Yerevan for overnight.

If you want to visit the self-declared Republic of **Nagorno Karabagh** then on the eleventh day, after visiting Tatev, continue to Stepanakert (see pages 274–6).

Registering with the Nagorno Karabagh Foreign Ministry, either in Yerevan or Stepanakert (see pages 269–70) is essential before visiting other parts of the territory. Gandzasar and Dadivank (see pages 277 and 277–9 respectively) can be combined in a single day and the opportunity should be taken to visit Shushi (see pages 279–80). If there is time, Khndzoresk (see page 258) is not far off the Goris to Stepanakert road.

Anyone wishing to travel to the **extreme south** of the country could do so on the twelfth day after visiting Karahunj. Travel via Goris (see pages 256–8), stay overnight in either Kapan (pages 258–9) or Kajaran (page 260) and visit Meghri (pages 260–1) for the day, possibly driving there on the older road via Kajaran and back on the newer one through the Shikahogh Reserve (see page 259).

i TOURIST INFORMATION

Much useful information is available from the website of **Armenia Information** (*www.armeniainfo.am*), a service provided by the Armenian Tourism Development Agency. (For full details see *Chapter 3, Tourist information*, page 107.)

The best **internet source** of information is www.armeniapedia.org which is reasonably comprehensive on sites (including those in Nagorno Karabagh) but patchy on practical information. There is practical information on www.tacentral.com (including useful guides to the State History Museum in Yerevan and to Metsamor) but much of the country is not covered. For more websites see *Further information*, page 295.

The most useful **maps** of the country are published in Yerevan by Collage Ltd (*4 Sarian St, Yerevan;* ℆ *+374 10 520217;* e *collage@arminco.com; www.collage.am*). The pocket atlas *The Roads of Armenia*, costing AMD2,500, covers the country together with Nagorno Karabagh at a scale of 1:400,000. It has small street plans of Yerevan, Gyumri and Vanadzor. The map's third edition corrects many, but not all, of the inaccuracies of previous editions and it shows the new road south from Kapan to Meghri. Roads, rivers, railways, mountain summits and historical sites are shown, and names are given in both Armenian and English. The atlas does not appear to be available outside Armenia.

Perhaps more useful, because it is more accurate in the position of some historical sites, is Collage Ltd's more recent *Armenia & Mountainous Karabakh*, also 1:400,000 and AMD2,500. Place names are shown only in English so the map is a little less cluttered. Both the above maps show distances between towns and *The Roads of Armenia* also gives road numbers. Collage Ltd also publishes the best map of *Yerevan* (AMD2,500). Unlike the road atlas, the other two maps are available from Stanfords (see below) but at several times what they cost in Yerevan. Collage Ltd also produces a *Yerevan Guide Map* (AMD1,300) to a slightly smaller scale than its main Yerevan map but this smaller one usefully includes building numbers (see page 79). Another map is that covering Armenia and Azerbaijan at a scale of 1:560,000 published by International Travel Maps (*530 West Broadway, Vancouver, BC V5Z 1E9, Canada;* ℆ *+1 604 879 362;* f *+1 604 879 4521; www.itmb.com*), on which some of the maps in this guide are based. (If using this map, note that it too has misplaced at least one important historic site, namely Noravank). It is also available through Stanfords (*12 Long Acre, London WC2E 9LP, UK;* ℆ *020 7836 1321;* e *sales@stanfords.co.uk; www.stanfords.co.uk*).

The Armenian Monuments Awareness Project (AMAP) (*www.ArmenianMonuments.org*; see *Travelling positively*, page 97) is behind the information boards now appearing at many sites in Armenia. The developing website has some useful information, including a guide to Noratus.

The following tour operators can make arrangements to travel to Armenia or else operate group tours themselves:

UK

Birdquest Two Jays, Kemple End, Clitheroe, Lancs BB7 9QY; ☏ 01254 826317; e birders@ birquest.co.uk; www.birdquest.co.uk. Specialists for serious, in-depth birdwatching. Sometimes includes Armenia in regional tours.

Explore Worldwide Nelson Hse, 55 Victoria Rd, Farnborough, Hants GU14 7PA; ☏ 0870 333 4001; e res@explore.co.uk; www.explore.co.uk. Offers a Land of the Golden Fleece trip. (The fleece was kept at Colchis, near present-day Batumi on the Black Sea coast of Georgia.) The 16-day trip spends 6 nights in Armenia & a 4-day Azerbaijan extension is available.

Kirker Holidays 4 Waterloo Court, 10 Theed St, London SE1 8ST; ☏ 020 7593 1899; e travel@ kirkerholidays.com; www.kirkerholidays.com. Offers an 11-day group tour, with lecturer, to Armenia & Georgia (7 days in Armenia). Can also arrange tailor-made itineraries.

Kudu Travel Teffont Manor, Teffont Ewyas, Salisbury, Wilts SP3 5RL; ☏ 01722 716167; e kuduinfo@kudutravel.com; www.kudutravel.com. Offers a 12-day tour which includes some walking.

Martin Randall Travel Voysey Hse, Barley Mow Passage, London W4 4GF; ☏ 020 8742 3355; e info@martinrandall.co.uk; www.martinrandall.com. Specialises in high-brow cultural holidays. Offers an 8-day historical group tour, with lecturer.

Regent Holidays Mezzanine Suite, Froomsgate Hse, Rupert St, Bristol BS1 2QJ; ☏ 0845 277 3317; e regent@regent-holidays.co.uk; www.regent-holidays.co.uk. Can organise any itinerary in Armenia & Nagorno Karabagh (combined with Georgia & Azerbaijan if required) for individuals or groups. They also offer a 12-day group tour to Armenia & Georgia with an optional 7-day extension to Azerbaijan. Also short city-break tours to Yerevan. The authors have had personal experience of this firm's efficiency, flexibility & helpfulness.

Silk Road & Beyond Unit 6, Hurlingham Business Park, 55 Sulivan Rd, London W6 3DU; ☏ 020 7371 3131; e sales@silkroadandbeyond.co.uk; www.silkroadandbeyond.co.uk. Can organise any itinerary for individuals but also offers a 17-day tour to Armenia, Georgia & Azerbaijan which spends 6 days in Armenia. Also an 8-day tour to Armenia.

Steppes East The Travel Hse, 51 Castle St, Cirencester, Glos GL7 1QD; ☏ 01285 651 010; e east@steppestravel.co.uk; www.steppestravel.co.uk. Offers tailor-made itineraries.

Sunvil Discovery 10–12 Upper Sq, Old Isleworth, Middx TW7 7BJ; ☏ 020 8758 4722; e discovery@ sunvil.co.uk; www.sunvil.co.uk. Offers a 10-day tour to Armenia or tailor-made itineraries.

The Traveller & Palanquin 10 Bury Pl, London WC1A 2JL; ☏ 020 7436 9343, 7269 2770; e info@ the-traveller.co.uk; www.the-traveller.co.uk. Formerly the tours & travel department of the British Museum, this company offers a 14-day tour, with lecturer, to Armenia, Georgia & Azerbaijan (6 days in Armenia). Also 4-day trips to Yerevan & individual itineraries.

USA In the USA three companies which offer arrangements to Armenia are based in Glendale, California, and there is another in Pennsylvania. Each also has an office in Yerevan and one of them has an office in Stepanakert, Nagorno Karabagh as well.

Levon Travel 1132 North Brand Bd, Glendale, CA 91202; ☏ +1 818 552 7700, +1 800 445 3866; e sales@levontravel.com; wwwlevontravel.com. It also has offices at 10 Sayat Nova Bd, Yerevan; ☏ +374 10 525210; f +374 10 561483 & in Nagorno Karabagh at 16a Yerevanian St, Stepanakert (use the Yerevan contact numbers).

Menua Tours 3467 Ocean View Bd, Glendale, CA 91208; ☏ +1 818 249 2222; e info@menuatours.com; www.menuatours.com. It also has an office at 9 Alex Manugian St, AUA Business Centre, 1st Floor, Yerevan; ☏ +374 10 512051/2/3; f +374 10 512011.

Sidon Travel 428 S Central Av, Glendale, CA 91204; ☏ +1 818 553 0777; e sales@sidontravel.com;

www.sidontravel.com. Yerevan office in lobby of Ani Plaza Hotel, 19 Sayat Nova Av; +374 10 522967; e sidon@arminco.com.

AUSTRIA
Biblische Reisen Stifsplatz 8, 3400 Klosterneuburg; +43 2243 353 770; e info@biblische-reisen.at;

GEORGIA
Georgica Travel 22 Shanidze St, Tbilisi; +995 32 25 21 99; e georgica@caucasus.net; www.georgicatravel.ge

GERMANY
Biblische Reisen Silberburgstrasse 121, D-70176, Stuttgart; +49 7116 19250; e info@biblische-reisen.de; www.biblische-reisen.de. Runs group tours concentrating on churches & monasteries.

ISRAEL
Breeza Tours 27 Lishanski St, Rishon Letzion; +972 3 9625020; e info@breeza.co.il; www.breeza-tours.co.il. Offers an 11-day trip to Armenia & Georgia with 6 days in Armenia. Group & individual tours.

ITALY
Metamondo Via Ca' Rosso 21a, 30174 Mestre (VE); +39 41 8899 211; e info@metamondo.it; www.metamondo.it. Group tours.

NETHERLANDS
Koning Aap Reizen Entrada 211, 1096 EE Amsterdam; +371 20 788 7700; e info@

Sima Tours 2064 Sproul Rd, Broomall, PA 19008; +1 610 359 7521; m +1 610 304 5948; e info@simatours.com; www.simatours.com. It also has an office at 50 Terian St, Yerevan; +374 10 589954, 584715; f +374 10 543465.

www.biblische-reisen.at. Runs group tours concentrating on churches & monasteries.

Ventus Reisen Krefelder Strasse 8, D-10155 Berlin; +49 3039 100 332/3; e office@ventus.com; www.ventus.com. Group tours & individual arrangements.

Eco-Field Trips 11 Nes Ziona St, Tel-Aviv; +972 3 5100454; e mail@eco.co.il; www.eco.co.il. Runs group tours & makes individual arrangements.

koningaap.nl; www.koningaap.nl. Group tours & individual arrangements.

LOCAL TOUR OPERATORS IN YEREVAN All tour operators in Armenia are based in Yerevan. Some hotels in the provinces can organise local excursions; this is noted under individual entries. Apart from the American agents mentioned above, the tourist office lists around 130 more travel agents in Yerevan, an excessive number given the actual number of tourists who visit the country. Visitors who do not speak Armenian are strongly recommended to deal with those who have experience in making ground arrangements for tour operators from the UK since they will have staff who speak reasonable English. Tour operators dealing mainly with the diaspora may not speak as good English since the members of the diaspora usually speak Armenian. Tour operators can arrange all types of accommodation, guides and interpreters, car hire with or without driver, special-interest and general tours. They can also help with theatre tickets and virtually anything else a visitor may want. Armenians are very flexible and most things are possible. Suggested agents include:

Armenia Travel + M 4 Vardanants St; ☏+374 10 563667, 545330; e info@armeniatravel.am; www.armeniatravel.am. The authors have had personal experience of this company's efficiency & flexibility over many years.
Arminius Tours 2 Arshakunyats, 11th floor; ☏+374 10 545658; e arminius-reisen@yahoo.de; www.arminius.am

Armintour 33 Sayat Av; ☏+374 10 582282, 581123; e armint1@arminco.com; www.armintour.info.am
Hyur Service 50 & 96 Nalbandian St; ☏+374 10 546040, 546080; e contact@hyurservice.com; www.hyurservice.com
Saberatours-Sevan 32–38 Hanrapetutyan St (at Europe Hotel); ☏+374 10 525555; e incoming@saberatours.am; www.saberatours.am

Special-interest visits

Armenia lends itself to special-interest visits and several agents offer hiking, trekking, camping, winter sports, archaeological and other special-interest tours. The agents below offer such a range of special-interest tours.

AdvenTour 125a Arshakunyats Av; ☏+374 10 539609, 482271; m 091 426745; e adventour@netsys.am, info@armeniaexplorer.com; www.armeniaexplorer.com
Armenia Travel Bureau 24b Baghramian Av; ☏+374 10 561327; m 093 885642; e info@atb.am; www.atb.am. As well as the above range of tours, also offers biking, eco-tours, wine & even casino tours!

Avarayr 1 Buzand St; ☏+374 10 563681, 524042; e avarayr@arminco.com; www.avarayr.am
Seven Springs Tour 45/15 Komitas St, Yerevan; ☏+374 10 232440; m +374 94 912008; e info@7springstour.am, incoming@7springstour.am; www.7springstour.am

A good **website** for information on activity holidays is the section on ecotours on www.tacentral.am.

Anyone interested in **birdwatching** should contact the Ornithological Society of the Middle East, Caucasus and Central Asia (see page 7).

The diversity of accessible vegetation zones means that **botanical tours** are very rewarding. These can be arranged either via the Botanical Institute in Yerevan (☏ *+374 10 568690*) or the Yerevan tour operator Armenia Travel + M (see above). Tours specifically to **watch mammals** such as wolves and bears do not exist but local arrangements may be possible through Armenia Information (see page 107).

Horseriding holidays are also available at a number of locations such as the southern slopes of Mount Aragats and near Ijevan. See page 114 for details of a Yerevan riding school and page 227 for information about the riding school near Ijevan, Tavush province.

Most of the country away from the Ararat Valley has huge **hiking** potential and visitors are free to wander where they like, the only problems being absence of detailed maps and the difficulty of avoiding hospitality at every cottage. *Adventure Armenia* (see *Appendix 2*, page 294) describes 22 day-hikes. A number of signboards indicating trails have appeared at some sites, for example at Haghartsin Monastery and Jukhtakvank but it is difficult to get information about these beforehand. **Mountain climbing and hiking** can be arranged through Ajdahag Mountain Hiking Club (e *ajdahag@yahoo.com; www.narod.ru*). Armenia has superb **caving** with more than 10,000 caves in most regions of the country often concentrated along the river gorges. Most of the caves are little known although there is an active Armenian Speleological Society (☏ *+374 10 582254, 10 620248*). The proprietor of the Vayots Dzor Tourism Centre and Hotel at Vaik (see page 235) leads caving expeditions and caving can also be arranged through Amtour (☏*+374 10 744226;* e *info@amtour.am; www.amtour.am*) a company specialising in caving tours. Reportedly some of the best caving, though only for the experienced, is in Vayots Dzor province. Magili Cavern is in the gorge which leads to Noravank and is 1.7km deep. Stone tools and artefacts have been discovered in the cave, as well as more recent ceramic fragments from the 9th century onwards. The cave is home to thousands of insectivorous bats. The passageway is horizontal and varies from just enough for a person to crawl through to a spacious 10–15m in width. This very warm cave is open and the very steep entrance has a hand line to assist visitors. Other caves are strictly for the expert. At 3.3km, Archeri ('Bear') cave near Yeghegnadzor is Armenia's longest with some of the most spectacular stalactites and stalagmite formations in Europe. Unlike Magili it is far from horizontal with a vertical range of 145m. The cave gets its name from the remains of bears found here. Mozrovi, about 7.6km west of Arpi, has fine speleothems (mineral deposits of calcium carbonate precipitated from solution).

Winter sports are available at Tsaghkadzor (see *Chapter 4*, page 185) and Jermuk (see *Chapter 6*, page 248).

Byurakan Astrophysical Observatory (see *Chapter 4*, pages 153–4) offers events for amateur **astronomers** (e *director@bao.sci.am, observ@bao.sci.am; www.bao. am*). A night tour can be arranged by Menua Tours (see page 54).

OTHER SERVICES Some agents offer a variety of services which may be of use to visitors, such as **Hyur Service** (see page 56) which offers apartment and house accommodation, house cleaning and laundry, interpreter services (1hr/1 day AMD8,000/25,000) and cell-phone rental (AMD5000/day) as well as organising tours and car rental. Likewise, **Menua Tours** (see page 54) also offers services beyond tours and car rental, including interpreter and shopping assistance (1hr AMD8,500) and apartment rental.

RED TAPE

All visitors require **visas** except passport holders of Azerbaijan, Belarus, Georgia, Kazakhstan, Kyrgyzstan, Moldova, Russian Federation, Tajikistan, Ukraine and Uzbekistan. Tourist visas are easy to obtain and there are three ways of so doing. The easiest and now the most common way is **on arrival in Armenia.** At Zvartnots Airport, where most visitors arrive, it is straightforward and quick. Single-entry tourist visas are available for 21 or 120 days. The fee must be paid in Armenian drams (AMD3,000 for a 21-day visa, AMD15,000 for a 120-day visa). It is easy to change money in the airport, but a considerable commission is charged, so only change the minimum required and get a better deal later at one of the many bureaux de change in the city centre. When coming down into the arrivals hall the exchange kiosk is straight ahead. To the left is an area where visa application forms can be completed. The visa issuing desks, usually well staffed, are opposite the form-filling area. Visas can also be obtained at the following border checkpoints: Ayrum railway station, Bavra, Bagratashen, Gogaven border with Georgia (but not at such minor borders as the crossing from Georgia near Khuchap Monastery on the road over the Wolf's Gates Pass) and at the Meghri land border with Iran. The procedure here may be slower, especially for those last off the bus. Border crossing points can only issue single-entry visas (3-day transit, 21-day or 120-day tourist visas).

The second method is to apply for a conventional visa through an **Armenian embassy.** The application form for a conventional visa can be downloaded from the Armenian Foreign Ministry website (*www.armeniaforeignministry.com*) and applications should be made to the appropriate embassy. Note that applications from residents of the US states of Alaska, Arizona, California, Colorado, Hawaii, Idaho, Missouri, Nevada, New Mexico, Oregon, Texas, Utah, Washington and Wisconsin should apply to the Consulate General in Los Angeles and not to the embassy in Washington DC and fees must be paid by certified cheque or money order. Cash, credit cards and personal cheques are not accepted. In the UK payment must be by cash or postal order. Visas are normally issued in two to three working days. Since 1 January 2010 the fees for a conventional visa are the same as for those obtained on arrival (see above). Visas for children under 18 are issued free of charge. Multiple-entry visas are only available through an embassy.

A third way of obtaining a tourist visa is to obtain **an electronic visa** over the internet. Simply go to the web page of the Armenia Foreign Ministry (see above), complete the application page and pay the fee by credit card. The visa is normally issued within two working days and confirmation that it has been issued is sent electronically. It can then be collected on arrival. A valid e-visa allows entry through Zvartnots Airport and the same land border crossing points as above. E-visas are currently US$15 for a 21-day visa and US$60 for 120-days (so more expensive than obtaining either a visa on arrival or a conventional visa through an embassy). It has the advantage that no paper is inserted into one's passport, a consideration if you intend to visit Azerbaijan in the future. Without a credit card, this method isn't an option.

For any type of visa other than a tourist visa an invitation is required. In the case of **business trips** it must be certified by the Consular Department of the Ministry of Foreign Affairs or for private trips by the Passport and Visa Department of the Ministry of Internal Affairs. Multiple-entry visitor visas are available and transit visas are required for stops in Armenia *en route* to other countries. (For full details see the website of the appropriate Armenian embassy below.)

Tourist visas can be extended at the Passport and Visa Department of Police of Republic of Armenia in Yerevan (*13A Mashtots Av*; +374 10 530182) for AMD500 per extra day. Failure to extend on time now carries a fine of AMD50,000–100,000. Previously, due to the inconvenience of the several visits needed to extend a visa, the advice given was to pay, on departure, the US$3 (approx AMD1,000) per day fine for overstaying, now a much less financially attractive option.

ARMENIAN EMBASSIES ABROAD

Argentina J A,Pacheco de Melo 1922, C1126AAD Buenos Aires 1035; +54 114 816 8710; f +54 114 812 2803; e armenia@fibertelcom.ar

Austria Neubaugasse 12-14/1/16, 1070 Vienna; +43 1 5227479; f +43 1 5227481; e armenia@ armembassy.at

Belarus 17 Kirov St, Minsk; +375 172 275153/270936; f +375 172 275153; e armrep@ cis.minsk.by

Belgium Rue Montoyer 28, 1000, Brussels; +32 2 348 4400/2; f +32 2 348 4401; e armembel@ skynet.be; www.armembassy.be

Bulgaria 11 Fl April 20 St 11, 1606 Sofia; +359 2 526046/547970; f +359 2 526046; e armembsof@omega.bg

Canada 7 Delaware Av, Ottawa, Ontario K2P 0Z2; +1 613 234 3710; f +1 613 234 3444;

e armcanadaembassy@mfa.am; www.armembassycanada.ca

China 4-1-61, Tayuan Diplomatic Apts, Beijing, 100600; +86 10 653 25677; f +86 10 653 25654; e armchinaembassy@mfa.am

Egypt Mohamed Mozhar 20, Cairo; +202 27374157/59; f +202 27374158; e armegyptembassy@mfa.am; www.armembegypt.com

France 9 Rue Viète, 75017 Paris; +33 1 42 12 98 00; f +33 1 42 12 98 03; e ambarmen@wanadoo.fr

Georgia 4 Tetelashvili St, Tbilisi; +995 32 951723, 964286; f +995 32 964287; e armemb@ caucasus.net

Germany Nussbaumallee, D14050, Berlin; +49 30 405 09120/11/15; f +49 30 4050 9125; e armemb@gmx.de

Greece 95 Konstantinou Paleologou Av, Khalandri 15232, Athens; \+30 210 683 1130; f +30 210 683 1183; e armemb@otenet.gr

India E-1/20, Vasant Vihar, New Delhi 110057; \+9111 24112851/52; f +9111 24112853; e armemb@vsnl.com

Iran 1 Ostad Shahriar Street Corner of Razi, Jomhouri Eslami Av, Teheran; \+98 21 66704838, 66704833; f 98 21 66700657; e emarteh@yahoo.com

Italy Via dei Colli della, Farnesina 174, 00194 Rome; \+39 06 329 6638/7764; f +39 06 329 7763; e embarmit@tin.it

Kazakhstan 579 Seyfulin St, Almaty 480075; \+7 3272 9177296; f +7 3272 917296; e akod100@hotmail.com

Lebanon Rabieh, Mtaileb, Jasmin St, Beirut; \+961 4 402 952; f +961 4 418 860; e armenia@dm.net.lb

Poland ulica Woziwody 15, 02-908 Warsaw; \+48 22 8408130/8620; f +48 22 642 0643; e main@embarmenia.it.pl

Romania Apt 2, Str Coloteşti 1, Bucharest; \+40 21 3197604; f +40 21 3197603; e armembro@starnets.ro

Russia Armiansky per 2, Moscow 101000; \+7 495 9241269/9244535; f +7 495 9245030/9244535; e info@armem.ru; www.armenianembassy.ru

Switzerland 28 Av du Mail, 1205 Geneva; \+41 22 320 1100; f +41 22 320 6148; e arm.mission@deckpoint.ch

Syria Malki, Ibrahim Hanano St, PO Box 33241, Damascus; \+963 11 613 3560; f +963 11 613 0952; e am309@net.sy

Turkmenistan Kioroghli St 14, Ashgabad; \+993 12 295 542/354 418; f +993 12395 538/49; e eat@online.tm

Ukraine 45 Volodimirska St, Kiev 01901; \+044 234 9005, 235 1004; f +044 235 4355; e despanut@voliacable.com; www.armembassy.com.ua

United Arab Emirates PO Box 6358, Abu Dhabi; \+971 2 4444196; f +971 2 4444197; e aremir@emirates.net.ae

UK 25A Cheniston Gdns, London W8 6TG; \+44 207 938 5435; f +44 207 938 2595; e armemb@armenianembassyuk.com, consular@armenianembassyuk.com; www.armenianembassy.org.uk

USA 2225 R St NW, Washington, DC 20008; \+1 202 319 1976; f +1 202 319 2982. Consular Section: \+1 202 319 2983; f +1 202 319 8330; e armpublic@speakeasy.net; www.armeniaemb.org. Consulate General also at 50 North La Cienega Bd, Beverly Hills, CA 90211; \+1 310 657 6102/7320; f +1 310 657 7419; e armconla@aol.com

For a list of embassies and consulates in Armenia, see *Chapter 3*, pages 115–16.

GETTING THERE AND AWAY

BY AIR Yerevan has two airports, at **Zvartnots** 10km west of the city and **Erebuni** (now used only by the military) closer to the centre on the south side. A new terminal has brought Zvartnots fully up to international standards with signage in English as well as Armenian. Trolleys are available; rates are AMD400 for a trolley or AMD2,500 for a trolley and a porter who will carry up to three items of baggage. Additional items of baggage are AMD250 each. Porters can be recognised by their distinctive red-and-blue tops with 'CART SERVICE' written in English on the back.

The new departure hall has a well-stocked **duty-free** area where there are typical Armenian specialities such as crafts, dried-fruit sweetmeats, coffee and herbal teas as well as the usual alcohol (including brandy which is cheaper than in central Yerevan), perfume, clothes, luggage, etc. There is a small range of books mostly in Armenian.

Several western European **airlines** fly to Yerevan. Three airlines fly four times a week: **BMI** (British Midland International) (*37 Moscovian St, Yerevan;* \ *10 521383, 528220; www.flybmi.com*) from London Heathrow on Tuesdays, Wednesdays, Fridays and Sundays; **Austrian Airways** (*9 Alek Manukian St, AUA Business Centre, Yerevan;* \ *10 512201/2/3; www.austrian.com*) from Vienna on Tuesdays,

2

Thursdays, Fridays and Sundays; and **Czech Airlines** (*2 Baghramian Av, Yerevan;* ✎ *10 564099, 522162, 563624; www.czechairlines.com*) from Prague also on Tuesdays, Thursdays, Fridays and Sundays. **Air France** (*9 Alek Manukian St, Yerevan;* ✎ *10 512277, 512288, 512281; www.airfrance.com*) flies thrice weekly from Paris on Mondays, Wednesdays and Saturdays. **Air Italy** (*5 Spendarian St, Yerevan;* ✎ *10 530608; www.airitaly.it*) flies from Verona on Tuesdays and Fridays.

Armavia (*3 Amirian St; 37 Sayat Nova Av; 1 Yekmalian St, Yerevan;* ✎ *10 564806, 564816, 564805, 593816; www.u8.am*), based at Zvartnots Airport, operates international flights to destinations in Europe and Asia – Aleppo, Amsterdam, Athens, Beirut, Berlin, Dubai, Ekaterinburg, Istanbul, Kharkov, Kiev, Krasnodar, Larnica, Marseille, Moscow, Nizhniy Novgorod, Novosibirsk, Odessa, Paris, Rome, Rostov, Samara, Simferol, Sochi, St Petersburg, Tehran, Volgograd and Zurich. Flights to many of the above are weekly but are thrice weekly to Paris, Rome, Dubai, Sochi and Zurich; twice weekly to Athens and St Petersburg; daily to Tehran and four times a day to Moscow.

Aeroflot (*12 Amirian St, Yerevan;* ✎ *10 522435, 532131; www.aeroflot.co.uk*) flies from Moscow to Yerevan twice daily.

At the time of writing most of the flights to Yerevan operated by western European airlines leave late in the evening, typically around 22.00, thus arriving in Yerevan around 07.00 local time. The only exceptions are Air France's flights (which leave Paris about 13.00, arriving in Yerevan around 22.00 local time, allowing a reasonable night's sleep) and two of BMI's flights which, while not as convenient as Air France's, do at least permit some sleep in Yerevan before embarking on sightseeing – the Wednesday and Thursday flights departing London at 16.00, arriving Yerevan at 01.00.

As airlines change schedules frequently, the above is only an indication of the situation at the time of writing. A **full timetable** for Zvartnots Airport, is available on the website of Armenia Information Service (*www.armeniainfo.am*).

Passengers transiting via Moscow, Ukraine or Georgia no longer require transit visas as was the case in the past. Note, however, that the Sheremetyevo Airport website (*www.svo.aero*) advises that while Russian transit visas are not needed for foreigners spending less than 24 hours at Sheremetyevo, they are required for a longer transit. They can be obtained from the consular office at the airport (⊕ *06.00–01.00 daily*) although the site strongly advises anyone who needs a Russian transit visa to obtain one before travelling.

A number of CIS airlines also fly to Yerevan, but many of them have no offices in either the city or at the airport and, while tickets can readily be booked through a travel agent, it is not possible to easily contact many of these airlines direct which are based in various Russian or Ukrainian provincial cities. Also many of these services operate only weekly so don't miss the plane; should you do so you won't get a refund. Lastly, most flights to CIS destinations are on Russian-built aircraft. These aircraft are now banned from western European airports on environmental grounds (too noisy) but are used almost exclusively by the plethora (around 350–400) of airlines operating within the CIS.

All air fares change frequently; the following is only an indication of cost at the time of writing. Prices quoted are the best available return public fares (including taxes) on the above Western airlines, in economy class, between London and Yerevan. As the flights fill over time and departure dates draw near prices will go up. Travel agents and tour operators normally have cheaper contracted fares but these can only be sold as part of a package holiday. BMI's London to Yerevan flights are direct; they are also the most expensive at £582. LOT tends to be cheapest and can sometimes, although rarely, be as low as £235. Other airline prices are in the region of £375–390.

Airport transfer The **city centre** can be reached by **minibus 108** (cost AMD200), but this is of no use to passengers arriving on flights from western Europe since it does not operate at night. However, Yerevan's **taxis** are cheap – expect to pay around AMD5,000 to the centre. The journey takes about 15 minutes. In the arrivals hall, after passing through passport control there is a desk where you can arrange a taxi. Note that on leaving the airport the tag on your luggage will be checked against that on your ticket or boarding pass, so do not discard it.

Other international airports Yerevan Zvartnots is not actually the only Armenian airport with international services. Shirak Airport (see page 197) at Gyumri has a service on Saturdays to Moscow. It is said that taxis meet arriving flights at this little-used airport.

BY TRAIN It is quite possible to arrive in Armenia by train. An overnight service operates from **Tbilisi** in Georgia on odd dates (though not on both the 31st and the 1st as these are consecutive dates) departing at 16.00 and arriving in Yerevan at 06.06 the next morning. The northbound service leaves Yerevan at 20.20 on even dates and arrives in Tbilisi at 08.15. *En route* the train calls at 12 intermediate stations, including Vanadzor and Gyumri, but mostly at inconvenient hours of the night. Trains have four classes: *obshi* (open seating on wooden benches), *plas* (reserved seats, possibly on wooden seats, more often on padded ones) and two types of compartments: *coupé* (compartments with sleeping berths for four), and *CB* (SV in English) or Luxe, a compartment for two. Prices, one-way, range from AMD2,782 for *obshi* to AMD12,098 for *CB*. Toilets on the train are not noted for their cleanliness, and food is not available so bring some with you rather than rely entirely on your fellow passengers to share their usually ample provisions. The ride is highly scenic but the best bits are hidden in the dark except, to some extent, in midsummer. Tickets are bought at the stations and can be purchased up to about ten days in advance; seats can also be booked.

BY BUS It is easy to travel by bus from either Georgia or Iran. There are also services from Turkey which operate via Georgia, but note that it is currently not possible to travel from Russia to Armenia via Georgia, as was previously the case. It is now illegal under Russian law for foreigners to enter or leave Georgia via land borders with Russia. In theory a Georgian transit visa should not be required for holders of Armenian visas spending less than 72 hours in Georgia. Georgian visas can now be obtained at the border if necessary. Tickets should be bought in advance if at all possible. The baggage allowance on buses is 20kg with excess being charged at AMD250 per kilo. Most buses to destinations outside Armenia leave from Kilikia Central Bus Station (*6 Isakov Av, just past the brandy factory on the road to Ejmiatsin;* +374 10 565370).

From Georgia direct buses leave Tbilisi at 08.00 and 10.00 daily, taking seven hours for the journey to Yerevan via Stepanavan and Ashtarak at a cost of about GEL44 (Georgian lari) (US$25). The return service also operates at 08.00 and 10.00 and takes seven hours; the cost is AMD6,500. Minibuses also travel between Tbilisi and Yerevan, hourly 10.00–16.00, taking six hours for the journey which costs AMD6,000. In both countries tickets are purchased at the bus stations (Ortachala bus station and at the main train station in Tbilisi; Kilikia Central bus station in

Yerevan) and can be bought a few days in advance. There is a bus from Batumi on Georgia's Black Sea coast leaving at 07.00 on Mondays and Fridays and taking 12 hours for the journey via Gyumri at a cost of GEL32/US$18.The return service leaves Yerevan also on Mondays and Fridays at 07.00 and costs about AMD7,000. (Note: times and days can change so check locally if intending to use these routes.)

From Iran the bus leaves from Tehran daily at 13.00 and is scheduled to arrive in Yerevan 26 hours later. The fare is US$25 (although note that some sources quote 34 hours and US$35). The southbound service leaves Yerevan at 10.00 daily; cost AMD17,000.

Coming **from Turkey**, a number of companies operate buses between Yerevan and Istanbul, all apparently leaving Istanbul on Thursdays between 09.00 and 10.00. From Yerevan buses depart on Saturdays at 10.00 or 11.00 or 'when it is full'. The journey is scheduled to take 41 hours and the fare is US$60. You may need to obtain a Georgian transit visa (available at the border) and travellers report being asked for an additional US$10 'entry fee' at the Georgian border at Batumi. The advice is to check details before travelling and to book a ticket three to seven days in advance either personally at the bus station or via Emniyet Kesebirler Turizm (*Hotel Erebuni, 3rd floor, room 21A;* \ +374 10 540756, 560638, 564993; e *eminet@ netsys.am*) in Yerevan or the same firm in Istanbul (*Kucuk Langa Cad. Emniyet, Oto Gari No. 5/A Aksaray-IST;* \ +212 632 78 74; e *rayaistanbulr@hotmail.com*).

✚ HEALTH   *with Dr Felicity Nicholson*

All travellers to Armenia should ensure that they are up to date with **immunisation** against tetanus, polio and diphtheria (now given as an all-in-one vaccine, Revaxis, which lasts for ten years), and hepatitis A. Hepatitis A vaccine (Havrax Monodose or Avaxim) comprises two injections given about a year apart. The course costs about £100 (but may be available on the NHS), it protects for 25 years and can be given even close to the time of departure. It is also sensible to be immunised against typhoid fever. In addition, some visitors, depending on what they are likely to be doing, may be advised to have protection against tick-borne encephalitis, malaria, hepatitis B and rabies (see page 64). Visitors should ensure that they take any essential medications with them as drugs can be difficult to access. Consider also taking antibiotics with you (available only on prescription in the UK). **Tuberculosis** is very common in

QUICK TICK REMOVAL   *Dr Jane Wilson-Howarth*

Asian ticks are not the prolific disease transmitters they are in the Americas, but they may spread Lyme disease, tick-bite fever and a few rarities. Tick-bite fever is a non-serious, flu-like illness, but still worth avoiding. If you get the tick off whole and promptly, the chances of disease transmission are reduced to a minimum. Manoeuvre your finger and thumb so that you can pinch the tick's mouthparts, as close to your skin as possible, and slowly and steadily pull away at right angles to your skin. This often hurts. Jerking or twisting will increase the chances of damaging the tick, which in turn increases the chances of disease transmission, as well as leaving the mouthparts behind. Once the tick is off, dowse the little wound with alcohol (local spirit, whisky or similar are excellent) or iodine. An area of spreading redness around the bite site, or a rash or fever coming on a few days or more after the bite, should stimulate a trip to a doctor.

Armenia, with an incidence of 73 cases per 100,000 people in 2008. The disease is spread through close respiratory contact and occasionally through infected milk or milk products. The vaccine is usually only recommended for those aged 16 or younger who will be spending three months or more living and working with the local population. For those aged 17 to 35, a case-by-case assessment needs to be done. The vaccine is not considered effective for those over the age of 35.

TICK-BORNE ENCEPHALITIS Caused by a virus in the same family as yellow fever, tick-borne encephalitis is spread through the bites of infected ticks which are usually picked up in forested areas with long grass and it can also be transmitted through the unpasteurised milk of infected livestock. Anyone liable to go walking in late spring or summer (when the ticks are most active) should seek protection. A vaccine is available against the disease and initial immunisation ideally consists of three injections. The second is given one to three months after the first and the third five to 12 months after the second. If time does not allow for the third dose, around 90% protection is given by the first two and, if time is shorter still, then the second dose can be done two weeks after the first. There is a different vaccine for children aged one to 15 (Ticovac Junior) but the schedule is the same. Taking preventative measures is also very important. When walking in grassy and forested areas, ensure that you wear a hat, tuck your trousers into socks and boots and your shirt into your trousers, have long-sleeved tops and use tick repellents. Ticks can more easily be seen on pale clothing and can be flicked off before they get a grip on you so consider your clothing carefully. It is important to check for ticks each time you have been for a long walk – this is more easily done by someone else. If you find a tick then slowly remove it (see box opposite), taking care not to squeeze the mouthparts.

MALARIA After being eliminated in the 1960s malaria reappeared in 1994 following the reduction in control measures. It was largely confined to a small area in the Ararat Valley, roughly from Khor Virap in the north as far south as Yeraskh, although in 1999 there were reported cases in the outer southern suburbs of Yerevan. The number of reported cases fell to only 29 in 2003 and since 2006, according to WHO, no cases due to local transmission have been reported. However, there is always the possibility that the disease could reappear. The main road to the south passes through the malarial area but as mosquitoes are mostly active after sunset it may be unnecessary to take precautions if simply passing through. Birdwatchers visiting the much-favoured Armash fish ponds were (until recently) recommended to take precautions and up-to-date advice should be sought. The risk time is from June to October. Malaria in Armenia is exclusively of the benign *Plasmodium vivax* form so the drugs currently recommended are Chloroquine or Proguanil.

HEPATITIS A AND B Vaccination against **hepatitis B** can take six months to become effective and as the disease is most likely to be picked up through inadequately sterilised needles or syringes the best way of avoiding it may be to take an emergency medical kit which contains these items. Do note, however, that a shorter course is available if there is no time for the full course. Three injections are needed for the best protection and can be given over a three-week period if there is time for those aged 16 or over. The shortest course for those under 16 is two months. **Hepatitis A** vaccine can be given in combination with hepatitis B, as Twinrix, although two doses are needed at least seven days apart to be effective for the hepatitis A component and three doses are needed for the hepatitis B. Hepatitis B vaccine is always recommended when working in medical settings and also with children.

Should diarrhoea occur it is important to maintain hydration by drinking plenty of fluids. Sachets of oral rehydration salts give a perfect biochemical replacement but other, less expensive, mixtures will do. Any dilute mixture of sugar and salt in water is beneficial; for example, Coke with a three-finger pinch of salt in a glass. Or make a solution of eight level teaspoons of sugar (18g) and one level teaspoon of salt (3g) to one litre (five cups) of safe water. A squeeze of lemon juice or orange juice improves the flavour and adds potassium which is also lost in diarrhoea. Drink two large glasses after each bowel action and more if you are thirsty. These solutions are still absorbed well if you are vomiting, but you will need to take just sips at a time. If you are not eating you need to drink three litres a day plus whatever is pouring into the toilet. If you feel like eating, take a bland, high carbohydrate diet.

If the diarrhoea is bad, or you are passing blood or slime, or you have a fever, you will probably need antibiotics in addition to fluid replacement. A dose of norfloxacin or ciprofloxacin repeated twice a day for three days may be appropriate. Note that antibiotics are only available on prescription in the UK.

RABIES Vaccination is essential for anyone likely to be in close contact with animals or for those who are going to be more than 24 hours from medical help. Pre-exposure vaccination comprises three doses over a minimum of 21 days, and all three doses are required to change the treatment needed should you be exposed. If you have had all three pre-exposure doses, then you still need two more doses of vaccine if you are bitten or otherwise exposed, the first ideally on the day of exposure (or as soon afterwards as possible) and the second post-exposure dose three days later. If you have not had the pre-exposure doses you will need rabies immunoglobulin (RIG), which is expensive (around US$800 a dose) and is often unavailable. Vaccine alone when you have not had the pre-exposure doses of vaccine is not effective. Post-exposure prophylaxis should be given as soon as possible although it is never too late to seek help as the incubation period for rabies can be very long.

Rabies is spread through an infected bite, scratch or lick over an open wound from any warm-blooded animal. Dogs are the most likely source in Armenia. If you think you have been exposed then wash the wound immediately and thoroughly with soap and running water for about ten minutes. Then douse the wound with iodine or a strong alcoholic solution (vodka may be the most immediately available) and go straight to medical help.

Note that it is important to seek medical help even if you have had the full three-dose course of pre-exposure immunisation, as explained above. Inform the medical staff of exactly what immunisation you have, or have not had – this can save a lot of worry, and unnecessary expense. Medications, including vaccines, have to be paid for in Armenia.

TRAVELLERS' DIARRHOEA Like anywhere else, travellers' diarrhoea can occur in Armenia and visitors should take the usual sensible precautions such as handwashing before eating. Tap water should not be drunk unless boiled (remember to avoid ice cubes) but the water from Armenia's many springs (see page 87) is safe. Bottled water is easily available. Where the water quality is dubious, brush your teeth with bottled or boiled water. Food such as fruit and cheese bought at markets for picnics should be well washed in the spring water which flows at most picnic sites. Food you have washed and peeled yourself, and hot foods, should be safe. Raw foods, cold cooked foods, salads which have been prepared by others and ice cream are potentially risky, and foods kept lukewarm in hotel buffets may be dangerous, but do keep a sense of proportion. In several lengthy visits to Armenia we were only afflicted once and we enjoyed vast quantities of delicious Armenian fruit, vegetables, salads and ice cream!

SUN Remember that Armenia is a sunny country and that the temperature at the higher altitudes can mask the strength of the sun. Sunscreen, hat and sunglasses should not be forgotten.

SNAKEBITE Snakes rarely attack unless provoked, usually preferring to get out of the way of humans as soon as they detect any vibration. Wear stout shoes and long trousers in areas where there may be snakes. Most snakes are harmless and even venomous species will dispense venom only in about half of their bites so even if you are bitten you are unlikely to have received venom. Many so-called first-aid techniques such as cutting into the wound or applying a tourniquet are dangerous and do not work. The only effective treatment is antivenom. If you are bitten by a snake which you think may be venomous:

- Keep calm. It is likely that no venom has been dispensed.
- Prevent movement of the bitten limb by applying a splint.
- Keep the bitten limb below heart height to slow the spread of any venom.
- If you have a crêpe bandage wrap it round the whole limb (eg: toes to thigh) as tightly as you would for a sprained ankle.
- Evacuate to a medical facility which has antivenom. If within an hour's drive of Yerevan go to the Republican Hospital, Department of Toxicology, 6 Makarian Street (*reception: +37410 340020; toxicology dept +374 10 343166*). Otherwise go to the nearest regional polyclinic.
- NEVER cut or suck the wound.
- NEVER give aspirin. Paracetamol is safe.
- DO NOT apply ice packs.
- DO NOT apply anything to the wound.

Treatment with antivenom requires identification of the snake. Ideally the snake should be killed, if that can be done safely, and taken to show the doctor. Beware! A dead or even a decapitated snake can still exhibit a bite reflex and can leak venom through its fangs. It is wise to handle it with a stick and transport it in a leak-proof container.

HIV/AIDS In 2008 UNAIDS/WHO estimated the prevalence rate at about 0.1% of the adult population. This compares with the prevalence rate in the UK of around 0.2%. If you must indulge, use condoms or femidoms, which help to reduce the risk of transmission.

TRAVEL CLINICS AND HEALTH INFORMATION A full list of current travel clinic websites worldwide is available on www.istm.org/. For other journey preparation information, consult www.nathnac.org/ds/map_world.aspx. Information about various medications may be found on www.netdoctor.co.uk/travel.

UK

Berkeley Travel Clinic 32 Berkeley St, London W1J 8EL (near Green Park tube station); ☏ 020 7629 6233; ⏱ 10.00–18.00 Mon–Fri; 10.00–15.00 Sat

Edinburgh Travel Health Clinic 14 East Preston St, Newington, Edinburgh EH8 9QA; ☏ 0131 667 1030; www.edinburghtravelhealthclinic.co.uk; ⏱ 09.00–19.00 Mon–Wed, 09.00–18.00 Thu & Fri. Travel vaccinations & advice on all aspects of malaria prevention. All current UK-prescribed anti-malaria tablets in stock.

Fleet Street Travel Clinic 29 Fleet St, London EC4Y 1AA; ☏ 020 7353 5678; e info@ fleetstreetclinic.com; www.fleetstreetclinic.com; ⏱ 08.45–17.30 Mon–Fri. Injections, travel products & latest advice.

Hospital for Tropical Diseases Travel Clinic Mortimer Market Centre, Capper St (off Tottenham Ct Rd), London WC1E 6JB; ☏ 020 7388 9600; www. thehtd.org; ⏱ 13.00–17.00 Wed & 09.00–13.00 Fri. Consultations are by appointment only & are only offered to those with more complex problems. Check the website for inclusions. Runs a Travellers' Healthline Advisory Service (☏ 020 7950 7799) for country-specific information & health hazards. Also stocks nets, water purification equipment & personal protection measures. Travellers who have returned from the tropics & are unwell, with fever or bloody diarrhoea, can attend the walk-in emergency clinic at the hospital without an appointment.

InterHealth Travel Clinic 111 Westminster Bridge Rd, London SE1 7HR; ☏ 020 7902 9000; e info@interhealth.org.uk; www.interhealth.org.uk; ⏱ 08.30–17.30 Mon–Fri. Competitively priced, one-stop travel health service by appointment only.

MASTA (Medical Advisory Service for Travellers Abroad) At the London School of Hygiene & Tropical Medicine, Keppel St, London WC1E 7HT; ☏ 09068 224100 (this is a premium-line number, charged at 60p/min); e enquiries@ masta.org; www.masta-travel-health.com. For a fee, they will provide an individually tailored health brief, with up-to-date information on

how to stay healthy, inoculations & what to take.

MASTA pre-travel clinics ☏ 01276 685040; www.masta-travel-health.com/ travel-clinic.aspx. Call or check the website for the nearest; there are currently 50 in Britain. They also sell malaria prophylaxis, memory cards, treatment kits, bednets, net treatment kits, etc.

NHS travel websites www.fitfortravel.nhs.uk or www.fitfortravel.scot.nhs.uk. Provide country-by-country advice on immunisation & malaria prevention, plus details of recent developments, & a list of relevant health organisations.

Nomad Travel Clinics Flagship store: 3–4 Wellington Terrace, Turnpike Ln, London N8 0PX; ☏ 020 8889 7014; e turnpike@nomadtravel.co.uk; www.nomadtravel.co.uk; walk in or appointments ⏱ 09.15–17.00 everyday with late night Thu. Also has clinics in west & central London, Bristol, Southampton & Manchester – see website for further information. As well as dispensing health advice, Nomad stocks mosquito nets & other anti-bug devices, & an excellent range of adventure travel gear. Runs a Travel Health Advice line on ☏ 0906 863 3414.

The Travel Clinic Ltd, Cambridge 41 Hills Rd, Cambridge CB2 1NT; ☏ 01223 367362; e enquiries@travelclinic.ltd.uk; www.travelcliniccambridge.co.uk; ⏱ 10.00–16.00 Mon, Tue & Sat, 12.00–19.00 Wed & Thu, 11.00–18.00 Fri

The Travel Clinic Ltd, Ipswich Gilmour Piper, 10 Fonnereau Rd, Ipswich IP1 3JP; ☏ 01223 367362; ⏱ 09.00–19.00 Wed, 09.00–13.00 Sat

Trailfinders Immunisation Centre 194 Kensington High St, London W8 7RG; ☏ 020 7938 3999; www.trailfinders.com/travelessentials/ travelclinic.htm; ⏱ 09.00–17.00 Mon, Tue, Wed & Fri, 09.00–18.00 Thu, 10.00–17.15 Sat. No appointment necessary.

Travelpharm www.travelpharm.com. The Travelpharm website offers up-to-date guidance on travel-related health & has a range of medications available through their online mini-pharmacy.

Irish Republic

Tropical Medical Bureau 54 Grafton St, Dublin 2; ☏ +353 1 2715200; e graftonstreet@tmb.ie; www.tmb.ie; ⏱ until 20.00 Mon–Fri & Sat

mornings. For other clinic locations, & useful information specific to tropical destinations, check their website.

USA

Centers for Disease Control 1600 Clifton Rd, Atlanta, GA 30333; ☎ (800) 232 4636 or (800) 232 6348; e cdcinfo@cdc.gov; www.cdc.gov/travel. The central source of travel information in the USA. Each summer they publish the invaluable Health Information for International Travel.

IAMAT (International Association for Medical Assistance to Travelers) 1623 Military Rd, #279 Niagara Falls, NY 14304-1745; ☎ 716 754 4883; e info@iamat.org; www.iamat.org. A non-profit organisation with free membership that provides lists of English-speaking doctors abroad.

Canada

IAMAT (International Association for Medical Assistance to Travellers) Suite 10, 1287 St Clair St West, Toronto, Ontario M6E 1B8; ☎ 416 652 0137; www.iamat.org

TMVC Suite 314, 1030 W Georgia St, Vancouver, BC V6E 2Y3; ☎ (604) 681 5656; e vancouver@ tmvc.com; www.tmvc.com. One-stop medical clinic for all your international travel health & vaccination needs.

Australia and New Zealand

TMVC (Travel Doctors Group) ☎ 1300 65 88 44; www.tmvc.com.au. 30 clinics in Australia & New Zealand, including: *Auckland* Canterbury Arcade, 174 Queen St, Auckland 1010, New Zealand; ☎ (64) 9 373 3531; e auckland@traveldoctor.co.nz; *Brisbane* 75a Astor Terrace, Spring Hill, Brisbane QLD 4000, Australia; ☎ (07) 3815 6900; e brisbane@traveldoctor.com.au; *Melbourne* 393

Little Bourke St, Melbourne, Vic 3000, Australia; ☎ (03) 9935 8100; e melbourne@ traveldoctor.com.au; *Sydney* 428 George St, Sydney, NSW 2000, Australia; ☎ (2) 9221 7133; e sydney@traveldoctor.com.au

IAMAT (International Association for Medical Assistance to Travellers) 206 Papanui Rd, Christchurch 5, New Zealand; www.iamat.org

South Africa

SAA-Netcare Travel Clinics ☎ 011 802 0059; e travelinfo@netcare.co.za; www.travelclinic.co.za. 11 clinics throughout South Africa.

TMVC NHC Health Centre, Cnr Beyers Naude & Waugh Northcliff; ☎ 0861 300 911; e info@ traveldoctor.co.za; www.traveldoctor.co.za. Consult the website for clinic locations.

IN ARMENIA Visitors at present still do a fair amount of **passive smoking** in spite of anti-smoking legislation. From the end of 2005 separate non-smoking areas were meant to have been designated in restaurants, while public organisations and state institutions had to allocate a separate room for smokers with the rest of the premises smoke-free. In 2006 smoking in hospitals, public transport, schools and colleges, and sports facilities was banned.

Enforcement of the ban is variable. Certainly in smaller restaurants it seems non-existent. Cigarettes are consumed in large quantities; around 70% of men smoke. Surveys show that 35% of Armenian smokers believe that smoking will do them no harm while 45% believe that passive smoking is harmless. Around 39% of Armenian doctors smoke, although no longer perhaps in front of their patients as was the case in the past! Nevertheless life expectancy remains among the highest in the CIS at 70.5 years for men and 74.5 for women (according to official statistics), but 69 and 77 respectively according to the American CIA.

Armenia's economic problems have had a serious impact on health care. The **fertility rate** of women plummeted to less than half its 1990 rate but has shown a small rise in recent years. Towns and villages are consequently often experiencing falling population although the country's abortion rate officially remains below the European average. Aid workers, however, claim that women are choosing to terminate pregnancy in unprecedented numbers. Preliminary indicators from a UNICEF-conducted nutrition survey in Armenia suggest that **malnutrition** has tripled to being found in 12% of children up to the age of five and the infant mortality rate is more than three times the average of EU member states, although it has more than halved between 1990 and 2008. Armenia's government can only now fund less than 30% of the nation's health budget and UNICEF reports that one hospital director freely admits that patients are illegally charged for drugs, 'since that is the only way that we can afford to keep our doors open'. The steep increase in **maternal mortality** is directly attributed to reduced health expenditure. Health workers, like teachers, report intermittent payment of salaries. The United Nations says that 26% of Armenia's population is still **living in 'extreme poverty'**, surviving on less than US$1 per day and classifies more than two-thirds of the population as 'poor'.

A **reciprocal health agreement** exists for British citizens which means that health treatment (including dental) is free on producing a UK passport. However, drugs still need to be paid for. Many US health insurance policies do not include Armenia so special cover needs to be purchased. The UK Foreign Office advises that medical facilities are generally poor. It is prudent for all visitors to ensure that their insurance will cover repatriation, or at least evacuation, in the event of serious illness or accident.

SAFETY

Most visits to Armenia are trouble free. Crime is increasing in Yerevan especially (though from a very low base level) and visitors should take sensible precautions. The risk of being a victim is, however, much less likely than in most western European and American cities. Far greater risks after dark are either tripping up on pavements in need of repair or else falling into holes dug during the pavement's reconstruction. Watch out, too, for missing manhole covers. These risks have reduced, at least in the centre of Yerevan, but can still be a problem elsewhere.

The military situation does mean that some areas along the 1994 cease-fire line should definitely be avoided because of the risk from occasional snipers on the Azerbaijan side. The old road from Ijevan to Noyemberian is a particular problem but there is no need to use it as a new road has been built further from the ceasefire line. There is a problem, particularly in Nagorno Karabagh, from minefields. To the best of the author's knowledge all places mentioned in this guide are perfectly safe to go and sights where the unresolved conflict means that safety is problematic have been excluded. However, visitors to Nagorno Karabagh should note that consular services are unavailable there if they do encounter difficulties.

Armenia's death rate in road-traffic accidents has historically been proportionately much higher than that in the UK despite considerably lower traffic levels. The Armenian figure is likely to deteriorate even further as the improved roads tempt drivers to higher speeds and increasing traffic levels mean that it is even more dangerous than it was previously to drive round blind bends on the wrong side of the road. In fact the old pot-holed tracks, where speeds were perforce low as drivers sought to avoid the deepest ruts, have undoubtedly helped to keep the accident rate down. The legislation dating from Soviet days making the wearing of seat belts compulsory is now actively enforced by the traffic police (see page 77).

Pedestrians should be extremely careful at pedestrian crossings. Often vehicles do not give pedestrians priority at such crossings, even though there is a hefty fine if caught disobeying. Be especially aware of traffic turning right.

Telephone numbers for the emergency services are:

As Armenia is a former republic of the Soviet Union, attitudes towards disabled travellers are still very much entrenched in the communist era. However, like other countries in the region, it is slowly changing to reflect outside influences as it tries to increase its tourist trade for those with disabilities.

PLANNING AND BOOKING There are few specialist travel agencies running trips to Armenia. Companies such as Visit Armenia (*www.visitarm.com*) may be able to offer trips to the area.

GETTING THERE The main airport in Armenia is Zvartnots International Airport and it has facilities for those in wheelchairs including disabled toilets and other amenities. However, Shirak Airport may lack the same facilities.

ACCOMMODATION A number of hotels in Armenia have wheelchair access, such as the Golden Tulip Hotel (*14 Abovian St, Yerevan;* ⎰ *+37410 591600; www.goldentulipyerevan.com*; see page 108) or Best Western Congress Hotel (*1 Italia St, Yerevan;* ⎰ *+374 10 59 11 99; www.congresshotelyerevan.com*; see page 108).

VISITING PLACES Armenia has a number of historical sites and many will be difficult for wheelchair users to gain access to. The Garni temple, for example, has a number of steps and may cause problems for those who struggle on their own unless they are accompanied by an assistant.

Unfortunately, public transport does not have full access which may cause problems if you are unable to board buses unaided.

TRAVEL INSURANCE There are a few specialised companies that deal with travel to Armenia. A number of operators deal with pre-existing medical conditions such as Travelbility (⎰ *0845 338 1638; www.travelbility.co.uk*) and Medici Travel (⎰ *0845 880 0168; www.medicitravel.com*).

Medical facilities within Armenia are limited. The main hospitals in Yerevan, such as the University Clinic, are somewhat basic but are able to cater for those travellers who are in wheelchairs or have impediments. Hospitals in other parts of the country, however, lack the facilities of those in the capital.

FURTHER INFORMATION A good website for further information on planning and booking any accessible holiday is www.able-travel.com, which provides many tips and links to travel resources worldwide.

It may be worth contacting the Armenian tourist board (*www.armeniainfo. am*) for further advice. There is also information available via the Ministry of foreign affairs in Armenia (*www.armeniaforeignministry.com*).

Practical Information   SAFETY

2

Ambulance ⎰ 103   **Police** ⎰ 102
Fire ⎰ 101

WOMEN TRAVELLERS There are no particular safety problems for women as the strongly traditional family values ensure that they will not receive unwelcome attention. It is true that a woman walking alone in the late evening is an uncommon sight but it does not imply that she would be vulnerable if she did. Women drivers are now seen in Armenia but they are still a small minority.

OTHER TRAVELLERS Armenia has very few facilities for the **disabled** although ramps for wheelchair access have appeared in one or two hotels.

Travelling with children is not a problem from the social aspect. They are welcome anywhere. Family life is important to Armenians – they would find the concept of a child not being allowed into a restaurant, for example, very strange. Nappies and baby food are available in Yerevan and other major towns, often from pharmacies. Most restaurants and hotels will respond to parents' requests about food preparation. In Yerevan, the Grand Candy café (see page 127) is specifically geared towards children and some other cafés have play areas. There are funfairs near the cathedral and in Victory Park and amusements for smaller children in Children's Park on Beirut Street. Some swimming pools have facilities for children, for example Waterworld, and good weather brings out street amusements in a number of towns. See below for advice on taking children to historical sites.

Homosexuality was decriminalised in 2003 but is still an unacceptable lifestyle in Armenian society. The British Foreign Office advises homosexual travellers to exercise discretion in Armenia. It is common in Armenian culture to see a mother and daughter or two female friends holding hands in the street and not uncommon to see two men hug each other in greeting; these signs of affection are not an indication of sexual orientation.

OTHER DANGERS AND ANNOYANCES The **traffic police** who used to spend much of their time stopping motorists for 'routine checks' (and who were reputed to seek bribes) are now more usefully employed enforcing the seat belt laws and even speed limits. They do still sometimes stop cars for routine checks of documents (see page 77), but I was assured by my driver that bribery was now much less common.

As mentioned elsewhere in this guide, there is danger from earthquakes, poisonous snakes, deep holes concealed by long grass at several monasteries and various other hazards ranging from the potential for dehydration when it's hot to the possibility of frostbite when it's cold. The vast majority of visitors suffer none of these, although it is rather difficult always to take precautions against earthquakes. Possibly the only sensible advice is to avoid Soviet-era flats. If visiting such flats, note that the staircases are often in poor condition with limited illumination.

It is, however, necessary to **supervise children** very closely at many historic sites. Apart from the deep holes concealed by long grass and the snakes, which find convenient lairs in the piles of fallen stones, much of the masonry of less frequented buildings is precarious and Armenian castle builders were adept at siting their fortresses on the top of precipices. Even at touristy places like Noravank the cantilevered steps which give access to the second floor of the mausoleum require considerable care – especially descending. Just to reach a few of the sites requires hill-walking skills and appropriate footwear – it may not be a long walk to Baghaberd for example but it is extremely steep and made difficult by unstable scree.

At one or two sites, notably Kirants, beware of giant hogweed *Heracleum mantegazzianum*. This is a tall plant of the family Umbelliferae whose white flowers are held in flat-topped umbels. Do not touch it with bare skin as it causes painful weals. Its hollow stems sometimes tempt children to use them as peashooters with the result that their lips and hands become affected and require treatment.

WHAT TO TAKE

Apart from obvious items like **walking boots** and a compass if you're going hiking or **binoculars** if you're birdwatching there are a few other items which are best brought into the country. Any **medications** that you may need should be brought as these may be difficult to obtain, particularly away from Yerevan. Bring a small **torch** and carry it around, as it is needed when visiting the subterranean rooms at a few sites and may also be useful on the stairs of Soviet-era flats and poorly lit subways. **Slide film** is difficult to obtain in the country and high-quality processing of slide film is impossible. (Film for prints is readily obtainable and processing is usually of good quality. **Memory cards** are likewise easily obtainable and printing of digital images readily available. **Digital camera batteries** are hard to find – the best place to look for them is at Zig Zag photographic chain, see page 115.) **Clothing** is largely dependent on the time of year and activities planned, but do note that Armenians recognise foreign tourists by their casual clothes. Armenians regularly dress much more smartly and stylishly than most Westerners. (By contrast they recognise members of the diaspora because they always look as if they are dressed for a special occasion.) If there is any likelihood of being invited for dinner into somebody's home, or even going to an orchestral concert or the opera, it is worth taking something smarter. Note that Armenian women do not have pierced parts of their body other than their ear lobes, men do not wear earrings, and neither sex sports tattoos.

Armenia's **electricity** supply is at a voltage of 220V and a frequency of 50Hz. It uses standard continental European plugs with two round pins. This means that British and Irish appliances need only a simple cheap **adaptor** to match their plugs with Armenian sockets. Such adaptors are easily bought at home but cannot easily be found in Armenia so they should be taken. However, in North America electricity is supplied at 110V and 60Hz. This means that American appliances require not only an adaptor (to cope with the different shape of the pins of the plug) but also a **transformer** to cope with the different voltage. These should be bought before leaving home. In addition American devices where the mains frequency is important (such as electric clocks) will not work correctly in Armenia. Also in the case of computers and hi-fi equipment it is necessary to check whether or not particular components will function correctly on frequencies of both 50Hz and 60Hz.

Very few Armenian sinks have **plugs**, even in Western-style, modern hotels. If you want to be able to fill a sink with water take a one-size-fits-all plug with you.

$ MONEY AND BUDGETING

Armenia's own economic problems, coupled with the disintegration of the financial markets of the former Soviet Union, reinforced the need for Armenia to have an independent monetary policy. The introduction of the dram (officially abbreviated to AMD) as a national currency on 29 November 1993 made an independent monetary policy possible. Each dram, which is simply the Armenian word for money, is made up of 100 luma, the Armenian word for a small part of anything. Initially the exchange rate was US$1 = AMD14. By the end of March 1994 it had reached US$1 = AMD230 and at the end of 1994 stood at US$1 = AMD400. It subsequently drifted down to US$1 = AMD585 and £1 = AMD850 but then appreciated, and in June 2006 stood at US$1 = AMD417 and £1 = AMD767. In February 2011 the rate was US$1 = AMD365, £1 = AMD586 and €1 = AMD498. There were originally five denominations of banknotes: AMD10, 25, 50, 100 and 200. Inflation subsequently forced the addition of AMD500, 1,000 and 5,000 notes. In 1997, these were superseded by a completely different design of banknote depicting famous Armenian males. The notes currently in use depict: AMD1,000 – the poet Eghishe Charents (1897–1937; see page 45); AMD5,000 – the writer and poet Hovhannes Tumanian (1869–1923; see page 44); AMD10,000 – the poet Avetik Isahakian (1875–1957; see page 126) and AMD20,000 – the painter Martiros Sarian (1880–1972; see page 47). Recently a 50,000 dram note was introduced, dedicated to the 1,700th anniversary of the adoption of Christianity, which depicts Ejmiatsin. Over the years notes up to and including AMD500 have been replaced by coins.

Armenia is very much a cash-based society. Some hotels and luxury shops aimed at Western visitors accept credit cards but many do not, cash or bank transfer being the only accepted form of payment in many hotels, especially outside Yerevan. Travellers' cheques can most easily be exchanged at HSBC branches in Yerevan, but they charge a significant fee for doing so on any cheques but their own. You will need to show your passport. Travellers' cheques issued by Thomas Cook or American Express are easiest to cash; ones denominated in US dollars are preferred, but those denominated in euro are also accepted. Armenia now has hole-in-the-wall cash machines in all major towns operated by various banks. Not all machines accept Western cards but many do. Look for the symbols by the machine advising what cards will work there.

By far and away the most usual way of obtaining drams, however, is by changing cash at one of the innumerable exchange offices in the country. Dollars are again the preferred currency though euros and roubles are widely accepted and a few places, mostly in Yerevan, will take British pounds. It is usually possible to exchange other currencies in the centre of Yerevan. However, as a general rule visitors to Armenia should bring most of their funds in cash US dollars, regarding other forms solely as an emergency reserve. This is even more the case outside Yerevan. The lack of crime makes doing so safer than might be imagined. There is less concern than formerly about accepting notes in less than pristine condition but it can still prove difficult to get rid of ones which are torn or marked. There is also considerable wariness about accepting the older design of US dollar notes owing to the number of forgeries in circulation.

Although all purchases in Armenia should be paid for in drams, there are a few places where dollars are welcome. Vernissage market is one: most of the stallholders even quote prices in dollars (though they will of course accept drams).

There seems to be a constant shortage of change in Armenia; small establishments may not be able to change the higher denomination notes.

BUDGETING Apart from Western-style hotels, which charge Western prices as indicated in the body of the text, and international phone calls, most things of interest to visitors are cheap. In particular, other than in establishments aimed at Westerners it is difficult to spend more than AMD5,000 on a meal, and a snack at a stall in the street will only cost AMD150–1,000. In a café an Armenian coffee will cost AMD200 or so while a half-litre of beer costs up to AMD500. When thirsty in the countryside, patronise free one of the excellent springs, but if in town you can buy a litre bottle of water for AMD200–300. A block of chocolate to keep you going will set you back AMD250 for the local stuff while an imported Mars bar is AMD350. A loaf of bread or some sheets of *lavash* for your picnic will cost AMD150–300.

Other tourist essentials: postcards cost between AMD300 and AMD500 with an additional AMD240 for postage; a 36-exposure 35mm film costs up to AMD3,000; memory cards for digital cameras start at AMD7,000 for a 4GB card, AMD260,000 for 16GB; a digital camera battery costs AMD6,600, a battery plus charger is AMD14,000; the T-shirt to prove that you've been to Armenia is priced between AMD3,000 and AMD6,000.

Public transport fares are low and the longest minibus journey from Yerevan (to Meghri) costs AMD6,000. The longest train journeys, such as: Yerevan to Gyumri, cost AMD950. Car hire with driver is cheaper than without, but don't necessarily expect a new vehicle. Typical rates are AMD25,500–27,300 per day for a private car or AMD32,760–35,600 for a 4x4 including fuel; prices will depend on the cost of fuel. The driver's expenses such as meals and accommodation must also be met if he is away from home.

Tipping is discretionary, but the etiquette is much the same as in the West with approximately 10% being added to the bill in restaurants and taxis. In Yerevan city centre where taxi journeys usually cost under AMD1,000 it is the norm to at least round up the amount given to AMD1,000. If you have engaged the services of a guide, interpreter or driver and are pleased with their performance you may wish to show appreciation with a tip – again 10% is standard.

GETTING AROUND

Note that all fares quoted are for a single journey unless stated otherwise. Return tickets are not sold; a notable exception is the cable car to Tatev.

BY TRAIN Virtually the whole of Armenia's rail network is electrified at 3,000V DC. The track has the standard Soviet gauge of 1.524m rather than 1.435m which is the norm in western Europe and North America. Apart from the passenger services round Yerevan, which are operated by multiple units, other trains are hauled by twin-unit locos of class VL10: VL stands for Vladimir Lenin. They were built at Tbilisi, Georgia, and Novocherkassk, Russia, between 1967 and 1977. A timetable, in Russian, is available on request at Yerevan's main railway station (see pages 131–2). To reach the main railway station take the metro to Sasuntsi Davit which adjoins the railway station.

There are only a handful of internal train services but some of them may be of use to visitors. A train leaves the main railway station in **Yerevan for Gyumri** (cost AMD950) at 08.00 arriving in Gyumri at 12.05. The return train leaves Gyumri at 17.30, arriving in Yerevan at 21.35. Another useful route is that from **Yerevan to Hrazdan** (AMD300), extended to Sevan and Shorzha in summer. Trains run daily except Wednesdays. They do not, however, leave from the main railway station but from Kanaker station in Yerevan's northeast suburb of Kanaker. The station is hidden down a narrow winding lane which goes eastwards off the northern part of Zakaria Kanakertsi Street. A small sign, in Armenian and Russian, attached to a gas pipe points the way. The train leaves Kanaker at 08.30, Hrazden at 10.00, Sevan at 10.50 arriving Shorzha at 12.10. The return train leaves Shorzha at 16.30, Sevan at 18.00, Hrazden at 18.40 and arrives at Kanaker at 20.20. (These times differ from those given for Kanaker and Hrazden in the printed timetable which was printed before the times of the extension to Shorzha were finalised. The above times were given to me by the person in charge of the train, so are likely to be correct but do check if intending to use the route.)

There is a morning **commuter train to Yerevan** from Yeraskh (the last station on the line to the south before the closed border with Nakhichevan) at 06.30, arriving in Yerevan at 08.21. The return train leaves at 17.20. There are also trains between Yerevan and Ararat on the same line, departing Yerevan at 09.30 and 14.40, arriving Ararat at 10.35 and 15.35 respectively. From Ararat trains leave for Yerevan at 11.05 and 15.50. Trains depart from Yerevan for Armavir (to the west) at 06.10, 11.30, 15.30 and 19.00. The journey takes 55 minutes. Return trains leave Armavir at 07.30, 13.00, 17.20 and 21.20.

There are trains **between Gyumri and Pemzashen** (south of Artik), departing Gyumri at 07.00 and 16.00, arriving Pemzashen at 08.07 and 17.17 (cost AMD250). Trains return from Pemzashen at 08.20 and 17.50. Of far more interest to visitors, however, is Armenia's remaining passenger train which offers a spectacularly scenic ride along the **Debed Gorge**. A train leaves Gyumri daily at 06.15 and runs via Vanadzor and Alaverdi to Ayrum, the last station before the Georgian border, where it is due to arrive at 11.05. The return journey departs Ayrum at 17.00. The section of route between Vanadzor and Alaverdi is particularly worthwhile and is seen best on the morning northbound service.

Travelling by train is cheap with the longest journeys, such as Yerevan to Gyumri and Gyumri to Ayrum, costing AMD950. Tickets are bought at stations and are

BUS AND MINIBUS DEPARTURES FROM YEREVAN

KILIKIA CENTRAL BUS STATION (*6 Admiral Isakov Av;* +374 10 565370)
Armavir (minibus) 07.30–21.30, every 15mins
Artik (bus) 15.30, 16.00; (minibus) 15.00, 16.00
Gyumri (bus) 12.30, 16.30
Jermuk (minibus) 15.00
Noyemberian (minibus) 09.30, 14.30, 15.30, 16.00
Sisian (minibus) 08.30, 10.30, 12.30, 14.30
Stepanakert (minibus) 07.00, 08.00, 09.00, 10.00
Stepanavan (bus) 13.00; (minibus) 09.00, 11.00, 14.30, 16.00, 17.00
Talin (bus) 12.45, 15.00, 16.00; (minibus) 13.00, 15.00, 16.00
Tashir (minibus) 09.30, 15.00
Vanadzor (bus) 16.00
Vardenis (minibus) between 07.00–19.00

NORTHERN BUS STATION (*1 Tbilisian Rd;* +374 10 621670)
Chambarak (minibus) 09.30, 10.30, 16.00
Dilijan/Ijevan (minibus) 09.00–18.00 hrly
Martuni (minibus) 10.00–18.00 approx hrly

ABOVIAN SQUARE
Zvartnots Airport (minibus) 108 (minibus 107 also goes to the airport but it leaves from the junction of Kassian & Komitas streets, near Barekamutiun metro station & does not go through the city centre)

AGATANGEGHOS/KHORENATSI STREETS CORNER (*behind Rosia trade centre*)
Alaverdi (minibus) 09.00, 14.00, 15.00, 16.00
Artik (minibus) 11.00–18.00 hrly
Gyumri (minibus) 07.30–20.30, every 20mins
Vanadzor (minibus) 07.30–20.00, every 20mins

ARSHAKUNIATS AV (*road south from south end of Grigor Lusavorich St*)
Yeghegnadzor (minibus) 08.00–19.00 hrly

always for a single journey; return tickets are not sold. Trains are, on the whole, efficient although relatively slow. It is possible to book tickets and seats a few days in advance although trains are rarely so busy that seats can't be found.

BY BUS Bus services proper have declined and no longer serve all main towns direct from Yerevan. All places are, however, linked by minibus (*marshrutka*) services. The maximum bus fare from Yerevan by bus is to Tashir (AMD1,300). Generally speaking minibuses cost around 50% more than buses. The maximum minibus fare is to Stepanakert or Meghri, both of which cost AMD6,000. Minibuses are driven much more recklessly than buses and are consequently considerably quicker. When travelling between the north and south of the country, it is invariably necessary to change at Yerevan. While it is probably possible to go almost anywhere you might want to go by minibus, the problem for the visitor is finding out where the bus leaves from and at what time. Timetables, as such, are not available and although many routes leave from the Kilikia Central bus station which is about

14/3 GAI STREET (*near Mercedes Benz showroom – formerly called Haik Av*)
Garni (bus) 08.45–21.30, every 50mins; (minibus) 10.00–20.30, every 50mins

28 ISAHAKIAN STREET (*in front of Drama Theatre*)
Dilijan (minibus) 11.00–18.00, approx every hr
Sevan (bus) 10.30, 14.30; (minibus) 08.00–18.00, every 40mins

KHORENATSI STREET (*behind Rosia trade centre*)
Artashat (minibus) 09.00–11.00, every 10mins
Dvin (minibus) 09.20–20.20 hrly
Goris (minibus) 07.30, 15.00
Kapan (minibus) 07.30, 12.00
Meghri/Agarak (minibus) 07.00

MASHTOTS AVENUE/SARIAN STREET CORNER
Ejmiatsin (bus) 07.20–22.00 every 20mins; (minibus) 07.30–22.00 every 10mins

PARONIAN STREET/MASHTOTS AVENUE CORNER
Ashtarak (bus) 09.10, 10.15, 13.10, 14.00, 17.00, 18.00; (minibus) 08.40–18.40 hrly

RAILWAY STATION
Khor Virap (bus) 09.00, 14.00, 18.00; (minibus) 11.00, 15.30, returning at 13.20, 15.20, 17.20

RAYKOM STATION (*24 Azatutyun Av*)
Gavar (minibus)check times before travel
Hrazden (minibus) 09.00–19.00, operates frequently, no fixed times

TIGRAN METS AVENUE
Spitak (minibus) 09.30–19.30 hrly

800m from Victory Bridge in the Zvartnots direction, many leave from other places and there are about 16 bus stations in Yerevan. The Armenians themselves, if they want to find out something such as where a bus goes from, will ask someone who knows or who knows someone else who knows. A visitor may be best to follow their example and ask at their hotel, homestay or the tourist information office in Yerevan, whose website (*www.armeniainfo.am*) has helpful details of routes and frequencies. Transport to a single destination can leave from several sites in the city. The central bus station can be reached by many minibus routes including 13, 15, 23, 27, 54, 67, 68, 75, 77, 90, 94 and 99. It is a large A-frame building and, although working 24 hours, the café is open only from 06.00 until 17.00. The left-luggage office is always open.

The details on pages 74–5 of the stations from which buses/minibuses of possible interest to tourists depart are an indicative guide only; changes are frequent. Note also that bus routes sometimes become minibus routes.

Other towns have minibus services to local villages – again, ask locally. Minibuses do not serve tourist sites per se: a taxi is often the best way to reach such sites.

BY TAXI Taxis in Armenia are plentiful and relatively cheap and are often a reasonable alternative to public transport, even for inter-city journeys. Bus stations usually have plenty of waiting taxis, they can be flagged down in the street and if you see a taxi stationary at the side of the road then it is probably available. Although there are no designated taxi ranks they do tend to wait in roadside bays. You should have no difficulty in finding a taxi! On the whole taxi firms and drivers do not speak English so if phoning for a taxi it is best to ask your hotel or host to do it for you. After the minimum charge of a few hundred drams, prices are in the order of AMD70–200 per kilometre. If you are hiring a private taxi for a long journey, be sure to agree the price before starting. In 2010 a taxi from Vanadzor to Yerevan, for example, cost AMD8,000, as did one from Goris to Tatev. Registered taxis in Yerevan charge AMD100 per kilometre. Most journeys within central Yerevan cost less than AMD1,000. Telephone numbers of some Yerevan taxi firms are given on page 107. Others can be found on Armenia Information's website (*www.armeniainfo.am*).

DRIVING Much improvement in the state of the roads has taken place in recent years but many roads are still full of deep **pot-holes** and, except in the very centre of major towns, assorted livestock. Drivers seek to avoid the worst of the pot-holes and the livestock by weaving to and fro and sometimes going off the road altogether. Traffic drives on the right-hand side of the road in Armenia, but on bad roads keeping to the right is only practised when passing another vehicle. Additionally many rural routes linking villages are unmade and can become seas of mud after rain. This applies even more to the roads within villages, where the daily passage of animals from their accommodation within the village to the fields and back ensures that village streets end up like farmyards. Drivers are adept at avoiding the livestock and so manage on the whole to avoid the human population as well. Do not assume that because a car is coming straight towards you that this represents danger as the driver is probably merely dodging the pot-holes and regards you as just another obstacle to avoid by swerving. However, the situation is different in the middle of towns, especially Yerevan, where it can feel as if drivers are completely oblivious to pedestrians. Drivers turning right are allowed to proceed at pedestrian crossings if there is no-one crossing but should give priority to pedestrians. Failure to do so carries a fine, if caught, of AMD30,000 but the risk of being caught must be slight, given the number of drivers who flout this law. Great care should be taken when crossing roads, even at 'green man' crossings. Vehicles can approach at high speed with apparently no intention of stopping. A new ruling allows a pedestrian to be fined AMD3,000 for jaywalking.

Speed limits are 60km/h within towns and 90km/h on rural roads. The traffic police have become more active in stopping drivers who break speed limits. There are on the spot fines of AMD12,000 for being up to 21km/h over the limit and a further AMD7,000 for every extra 10km/h above that. **Seat-belt compliance** is also being enforced. There is an on the spot fine of AMD5,000 for any driver or front-seat passenger not wearing a seat belt. Rear seat belts are not compulsory.

Drivers must carry their licence and proof of car ownership at all times. Drivers must give way to traffic from the right, even on roundabouts.

Petrol is available in two categories: regular (93 octane) and premium (95 octane). At the time of writing regular cost AMD400 per litre and premium AMD420. Unleaded fuel is unavailable but diesel is widely sold. Gone are the days when much fuel was dispensed in cans from parked roadside tankers although this can still occasionally be seen in the more remote areas. Many vehicles in Armenia are dual-fuel, petrol and gas (CNG, compressed natural gas), gas being significantly cheaper at AMD200 per cubic metre. When filling up with gas all occupants must leave the vehicle: a waiting area, of varying comfort, is usually provided. Petrol and gas are readily available in towns and on main routes leading out of towns but stations are less frequent when off the main roads. As everywhere, it is sensible to fill up before embarking on a long journey.

Car hire Cars can be hired with or without a driver. Many local tour operators (see page 56) can arrange private car hire with driver, tailoring car and driver to particular requirements. For all car rentals, a valid driving licence and passport must be presented, a refundable deposit is required and payment is by credit card. Other terms and conditions, including minimum age, vary between firms.

Several **international car-hire companies** are established in the country and have offices in Yerevan, but not at the airport although pick-up and drop-off at the airport can be arranged in advance. Rates range from AMD19,000–75,000 per day and 4x4 is available.

Avis 33 Sayat Nova Av & 4 Abovian St; +374 10 516363, 584555; www.avis.com.am
Hertz 7 Abovian St; +374 10 584818; info@ hertz.am; www.hertz.am. Website covers terms & conditions clearly.

Sixt 42 Acharian St; +374 10 234760; info@ sixt.am; www.sixt.am

Local firms Local competition is provided by an increasing number of companies. All are based in Yerevan and are geared to foreign visitors. It is very rare for Armenians to hire a car. All firms must ensure that their cars comply with regulatory standards including MOT. Two local companies are:

Avanguard 7/3 Mashtots Av; +374 10 500809; contacts@avanguard.am; www.avanguard.am

Beau Monde 6 Sarian St; +374 10 569256; info@beaumonde.am; www.beaumonde.am. Has a good website with a clear exposition of terms & conditions. They also rent bicycles.

Other companies can be found on Armenia Information's website (*www.armeniainfo.am*).

An ambitious building programme has resulted in Yerevan being well provided with upmarket hotels. There is a wide choice of hotels within the central area although some visitors might prefer, particularly in midsummer, to stay outside the central district. Expect to pay Western prices at these hotels. There are also some less expensive hotels, mostly built in the Soviet era for tourist groups and since renovated. Budget travellers are much better seeking homestays rather than hostel accommodation with the exception of the Envoy Hostel in Yerevan. Information about Yerevan accommodation is given on pages 107–10.

Outside Yerevan accommodation has now improved enormously and good hotels are available in most of the places tourists are likely to want to stay. Some of these hotels are new-builds while others are **renovated Soviet-era hotels**. The latter vary from very acceptable to excellent. There are still some Soviet-era hotels that were used to house refugees in the early 1990s, have never recovered, and are not recommendable. Soviet-era hotels tend to be renovated floor by floor. Renovated floors are usually fine, but avoid those which are not. A chain of **Tufenkian hotels** (*www.tufenkian.am*) aimed at Western tourists is being developed in restored buildings. The first outside Yerevan were on Lake Sevan and in the Debed Valley. Others are promised for Areni, Dilijan and Karabagh but construction has not yet started.

Some hotels have **self-catering facilities**. These may be in the form of so-called **cottages** – separate small buildings which can accommodate between four and eight persons, although the number is flexible as extra beds can often be erected. Such cottages in Soviet times tended to be in hotels with large grounds and were originally for families spending the whole of their holiday in one place. However, the concept of cottages has been happily adapted to new establishments and it is quite common for a hotel to comprise several small buildings rather than one large building. This preference for individual units can also be found in restaurants where instead of one large dining room there are multiple rooms with a single table.

Another feature of the Soviet era was the **guesthouses** run by various bodies to provide accommodation for their members while on holiday. They are therefore usually in pleasant surroundings. Some of these have been sold off, while in other cases they remain in the hands of the original owner. It is possible to stay at most of them and they are generally inexpensive. The standard varies enormously. The privatised ones are usually well managed, some having been upgraded, some still needing a lot of new investment. Those still in the hands of the original owners vary from the fascinating and pleasant, to one in which it was necessary to sleep with the window open to avoid choking on the dust, and where the wealth of dead insects in the bedroom provided an interesting identification challenge. (It isn't mentioned in this guide.) Soviet-era guesthouses were usually large establishments offering a variety of activities as well as accommodation. Now renovated, such establishments often call themselves 'hotel resorts'. This slightly puzzling term usually means that the hotel offers a number of facilities (such as sauna and swimming pool) as well as activities (various sports, horseriding, etc) all within the hotel complex.

Yet another feature of the Soviet era was the **spa hotels** which provided

HOTEL PRICE CODES	
$$$$$	£100+
$$$$	£75–100
$$$	£50–75
$$	£25–50
$	< £25

Addresses in Armenia can be confusing, at least to visitors from the UK. It is the whole building, sometimes covering a large area, which is numbered rather than individual premises or entrances. Thus, several shops may all have the same address because they are in the same building and two addresses, eg: numbers 2 and 6 on the same street which look as if they will be fairly close together, can be a surprising distance apart. If a building occupies a corner site with wings on two (or more) streets the whole building has a number relating to one of the streets on which it stands. Premises in that building, even if their entrance is from another street, will still give the first street as their address. It is quite common therefore to have to go round the corner to get in. For example, the Jazzve café with an address of 8 Moscovian Street in Yerevan is actually on parallel Isahakian Street, as the building stretches round three sides of a square. If an address number has a suffix, such as 4a or 4/1, it is possible that it is round the back of the building. Most large blocks have courtyards round the back and many premises are entered via these courtyards, particularly residential apartments in buildings where shops occupy the ground floor. The address may even be in a separate building within a courtyard.

However, the familiar pattern of even and odd numbers on opposite sides of the street is used, as is numbering buildings from the town centre outwards.

various therapeutic treatments for their guests. Several of these have been upgraded and combine their medical and hotel functions. It is perfectly possible to stay there without being a patient but prices usually include treatment whether you take it or not.

Motel-type accommodation, often associated with roadside eating places on the main routes, is increasing rapidly. Such accommodation is often newly built and pleasant. **Hostel** accommodation in Armenia is limited. There is one excellent hostel in Yerevan (see page 109) and YMCA accommodation in Spitak is scheduled to open at the end of 2010. The seedy rundown **dormitories** at the bus and railway stations are not recommended for any but the destitute and not for women under any circumstances.

Homestays (Armenia's term for bed and breakfast establishments) are available throughout the country and provide a real insight into Armenian family life particularly as generally excellent meals can be organised. The one real snag is, of course, the language barrier but many visitors enjoy homestays in spite of this. Homestays, invariably safe and usually very comfortable, can be arranged through one of the Yerevan travel agents (see pages 55–6), Armenia Information (see page 107) or one of the regional information centres. (It is not unknown for tourists simply to ask around when they arrive in a village, but of course there is an element of potluck in this method.) There will be only one bathroom for everyone, both you and the household. Expect to pay AMD10,000 per person for a twin room including breakfast plus about AMD3,000 per person for dinner – including drinks. You will need to give the hostess enough time to prepare an evening meal – she'll often think that she needs 48 hours' notice – but you'll get a feast. Also, it's usually best to buy some wine yourself, or you'll probably end up with a choice of vodka or sweet red wine. Even if you cannot manage to stay, do try to fit in one or two home-

Practical Information   ACCOMMODATION   2

cooked meals. As with homestay accommodation, such meals can be organised through one of the Yerevan travel agents. While the water situation (see *Chapter 1, Life in Armenia*, page 29) has improved greatly in most parts of Armenia, some rural places still face difficulties and water may only be available for limited periods each day. Occasionally you may have to fill the WC cistern by ladling water stored in the bath. Hot water may not be continuously available everywhere.

Rented accommodation can be arranged through Yerevan travel agents and is a good option for those wishing to stay for more than a day or two. The price varies according to the standard of apartment; expect to pay AMD10,000–30,000 per day. Many Soviet-era flats have an unpromising approach, with dark, dilapidated stairways and lifts that do not always function, but the flats themselves are usually spacious and comfortable.

It is possible to **camp** anywhere except on private property and in the national reserves (see page 10). There are no permanent campsites as found in the West. Some tour operators (see page 56) do include camping during their treks and one enterprise (see page 227) in Tavush province offers a riverside campsite.

The **accommodation price codes** (see box, page 78) used in this guide are based on the price of a double room in peak season, usually late May/June to the end of September, although for accommodation in winter sports areas winter is the peak season (and here, at weekends, it can be very busy). Even in the peak summer season it should not be difficult for individual visitors to find accommodation somewhere although the choice is obviously greater if you book in advance. Groups do need to book in peak season. Prices usually include **breakfast** although in a significant minority of establishments, both small and large, breakfast is extra. Where this is the case the cost is stated in individual accommodation entries. Breakfast rarely costs more than AMD1,000. A few hotels do not include tax in their price; this is noted in the listings. As explained on page 72, Armenia is a cash-based society and most accommodation (apart from big hotels in Yerevan and some other towns) has to be paid for in cash or by bank transfer. Establishments which accept cards are noted under individual entries. Although the position may change, it should be assumed that cards are not accepted unless it is positively stated that they are. Some hotels offer lower prices outside their peak season.

EATING AND DRINKING

Two points need to be made about eating in Armenia. Firstly, Armenian cuisine has much more in common with Turkish, Persian or Arab cooking, all of which countries at one time ruled Armenia, than it does with the cooking of Russia, which also ruled Armenia, or that of western Europe. Secondly, given the range and interest of dishes which can be experienced in an Armenian household, the menus of restaurants and hotels tend to be repetitive and predictable. Very sadly, almost all restaurant menus, especially away from Yerevan, have been reduced to a few salads followed by grilled or barbecued meat and vegetables. Armenian thinking is quite different from that in Britain or France, for example, where one goes to a restaurant for a good meal. In Armenia one goes to a restaurant to give the wife of the family a rest and accepts that the food will be worse than at home. The only way most tourists can begin to appreciate the range of Armenian cookery is to get a travel agent to organise for them some homestays with dinner included or else to book a meal in a private house – this can be arranged at houses which provide homestays as long as notice is given. The hostess is highly likely to outshine any restaurant in the vicinity. I personally have never eaten better in Armenia than in private houses.

Having said that, it is also true that the quality and variety of restaurants, especially in Yerevan, has improved out of all recognition since Soviet days when surly staff glumly informed customers that everything they asked for from the menu was unavailable and meals took hours as the staff frequently vanished to enjoy a long rest. Nowadays one problem for foreigners who are not used to it is quite the reverse: meals are served quickly with the second course arriving before the first is half eaten. (It is the normal Armenian custom to serve everything at once. Avoid this if you wish by only ordering one course at a time.) It is perfectly acceptable to order a number of main dishes and have these placed in the middle of the table so everyone can sample a little of each.

The quality of the ingredients is extremely high because Armenia produces a wide range of excellent fruit and vegetables as well as meat: pork, chicken and lamb. The only exception is beef which tends to be less satisfactory because it is predominantly from Caucasian brown cattle, a breed developed between 1930 and 1960 by crossing Swiss brown bulls with cows of the local lesser Caucasus breed. The resulting beef does not compare to Aberdeen Angus, Beef Shorthorn or Hereford. Also the Armenian practice of eating beef and lamb fresh rather than hanging it for up to three weeks after slaughter tends to make it tougher and less flavoursome than in the West.

The quality of Armenia's **fruit and vegetables** is so high, partly because the climate favours them, partly because they have not been bred to survive transport to a supermarket in another continent and partly because they do not have to appear absolutely identical to every other example of that fruit or vegetable which the supermarket sells. Probably apricots, native to Armenia, are the most famous produce, but in season markets and the ubiquitous roadside vendors pile their stalls with peaches, cherries, apples, pears, quinces, grapes, figs, pomegranates, plums, oranges, lemons, melons, watermelons, tomatoes, squashes, aubergines, peppers, asparagus, cucumbers, courgettes, onions, potatoes, carrots, peas, beans, cabbages, okra, a whole range of mushrooms, almonds, walnuts and hazelnuts.

A staple ingredient of Armenian cookery is **bulghur**. Traditionally it is made by boiling whole grains of wheat in large cauldrons until they begin to soften, upon which they are removed and dried in the sun. The grains are cracked open and the kernels divided into categories depending on size. This process ensures that they will keep for years without deteriorating. Fine bulghur is preferred for *keufteh* (see below) while coarse bulghur is preferred for pilaffs and soups.

Warning to **vegetarians**: although it is extremely easy to have a meat-free diet in Armenia some Armenian dishes may not be what they seem from the menu. For example, mushroom salad may contain as much chicken as mushroom and, because the ingredients will be chopped fine and mixed up together, it will be impossible to avoid the chicken. Always ask before ordering.

BREAKFAST Most Armenians make do with a cup of coffee (*soorj*) or tea (*tay*) together with bread (*hats*), butter (*karog*), jam (use the English word), honey (*merr*) and possibly cheese (*paneer*). Another preserve which may appear at breakfast is *muraba*, various whole fruits in a thick syrup, although it can also be offered as a sweetmeat with coffee. Occasionally a **tomato omelette** (*loligov dzu*) will be offered, in the Armenian version of which onions are first gently fried, then chopped tomatoes are added and finally whipped eggs are poured on (sometimes with a little cream and curry powder added) for the final cooking. Yoghurt (*madzoon*) is also likely to be offered. In smaller establishments you will be asked the evening before what you will want and when. In homestays the uneaten food from the night before (of which there will be a great deal since Armenian cooks greatly overestimate visitors' appetites) will also be laid out. It is not unknown for the evening's undrunk brandy also to be proffered at breakfast. The main **Yerevan hotels** offer something considerably more than this (though minus the brandy) with a whole buffet breakfast available and a variety of omelettes but this is pandering to Western hotel eating habits rather than authentically Armenian. Nor can one or two Soviet-style guesthouses which offer semolina and boiled beef be regarded as remotely Armenian. Breakfast is often served relatively late by Western standards, rarely before 08.00 and frequently not until 09.00. In fact the whole day is shifted somewhat towards evening.

For breakfast in winter visitors may encounter **khash**, which can perhaps be translated as 'cowheel soup'. Most visitors detest it, but a *khash* party is a unique Armenian ritual. Apart from the (acquired?) taste, it also makes the breath smell foul! *Khash*, which traditionally is never eaten by one person dining alone, is sometimes served in restaurants but usually it is a ritual for a group of friends who will have fasted the previous evening. The cowheels (and sometimes other parts of the animal such as the head or stomach) are boiled all night with neither salt nor herbs. By morning a thick broth has been produced and the meat has flaked off the bones. Just before serving at breakfast time, crushed garlic and salt are added. The broth is then eaten by dipping *lavash* in it. The soaked *lavash* is transferred to the mouth using hands alone. It is always accompanied by greens, radishes, yellow chilli peppers, mineral water, and sometimes by red chillies and pickles as well. It is also accompanied by vodka, ideally mulberry vodka, of which considerable quantities are drunk in a series of toasts, the first of which is '*Bari luys*' ('Good morning') and the last of which is to the maker of the *khash*.

LUNCH Many restaurants start serving meals by 12.00 and service is continuous until late evening. Armenians argue that one should eat when one is hungry rather than be guided by the clock. Traditionally though, lunch is a fairly light meal with the main meal being taken after work. For visitors, lunch is often an excuse to buy some fresh produce at the market. The basis for the picnic is **lavash**, Armenia's classic flatbread; see box opposite. Although it's traditionally unleavened, some present-day cooks cheat and use yeast. It is baked rapidly in an oven set into the ground called a *tonir* and comes in the form of thin sheets which can be readily stored since *lavash* is successfully freshened even after it has dried out by sprinkling a little water on it. In villages where there is no market people still bake it in their own houses, often several women saving on fuel and having a social morning by baking bread together, each making enough to last her family for a few days or longer.

Tomatoes and cucumbers together with cheese and sour cream make an excellent filling. Other possibilities obtainable at any market are the spiced dried meats such as *basturma*, which is dried, salted and flattened beef surrounded by a dried mixture of paprika, garlic and cumin, or *sojuk* which is spiced and salted minced beef (sometimes mixed with pork or lamb) formed into a sausage and then dried. In the Sevan area smoked fish can be bought to make another variant.

An alternative lunch would be to call at one of the roadside **barbecue** stalls which are common on the main roads in summer. They offer the ubiquitous Armenian menu of *khorovats* (barbecued meat, usually pork but sometimes chicken or lamb, together with salads, vegetables and *lavash*). Seeing and smelling the food cooking and then eating it either in the open air or under an awning is one of the pleasures of travelling in Armenia. Prices are usually a little less than you would pay for a

The *tonir*, or oven, in which *lavash* is baked is a large cylindrical clay structure sunk into the ground. A fire is lit in the bottom of the *tonir* and baking begins when the walls of the oven are hot enough, as *lavash* is cooked on the actual wall of the oven. When meat is being cooked it is suspended within the *tonir* over the glowing fuel.

Traditionally *lavash* dough consists simply of flour, salt and water although nowadays some cooks add yeast or other ingredients such as buttermilk. When several women from the same family or same village join together to make a large batch an efficient mini production line ensues, with one woman rolling out pieces of dough on a floured baking board, a second skilfully stretching the dough into very thin sheets by throwing it to and fro in the air and then laying it on a special padded implement, a *batat*, which has a handle on the non-padded side. It is said that the dough should be stretched to about 24 by 12 inches (30x60cm) and should be no more than $^1/_{16}$-inch (1½mm) thick. The dough is then swiftly and firmly applied by means of the *batat* to the wall of the *tonir* to cook. This takes only a brief time. It is then removed from the *tonir* with a long metal hook, often by a third member of the group, and added to the pile of cooked *lavash*. The skill lies in judging the correct moment to remove the *lavash* from the *tonir* and the oldest member of the group is often granted this important task. The surface of the blisters which form when the dough comes in contact with the heat should be nicely browned.

similar meal in a restaurant. Of course, the restaurants are open if it's either raining or else too hot. In towns it might be possible to find a café selling the traditional Armenian fast food **lahmadjoun**. This tasty speciality comprises a thin dough base covered, in similar style to a pizza, with tomato, herbs, spices and very small pieces of meat. It's normally rolled up and eaten like a sandwich.

DINNER The main meal is eaten in the evening. **Bread** will certainly be provided, usually *lavash*, but some restaurants, particularly in Yerevan, have taken to giving foreigners ordinary bread and reserving the *lavash* for Armenians unless foreigners specifically ask. The meal usually begins with a selection of **salads** which can incorporate both raw and cooked vegetables, peas, beans, herbs, fruits, nuts, bulghur, eggs and meat. In season romaine lettuce is used but in winter cabbage is substituted. Often the salads will double up as an accompaniment to the main course. Popular salads include cucumber and tomato salad (*varounki yev loligi aghtsan*), green bean salad (*kanach lobov aghtsan*), kidney bean salad (*karmir lobov aghtsan*), aubergine salad (*simpoogi aghtsan*) and potato salad with sour cream (*titvaserov kartofili aghtsan*).

The second course would traditionally have been **soup**, although this is not now commonly served in summer, and restaurants frequently have none available. Some of the soups are actually so substantial as to be main courses while others are cold concoctions for summer. Armenian soups are excellent so take any opportunity to try one – if you can manage yet more food. A popular summer soup is *jajik*, chilled yoghurt and cucumber soup, which can either accompany the main course or precede it. Other cold soups made with apricots, cornelian cherries *Cornus mas*, currants, mulberries, or sweetbrier *Rosa rubiginosa* can be served as either a

Practical Information EATING AND DRINKING 2

first course or a dessert. More substantial soups for winter include *targhana abour* made with yoghurt, mint and onion, *shoushin bozbash* (lamb soup with apple and quince) and *missov dziranabour* (lamb soup with apricots). More homely soups, often offered in homestays, are *spas* (yoghurt and bulghur) and *aveluk* (wild sorrel). *Harissa*, a thick soup of bulghur and chicken which is filling if rather unexciting, may be offered in homestays.

The main course would usually be based on meat or fish. **Fish** is obviously less common than in countries which are not landlocked but whitefish from Lake Sevan is sometimes available and also trout from Armenia's rivers. Trout and sturgeon are available from the Armash fish ponds. Beware some of Yerevan's restaurants which offer sea fish, smoked salmon or shellfish imported from goodness knows where. Leave such dishes to the expatriates who want to be reminded of home.

Unfortunately restaurants rarely offer dishes which have been cooked by braising or casseroling although such dishes certainly form part of traditional Armenian cookery. **Chicken** is far more likely to be roasted, perhaps with a stuffing (*pilavov letzvadz hav*) based on rice or bulghur and with some vegetables or dried fruit, or else it might be barbecued (*khorovats varyag*) or fried (*tapakatsi*). A really upmarket restaurant might offer a more imaginative stuffing such as would be used in Armenia on festive occasions. **Game** is very rarely offered, probably because so little of it survives. **Lamb** is immensely popular and a huge variety of lamb stews are cooked in the country with ingredients from quinces (*missov sergevil*) and apricots (*missov dziran*) to artichokes (*missov gangar*) and leeks (*missov bras*). They are fascinating, delicious dishes, usually served with a rice pilaff (*printzi pilaff*) or bulghur pilaff (*tzavari pilaff*), but the chance of finding one on a restaurant menu is slight. You will, however, find lots of **barbecues** (*khorovats*) using lamb (*gar*), pork (*khoz*), beef (*tavar*), chicken (*hav*) or, occasionally, veal (*hort*). The meat will come with vegetables, of very high quality but not prepared or cooked with the flair and imagination shown in an Armenian household. A popular way of cooking green vegetables, such as asparagus and beans, is to fry them and then add whipped eggs. The result is rather like scrambled eggs with vegetables and could form a meal in itself although it is usually served as a vegetable.

Other dishes occasionally encountered include **dolma** of which there is a whole range. They comprise vegetables or occasionally fruits which have been stuffed with meat or rice. Vine leaves or cabbage leaves are most commonly used depending on the season but the range of vegetables used in Armenian homes is staggering: artichokes, chard, aubergines, peppers, courgettes, onions, tomatoes, apples, melons and quinces. The stuffing could be made from some combination of minced beef or lamb, rice, bulghur, dried fruits, chopped vegetables, yoghurt, and a mixture of herbs and spices. Needless to say a visit to an Armenian home is necessary to encounter this kind of range but some restaurants do include one of the more common ones on the menu.

Keufteh is another classic style of Armenian cookery. It is bulghur which has been mixed with finely chopped vegetables and herbs and often with lamb as well. Again there are innumerable variations depending on the cook and the availability of seasonal ingredients. It can be cooked or uncooked, hot or cold, and some have two separate mixtures, one for the core and one for an outer shell. In the popular *sini keufteh* the inner stuffing is made from butter, onions, minced lamb, pine nuts and spices while the outer shell comprises bulghur, more lamb, onion and other spices. It is prepared in a baking dish before being cut into squares and then baked. It can be eaten hot or cold with vegetables or salad.

DESSERT AND PASTRIES Dessert as often as not consists of **fresh fruit** accompanied by cheese (*paneer*). In summer **ice cream** (*parrparrak*) is served but is always factory rather than artisan produced. **Pastries** are more often eaten with a cup of afternoon tea or coffee or in the late evening. Armenia's best pastries, and very good they are too, are those which exploit its fruit and nuts. *Baklava* is widely available and exists in many forms. Layers of buttered filo pastry stuffed with some combination of nuts, apples, cheese and cream is formed into rolls or diamonds and then baked. Afterwards it is covered either with honey or with a sugar and water syrup that has been flavoured with lemon. Also excellent are the **dried fruits** such as apricots, peaches or plums which have been stuffed with nuts. Another interesting and enjoyable novelty is **fruit or sour** *lavash*, thin sheets of dried fruit *purée*. Plum was the classic fruit to use but nowadays a wide range of fruits is employed.

EATING OUT IN ARMENIA It is relatively cheap to eat out in Armenia except for the few places in Yerevan aimed at the more expensive end of the tourist trade which charge Western prices. Main courses usually cost somewhere between AMD2,500–4,000 and it is easy to have a full meal (which in Armenia usually comprises salads and a main course) for AMD5,000 per person. A bottle of wine will add somewhere between AMD2,500–5,000, half a litre of beer AMD500 and two coffees AMD400. There is not usually a significant price differential between restaurants and cafés. Restaurants which fall outside this price range are noted under their individual entries. A light course, such as an omelette, may well cost under AMD1,000 and a savoury street snack can be had for as little as AMD150. Most restaurants open at noon and cafés about 10.00. Most will stay open until midnight or until the last customer has gone. For picnics or for those self-catering, markets provide a wide range of food at budget prices. Another option is to patronise the roadside stalls which sell seasonal fruit and vegetables (see page 81).

DRINKS Armenia is justly renowned for its **brandy**, its **coffee** and its **spring water**. Other drinks, such as some of the **herbal teas** – particularly the thyme tea – are well worth trying and certain of the **wines** are passable without quite threatening the industries of Chile or Australia just yet. Armenian alcohol consumption is at the bottom end of the European range. Although beer can be drunk freely, social etiquette has established formal rules for the drinking of wine and spirits. They may only be drunk when eating and each table has its *tamada* who is responsible for making toasts: no-one drinks without a toast. Toasts can be extremely long, with persons around the table requesting the *tamada* to be allowed to toast. The theory is that the *tamada* is able to regulate the alcohol intake of those present and stop people getting drunk. Unfortunately it doesn't always work because the *tamada* himself sometimes ends up inebriated forcing everyone else to keep going. For most Westerners anyway this ritual is irksome since they are both forced to swig a glass of brandy or vodka when they don't want one just because a toast is proposed or else they are forbidden to enjoy a sip of wine with the food because no toast is then coming to an end. Women will be let off drinking at every toast but it is considered unacceptable for men not to drink every time. It should be noted that Armenians themselves often prefer to drink brandy or vodka with meals rather than drink wine, quite contrary to Western habits. Indeed while one often sees Armenians drinking vodka, drinking even Armenian wine is largely the prerogative of foreigners.

Armenia's drinks industry suffered from two heavy blows in the late 1980s. Firstly, Soviet president Gorbachev launched a strong anti-alcohol campaign and then during the blockade years in the early 1990s goods could not get to the main market in the rest of the CIS. As markets could not import Armenian products other, often inferior, suppliers were only too happy to step into the void. As a result of both these factors production and sales fell considerably, eventually bottoming out in 1996, since when there has been some recovery, especially since 2005.

Armenian **brandy** (*konyak*) sprang to prominence at the Yalta conference in 1945 when Stalin plied Winston Churchill, the British prime minister, with it and Churchill declared that it was better than any French brandy. Many would still agree. Although called cognac in Armenia and the rest of the former Soviet Union, this is forbidden under Western trade rules which specify that cognac must be produced in the Cognac region of France. Armenian brandy comes in a variety of qualities. At the bottom of the range is three star, so called because it has been kept (in oak casks) for three years after fermentation. Up to six years the number of stars indicates age but beyond six years special names are given. The Ararat factory in Yerevan, founded in 1887 and now owned by Pernod Ricard, offers Ani (six years old), Select (seven years old), Akhtamar (ten years old), Celebratory (15 years old), Vaspurakan (18 years old) and Nairi (20 years old). Prices range from AMD3,500 for a 500ml bottle of three star to AMD12,500 for Akhtamar and AMD22,500 for Nairi. Prices in the duty-free at Yerevan Zvartnots Airport are lower – for example AMD8,815 for a bottle of Akhtamar (my favourite) and AMD21,730 for Nairi. About 70% of production is exported to Russia. Other quality producers are Great Valley and MAP and they also export a large proportion of their production. There are around a dozen smaller firms producing inferior products.

Vodka (*vodka* or *oghi*) is distilled by more than 45 small and medium-sized companies in Armenia, including Avshar, Vedi-Alco, SGS (based in Nagorno Karabagh), Garib and Artashat-Vincon. Production has been increasing steadily since 1996 and in 2000 Armenia began exporting its vodka, mainly to the United States and Cyprus. As well as ordinary vodka, several traditional Armenian varieties are made in people's homes, such as mulberry (*t'ti*) vodka, grape (*khagho*) vodka and apricot (*tseeran*) vodka. Many of the vodkas are pleasant enough but they do not compare in quality to the brandy though they are popular in Armenia. The price of vodka (AMD800–10,000 for 500ml) depends on the quality and what it is made from. Armenian vodka is cheaper than Russian and fruit vodkas more expensive than ordinary vodka. You can buy a 500ml bottle of decent fruit vodka for AMD2,500–5,000.

Armenia grows a range of grape varieties but the climate does not lend itself to the 'cool climate' grape growing such as is becoming more popular in the New World, and the **wineries** (more than 15 in Armenia) have had insufficient funds to be able to invest in temperature-controlled fermentation. A considerable number of different white and red wines are available, many of the reds being sweet or semi-sweet. Although the best-known grape variety in Armenia is Areni, used for making dry red wines, the most enjoyable white Armenian wines are those made by the Ijevan winery from the Georgian Rkatsiteli grape. Although some very cheap wine is available, the more drinkable bottles cost about AMD1,800 to AMD2,000 and a good red wine about AMD4,000, slightly more in a restaurant whose mark-ups, other than in Western-style hotels, rarely exceed 25%. The Armenian for wine (*ginee*) can be preceeded by the appropriate adjectives: red (*karmir*); white (*spitak*); dry (*chor*); sweet (*kaghtsr*).

Although imported **beer** (*garejoor* but mostly people use the name of the brand they want rather than the generic word for beer) is occasionally encountered, usually from Heineken or Russia's Baltika brewery, two indigenous brands are ubiquitous throughout the country: Kilikia (brewed in Yerevan) and Kotayk (brewed in Abovian). Local connoisseurs tend to prefer the Kilikia brand but many visitors opt for Kotayk. A third brand, Erebuni, is in fact brewed at the Kotayk brewery and a fourth, Gyumri, is brewed in Gyumri. Beer costs around AMD290–340 for a 500ml bottle bought from a supermarket but this rises to AMD500 for one in a popular pavement café in central Yerevan.

Haikakan soorj, **Armenian coffee** (also called *sev soorj*, black coffee), is excellent and the perfect end to a meal, ideally accompanied by a glass of brandy. It is brewed in small long-handled copper pots using very finely ground beans and served in small cups in a similar way to Turkish coffee. It is usually served slightly sweetened (called *normal* with the stress on the second syllable) and even visitors who drink coffee without sugar at home may prefer it this way. If coffee is desired without any sugar then ask for it *soorj arants shakari*. In a café, coffee costs around AMD200. Instant coffee is also available and tastes just like it does everywhere else. **Tea** (*tay*) in Armenia can be either a standard brand of tea bag dunked in a cup or herbal. Some wonderful teas, especially thyme tea (*oortsi tay*), may be encountered made from a whole gamut of different herbs collected from Armenia's hillsides during the summer and then dried.

Water (*joor*) is another joy in Armenia. The water from Armenia's springs is delicious and always safe to drink. Many of these springs are located by the sides of roads or tracks or at monastic sites and, quite often, picnic tables are provided. It may seem bizarre to recommend spring water but all visitors should make an effort to try it. **Bottled water** (*hankayeen joor* – literally mineral water) is also available. Jermuk is the most common source but Dilijan, Bjni, Byurakan, Byureg and Noy may also be encountered. Carbonated and still are both now widely sold. If you ask for bottled water it will be assumed that you want sparkling; if you want still water ask for it without gas (*arants gazi*).

A drink popular with Armenians and often drunk with meals is **tan**, a mixture of yoghurt, sparkling or still mineral water and salt. I am told it is most refreshing.

Pasteurised fruit juices are generally available, normally in cartons, as is the usual international range of bottled soft drinks together with some local competitors. A particular joy which might be encountered during a homestay is fruit juice made from the family's own fruit trees. Cornelian cherry juice is especially recommended. Occasionally one of the more traditional restaurants will have a novel juice on offer: sea buckthorn juice is one possibility. Despite its name, sea buckthorn *Hippophae rhamnoides*, a small tree of the oleaster family, grows in Armenia.

PUBLIC HOLIDAYS AND FESTIVALS

PUBLIC HOLIDAYS

New Year's Day	1 January
Christmas Day	6 January
Army Day	28 January
International Women's Day	8 March
Good Friday	March/April
Easter Monday	March/April
Day of Motherhood and Beauty	7 April
Genocide Memorial Day	24 April
Victory and Peace Day	9 May
First Republic Day	28 May
Constitution Day	5 July

Independence Day	21 September
Earthquake Memorial Day	7 December
New Year's Eve	31 December

Genocide Memorial Day and Earthquake Memorial Day are called 'commemoration days' rather than public holidays. On Genocide Memorial Day everything is shut as on a public holiday. Earthquake Memorial Day is now a working day, although with civic commemoration ceremonies.

FESTIVALS

Vardevar The Vardevar Festival, held on a Sunday in summer, is a date for which visitors should be well prepared. The precise date is fixed according to the Church calendar and varies from year to year. Being 14 weeks after Easter, it usually falls in July. Vardevar nowadays commemorates the Transfiguration, the incident described in St Matthew's Gospel, chapter 17, when Christ took three disciples up Mount Sinai where his appearance was transfigured as he talked with Moses and Elijah. Its origins, however, are pre-Christian: Vardevar was formerly associated with Aphrodite (Anahit) and rose petals were scattered on the worshippers. (*Vard* is the Armenian word for 'rose'.) Nowadays in place of rose petals the festival involves children collecting water, stalking passers-by, and then throwing it over them. That the more water-affluent children will have managed to stockpile many buckets-worth means that nobody that day should wear smart clothes or indeed any clothes which might be damaged by water. Inevitably Vardevar is therefore a risky day to get married. It is also most unwise, despite the temperature in summer, to drive around with car windows open unless certain that no children are lurking out of sight behind a tree or wall. Adults can and do retaliate against the water throwers, for example by using their own stockpiled supplies to effect revenge on the miscreants below by aiming at them from the safety of the balconies of their apartments. Armenia is not the only country to have such a festival – Thailand and Myanmar (Burma) both have similar festivals to celebrate the Buddhist New Year. In Poland and Hungary water throwing is practised on Easter Monday when the boys throw it on the girls – the more gallant married men spray perfume on their wives but this variant has not yet reached Armenia.

New Year and Christmas In Armenia, as in all Eastern churches, Christmas (which falls on 6 January) is celebrated after New Year. In fact the two weeks from 31 December are a period of continuous family and church-centred celebration. In the weeks before New Year the shops are busy with people shopping – principally for food although also for presents. Food, especially family meals, forms the important focus of the festivities. For three days before New Year's Eve so much food is prepared that you would think there was going to be a two-month siege! Everyone wants to make sure that there are generous helpings for all the extended family members who will visit. Everyone visits everyone else. Even if your aunt has visited you one day, you will still go and see her the next. On New Year's Eve a large piece of meat is cooked, often roast leg of pork, as well as numerous accompanying dishes and desserts, in preparation for visitors who start to arrive after the midnight bells. A small gift is always taken for whoever you are visiting, often a box of chocolates or a bottle of wine or vodka. Presents are given on New Year's Eve rather than at Christmas and it is Kaghand Papi, Grandfather Kaghand (see box opposite), who brings them for small children. Both the birth of Jesus and his baptism are remembered on 6 January. At the church service water is blessed, consecrated oil (chrism or, in Armenian, *meron*) is poured into the water and a Cross is dipped into

In Russia, and some other Slavic cultures, the traditional character of Ded Moroz (the literal meaning of the Russian being 'Grandfather Frost' but often translated as 'Father Frost') played a similar role to that of Santa Claus or Saint Nicholas in the west. Ded Moroz has his roots in pagan beliefs and was originally a wicked sorcerer who stole children, but under the influence of Christian Orthodox tradition he became a kind person who gave gifts to children at New Year. In the officially atheist Soviet Union the celebration of Christmas was discouraged and New Year celebrations, which included the arrival of Ded Moroz with gifts, were promoted. He, or a local counterpart, was introduced into other parts of the Soviet Union and into eastern European counties in the Soviet bloc, despite his being alien to them. Since the collapse of the Soviet Union countries such as Slovenia, Bulgaria, Poland and Romania have reverted to their traditional characters associated with Christmas.

In Armenia it was Dzmer Papi (literally 'Grandfather Winter' but usually more euphoniously translated as 'Father Frost') who was introduced during the Soviet period. There seems not to have been a pre-Soviet equivalent. Since independence, Dzmer Papi has been replaced by Kaghand Papi (Grandfather New Year) – possibly based on a figure from ancient mythology.

the water to symbolise Christ's baptism. This water is then distributed to the faithful who will either drink it or wash their hands and faces in it.

Christmas is a religious festival. The family go to church on either Christmas Eve or Christmas Day, the main family meal taking place on the other day. Again large amounts of food are prepared for the many visitors who will come. A pilaff and baked fish are always included.

Easter A night-time Easter Eve church service is attended followed by a family meal on Easter Sunday. As with Christmas, fish forms the centrepiece of the meal and there will also be green vegetables cooked with whipped eggs and a sweet pilaff. There are egg fights for the children, with hard-boiled eggs which they have painted or dyed the previous day. The pointed ends of the eggs are engaged first then, when they have all cracked, the blunt ends are tested. The winner is the one whose egg lasts the longest without breaking. The eggs are then made into an Easter sandwich with *lavash*, greens (usually tarragon) and cheese.

SHOPPING

In town centres most shops open at 09.30 or 10.00 and then remain open until 19.00. Shops rarely close for lunch. Some shops, especially food shops and markets, open daily but many specialist shops such as bookshops remain closed on Sundays. In residential areas small shops and kiosks are open for very long hours – often till after midnight – while roadside stalls on main routes are sometimes open 24 hours.

Also open 24 hours are branches of the supermarket chains which have appeared in the last few years. These supermarkets, and indeed all shops in Armenia, are well stocked and visitors should be able to buy most of what they need, especially in the towns. (See page 7 for items which should be brought from home). Shopping, apart from the Western designer shops on Northern Avenue in Yerevan which charge Western prices, is relatively inexpensive.

By law, exporting any work of art which is more than 50 years old from Armenia requires approval from the government's Department of Cultural Heritage Preservation at 51 Komitas Avenue, third and fourth floors. For those without linguistic skills, it is advisable to get the dealer to sort it out. You need to take the item, together with two photographs, to the third floor – the Department of Expertise – and pay AMD2,000. You then go to the fourth floor – the permit department – with the photographs and the papers issued on the third floor. You pay a further sum which depends on the valuation of the expertise department. For an item valued up to AMD250,000 you pay AMD5,700; for one valued up to AMD500,000, you pay AMD15,700, etc. Generally the permit is then issued on the spot. However, if the item is considered to be of national importance museums and art galleries have a month to exercise the option to buy it. If none want it an export permit will be issued. This procedure is not required for items less than 50 years old, but the date, name of the author and his/her signature should be appended.

This may be rigorously enforced in the case of paintings (sometimes even those painted last week by an unknown artist and bought at Vernissage) and handmade carpets, but often less so in the case of other items such as carvings or embroideries. In the past, there were reports of customs officers at the airport citing rules written and unwritten and refusing to allow the export of paintings in particular, despite the purchaser having the correct paperwork. Bribery was reported to work in these cases.

The widest range of **souvenirs** is to be found in Yerevan. Obvious items to take home include the increasing number of books of photographs of Armenia (see *Bookshops*, page 115), Armenia's highly regarded brandy (easily obtainable in markets, shops and specialist brandy outlets) and craft items. There is no doubt that the best place to buy crafts is at Vernissage in Yerevan (see page 122), but they can also be found on souvenir stalls at some of the more popular tourist sites and in other outlets in Yerevan. (See *Shopping, Chapter 3*, pages 114–15.) The cathedral shop at Ejmiatsin also has a good range of articles. Typically Armenian are carpets (and for those who want something cheaper than a full-sized floor covering, bags and waistcoats made from carpet offcuts), wood and stone carving, embroidered articles (from large tablecloths to handkerchiefs; see page 123) and jewellery incorporating Armenia's semi-precious obsidian (see page 3). Paintings for sale are displayed at weekends in the small park to the northwest of the Opera House in Yerevan and at Vernissage.

 ARTS AND ENTERTAINMENT

As in most countries, but perhaps more so than in many, access to the arts and to formal entertainments is concentrated in the capital. All the major **museums and art galleries** are in or near Yerevan (see pages 138–44). Other towns do have small museums and art galleries but they do not compare to those in Yerevan. Labelling, even in important Yerevan museums, often makes no concession to non-Armenian speakers.

Entrance fees are low by Western standards, rarely being more than AMD1,000 and often much less. The entrance fee for children is usually lower than the adult rate. If an English-speaking guide is available, this costs about an extra AMD2,500–5,000. The most commonly encountered foreign-language guided tours are English and Russian. Other languages are much rarer; if available they are noted under individual entries. Most museums are closed on Mondays, a few on other days. Opening hours and days are stated in individual entries.

Theatres and concert halls are also concentrated in Yerevan (see page 113). Performances are usually in Armenian, apart from opera which may be sung in the original language. Theatre tickets cost AMD1,500–15,000 and are usually bought from the venue although tickets for one venue, especially if it is not in the town centre, may sometimes be sold at another. Box offices display posters showing which tickets they are selling. Tour operators can arrange tickets.

In Soviet days most towns had a **cinema** but this is no longer the case; only Yerevan has cinemas, including two refurbished ones (see page 113) which show films in English. Tickets cost AMD1,000–5,000. The annual **Golden Apricot International Film Festival** (*3 Moscovian St, Yerevan;* `\` *10 521042; *e* info@gaiff.am; www.gaiff.am*) takes place in Yerevan during July. The first festival in 2004 attracted 148 films by 70 film-makers from 20 countries. By 2009 it had grown to 450 submitted films, from 67 countries, and in 2010 there were 500 entries out of which 120 were chosen. The festival takes as its theme 'Crossroads of Cultures and Civilisations' and welcomes films representing various nations, ethnicities and religions, collectively depicting the richness of the human experience. The opening of the festival is marked by a traditional blessing of Armenia's famous apricots.

Armenia is a country of **statues**. This is an active art form, perhaps not surprising in a land with such a long history of carving; witness the thousands of khachkars. New statues appear regularly throughout the country. Some statues are described in this guide (see pages 117–34 and 224) but visitors are likely to see many more. Khachkar carving continues to be an active art form.

More modern forms of entertainment such as **casinos** and **nightclubs** are on offer in Yerevan (see page 113), as are some **sports** (see page 114). The Armenians are good at entertaining themselves. They have certainly taken to the café culture; witness the large numbers of busy cafés in Yerevan's city centre. Very few bars, as such, exist; cafés and restaurants are the places to relax, have a drink and enjoy company. Strolling, a pastime which seems to have disappeared from much of Western life, is alive and well in Armenia and visitors may enjoy rediscovering this art.

HISTORIC SITES

In this guide, prices and opening hours are included where they apply. Otherwise assume the site is free and always open or, in the case of churches, open all day. Most historic sites are free.

There may appear to be some confusion between the terms **church** and **monastery** at times. This is because at some sites only the church of a monastery survives but the site is still referred to as a monastery. With more and more churches becoming active places of worship, it is now common for the church itself to be locked at night although the site as a whole may still be accessible. Non-active churches may be open all the time.

The great majority of churches and monasteries are either open all the time or else open all day (09.00–18.00 at least) with the caretaker or keyholder selling candles to visitors. Even if a locked door greets you, there is a strong possibility that the caretaker, having seen visitors arriving, will soon appear. In only three cases (St John the Baptist near Lanjar; the Mother of God Church at Garni; Holy Apostles at Sevanavank) have I regularly failed to get in. This is very unlikely at the more popular sites.

Most other sites (**fortresses, caravanserais, prehistoric monuments**) are always open. Where there are opening hours they are stated in the text.

❯MEDIA AND COMMUNICATIONS

MEDIA Armenia has two **television** stations: Armenia First (public television) and Armenia TV (commercial) and over 40 private television companies, mostly owned by wealthy individuals with government connections. They are of little interest to those who do not speak Armenian and, indeed, many Armenians themselves prefer to watch Russian television. The independent television station A1+ is closed down from time to time by the government but posts news on its website (*www.A1plus.am*) in both Armenian and English. The **press** is likewise almost entirely in Armenian with the exception of the weekly *Noyan Tapan Highlights* (*Noah's Ark Highlights*) which gives an English-language résumé of contemporary events as well as listings of what's on at the theatres. It isn't particularly easy to obtain but can be picked up in Yerevan at the Armenia Information office (see page 107) and is on sale at Artbridge bookshop (*20 Abovian St*) and Salt Sack (*3/1 Abovian St*). Investigative journalists in Armenia are periodically assaulted by thugs employed by those who have vested

---

PHOTOGRAPHIC TIPS   *Ariadne Van Zandbergen*

EQUIPMENT An SLR camera with one or more lenses is recommended for serious photography. The most important component in a digital SLR is the sensor, either DX or FX. The FX is a full-size sensor identical to the old film size (36mm). The DX sensor is half size and produces less quality. The type of sensor will determine your choice of lenses as the DX sensor introduces a 0.5x multiplication to the focal length. FX ('full frame') sensors are the future, so I will further refer to focal lengths appropriate to the FX sensor.

Always buy the best lens you can afford. Fixed fast lenses are ideal, but very costly. Zoom lenses offer good flexibility with composition. If you carry only one lens a 24–70mm or similar zoom should be ideal. For a second lens, a lightweight 80–200mm or 70–300mm or similar will be excellent for candid shots and varying your composition. Wildlife photography requires at least a 300mm lens. For a small loss of quality, teleconverters are a cheap and compact way to increase magnification: a 300 lens with a 1.4x converter becomes 420mm, and with a 2x it becomes 600mm. NB 1.4x and 2x teleconverters reduce the speed of your lens by 1.4 and 2 stops respectively.

For ordinary prints a 6-megapixel camera is fine. For better results, the possibility to enlarge images and for professional reproduction, higher resolution is available up to 21 megapixels.

It is important to have enough memory space. You should calculate how many pictures you can fit on a card and either take enough cards or take a storage drive onto which you can download the cards' content.

Remember that digital camera batteries, computers and other storage devices need charging. Make sure you have all the chargers, cables, converters with you.

DUST AND HEAT Keep your equipment in a sealed bag, and avoid exposing equipment to the sun when possible. Digital cameras are prone to collecting

interests to protect. Censorship was prohibited under a 2004 media law but libel and defamation are punishable by prison terms and journalists have been sentenced under these laws. The US-based NGO Freedom House reports that self-censorship is common, particularly in regard to reporting corruption and the Nagorno Karabagh situation. **Radio** does not play a large part in the life of Armenians, being mostly listened to in the car. Public Radio of Armenia is the national, state-run station. There are also many private radio stations; I am told that the quality is not good.

TELEPHONE In 2006 the large Russian **mobile** telephone operator VimpelCom acquired the 90% share of Armentel which had been owned since 1998 by the Hellenic Telecommunications Organisation; the remaining 10% remained in the hands of the Armenian government. There had been widespread dissatisfaction with Greek-owned Armentel which levied high charges for poor service. Enormous strides have now been made in modernising the outdated Soviet-era system. In 2008 Armentel was rebranded as Beeline. Beeline holds all landlines and 30% of the cellular network. There are two other phone companies, VivaCell which holds 70% of the cellular market and Orange, a relative newcomer. Mobile phones are ubiquitous and there is good coverage throughout the country. If you need to hire a mobile phone this can be done through Hyur Service (see *Tour operators*, page 56) for AMD500 per day.

dust particles on the sensor which results in spots on the image. The dirt mostly enters the camera when changing lenses, so be careful when doing this. You can have your camera sensor professionally cleaned, or you can do this yourself with special brushes and swabs, but note that touching the sensor might cause damage and should only be done with the greatest care.

LIGHT The most striking outdoor photographs are often taken during the hour or two of 'golden light' after dawn and before sunset. Shooting in low light may enforce the use of very low shutter speeds, in which case a tripod/ beanbag will be required to avoid camera shake. The most advanced digital SLRs have very little loss of quality on higher ISO settings, which allows you to shoot at lower light conditions. It is still recommended not to increase the ISO unless necessary.

Generally, it is best to shoot with the sun behind you. When photographing animals or people in the harsh midday sun, images taken in light but even shade are likely to look nicer than those taken in direct sunlight or patchy shade.

PROTOCOL In some countries, it is unacceptable to photograph local people without permission, and many will refuse to pose or will ask for a donation. Don't try to sneak photographs. Even the most willing subject will often pose stiffly when a camera is pointed at them; relax them by making a joke, and take a few shots in quick succession to improve the odds of capturing a natural pose. For comments on photographing Armenians, see page 96.

Ariadne Van Zandbergen is a professional travel and wildlife photographer specialised in Africa. She runs 'The Africa Image Library'. For photo requests, visit the website www.africaimagelibrary.co.za or contact her direct e ariadne@hixnet.co.za.

2

Both Beeline (*www.beeline.am*) and VivaCell (*www.vivacell.am*) have 24-hour desks in the arrivals hall at Zvartnots Airport where a free Armenian SIM card can be obtained. Note that an identification document is required of both Armenians and foreigners when registering a SIM card so your passport will be needed. Both companies have multiple outlets in Yerevan and throughout the country where pre-paid or post-paid cards are available and they can also be bought at numerous supermarkets, shops and kiosks. They both produce leaflets in English detailing their products and tariffs (of which there are many), but VivaCell has the better website. It is in English as well as Armenian and Russian whereas Beeline's is only in Armenian and Russian.

Your own mobile phone will work in Armenia on a roaming basis if you arrange this with your provider before leaving home. The advantage is that you can keep your own mobile number; the disadvantage is that it is significantly more expensive than using an Armenian SIM card and number.

Dialling Armenia from abroad the country code is 374 followed by the local city code. If **dialling within Armenia**, insert an additional 0 before the city code. In this guide, town codes are given where relevant and a list of the main ones are included in the box below. Elsewhere, the appropriate code is included with the individual phone number.

International calls from Armenia can of course be made from landlines or mobiles as elsewhere. If using a landline, a cheaper option than direct dialling is to purchase an **international call card** available from shops, kiosks, newspaper stands, etc. Instructions are on the card but essentially you dial the number on the card, followed by the scratch number then follow the voice instructions.

In Yerevan and a few other places calls can be made from **public card phones** in the streets, these cards also being on sale at numerous outlets. In the pre-mobile-phone era and in the many towns which did not have card phones it was necessary to go to the main post office to make a call. The procedure involved writing the number required on a form, handing it to the clerk, and then waiting to be connected manually. Apparently in some regions this method is still available but for how much longer is unknown.

INTERNET Internet services have also improved greatly in recent years. Domestic connection is usually **dial-up**, other methods being very expensive although Wi-Fi is available in many hotels. There are internet cafés on almost every corner

---

TELEPHONE CODES

Alaverdi 253	Gyumri 312	Talin 2490
Aparan 252	Hrazden 223	Tsaghkadzor 223
Armavir 237	Ijevan 263	Vaik 282
Artik 244	Jermuk 287	Vanadzor 322
Ashtarak 232	Kapan 285	Vardenis 269
Chambarak 265	Meghri 2860	Yeghegnadzor 281
Dilijan 2680	Sevan 261	Yerevan 10
Ejmiatsin 231	Sisian 2830	
Goris 284	Stepanavan 256	

For Karabagh phone codes, see page 274. There are several codes for mobile phones but people will give you this with their phone number.

in Yerevan and other towns, charging about AMD300 per hour. Most hotels offer internet access, usually included in the room price. A curious feature of previous Armenian use of the internet was that it could not cope with the Armenian alphabet and, surprisingly, not even the Cyrillic alphabet with any reliability. Therefore Armenians emailing each other tended to transliterate these languages into Roman letters. Having got used to doing this many Armenians continue to do so, although using the Armenian alphabet is no longer a problem. Problems can arise, however, if you're carrying out internet searches because of the lack of standardisation of transliteration (see *Note on transliteration*, page VIII).

POSTAL SERVICES The national postal service Haypost (*www.haypost.am*) is now under Dutch management. Post offices throughout the country are being modernised and new services introduced. Post offices are widespread; even quite small villages have one. At last postal services to Armenia appear to be improving. Recent letters from the UK have arrived three to four weeks after being posted, much better than the past when they often never arrived at all. Postal services from Armenia to the West are usually reliable. Items have taken as little as six days from Yerevan to Scotland but two weeks is average. It can be slower from the provinces. Other than at the main post offices in Yerevan, counter clerks may not be familiar with the correct postage for letters. There is a standard charge of AMD240 for postcards sent abroad. Letters are charged by weight; for those going abroad the cost is AMD375 for letters up to 20g, AMD875 for 20–100g, etc.

BUSINESS

Even after over 70 years of Soviet rule, Armenians have maintained an entrepreneurial spirit. However, corruption in official bodies is widespread, though less of a problem than in Russia, for example. Business practices as such are not widely different from those in the West but it is absolutely vital to be certain of the competence of interpreters when translating between Armenian and Western languages: many problems arise because what is apparently the same word or phrase does not mean precisely the same in two different languages. Business hours are 09.00–17.00. At work men and women are on an equal footing although, as explained on page 33, it is customary for a married woman to stay at home to look after the couple's children while they are young. On a semi-social level, most business visitors find themselves being taken out to restaurants by their hosts for lengthy meals and numerous toasts (see *Drinks*, page 85, for the rules on toasting). They may also be taken to historic sites, particularly at the weekend.

BUYING PROPERTY

It is easy to purchase property in Armenia. Foreigners can buy an apartment or house outright although they cannot buy land outright unless they are either of Armenian descent or else buy it through a company (which can be foreign-owned). Foreigners can only lease land, which can be for up to 99 years. Prices are highest in central Yerevan at about US$5,000/m², while one of the newly built apartments on Northern Avenue currently costs US$2,500/m². Prices drop gradually the further from the centre one travels, with suburban prices being about half this. Prices in towns near Yerevan tend also to be relatively high with prices in other towns considerably lower. The smallest house in the new Vahakni residential community on the northwest outskirts of Yerevan will cost you 141 million drams plus a 'homeowner's fee' of

AMD45,000 per month. When looking for anywhere to buy, only ever consider stone-built property: the poor quality of Soviet prefabricated construction was demonstrated vividly in the 1988 earthquake. Property is widely advertised in the local press, including the English-language *Noyan Tapan Highlights*, or you could use a broker to find you something though they rarely speak English. A broker's fee is typically 3% of the purchase price. Brokers will also handle the paperwork, whether or not you purchase through them, for a fee of around US$250.

Sound advice on buying a property in Armenia can be found at www.armeniapedia.org. A broker with a satisfactory website is ESCo (*13 Sayat Nova Av, Yerevan;* \ *+374 10 520302; www.esco.am*).

CULTURAL ETIQUETTE

As is made clear throughout this guide, Armenians are extremely hospitable and, especially in rural areas, visitors will often be invited into people's houses for coffee. Accept with good grace, however poor the family; the invitation is sincere and the family will be genuinely pleased to see you. If dining with a family, including on a homestay, expect to be plied with far more food than it is humanly possible to eat. It is polite to at least try every dish. See the section on drinks (page 85) for the rules on toasting and the section on breakfast (page 82) if you have the (mis)fortune to be invited to a *khash* party.

If invited to someone's home for a meal a small gift for the hostess, who will have spent very many hours preparing the meal, is appropriate – a box of chocolates or flowers (but always an odd number of flowers, an even number is for the cemetery).

When visiting churches it is customary to buy candles (expect to pay AMD60–100 each) and then light them before sticking them in the trays of sand. Matches are provided. There is no particular need to dress more conservatively than elsewhere in Armenia, but women should wear a headscarf if intending to take communion. It is correct to leave a church walking backwards (so as not to turn one's back on God) but some people don't.

Armenians do tend to dress more smartly than Westerners and also more formally. In particular going to someone's house for dinner, or to the theatre, is an occasion for formality (suit or dress) rather than for dressing down. Shorts are worn by both sexes in summer but are not particularly common.

It is normal to greet people any time you meet them outside a town. Just say '*Barev dzez*' – 'Hello'. Expect people in rural areas to be very curious about where you come from, what you are doing, and what you think about Armenia. It is very hard not to interact with local people, although the language barrier is considerable unless you speak either Armenian or Russian. Very few people speak English and even those who do, including English-language teachers, may not understand what is said to them since they are unaccustomed to hearing English spoken by native speakers of the language.

With very few exceptions, Armenians of all ages love having their photograph taken, although it is of course polite to ask before taking a portrait shot. In general, people will happily pose and, if your language is up to it, you can even, for example, persuade a shepherd to move his sheep to a more photogenic position. You may well be remonstrated with by old ladies if you fail to take their photograph while photographing the monument by which they are sitting, and children will quite often pester you to take their picture.

In the West, although we are not necessarily conscious of it, we often smile at someone we are speaking to, even if we do not know them and are encountering them in a superficial business situation, as in a bank or enquiry office. However, this is not always the case in Armenia and it can be surprisingly disconcerting for a foreigner. It is not that the person is surly or doesn't want to see you, it is just that Armenians tend not to smile unless they know you or there is something to smile at, such as a joke.

Again, in the West, we are accustomed to think that if a door is firmly shut it probably means that the place is either closed or one is not meant to enter. This is not the case in Armenia. If the place looks shut it is worth trying the door: the premises may well be fully open for business. For example, the ticket office for the Matenadaran can look very shut when it is in fact open. Even in the National Gallery the large forbidding doors to some of the rooms may be firmly shut (sometimes for so prosaic a reason as to keep the cold out) but one is meant to open them to continue the tour of the art gallery.

Some large hotels have an entry hall devoid of furnishing or people. Go up to the next floor and you will find a fully functioning hotel. There may be a couple of burly men sitting in the entrance hall: they will direct you to where you need to go. If a hotel looks deserted when you arrive, don't panic, someone will soon appear.

TRAVELLING POSITIVELY

Armenia's economic situation means there is much poverty, although this is not always evident. The country is very dependent on assistance from outside and help is always welcome, both large and small scale.

ARMENIAN MONUMENTS AWARENESS PROJECT (AMAP) (*101 Pavstos Buzand St, Door 1, Apt 6, Yerevan;* \ *+374 10 532455;* e *contact@ArmenianMonuments. org; www.ArmenianMonuments.org*) An NGO which aims to stimulate sustainable economic development arising from tourism at Armenia's historical, cultural and natural monuments. It also aims to assist in monument preservation and is the body behind much of the welcome recent increase in information at historic sites. Donations can be made via the website.

HALO TRUST A non-political, non-religious NGO and the largest humanitarian mine-clearance organisation in the world, undertakes mine clearing in Nagorno Karabagh (see box, *Chapter 7*, page 268). Some governments are withdrawing funding from Nagorno Karabagh; for example, the UK's Department for International Development has excluded Nagorno Karabagh from its mine-action strategy for 2010–13, despite previously funding mine clearing there. Governmental monies can only be used within the pre-1991 boundaries of Nagorno Karabagh so mine clearance outwith these boundaries is entirely dependent on other sources. All donations, whatever the size, are welcome and can be made via the website (*www.halotrust.org/help.html*). Alternatively, donations may be sent to the HALO Trust's headquarters (*Carronfoot, Thornhill, Dumfries DG3 5BF, UK*). Anyone wishing their money to be used specifically for Nagorno Karabagh should state this.

HAYASTAN ALL-ARMENIAN FUND (*www.himnadram.org*) Founded in 1992 as a means whereby all Armenians worldwide could contribute to the development and stability of newly independent Armenia. Help is given where it is most needed whether that be infrastructure, economic development, job creation or humanitarian relief. Projects range in size from a new classroom for a village school to 150km of new road, and they also cover green projects such as the planting of trees to replace those cut down for firewood during the electricity shortages of 1992–95.

All contributions to programmes great and small are welcome, and not only from members of the diaspora. Donations can be made via the website or through one of the local branches. The UK address is Hayastan All-Armenian Fund Great Britain, c/o Armenian Vicarage, Iverna Gardens, Kensington, London W8 6TP. Donors can be certain that their money will be used to fund the project specified. It will not end up in some corrupt politician's pocket: the diaspora go to see how their money has been spent and would never tolerate corruption.

ORRAN (*6 First Yekmalian St, Yerevan;* \ *535167;* e *orran@orran.am; www.orran.am*) A charity established in 2000 with its headquarters in Yerevan. It aims to help the poorest in society, mainly children and the elderly. Visitors are welcome. Donations can be made via their website or by cheque in US dollars to 2217 Observatory Avenue, Los Angeles, CA 90027, USA.

OXFAM Oxfam has worked in Armenia since 1998 to support refugees who fled to Armenia during the Karabagh conflict and the communities in which they settled. It now assists small farmers and women's groups and monitors the impact of government policies on the poor. A visit to Oxfam's projects can be arranged via Margarita Hakobyan at Oxfam's office in Yerevan (*Apt 10, 3a Terian St;* \ *+374 10 538418, 501464*). Donations can be sent to Oxfam House (*John Smith Dr, Cowley, Oxford OX4 2JY, UK*). Anyone who wishes their donation to go specifically to Armenia should state this when donating.

STUFF YOUR RUCKSACK (*www.stuffyourrucksack.com*) A website set up by television's Kate Humble which enables travellers to give direct help to small charities, schools or other organisations in the country they are visiting. Although there are no Armenian organisations listed on this website at present the sorts of gifts envisaged would be welcome in Armenia. Some of the other charities listed above may be able to give information about the best means of directing help to where it is needed.

Part Two

THE GUIDE

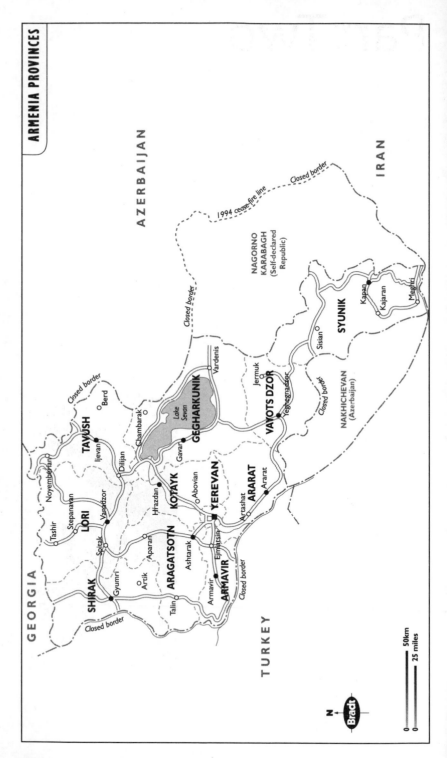

GEORGIA

AZERBAIJAN

TURKEY

IRAN

Closed border

1994 cease-fire line

Closed border

NAGORNO
KARABAGH
(Self-declared
Republic)

Closed border

SYUNIK

Kapan

Kajaran

Meghri

Sisian

NAKHICHEVAN
(Azerbaijan)

Closed border

SHIRAK

TAVUSH

LORI

KOTAYK

ARAGATSOTN

ARMAVIR

YEREVAN

ARARAT

GEGHARKUNIK

VAYOTS DZOR

Berd

Noyemberian

Tashir

Ijevan

Stepanavan

Dilijan

Vanadzor

Chambarak

*Lake
Sevan*

Vardenis

Spitak

Hrazdan

Gavar

Gyumri

Artik

Aparan

Abovian

Jermuk

Yeghegnadzor

Ashtarak

Artashat

Ararat

Talin

Armavir

Ejmiatsin

Closed border

Closed border

N

50km

25 miles

0

0

Bradt

3

Yerevan

Telephone code 10

Armenia's capital stands on the Hrazdan River which flows south from Lake Sevan to join the Arax south of the city. The river in its deep gorge skirts the centre of the city on its western side and consequently many visitors only ever see it as they cross Victory Bridge (so called because it was built in 1945) on the drive into the city from Zvartnots Airport. Yerevan's lower parts are at an altitude of around 900m above sea level but the higher parts up on the plateau are around 1,200m. Precipitation is light at 277mm per annum with May being the wettest month (43mm) and August the driest (8mm). The average temperature (measured over 24 hours) varies from −3°C in January to 26°C in July though these averages mask considerable diurnal variation: night-time lows in January are around −15°C while daytime highs in July reach 44°C. Yerevan is a very sunny place with an average of 2,579 hours of sunshine annually (there are 8,760 hours in a year) and only 37 days classed as non-sunny.

Yerevan's centre, Republic Square, boasts some of the finest Soviet-era buildings in the whole of the former USSR and there is a surprising range of architectural styles within the whole central area owing largely to the fusion of Armenian and Russian styles. Outside the central core of the city, Soviet influence is rampant owing to the rapid expansion of the city during that epoch when its population increased 30-fold.

HISTORY

Although Yerevan's fortunes have waxed and waned considerably over time, and it was never the capital of Armenia prior to 1918, it is actually a very old city. The Urartian King Argishti I (ruled c785–c762BC) established a garrison of 6,600 troops at Erebuni in the southeast part of the present city in 782BC, thus making Yerevan older even than Rome which is traditionally claimed to have been founded in 753BC. About a century later, the Urartian King Rusa II (ruled c685–c645BC) chose a different site, Teishebai Uru ('City of [the God] Teisheba') overlooking the Hrazdan River which he believed would be less vulnerable to attack by the Scythians. It is now known as Karmir Blur ('Red Hill') in the western part of the modern city. Erebuni had grown within 100 years to be a substantial settlement but the establishment of Teishebai Uru caused its rapid decline.

Proximity to the fertile plain ensured that Yerevan remained a significant settlement as, along with the rest of Armenia, it was caught up over the centuries of turmoil, its size fluctuating considerably as the degree of urbanisation in the country varied. Eventually it was almost totally destroyed by an earthquake in 1679. The collapsed bridge over the Hrazdan was quickly replaced by a new four-arch structure and Yerevan's importance began to rise again as it found itself close to the frontier line where the Persian, Turkish and Russian empires were jostling for supremacy. At the time of the earthquake, Yerevan itself was under Persian rule, with a mixed Christian and Muslim population. In 1684, at the request of the French king Louis XIV, Shah Suleiman II permitted French Jesuits to establish a mission there to try to persuade the Katholikos to accept the supremacy of the Pope and bring the Armenian Church into the Roman Catholic fold. The missionaries achieved little and greatly lamented the loss of the excellent Yerevan wine when Shah Hussein, who had succeeded his father, banned all wine throughout the Persian Empire in 1694. A new main church to replace those destroyed in the earthquake was erected in 1693–94 and a new central mosque in 1765–66.

Russian southward expansion into the Caucasus began under Peter the Great in 1722, ostensibly with the object of protecting Orthodox believers. It was a fairly gradual process. In 1801, Russia formally annexed eastern Georgia as the new Russian province of Tiflis and installed Prince Paul Tsitsianov, Georgian born but Russian educated, as governor. In 1804, Tsitsianov led a 5,000-strong Russian army south and attacked Yerevan on 1 May. Despite besieging the town from 2 July until 3 September he was forced to withdraw but the following year he was asked by two Armenian notables to try again so as to save the Christian population of Yerevan from Muslim oppression. His haughty reply was to the effect that he did not care even if the Christians at Yerevan were 'dying in the hands of unbelievers' because 'unreliable Armenians with Persian souls' deserved in his view to 'die like dogs' since they had done nothing to help him when he was besieging the city. Tsitsianov was killed at Baku in 1806 and in 1808 Russia made a second attempt, this time under Field Marshal Ivan Vasilievich (1741–1820) but had no more success. Eventually General Ivan Paskevich (1782–1856), a veteran of the Battle of Borodino, succeeded and led victorious Russian troops into Yerevan on 2 October 1827. On this occasion the Tsar awarded him the title Count of Yerevan but he subsequently gained the additional title Prince of Warsaw as a further token of the Tsar's appreciation when he was responsible for killing 9,000 Poles during the second Polish uprising against Russian rule in 1831.

The Russian conquerors found a town which in 1828 had 1,736 low mud-brick houses, 851 shops, ten baths, eight mosques, seven churches, seven caravanserais and six public squares all set among gardens surrounded by mud walls. On the one and only visit to Yerevan by a Tsar, Nikolai I in 1837 described the city as a 'clay pot'. Matters changed only slowly in what was still a garrison town; the principal Russian settlement in Armenia was Alexandropol (Gyumri) rather than Yerevan. Occasional traces of 19th-century Yerevan can still be found, although Yerevan's importance was to change out of all recognition with its proclamation as capital of the First Armenian Republic on 28 May 1918. The brilliant Armenian architect Hovhannes Tamanian (1878–1936) drew up a master plan in 1924–26 for what was now the capital of Soviet Armenia. It envisaged the creation of a large central square surrounded by imposing buildings constructed of tuff (see page 3). From this square would lead broad avenues, and encircling the whole central area would be a green ring of parkland. Quite a large part of this did in fact come to pass and is described in the following section.

Tamanian did not, of course, foresee the 30-fold expansion of the city's population during the Soviet era to an estimated 1.2 million with its dreary urban sprawl of apartment blocks. There was in practice considerable local enthusiasm for expanding the city since any Soviet city with a population exceeding one million was considered to be of 'all Union importance' and entitled to benefits which included a metro system and a crematorium. Economic problems since independence have resulted in a fall in Armenia's population so the main focus in building, apart from the new cathedral, is on luxury houses for the new elite together with the paraphernalia of hotels, embassies and accommodation for expats which any capital city attracts. There is also underway considerable necessary and welcome refurbishment of the infrastructure, such as roads and pavements, which is largely being paid for by the diaspora. By contrast the erosion of the green belt by an amazing number of cafés is rather sad.

GETTING THERE AND AWAY

Most visitors to Armenia begin their stay in Yerevan, the vast majority arriving **by air** at Yerevan's Zvartnots Airport. For information about arriving by air, including airlines, the airport and transport to the city centre, see *Chapter 2, pages 59–61.* Even those arriving **by bus** from Iran, Georgia or Turkey (via Georgia) (see *Chapter 2, page 61*) or **by train** from Georgia (see *Chapter 2, page 61*) usually start their tour in Yerevan. Apart from the fact that most transport delivers passengers to the city, there is much to be said for starting in the capital, which has the best sources of information, much of the cultural life and is where bookings (for accommodation, hire cars, etc) can most easily be made if not arranged in advance. Many of the important historical sites can be reached in day trips from the capital and all transport to the provinces goes through Yerevan.

Hiring a car, with or without driver, gives most flexibility, especially if wishing to reach off-the-beaten-track places (see *Tour operators, pages 55–6; Driving, pages 76–7; Car hire, page 77*). Rates range from AMD19,000–75,000 per day.

It is possible to reach most places by **public transport** but note that the transport serves local communities, so if a tourist site is not near a town or village it will not be served per se, apart from one or two exceptions. Most public transport is in the form of buses or minibuses (see *Chapter 2, pages 75–6*) which are cheap, the longest journeys in the country costing AMD6,000. Trains are even cheaper, the most expensive journey costing only AMD950, but much of Armenia is not covered by rail. There are, however, some routes which may be useful to visitors (see *Chapter 2, pages 73–4*).

Taxis (see *Chapter 2, page 76*) are also relatively cheap, are abundant and can provide a viable alternative to a hire car or public transport. For example, a taxi for the 120km from Vanadzor to Yerevan costs around AMD8,000. They are the only option for getting to some places not served by public transport, apart from walking or cycling.

GETTING AROUND

BY METRO The metro consists of one line together with a short branch in the southern suburbs. It is safe, efficient and cheap. The main line runs from the north side of the city across the central district and out to the south. The stations most likely to be of interest to visitors are, from north to south: Marshal Baghramian [118 C1] (near the British embassy); Yeridasardakan ('Youth') [119 G2] on the green belt east of the Cascade; Hanrapetutian Hraparak ('Republic Square') [119 F5] which is not actually on Republic Square but is behind the art gallery at the west end of Vernissage; Zoravar Andranik ('Commander Andranik') [119 E7] opposite the foot of the slope leading up to the cathedral; and Sassountsi Davit ('David of Sassoun') [104 D5] adjacent to the main railway station. The first section from Baregamatyun

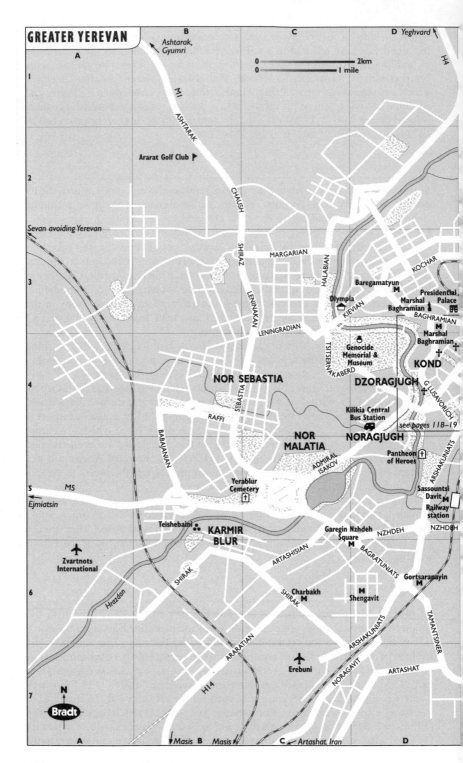

GREATER YEREVAN

Ashtarak, Gyumri

Yeghvard

0 ——————— 2km
0 ——————— 1 mile

Ararat Golf Club ▶

Sevan avoiding Yerevan

MARGARIAN

KOCHAR

Baregamatyun Ⓜ

Olympia

Marshal
Baghramian

Presidential
Palace

BAGHRAMIAN

Ⓜ

Marshal
Baghramian

KIEVIAN

Genocide
Memorial &
Museum

KOND

NOR SEBASTIA

DZORAGJUGH

Kilikia Central
Bus Station

see pages 118–19

NOR
MALATIA

NORAGJUGH

Pantheon
of Heroes

Yerablur
Cemetery

Sassountsi
Davit Ⓜ

Railway
station

Ejmiatsin

Teishebaini

KARMIR
BLUR

Garegin Nzhdeh
Square Ⓜ

NZHDEH

NZHDEH

Gortsaranayin
Ⓜ

Zvartnots
International

Charbakh
Ⓜ

Ⓜ
Shengavit

Erebuni

N

Bradt

Masis *Masis* *Artashat, Iran*

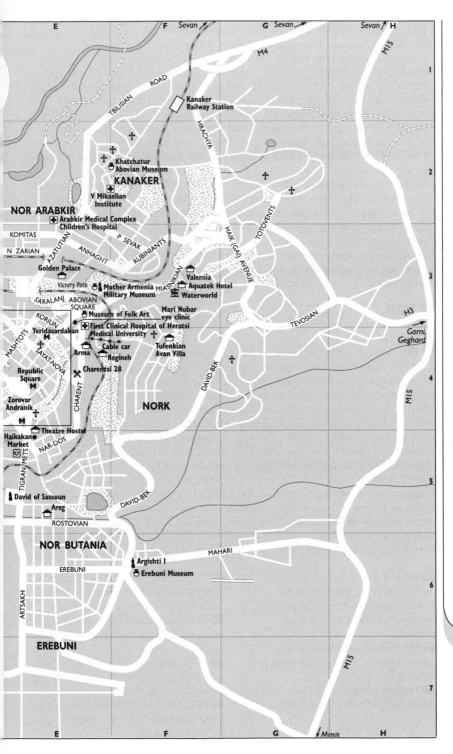

('Friendship') [104 D3] in the north to Sassountsi David was opened on 7 March 1981. The system was then extended south to Gortsaranayin ('Factory') [104 D6] in 1983, Shengavit [104 D6] in 1985 and Garegin Nzhdehi Hraparak ('Garegin Nzhdeh Square') [104 C6] in 1987. The branch to Charbakh [104 C6] was opened after independence in 1996 to make a total of 13.4km of route with ten stations. An extension into the northwestern suburbs is under construction which will cross the Hrazdan River on a bridge, but no work has been carried out on it since 1989. Most of the existing route is underground with only two stations, Sassountsi Davit and Gortsaranayin, built above ground. Trains are usually formed of two coaches although the platforms were built to accommodate five-coach trains, and run every five minutes from 06.30 to 23.00. A flat fare of AMD50 is charged and entry to the platforms is by plastic tokens which can be purchased from the ticket office at any station. The maps of the route can be confusing since they show not only the operating part of the system in red but also some projected extensions in blue. When on a train it is impossible to read the names of stations since the signs are carefully positioned so as to be invisible from the trains. It is therefore necessary to listen to the announcements or else count the number of stops. The entrances to stations are marked on the surface by the blue letter Ս which is capital M (for Metro) in the Armenian alphabet.

BY TRAM Yerevan had trams as far back as Tsarist days but a more extensive network started to be developed in 1933. The final tram route closed in 2004.

BY BUS Introduced to the city in 1949 to supplement the trams, **trolleybuses** charge a flat fare of AMD50. More recently conventional diesel **buses** have been added for which the fare is also AMD50 within the city. No further vehicles were purchased after independence until 2003, since when secondhand vehicles from Marseille, Lyon and Florence have appeared as well as new MAN buses from Germany and smaller Isuzu vehicles from Japan. The new vehicles are bright yellow but the secondhand ones still sport the livery of their previous operator. The most conspicuous means of transport is **minibuses** (*marshrutny* or *marshrutkas*). A network of routes covers the city with the vehicles operating at frequent intervals until the small hours. To board one simply wave it down in the street and then indicate to the driver when you wish to alight. It is normal to pay when getting off. A flat AMD100 is charged. The city government wishes to get rid of the minibuses, replacing them with conventional ones, but this seems unlikely to happen any time soon. There are some 125 *marshrutka* routes within Yerevan; full details of each is available at www.armeniainfo.am. The following is a small selection of routes which may be of interest to tourists:

108 Abovian Sq to Zvartnots Airport via the following streets: Abovian, Moskovian, Khanjian, Tigran Mets, Artsakh, Garegin Nzhdeh, Bagratuniats, Admiral Isakov & Ejmiatsin crossroads.

107 Marshall Baghramian metro station to Zvarnots Airport, via a westerly route which avoids the city centre.

109 Victory (Haghtanak) Park to main railway station via Sayat Nova & Tigran Mets avenues.

11 Central bus station to Erebuni Museum via Victory Bridge, Mashtots Av, Amirian St, Republic Sq, Tigran Mets Av & the main railway station.

85 Also runs between Erebuni Museum & the railway station, before heading into the western suburbs.

75 Ejmiatsin crossroads to the Pantheon via Admiral Isakov Av, Mashtots Av, Republic Sq, Tigran Mets Av & the railway station.

23 Railway station to the Pantheon via Tigrans Mets Av, Khorenatsi St, Mashtots & Admiral Isakov avenues & Sebastia St.

BY TAXI (See also *Chapter 2, Getting around,* page 76.) Taxis are plentiful and relatively cheap. Fares within central Yerevan are usually under AMD1,000. There are no designated taxi ranks but taxis can always be found at places such as the train and bus stations, the main markets and near many road intersections. They can be flagged down in the street and if you see a taxi stationary at the side of the road then it is probably available. On the whole taxi firms and drivers do not speak English so if phoning for a taxi it is best to ask your hotel or host to do it for you. There are dozens, if not hundreds, of reliable taxi firms in Yerevan including the following:

🚗 **Alex** ☏ 10 209090
🚗 **Busy** ☏ 10 211000

🚗 **Elite** ☏ 10 245999
🚗 **Super** ☏ 10 534110, 531410

ON FOOT For those who are reasonably fit central Yerevan is best explored on foot, not least because it can be quicker and pleasanter than sitting in a vehicle (especially a crowded minibus in the heat of summer) in a traffic jam. Those unaccustomed to walking may find that some of the distances, especially when going uphill, stretch them. Personally, I have found it perfectly easy to cover the whole of the area within the circular green belt and somewhat beyond (the area shown as central Yerevan on most maps) on foot.

Envoy Hostel (*www.envoyhostel.com*) organises free daily (morning and evening) guided walking tours of Yerevan (see page 109).

TOURIST INFORMATION AND LOCAL OPERATORS

A wealth of useful information is available from **Armenia Information** [119 F5] (*3 Nalbandian St;* ☏ *542303/6;* e *help@armeniainfo.am; www.armeniainfo.am;* ⊕ *09.00–19.00 daily*), a service provided by the Armenian Tourism Development Agency. They have a library of books which can be consulted, sell various publications and maintain registers of all types of accommodation, including bed and breakfasts (homestays). These can also be viewed on their website. The office won't make bookings itself but will tell people to contact the establishment direct or else go to a travel agent. The office may move during the lifetime of this book from Nalbandian Street to Republic Square, probably at the State History Museum.

A number of maps and free leaflets are available from the information centre and hotels. Two booklets are particularly useful: *Yerevan Scope,* which can be viewed online at www.yerevanscope.am, has information about Yerevan and the provinces as well as a wealth of practical information. *Yerevan Guide* (*www.accea. inf*), published quarterly, also has a wealth of practical information.

TOUR OPERATORS For a list of tour companies in Yeravan, see *Chapter 2,* pages 55–6.

Tour operators can arrange all types of accommodation, guides and interpreters, car hire with or without driver, special interest and general tours for groups and individuals, help with theatre tickets and virtually anything else a visitor may want.

A small number of hotels arrange tours for their guests. Where applicable this is noted under individual hotel entries.

🏠 WHERE TO STAY

The development of new hotels in Yerevan, particularly upmarket ones, has been considerable in recent years, but there are fewer available at the lower end of the market. In February 2006 a new official voluntary grading system (from one to five stars) for hotels, motels and spas was introduced by the Ministry of Trade and Economic Development. The grading can be shown either as five-pointed stars or in Roman numerals. During the winter most hotels charge a lower rate although in winter sports areas summer may be low season. It is now required by law that hotels quote their prices in AMD but note that a few tend to quote their prices excluding Armenia's 20% VAT. Many hotels away from the central area provide free transport to and from the centre. This can be quite a pleasant option in the heat and humidity of midsummer but the inconvenience would probably outweigh the bonuses for most visitors.

In October 2005, Armenia's first **backpacker hostel**, Envoy (see *Hostels*, page 79), opened charging US$15 per night – it has become understandably popular.

Another good option for the budget traveller is undoubtedly a **homestay** (bed and breakfast), particularly as dinner can be requested and will prove to be a much more authentically Armenian experience than most restaurants will provide. Homestays, invariably safe and usually very comfortable, can be arranged either through Armenia Information (see page 107) or through Yerevan travel agents (see pages 55–6). It's best to buy a street plan beforehand and then ask the tourist office to show you where you are going as the biggest problem is often finding the right place. Take a note of the address in Armenian so that you can enquire of people, and also ask which minibus goes in the right direction: or 'splash out' on one of Yerevan's very inexpensive taxis. See pages 79–80 for more information on homestays.

For an overview of hotel prices, see page 80.

CENTRAL AREA HOTELS

🏠 **Armenia Marriott** [118 D5] (226 rooms) 1 Amirian St; ☎ 599000; e armenia.marriott@ hotelmail.r.am; www.marriottarmenia.com. Absolutely central with an attractive façade on Republic Square. The building dates from 1954 but has been completely modernised & the formerly small rooms have been greatly enlarged. Marriott beds are described thus '8.5-inch foam mattresses, down comforters, fluffier pillows'. All rooms have separate living & sleeping areas. Wi-Fi. Cards accepted. Prices exclude tax & b/fast. B/fast AMD5,000–8,400. $$$$$

🏠 **Golden Tulip Yerevan** [119 F4] (104 rooms) 14 Abovian St; ☎ 589400; e info@ goldentuliphotelyerevan.com; www.goldentuliphotelyerevan.com. Yerevan's oldest hotel. It was built in 1927 & refurbished in 1998 but the rooms are surprisingly small. On the main shopping street about 5mins from the centre. Rooftop swimming pool. Accepts cards. B/fast extra AMD5,600 pp. $$$$$

🏠 **Ararat** [118 C7] (46 rooms) 7 Grigor Lusavorich St; ☎ 510000; e info@ararathotel. am; www.ararathotel.am. This pleasant, colourfully decorated hotel was built in 1990 & has helpful staff, disabled access & a roofed central courtyard with plants & water feature.

Swimming pool. Price includes 1 horseriding session & 2hrs at Hayastan Sports Complex. Accepts cards. $$$$

🏠 **Ani Plaza** [119 G4] (250 rooms) 19 Sayat Nova Av; ☎ 589500, 589700; e info@ anihotel.com; www.anihotel.com. A 14-storey tower block built in 1970 & partially renovated since 2002. The renovated rooms, on the higher floors (better views & quieter), are very much improved & quite pleasant. Has non-smoking rooms. Live music (classical & jazz) every day in whisky bar. 10mins' walk from the centre. Accepts Visa & MasterCard. Wi-Fi. Unrenovated rooms cheaper than renovated. Prices reflect the central location. $$$$

🏠 **Best Western Congress Hotel** [118 D7] (126 rooms) 1 Italy St; ☎ 591199; e congress@congresshotelyerevan.com; www.congresshotelyerevan.com. Built in 2001. Pleasant, brightly decorated hotel with 2 non-smoking floors. Wi-Fi. Fitness centre & sauna. Outdoor swimming pool. Cards accepted. Tax & b/fast not included. $$$$

🏠 **Aviatrans Hotel** [119 F5] (55 rooms) 4 Abovian St; ☎ 567230; e hotel@aviatrans.am; www.aviatrans.am. A comfortable, relatively small, central hotel with very helpful reception staff. Built in 1998, renovated 2008. Currency exchange, Avis car rental & gift shop within hotel. Wi-Fi. Cards accepted. **$$$$**

🏠 **Europe** [119 F6] (47 rooms) 32/88 Hanrapetutian St; ☎546060; e sales@ europehotel.am; www.europehotel.am. Attractive central hotel opened in 2003. French spoken. Brochure states hotel is of French design. Accepts cards. **$$$$**

🏠 **Shirak** [118 D6] (104 rooms) 13a Khorenatsi St; ☎529915; e shirak_hotel@cornet.am; www.shirakhotel.com. Large 14-storey tower block built in 1981 with renovation continuing. Rooms & shower rooms well renovated. Looks fresh & clean in pale cream. Basic but very acceptable. Cards accepted. **$$$**

🏠 **Erebuni** [119 E6] (36 rooms) 26/1 Nalbandian St; ☎564993, 580505; e info@ erebunihotel.am; www.erebunihotel.am. Renovation has transformed this hotel which dates back to 1980, bringing it completely up to date.

HOTELS OUTSIDE THE CENTRE

🏠 **Aquatek Hotel** [105 F3] (28 rooms) 40 Miasnikian Av; ☎588888; e info@aquatek.am; www.aquatek.am. In Nork district about 15mins from the centre by taxi. The hotel is an integral part of the Aquatek building which also houses the aquapark (swimming pools, other water amusements, gym & sauna) to which hotel guests have free access. Rooms are bright, modern & overlook the swimming pool. Note that part of the cost is entry to aquapark. Accepts cards. Prices vary greatly depending on season, but during peak times: **$$$$$**

🏠 **Golden Palace** [105 E3] (66 rooms) 2/2 Azatutian Av; ☎219999; e info@ goldenpalacehotel.am; www.goldenpalacehotel.am. In a pleasant location overlooking the city near the top of the Cascade: not a long way out but too far to walk – though you can use the Cascade escalator. Opened in 2005 the hotel is aimed at business executives. Sauna, swimming pool, several restaurants. Wi-Fi. Accepts cards. **$$$$$**

🏠 **Metropol** [118 B6] 2/2 Mesrop Mashtots Av; ☎510700; e metropol@metropol.am; www.metropol.am. Close to Victory Bridge about 20 mins' walk from the centre, this hotel opened in 2001 with 40 rooms but has since been extended & was undergoing further refurbishment in 2010. The hotel refused to divulge how many rooms it has

Helpful staff. Discounts for swimming pool next door. Accepts cards. **$$$**

🏠 **Guest House of the University** [119 G2] (40 rooms, various permutations of sgl, dbl & trpl) 52 Mesrop Mashtots St; ☎560003; e ysugh@ xter.net. Refurbishment has turned it into a pleasant, if basic, hotel which will accommodate tourists. 3 floors, no lifts but porterage available. No credit cards. Meals are available but groups should order in advance. **$$**

🏠 **Envoy Hostel** [119 E3] (2 rooms with 8 beds, 6 rooms with 4 beds) 54 Pushkin St – entrance round the corner, from Parpetsi St; ☎530369; e info@envoyhostel.com; www.envoyhostel.com. Everything a hostel should be. This clean, well-organised central hostel has 24hr reception, spacious toilet/shower rooms (separate male/female), common room, kitchen & Wi-Fi. Arranges tours to popular Armenian sites & to Nagorno Karabagh (*www.envoytours.am*) & free daily walking tours of Yerevan. Cash only. B/fast inc. **$**

at present, implying it was a commercial secret. It offers 'luxurious comfort & classic sophistication' & has a somewhat ponderous feel, reminiscent of Soviet luxury. Cards accepted. **$$$$**

🏠 **Tufenkian Avan Villa Yerevan** [105 F4] (14 rooms) 13 Nork Marash St, bldg 16; ☎655877; e hotels@tufenkian.am; www.tufenkian.am. In Nork about 15–20mins from the centre by taxi. Free transportation available. One of the new Tufenkian Heritage Hotels decorated in traditional Armenian style. The website also claims: 'Sealy crown jewel mattresses, wool duvets, walnut & wrought iron fixtures & famous handmade Tufenkian Armenian carpets'. (The owner of the chain is involved in carpet manufacture.) Very good Armenian cooking indeed. Price depends on size of room & view: **$$$** (small room). **$$$$**

🏠 **Hrazdan** [118 B3] (58 rooms) 72 Dzorapi St; ☎535332; e hrazdan@hotelhrazdan.am; www.hotelhrazdan.am. As the name implies, situated on the west side overlooking the gorge of the river. About 20mins' walk or 5mins by taxi to the centre. A 15-storey tower block built in 1976 & now renovated. The lift lobbies are box-like but the rooms themselves have lots of windows. A bright, cheerful, marble entrance hall. Outdoor swimming pool. Cards accepted. **$$$**

3

🏨 **Bass** [118 C1] (14 rooms) 3/1 Aigedzor St; ☎ 222638, 261080, 262751; e hotelbass@lans.am, bass@lans.am; www.bass.am. Located on the west side of the city near the American University about 20mins' walk or 5mins by taxi from the centre. 100m from Marshal Baghramian metro station. Built in 1995, it was the first new hotel to be opened after independence. Quite small with very pleasant staff & very good food. Wi-Fi. Accepts cards. **$$$**

🏨 **Arma** [105 E4] (34 rooms) 275 Norqi Ayginer St; ☎ 546000; e hotel@arma.am; www.arma.am. Overlooking the city from the northeast, the views over Yerevan towards Ararat are stunning. It is particularly enjoyable to dine on the terrace watching the sun sink below Mount Ararat. This hotel opened in 1996. Not too far from the city centre but it's a steep climb. Accepts cards. **$$$**

🏨 **Valensia Hotel** [105 F3] (58 rooms & cottages) 40 Miasnikian Av; ☎ 524000; e valensiareservation@xgroup.am; www.xgroup.am. In Nork district, 15mins from centre by taxi. Rates include free admission to next-door-but-one Waterworld (not next door Aquatek) which has various facilities for cooling off during the summer including a wave pool. This makes it a good option for families. Opened in 2001. Accepts Visa & MasterCard. (Cottages, which smelt a bit musty, sleeping 4–6 persons AMD50,000.) **$$$**

🏨 **Olympia** [104 C3] (12 rooms) 56 Barbyus St; ☎ 271850; e info@olympia.am; www.olympia.am. Overlooking the Hrazdan River on the northwest side about 15mins by taxi from the centre. Small with an outdoor café. Claims to have the most flexible discount system in Armenia. Cards accepted. B/fast not inc. **$$$**

🏨 **Regineh** [105 E4] (60 rooms) 235/1 Norki Ayginer; ☎ 654020; e reservation@ hotelregineh.am; www.hotelregineh.am. New, pleasantly airy & bright hotel. A stiff climb up from the city but with good views towards Mount Ararat. Dedicated to the memory of the owner's wife. Non-smoking rooms. Wi-Fi. Swimming pool. Accepts Visa & MasterCard. **$$$**

🏨 **Areg** [105 E5] (14 rooms) 80 Bournazian St; ☎ 456213; e anazo@web.am; www.areg.am. Located near the main railway station & hence easily accessible by metro. Small family-run hotel which can also arrange tours. Cash only. **$$**

🏨 **Theatre Hostel** [105 E4] (2 rooms, 12 beds) 27 Tigran Mets Av (entrance at back of bldg; go through alley next to Beeline office); ☎ 545676; e info@theatre.am; www.armeniahostel.am. Claims to be 5mins' walk from Republic Square. A rather cramped hostel with bunk beds lining the walls of 1 (windowless) room (8 beds) which acts as a corridor to the 2nd room. Showers: 2 in same room; 1 toilet. B/fast inc. **$**

✕ WHERE TO EAT AND DRINK

Yerevan has innumerable eating places, many of which, especially away from the centre, are very cheap. On the whole, Armenia does not have separate bars (although large hotels have bars); cafés are really the places to drink as well as eat. The following is merely a selection of interesting and popular places. Apart from these it is worth looking at **Proshian Street**, known locally as Barbecue Street because it is lined with places to eat in the reasonably priced range. There are lots of open-air cafés along Yerevan's green belt (now less green because of their number) and also around the opera house. Note that some charge a premium for sitting in areas with comfortable armchairs. Several small restaurants are clustered at the foot of the Cascade. Main courses usually cost somewhere between AMD2,500–4,000 and it is easy to have a full meal (which in Armenia usually comprises salads and a main course) for AMD5,000. Restaurants which fall outside this price range are noted under their individual entries. A light course, such as an omelette, may well cost under AMD1,000 and a savoury street snack can be had for as little as AMD150. Most restaurants open at noon and cafés about 10.00. The exception is Artbridge which opens at 08.30 (see opposite). Most will stay open until midnight or until the last customer has gone. Few restaurants have websites; those which do exist are often not informative. There are exceptions though and websites which are useful have been listed. Outside the central area of Yerevan there are innumerable small places where you can get a cheap snack and most districts of town have an acceptable restaurant (which has three or four bedrooms attached, payable by the hour). If you need to find somewhere to eat, then ask anyone 'Where is there a restaurant?' (*Vorterr e restoran?*).

Note that **restaurants in hotels** are not included in the list below. All the hotels listed above have restaurants.

✘ **Ai Leoni** [119 E2]40 Tumanian St; ☎538331, 530892. Expensive Italian cuisine.

✘ **Aragast** [119 G2]41 Isahakian St; ☎545500. An imitation boat with a pleasant view over a small artificial lake with boats. Inexpensive. Jazz in evenings.

✘ **Ararat** [119 E5] Republic Sq, Government Bldg #2; ☎527933, 527382, 567634. Yerevan's best restaurant in Soviet days. Live Armenian music in the cellar part in the evening.

✘ **Artbridge Bookshop Café** [119 F4] 20 Abovian St; ☎581284, 521239; www.artbridge.am; ⏰ 08.30–midnight. (See also *Shopping,* page 115.) One of the few places open early in the morning so useful for b/fast which is available all day. Also soups, salads & pastries.

✘ **Arya** [119 F2] 1/17 Tamanian St (entrance from Isahakian St); ☎568013. Iranian restaurant with genuine Persian cuisine. Enjoyable.

✘ **Beerloga Pub** [118 C3] 24 Sarian St; ☎527840. Typical pub menu which includes pizza, salads, *lahmadjoun* (see *Chapter 2,* page 83) & main courses. One of its attractions is that it also serves crayfish (AMD500–1,500 each depending on size).

✘ **Blackberry** [119 F4] 3 Abovian St; ☎033838. Although this lounge bar serves adequate meals it is not particularly recommended for eating but it is a very civilised, quiet place to relax over a drink. Its entrance hall is lined with bookcases full of Russian books which can be read by customers; indeed regulars can borrow a book to read at home.

✘ **Café Central** [119 G4] (pronounced the French way) 30 Abovian St; ☎583990; www.cafecentral.am. Deservedly popular. Good salads & interesting desserts, as well as main courses. Also sells coffee beans/ground coffee.

✘ **Café la Bohème** [119 F2] 2/1 Tamanian St; ☎545857; www.cafelaboheme.am. A pleasant small café near the foot of the Cascade. European cuisine includes tasty baked trout.

✘ **Caucasus** [119 H5] 82 Hanrapetutian St; ☎561177. Separate section for Armenian & Georgian food but not everything on the extensive menu is always available. Live folk music evenings in the side decorated in Armenian style; you can hear it wafting through to the Georgian side. Reservations advisable.

✘ **Charentsi 28** [105 E4] 28 Charents St; ☎572945; www.charentsi28.com. A relative newcomer to the restaurant scene, just beyond the central area but worth seeking out. In a fully restored old house with an ambience, as they say, of 'casual elegance'. A very informative website.

✘ **Dolmama** [119 F5] 10 Pushkin St; ☎568931. Good but very expensive indeed by Yerevan standards. Whether it's worth the money depends on who is paying. Main course AMD10,000.

✘ **Jazzve** [119 E3] 35 Tumanian St; ☎533663; www.jazzve.am. Also at 18 Abovian St (inside Moscow cinema), 8 Moscovian St (entry from Isahakian St) & amongst the open-air cafés in front of the opera house. Established in 2003, this chain of coffee shops is decorated in literary style, with menus in the form of newspapers. Reliably good coffee, desserts & a full meals menu. There is no jazz, *jazzve* being the Armenian word for the long-handled copper pot in which Armenian coffee (*sev soorj*) is traditionally made.

✘ **Jingalov Hats** [119 G3] 62 Terian St; ☎582205. Nothing to do with headwear; *jingalov hats* (see *Chapter 7,* page 273) is the typical herb bread from Nagorno Karabagh. This café, which serves only this one dish, is good for when you want a quick, filling, tasty snack without having to spend time deciding what to choose. The next best thing to eating it in Karabagh. Also good for vegetarians – no meat served at all. One *hats* costs AMD500 & is ample unless you are very hungry.

✘ **Khinkalis** [119 F4] 21/1 Tumanian St; ☎582352. This basement restaurant doesn't really have a name but is known by its speciality, Georgian *khinkali*, ravioli-like dumplings. Indeed the sign outside simply says 'Ravioli'. An extensive area, decorated in large country-house style. Especially busy in winter.

✗ **Kilikia** [119 G5] 78 Hanrapetutian St; ☎548808. Pleasant restaurant with traditional Armenian music played at a sensible volume. Reservations advisable.

✗ **Marco Polo** [119 E5] 1/3 Abovian St; ☎561926. A popular café with a wide range of dishes. It is possible to have a tasty snack for under AMD1,000.

✗ **Milagro** [119 G3] 69 Terian St; ☎510404. Restaurant/bar, rather than a café. European dishes. Wines are mainly French. Live classical piano music at w/ends. Relatively expensive by Armenian standards. Main course AMD7,000.

✗ **Natura Gold** [119 F4] 11 Abovian St; ☎582184. Originally a tea house serving speciality teas & desserts, it now serves snacks & main courses too.

✗ **Old Yerevan** [119 E3] 2 Northern Av; ☎540575, 588855. Live performances of Armenian song & dance from 20.00 but excruciatingly loud. Adorned with photographs of famous official visitors brought here by their Armenian government hosts. Reservations advisable.

✗ **Our Village** [119 F3] 5 Sayat Nova Av; ☎548700. In a basement decorated with old coffee pots, radios, etc. Serves only Armenian produce & drinks. Live folk music in the evenings. Waiting staff wear traditional costume & menus (singed at edges) have carefully placed holes burnt in them. An experience. Reservations required.

✗ **Pascucci** [119 F3] 42 Terian St; ☎568969. Italian, combining café & jewellery shop.

✗ **Pizza di Roma** [119 E5] 1 Abovian St, with smaller branches elsewhere; ☎587175. Forget the name, this place serves a wide range of food. Excellent quality & value.

✗ **Rembrandt** [119 F4] 14 Abovian St; ☎567765. Essentially a seafood restaurant with fish imported from as far away as France. Decorated with reproduction oil paintings. Old-style British bar area. Relatively expensive. Note that fish is sold by weight. For example: Dover sole from the Netherlands costs AMD7,000 per 100g.

✗ **Sayat-Nova** [119 H5] 33a Sayat Nova Av; ☎580033, 541336. Good food. The top storey is a café. In summer there are often concerts in the largest of the 3 halls, which is called Coliseum – see the poster outside for details. Sometimes there are discos.

✗ **Sherlock Holmes** [118 C1] 25 Marshall Baghramian Av; ☎260100. Claims to be English-style. Hmmmm… Opposite the British embassy.

✗ **Square One** [119 E5] 1/3 Abovian St; ☎566169. Serves European & American food. Very popular both with diaspora & locals – perhaps it's the English b/fast or (more likely) the American-style apple pie & chocolate cake. Music can be loud.

✗ **Tashir Pizza** Branches at 29 Komitas St, 33 Khorenatsi St, 16 Gai St, 50 Mesrop Mashtots Av [119 G2],15 Tumanian St [119 G4], 50 Khanjian St [119 H4], 69 Terian St [119 G3], 27/4 Nzhdeh St; ☎511111/2/3/4/5/6/7/8 respectively. A chain producing high-quality pizzas. It is possible to buy portions rather than a whole pizza. Eat in & take-away.

✗ **Tbilisi Tavern** [119 F4] 3 Abovian St; m 099 638990. Serves Armenian & Georgian dishes. Live music

✗ **The Club** [119 E2] 40 Tumanian St; ☎531361; www.theclub.am. Extremely good food in this basement restaurant which also incorporates a souvenir shop & bookshop with some titles in English. Forget the name as it's not a club at all. Reservations advisable. Occasional concerts. Has probably the most informative website of any restaurant in Yerevan which includes the menu, with prices, plus details of concerts.

✗ **The Colour of Pomegranates** [118 C5] 6/44 Zakian St (cnr of Zakian & Khorenatsi sts); ☎525095. Pleasant, small restaurant, named after the iconic 1968 film, directed by Sergei Parajanov. Georgian & Armenian cuisine. The proprietor makes his own apricot vodka which is very good & explosively alcoholic.

✗ **Thomas Tea** [119 G4] 22 Abovian St; ☎543330; www.thomastea.am. A basement café cheerfully decorated with all the appurtenances of tea making. Also sells its teas. Serves a vast range of teas, all well described on the menu. Also snacks such as crêpes, savoury & sweet (AMD900–1,400), as well as main courses.

Details of what is on can be obtained from Armenia Information's (see page 107) office or website, and are published in *Noyan Tapan* (see page 92).

CINEMA Two cinemas show **films in English** most evenings. **Kino Nairi** [119 G2] (*50 Mesrop Mashtots Av;* ℡ *542829*) shows films in English at 22.00. **Kino Moscow** [119 F4] (*18 Abovian St;* ℡ *521210*) shows the same film in English and dubbed into Russian in separate auditoria. The week-long annual Golden Apricot International Film Festival (see *Chapter 2*, page 91) takes place in Yerevan during July.

CASINOS All Yerevan's casinos have been closed and moved outside the city boundary. The road to the airport is thickly populated while there are quite a few on the Sevan highway. Armenia Information's website (*www.armeniainfo.am*) gives details of eight casinos but there are many more lining the above roads.

CLASSICAL MUSIC The **National Academic Opera and Ballet Theatre of Armenia** [119 F3] (*54 Tumanian St;* ℡ *527992, 533391;* e *info@opera.am; www.opera.am*) stages regular opera and ballet except during July and August. However, it is worth seeing the building for its own sake although it can only be viewed during performances. Unfortunately schedules of performances are only ever announced two or three weeks in advance. Tickets (AMD1,500–15,000) are best bought in person from the ticket office just behind the theatre, to the northeast. Although it is theoretically possible to book by phone and pick up the tickets just before the performance starts, it has been known for the tickets no longer to be available for collection. The **Aram Khachaturian Concert Hall** [119 F3] (*46 Mesrop Mashtots Av;* ℡ *560645, 564965;* e *philharmonic@apo.am, concert@apo.am; www.apo.am*), in the northern half of the building whose southern half is the opera and ballet theatre, is the home of the Armenian Philharmonic Orchestra and hosts concerts throughout the season. Finally, the **Komitas Chamber Music Hall** [119 H3] (*1 Isahakian St;* ℡ *526718*) presents regular concerts by the Armenian Chamber Orchestra.

Other theatres Apart from the National Academic Opera and Ballet Theatre (see above) there are at least 15 other theatres in Yerevan. Armenia Information (*www.armeniainfo.am*) lists them all and the free publications *Yerevan Scope* and *Yerevan Guide* also give details. All, except the **Stanislavsky State Russian Drama Theatre** [119 F4] (*7 Abovian St;* ℡ *569199*), which performs in Russian, perform exclusively in Armenian. There are two puppet theatres which may appeal to non-Armenian speakers: the **Yerevan State Theatre of Marionettes** (*43 Mesrop Mashtots Av;* ℡ *562450*) and the **Hovhannes Tumanian State Puppet Theatre** (*4 Sayat Nova Av;* ℡ *563244*).

JAZZ The main jazz club is **Poplovak** [119 G2] (*41 Isahakian St;* ℡ *52230, in Aragast restaurant, see page 111*) where reservations are always required. It is well known for the murder of a Georgian Armenian by presidential bodyguards in the men's lavatories (see page 25). Quite good for food though drink prices are high. The **Malkhas Jazz Club** [119 E3] (*52 Pushkin St;* ℡ *531778*) is a bar/restaurant serving Armenian and European cuisine but which also stages live jazz. It is owned by Levon Malkhasian who is considered to be the godfather of Armenian jazz. **Cafesjian Centre** (see page 141) hosts concerts, including jazz and classical.

Yerevan ENTERTAINMENT AND NIGHTLIFE **3**

NIGHTCLUBS For those who wish to sample Armenian nightclubs, Armenia Information (*www.armeniainfo.am*) lists 28 such venues, giving contact details.

SPORT Although facilities are slowly increasing they remain limited. During good weather billiard and table-tennis tables appear in parks and can be hired by the hour. Tennis courts can be hired by the hour at the **Ararat Tennis Courts** [119 H4] (*2 Alek Manukian St;* 570648) in Yerevan's green belt near Yerevan State University. Equipment can be hired and coaching is apparently always available. There is an adjacent clubhouse and café. Tennis, basketball, golf and mini-golf are available at **Ararat Golf Club** [104 B2] (see below). At **Play City** (*35 Acharian St;* 288377; e info @ playcity.am; www.playcity.am), in Yerevan's northeast suburb of Avan, you can play bowling, karting, paintball, billiards and mini-golf. There is a bar/restaurant in the complex.

Riding Riding lessons and hire of horses can be arranged at **Yerevan Riding School** which is located to the north of the city at the Ten out of Ten shooting club (*1st bldg, 3rd Gorge, Yeghvard Highway, Davtashen;* 361010; www.xgroup.am). A course of ten 45-minute lessons costs AMD15,000. Hire of horses without instruction costs AMD3,000 for 45 minutes rising to AMD3,500 at weekends.

Swimming Several of the larger city-centre hotels have swimming pools to which non-residents can go – at a price. Among the other venues are:

Aquatek [105 F3] See page 109 for contact details. ⊕ 08.00–23.00; Mon–Fri child/adult: AMD3,000/5,000, Sat & Sun: AMD3,500/6,000. Other facilities extra. Non residents can visit the swimming pools & other water amusements, **Ararat Golf Club** [104 B2] 50 Gevorg Chaush St; 10 94085; ⊕ swimming pool: Jun–Sep 10.00–20.00; child/adult Tue–Fri AMD3,000/4,000, Sat & Sun AMD4,000/6,000. The Ararat Golf Club has a very pleasant swimming pool area to which non-members are admitted. A couple of hours spent relaxing here can be recommended. The club also has facilities for tennis, basketball, football, mini-golf &, of course, golf (9 holes). **Waterworld** [105 F3] 40 Miasnikian St; 10 638998; ⊕ Jun–Sep 13.00–20.00; admission price is by height, adult approx AMD5,000. It is popular with Yerevan residents during the heat of summer so it can be busy. It is especially suitable for families with children as there is much to keep them entertained.

SHOPPING

Yerevan has every type of retail outlet imaginable, from expensive shops on Northern Avenue selling internationally known designer brands, to that part of Vernissage specialising in secondhand nuts and bolts. There is even a subterranean department store (see *Abovian Street from Tumanian Street*, page 126). For cheap clothes try the Ararat covered clothing market (sometimes marked on maps as 'Rosia'), opposite the foot of the steps to the cathedral. The street market to the south of Rosia sells most things from budgerigars to coffee beans and is useful for any small item you may have forgotten to pack. For fresh food shopping (and dried fruits) it is worth visiting the covered markets on Mesrop Mashtots Avenue (see page 129) and the Haikakan market on Khorenatsi Street off Tigran Mets Avenue about 500m south of the cathedral. Those with a sweet tooth may wish to patronise the Grand Candy store and pastry shops near the Matenadaran (see page 127). There are also plenty of vendors of ice cream on Yerevan's streets.

Craft items are best bought at **Vernissage** [119 F6] (see page 122) if in Yerevan at the weekend. Similar items, although a much smaller range, can be found on the first floor of **Disc Planet** (*1/3 Abovian St* [119 E5]; ✆ *542334; 33 Abovian St* [119 H2]; ✆ *582098*). **Made in Armenia Direct** (*www.madeinarmeniadirect.com*) has outlets in Marriott Armenia [118 D5] and Congress [118 D7] hotels. Another good souvenir shop is **Salt Sack** [119 F4] (*3/1 Abovian St*). One of Yerevan's biggest **bookshops** is **Noah's Ark** [119 E5], Republic Square. It has a good selection of books in English but note that some titles available at, for example, the cathedral bookshop at Ejmiatsin, are unavailable here. **Artbridge** bookshop/café [119 F4] (*20 Abovian St;* ✆ *581284; www.artbridge.am;* ☉ *08.30–midnight*) specialises in foreign-language publications and has a wide selection of English-language books on Armenia. It also sells handmade crafts and the café does a very good *café glacé*. **Bookworld** [118 D4] (*20 Mesrop Mashtots Av*) is a large bookshop mostly stocking books in Armenian and Russian but there is an English section. **Secondhand books** are to be found displayed in the pedestrian underpass at the junction of Abovian and Moscovian streets, in a shop at the top of Mesrop Mashtots Avenue and at Vernissage. **Brandy** can be bought from numerous outlets in markets and supermarkets but specialist dealers are to be found at 14 Abovian St, 45 Mesrop Mashtots Avenue, 12 Amirian Street and at Yerevan brandy distillery [118 A6] (see page 134). A good **photographic** dealer with several branches is **Jupiter Photo Express** (*15 Vartanants St, 33 Khorenatsi St, 21 Baghramian Av & 50 Terian St; www.jupiter-photo.info*). Another is the **Zig Zag** chain (*24 Mesrop Mashtots Av & 20 Sayat Nova Av*).

Small **supermarket chains** have arisen in recent years and many branches are open 24 hours. They are well stocked and in addition have 24-hour currency exchange kiosks. One such chain is **SAS** (*18 Mesrop Mashtots Av; 31 Tumanian St; 85 Baghramian Av; 52 Komitas Av; 35 Isahakian St; www.sas-grp.com*).

OTHER PRACTICALITIES

BANKS AND EXCHANGING MONEY There are several banks in the centre of Yerevan, for example on Vazgen Sargsian and Nalbandian streets. HSBC, just round the corner from the Marriott Hotel, is popular but it is always busy and the queues move slowly. If all you want to do is change some cash it is much quicker to go to one of the currency exchanges which can be found on Tigran Mets Avenue (where there is a good chance of being able to change even such exotica as New Zealand dollars or Swedish krone) or in the small supermarkets (see above).

EMBASSIES AND CONSULATES IN YEREVAN For a list of Armenian embassies abroad, see pages 58–9.

🄴 **Belarus** 12 Nikol Duman St; ✆ 220269, 275611; e armenia@belembassy.org
🄴 **Brazil** 57 Simeon Yerevantzu St; ✆ 500210; f 536955
🄴 **Bulgaria** Nor Aresh, 16 Sofia St; ✆ 458233; e bularm@arminco.am
🄴 **Canada** Marriott Hotel, Room 306, 1 Amirian St; ✆ 567990; e concda@gmail.com
🄴 **China** 12 Baghramian Av; ✆ 560067, 561234; e chiemb@arminco.com

🄴 **Egypt** 6a Sepuh St; ✆ 226755/220117; e egyemb@arminco.com
🄴 **Estonia** 43 Gyulbekian St; ✆ 263973, 220138; e aries@arminco.com
🄴 **Finland** 6 Tamanian St; ✆ 265587
🄴 **France** 8 Grigor Lusavorich St; ✆ 561103, 564667, 583511; e admin@ambafran.am; www.ambafrance-am.org
🄴 **Georgia** 42 Arami St; ✆ 564183, 585511, 523567; e geoemb@netsys.am

🅔 **Germany** 29 Charents St; ✆523279, 524581, 586591; e germemb@arminco.com; www.eriwan.diplo.de

🅔 **Greece** 6 Demirchian St; ✆530051, 536754; e grembarm@arminico.com

🅔 **Hungary** 2 Zakian St; ✆538957

🅔 **India** 50/2 Dzorapi St; ✆539173, 538288; e inemyr@arminco.com, interpreter@embassyofindia.am

🅔 **Iran** 1 Budaghian St; ✆232920, 234900, 232952, 280457; e info@iranembassy.am; www.iranembassy.am

🅔 **Italy** 5 Italy St; ✆542335, 542336, 542301; e ambitaly@arminco.com; www.ambitarm.am

🅔 **Kyrgyzstan** 67 Arshakuniats St; ✆440044; e kyrgyzcon@netsys.am

🅔 **Lebanon** Dzoragyugh 13–14; ✆583403, 527463; e libarm@arminco.com

🅔 **Norway** 50 Khandjian St (Tekeyan Centre); ✆571798, 551582; e admin@nrc.am

🅔 **Nagorno Karabagh** 17a Zarian St; ✆249705, 249928; e ankr@arminco.com

🅔 **Poland** 44a Hanrapetutian St; ✆542493/5; e polemb@arminco.com

🅔 **Romania** 15 Barbius St; ✆275332, 277610

🅔 **Russia** 13a Grigor Lusavorich St; ✆567427, 582521, 545218, 589843; e russia@arminco.com; www.armenia.mid.ru

🅔 **Slovenia** 22 Ghazar Parpetsi St; ✆531500, 538796; e consul.slovenia@netsys.am

🅔 **Syria** 14 Baghramian Av; ✆524028, 524036; e syrembar@intertel.am

🅔 **Thailand** 8 Amirian St; ✆560410, 542331; e info@thaiconsulate.am

🅔 **Turkmenistan** 52 Yerznkian St; ✆221029, 221039; e serdar@arminco.com

🅔 **Ukraine** 5/1 29 Arabkir St; ✆229727; e ukremb@aatv.am

🅔 **UK** 34 Baghramian Av; ✆264301; e enquiries.yerevan@fco.gov.uk; www.ukinarmenia.fco.gov.uk

🅔 **USA** 1 American Av; ✆464700, 521611, 543900; e usinfo@usa.am; www.usa.am

INTERNET Internet cafés seem to be on every corner in Yerevan but they do tend to come and go. At the time of writing the following were among the many: **Erudit** [119 G7] (*13 Khanjian St*), **Max Power** [119 E5] (*3 Arami St*), **Remcon** [119 G3] (*36 Abovian St*) and **Nornet** [105 F5] (*18/20 Tigran Mets Av*). Expect to pay about AMD300 per hour.

MEDICAL ISSUES Most hotels can help with finding a **doctor** and embassies may have lists of specialists. **Hospitals** have 24-hour emergency departments; there is a rota for receiving patients. To call an **ambulance** in an emergency, dial ✆ 103; patients needing hospital admission will be taken to the receiving hospital.

Hospitals also have casualty departments where patients can self-refer if needing immediate treatment. Possible hospitals include:

✚ **Arabkir Medical Complex Children's Hospital** [105 E2] 30 Mamikoniants St; ✆231352, 236883

✚ **First Clinical Hospital of Heratsi Medical University** [105 E3] 58 Abovian St; ✆561778, 563508

✚ **Nairi Medical Centre** [118 A3] 21 Paronian St; ✆537742

✚ **V Mikaelian Institute** [105 E2] 9 Hasratian St; ✆281790, 281990

There is also a 24-hour emergency dental service but apparently it is staffed by relatively inexperienced newly qualified dentists so anyone with a problem may prefer to attend one of the many private dental clinics, some of which have 24-hour cover. Again embassies may hold lists of dentists. A clinic which has at least one dentist who speaks good English is **Agat-dental** (*33a Baghramian Av*; ✆ *272623 – ask for Hasmik*). I have no personal experience of treatment at the clinic. **Pharmacies** abound and are indicated by the (Russian) word '*apteka*'. **Natali Pharm** is a chain which has 24-hour branches throughout the city including, in central Yerevan, at 3 Mashtots Avenue [118 B5] and 10 Tigran Mets Avenue [119 E7]. (A full list can be found at *www.spyur.am/natalipharm*.)

POST OFFICE The most convenient post office is that on Republic Square [119 E6] (see below, page 120; ☉ *08.00–19.00 Mon–Sat, 10.00–16.00 Sun*). It has a Philatelic Corner for anyone interested in stamp collecting. See also *Chapter 2, Postal services,* page 95.

WHAT TO SEE AND DO

A WALK AROUND YEREVAN
Around Republic Square Visitors to Yerevan are inevitably drawn to the large and imposing **Republic Square** [119 E5–E6] and it is an appropriate place to start this walk: in Soviet times the square was called Lenin Square. It is certainly one of the finest central squares created anywhere in the world during the 20th century. The building on the northeast side with fountains outside is the **State History Museum** [119 E5] (see page 139) of 1926 with its white symmetrical colonnades to which the **National Gallery of Art** (see page 140) storeys in a similar colour were added in 1950. It formerly also held the Museum of the (Bolshevik) Revolution. The marriage of the 1926 original with the 1950 addition produces a curious effect looking like two quite separate buildings, one behind the other. It is sometimes claimed that Yerevan needed a large new art gallery after 1945 because many valuable works of art were brought here for safe keeping during the war years from other Soviet cities and never subsequently returned; the collection is almost certainly the finest in the former USSR apart from those of Moscow and St Petersburg. The water of the **three fountains** outside the museum sometimes dances in time to classical music on summer evenings while changes to the lighting are used to enhance the effect. This unusual spectacle was invented by Abraham Abrahamian, a professor in the electronics department of Yerevan University.

Underneath the square is a **large bunker** constructed during the Cold War to protect officials from danger in the event of a nuclear attack. Since independence, suggestions have been made that it could be handed over to the museum as an additional display area but lack of funding together with renewed tensions in the Middle East will probably ensure that it retains its original purpose for the time being.

To the left of the museum across Abovian Street on the northwest side of Republic Square is a **government building** designed by Samvel Safarian (1902–69) and built in the 1950s. It incorporates much Armenian detail but although built to harmonise with the earlier buildings it is somewhat more massive. It now houses the Ministry of Foreign Affairs. By contrast the ground floor is occupied by one of Yerevan's best bookshops called **Noah's Ark** [119 E5]. Continuing anticlockwise, across Amirian Street is the curving façade of the **Hotel Armenia** [118 D5] (see page 108), possibly Yerevan's best hotel after its opening in 1954 and very popular with the diaspora. It has now been extensively refurbished by the Marriott chain. During the rebuilding work a secret floor was discovered with a 1.5m-high ceiling: it was used by the KGB to spy on the guests. The pavement café outside is crowded by the diaspora from 08.00, when it opens, until late at night, when it closes, and they are certain to meet many of their acquaintances from home if only they sit here long enough.

Still continuing anticlockwise, a broad street with fountains down the middle is crossed. In the centre of the street formerly stood the statue of Lenin designed by Sergei Merkurov (1881–1952), erected in 1940 to mark the 20th anniversary

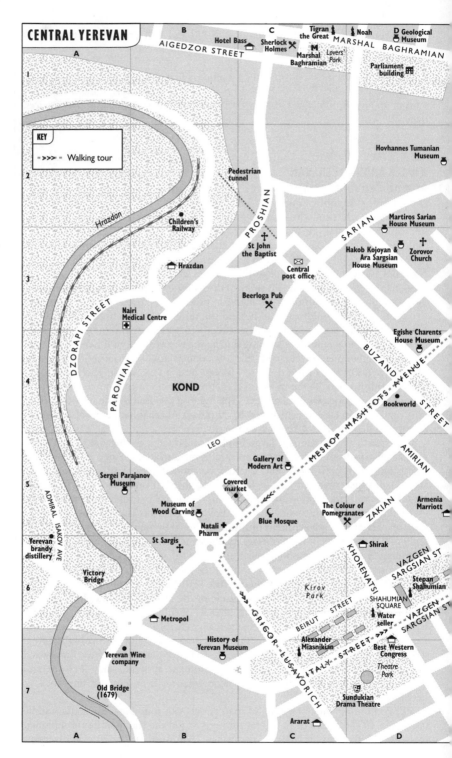

CENTRAL YEREVAN

KEY

- ⇢>>> = Walking tour

AIGEDZOR STREET

Hotel Bass
Sherlock Holmes
Tigran the Great
Noah
Geological Museum
Marshal Baghramian
Lovers' Park
MARSHAL BAGHRAMIAN
Parliament building

Pedestrian tunnel

PROSHIAN

Hrazdan

Children's Railway

Hrazdan

St John the Baptist

Central post office

Beerloga Pub

Hovhannes Tumanian Museum

SARIAN

Martiros Sarian House Museum

Hakob Kojoyan & Ara Sargsian House Museum

Zorovor Church

Egishe Charents House Museum

DZORAPI STREET

Nairi Medical Centre

PARONIAN

KOND

LEO

BUZAND STREET

MESROP MASHTOTS AVENUE

Bookworld

AMIRIAN

Gallery of Modern Art

Sergei Parajanov Museum

Covered market

Museum of Wood Carving

Natali Pharm

Blue Mosque

The Colour of Pomegranates

ZAKIAN

Armenia Marriott

Shirak

ADMIRAL ISAKOV AVE

Yerevan brandy distillery

St Sargis

VAZGEN SARGSIAN ST

Kirov Park

KHORENATSI

SHAHUMIAN SQUARE

Stepan Shahumian

Victory Bridge

Metropol

BEIRUT STREET

Water seller

VAZGEN SARGSIAN ST

History of Yerevan Museum

Alexander Miasnikian

Best Western Congress

GRIGOR LUSAVORICH

ITALY STREET

Theatre Park

Yerevan Wine company

Old Bridge (1679)

Sundukian Drama Theatre

Ararat

A   B   C   D

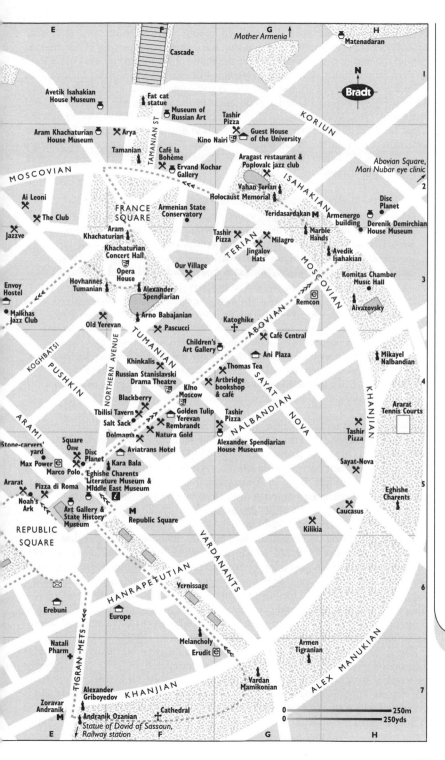

E   F   G ↑   H

Mother Armenia

Cascade

Matenadaran

Bradt   N

Avetik Isahakian
House Museum

Fat cat
statue

Museum of
Russian Art

Tashir
Pizza

Kino Nairi

Guest House
of the University

KORIUN

Aram Khachaturian
House Museum

✗ Arya

Tamanian

Café la
Bohème

Ervand Kochar
Gallery

Aragast restaurant &
Poplovac jazz club

*Abovian Square,
Mari Nubar eye clinic*

MOSCOVIAN

Vahan Terian

Holocaust Memorial

Disc
Planet

Ai Leoni

FRANCE
SQUARE

Armenian State
Conservatory

Yeridasardakan M

Armenergo
building

Derenik Demirchian
House Museum

✗ The Club

Aram
Khachaturian

Tashir
Pizza

Milagro

Marble
Hands

Jazzve

Khachaturian
Concert Hall

Our Village

Jingalov
Hats

Avedik
Isahakian

Komitas Chamber
Music Hall

Envoy
Hostel

Opera
House

Hovhannes
Tumanian

Alexander
Spendiarian

Remcon

Aivazovsky

Malkhas
Jazz Club

Old Yerevan

Arno Babajanian

Pascucci

Katoghike

Café Central

Mikayel
Nalbandian

Children's
Art Gallery

Ani Plaza

KOGHBATSI

PUSHKIN

Khinkalis

Thomas Tea

Ararat
Tennis Courts

Russian Stanislavski
Drama Theatre

Artbridge
bookshop
& café

ARAMI

Blackberry

Kino
Moscow

Tbilisi Tavern

Golden Tulip
Yerevan

Tashir
Pizza

Salt Sack

Rembrandt

Dolmama

Natura Gold

Alexander Spendiarian
House Museum

Tashir
Pizza

Square
One

Disc
Planet

Aviatrans Hotel

Max Power

Kara Bala

Marco Polo

Eghishe Charents
Literature Museum &
Middle East Museum

Sayat-Nova

Ararat

Pizza di Roma

Caucasus

Eghishe
Charents

Noah's
Ark

Art Gallery &
State History
Museum

M

Republic Square

Kilikia

REPUBLIC
SQUARE

VARDANANTS

HANRAPETUTIAN

Vernissage

Erebuni

Europe

Natali
Pharm

Melancholy

Erudit

Armen
Tigranian

TIGRAN-METS

Alexander
Griboyedov

KHANJIAN

Vardan
Mamikonian

Zoravar
Andranik M

Andranik Ozanian

Cathedral

Statue of David of Sassoun,
Railway station

0   250m
0   250yds

E   F   G   H

Yerevan WHAT TO SEE AND DO

3

of Soviet power and speedily removed, along with its huge pedestal, after independence. Standing where the statue once stood and looking at the hillside behind the museum it is possible to see the statue of **Mother Armenia** [105 E3] on an even larger plinth, 34m high, constructed in 1950 as the Victory Memorial in memory of the Great Patriotic War. The forged copper statue of Mother Armenia, a heroic figure holding a sword, was designed by the sculptor Ara Harutyunian and erected in 1967. Very provocatively for this date, the statue with sword takes the shape of the Cross. Mother Armenia actually stands in the space occupied from 1950 until 1962 by a 16.5m-tall statue of Stalin; at 21m Mother Armenia is, perhaps symbolically, taller than Stalin used to be. A Soviet writer in 1952, one year before Stalin's death, claimed:

Topping the Memorial Building is a statue of Stalin in a long greatcoat of which one lap is thrown open, showing the figure caught in a forward stride. In this statue wrought in Armenian bronze, the sculptor S. Merkurov (NB: The same who was responsible for Lenin), has depicted Stalin in a characteristic pose of dynamic movement, supreme composure and confidence. Stalin stands with one hand in his coat-breast and the other slightly lowered as though his arm, swung in rhythm with his step, has for one brief moment become frozen in space. Stalin's gaze rests upon the splendour of the new Armenian socialist capital, upon its new handsome buildings, its wide green avenues, upon the central square in the opposite end of the town. There, Lenin, in his ordinary workday suit, has swung abruptly around in that characteristic, impetuous, sweeping way of his, so dear and familiar to every Soviet man, woman and child. The statues are very tall and the impression is that the two great leaders exchange glances of deep understanding as they survey the prospering life around them, so much of it the handiwork of their own genius, their self-abnegating labours, their perspicacity, the wisdom that enabled them to see far into the future.

A flower bed has replaced Lenin whose statue, with head detached, lies stored in the courtyard behind the History Museum. The sculptor of the vanished Lenin and Stalin as well as of Stepan Shahumian, Sergei Merkurov (1881–1952) (see page 197), was no incompetent hack who devoted his whole working life to immortalising (?) communist leaders. Born in Alexandropol (present-day Gyumri), Merkurov studied in Paris where he was much influenced by Rodin before going on to sculpt many of the leading figures of his day as well as to create striking monuments to such figures as Chekhov and Pushkin.

The next building on the square, also built in 1950 and with a curving façade, houses a **post office** [119 E6] which is accessible through the left-hand door. Although not the main post office of Yerevan this one has a pleasing stained-glass window behind the counter depicting a woman in Armenian costume holding a telegraph tape. It is useful for buying stamps, especially as the staff actually know the postal rates for letters and cards sent abroad which is not always the case in Armenia. The building also houses the Ministry of Transport and Communications. In Soviet times it held the Council of Trade Unions.

The final building, on the southeast side of the square, was partly built under Tamanian's direction in 1926, though only completed in 1941. An irregular pentagonal structure with one curved side, it is possibly Tamanian's masterpiece. An elegant colonnade above arches forms a gallery along the whole façade and is combined with Armenian detail in the capitals. The archway to the inner courtyard is surmounted by a clock tower which usually flies the red, blue and orange Armenian flag (the building is home to the offices of government ministers) – one of the relatively few places in Yerevan where it is commonly seen. In Soviet days the flag which flew here was of course that of the Armenian Soviet Socialist Republic which actually went through four different designs. The last version, adopted in 1952, was red with a horizontal blue stripe across the middle and a yellow hammer and sickle together with a five-pointed star in the top left corner of the front.

To the cathedral Leave Republic Square along the street that runs between the post office and the government buildings. It is named **Tigran Mets Avenue** in honour of King Tigran II (the Great) who ruled Armenia from c95BC until 55BC. The street bends right after a few yards between buildings which mostly date from the 1920s and 1930s.

Emerging from Tigran Mets Avenue, to the left on the corner of **Khanjian Street** is a **bronze statue** [119 E7] dating from 1974 of Alexander Griboyedov (1795–1829), the satirical playwright whose best-known play, *Woe from Wit*, was only performed and published posthumously. Its hero is branded a lunatic when he arrives in Moscow full of liberal and progressive ideas – a dangerous practice in either the Tsarist or the communist era. Griboyedov was also a diplomat and instrumental in Russia's peace negotiations with Turkey following the war of 1828–29 when Russia gained control of much of Armenia. After that he was appointed Russia's ambassador to Persia but while Griboyedov was in Teheran negotiating with Persia an angry mob stormed the Russian embassy and killed him.

Just past the statue, the striking building on the right with a two-part roof is the former Russia cinema, now the **Ararat clothing bazaar** (sometimes marked as 'Rosia' on maps): the two parts of the roof symbolise the two peaks of Mount Ararat. Underneath it is the **metro station** originally called Hoktemberian ('October' in honour of the October revolution of 1917), but now renamed Zoravar Andranik ('Commander Andranik') in honour of Andranik Ozanian (1865–1927). Born in western Armenia, Ozanian became head of the Armenian self-defence troops in the 1890s until in 1905 he moved west to seek assistance for the Armenian cause. He subsequently participated in the liberation of Bulgaria from Ottoman rule in 1912–13 before organising Armenian units to fight alongside the Russian army against Turkey during World War I. Being more in sympathy with socialist ideals than the new Armenian government led by the Dashnak Party he left in 1918 for Bulgaria and then moved to the USA, dying in Fresno, California. His last expressed wish was to be buried in Armenia. Although he was originally interred in Fresno, after a few months his coffin was moved to Europe and he was reinterred among the renowned in the cemetery of Père Lachaise in Paris. He was finally brought to Armenia in 2000 and now rests in the Yerablur Cemetery in Yerevan where the dead from the Karabagh war are buried. His **statue** [119 E7], unveiled in 2003, can be seen at the foot of the slope leading up to the cathedral. It depicts him brandishing a sword while rather uncomfortably riding two horses at once, one of which is crushing a snake beneath its hoof.

The **cathedral** [119 F7], straight ahead up the slope to the left, is dedicated to St Gregory the Illuminator (as he is always called, although St Gregory the Enlightener would be a better translation since his achievement was converting Armenia into a Christian country). It was consecrated in September 2001 to celebrate what was officially the 1,700th anniversary of Christianity becoming the state religion and to this end symbolically has seating for 1,700 people in the main church although a further 300 can be accommodated in the smaller chapels dedicated to St Trdat, the king who adopted Christianity as the state religion, and his wife St Ashken. There is also a *gavit* (see page 39) and a bell tower. The cathedral may well be the

3

first church in Armenia which visitors see but, even apart from its modernity, it is in several respects atypical. Firstly, there are seats: it was one of the first churches in Armenia to introduce them. Traditionally there were no seats in Armenian churches as the congregation stood throughout the service. Secondly, there are no candles. It is normal on entering an Armenian church to buy candles and then to light them. Here candles are forbidden and may only be lit in a separate building on the southeast side. Thirdly, there is an organ. Fourthly, the church is well lit, having many windows as well as a large metal chandelier. Fifthly, by Armenian standards it is enormous with a total area of 3,500m^2 and a height of 63m. It has been described as having more the atmosphere of a concert hall than a place of worship but it is conspicuously busy with numerous Armenians of all ages visiting and a constant succession of weddings, particularly at weekends. (See pages 33–4 for information about Armenian wedding customs.) Rather incongruously, near the entrance is a panoply brought from the church of St Gayane at Ejmiatsin, underneath which is a casket containing some of the relics of St Gregory which were brought here from the Church of San Gregorio Armeno, Naples, where they had been kept for more than 500 years. They were a gift from Pope John Paul II on the occasion of the cathedral's dedication. Other relics of the saint have been built into the cathedral's foundations.

Leave the cathedral by the main door through which you entered and walk back down the slope. At the foot of the slope do a U-turn to the right into the part of the **circular green belt** in Tamanian's 1926 plan which was actually created. This part in summer now holds a children's funfair; beyond it, walk through trees and cafés until a radial road crosses the green belt. Here there is another **statue** [119 G7] of a warrior on horseback. It is Vardan Mamikonian, the leader of the Armenian forces killed at the Battle of Avarayr (see *Chapter 1, History,* page 16) in AD451 when his troops were overcome by a much larger Persian force. Made of wrought copper and unveiled in 1975, it is by Ervand Kochar (1899–1979), other examples of whose work include the fine statue of David of Sassoun outside the main railway station and several paintings in the National Gallery of Armenia.

Vernissage [119 F6] Instead of continuing along the green belt, turn left across Khanjian Street and take the left hand of the two streets, **Buzand Street**, heading back towards the art gallery. If you are here during the week you will see a broad street with some non-functioning fountains down the middle and a handful of stalls. At the weekend you will, by contrast, be confronted by the justly celebrated **market** of Vernissage. (*Vernissage* is a French word, literally meaning 'varnishing' or 'glazing' but also used in the sense of 'preview', or 'private viewing', at an art gallery.) Vernissage is unquestionably the best place in Armenia, and possibly in the Caucasus, to buy souvenirs and craft items with a huge range of items being sold, for the most part by the people who made them. The range covers carpets, embroideries, wood and stone carvings, paintings, metalwork, etc and the quality ranges from the superb to the tacky. It is generally possible to pay in either drams or US dollars and, while bargaining is acceptable, you may feel that the low prices do not really reflect the work that has gone into some of the items for sale and that if a stallholder is only asking £100/US$150 in the first place for something which has clearly involved 200 hours of highly skilled work then it is unreasonable to demand any reduction in price. As well as craft items there are also stalls selling various antique items, from old radios and Soviet-era medals to secondhand books.

Continue the length of Vernissage, repeatedly doubling back so as to visit each of the aisles. Outside the **Experimental Art Complex** (*1/3 Buzand St*) is another

Visitors will probably be most aware of embroidery during their visit to Vernissage, Yerevan's weekend market (see opposite). Here many colourful hand-embroidered articles are on sale, ranging from small items such as handkerchiefs to larger-scale works such as tablecloths. Much of the embroidery is based on the celebrated Armenian illuminated manuscripts, one of the most popular subjects being letters of the Armenian alphabet in the form of birds. The technique used is known as free-style embroidery or needle painting and some of the results are exquisite. Other styles of Armenian embroidery, such as Aintab, are types of drawn thread work or cut work, akin to Hardanger embroidery. Yet another variety is an interlaced embroidery technique, also known as Marash or Maltese Cross embroidery.

One theory is that these various types were introduced into Europe from Armenia at the time of the Crusades (1096–1270) as a result of the known commercial, military and social contacts between the Armenian kingdom of Cilicia on the Aegean coast of Turkey and the Crusaders.

A technique which may be less familiar to visitors is Armenian knotted needlelace. Superficially this resembles crochet in appearance but the loops are knotted together rather than looped together, thus making it more robust because even if some threads are damaged the whole will not unravel. The stitches are made with an ordinary sewing needle, not with a crochet hook. Once the basic knotting technique is mastered, the skill lies in regulating the size and shape of the loops and many different patterns are known with evocative names such as Ararat, Yerevan and Arek, the last based on the circular sun design common in other Armenian art forms and often seen on khachkars.

There is a good display of Armenian embroidery in the Museum of Folk Art in Yerevan (see page 142) and in the ethnographical museum at Sardarapat (see page 170). Ejmiatsin Cathedral Museum (see page 165) houses examples of ecclesiastical embroidery.

statue [119 F6] by Ervand Kochar, his bronze *Melancholy*. At the far end, on the left, is the side of the art gallery whose front is on Republic Square. To the right, down some steps, is **Hanrapetutian Hraparak** [119 F5] ('Republic Square') underground station. Depending on the weight or bulk of any purchases made at Vernissage, this may be a good place to break the walk.

Abovian Street from Republic Square to Tumanian Street
If you decide to keep going, continue straight on along the back of the art gallery. Before turning right into Abovian Street, look first at the two buildings to the left which are at the bottom end of Abovian Street adjoining Republic Square. **Abovian Street** is probably Yerevan's most important shopping street and also has its best Tsarist-era buildings. It is named after Khatchatur Abovian (1805–48), a teacher and writer whose best-known novel, *Armenia's Wounds*, is based around the events of the Russo–Persian war of 1826–28. **Number 2** Abovian Street, on the left-hand side as one faces Republic Square, is a red-and-black neo-Classical building constructed in 1880 as a boys' secondary school on a site where it had originally been planned to build Yerevan's cathedral. In Soviet times the building was adapted for chamber music concerts and is now the Arno Babadjanian Concert Hall. **Number 1** on the

3

opposite side is slightly newer having been built between 1900 and 1914 to house a trading business; it is also constructed of red-and-black tuff but is in the then fashionable Art Nouveau style.

Before continuing up Abovian Street it may still be worth walking about 300m down **Arami Street**, opposite to the road you have walked from Vernissage, although at the time of writing most of the old houses with balconies were in various stages of demolition to make way for tall blocks of flats. Passing the Georgian embassy on the right, the object of the detour is a **stone-carvers' yard** [119 E5] on the left where khachkars and other items are still created from tuff in the traditional way. To see these carvers at work is to witness the successors to over 1,000 years of tradition and it will be sad if this workshop is, in its turn, removed. Return to Abovian Street and turn left up the hill. On the left is the start of the new **Northern Avenue** linking Republic Square with the Opera and Ballet Theatre, part of Tamanian's master plan of 1926 which was not then realised, but on which construction finally started amidst much controversy in 2002. Either walk up Northern Avenue at this stage or walk down later from the theatre. The eight- and nine-storey buildings on Northern Avenue built in tuff of various colours combine modernity with a definite Armenian character. Internationally known retailers occupy the ground-floor shops while overhead the screaming swifts have happily colonised the high buildings.

Formerly located in the middle of the intended path of the North Avenue, but now on the pavement of Abovian Street opposite the lower end of Northern Avenue, is a **statue** of an old man holding a bunch of roses. Created by the sculptor Levon Tokmajian and erected in 1991, it originally marked the exact spot where the old man it portrays used to stand in the 1930s. His real name was Karapet, but the locals gave him the name '**Kara Bala**' [119 F5], Turkish for 'black boy', because of his dark complexion. See box text, below.

Number 8 on the right-hand side of Abovian Street was built in the 1880s, again in neo-Classical style. After 1937, the building housed the Soviet Central Committee and the office of Comsomol, the Soviet youth organisation, and it was

KARA BALA

Kara Bala was said to have come from a well-to-do family and was married to a beautiful wife; they had a son. Kara Bala grew roses. He would take his roses to Astafian Street (as Abovian Street was then known) where he would stand and give them to girls. In particular he was said to be passionately in love with the famous actress Arus Voskanian who used to walk along Abovian Street to the theatre, and he gave her one red rose every morning. However, she had another admirer, a Turkish man, and this made Kara Bala so jealous that he murdered his rival, for which he was subsequently tried and imprisoned.

On his eventual release he found that his wife and son had left him, that he didn't have a house and a garden any more and that his roses had been uprooted. 'I am not Kara Bala any more, I'm Dardy Bala' ('dard' means sorrow in Armenian), he kept saying, wandering sadly around the town with a bottle of wine. However, he didn't stop giving flowers. Whenever he came across flowers he gave them to women and many in Yerevan still remember him going up to young couples in the 1960s to present the girl with a bunch. Eventually he died and his frozen body was found one morning sitting on a rock.

(until recently) still possible to detect where there was formerly a red star in the top arch of the masonry. It retains one of its original wooden doors. On the opposite side of the street at **number 1/4** is the dark façade (at the time of writing being incorporated into a new building) of the Gabrielian mansion, built in 1910 by the architect Meghrabian and combining Classical and Art-Nouveau elements.

Continue uphill across **Pushkin Street**. The **first building** on the right, with salmon-coloured stucco and red trim, dates from the 1870s. A plaque on the wall commemorates the playwright Maxim Gorky's one-night stay in the building in 1928. Opposite it, on the left, is the red-tuff **Khanzatian mansion** and just above that is the **Hovhannissian mansion**, a large building dating from 1915–16 which incorporated a hospital on the ground floor. It now houses the Armenian Society for Friendship and Cultural Relations with Foreign Countries. Note the windows which incorporate a Star of David in the framework. The Tbilisi Georgian restaurant is in the basement; entrance on the corner at the left.

Slightly higher up the hill, still on the left, is the **Russian Stanislavski Drama Theatre** [119 F4] built in 1937 in Constructivist style but considerably altered in 1974 when it gained a façade of yellowish tuff. Its architect Karo Alabian (1897–1959) worked on several interesting Soviet-era projects including Krasnopresnenskaya metro station in Moscow and the post-war reconstruction of Stalingrad.

Opposite the Stanislavski Theatre is the small square called, until recently, Zodiac Square because its fountain incorporates each sign of the zodiac. However, in 2001 it was renamed **Charles Aznavour Square** in honour of the composer, singer and actor who was born in Paris in 1924 to Armenian parents who had fled the Turkish massacres. The square was created in the 1920s by demolishing a 17th-century Persian mosque together with the Church of Sts Peter and Paul which also dated to the 17th century. The Hotel Yerevan (now the Golden Tulip Hotel; see page 108), designed by Nicoghayos Buniatian (1884–1943) has its entrance on the square. It dates from 1926. At one time Yerevan's most elegant hotel, it once again boasts five-star status. Its red-tuff construction with wrought-iron balconies in traditional Armenian style contrasts oddly with the grey stonework of the entrance surmounted by white Ionic columns. Across the square is the **Moscow Cinema** [119 F4] which dates from 1933. Between the hotel and the cinema is the **exhibition hall of the Painters' Union** used for temporary shows. The square is host to occasionally changing statues of creatures made from bits of machinery. On my last visit there was a surprisingly life-like bull and an enormous spider.

Abovian Street from Tumanian Street to the green belt
Continue uphill across **Tumanian Street** beyond which Abovian Street widens considerably and is lined with trees. Most of the buildings here date from the 1940s. On the right just after crossing Tumanian Street is a **statue** of two men who look as if they have imbibed the contents of the wine jar on which they sit. **Artbridge bookshop/café** [119 F4] (see pages 111 and 115), a little higher on the right at number 20, has an excellent range of English-language books, guides, maps and newspapers. The café is a good place for coffee, especially as it is one of the few places which opens early, at 08.30. Higher up on the left is the superb **Children's Art Gallery** [119 G4] which is well worth visiting (see page 142). Continue across **Sayat Nova Avenue**.

In the first block on the right is the 16-storey Ani Plaza Hotel built in 1970 (see page 108). On the left is the remaining part of the only one of Yerevan's churches to have at least partially survived the 1679 earthquake. Known as the **Katoghike** [119 G3] (literally 'cathedral', singularly inappropriate for the tiny building still standing), its current form dates from 1936 when the main church, a substantial basilica without a dome rebuilt in 1693–94, was demolished in the name of urban redevelopment. It was known that there had been a church on this site since the 13th century but until the demolition was underway nobody realised that the apse and sanctuary actually comprised this old church. Inscriptions of 1229 and 1282 on the newly revealed southern façade as well as one of 1264 on the wall proved this to be the case. Public and scientific outcry won the newly revealed church a reprieve, although until recently it was tucked away behind the 1930s buildings for which the 17th-century church was demolished. These buildings have, in turn, now been demolished and there are plans to rebuild the larger church, although this time beside the small one rather than around it. Since independence it has resumed a religious function and services are held there although it is so tiny that there is hardly room for the officiating priest let alone any congregation. To either side of the *bema* (see page 39) are carvings, some of which appear to have been defaced. In front of the church is a small collection of khachkars and other sculpted fragments from the core of the destroyed basilica.

Continue up the hill. On the right, plaques on numbers 28, 30 and 32 commemorate residents of these buildings which were put up in the 1930s to house artists and intellectuals: trying, however, to get biographical details of these individuals named on the plaques, I drew an almost complete blank. Slightly higher up, also on the right, is a 1930s Art Deco building sporting the Russian word for bread. Continuing uphill Abovian Street meets the circular green belt. Steps lead down to a **pedestrian underpass** beneath Moscovian Street which on closer inspection proves also to house a large **subterranean department store** as well as a considerable part of Yerevan's secondhand book trade, including a selection of often unexpected titles in English. The continuation of Abovian Street uphill is dealt with in the *Elsewhere in Yerevan* section on pages 132–3.

The green belt The walk round Yerevan continues by ascending the steps on the left-hand side halfway along the underpass to emerge into the circular green belt with Moscovian Street on the left and Isahakian Street on the right. The first **statue** [119 H3] encountered, an old man with a walking stick, dates from 1965 and is of the poet Avedik Isahakian (1875–1957) whose early work reflected sorrow and anguish for the fate of humankind. He left Armenia in 1911 as a result of Tsarist oppression but returned in 1936. The statue is by Sergei Bagdasarian. To the right just past the statue, the building which looks like a large upside-down spaceship is **Yeridasardakan** [119 G2] ('Youth') metro station which opened in 1981: the name reflects the number of students in this part of the city owing to the proximity of the university.

Further along is a large pair of **marble hands** [119 G3], a gift from Yerevan's twin city of Carrara in Tuscany; Yerevan achieved its first twinning in 1965 when it was linked with both Carrara and Kiev. Yerevan's response to the gift was to send in return a model of a spring of water carved in tuff and decorated with Armenian motifs – an exact copy also stands a little further on across Terian Street. Immediately across **Terian Street** is a new **memorial** [119 G2] to the victims of both the Jewish Holocaust and the Armenian genocide which seems to have replaced that to the Jewish Holocaust which stood a little further on. Uniting the two khachkar-like halves of the memorial is a brass representation of the eternal flame. The Armenian inscription reads 'Live but do not forget', presumably the Hebrew reads likewise.

Continuing along the green belt, the next **statue** [119 G2] is of a pensive-looking individual. This was erected in 2000 of the poet Vahan Terian (1885–1920) after whom the street was named. There is a small lake on which it is possible to hire battery-operated boats: the Aragast restaurant on the north side is itself built in imitation of a boat (see page 111). One of the cafés here may be a pleasant place to break the walk, partly because, unlike most, they do not (yet?) blast excessively loud music at customers and partly because the remaining section of Tamanian's planned circular green belt back to Republic Square was never built so that this tour must revert meanwhile to city streets. At the end of the green belt to the left is the **music school** named after Sayat Nova (1712–95), composer and poet in Armenian, Georgian and Persian languages. Outside the music school is a bust of Sayat Nova and to the left in front of the **Armenian State Conservatory** [119 F2] is a 1986 **statue** of a man leaning back on a tree: he is the composer **Komitas** (1869–1935) whose career is outlined on page 41. The conservatory itself has busts outside of Bach, Shostakovich, Khachaturian and Beethoven. At the northeast corner of **France Square** stands the **statue** of a rather consumptive-looking William Saroyan (see *Chapter 1*, page 46).

The Cascade [119 F1] A visit to the **Matenadaran** [119 H1] (see page 140) can conveniently be made from here by turning right up **Mesrop Mashtots Avenue**, formerly Lenin Prospekt but renamed in honour of the inventor of the Armenian alphabet; the museum faces down the street with a **statue** of Mesrop Mashtots outside. At the bottom of the slope leading up to the Matenadaran, to the left as one faces the museum, is a group of **pastry shops** selling mouth-watering Armenian cakes and pastries. Also, for those with a sweet tooth, on the opposite corner is the shop of Grand Candy, Armenia's best-known brand of sweets, plus the adjacent doughnut café. The walk continues straight on across Mesrop Mashtots Avenue as far as the park at the foot of the Cascade. The **Cascade** was designed to be a large artificial waterfall tumbling down from the monument commemorating 50 years of Soviet rule but it was left uncompleted at the demise of the Soviet Union. Funding from the Cafesjian Family Foundation has allowed revitalisation of the project and the establishment within the Cascade complex of the **Cafesjian Centre for the Arts** (see page 141). Renovation started in 2002, with the Centre for the Arts opening at the end of 2009. Work continues to extend the Cascade up to the plaza at the top, from where there is an excellent view of the city. The plaza can be reached by steps alongside the Cascade or by road from the city centre. There is also an escalator under the steps and this started to operate again in November 2002 after being out of use since 1997, thus saving the residents living at the top of the hill a climb up around 500 steps. It operates from 07.00 until 23.00. The occasion of the escalator's reinstatement was the unveiling of a **statue** [119 F1] of a fat cat. The self-satisfied-looking, well-fed (and to my mind rather ugly) cat, 2.5m high in bronze covered in black, is the work of the Colombian artist, Fernando Botero (born 1932), and one of several of his cats located in capital cities. It was a gift from Gerard Cafesjian and was the first exhibit of the arts centre to arrive. It was reported in the local press that while the cat was greeted with smiles by the local residents, accustomed to statuary of Soviet dimensions, the loudest cheers were for the reactivation of the much-missed escalator. Another Botero **statue**, of a fat, naked, stunted gladiator wearing a helmet, has joined the collection of statues in the **Tamanian Sculpture Park** at the foot of the Cascade after originally being placed at the top when it arrived in 2005. Much more appealing are some sculptures by British artists. There are three works by Lynn Chadwick (1914–2003) – the one entitled *Stairs* is particularly appropriately located – and two by Barry Flanagan (b1941) including an especially attractive *Hare on Bell*. Other sculptures are *Shadows* by Jaume Plensa (b1955) and *A Surprise for Fabricius Luscinus* by Jim Unsworth (b1958).

3

On the **plaza** above the Cascade, as well as the tall monument commemorating 50 years of Soviet rule, there is also a low square grey building, a monument to Stalin's victims. This has now acquired a pink tuff tambour-like hat. Across **Azatutian Avenue** is the entrance to **Victory (Haghtanak) Park** [105 E3], at the east end of which stands Mother Armenia (see page 120). In the centre of the park is a statue inscribed 'No to war'. Within the park are various fairground amusements and a boating lake.

Around the opera house In the gardens below the Cascade is a **statue** [119 F2] of Alexander Tamanian, much of whose work has already been seen on this walk. Carved from a single block of basalt and mounted on a marble plinth, his hands are resting on a plan of the city in this work by Artashes Ovsepian. It has been suggested that this was the first statue of an architect in the entire world. Tamanian, author of the original plan for the Cascade, stands with his back to it and, rather surprisingly, he is facing the back of one of his finest buildings; opened in 1933 as the Yerevan State Opera House, it was renamed two years later, the **Spendiarian Armenian Theatre of Opera and Ballet** [119 F3]. Note that the oval building also houses the **Khachaturian Concert Hall**. The entrance to the theatre is on the south side whilst that of the concert hall is on the north side of the building. (See box text below for information on Spendiarian himself.)

At the back of the opera house (ie: on the side nearer the Cascade) is a **statue** [119 F3] of the Armenian composer who is the best known outside the country, Aram Khachaturian (1903–78); see page 41 for biographical details. Round the front, the **right-hand statue** [119 F3] is the eponymous Spendiarian while to the **left** [119 E3] is Tumanian, a second of whose poems was the source of the most-famous Armenian opera, *Anoush*. With music by Armen Tigranian it is another gloom-laden tale typical of the time when it was composed although it does contain much attractive Armenian dance music; it was first seen at Alexandropol (Gyumri) in 1912. The piece ends with Anoush leaping off a precipice after her brother has killed her lover for breaking a village taboo.

A **sculpture** [119 F3] of composer and pianist Arno Babajanian (1921–83) was erected next to the small pond (known, rather appropriately, as Swan Lake) in front of the opera house in September 2002 but had to be removed before its official unveiling because its expressionistic style met with far from universal approval. Passers-by said that the work of sculptor David Bejanian was 'an insult' and even the Armenian president, Robert Kocharian, questioned whether it was appropriate. The main objections were to the exaggerated facial features and the long fingers which, it was claimed, made Babajanian look almost like a bird. Bejanian did agree to take the work away to make the hands more realistic and to 'correct' the face, but he said that his new and unrealistic approach had made his sculpture different from other monuments in the city. He said that 'All the monuments in Yerevan are done in a similar style and if we change heads of all the monuments within one night – for example replace Tumanian's head with Spendiarian's, Sarian's with Komitas's – perhaps only the subjects will feel the change. Arno was done to be in an expressive manner so that his head couldn't be placed on the shoulders of anyone else.' When the statue was returned after its 'correction' any changes were imperceptible.

Mesrop Mashtots Avenue The small **park** to the northwest of the opera house contains a **statue** of the painter Martiros Sarian (1880–1972). Rather appropriately the park is used at weekends for the sale of paintings in a similar way to Vernissage. A little to the south is the sculpture *The Men* depicting well-known characters from a Soviet-era film of the same name directed by Edmond Keosayan and popular with Armenians. At this point a detour can be made to visit **Zoravor Church** [118 D3] which is hidden behind Soviet apartment blocks. Turn right from Mesrop Mashtots Avenue along Tumanian Street, then left along Parpetsi Street, then first right into a narrow side street. The church is at the end of this small street, surrounded by trees. It dates from 1693 with renovations in the late 18th century and 1990s. If you're in need of refreshment, there is a Jazzve coffee shop at 35 Tumanian Street. From the back of the opera house continue down tree-lined Mesrop Mashtots Avenue. It is not for the most part architecturally interesting, being lined by office blocks containing shops at street level, but at the top of Mashtots on the right are two shops which may be of interest. One is a well-stocked secondhand **bookshop** and next door is a **brandy shop** belonging to the Ararat distillery (see page 134). As well as brandy it has good selections of imported and Armenian wines. The first interesting building encountered is in the fifth block from the opera house. Behind elaborate doors on the left lies the **Blue Mosque** [118 C5], built in 1765 and the only one surviving in Yerevan. During Soviet days it was the museum of the city of Yerevan but in 1999 it was renovated in Persian style at the expense of the Iranian government and is now functioning as a mosque once more. The grounds are quite pleasant with shrubs and trees, and access to the interior is possible through the main gate which is usually open. The other interesting building is just past the mosque on the opposite side. It is the 1940s-built **covered market** [118 B5]. Designed by Grigor Aghababian (1911–77), it is immediately recognisable by its arching roof and Armenian decoration on the façade. It is a good place to buy both fresh produce and the superb Armenian dried fruits including those stuffed with nuts. (See box, page 130.) A few metres further along Mesrop Mashtots, beyond the market and mosque go straight ahead through the underpass beneath Grigor Lusavorich ('Gregory the Illuminator') Street. You quickly reach the Hrazdan Gorge close to **St Sargis Church** [118 B6]. The present church replaces the one destroyed in the 1679 earthquake. It was built during the period 1691–1705 and rebuilt between 1835 and 1842. Further extensive rebuilding including a taller cupola took place from 1971 onwards and was completed in 2000. From the church there are good views over the Hrazdan to Victory Bridge, Ararat, the stadium and the Genocide Memorial.

Italy Street and Beirut Street Return to Grigor Lusavorich Street and turn right in the underpass to emerge on the east side of this street facing south. After one block there is a **park** on the left, formerly called Kirov Park (see *Chapter 5*, page 205 for information on Kirov) and now **Children's Park** [118 C6]. In it is a **bust** erected in 1950 of Soviet war hero Nelson Stepanian (1913–44). Keep straight on past the park as far as the next street on the left. To the right across the road is a striking new building complete with a clock tower. Finished in 2005, it houses the municipal offices for the city government and the **History of Yerevan Museum** [118 B7] (see page 141). The carvings on the southern façade represent the 12 capitals of Greater Armenia, from Urartian Van to present-day Yerevan. The carving over the entrance to the museum is a plan of Yerevan, and that over the entrance to the municipal offices is the tree of life over the circular symbol of eternity.

Turn left from Grigor Lusavorich Street into what was in his lifetime called Stalin Street but is now called Beirut Street. In the middle of this street is a 1980 granite **statue** [118 C7] of Alexander Miasnikian (1886–1925), a professional Bolshevik revolutionary who was appointed Commissar for Armenia in 1921. He was reported to have died in an air crash although rumours arose that he had really been poisoned on the orders of Stalin because of disagreements over western Armenia. There are rose gardens and fountains in the middle of the street behind the statue. The opposite side of the street is actually called Italy Street rather than Beirut Street; the Italian embassy is on the corner.

Walk along **Beirut Street**. Cross over to **Italy Street** after a few metres to visit the **Theatre Park** [118 D7], formerly named the Park of the 26 Commissars in honour of the 26 Bolsheviks who set up a short-lived government in Baku which was deposed as the Turkish army approached. They fled to Turkmenistan but were captured and executed in September 1918. The park has been renamed Theatre Park, as the park is home to the **Sundukian Drama Theatre** [118 D7]. Its company was created in 1925. The inaugural performance was of the play *Pepo* by Gabriel Sundukian (1825–1912), a story about love versus exploitation set in Tiflis (Tbilisi) and first performed in 1871. There is a statue dating from 1976 of the eponymous Pepo in the park as well as a bust of Sundukian which dates from 1972. The present 1,140-seat building was built in 1966 and was reopened after renovation in 2004. Just beyond the entrance to the park in the central reservation is a bronze **statue** erected in 1970 of a boy holding a large jug of water. It is a reminder of the days when such youths used to sell water along the dusty streets of the old town.

Continuing along Beirut Street or Italy Street, depending on which side you care to walk, just past the next intersection is another **statue** [118 D6], this time of Stepan Shahumian, again created by the same Sergei Merkurov who was responsible for the now-vanished Lenin and Stalin. Stepan Shahumian (1878–1918) was an Armenian who was instrumental in imposing Bolshevik rule in Azerbaijan and one of the 26 commissars after whom the park was named. He is further commemorated in having two towns named after him: Stepanavan in Lori province and Stepanakert in Nagorno Karabagh. The granite statue, erected in 1931, is the oldest on this walk. Behind it, in the middle of the street, is a **fountain** with 2,750 jets, one for every year of Yerevan's existence up to the time that the fountain was installed in 1968. It extends as far as Republic Square which is where the walk started and, when the fountain is operating, the cafés lining it make it another pleasant place to rest after walking the streets of central Yerevan.

The western part of the green belt The part of the green belt not already covered in this walk is perhaps not as attractive as the northern section but it nevertheless has some worthwhile sculptures and offers the opportunity to see a slightly less sophisticated side of Yerevan life – men playing chess or backgammon and children playing open-air table tennis, for example. From the **statue of Mamikonian** [119 G7] continue along the green belt instead of turning left to Vernissage as described on page 122. The first sculpture encountered is a **basalt statue** [119 G7], by Artashes Hovsepian, of the composer Armen Tigranian (see *Chapter 1, Music*, page 41), holding perhaps the musical score of his best-known opera *Anoush*. The next, after walking through an area of cafés and across Sayat Nova Avenue, is a **bronze monument** [119 H5] by Nikoghayos Nikoghosian to the poet Eghishe Charents (see *Chapter 1, Literature*, page 45), the pain depicted in the sculpture echoing his life. Shortly after this on the right is the **Yerevan State University**. It is probably best to stay on this side and use the underpass to negotiate the new road which crosses the green belt before returning to it to find the **bronze statue** [119 H4], also by Nikoghayos Nikoghosian, of Mikayel Nalbandian (1829–1866) who looks out across the street bearing his name. Nalbandian – writer, philosopher, journalist and poet (the words of Armenia's national anthem are adapted from one of his poems) – was a revolutionary democrat who travelled widely throughout Europe, visiting Warsaw, Berlin, Paris, London and Constantinople. Returning to Russia he was imprisoned in the Peter and Paul fortress in St Petersburg by the Tsarist government, spending three years in solitary confinement. He was subsequently exiled to a remote area 500 miles southeast of Moscow and died of TB in prison aged 37. In *A Reference Guide to Modern Armenian Literature*, Kevork Bardakjian (Professor of Armenian Language & Literature, University of Michigan) described Nalbandian as 'an outspoken publicist whose lively and bold style, at times crude and arrogant, was almost invariably laced with irony'. The sculptor seems to have caught the essence of the man. The **final statue** [119 H3] on this part of the green belt is by Yuri Petrosian. Set in bronze it depicts the painter Hovhannes Aivasovsky (see *Chapter 1, Painting*, page 46), well known for his dramatic seascapes. He stands, palette in hand, amongst the waves.

ELSEWHERE IN YEREVAN Some of the sights covered in this section can be easily reached on foot. Others probably require transport, unless you are a keen walker, and these are noted under individual entries.

Around the railway station [104 D5] (*The easiest way to get here is to catch the metro to Sassountsi David ('David of Sassoun') station*) Tamanian's plan was for a new central railway terminus but this was never realised and the main station is in an industrial area south of the centre. The fine station building dates from 1956 and is a striking structure though it now sees much less traffic because of the closure of the border with Azerbaijan; there are now only nine departures each day and consequently few visitors ever come here. The long façade has, uniquely for Armenia, a tall central spire that would not be out of place in St Petersburg. The finial of this spire is, equally unusually, still topped by a purely Soviet symbol being a form of the design of the coat of arms of Soviet Armenia adopted in 1937 and replaced after independence in 1992. The coat of arms was based on a design by the well-known Armenian artist Martiros Sarian and depicts the five-pointed Soviet star above Mount Ararat with a bunch of grapes and ears of wheat below. The coat of arms also bore the well-known slogan 'Proletarians of all lands, unite!' but the railway station does not appear from ground level to enjoy this embellishment.

In front of the station is Ervand Kochar's very fine equestrian **statue of David of Sassoun** [105 E5] mounted on his horse Dzhalali. (See *Chapter 1*, page 48 for further information on Ervand Kochar.) The epic stories of David of Sassoun date back to the 10th century though they were not written down until 1873. They recount the fortunes of David's family over four generations, Sassoun symbolising Armenia in its struggle against Arab domination. The statue shows David brandishing a sword which is ready to fall on the invaders while water flows from a bowl over the pedestal, symbolising that when the patience of the people is at an end there will be no mercy for the oppressors. David's crest of honour was a sword of lightning, belt of gold, immortal flying horse and sacred cross.

More prosaically, on one of the tracks away from the station platform is positioned a steam engine. It is E^u class number 705–46, built in 1930 and one of around 11,000 E class 0-10-0s built between 1912 and 1957 as the standard design for hauling heavy freight trains. This is the largest number of any steam locomotive design ever constructed. In the E^u variant, to which this particular example belongs, the superscript U stands for *usilennyi* – 'strengthened'. The last driver of the train, born in 1927, has a collection of personal memorabilia, including photographs of Stalin, in the train which he is happy to show anyone who is interested. Like many Armenians he is more than willing to pose for photographs: he insists on wearing his uniform jacket with his medals for the occasion. A small **railway museum** has been established in the station building. Only railway enthusiasts would make a special journey to see it but it might be worth a quick look while waiting for a train. If it is closed, ask at Enquiries.

The far end of Abovian Street

Abovian Street has some worthwhile buildings beyond Isahakian Street where it crosses the green belt. On the left corner of Abovian and Isahakian is the **Armenergo building** [119 H2] housing Armenia's main electricity utility. Constructed in 1930 of black tuff, it was designed by Hovhannes Margarian (1901–63) who was also responsible for the Yerevan brandy distillery.

Passing numerous vendors whose prices are among the lowest in the city and then crossing Koriun Street, the building of black tuff on the right corner is the **Yerevan Medical University**. Anyone wishing to see Yerevan's **cable car** [105 E4] should turn right into Koriun Street and walk along it for one block to the lower terminus. It used to take travellers up to the Nork Plateau and operated daily except Sundays from 08.00 until 19.00. However, in 2004 one of the cars plunged to the ground killing five passengers and it has since been out of use. The accident was blamed on poor maintenance. A new footbridge to the lower terminus has been built across a recently built slip road; are there plans to reinstate the cable car?

Otherwise, continue uphill along Abovian Street. On the left side of the street is a small park housing the **original university observatory** designed in the 1930s by Tamanian but superseded by the Byurakan astrophysics observatory (see *Chapter 4*, pages 153–4) on Mount Aragats. At the entrance to the park is a **statue** of Victor Hambartsumian (1908–96), a prominent astrophysicist and one of the founders of the observatory. On the right-hand side of Abovian Street there is a neo-Classical building of 1880 which originally housed the Guyanian Mirzorian School for Girls but now houses the university faculty of theology. After an elaborate wrought-iron fence (still incorporating a hammer and sickle design, alternating with the staff of Aesculapius) complete with stone posts and flower pots enclosing a hospital courtyard, is a particularly interesting building. It is the **Mari Nubar children's eye clinic** [105 E3] which includes a series of pyramids in the frieze below the cornice. This building stems from an initiative in Egypt taken on Easter Sunday (15 April) 1906. Armenians had been prospering in Egypt, and particularly so since the British occupied the country in 1882. Numbers of Armenians there were also being swelled by refugees from Ottoman oppression as well as from the Armenian–Azeri conflicts. The driving force behind the initiative was Boghos Nubar Pasha (1851–1930), an Armenian whose father, Nubar Pasha, had been prime minister of Egypt on five separate occasions between 1872 and 1895. The initiative saw the founding of the Armenian General Benevolent Fund whose mission was to establish and subsidise schools, libraries, workshops, hospitals and orphanages for the benefit of Armenian communities throughout the Middle East and adjacent regions and the Yerevan children's eye hospital was built under the auspices of this organisation. Later Boghos Nubar Pasha was to be leader of the Armenian delegation at the Paris peace conference of 1919. The newly decorated building is still an eye clinic but no longer just for children.

Abovian Street opens out into **Abovian Square** [105 E3], in the centre of which is a statue of Abovian himself sculpted by Suren Stepanian and unveiled in 1950. This was not the statue of Abovian originally intended for this site. That statue, made of bronze, was sculpted in Paris in 1913 by Andreas Ter-Marukian, packed up for shipment, but then, owing to some misunderstanding, it was forgotten and lay undisturbed for 20 years. When it was finally delivered in 1935 it was first erected on Abovian Street near the Moscow Cinema, then moved to the children's park by the Hrazdan River, before finally in 1964 being taken to the Abovian House Museum where it remains.

The building on the right as you enter the square is a hospital of the 1930s. The Folk Art Museum is just beyond that (see page 142).

Marshal Baghramian Avenue to the American University (*It is convenient to walk up one side & back down the other side of this broad street*) The street has some striking buildings and provides a contrast to the centre of Yerevan. It is home to a number of foreign embassies as well as to Armenia's parliament building and presidential palace. (Note that it is not advisable to stop outside these two buildings; see below, page 134.) Starting from the northwest corner of the newly named **France Square** [119 F2] (so named following the French president's visit in 2006) walk up the south side of the street. Near the bottom on the left is the **Union of Writers building**, renovated in 2010. Higher up is the imposing **parliament building** [118 D1] (designed by Mark Gregorian in 1950) set in beautifully kept grounds behind tall railings. Across the next side street is **Lovers' Park** [118 C1] (⊕ *Mar–Nov 07.00–02.00, Dec–Feb 07.00–01.00*) which has been renovated by the Boghossian Foundation. It is favoured not only by couples but also by young mothers and older

folk enjoying a rest on one of the benches in the shade. There are also a couple of cafés so it is a good place for a cool drink before continuing. A little higher up, across the road, are the **British embassy**, steps leading up to the American University and the **bronze statue** [118 C1], by Norayr Karganian, of Marshal Baghramian after whom the street is named. Hovhannes Baghramian was born in Russia to Armenian parents. He fought in World War I, in the Turkish–Armenian war, taking part in the Armenian victory at Sardarapat (see *Chapter 1, History,* page 20) – and in World War II commanding forces which expelled the Nazis from the Baltic states. He is buried at the Kremlin Wall Necropolis in Moscow. Turn round at this point to walk back down to the centre of town. Opposite Lovers' Park the **presidential palace** [104 D3] is on the left. Just within its grounds are **two marble statues** by Levon Tokmajian, Tigran the Great on the left and Noah on the right. Admire the statues as you walk. If you stop you will rapidly be told to move on by police guarding the palace. Apparently after the post-election protests in 2008 (see *Chapter 1, History,* page 26) a ruling allows people to walk past the parliament and presidential palace but forbids them to stop there.

Kond The district of Kond, on the west side of central Yerevan, is the only place where it is still possible to see a few of the **old houses** which, until the early 20th century, were typical of the whole of Yerevan. The easiest way to find the remaining (as of 2010) old houses is to enter Kond up the steep cobbled slope from Sarian Street, just below building 24. For the church, turn right at the top of the slope, then left, and the church comes into view. The area of small houses with their flat roofs, narrow alleys and small courtyards was earmarked for conservation during Soviet times but little was done and much has now been demolished to make way for taller modern buildings. Within Kond is **St John the Baptist Church** [118 C3], a medieval church destroyed in the 1679 earthquake and rebuilt in 1710 and again in the 1980s. The busy pink and grey tuff church has an interesting carving (presumably modern) over the north door by which one enters.

By Victory Bridge [118 A6] The high-level Victory Bridge dates from 1945, its name celebrating victory in World War II. Victory Bridge, 200m long and 34m above the river, supersedes the red-tuff bridge constructed following the collapse of its predecessor in the 1679 earthquake and rebuilt in 1830 after the Russian conquest of Yerevan. The four arches of the 1679 bridge, 80m long and 11m above the river can be seen to the south of Victory Bridge, the central two arches spanning the river itself; the smaller side ones originally crossed irrigation canals. Most visitors see the **Hrazden Gorge** through which the river flows only as they cross Victory Bridge. In spring, when all is green and the poppies are flowering, driving or walking in the gorge is pleasant, but in the summer it can be hot. Restaurants and cafés have taken over one stretch of the gorge but, thankfully, much remains unspoilt. The **Children's Railway** (see box, opposite) is down in the gorge (↖ 527263; ⊕ 10.30–23.30 daily summer only – from late April, depending on the weather; child or adult AMD300).

At each end of Victory Bridge are prominent buildings associated with Yerevan's alcohol business. At the west (airport) end is the **Yerevan brandy distillery** [118 A6] (*2 Isakov Av;* ↖ 510149/150; www.ybc.am; tours approx AMD3,000) which stands on a plateau high above the bridge. The distillery was founded in 1887 but the present building was designed by Hovhannes Margarian, the same architect as was responsible for the Armenergo building in upper Abovian Street. Its façade displaying nine arches can be best appreciated when approached by the long flight of steps from the valley below. Guided tours of the storage facilities and museum, with sampling of the products, can be arranged but the actual production is not shown. It is now owned by the French Pernod Ricard company. Unfortunately its excellent products are difficult to obtain in western Europe; presumably its owners see little point in competing with their French products.

At the other (city) end of the bridge the large rather forbidding building constructed of basalt which faces the bridge, houses the **Yerevan Wine Company** [118 A7]: built about 1930, its shape and dimensions are exactly those of the former citadel that occupied the site, which is the reason for its appearance. Its architect Rafael Israelian (1908–73) was also responsible for the very fine memorial commemorating the Battle of Sardarapat in Armavir province. It is often stated that the first performance of Griboyedov's *Woe from Wit* (see page 42) was actually given in a room of the fortress by Russian army officers in 1827 but it is not clear what evidence exists for this claim. It seems unlikely that army officers would have acted in a play which was prohibited by the Tsarist authorities and which was not published until seven years later.

The Genocide Memorial and Museum [104 D4] The Genocide Memorial and Museum at Tsitsernakaberd ('Swallow Castle') are among the few points of interest on the west side of the Hrazdan River. Visiting them is strongly recommended for anyone wishing to understand Armenia and its people. In 1965, Armenians throughout the world commemorated the 50th anniversary of the 1915 genocide, and the lack of any tangible symbol in Armenia itself was conspicuous to the extent

THE CHILDREN'S RAILWAY [118 B2]

Children's railways were a Soviet Union phenomenon although a few were built in other cities of the Soviet bloc such as Budapest. They were not built as fairground amusements but to train children aged from nine to 15 in the operation of real railways. The first opened at Tbilisi, Georgia, in 1935. Yerevan's opened in 1937 and was extensively renovated in the late 1950s. (The second children's railway in Armenia, at Leninakan (Gyumri), never reopened after being damaged in the 1988 earthquake.) It operates during the summer when children are not at school, the first day of operation usually being Genocide Memorial Day (24 April). It is now simply a recreational amusement; children no longer perform all the tasks under adult supervision. Both children and adults can ride on the train. The line is 2.1km long along the Hrazdan Gorge and starts from a gaily painted station whose architecture was clearly influenced by Yerevan's main railway station. It also incorporates stained-glass windows depicting birds. To reach it from the city, walk west from Mashtots Avenue along the broad street which has defunct fountains down the middle (called Aram Street to the north and Buzand Street to the south). From the far end a long pedestrian tunnel leads to the gorge and the children's railway.

All children's railways have a track gauge of 750mm. The original steam locomotive, coal-burning 0-8-0 number 159-434, is of a design built in the 1930s mainly for forestry work. Although still on view, it is apparently unserviceable. The usual motive power is a diesel hydraulic, currently number TY2 096 dating from 1958. The route is a single track towards Victory Bridge. There are no facilities for the locomotive to run round the train at the far end and the coaches are therefore hauled out but propelled back.

that the Genocide Memorial was created and completed in 1967. The architects Kalashian and Mkrtchian have succeeded in creating a striking and appropriate monument. Although the ideal approach is to mount the flight of steps leading up to it, most visitors are likely to approach instead from the car park, in which case the first thing they will notice is the collection of trees, each of which has been planted by a distinguished visitor. Separating the museum from the monument is a 100m-long memorial wall of basalt carved with the names of villages and towns where massacres of Armenians by Turks are known to have taken place. The monument itself has two parts. There is a 44m-tall stele reaching to the sky symbolising the survival and spiritual rebirth of the Armenian people. It is riven, however, by a deep cleft which symbolises the separation of the peoples of western and eastern Armenia while at the same time emphasising the unity of all Armenian people. Adjoining the stele is a ring of 12 large inward-leaning basalt slabs whose shape is reminiscent of traditional Armenian khachkars. The 12 slabs represent the 12 lost provinces of western Armenia and their inward-leaning form suggests figures in mourning. At the centre of the circle, but 1.5m below, burns the eternal flame. The steps leading down are deliberately steep, thus requiring visitors approaching to bow their heads in reverence as they descend.

The **museum** (*www.genocide-museum.am;* ⊕ *(museum) 11.00–16.00 Tue–Sun; free guided tour in Armenian, English, French or Russian; entrance free, there is a container for donations*) was added in 1995 to commemorate the 80th anniversary of the massacres. The museum is a circular subterranean building and was designed by the same architects as the memorial. The museum is well labelled in Armenian, English, French and Russian. Much information is given on the number of victims in different parts of western Armenia and there are many photographs taken by German army photographers who were accompanying their allies the Turks during World War I. There are also examples of foreign publications about various aspects of the genocide including reports by British, American and German officials on the maltreatment of the Armenians by the Turks. One typical exhibit reproduces the letter sent by Leslie A Davis, the American consul at Harput (west of Lake Van) to his boss, the American ambassador at Constantinople on 24 July 1915. It reads:

> I do not believe that there has ever been a massacre in the history of the world so general and thorough as that which is now being perpetrated in this region, or that a more fiendish, diabolical scheme has ever been conceived in the mind of man.

Erebuni

Erebuni, on a hilltop in the southern part of the city, is the original site of Yerevan. It can be reached by *marshrutkas* 11 and 85 (see *Getting around,* page 106). Visitors can see the partially excavated remains of the site of the city together with interesting objects found there which are now housed in a worthwhile museum at the bottom of the hill. Erebuni was discovered by chance in 1950 during exploration of Arin Berd Monastery which had later been built on the site. A cuneiform inscription was uncovered which can be dated to 782BC. It states: 'By the greatness of [god] Khaldi, Argishti, son of Menua the powerful king of Biaini and ruler of Tushpa city built this splendid fortress and named it Erebuni, strength to Biaini.' (Biaini was the Urartian name for their country. Urartu is the Assyrian name.) Argishti was the Urartian King Argishti I (ruled c785–c762BC) who established a garrison here of 6,600 troops, the first Urartian settlement on this side of the Arax. Its heyday lasted for only about a century until the Urartian King Rusa II (ruled c685–c645BC) chose a different site, Teishebai Uru (literally City of [the God] Teisheba), see page 101, overlooking the Hrazdan River which he believed would be less vulnerable to attack by the Scythians. However, Erebuni remained occupied as is testified by archaeological finds from later periods.

When visiting the site go to the **museum** (*38 Erebuni Av;* \ *458207;* ⏰ *10.30–16.30 Tue–Sun; guided tour in Armenian AMD2,000, in English AMD2,500; adult/child AMD1,000/300*) first as the model of Erebuni there gives a good idea of the general layout. An English-speaking guide is available, as well as a booklet giving a brief description in five languages. Particularly interesting are three silver rythons (drinking horns in the form of animals), one of which is shaped like a horse, one like a bull's head and one like a man on horseback. The helmet of King Sarduri II (ruled c763–c734BC) is on display together with a large jug, possibly a funerary urn, with bulls' heads. There is also a good selection of jewellery, ceramics and weapons found on the site. The central courtyard of the museum is a reconstruction of the palace courtyard. Of particular interest is the stone, actually found at Tanahat Monastery, Syunik (not the better-known Tanahat Monastery, Vayots Dzor). It has a cuneiform inscription dedicated to the Urartian King Argishti II (ruled 714–685BC) but the stone was made into a khachkar in the 11th century by which time no-one of course could read the inscription. A tuff **statue** of Argishti I on his chariot, by Levon Tokmajian, stands on the street outside the museum.

The shape of the hill on which Erebuni is built necessitated a triangular shape for the **citadel**. It had walls around 12m high, the lower 6m being formed of two parallel walls of large stone blocks with rubble filling the space in between the rows and large buttresses providing additional strength. Above the stone blocks clay bricks were used which were then covered with plaster. Within the citadel was the royal palace, temples and service premises, everything being connected by stairways because the slope of the hill necessitated the buildings being constructed at different levels. A **good view** of the walls can be had from below and it is worthwhile walking along the path which follows them right round the outside. It can be accessed from near the vehicle entrance to the site or from steps which lead up from the left side of the museum.

Entering the site from the access road and car park the first building on the left is the reconstructed **Hall of Columns** used to greet dignitaries. It has a blue wall with a frieze and the present roof is supported by six wooden columns. Continuing up the main entrance slope and steps, near the top of the steps is a copy of the **Argishti stone** (the original is kept in the museum) erected in 782BC and referred to above. Just after going through the entrance way a narrow alley goes off right to the **necropolis**. To the southwest of the central square was the **temple of Khaldi**, the chief god. It was crowned by a tower with a flat top that was probably used for sending smoke signals which would have been visible from far across the plain. Following the collapse of the Urartian kingdom and the installation of a Persian viceregent at Erebuni, the temple was converted for use as a 30-column *apadana* (**reception hall**). Part of this has been reconstructed and the design of frescoes can be seen generally with figures of gods between horizontal bands in contrasting colours.

Northwest of the Khaldi temple was a **pillared courtyard**, probably used by the king for important meetings, together with a **small temple** devoted to Sushi, another of Urartu's 69 gods (of whom 55 were male) and used by the royal family. At its entrance is another cuneiform inscription. The palace's **main reception hall** was northeast of the central square. Surrounding the main buildings were living quarters for the garrison and for servants, together with buildings for storing produce such as meat, fruit, wine, sesame seed oil, and milk products in *pithoi* (large urns) sunk into the ground to keep them cool. Different parts of the site are stated to have had different functions but this is not obvious when walking round the ruins.

Haik Avenue (also known as Gai Avenue) in the northeast of Yerevan is the main road out towards Garni and visitors heading there frequently notice the four statues alongside the road. The **first**, on the left, made of copper and dating from 1975, is of a man wearing a lion skin and aiming his bow either at Turkey or at the block of flats opposite. This is Haik, great-great grandson of Noah and legendary founder of the Armenian people. The **second** statue, by the well-known sculptor Ervand Kochar (see page 48) is of another Haik. The figure on horseback to the right of the road brandishing a sword and looking back towards Turkey is Haik Bzhshkian (1887–1937). Born in Tabriz (Persia) he was active in revolutionary movements and also in World War I when he commanded Armenian troops. Subsequently he supported the Bolshevik cause and after service in Siberia became commissar of the military forces in Soviet Armenia. His military career continued but he succumbed along with 40,000 others, to Stalin's purge of the Red Army. The victims were variously accused of being 'spies', 'Fascists', or 'Trotskyite-Bukharinite'. The bronze statue was erected in 1977, a time when the true cause of death was not acknowledged.

The **third** statue, on the left and opposite a market, is a 2003 marble statue of King Tigran II (the Great) who ruled from c95BC to 55BC. The **fourth** statue, also on the left and dating from 1982 is of Tork Angegh ('Ugly Tork'). He is shown standing on a pile of boulders, carrying an enormous rock on his shoulders, and with a grotesque expressionistic face. In legend he was a very kind giant and a skilled artist. Eventually, despite his ugliness, he was able to marry the woman he loved after defeating her 20 other suitors.

Karmir Blur [104 B5] The site of Teishebai Uru to which the Urartian King Rusa II moved his capital from Erebuni is now known as Karmir Blur (Red Hill) or Teishebaini. It is in the southwest suburb of Karmir Blur on the south side of the Hrazden Gorge and is probably most easily found by taking a taxi. There is not a lot to see apart from the bases of the massive megalithic walls which surrounded the citadel but the situation, on the edge of the gorge, is impressive. Walking around the hill not only gives an impression of how huge a city Teishebaini must have been but also affords excellent views of the gorge itself. Many of the articles unearthed during excavation are on display at the State History Museum (see opposite).

YEREVAN'S MUSEUMS AND GALLERIES Yerevan has many museums, several of which have already been covered. There are some which most visitors agree are 'must-sees' and should be fitted in if at all possible. Others are very worthwhile even for those without a special interest in the subject covered. Yet others will probably appeal only to those with a special interest. I have tried to give some indication of these groups in the entries below although it is inevitably subjective. Non-Armenian speakers should note that many museums, particularly some of the smaller house museums, have information only in Armenian.

Most museums charge Western visitors around AMD500–1,000 per person although some (including the Genocide Museum and the Military Museum) are free. For more information on entry fees and opening hours, see *Chapter 2*, pages 90–1.

Must-sees

State History Museum [119 E5] (*Republic Sq;* ✆ *582761; www.historymuseum.am;* ⊕ *11.00–18.00 Tue–Sat, 11.00–17.00 Sun, last entry 1hr before closing; guided tour in English AMD5,000; adult AMD1,000*) Apart from the exposition 'Palaeolithic to Bronze Age' which opened in 2010, the museum is virtually devoid of labelling in any language but Armenian. This is a great pity as it is a well-displayed excellent collection. There are no brochures or floor plans. English-speaking guides are available but it can be difficult to persuade them to concentrate on the items in which you're particularly interested rather than to follow the standard tour. However, for the lower two floors of the museum public-spirited individuals have provided a **guide** which can be freely downloaded from www.tacentral.com. It is strongly recommended that you do so before visiting. Their advice – to save your visit to the museum until the end of your trip – is sensible; the most important exhibits can then be put into the context of sites with which you are already familiar.

The ticket office is to the right as you go in. Go up to the third floor, through the glass doors which lead to the art gallery, and up the stairs on your left to reach the **new display** covering two million–1000BC. These four rooms contain a fascinating collection of items showing the enormous wealth of historic objects unearthed in Armenia. The collection certainly brought to life for me the ancient history of the country, with finds from so many well-visited sites such as Garni, Lake Sevan, Metsamor and Dvin. There are introductory explanations in English although the English is often surprisingly poor, ending up with contortions such as 'The making of tools was a peaceful and trustworthy dialogue of the prehistoric man with materials to realise and obtain the spiritual energy of the image enclosed in stone.' Furthermore, whilst much is labelled in English, it's usually the obvious articles such as knives, beads, etc, and where labels would actually be useful and interesting they are often sadly lacking. Favourite items of mine include finds from Karmir Blur such as Argishti I's ritual helmet and decorative shield of the 8th century BC, jewellery from various pre-Christian sites, and the Bronze Age chariot burial from near Lake Sevan. Also on display is the world's oldest shoe found in a cave near

YEREVAN'S CEMETERIES

Yerevan has two cemeteries of interest. The **Pantheon** [104 D5], Arshakuniats Avenue in the southeast suburbs of Yerevan, is where Armenia's famous deceased are interred. The inmates most familiar to visitors are likely to be the composers Komitas and Aram Khachaturian together with the writer William Saroyan. Presumably the reason that only the upper half of Saroyan's body is shown in the 1984 sculpture on his tombstone, is that only half his ashes are here: the other half are in Fresno, California.

The cemetery of **Yerablur** [104 C5], Sebastia Avenue, to the right off the road to Zvartnots, houses the dead from the Nagorno Karabagh war together with Andranik Ozanian, fighter against Turkey in the late 19th and early 20th centuries, and Vazgen Sarkisian, the prime minister who was assassinated in parliament in 1999. To visit this cemetery, particularly on one of the traditional Armenian days for visiting graves such as Easter Monday, is even more poignant than with most war cemeteries because the war in which they were killed is so recent (1989–94) and many of the figures tending the graves are the mothers or other close relatives of those who died. Most of the graves carry a picture of the deceased.

Areni and radiocarbon dated to about 3500BC by laboratories in Oxford in the UK, and California, USA.

On descending to the **second floor** English disappears and it is here the online guide is helpful, at least in part although things have inevitably changed with the opening of the third floor. In the rooms to the right of the staircase the guide still (2010) corresponds exactly to the displays. However, the rooms to the left, from where many exhibits have been moved upstairs, now display items from the Armenian kingdom of Cilicia and information about 20th-century events. The **first floor** has also changed but there is still an extensive display of carpets and religious artefacts.

National Gallery [119 E5] (*Republic Sq;* \ *580812;* e *galleryarmenia@yahoo.com; www.gallery.am;* ⊕ *11.00–17.00 Tue–Sun; guided tour in English AMD5,000; adult AMD800*) The third-best collection in the former Soviet Union. Go straight ahead after entering the building and up the stairs to the **first floor** where the ticket office is on the left. (Do not go to the ticket office on the ground floor – that's for the historical museum.) A **helpful floor plan** leaflet in English is available for AMD300, but you will have to ask for it; it is kept under the counter. After buying a ticket take the lift to the **seventh floor** to start viewing. Trying to do anything else, such as going directly to the Armenian paintings on the fifth floor, is possible but causes total bewilderment among the staff. Apart from some Asian porcelain and copies of Sri Lankan cave paintings the collection largely comprises paintings from the main European schools as well as works by the major Armenian painters. Italian artists represented include Bicci di Lorenzo (*The Betrothal of St Catherine*); Benvenuto Garofalo (*Virgin Mary with the Christ Child*); Jacopo Tintoretto (*Apollo and Pan*); Jacopo Bassano (*Adoration of the Shepherds*); Leandro Bassano (*Good Samaritan*); Francesco Guardi (*Courtyard with Stairs*). Flemish painters include: Hans Jordaens III (*The Jews Crossing the Red Sea*); and David Teniers the Younger (*Kegl Players and The Village Feast*). Dutch painters include Jan van Goyen (*View of Dordrecht*); Pieter Claesz (*Still Life*); Jan Wijnants (*Landscape with Broken Tree*). French artists include Louis le Nain (*The Nest Robbers*); Jean Baptiste Greuze (*Head of a Girl*); Eugène Boudin (*Sea Harbour*). Among the Russian works Ilya Repin's *Portrait of Teviashova* and Isaac Levitan's *Reaped Field* particularly stand out. The collection of Armenian works includes all the greatest Armenian painters with a good collection of Aivasovsky's seascapes and works by Martiros Sarian.

Matenadaran [119 H1] (*53 Mesrop Mashtots Av;* \ *562578; www.matenadaran.am;* ⊕ *10.00–16.00 Tue–Sat; closed Sun & Mon; guided tour in Armenian AMD1,500– 3,500, in English, French, German or Russian AMD2,500–6,500 depending on group size; adult/child AMD1,000/100*) The Matenadaran was purpose built in 1957 to house 14,000 Armenian manuscripts but the original single display room could show fewer than 1% of them. A second room was opened in 2006 to show manuscripts from the Armenian kingdom of Cilicia. The museum provides virtually the only opportunity in Armenia to see examples of this important art form. The **ticket office** is entered from the outside to the right of the main entrance steps and the **gift shop** to the left – it is worth paying for the English-speaking guide. Items include the oldest-surviving manuscript (dating from 989), the earliest Armenian printed book (printed in Venice in 1512) and translations of many important works into Armenian. Armenians are particularly proud of the copy of Ptolemy's map which shows Armenia extending from the Black Sea to the Caspian.

Genocide Museum [104 D4] See pages 135–6.

Erebuni Museum See pages 136–7.

Cafesjian Centre for the Arts [119 F1] (*Cascade;* ☎ *541932;* e *info @cmf.am; www.cmf.am;* ⊕ *10.00–17.00 Tue–Thu, 10.00–20.00 Fri–Sun; adult AMD1,000, 13–17yrs AMD700, children under 12 free; several categories of annual membership available*) The Centre, opened in 2009 within the Cascade, aims to bring the best of contemporary art to Armenia. The exhibits are from the personal collection of the founder, Gerard L Cafesjian, and include items from one of the most comprehensive glass collections in the world. The gallery is on six levels of the Cascade with a dedicated lift from each floor. The Cascade escalators between floors function between 07.00 and 23.00. A fascinating and eclectic collection of objects is displayed with excellent information labels in English. A visit here, together with the sculpture park in front of the Cascade, is strongly recommended. (For information on the Cascade itself and the sculpture park, see page 127.)

History of Yerevan Museum [118 B7] (*1 Argishti St;* ☎ *568185; www.yerevanhistorymuseum.am;* ⊕ *11.00–17.30 Mon–Sat, closed Sun; adult/child AMD500/250*) Located in the new City Hall (see page 130); enter the History of Yerevan Museum by the far left-hand door. This well-laid out museum on three floors traces the history of Yerevan from ancient times to the early 21st century. Most items are labelled in English as well as Armenian but signs indicating which period each floor covers are only in Armenian. The first floor is ancient and medieval although the model in the centre shows 19th-century Yerevan, with archaeological sites at each corner; the second covers the 19th century whilst the third focuses on the 20th century. The third floor shows domestic scenes, including traditional Easter and New Year decorations.

Worthwhile

Martiros Sarian House Museum [118 D2] (*3 Sarian St;* ☎ *581762; www.saryan.com;* ⊕ *10.00–18.00 Fri–Tue, closes at 17.00 on Wed, closed Thu; AMD600*) The house museum of one of Armenia's greatest 20th-century artists housing around 170 of his works and showing their brilliant colours reflecting a sunny climate.

Ervand Kochar Gallery [119 F2] (*39/12 Mesrop Mashtots Av;* ☎ *580612;* ⊕ *11.00–17.00 Tue–Sat, 11.00–16.00 Sun; guided tour in foreign languages AMD2,000; AMD600*) See page 48 for biographical details of this interesting artist. As well as paintings from all parts of his career, including the Tiflis, Paris and Yerevan periods, there are also photographs of some of his monumental sculptures. This excellent museum gives a very good idea of the range of work of this talented artist who was persecuted in Stalinist times. A visit is strongly recommended. English-speaking guide available.

Aram Khachaturian House Museum [119 E2] (*3 Zarobian St;* ☎ *589418; www.khachaturyanmuseum.armeniatour.am;* ⊕ *11.00–16.00 Mon–Sat, closed Sun; AMD500*) Contains personal memorabilia of Armenia's best-known composer as well as props and costumes from his ballet *Spartacus* and photographs of Khachaturian with many well-known people including many non-musicians such as Che Guevara, Ernest Hemingway, Sophia Loren, U Thant and Charlie Chaplin. There is an astonishingly vivid painting by Edman Aivazian of Khachaturian conducting at the EMI studios in London. Painted in 1977, a year before Khachaturian's death, few paintings have ever captured so well the spirit of music making and the museum is worth visiting to see this alone. The museum makes no reference to the composer's falling foul of the Soviet authorities in the late 1940s. Also in the building are a concert hall and a collection of CDs of Khachaturian's music. An English-speaking guide is available.

Museum of Folk Art [105 E3] (*64 Abovian St;* \ *569387; www.folkartmuseum.am;* ⊕ *11.00–17.00 Tue-Sun; AMD500*) A wide range of embroidery, lace, silver jewellery, stone carving, wood carving, carpets, ornamental metalwork and ceramics. There are numbers of salt containers in the shape of women, a traditional Armenian symbol of the woman as being the essence of the home. Other interesting exhibits include shawls from the Lake Van area (now in Turkey) which are similar in style to those from the Scottish Shetland Isles. The museum is particularly strong on wood carving.

Mother Armenia Military Museum [105 E3] (*Victory Pk, 2 Azatutian;* \ *201400;* ⊕ *10.00–17.00 Tue-Fri, 10.00–15.00 Sat & Sun; admission free*) The museum is located inside the structure, which from 1950 to 1962 supported the statue of Stalin, but now supports the statue of Mother Armenia. Originally the whole was devoted to World War II but the upper floor is now devoted to the Nagorno Karabagh conflict. The displays of uniforms, portraits of marshals, etc are not particularly interesting although camouflage netting is successfully used to create atmosphere on the lower floor. The museum is notable for succeeding, even in a Stalin-era building, in creating the atmosphere of a church as one enters and this is echoed in the statue of Mother Armenia, a young woman holding a sword horizontally and thus forming the shape of the cross. The labels show no concession to those who do not speak Armenian.

Children's Art Gallery [119 G4] (*13 Abovian St;* \ *520951;* ⊕ *11.00–16.00 Tue-Sat, 11.00–15.00 Sun; guided tours in English, German & Russian AMD2,500; adult/child AMD500/200*) This fascinating gallery has two parts to its exhibits. There is a permanent collection of works of art by children from around the world and there are temporary displays of work by Armenian children on various themes such as Europe, the Bible, or Armenian folk stories. The standard of the exhibits, which include other art forms such as embroidery, metalwork and carving, is excellent. The children are given instruction in art and craft techniques and then given a theme to tackle. It is worth having a guide especially for the themed Armenian section. Attractive books of the children's work are on sale and they make excellent souvenirs. Strongly recommended.

Sergei Parajanov Museum [118 A5] (*15 Dzoragyugh St;* \ *538473; www.parajanovmuseum.am;* ⊕ *10.30–17.00 daily; guided tours in English, French, German & Russian AMD2,500; AMD700*) Dedicated to the artist and film director known in Armenian as Sargis Yossifovich Paradjanian (1924–90), this museum is a must-visit for anyone with the slightest interest in 20th-century culture. It's best to get the English-speaking guide to show you round first, and afterwards to wander round on your own. Parajanov essayed a range of art forms from films (mostly silent, more like a series of still scenes one after another) to collages to pen drawings. He seems to have been either egocentric or megalomaniacal – witness his showing himself in the central place in *The*

Last Supper. There is a fish made from broken combs and a representation of blue irises made from broken glass. Mosaics also feature prominently. All in all, it's an extraordinary museum.

And if there's still time ...
Geological Museum [118 D1] (*24a Baghramian Av;* m *091 669061;* ⊕ *Mon–Fri 11.00–16.00, closed Sat & Sun; admission free*)

Gallery of Modern Art [118 C5] (*7 Mesrop Mashtots Av;* ↖ *535359;* ⊕ *11.00– 16.00 Tue–Sun; AMD500*) Founded in 1972, it was the only such gallery in the entire USSR. With additional funds provided by the diaspora it has built up a representative collection of 20th-century Armenian painting and sculpture.

Hovhannes Tumanian Museum [118 D2] (*40 Moscovian St;* ↖ *560021;* ⊕ *11.00–16.00 Mon–Sat; AMD500*) Dedicated to the writer (see page 44). The ground floor houses personal items and upstairs is a re-creation of his apartment.

Eghishe Charents Literature Museum [119 E5] (*1 Arami St;* ↖ *581651;* ⊕ *10.00–17.00 Tue–Sat, 10.00–16.00 Sun; AMD300*) Dedicated to the writer (see page 45). In the writer's former house but more an archive of papers associated with many different writers than a museum devoted entirely to Charents. There is a separate **Eghishe Charents House Museum** [118 D4] (*17 Mesrop Mashtots Av;* ↖ *535594;* ⊕ *10.30–16.00 Tue–Sat, 10.00–15.00 Sun; AMD500*).

Khatchatur Abovian Museum [105 F2] (*4 2nd St, Kanaker;* ↖ *248686; www.abovyanmuseum.com;* ⊕ *10.00–17.00 Tue–Sun; adult/child AMD500/300*) Dedicated to the novelist (see page 44) and in his parents' house now in the northeast suburbs. Exhibits cover various parts of his life such as an ascent of Mount Ararat, the Russo-Persian war of 1828–30 and his mysterious sudden disappearance, possibly at the hands of Tsarist agents.

Derenik Demirchian House Museum [119 H2] (*29 Abovian St;* ↖ *527774;* ⊕ *10.30–16.00 Tue–Fri, 10.30–15.00 Sat & Sun; AMD500*) Dedicated to the writer (1877–1956) who was best known for his play *Nazar the Brave* (1923). Among the personal effects is the writer's Stradivarius violin.

Avetik Isahakian House Museum [119 E1] (*20 Zarobian St;* ↖ *562424; www.isahakyanmuseum.am;* ⊕ *11.00–16.00 Tue–Sat, 11.00–15.00 Sun; AMD500*) Dedicated to the poet (1875–1957) who, after his return from study at Leipzig University, was arrested by the Tsarist police and banished because of his involvement in the Armenian freedom movement. Very much an establishment figure in Soviet days, he was awarded two Lenin prizes and became a deputy to the Armenian supreme soviet. The museum contains personal effects and memorabilia.

Hakob Kojoyan and Ara Sargsian House Museum [118 D3] (*70 Pushkin St;* ↖ *561160; www.arasargsyan.com;* ⊕ *10.00–16.00 Tue–Sun; AMD300*) Dedicated to the artists (1883–1959 and 1902–69 respectively); Sargsian was a sculptor, producing works such as *Hiroshima* and *Mother Armenia*. The ground floor is dedicated to him and contains a reconstruction of his studio as well as examples of his work. Upstairs is devoted to Kojoyan with examples of his work and personal effects. He was a talented book illustrator as well as a painter and is credited with the first Soviet Armenian painting *The Execution of the Communists at Tatev* (1930 – now in the National Gallery of Armenia).

Alexander Spendiarian House Museum [119 G4] (*21 Nalbandian St;* ☏ *580783; www.spendaryanmuseum.am;* ⊕ *11.00–16.30 Tue–Sun; AMD400*) Dedicated to the composer (see page 128); as well as manuscripts and personal effects, there is a display about his best-known work, the opera *Almast*.

Middle East Museum [119 E5] (*1 Arami St;* ☏ *563641;* ⊕ *11.00–17.00 Tue–Sat, 11.00–16.00 Sun; AMD300*) Based on the collection of the painter Marcos Grigorian, it has an excellent collection of Persian applied arts with pottery, bronzes and ritual figurines dating back five millennia. Included are exhibits from Persia's pre-Islamic Zoroastrian culture. Not always open when it should be.

Museum of Wood Carving [118 B5] (*2 & 4 Paronian St;* ☏ *532461; www.artwood.am;* ⊕ *12.00–18.00 Tue–Sun; AMD400*) An interesting small museum. Separate sections cover the history of Armenian wood carving, applied carving and sculpture. The small sign outside is, somewhat perversely, carved in stone.

Museum of Russian Art [119 F1] (*38 Isahakian St;* ☏ *560872;* ⊕ *10.00–17.00 Tue–Sat, 10.00–15.00 Sun; AMD500*) Mostly late 19th- and early 20th-century works. Founded in 1984 and based on the collections of Professor Aram Abrahamian. An attractive gallery and well worth a visit.

DAY TRIPS FROM YEREVAN See *Chapter 4, Central provinces,* for suggested day trips from Yerevan.

4

The Central Provinces

Any place in the five central provinces of Aragatsotn, Ararat, Armavir, Gegharkunik and Kotayk can be visited on a day trip from Yerevan except for the eastern parts of Gegharkunik. The most popular excursions are the **town of Ashtarak** together with the **fortress and monastery at Amberd** in Aragatsotn; the monastery of **Khor Virap** in Ararat with its stunning views of the mountain in clear weather; the **churches of Ejmiatsin** and the **monument and museum at Sardarapat** in Armavir; **Lake Sevan** and the **Sevan Monastery** in Gegharkunik; and the temple at **Garni** and **monastery at Geghard** which are close to each other in Kotayk. All of these are standard places on most visitors' itineraries. The following pages make numerous other suggestions but, if I had to choose just one, it would be the amazing field of **khachkars at Noratus**.

ARAGATSOTN PROVINCE

The province whose name means 'foot of Aragats' comprises the land around **Mount Aragats**, at 4,090m (13,419ft) the highest mountain in the present-day republic. The province's geography is extremely varied and it is probably best thought of as being three separate zones: the mountain itself, arid steppe to the west, and the land bordering the gorge of the Kasagh River to the east. Each of these zones has its different attractions. Ashtarak ('Tower'), the provincial capital, is in the Kasagh Gorge in the southeast of the province and only 22km from Yerevan.

Accommodation in the province is limited apart from homestays, but since everywhere can be reached as a day trip from Yerevan this shouldn't prove a problem. There are **minibuses** from Yerevan to Ashtarak and Talin (see *Chapter 2*, pages 75–6) and from Ashtarak local minibuses go to some villages, although it is probably easier to hire a taxi in Ashtarak, or even in Yerevan. See *Chapter 2, Taxi*, for information about taxi fares, page 76. The main roads in the province are good. Most places are accessible by car and a 4x4 is only necessary if you are intending to explore very minor roads or are trying to reach Amberd before the snow has fully melted.

 WHERE TO STAY AND EAT

Ashtaraki Dzor Centre ('Astarak Gorge') ╲ 232 36778. The most comfortable accommodation option situated just upriver from Ashtarak town on the other side of the river beyond the high viaduct. There is often live music & w/ends especially can be very noisy with wedding parties. Unfortunately the beautiful setting is marred by the tiny cages in which animals are kept. No credit cards. Charges by the hour. It is perfectly possible to stay the night although the staff may be a bit surprised. **$$**

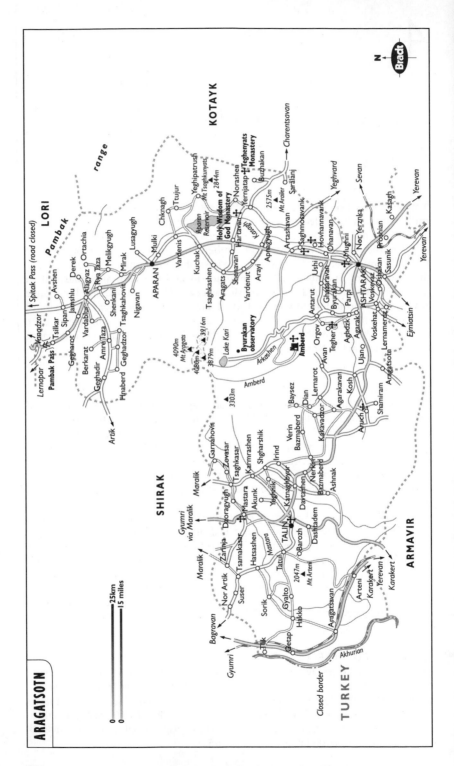

ARAGATSOTN

There is a good **bakery** at Aparan (see page 152) which sells excellent snacks and a **café** at Amberd (see page 154). The road out of Yerevan is lined with stalls selling seasonal produce and barbecue stalls. Or take food from Yerevan for a picnic.

PRACTICALITIES Most visitors will rely on Yerevan for any facilities needed. Astarak is the only other sizeable place in the region although Aparan and Talin can supply most things. Larger villages will have a shop where basic supplies can be purchased and some petrol stations also have small shops attached.

Main roads have fuel stations, particularly plentiful between Yerevan and Agarak.

ASHTARAK *(Telephone code 232)* Ashtarak is situated on the **Kasagh River**. This river rises in the southeastern corner of Shirak province and then flows south through Aragatsotn to join the Arax south of Yerevan. Ashtarak is a pleasant town with some older buildings including some fine medieval churches. It is now rather dominated by the modern bridge carrying the Yerevan to Gyumri main road high over the gorge, bypassing the city and considerably reducing traffic over the older three-arch bridge of 1664. This older bridge has a rather unusual appearance in that the three arches are unequal in size with the southernmost arch almost twice the height of the northernmost. Prominently perched atop an outcrop on the east bank of the river between the new and old bridges is the small red-tuff **church of St Sargis**, a modern construction on early foundations. The main part of the city, however, is on the west bank.

Legend states that three sisters lived here who all loved the same prince – Sargis: the elder two decided to kill themselves to leave the way free for the youngest. One of the elder sisters dressed in an apricot-coloured dress and the other in a red dress and then they both threw themselves into the gorge. The youngest sister learned what had happened, put on a white dress, and threw herself into the gorge after them. The prince became a hermit but three churches appeared at the edge of the gorge: one apricot-coloured, one red and one white. The problem with this legend is that the present colour of these churches doesn't correspond with it, although the names do. Karmravor ('Reddish'), the church of the sister wearing the red dress, is apricot coloured (though it does have a red roof); Spitakavor ('White-ish'), the church of the sister wearing the white dress is red; while Tsiranavor ('Apricot-ish'), whose sister wore the apricot-coloured dress, is actually white!

By far the best preserved of the three is the small 7th-century **Karmravor Church** dedicated to the Mother of God. It is one of the few Armenian churches of this period to have survived unaltered, even retaining a roof of tuff tiles and a tiled octagonal cupola. A single aisle cross-dome church, it is one of Armenia's most appealing town churches. An extensive cemetery with khachkars lies to the north and east of the surrounding walls. The other two churches in the legend, 14th-century **Spitakavor** and 5th-century **Tsiranavor**, are both roofless and forsaken but are only a short walk away and the views of the gorge are pleasant. The large storage jars decorating the gardens passed on the walk are often unearthed in the district. The churches of the legend are on the northeast side of the city but Ashtarak's biggest church, **St Marina**, is in the city centre. Built in 1281, it is again a cross-dome church with octagonal tambour but the tambour and cupola here are unusually high. The tambour features attractive decoration in contrasting colours of tuff but the appearance of the whole is seriously marred by a Soviet-era addition which looks more like a large derelict shed than part of a church.

Eight kilometres southwest of Ashtarak is the village of **Oshakan** whose **5th-century church** was most unattractively renovated in 1875 and then had unappealing frescoes foisted on it in 1960. It is famous as the burial place of Mesrop Mashtots and the alphabet is spelled out in grass which must take an awful lot of cutting. A new **stele** stands at the entrance to the church, commemorating the 1995 visit of Katholikos Karagen I. Near the top is a **sundial** with the traditional Armenian use of letters for numbers. However, whether due to unfamiliarity with the old letter/number system or because of Oshakan's association with the alphabet, the hours are uncharacteristically numbered with a continuous sequence of the first 12 letters of the alphabet (see box, *Sundials*, page 36). In the grounds of the church is a collection of **modern khachkars** carved by Ruben Nalbandian. There are 36 of them, each a letter of Mashtots's original alphabet, carved with images appropriate to the letter as well as a typical Armenian cross and the circular symbol of eternity. A visit is enhanced by the company of an Armenian speaker but, armed with a copy of the Armenian alphabet (see *Appendix 1*, page 284), it is possible to appreciate the ideas behind some of them. For example, the Armenian letter 'E' bears an image of Ejmiatsin, 'M' depicts Mesrop Mashtots, and on 'J' water flows from the eternity symbol, *joor* being the Armenian word for 'water'. The first rank of nine can be read as (Ch)rist, (E)jmiatsin, (S)aint, (M)(A)(SH)(T)(O)(TS).

MOUNT ARAILER – A BOTANICAL FORAY

The extinct volcano of Mount Arailer, about an hour's drive north of Yerevan, makes an ideal botanical excursion. The trip takes in semi-desert, mountain steppe, forest, meadows and agricultural ecosystems. There are several trails and tracks for a 4x4 but it is not necessary to climb to the 2km-diameter crater at the top; the lower slopes afford much of interest. More than 650 species of vascular plants grow on Arailer, almost 20% of the whole Armenian flora.

Timing a visit for flowers is always going to be a compromise. Arailer has snow cover from December which may not fully melt until late May. The first flowers to appear in February/March are *Merendera trigyna* and *Crocus adamii*. Irises, tulips and other spring flowers follow. The most luxuriant growth is in May/June including the scented white flowers of *Crambe orientale*, aromatic thyme, crimson poppies and the dark red bugloss *Echium russicum*. You should also see spectacular fields of agricultural weeds, cornflower, poppy, chamomile and blue larkspur. In the moister meadows are lovely violet-purple, almost black *Gladiolus atroviolaceus*, brilliant blue *Anchusa azurea*, white *Anthemis* daisies, the white foam of *Filipendula hexapetala*, various star of Bethlehem, *Ornithogalum*, species and much more.

Arailer's northern slopes have remnant forest, remains of much wider cover in the past. Over 40 species of shrubs and trees are present including Caucasian oak, *Quercus macranthera*, birch, maple, aspen, cherry, apple, pear and several species of *Sorbus*. There is also a subalpine crook-stem forest, where trees have been weighed down on their sides by heavy snow and then new growth has grown upwards before the snow melted. On the lower slopes can be found the orchid *Dactylorhiza romana*, an inflated cowslip *Primula megacalyx*, *Veronica gentianoides*, beloved by UK cottage gardeners, and a little later the large-flowered violet-blue *Iris demetri*.

To reach the southern slopes of Mount Arailer take the Ashtarak road from Yerevan, turn off before Ashtarak for the village of Nor Yerznka, from where the asphalt road takes you to the southern slopes. To reach the crater it is better to take the Mughni exit, go as far as the village of Karbi and walk from there.

In the **gorge** at Oshakan a **five-arch bridge** dating from 1706 spans the Kasagh. Any vehicles which look as if they are attempting an impossible fording beside the bridge are simply using the river as a free car-wash.

NORTHWARD ALONG THE KASAGH The main road north from Ashtarak towards Vanadzor and the Georgian border keeps, for the most part, to the west bank of the Kasagh. The section of road crossing directly over the Pambak range into Lori province by the **Spitak Pass** (2,378m) is now impassable owing to washouts, and the modern road deviates to the west over the slightly lower **Pambak Pass** (2,152m). The view from the road north from Ashtarak is dominated by Mount Aragats to the west; to the east the conical **Mount Arailer** (2,575m) is prominent on the southern part of the route but further north the Pambak range rises to 3,101m at **Mount Tegh**. A whole succession of monasteries lie along the river, many of which are interesting and attractively sited.

Mughni The village of Mughni, nowadays within the Ashtarak city limits, lies just to the north of the main Yerevan to Gyumri road at the west end of the high viaduct over the Kasagh Gorge. The 14th-century **Monastery of St George** was completely rebuilt between 1661 and 1669 during the period when eastern Armenia saw a revival of church building thanks to the stable conditions enjoyed under the Safavid shahs of Iran. It is unquestionably one of the finest buildings of this renaissance and it is now surrounded by well-tended gardens. It is notable that the church withstood the earthquake of 1679 which flattened Yerevan and badly damaged the Monastery of Hovhannavank to the north. The main cross-dome church has a distinctively striped circular tambour supporting the conical umbrella cupola and different colours of tuff are also used to decorative effect on the gable ends. The *gavit*, most unusually, has three arches at the west surmounted by a belfry whose cupola is supported by 12 columns. The south doorway is especially notable with elaborately carved tuff of different colours and fine carved wooden doors. Inside the church, fragments of 17th-century murals survive, notably one showing the baptism of Trdat on the north wall. There is an altar screen, unusual in Armenian churches. The fortress wall of the monastery survives with small towers at the northwest and southwest corners. At the northeast corner the original service buildings have been restored: they originally housed the living quarters of the monks together with the refectory. St George's should be additionally commended for being the first church in Armenia to produce for visitors a well-written useful guide in English. Presumably this commendable initiative was thanks to the Armenian Prelacy Ladies' Guild (New York) who funded the (well carried out) restoration.

Hovhannavank (monastery) Situated about 5km north of Mughni, Hovhannavank ('Monastery of John') is the southernmost of two sizeable monasteries that are perched on the edge of the gorge and linked by a path which makes a pleasant, though potentially rather hot, walk: it is about 5km from Hovhannavank to Saghmosavank and there is little shade. The oldest part of Hovhannavank, perhaps the more appealing of the two monasteries, is a **basilica** structure dating from the 5th century though extensively rebuilt since then. On the south side of this early basilica stands the **main church,** dedicated to John the Baptist, and erected by Prince Vache Vachutian in 1216–21; the prince was Governor of Ani from c1213 until 1232. The corner rooms of this church are two-storey and those at the west have cantilevered steps. As at some other churches of

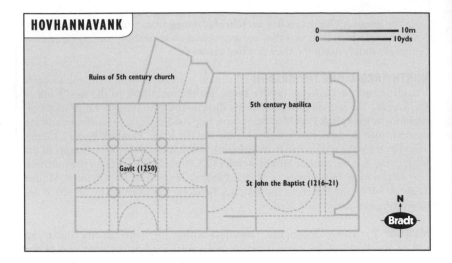

0 ——————— 10m
0 ——————— 10yds

Ruins of 5th century church

5th century basilica

Gavit (1250)

St John the Baptist (1216–21)

N

Bradt

this period, the front of the altar dais was originally decorated with stars, pentagons and diamonds and some of this decoration survives. The *gavit* was built in 1250 to serve both the churches and is consequently off-centre. Four pillars divide it into separate sections, each of which is differently decorated; the belfry supported by 12 columns was probably added in 1274.

The cupola of the main church collapsed following an earthquake in 1679 and then again, following another one, in 1919; the latter also damaged the south façade and still more damage resulted from the 1988 earthquake. However, the 12-sided tambour and cupola were reconstructed in 1999 and repairs are continuing. Particularly strange is the tympanum of the south door. Christ can be seen apparently blessing the five wise virgins with His right hand and rebuking the five foolish virgins with His left. Except that the virgins have beards so are they really meant to be the Apostles and in that case why are there only ten? The church is surrounded by a fortified wall, originally constructed in the 13th century and rebuilt in the 17th. To the north is an extensive graveyard with khachkars.

Saghmosavank (monastery) The monastery was, like Hovhannavank, built by Prince Vache Vachutian. Not surprisingly the two monasteries have many similarities, not least in their situation on the rim of the gorge and in the stone used in their construction, although the architectural details are quite different. The oldest part of Saghmosavank ('Monastery of Psalms') is the **Zion Church** of 1215 with its round tambour and conical cupola. Inside there are frescoes on the arch over the apse and carved angels over the sanctuary. The smaller **Mother of God Church** to the south was built in 1235 and was followed by the large *gavit* which has an impressive entrance doorway similar to those found at the entrance to mosques. Whether this simply reflects the previous experience of the architect or had some other significance is not clear. The layout of the existing buildings required the **library** to be L-shaped when it was added in 1255; there is a fresco of St Gregory over the door to the Mother of God Church. Unfortunately this door is usually locked as the church is, according to the caretaker, 'only a store room'. As at Hovhannavank, a **fortified wall** surrounds the complex: the local goats enjoy standing on top of this one to keep an eye on the tourists.

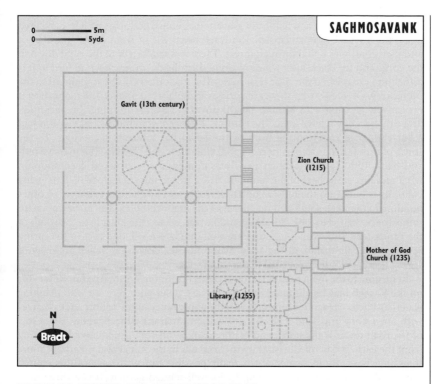

0 ————— 5m
0 ————— 5yds

Gavit (13th century)

Zion Church
(1215)

Mother of God
Church (1235)

Library (1255)

N

Bradt

NORTH TO APARAN AND THE PAMBAK PASS With the four peaks of Mount Aragats to the west, the road continues north through fields of cabbages and past herds of cattle. In 2005, the 36 letters of the original Armenian alphabet carved out of tuff were placed on a hillside some 2km north of Saghmosavank, just north of the village of **Artashavan**. They are plain and, with their random positioning on a litter-strewn hillside, they compare unfavourably with the interesting and elaborately carved modern alphabet khachkars at Oshakan church (see page 148). Ten kilometres north from Saghmosavank at the village of Hartavan a road goes off right to **Yernjatap**: in about 4km the road starts to wind down towards the Kasagh. Turn left onto a minor dirt road which similarly winds down but slightly upstream. Standing on a knoll just before the bridge over the river are the ruins of the **Monastery of the Holy Wisdom of God**, founded in the 5th century and renovated in 1244. It is a peaceful and isolated spot. The church is swathed in wooden scaffolding within and without and a little work has been done on the roof to keep out the elements. The *gavit* with its massive columns is roofless. Some decoration survives on the altar dais and the remains of a red-painted frieze are discernible. The doorway from the *gavit* into the church has carved black-and-red tuff decoration.

Continuing through Yernjatap, about 5km beyond the village, take the road branching left to the village of **Buzhakan**, a resort centre in Soviet days and an excellent centre for walking. Keep straight on through the village, ignoring the track which goes off right soon after entering the village, until the main asphalt road forks left and a dirt road continues straight ahead. In dry weather it is possible to drive all the way up to the monastery but parking at the start of the track and walking the last 3km to **Teghenyats Monastery** makes a very beautiful walk. The first section is between fields as far as a half-built guesthouse, construction of which was halted when the Soviet Union collapsed. The track bears left in front of the guesthouse and then continues uphill through forest. There is a small river to the right down in the gorge and the track, after winding along the hillside, drops down to ford it. It is difficult to cross when the river is in spate. The track then climbs straight up to the monastery. On the way up there are springs and places to picnic. The monastery is evocatively situated with **Mount Tsaghkunyats** (2,844m) forming the backdrop. The ruins occupy a large area. The ruinous 10th-century church looks as if it had a barrel-vaulted roof and the front of the *bema* has interesting carvings. To the south of the church is a collection of small chambers and chapels. The massive red-and-black 12th- to 13th-century *gavit* was domed; there is carved decoration on what remains of the base of the tambour. The 13th-century refectory with its many columns is built into the hillside north of the *gavit* and there is evidence of other building to the west, south and northeast of the main complex. The graveyard, with tombstones shaped to look like sheep and horses, covers the hillside to the south of the monastery. Snow can linger up here well into late April; one visit in the spring revealed bear footprints in the snow while further down the valley an array of spring flowers rapidly succeeded the melting snow.

Returning to the main road at Hartavan and continuing north, **Aparan Reservoir** on the Kasagh may be glimpsed over to the east: it supplies Yerevan with drinking water. Just before reaching **Aparan** town the appearance of the countryside changes with open stony grassland replacing cultivation. Aparan's **church**, about 100m east of the road towards the north end of the town, is one of Armenia's oldest, dating from the earliest days of Christianity in Armenia in the 4th century. Perhaps more than anywhere else in Armenia it is really possible to feel the age of this church built of dark grey tuff and standing in its well-tended garden, It is a three-nave basilica without a cupola, the naves being divided by T-shaped pillars; the roof is barrel-vaulted. At the apse a modern stained-glass window is virtually the church's only decoration. An unusual feature is the row of four large stone blocks, a little like khachkars, which form a sort of half barrier across the chancel in front of the altar dais. The stepped base on which the church stands is larger than the present church and there are the remains of two other churches to the north.

It is worth being in Aparan at lunch time. On the right, immediately after entering the town from the south, is a new metallic grey building which houses a **bakery**; the smell of freshly baked bread will help to guide you there and tempt you to try one, or two, of their delicious snacks (eat-in or take-away). Highly recommended.

Leaving Aparan a striking **monument** can be seen on a hill to the west. This commemorates an Armenian victory over Turkey in 1918. The remains of the Armenian General Dro were returned here from Massachusetts in June 2000. The countryside becomes greener as rainfall in this area is higher than in the lower-lying areas further south. The road passes several villages inhabited by Yezidi people. Working mostly as shepherds, they are fire-worshipping Zoroastrians and recognisable (to the Armenians) as being racially different with darker skin; the women also tend to wear more colourful clothes and a scarf over the head. As they joined the Armenians in fighting the Turks they are seen as natural allies and there is no racial discord. Modern Yezidi cemeteries are distinctive with graves that look almost like small houses. An older cemetery is by the road in the village of **Rya Taza** where there are tombstones in the form of horses for the men though much simpler ones, sometimes depicting a cradle, for women. Constructing tombstones in the form of animals was not associated solely with Yezidis in Armenia as the tombstones of Armenian nobility were sometimes in the form of sheep.

top   Armenian brandy (*konyak*) sprang to prominence at the Yalta conference in 1945 when Stalin plied Winston Churchill with it and Churchill declared that it was better than any French brandy (VDB) page 86

above left   Selling homemade cakes at Geghard Monastery (DH) page 188

above right   Armenia's dried fruits are excellent; particularly apricots, peaches or plums which have been stuffed with nuts (AB) page 85

below   Tomato vendor's car, Ijevan market — the quality of Armenia's fruits and vegetables is extremely high (NH) page 81

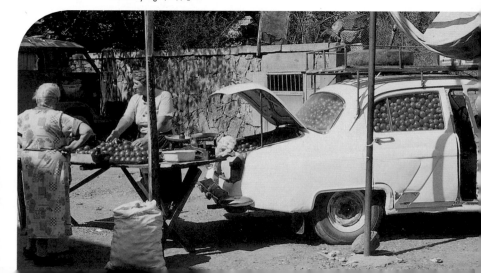

left Noravank is one of Armenia's best-known and best-loved tourist sights (SS) page 237

below Dadivank in Nagorno Karabagh is traditionally believed to be on the site of the grave of St Thaddeus, who was martyred in the 1st century for preaching Christianity (L/D) page 277

bottom Ejmiatsin became the spiritual centre for Armenia's Christians shortly after the country's conversion in the early 4th century (WK/A) page 163

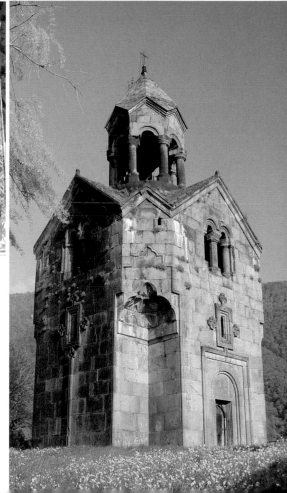

top   The lower tympanum of the *gavit* at Noravank is one of two remarkable tympana set above the doorway of the John the Baptist Church (NH) page 238

above left   Wall painting at St Sargis Church, Meghri (DH) page 261

right   The ingenious three-storey bell tower at Haghpat Monastery (Sh/D) page 216

above   Women making *lavash*, the traditional Armenian flatbread (SS) page 83

left   Men playing chess (DH)

below   Handmade carpets make a typically Armenian souvenir (SS) page 90

above Fortune telling from coffee grounds, Areguni (NH)

right Priest of the Armenian Apostolic Church; training for the priesthood lasts seven years (DH) page 30

below Many families in Armenia rely on subsistence agriculture and often keep their own livestock (AB) page 29

above   Lake Sevan's beaches
are very popular with Armenians
(I/A) page 173

left   The dormant volcano of Mount
Aragats is the highest peak in
Armenia at 4,090m
(PC/A) page 153

below   The spectacularly beautiful site of
Hnevank is found in a gorge close
to the confluence of the Dzoraget
and Gargar rivers (d/A) page 220

above   **Countryside near Makaravank**
(SS) page 225

right   **Caucasian agama (*Laudakia
caucasia*); Armenia is very rich
in reptile species, boasting a
total of 50** (NB/FLPA) page 7

below   **There is a conspicuous
abundance of butterflies in
Armenia** (AB) page 9

The road climbs up through rolling hills and over the pass into Lori. Although the old road via the Spitak Pass is unusable by vehicles it would probably make an interesting walk. The whole distance from Alagyaz, where the new road branches off, to Spitak is about 25km but anyone with a driver could be taken as far as Sipan on the old road and then picked up at Lernatsk, about 5km south of Spitak, leaving about 16km to walk over the pass itself.

MOUNT ARAGATS Mount Aragats has four separate peaks, the highest being the northernmost one at 4,090m. The four summits are situated around the rim of a volcanic crater, broken between the southern and eastern peaks by an outflowing stream. Any reasonably fit person can walk to the southern peak once the snow has melted, although it is always necessary to remember that even those accustomed to walking at home will take longer here unless they are acclimatised to the altitude. It is obviously essential to take the same precautions here as are necessary when ascending any mountain. Do not consider going without walking boots, compass, waterproofs, warm clothing and water. The easiest approach is to take the road, often closed well into June, which ascends the southern slope of Aragats as far as the cosmic ray station situated by (artificial) **Lake Kari** at 3,190m. The cosmic ray station was inaugurated in 1943 to study astroparticle physics. According to the station's brochure, work currently concentrates on monitoring solar activity as well as on studying the physics of extensive air showers and measuring the incident flux of galactic cosmic rays.

From the end of the road it takes about two hours to walk up to the southern peak (3,879m) by heading for the northwest corner of the summit until a rough track is encountered which leads to the top. For those wishing to reach the highest point in Armenia it takes about four hours from the end of the road and should be attempted only by those accustomed to mountain walking. Because clouds often gather round the crater from mid morning, an early start is recommended to maximise the potential for spectacular views and to minimise the risk of becoming disorientated in cloud. Apart from the break between the southern and eastern summits the peaks are linked by high saddles and a ridge descends south from the southern peak.

South of the cosmic ray station at an altitude of 1,405m is **Byurakan Astrophysical Observatory**, founded in 1946. Visits to the observatory and cosmic ray station can be arranged (see *Chapter 2, Special-interest visits* page 57). The original equipment included a 45cm Cassegrainian telescope (a reflecting telescope in which incident light is reflected from a large concave mirror onto a smaller convex mirror and then back through a hole in the concave mirror to form an image) and a 52cm Schmidt telescope (a reflecting telescope incorporating a camera and consisting of a thin convex glass plate at the centre of curvature of a spherical mirror which thus corrects for spherical aberration, coma and astigmatism). Radio telescopes were added in 1950. In 1960, a larger Schmidt telescope with a 102cm glass plate and 132cm mirror was installed and, in 1965, an important programme began looking for UV-excess galaxies. It continued for 15 years and achieved considerable international renown with 1,500 such galaxies being identified. (In 1968, the observatory was awarded the Order of Lenin.) A larger 2.6m telescope was installed in 1976 and a second survey was started which was also to achieve major international recognition. The object this time was to obtain baseline data for an ongoing survey of 600 quasars, emission-line and UV-excess galaxies although the detailed work ended up providing information about 3,000 varied objects. Since independence the 2.6m telescope has been refurbished and in 1998 the observatory was named in

4

honour of Viktor Hambartsumian (1908–96), its founder in 1946, whose face used to be familiar to visitors because his picture appeared on the AMD100 banknote until the note was replaced by a coin.

The **road to Lake Kari** holds much of botanical interest. In early June, look out for *Draba, Crocus adami, Scilla siberica, Pushkinia scilloides* and the delightfully downy *Ajuga orientalis*. July and August see the alpine meadows in full flower.

The southern slopes of Mount Aragats
The fortress and church of **Amberd** are beautifully situated on the southern slope of Aragats at an altitude of over 2,000m between the gorges of the Amberd and Arkashen rivers but may be inaccessible because of snow as late as May. In late May/June, the fortress and church are surrounded by expanses of bright red oriental poppies, geraniums, various peas including the Persian everlasting pea *Lathyrus rotundifolius*, a relative of the garden-popular perenial pea, and the tall *Nectaroscordum siculum*, an onion relatively rare in the wild but often grown in UK gardens. In nearby grassland grows the striking borage relative *Solenanthus circinatus* with its metre-high stems of bluish-purple flowers. **To reach Amberd**, turn left off the road to the cosmic ray station. In clear weather spectacular views of the two buildings can be obtained from the approach road with Mount Ararat in the background, a view all the more impressive because the café does not obtrude when viewing from this direction, although inconsiderately parked tourist buses might. (The buses, on day trips from Yerevan, rarely arrive before 10.30 so it's quite easy to beat them.) The owner of the **café** (⊕ *May–end Oct, depending on weather*) lives on site so opens the café when tourists arrive and closes when they have all gone. (*Snacks start at about AMD2,500; a mug of herbal tea is AMD200; the car-park attendant expects a discretionary tip & the toilets are AMD100pp.*) The church, a typical cross-dome structure with an umbrella cupola, is older than the present fortress, having been built in 1026 by Prince Vahram Pahlavuni, leader of the Armenian forces who fought against the incorporation of Ani into the Byzantine Empire. The present fortress dates from the 12th century although there had been a stronghold here since the 7th century which changed hands several times according to the fortunes of war. The final phase of building took place after the brothers Ivane and Zakare Zakarian captured it from the Seljuk Turks in 1196. Acquired by Prince Vache Vachutian in 1215, it withstood Mongol invaders in 1236 but was finally abandoned in 1408.

The approach to the fortress is from the west, the side least protected by natural defences, and the windowless west wall has defensive towers and steps inside the castle up to what would have been a walkway on top of the wall. The eastern side of the fortress is more domestic in appearance. Inside there is evidence of at least three storeys of small rooms and the many windows of differing styles, looking out towards the church, suggest various phases of rebuilding.

Three small buildings at the foot of the fortress on the east have been restored. That nearest the castle (the **cistern** on the site plan) certainly has evidence of a water-related function. The middle building is a small **chapel** while the easternmost, the 13th-century **bathhouse**, has two rooms each with a dome. Grooves in the wall would have held clay water pipes, similar to those visible at Lori Berd near Stepanavan. A path around the outside of the fortress affords good views of the gorge of the Amberd. It is possible to go inside the castle. Many people scramble up the steep scree-like slope visible from the car park but the easiest (and official) way in is through the door in the east wall; a path goes off between the chapel and cistern. (Note that, inside, some of the walls don't seem too stable.)

Another attractive and interesting church is **Tegher**, founded by Prince Vache Vachutian's wife Mamakhatun in 1213. Constructed of basalt and commanding extensive views over the plains below, it is south of Amberd. Note: the road map, *Roads of Armenia* (see page 53), implies that it is necessary to drive via Agarak between Amberd and Tegher; this is certainly true for large vehicles. However, for cars, in good weather, a shorter route (shown on the *Armenia and Mountainous Karabakh* map; see page 53) is possible. It goes west from the Byurakan road at Antarut then via Orgov to join the road to Tegher. It is an attractive route, dropping down to cross the Amberd (a popular spot for fishing) and back up the far side.

The oldest part is the **Mother of God Church** with round tambour and conical roof. The front of the altar dais shows seven arches, said to symbolise that this was the seventh church built by the family. To its right is a now-blocked-off secret passage down into the river gorge for water and escape. The large *gavit* of 1232 is particularly attractive with pleasing decoration around the base of its cupola: the pillars supporting the roof were brought from 10km away. Set into the floor is the grave of the founder and her husband and, more unusually, one grave depicting the deceased as having only one leg and another indicating that the deceased had been buried with feet pointing west rather than east. Two-storey **corner rooms** at the west end give the external appearance of two small chapels perched on the roof of the *gavit*. In the vicinity are the remains of other buildings including a **bread oven** just below the church. Behind the church is a **picnic area** and some visitors **camp** here then walk the 12km over the hills to Amberd.

Continuing south from Tegher the road descends through the village of **Aghdzk**. On the east side of the village street are the ruins of a 4th-century three-aisle **basilica church**, to the south of which is a **mausoleum**, originally of two storeys but with only the subterranean part now intact. According to the early historians Movses Khorenatsi and Pavstos Buzand, the mausoleum was built in 364, in the period of the Armenia–Persian war to house the bones of the kings of the Arshakuni dynasty which had been seized by the Persians but were then recaptured by the Armenian leader Vasak Mamikonian. The carvings in the chamber date from the late 4th or early 5th century and are unique in early Armenian Christian art. On the north wall is Daniel in the lions' den while on the south is a boar hunt. A torch is essential for seeing the carvings.

THE WESTERN STEPPES OF ARAGATSOTN

The arid steppe which forms the western part of Aragatsotn is a complete contrast to the eastern and central parts of the province and is crossed by the main Yerevan to Gyumri road. For convenience the western slopes of Aragats are included here as they too are best accessed from that highway.

Agarak

Heading west along the main road, some 8km from Ashtarak is the village of Agarak where a large site, thought to be early Bronze Age, was excavated during the first decade of this century. The site occupies 200ha on an extensive outcrop of tuff. It is signposted on the left just after leaving the village. After an information board the track veers right, uphill. Keeping close to the weather-beaten cliff-like rock on your right you reach a 1m³ cavity in the white tuff. At the bottom is a small passageway, 50cm long, which leads into an underground 2m³ chamber. Carved into the walls are large rectangular niches. Apparently a complete skeleton and weapons, thought to be Urartian, were found here. A torch is essential if you wish to explore. On the top of the rocky outcrop removal of the thin layer of topsoil has revealed numerous pits carved into the rock. Some are deep and either rectangular or circular, others are shallow and have an obvious channel running from them. Some are now filled with water creating small ponds in which irises and frogs flourish. Yet others look very like the rock-hewn coffins in places such as Lmbatavank.

Kosh 20km from Ashtarak a road leads right to the village of Kosh. Behind the village is a cemetery dominated by a hill on which are the remains of a small 13th-century castle built on an earlier foundation. It is rectangular in shape with round corner towers. In the cemetery itself are the 13th-century **Church of St Gregory** complete with sundial, and the 19th-century **Church of St George**. More interesting than either, however, is the 7th-century **Church of St Stephen**. It is reached by taking the road out of Kosh towards Sasunik (turn right in the village by a blue sign which contains information about the water and sewage system; the main road bears left and if you reach the prison you have missed the turning). Follow it for a short distance up the hill until the church is seen in a gorge to the right. A track leads over to the church and the short walk from the road is pleasant and interesting, passing old khachkars and caves apparently formerly used by the monks. The well-preserved church itself is perched on a ledge so narrow in the side of the gorge that the shape of the roof had to be adjusted to avoid an overhanging rock. One of the church's corners is supported by a pile of rocks, more dramatic before the recent path around the church was laid but still visible. Inside can be discerned the remains of frescoes.

Aruch and Talin Further west and just south off the main road is the much more important but much less appealingly situated monastery of **Aruchavank** situated in the village of Aruch. The large **Cathedral Church of St Gregory** was built of red and grey tuff in 666 when Aruch was the seat of Grigor Mamikonian, a prince who enjoyed local autonomy during the period of Arab rule. The cupola of the church has collapsed, remaining unrestored when some work was carried out between 1946 and 1948. Further work has been carried out recently and the church, having been locked for many years, is now open. The windows have been glazed but the cupola is still missing. The church is unusual for one so large in having only a single nave. There are the remains of the frescoes in the apse and in the southeast corner room. A cemetery with recumbent 19th-century gravestones surrounds the church and in the south of the precinct are the remains of Grigor Mamikonian's palace and another basilica church. Away from the centre of the village Aruch also has a **ruined caravanserai**, possibly Armenia's most frequently noticed as it is just a few metres from the main Yerevan to Gyumri road on the south side. When built it was on the main route linking the then important Armenian cities of Tabriz (in present-day Iran), Dvin and Kars. The caravanserai is commended as a stop for birdwatchers as it is an excellent location for the larks, wheatears and other birds of this arid plain.

The next point of interest heading west is **Talin** (*telephone code 2490*), also just south of the present main road. The **cathedral** here is more ornate than that at Aruch but the setting is spoilt by piles of rusty scrap metal lying around. The large church is surrounded by an extremely large area of tombstones. Like Aruchavank it was built in the 7th century. It has, however, three naves and is an altogether more impressive building of red and grey tuff with a 12-sided tambour decorated with arches into which windows are set. There is good 7th-century decoration around some of the windows. The remains of frescoes can be seen. The one in the apse probably depicts the Transfiguration while on the south wall can be seen a portion of the entry into Jerusalem. Talin lost its cupola in an earthquake in 1840 and was further damaged by another in 1931 although some restoration was carried out in

1947 and again between 1972 and 1976. The smaller church in a corner of the large site is roughly contemporaneous. An inscription records that Nerseh built it 'in the name of the Holy Mother of God for her intercession for me and my wife and Hrapat my son'. Unfortunately it isn't clear which of several Nersehs was involved.

Dashtadem A road runs south from Talin across the Talin Plateau eventually to drop down into the plains of Armavir province. Leaving Talin there is a very large **ruinous caravanserai** on the left: its sheer size is testament to the importance of the trade routes across Armenia. In about 6km the road reaches the village of Dashtadem. In the centre is a large **fortress** whose perimeter walls are entered through an arched gateway over which are interesting carvings of animals. Built according to the best theories of castle building, the gateway requires anyone entering to turn through a right angle thus preventing horsemen charging the entry. Within is a keep of the 9th or 10th century to which half-round towers have been added at some later date and under which large cellars can be explored. An Arabic inscription of the month of Safar 570 (ie: September 1174) on the fortress records that it was then under the control of Sultan Ibn Mahmud, one of the Shaddadid Seljuk princes who ruled in Ani. Five years ago we wrote 'amazingly this is not some preserved monument but home to several farmers who pile their hay up against medieval walls and also keep their livestock here. Dusk presents the extraordinary spectacle of the fortress's sheep arriving back from the fields to be followed by the fortress's cattle, a continuation of a routine seen throughout Europe in medieval days but where else now?' However, things have changed greatly. All but one of the houses lie derelict, some half demolished. There are no animals. The keep has been restored, not entirely felicitously, and the small 10th-century chapel against its inner wall has been rebuilt. It is possible to scramble up onto the walls of the keep from where there are good views but care is needed; there are no safety precautions. Rubble and metal barriers litter the site. It is to be hoped that the families displaced from the fortress now live in the new houses in the village outside. I wonder what the future plans for Dashtadem are. Work seems to have stopped, leaving the fortress in limbo, no longer a living community but not an appealing ancient monument either. Good views of the fortress on its hill can be obtained by continuing past the village along the main road. About 2km along this main road a khachkar marks a track going off left which leads to the restored 7th-century **Church of St Christopher**, built of rather forbidding grey stone, and with a more recent (13th-century) detached bell tower. Around the church is an extensive graveyard in use from the 6th century to the present day.

Mastara Mastara is yet another village now bypassed by the main road but the **church** here definitely warrants the short detour necessary to see it. Constructed of red tuff, most of the present structure dates from rebuilding carried out in the 7th century: it has never suffered significant earthquake damage. A surprisingly large construction, it has a massive octagonal tambour supporting a 12-panel cupola invisible externally because of its covering of grass. The tambour in turn is supported by eight large arches, or squinches, and eight smaller ones. This unusual design is found in other 7th-century churches which are referred to as being of the Mastara-type. Inside the church there is a great feeling of height – it is 21m from floor to cupola: the rather incongruous balcony on the west side dates from the building's use as a grain store for the local collective farm from 1935 until 1993. Unfortunately no money has yet been forthcoming for repairs to this important church. Over at the edge of the village the graveyard has a few gravestones in

4

the form of sheep together with what is claimed to be the largest khachkar in Armenia. The caretaker's young son accompanied us on one visit. I asked him why the cemetery had street lights. So, he said, people could visit the graves at night. Armenians normally consider it unlucky to visit a cemetery at night so I'm not convinced that his explanation is correct.

ARARAT PROVINCE

Mount Ararat is now in Turkey but the name of this province recognises that it is the part of present-day Armenia which approaches nearest to the biblical mountain: it is only some 33km from Khor Virap Monastery to the 5,165m (16,946ft) peak, separated from the lower 3,925m summit by the Anahit Pass. The whole massif looms high and spectacular above the plain, which is only around 900m above sea level, and the views are particularly stunning during the months of early summer (late May and early June) and autumn (late September and October) when visibility is at its best. Mount Ararat is especially beautiful in early morning and late evening. Armenians liken the snow-capped peak to a bride covering her head with a veil.

Ararat province has two distinct parts. There is fertile plain along the Arax Valley but most of the province is mountainous, rising to 2,445m at Mount Urts. Several fairly large areas within these mountains comprise the **Khosrov Reserve** and advance permission needs to be obtained either from the Ministry of Nature Protection in Yerevan (*Government Bldg 3, Republic Sq;* ↘ *10 521099, 519182;* e *info@mnp.am; www.mnp.am*) or from the reserve director (↘ *285 60655*) to visit them. **Tickets** (*entrance AMD3,000, guide AMD5,000, horse AMD5,000*) are also issued at the entrance to the reserve in Garni Gorge (see page 187). To the south the province is bordered by the detached Azeri region of Nakhichevan; the main road and rail links are of course closed at the border. The much smaller (a mere 7km²) Azeri enclave of Karki, astride the main road linking Yerevan with the south, was the scene of fierce fighting in the early 1990s, but the Azeri population has gone and the village is now inhabited by Armenians dispossessed from Azerbaijan. Karki has since been renamed Tigranashen.

The provincial capital of **Artashat**, 29km from Yerevan, is on the edge of the plain. It was established in 180BC by King Artashes I as his capital and retained that role until the reign of Khosrov III (AD330–38) when the capital was moved to Dvin. There is, however, little in the modern city to warrant a visit.

PRACTICALITIES There are no reasonable hotels in the province. Apart from visiting the main sights of Khor Virap and Dvin there is little to detain most visitors in Ararat. The towns of Artashat and Ararat have shops and eating places but none of note to warrant a detour. For details of minibuses to Artashat, Dvin village (not Dvin Museum) and Khor Virap see *Chapter 2,* page 75.

The main road between Yerevan and Yeraskh is flat and uninteresting but it can be an excellent place to buy fresh local produce and the first apricots to appear for sale are often found here. Fish from the Armash fish ponds can be bought on the main road near Yeraskh.

DVIN (*The site & museum* ⊕ *whenever the resident caretaker is at home (which he usually is); no entrance fee*) Heading south from Yerevan along the main road, the excavated ruins of the former capital Dvin lie about 10km to the east. Note that the position of Dvin on some maps is misleading. To **get there**, take the turn off for Artashat from the main road (M2) south. At the T-junction in Artashat turn left,

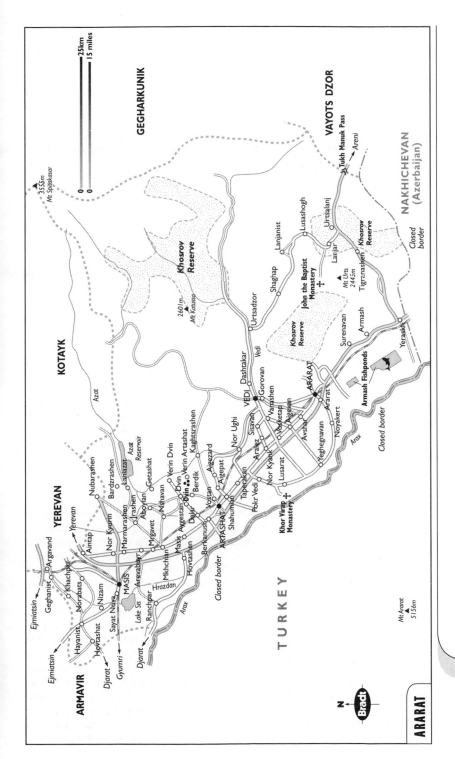

go through Mrgavan (now continuous with Artashat) and turn right in Berkanush onto the H9, signposted to Dvin. Do not go as far as the village of Dvin. Turn right 1km after leaving Aygestan (and 5.5km after turning right in Berkanush) onto the road for Hnaberd. Soon after leaving Hnaberd you come to a metal fence on the left. This is the fence around the site of Dvin and the entrance gate is a little further on. If asking locally for directions, be sure to ask for Hnaberd rather than Dvin. Simply push open the gate in the boundary fence and walk into the site.

Dvin served as the capital until the Arab conquest in AD640 when it became the seat of the governor. It was badly damaged by earthquakes in 863 and again in 893 but remained a significant town until the 13th century with a population, at its peak, probably of the order of 100,000. The second of these earthquakes destroyed what had been **Armenia's largest church**, dedicated to St Gregory and 58m long by 30m wide. Its foundations can be clearly seen, including the layout from at least two of its three rebuildings. Originally a pagan temple, it was rebuilt as a three-nave basilica with an east apse in the late 4th century. It acquired external arcaded galleries, of the sort which can be seen at Odzun, in the 5th century. Then in the 7th century it was rebuilt as a winged three-nave domed basilica, with apses also on the north and south. This church was slightly shorter, hence the double east apse seen today. Mosaics from its floor are now in the museum. North of the church are the foundations of the 7th-century **palace of the Katholikos** and a capital from one of its columns is now Dvin's best-known exhibit. East of this palace lay a single-nave **5th-century church**. An **earlier palace** (5th century) lay southwest of the main church. The small museum is surrounded by the caretaker's fruit trees. Its contents include finds from the site including examples of the glassware for which Dvin was renowned particularly in the 7th century. Outside are two large phalluses, one of which the caretaker uses as a stand over which to hang his jacket while the other serves as a towel rail thus combining utility with good taste. The extent of trade is evident in the finding here of coins minted in Byzantium while, conversely, coins minted at Dvin have been found in the Baltic states and Scandinavia. Behind the museum a path leads up the hill to the ruins of the **citadel** but it is difficult to form an idea of Dvin's historic appearance.

KHOR VIRAP MONASTERY (⊕ *09.00–18.00; free; minibuses from main railway station in Yerevan at 10.00 & 15.30, returning at 13.20, 15.20 &17.20; fare AMD400*)

Khor Virap ('Deep Dungeon'), prominently situated on a small hill in the Ararat plain, can be seen in the distance from the main road which passes 5km to the east. In contrast to Dvin, where few visitors ever go, Khor Virap receives so many that there are even souvenir stalls. They sell not only conventional souvenirs but also 'doves' – in reality homing pigeons – which the purchaser can then release to 'fly to Mount Ararat'. At any rate that's what the vendor claims they will do. In reality they fly straight back to him.

Khor Virap's historical significance is considerable, and there are, in clear weather, superb views of Mount Ararat, but architecturally the monastery is not particularly interesting. It is famous above all as the place where King Trdat III imprisoned St Gregory the Illuminator for 13 years in the late 3rd and early 4th centuries, and it is still possible to visit the subterranean cell where he was kept. However, although there was a monastery here by the 5th century, the present buildings are much more modern. Construction started in 1669. A large perimeter wall surrounds the **main church** with its 12-sided tambour and cupola. It is dedicated to the Mother of God. Rather plain otherwise, it has an elaborately decorated front to the altar dais. High on the eastern façade is a carving of St Gregory curing the possessed King Trdat.

Access to the cell where Gregory was imprisoned is from the smaller **St Gregory's Church** which is the barrel-vaulted structure at the southwest corner of the walls. To the right of the altar dais is the entrance hole from which a long ladder with 27 steps leads 6.5m down to the surprisingly large underground chamber; the first 2m of descent is very narrow, after which the hole widens. It tends to be stuffy in the chamber because of a lack of air circulation combined with the number of burning candles. It should be shunned by the claustrophobic and those who do venture down should take a torch. (Do not be confused by a second hole to the right of the door of the church. This leads to a separate underground chamber, possibly another prison. The entrance shaft is even narrower than that of St Gregory's prison, but children have been known to climb down.) A path goes uphill on the north side of the monastery. From the top of the hill it is possible to see minor evidence of the archaeological digs about which much detail is given on the USAID information boards; there are extensive views over the plain.

On a hillock to the left of Khor Virap as one approaches is a statue of Gevorg Chaush (1870–1907) who led Armenian *fedayi* (armed volunteers) in their struggle against the Turks in Sassoun province, the area in western Armenia around the source of the Tigris. He was killed in battle.

SOUTH FROM KHOR VIRAP The main road passes the town of **Ararat**, dominated by a large cement factory. Beyond Yeraskh the former main road and railway are both closed at the border and traffic must turn left at the roundabout to continue southward. Two passenger trains each day still travel this far from Yerevan, departing at 09.30 and 14.40. From here the present-day road turns east and starts to climb towards the **Tukh Manuk Pass** (1,795m) where it enters Vayots Dzor province. About 12km from Yeraskh the road crosses a former enclave of Azerbaijan: the Azeri village of Kharki, just south of the road, which is now the Armenian village of **Tigranashen**. Nineteen kilometres from Yeraskh a road branches left for **Lanjar**. Just beyond Lanjar tracks go left off this road as it crests a hill. Take the track which keeps to the right of the mountain, which in 7km reaches a **monastery** built in 1254 and dedicated to John the Baptist (older maps mark it as St Stepanos). The track passes the site of a summer village used by villagers pasturing their animals. Hospitality is impossible to avoid if on foot and difficult in a vehicle. The monastery is attractively situated but unfortunately seems always to be locked. It has a circular tambour and umbrella dome with a carving of the Holy family over the door. Above it is a second carving, presumably of God the Father.

ARMAVIR PROVINCE

The province is named after its capital, Armavir city, which is 46km west of Yerevan along a good dual carriageway. It is unlikely that anyone would choose to stay here as the main concentration of sights is in **Ejmiatsin**, or Vagharshapat as the city is now officially called, only 20km from Yerevan. The churches of Ejmiatsin together with the ruins of the one at Zvartnots were added to the UNESCO World Heritage List in 2000. The eastern part of the province merges imperceptibly with Yerevan's western sprawl where it includes Armenia's main international airport at Zvartnots. To the west the province comprises part of the flat and, in summer, hot plain of the broad Arax Valley. The Arax forms the border with Turkey in the south of the province while to the west the border is formed by the Akhurian River. There is little good hotel accommodation in the province but limited reason to stay here rather than in Yerevan anyway.

ARARAT

ARAGATSOTN

TURKEY

Yerevan

Sevan

Norakert

Zvartnots
Airport

Zvartnots
Church of
St George

Ashtarak

Amberd

Dasht

Shahumian

EJMIATSIN

Tsaghkunk

Artimet

Khorunk

Voskehat

Gai

Araks

Haykashen

Lernamerdz

Aghavnatun

Aragats

Tsaghkalanj

Samaghar

Haytagh

Arshaluys

Artashen

Griboyedov

Apaga

Jrarat

Yeraskhahun

Doghs

Taronik

Metsamor

Zartonk

Yeghegnut

Nuclear
power
station

METSAMOR

Aknalich

Arevik

Argavand

Argavand

Aigeshat

Tandzut

ARMAVIR

Mrgashat

Haykavan

Armavir

Noravan

Lukashin

Bambakashat

Nor
Armavir

Nor
Artages

Khanjian

Battlefield (1918) &
ethnographical museum
Sardarapat

Araks

Larughi

Nalbandian

Shenavan

Hatsik

Miasnikian

Arevadasht

Hushakert

Nor Kesaria

Dalarik

Baghramian

Koghbavan

Vanand

Talin

Karakert

Gyumri

Arteni

Argina

Shenik

Bagaran

Akhurian

Closed border

Closed border

Arax

Arax

Arax

Arax

Masis

N
Bradt

25km
15 miles

0
0

162

PRACTICALITIES The sights in the province are usually visited as day trips from Yerevan. Ejmiatsin has places to eat and there is a **restaurant** opposite St Hripsime Church (*Vargharshapat: 48 Mashots St, Ejmiatsin;* \ *231 49999;* m *091 216575. Restaurant is on the 1st floor, with good views across the road to St Hripsime. Wedding parties sometimes held here*). There is a café and a **restaurant** at Sardarapat (see page 170). If you are planning to spend time at Sardarapat in the heat of summer it would be wise to take something to drink with you.

EASTERN ARMAVIR

Zvartnots Cathedral (⊕ *10.00–17.45; guided tour in English AMD2,500; car parking AMD100; adult AMD700*) Leaving Yerevan along a road lined with furniture shops whose wares are hauled outside each morning and then hauled back at the close of business, the first point of less commercial interest is the ruin of the huge **Church of St George** at Zvartnots ('Celestial Angels'). It lies to the south of the road and the entrance driveway is marked by elaborate gates and an eagle with a ring in its beak gazing back over its shoulder, the work of the famous artist and sculptor Ervand Kochar. The church, built between 643 and 652 by Katholikos Nerses III, is believed to have been a three-storey structure but modern artists' impressions of its appearance are inevitably conjectural. Intended to surpass even Ejmiatsin Cathedral by its grandeur, it is usually thought of as having been circular but in reality had 32 equal sides. Decorated with frescoes, it was destroyed, probably by an earthquake in 930, to be lost under layers of dirt and debris and even the location was forgotten until its rediscovery in the early 20th century. Some limited reconstruction has been carried out, but protests have caused plans for a more thorough one to be held in abeyance. Inside the church the apse is now at a lower level than the main floor and there is what appears to be a baptistry in the floor reached by going down some steps, although it is now labelled as the reliquary of St Gregory Lusovorich, ie: the Illuminator.

At present the area on the east side is being used for laying out various stones according to which storey of the building they are thought to belong. There is some interesting sculptured decoration amongst the ruins, including one capital on the southeast pillar carved with a fine representation of an eagle; beyond the ruins can be seen the remains of other buildings including **Nerses's Palace** and a winery with vats sunk into the ground. To the west, walls stand to a height of 1.5m. At the southwest corner of the site is the **museum** (m *093 373928;* ⊕ *10.00–17.00 Tue–Sun; guided tours in Armenian AMD1,000 & English AMD2,500; adult/child AMD700/100*).

EJMIATSIN (*Telephone code 231*) The central square of the town is Komitas Square and a statue of Komitas by the same Ervand Kochar responsible for the eagle at Zvartnots was erected here in 1969.

Cathedral Ejmiatsin became the spiritual centre for Armenia's Christians shortly after the country's conversion in the early 4th century.

On the basis of archaeological evidence the first monastery at Ejmiatsin was of the basilica form but it was rebuilt in the 480s on a cruciform plan with four free-standing piers, four projecting apses which are circular on the interior and polygonal on the outside, and with a cupola. It was this second church, with cupola, which corresponds to Agathangelos's report of Gregory's vision (see box page 166), a report which fixed in Armenian culture the idea that churches should be cruciform in shape and should have cupolas. Further rebuilding was carried out in the 7th

Some Armenian sources claim that Zvartnots Church is depicted upon Mount Ararat on one of the frescoes in the Church of Ste Chapelle in Paris. This is fanciful as Ste Chapelle is noted not for its frescoes but rather for its stained glass which does indeed portray biblical stories including that of Noah's Ark. However, Ste Chapelle was not built until the 1240s and it seems unlikely that the French still had a record of what Zvartnots had once looked like some 300 years after its destruction. In the undated booklet on Zvartnots in the series *Historical Monuments of Armenia* (a series of small, cheap and possibly old, booklets on architectural ensembles, occasionally encountered at monuments but not always at the monument the booklet describes) it says 'Zvartnots is depicted in the relief devoted to the flood on the wall of St Chapel [*sic*] church in Paris'. Two pictures are shown of a carving of a boat, the superstructure of which resembles the appearance of Zvartnots proposed by Toromanian in 1909 but the above argument would apply equally to carved reliefs as to frescoes or stained glass. Another source suggests that it is St Grigor in Ani which is depicted on the reliefs although photographs of the ruins of St Grigor do not match the relief, apart from the fact that both are round. Anyway, it was actually King Gagik's church (not St Grigor) in Ani which was built, in AD1000, as a copy of Zvartnots but being unstable it collapsed some 25 years later. By the time Ste Chapelle was being built 200 years later the site of King Gagik's church was covered by houses and was presumably also forgotten.

century and Ejmiatsin remained the seat of the Katholikos until 1065 when the then Katholikos Gregory II was forced to flee by the Turkish Seljuk invaders who were ransacking monasteries. He moved to the Armenian principality of Cilicia (roughly the region of present-day Turkey around Adana and Tarsus at the extreme northeast corner of the Mediterranean Sea) and the seat of the Katholikos remained there even after Cilicia fell to the Egyptian Mamluks in 1375. Ultimately in 1441 a council decided that the seat of the Katholikos should return to Ejmiatsin. There are no records of any immediate reconstruction but the monastery was certainly in a very dilapidated state, with the roof in ruins and some facing stones having fallen, when in 1627 renovation eventually started. A wall was built around the precinct at this time and numerous service buildings were added. However, these were mostly destroyed in 1635–36 during the wars between Persia and Turkey for domination over Armenia and further rebuilding was required. The large three-storey bell tower was built in 1654 over the western doorway. Three smaller six-column rotundas were added at the beginning of the 18th century; that at the southern apse collapsed in 1921 to be replaced by a new structure.

Accordingly what visitors see now is the site of a pagan temple used as the site for a new Christian monastery in the 4th century, rebuilt in a quite different style in the 5th century and then very extensively renovated in the 17th. The tambour with its decorative medallions and cupola, the elaborately carved bell tower, surrounding wall, service buildings and much of the exterior carving are pure 17th century. The cathedral is surrounded by gardens in which khachkars brought from different parts of greater Armenia have been erected. Entered from the north perimeter wall is an attractive new (2010) **baptismal chapel** with provision for both infant and adult baptism (by immersion). The **Treasury Museum** (as opposed to the museum in

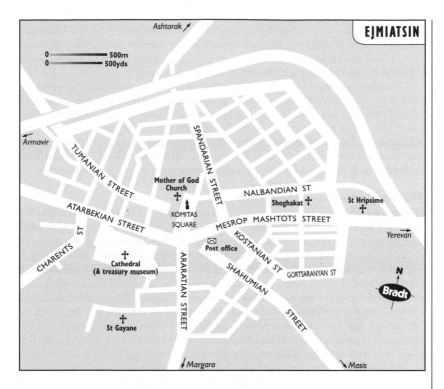

the cathedral) dates from 1869 and is one of the few Tsarist-era buildings here; the nearby seminary, closed during the Soviet period but reopened in 1997, is another. The carved wooden doors are also Tsarist-era and were made at Tbilisi in 1888. The oldest wall of the cathedral is the northern, which is 5th-century original. The exterior retains two 5th-century figured reliefs with Greek inscriptions, one showing St Thecla and St Paul, the other a cross flanked by two doves. The new gateway to the cathedral precinct commemorates the visit of Pope John Paul II in 2001.

In 1720, frescoes were added inside the cathedral but they were removed in 1891 only to be reinstated in 1956. The interior is still, as in AD480, dominated by the four massive free-standing pillars supporting the tambour. In the very centre is a stepped holy table bearing many candlesticks and crosses. Surrounded by a framework from which hang lamps and incense burners, it is said to mark the spot where the 'Only Begotten' appeared to St Gregory, telling him to build a church. The frescoes, the use of marble for floor and balustrade, the embroidered curtains, and the candles and crosses on the holy table give a much more decorative feel to the building than exists in any other church in Armenia.

The **Cathedral Museum** (⏰ *10.00–17.00, closed Mon, Sun it opens only after the end of the service – usually around 13.30 but later if there is something special such as an ordination; guided tours only; AMD1,500*) is reached through a door to the right of the altar dais. The museum isn't well labelled but English-speaking deacons are available who will also take visitors down to the old altar of the original pagan temple before requesting a donation. The treasury contains some curious items including what is claimed to be the lance which pierced the side of Christ, brought to Armenia by the apostle Thaddeus and long kept at Geghard, the hand of St Gregory the Illuminator, wood from Noah's Ark (carbon-dated to 6,000 years old), a drop of St Hripsime's blood and similar relics as well as more ordinary ecclesiastical pieces. Interested visitors can also arrange in advance (through a tour operator in Yerevan; see pages 55–6) for admission to the separate Treasury Museum in the Old Residence where a similar collection of historic ecclesiastical items is displayed.

The **cathedral shop** (⊕ *09.00–18.00 daily*), on the left as one enters the precinct, has a wide range of books and a selection of tasteful souvenirs. At the time of writing several buildings were under construction in and around the cathedral grounds: a tower-like chapel to the northwest (to be dedicated to the archangels Gabriel and Michael) for the use of seminary students, a guesthouse and charity hospital on land between the cathedral and St Gayane and, to the southwest, an educational building which will also house a display of manuscripts from the Matenadaran.

The other churches at Ejmiatsin

St Hripsime St Hripsime was one of the refugee nuns from Rome in the late 3rd century who were persecuted under the rule of King Trdat III and the king himself tried to rape her. This 7th-century church dedicated to her is unquestionably one of Armenia's architectural gems. Built by order of Katholikos Komitas in 618 it now unfortunately finds itself surrounded by undistinguished buildings between the main road in from Yerevan and the bypass. The present church is built over the mausoleum of the saint, which was constructed in 395. The church has proved more resistant to earthquake damage than many more modern buildings and its appearance has remained almost unchanged apart from the addition of a small portico on the west side and a cross on the roof in the 17th century. The separate bell tower was built in 1790. Standing on a raised paved area above the road and with the old fortified wall on the west side, the very pale pink tuff church is essentially a cross-dome church, with a 16-sided tambour, although it is more square than most. It has four apses with a corner room between each apse. Each corner room is, unusually for Armenia, separated from the central part of the church by a circular chamber. As so often, the cruciform shape of the church itself is not obvious from the exterior. It is also unusual in that the northeast corner room is reached by going down steps and that there is a mosaic depicting the Virgin and Child behind the altar. A **souvenir shop** is to the left of the steps going up to the paved area which is likely to be open whenever there is the chance of a visitor buying something.

LEGENDARY ORIGINS OF EJMIATSIN CATHEDRAL

According to Agathangelos's *History of the Armenians*, written in about 460, St Gregory the Illuminator saw a vision in which the heavens opened and a blaze of light shone upon the earth. Through the light a procession of angels came down to the earth headed by the tall and glorious figure of Christ. Carrying a golden hammer, he came down and struck the ground three times with it. A column instantly arose with a circular base of gold and a tall column of fire with a capital of cloud and cross of light. Similar visions appeared at three other sites where Hripsime, Gayane and another of their companions were martyred. The columns transformed themselves into churches covered by clouds whose shape was that of a cupola. After the vision faded, Gregory founded the Monastery of Ejmiatsin ('Descent of the Only Begotten') on the spot where Christ had struck the hammer. In reality the monastery was founded, like many others in Armenia, on the site of a pagan temple whose altar can still be visited.

St Gayane St Gayane was the abbess of the fleeing nuns persecuted by Trdat III. Her church is slightly later, rather more pleasantly situated, and of quite different style. The present church was built by order of Katholikos Ezr in 630 on the site of Gayane's martyrium. By the early 17th century it was forlorn, the roof having collapsed to leave just the walls and piers standing. Major reconstruction was therefore carried out in 1651–53 and a chapel was constructed under the east apse for the saint's relics. Unlike St Hripsime's church, St Gayane's is of the longitudinal basilica style and with an apse and corner rooms only at the east end. Free-standing pillars support the octagonal tambour. In 1683, a gallery was added at the west end: the three central arches are open while the smaller side ones built to house the remains of dignitaries of the church are blanked off and topped with six-column belfries. This gallery, prominent as one walks from the gate, gives the church a 17th-century appearance even though the main part of the building is older. On Sundays St Gayane's church is a popular place for sacrifices. The *orhnakar* is to the right of the main path leading to the front door while the *mataghatun* is in the southwest corner of the grounds.

Shoghakat This church was built in 1694 by Prince Aghamal Shorotetsi on the site of a chapel dedicated to one of Hripsime's and Gayane's anonymous companions. Coming here after visiting Ejmiatsin's other churches gives a clear picture of both continuity and change in Armenian church architecture. In particular the continued presence of a cupola atop a tambour, octagonal in this case, follows a tradition going back to the 5th century, but a prominent six-column belfry over the porch is evidence of 17th-century ideas. Similarly, the detailed ornamental carving in geometrical patterns could have been created at almost any time in the last 1,500 years. Few tourists ever go to Shoghakat, and certainly it does not compare to the main cathedral or St Hripsime, but it does provide interesting insights and locals claim that it marks the fourth place where St Gregory the Illuminator saw a vision of a column of fire.

Mother of God Church If few visitors go to Shoghakat, even fewer come here yet it has a Rococo-style altar which is unique in Armenia. The original church of 1767 was wooden and the present stone building dates from the 19th century. It was built as the village church for the ordinary people of Ejmiatsin as opposed to the members of the Holy See or of the monasteries and seminaries. Even now it is near a small market and overlooked by blocks of flats. A three-aisle basilica, it has paintings on the square columns depicting Christ, the Holy family and saints. The altar, painted sky blue and white and decorated with gold leaf is made of marble and wood and in an Italianate style. Outside, the bell tower was added in 1982.

CENTRAL ARMAVIR
Metsamor (Museum, archaeological site and ancient observatory)
(⊕ *Site always; museum: see below*) Given the lack of English at Metsamor a visit can be significantly enhanced by downloading beforehand the informative description of the site and museum from TourArmenia's website www.tacentral.com. Heading west from Ejmiatsin across the fertile plain, Metsamor nuclear power station can be seen to the right (see box, page 168). About 2km from the junction of the bypass with the turn off for Ejmiatsin a conspicuous monument to the left marks the spot where a Yugoslav plane bringing relief supplies for the victims of the 1988 earthquake crashed as it approached Zvartnots Airport killing all seven on board. Four kilometres beyond that a road leads off left towards the village of Taronik, with its many stork nests. Take this road and continue through the village until a

T-junction of surfaced roads. Turn right, continue through the village, then turn left immediately before the village cancellation sign. Follow this track through an area of fish ponds (and consequently quite good for little bittern, squacco heron and other birds favouring this habitat) towards the red tuff museum of Metsamor ('Black Swamp') which opened in 1971.

The small **museum** (⊕ *10.00–17.00 Tue–Sat, 10.00–15.00 Sun; guided tours, only in Armenian & Russian, are included in the price, but given how poorly the staff are paid, visitors may feel a tip is appropriate; AMD700*), which is badly in need of money being spent on it, is well worth visiting. It shows finds from the excavations at the site but there is minimal labelling in English and the staff do not speak English. Of particular interest is the basement where there is an exact reconstruction of one of the excavated royal tombs. The excavation of royal tombs has shown that the deceased were buried with feet to the east, presumably to face the rising sun, and in the foetal position within a sarcophagus in the early tombs but later lying within a casket. Royalty was buried not only with their jewellery and a supply of food and wine, but also with the domestic animals and decapitated human beings, presumably their slaves, who were slaughtered for the occasion. Also exhibited are some superb examples of gold jewellery, belt decorations in the form of lions, and a weight in the form of a frog made from agate and onyx. This weight, found around the neck of a woman, bears an inscription in Babylonian cuneiform. The ground and upper floors of the museum show examples of ceramics, jewellery, tools and other items including a very large phallus.

METSAMOR NUCLEAR POWER STATION

Metsamor nuclear power station is an early Soviet design, the first of its two 440 MW units being commissioned in 1976 and the second in 1980. In the immediate aftermath of the December 1988 earthquake there was concern lest Metsamor might have been damaged. It hadn't but nevertheless it was closed in March 1989 as a safety precaution. The energy blockade by Azerbaijan, imposed as part of the war over Nagorno Karabagh, resulted in catastrophic power shortages during the winters of 1992/93, 1993/94 and 1994/95. This was not only because electricity could not be imported but also the Armenian thermal power stations were dependent on imported gas supplies; those from Azerbaijan were cut off and the pipeline from Georgia was subjected to repeated guerrilla attacks within Georgia. Eventually in 1994 Armenia signed an agreement with Russia providing for Metsamor to be restarted with Russian help and one of the generating units was recommissioned in November 1995.

The main technical problem with Metsamor, apart from uncertainty over the quality of Soviet materials and workmanship, is the lack of a concrete containment vessel to contain radioactive leakage in the event of an accident. A plant spokesman is quoted as saying that it could withstand an earthquake of magnitude 9.0 on the Richter scale. The Armenian government, under considerable pressure from abroad, agreed to close it by 2004 provided other sources of generation could be developed. However, not surprisingly, other sources of generation did not materialise and the plant continues to function. A number of small hydro-electric stations are under construction throughout the country and the reliability of gas supplies has been increased by construction of a pipeline linking the Armenian and Iranian networks facilitating the import of gas not only from Iran but from Turkmenistan via Iran. The Armenian and Iranian electricity grids have also been linked. However, whether this will be sufficient to allow closure of Metsamor is

The small hill on which the museum stands is the site of an important Bronze Age **citadel**, around 30% of which has been excavated. Although there was occupation here much earlier the important remains and finds date from around 2000BC. Excavations have revealed an important metalworking industry, an astronomical observatory and considerable evidence of international trade.

The **excavated part of the site** lies just beyond the museum. The path from the museum crosses an extremely decrepit bridge and care is essential. The walls built in the second millennium BC can be seen; they were strengthened in the Urartian era. Up on the plateau are chambers and pits (those with runnels thought to be related to the metalworking industry) hewn into the rock. However, it is the ancient **observatory** where various markings can be seen on the stones which is likely to be of greatest interest. Archaeologists have suggested that it was used around 2800–2500BC to detect the appearance of Sirius, the brightest star in the sky, which may have been worshipped and which possibly marked the start of the year and indicated the time to start planting crops: at that epoch Sirius was visible in summer rather than in winter as it now is. If there is no-one from the museum free to show you the markings, walk along the path beside the megalithic walls in the direction of the power station, heading for a small outcrop of reddish rocks. By scrambling around on the far side of the rocks you will come across steps carved into the rock and it is in their vicinity that the markings are to be found. The easiest ones to see comprise a series of converging lines.

doubtful, particularly as Armenia's thermal generating plants are elderly and of low thermal efficiency. Metsamor was built with a 30-year design life and, since it had six years out of use, claims have been made that it could operate until 2016. Whether or not it does so may well depend on Armenia being able to fund a replacement able to supply the 40–45% of Armenia's electricity requirement which Metsamor currently satisfies.

Comparisons are sometimes made between Metsamor and the Chernobyl nuclear reactor in Ukraine which suffered a catastrophic accident with huge loss into the atmosphere of radioactive material while tests were being carried out in 1986. Such a comparison is misleading. Metsamor is a Pressurised Water Reactor (PWR) and uses light (ie: ordinary) water to cool the reactor and to generate steam. Water is also used as the moderator, the medium which slows down the neutrons to increase the chance of fission. It is therefore completely different in concept from the Graphite Moderated Water Cooled Reactor (RBMK is the Russian acronym) which failed at Chernobyl. The essential difference between the two is what happens if pockets of steam form in the coolant. In an RBMK reactor the excess steam does not lead directly to a change in the level of nuclear fission since that is controlled by the graphite moderator. Instead it leads to an increase in power generation which in turn leads to a further increase in steam, and a runaway cycle develops which is exacerbated because steam is also less effective as a coolant than water. (This is essentially what happened at Chernobyl when the normal link in the control system between thermal output and the degree of moderation had been temporarily disconnected for test purposes.) In the case of a reactor like Metsamor where water is the moderator as well as the coolant, the steam pockets increase the effect of the water in its role as moderator and so the level of nuclear fission declines.

4

Sardarapat A *marshrutka* from Yerevan to the village of Hushakert passes the entrance to the monument but it is one of many instances where the route is not listed in what schedules there are available. If using public transport a better option might be to travel to Armavir (see *Chapter 2,* page 76) then take a taxi. There are no taxis at Sardarapat so you would have to negotiate a price for waiting. Allow several hours.

The monument (⊕ *always*) To reach Sardarapat continue along the main road westwards as far as Armavir city. Just after what used to be a large brandy factory on the right (taken over by the French Pernod Ricard company and then closed) there is a flyover. It is necessary to turn left but to do so requires turning right and then right again over the flyover. Leaving the flyover the main road turns right at the T-junction. After leaving the suburbs of Armavir the road becomes dual carriageway again as far as Sardarapat whose striking **red tuff monument**, in the form of two Assyrian bulls facing each other separated by a structure from which bells are hung, can be seen straight ahead. This 35m-tall structure, contrasting with the massive bulls, is built in a form inspired by the stelae at Odzun, Lori province, and Aghudi, Syunik province.

The monument commemorates the victory by Armenian troops and irregular forces commanded by Daniel-Bel Pirumian over attacking Turkish troops who were coming down the railway from Alexandropol (Gyumri). The Battle of Sardarapat lasted from 22 May to 26 May 1918 and was a decisive victory resulting in the declaration of an independent Armenia on 28 May 1918. The monument was unveiled in 1968 to commemorate the 50th anniversary and each year on 28 May celebrations are held here: the bells are tolled and there are performances by folk song and dance groups.

The area surrounding the monument is meticulously well kept, perhaps because it has since 1998 come under the control of the Ministry of Defence: older women sweep the paths with besoms while younger ones weed the rose beds. The monument is on a small hill and is approached from the main road up a slope with steps. This commemorative monument is probably unique among those erected anywhere in the former Soviet Union in its appropriateness, stylishness and thankful absence of banal pseudo-heroic bombast. Its designer was the evidently gifted People's Architect of the USSR, Raphael Israelian (1909–73). At right angles to the approach slope, broad paths through gardens and flanked by eagles lead to a memorial wall covered with symbolic reliefs and penetrated by an arch. There is now also a memorial garden for the dead in the conflict over Nagorno Karabagh.

The ethnographical museum (⊕ *10.00–18.00 Tue–Sun; parking AMD100; guided tours in English, French, German & Russian AMD3,500; guidebook, with separate English supplement, AMD5,000; child/adult AMD300/700. Admission to the war museum hall costs an extra AMD300*) Sardarapat has a second, adjacent point of interest. There is an excellent museum which also includes some material about the battle. A path leads down to it from the memorial wall. Halfway along there is a **café** and to one side a **restaurant** (*both* ⊕ *12.00–18.00 in summer, approx late Apr/early May–Oct, depending on the weather*). While the food may not be Armenia's best they do at least provide a refuge from the midday heat. It can be extremely hot in the Arax plain in summer and there is very little shade at Sardarapat. Symbolically the museum has only two windows: one looking east towards Aragats and the other west towards Ararat. Apart from displays connected with the battle, it has good displays about life in the Arax Valley including finds from various archaeological sites in the valley along with displays of crafts such as carpet weaving, embroidery and lace making. There are also displays explaining the traditional farm tasks like butter making and other occupations such as armourer, blacksmith and goldsmith. A hall of contemporary sculpture, nothing more than 15 years old, has many intriguing pieces. The whole museum is well presented with good labelling, including in English.

GEGHARKUNIK PROVINCE

Gegharkunik comprises the area surrounding **Lake Sevan**, a large high-altitude lake whose surface level was originally 1,915m above sea level, and which formerly occupied almost 5% of the total surface area of the country. It is 78km long and 56km wide at its broadest point. Historic Armenia was a land of three large lakes but Lake Van is now in Turkey and Lake Urmia in Iran. The province also includes the beautiful and little-known valley of the Getik River which lies to the north of the lake. The Getik rises close to the Azerbaijan border and then flows northwest, roughly parallel to the lake shore but separated from it by the Areguniats range of mountains whose highest peak is **Mount Karktasar** (2,743m). The Getik flows into the Aghtsev River about 15km east of Dilijan.

The name Gegharkunik recalls early legends. Gegham was the great-great-grandson of Haik, the legendary founder of Armenia (see pages 11–12). Gegham left Armavir and moved north to Lake Sevan where he established a city which he called Gegh. The lake he called Geghamalich ('Gegham's lake'). The name of the province translates as 'Gegham's seat' since this is where he established his capital. The whole area around the lake is rich in prehistoric and historic remains. It seems that almost every village has a nearby Bronze or Iron Age fortress, megalithic tomb, medieval settlement or something else of interest,

Minibuses from Yerevan go to Sevan, Martuni, Chambarak and Vardenis (see *Chapter 2*, pages 74–6).

WHERE TO STAY AND EAT There is a lot of accommodation, mostly at the northwestern end of the lake, including many Soviet-era guesthouses run by various unions but at which anyone can stay and more recent small motel-type establishments. Some accommodaion is only open in the summer holiday season. The Tufenkian hotel at Tsapatagh on the eastern shore is a very pleasant hotel but not well located for the main tourist sights, although improvement in the road on that side of the lake has made the journey there much easier than it was. Apart from the hotels and restaurants listed below, summer sees many eating places opening around the lake, especially on the western side.

Harsnaqar (34 rooms) Tsamagaberd, Sevan; 261 20450, 20092, 22400, 23434; e reservation@harsnaqarhotel.am; www.harsnaqarhotel.am. One of the few hotels at the west end of the lake open all year. Built 2005. It has very pleasant rooms, & cottages (AMD90,000–100,000), which sleep up to 8 people, are also available. Entrance to Water World AMD1,500–2,000, depending on height. **$$$$**

Avan Marak Tsapatagh (34 rooms) Tsapatagh, Lake Sevan; contact via Tufenkian central office in Yerevan, 10 655877; e hotels@tufenkian.am; www.tufenkian.com; all year. This hotel opened in Dec 2002 & is a luxurious Tufenkian hotel situated further east at Tsapatagh. Its construction incorporates old stone barns. Outdoor swimming pool. The restaurant is in a separate building a few mins' walk away round the edge of the village but transport is available. Very pleasant hotel but not well located. It is 57km from Sevan town. The lake shore is about 10mins' walk away, crossing the railway (only 1 train daily each way – the freight train to & from

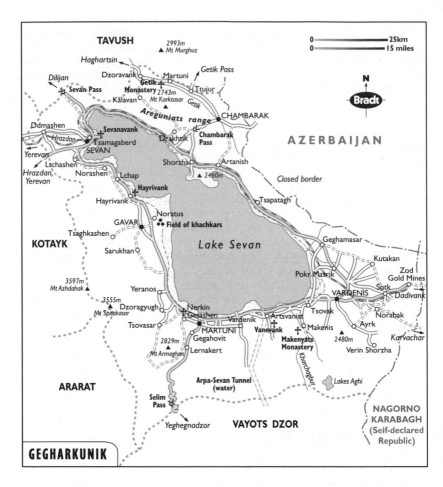

GEGHARKUNIK

the Zod gold mines), the road & an area which was formerly lake but is now sea buckthorn *Hippophae rhamnoides* scrub. A small area of scrub on the shore itself has been cleared for the benefit of guests. Prices vary depending on size of room & view of lake. **$$$–$$$$**

🏠 **Blue Sevan** (49 rooms) Chambarak; ☎ 10 288277 (Yerevan number), 261 60021/2; e bluesevan@ymail.com; www.bluesevan.com; ⏰ May–Oct. Note that although the postal address is Chambarak, this hotel is not in the town of Chambarak but is on the north shore of Lake Sevan. A well-renovated pleasant hotel set in wooded grounds. Helpful staff. Geared to families from Yerevan. Price varies with floor (cheapest on ground floor) & view of lake. Cards only accepted at Yerevan office. Also has cottages, AMD150,000, which sleep up to 6 people. **$$**

🏠 **Ashot Yerkat Restaurant/Hotel Complex** (8 rooms) Sevan Peninsula; ☎ 261 25000; m 091 025000, 091 500043; ⏰ all year. Near the car park for peninsula monasteries. Mainly a restaurant, one of the best. & ideal for coffee & pastries (their baklava is delicious) when visiting Sevanavank. **$$**

🏠 **Arevik** (8 cottages) Near Harsnaqar, Lake Sevan; m 094 210534; ⏰ closed in winter (Nov–Mar, depending on the weather). Each cabin-like cottage has 2 dbl rooms. B/fast extra, approx AMD2,000 pp. **$**

🏠 **Khrchit Restaurant/Hotel** (3 rooms) 100 Kamo St, Martuni (see comment on Martunis, page 179); ☎ 262 42964; m 091 228881, 094 030810; ⏰ all year. This restaurant, our favourite of several in Martuni, now has 3 very nice en-suite dbl rooms, with the advantage of readily available meals. B/fast extra, approx AMD1,000 pp. **$**

Homestays are of course available and were the only real option for places like Martuni until the recent availability of a small number of rooms at the Khrchit restaurant; see opposite. I have personal experience of one homestay:

🏠 **Artem & Nara Barseghian** (2 rooms) 34 Andranik St, Vardenis; 269 23147; m 094 769876; e 34.andranikst-artbar@rambler.ru; http://vardenis.free.fr (in French). The meals at this welcoming homestay are excellent with much homegrown produce, including the preserves at b/fast. Don't be surprised if a tot of brandy in your mug of tea is suggested: it's actually not bad at all! The house occupies 2 buildings, bedrooms in one, bathroom & dining room in the other. Lunch or evening meal AMD4,000 pp. **$**

OTHER PRACTICALITIES The towns in the province are small but like all small towns in Armenia they have all basic facilities. Lake Sevan's beaches are very popular with Armenians and in summer, particularly at weekends, it can be very busy.

LAKE SEVAN

History Lake Sevan, which now enjoys national park status, is fed by 28 rivers but there is only one flowing out, the Hrazdan which flows out of the lake at the western end to become a tributary of the Arax. In 1910, the Armenian engineer Soukias Manasserian published a book entitled *The Evaporating Billions and the Stagnation of Russian Capital* in which he proposed reducing the depth of the lake from 95m to 45m, using the water for irrigation and hydro-electric generation. The reference to 'evaporating billions' is a comment on the fact that 90% of the lake's water is lost through evaporation. (Manasserian also produced a plan to reduce the level of the Aral Sea, a much better-known environmental disaster.) Manasserian's scheme was developed in the Stalin era and approved by the then Armenian Soviet government though inevitably without any consultation with local people. The plan was later changed to reduce the level of the lake by 55m which would result in a reduction in its perimeter from 260km to 80km and its volume of water from 58km³ to 5km³. With breathtaking lack of realism it was planned that this drastic reduction in size would be accompanied by an equally drastic increase in the yield of fish caught in the lake of between eight and ten times to be achieved by releasing trout fry from hatcheries into the remains of the lake. A typical Stalin-era writer stated that Lake Sevan's 'scraggy, barren shores will be turned into sweet-smelling meadows, groves of nut trees and oak trees ... Around it beautiful roads and promenades will be laid ... There could be no objection to diminishing the size of the lake for it would merely mean diminishing the annual evaporation of a vast quantity of moisture that rose uselessly into the air.'

Work began in 1933 to implement the scheme when the Hrazdan was deepened to increase the discharge from the lake. A tunnel was also bored 40m below the original lake level but, because of delays caused by the war, it was not inaugurated until 1949 and was then trumpeted as a major achievement of the Soviet era. The lake level started to drop by more than 1m per year.

After Khrushchev's speech criticising Stalin at the 20th congress of the Communist Party of the Soviet Union in 1956, the wisdom of the Sevan venture started to be questioned. Already problems were starting to become manifest such as the difficulty of growing the promised nut trees and oak trees on the newly exposed shore together with a reduction in catch of the four subspecies of the endemic Sevan trout *Salmo ischachan*. In 1958, a 'Sevan Committee' was formed and the Soviet government decreed that the lake level was to be kept as high as possible with new thermal power stations replacing two of the originally projected eight hydro-electric ones. The new power stations were to be completed by 1970 but removing water for irrigation purposes was to cease by 1965. As a result of the action then taken the water level stabilised in 1962 at 18m below the original level but then eutrophic algal blooms started to occur, for the first time in 1964. A new tunnel, 49km long, was also constructed, intended to bring 200 million cubic metres of water each year north from the Arpa River into the lake. Completed in 1981 the tunnel only succeeded in raising the water level by 1.5m and a second tunnel 22km long was considered necessary to divert a further 165 million cubic metres each year from the Vorotan into the Arpa and thence to the lake. (This tunnel was only completed in 2003.) Matters deteriorated after 1988 as a consequence of the economic blockade of Armenia during the war over Nagorno Karabagh and the simultaneous closure of Metsamor nuclear power station. The Hrazdan River hydro-electric stations had to be operated more to maintain at least limited electricity supplies in Armenia and the level of the lake fell 20m below its original level with a surface area of 940km^2 in comparison with the former 1,360km^2.

Common whitefish *Coregonus lavaretus*, known as *sig* in Armenia, were introduced in the 1920s from Lake Ladoga. This species is also found as a relict species in various lakes in western Britain where it is called the powan, though another closely related fish also shares that name. The idea was that, as the whitefish were shallow-water feeders and the trout fed in deep water, the two could co-exist. In reality, the whitefish did not at first thrive, but changes in the lake caused by the reduction in level with an associated rise in temperature, and the use of agricultural fertilisers in the area round the lake gave rise to conditions which favoured the whitefish but not the trout. The trout are now on the verge of extinction in Armenia although they survive in Lake Issyk-kul in Kyrgyzstan where the species was introduced. Catching the endemic trout has been prohibited since 1976 but the ban is poorly enforced. It is also possible that the introduced crayfish *Astacus leptodactylus* is another competitor and goldfish *Carassius auratus* have also been accidentally introduced.

So far as the whitefish are concerned, falling numbers are giving cause for concern and the Ministry for Nature Protection now imposes a quota on the weight which can be caught each year together with a complete ban during the spawning season which runs from late November to mid December. There is, however, no way of enforcing the quota, and the local fishermen say that there is no way they can afford to cease fishing for the three or four weeks of the spawning season. There is a proposal to ban the netting of fish completely for three to four years. Fish can still be bought on the lakeside but they are no longer openly displayed. Instead the fisherman indicates to likely passing cars that he has fish for sale with the same gesture usually used to show the size of the one that got away. If crayfish are for sale the hand is held in a mimetic position, thumb, ring and little fingers together with index and middle fingers wiggling like the antennae of the creature. The decline in numbers is largely caused by overfishing but common carp *Cyprinus carpio* which appeared in the lake in the 1980s also compete with the whitefish for food.

The Armenian government's policy is to raise the lake level to 1,904m (a level last seen in 1957 but still some 11m lower than the original 1,915m) by the year 2031. To take the level higher than this would cause great problems because of the building and construction which has taken place on the drained land. By late 2009 a level of 1,899m had been reached. The newly flooded areas are conspicuous at all points around the lake. If the government's target is reached some 1,697 buildings and structures on the lakeside will be submerged, according to the chairman of the Lake Sevan Commission. Only 481 of these buildings are legally authorised and for these compensation will be paid. The rest will be demolished without compensation. A 15km section of the main road around the lake will also be submerged and will have to be rebuilt elsewhere. Already on the west side of the lake vehicles have to negotiate a considerable stretch of temporary dirt causeway across an area being inundated.

Visiting the lake today To those accustomed to the lakes of Switzerland or the lochs of Scotland, Lake Sevan with no mountains tumbling down to the water's edge will initially seem bare and windswept. Its real attraction lies in the ever-changing colours of its surface and in the skies above it. It is also, particularly on its southern side, an area with a long history and with a great many interesting places to see. Even these historical sites bring forcibly home the problems of the lake: the best known, the monastery of Sevanavank, was formerly on an island but falling water levels have turned the island into a peninsula and visitors travel there by road rather than by boat. Other attractions of the lake, for Armenians at least, are the beaches, the only ones in Armenia. While Western visitors would be unlikely to consider landlocked Armenia as a possible destination for a beach holiday, the beaches do provide a unique experience within the country for Armenians. Privatisation has resulted in visitors having to pay to use some of those adjacent to hotels but, in compensation, they are now looked after properly and kept clean.

Many buildings are springing up on the lakeside. There is no robust planning-permission system and an owner of land can build more or less anything regardless of how inappropriate it might be. Perhaps the owners hope to make enough of a profit before lake levels rise and their buildings are demolished. One hopes that the shores of Lake Sevan will not suffer the same fate as Yerevan's green belt.

THE WESTERN SIDE OF LAKE SEVAN
Sevanavank (monastery) This monastery is one of Armenia's most-visited tourist sights. The reduction in the level of the lake has both reduced the picturesqueness of the setting – it is now on a peninsula rather than an island – and boosted the number of tourist buses arriving. Although worth visiting, it is not really one of Armenia's most appealing places and owes its popularity largely to its proximity to the lake and to its accessibility from Yerevan. It is on the southwest slope of a hill overlooking the west end of Lake Sevan. The surviving buildings comprise the Mother of God Church, the smaller Holy Apostles Church, together with a ruined *gavit*. An inscription on the **Holy Apostles Church**, the oldest of the churches and situated at the northeast of the complex, states that the monastery was founded in 874 by Princess Miriam, wife of Prince Vasak of Syunik, and daughter of the Bagratid King Ashot I. This was a time when Armenia was emerging from subjugation under the Arab caliphate and the church was one of the first to be built in Armenia after more than 200 years of Arab Islamic domination. Not surprisingly the architects resorted to 7th-century practice in developing the design. Despite what the inscription says about Ashot being king, in 874 this was a little premature. By judicious exploitation of others' enforced absence at the caliph's court in Samarra, Ashot was able to amass great power and in 862 the caliph awarded him with the title Prince of Princes. Ashot managed to remain neutral in the wars between the caliph's Arab forces and the Byzantine Emperor Basil I which were being waged when Sevan Monastery was built. The caliph was only to give Ashot the title King in 884, ten years after the date of the inscription; he was later followed in doing so by the Byzantine emperor.

Holy Apostles is a typical and plain cross-dome church and, in the absence of corner rooms, its interior shape can be seen from the outside. There is a large doorway between the south and west arms and a small chapel with an apse between the south and east arms. The octagonal tambour has four small windows. Pending renovation it is kept locked.

The larger **Mother of God Church** is in similar style and lies to the southeast of the Apostles Church; it too has an octagonal tambour. The small chapels were probably later additions. There are two features of particular interest. One is an extremely elaborate 13th-century basalt khachkar. At the top right is God the Father with right hand raised in the Armenian style of blessing – tips of thumb and ring finger touching with the other three fingers upright representing the Trinity. He is surrounded by the symbols of the four evangelists – eagle, bull, ox and angel. At the top left is God surrounded by angels. The central panel shows Jesus on the cross flanked by Mary and St John. To the right of Jesus are panels showing his birth, the ox and ass, and the three kings. To his left are panels showing scales weighing good and evil, three figures and abstract decoration. Below Jesus, God is shown expelling Adam and Eve from Eden. The other notable feature is the wooden altar screen, part carved and part painted. It is most un-Armenian, being a gift in 1824 from the Monastery of St Thaddeus, south of Maku in present-day Iran.

Off the Mother of God Church is a ruined *gavit* in which are displayed pieces of khachkars found hidden in the cupola of the church. Its roof once rested on six detached wooden columns. The finely carved wooden capitals from the *gavit* depicting a chalice and the tree of life flanked by two doves are now in the Historical Museum in Yerevan, as are two carved walnut doors also from the *gavit*, one dating from 1176 and the other from 1486.

The monastery was one of the first seminaries to reopen in Armenia after the Soviet period. In the past being here was not necessarily a matter of choice. The French expert on the Caucasus Jean-Marie Chopin who visited the island monastery in 1830 reported that the regime was extremely strict with no meat, no wine, no youths and no women. It therefore served as a reformatory for those monks banished for their misdemeanours from Ejmiatsin. Another visitor reported that as late as 1850 manuscripts here were still being copied by hand. On the peninsula today is also the guesthouse of the president.

Ddmashen The village of Ddmashen, 12km west of Sevan, though probably more easily reached from Hrazdan in Kotayk province, has an interesting **7th-century church** of domed basilica construction. Its incongruous appearance is the result of a new 16-sided tambour being built in a different coloured stone in 1907 following earthquake damage. Very plain inside, it has a surprising number of windows, presumably added at a later date but not marring the feel of this early church.

Hayrivank (monastery) Heading southeast from Sevan along the south side of the lake the road passes through Ltchashen, site of the discovery of the Bronze Age burial chariot now on display in Yerevan's State History Museum. It is about 22km to the Monastery of Hayrivank; it can be seen on a knoll to the left of the road overlooking the lake. The monastery and surrounding rocks are all conspicuously covered with reddish-orange lichen. The monastery consists of a church from the end of the 9th century, a *gavit* from the 12th and a small chapel. The topography of the rather cramped site with the ground falling away quite steeply has resulted in the south and west arms of the church being no longer discernible from the outside, as the *gavit* and chapel had to be built forming one continuous wall with them. As with the churches at Sevan the tambour is octagonal but here the church exhibits some fine interior carving and the multi-coloured interior of the dome is also striking. Every interior wall of the *gavit* is covered with carved crosses. There are several attractive khachkars at the monastery and just north of it can be seen the scanty remains of a fortress occupied from the Bronze Age until medieval times.

Gavar   Not far beyond Hayrivank the main road bypasses the rather uninteresting provincial capital of Gavar which was founded as Nor Bayazit (ie: New Bayazit) in 1830 by Armenian migrants who had left Bayazit, Turkey, following the Turkish defeat by Russia. In 1959, it was renamed Kamo, the *nom de guerre* of Simon Ter-Petrosian (1882–1922), one of a number of Bolshevik supporters who raised money for the party by robbing banks in particular, but also post offices and railway ticket offices. He died in a road accident in Tbilisi. The city changed its name again following the Soviet collapse. Most of Gavar's industry has closed but the hosiery factory survives, exporting to the other CIS countries and seeking niche markets elsewhere. There is a Soviet-era **hotel** in Gavar, reported to be not as clean as it might be but which apparently serves a good dinner.

Noratus field of khachkars (⊕ *always*)   After the Gavar turn-off the main road heads south and skirts the edge of Noratus, home to one of Armenia's most amazing sights – the **field of khachkars**. Turn left off the main road at one of those preposterously over-engineered Soviet-era road junctions that must originally either have had some military rationale or else have been designed by someone with a penchant for grandiosity. On the eastern edge of the town is a huge **cemetery** with a modern section which is quite interesting but with an array of stones from the medieval period onwards where the range and fascination of the khachkars are overwhelming. Although there are many groups of khachkars in Armenia, nowhere can rival the impression which the approximately 900 here make. It is quite impossible to do justice to the carved stones on a single visit and one can merely wander across the site gazing in amazement at a row of 15 erect ones here, an area of recumbent ones there, no two alike. Stones with single crosses, stones with multiple crosses, geometric patterns, naturalistic ones: it is quite impossible to take in the riot of carved detail. Perhaps the sheep who graze here every day eventually learn to appreciate the detail but mere tourists don't have a chance. (The old women who tend the sheep like having their photographs taken and will remonstrate if you neglect to do so, sometimes persisting to such an extent that it can become a problem. They have hand-knitted socks and gloves for sale.) Quite why so many khachkars were erected here is not clear; possibly not all are tombstones and some may mark events other than death. A useful description of the Noratus cemetery walking tour recently instituted by the Armenian Monuments Awareness Project can be found on their website (see *Chapter 2, Tourist information*, page 53). Visitors should note that, like all khachkars which are still in their original positions, these face west and can therefore most easily be photographed in the afternoon.

Nearby, in the centre of the village of Noratus stands the small white 9th- or 10th-century **Church of St Gregory** with its relatively high cylindrical tambour. The narrow front of the church combines with the small rooms on the outside, which look as if they were built as later additions, the high tambour and the conical dome to give the appearance of a space rocket. There is, however, typical Armenian carving over the doorway and the altar dais inside is conspicuously large for the size of building.

Dzoragyugh and Nerkin Getashen   These two villages which lie south of the main road have interesting historic churches and also provide a picture of Armenian village life in the 21st century. **Dzoragyugh** ('Gorge Village') is home to two churches, both of which were founded in the late 9th century shortly after Sevanavank. The larger, ruinous one, Shoghagavank, dedicated to St Peter, is situated on a hill at the western end of the village. To reach it, having taken the Dzoragyugh turn-off from the main road, go straight ahead through the village; the church can be seen from afar. It was built between 877 and 886 and its founder was the same Princess Miriam who founded Sevanavank. The site again has a good array of khachkars, and is where local royalty are thought to be buried, but it is no rival for Noratus. Dzoragyugh's other church is harder to find. Near the entrance to the village, 3km from the main road, bear left at the post office onto a track which does a big loop to cross a small river. Keep the wooded river gully on your left and eventually the church will be seen among houses. It still functions as the village church today and is extremely well cared for. Its interior, one of the first to have carpets on the floor and on the altar dais, is decorated with, among other things, a carpet hanging on the wall depicting the Last Supper (and owing its composition to Leonardo da Vinci) as well as various embroideries. A large wrought-iron chandelier hangs from the ceiling. Originally built as the Masruts Anapat ('Hermitage of Masru') it was subsequently extended and now presents a plain, square appearance. Today it is known as St John the Baptist. The cupola and tambour are octagonal. The lower, older parts of the building are constructed of dark grey, rough-hewn basalt blocks, and contrast rather startlingly with the upper parts and tambour which are formed of red tuff, and some modern repairs effected with concrete blocks.

The next village, **Nerkin Getashen** ('Lower Getashen') was at one time the summer residence and administration centre of the Bagratid dynasty. It can be reached either from the Sevan–Martuni road or the road south from Martuni; although it's not signposted from either road. On the road south turn first right in Martuni, at traffic lights. A new asphalt road leads through the village and up to the cemetery. The large Mother of God Church (part of what was Kotavank), built of dark grey basalt was founded, again in the late 9th century, but this time by Miriam's son, Gregory Supan. It is almost square in external appearance thanks to the large corner rooms which conceal the internal cross shape. The dome and parts of the walls collapsed during the 17th century and only the east façade remains intact. Nonetheless the building still presents an impressive appearance today. However, the local Christian community opted to build a new church, at the foot of the hill below the old one, rather than seek to repair the damage of more than three centuries. Many interestly carved tombstones and khachkars stand around the church and the adjacent hill is likewise covered.

THE SOUTHERN SIDE OF LAKE SEVAN

Martuni and beyond The main road passes through Martuni where the road over the **Selim Pass** (2,410m) branches off right and goes south into Vayots Dzor province, being the only road linking northern and southern Armenia which avoids the capital. It has been upgraded and can now be used by all vehicles although it is impassable during much of the winter because of snow. Upgrading has taken away some of the pass's charm and has also reduced sightings of steppe eagles, black vultures and griffon vultures which were characteristic of the rolling uplands on this northern side. One of Armenia's most interesting sights, the intact 14th-century **Selim caravanserai**, is adjacent to the road but over the provincial border in Vayots Dzor. On the north side of the pass within Gegharkunik there is at **Geghovit**, the first village south from Martuni, a ruined 5th-century church dedicated to St George, and there are **petroglyphs** on Mount Sev Sar to the east of the road.

Martuni acquired its present name in 1926: Martuni was the *nom de guerre* of Alexander Miasnikian, the first prime minister of Armenia in Soviet days. The renaming of towns here manages to create particular confusion as there is another Martuni, also in Gegharkunik province but in the Getik Valley north of the lake. It is always necessary therefore to specify which Martuni one means: the northern one seems usually to be called Martuni Krasnoselsk region even though Krasnoselsk (Russian for 'red village') has officially reverted to its former name of Chambarak. Just to add to the confusion there is a third Martuni in Nagorno Karabagh.

Beyond Martuni the road swings east. After about another 20km it crosses the short channel which links the hydro tunnel bringing the water from the Arpa River to Lake Sevan and immediately afterwards the village of **Artsvanist** lies to the south of the road. Of the two roads into Artsvanist, the easternmost one is better and shorter. In a gorge on the southern side of the village is the secluded and appealing **Monastery of Vanevank**. It's probably best to park at the post office and walk down the track which is initially on the right-hand side of the river, then crosses to the left. The main church, dedicated to St Gregory and at the left-hand side, was built in 903 by Prince Shapuh Bagratuni together with his sister Miriam, the same Miriam who was also responsible for other churches in the district already mentioned. It was restored at the end of the 10th century by King Gagik I Bagratuni when the surrounding wall was built, parts of which can still be seen, notably on the hillside above and behind the monastery. The rather plain church building is itself basalt but the octagonal tambour is of contrasting red tuff. The right-hand church is barrel-vaulted and without a dome. It has a somewhat elongated appearance and is also built of basalt but has contrasting red tuff at the top of the gable ends. The *gavit* between the two churches was added at a later date. It has a bell tower and in the east part is what appears to be a burial vault.

Makenis Makenis is reached by continuing east from Artsvanist for about 6km and then turning right to head south for another 5km. The road to Makenis is in poor condition. Once in Makenis, bear left, then just before reaching the large school building turn sharp right and then left at the post office to reach the main gate of **Makenyats Monastery**, picturesquely situated at the edge of the village overlooking the Karchaghbur River. Quite apart from the monastery, Makenis is an evocative village with its livestock, dirt roads and dung drying for fuel. According to 13th-century chroniclers, the monastery was founded by Prince Gregory Supan in 851. This seems slightly early and a date later in the 9th century seems more plausible. It is a three-apse cross-dome church built of basalt with a circular tambour and surrounded by a substantial wall. There are large chapels on both sides of the altar dais with carved doorways and through the northern one water runs. At the west end there are large high corner rooms. Carvings of horses decorate the base of the southern pillar and the inside of the lintel of the main door. At the west gable is a small belfry. There is also a baptismal font. The *gavit* is now ruined but there is a small chapel to the southwest. The river must have changed its course slightly since the monastery was built, as the conspicuous latrine in the perimeter wall is now a few metres from it. There is a good collection of khachkars, some of which have been incorporated into garden walls and one of which has been removed to act as a bridge over a modern irrigation channel.

Vardenis and Ayrk Vardenis is the principal town in the eastern part of Gegharkunik and looks as though it experienced better days before it became almost a dead end following the closure of the border with Azerbaijan. After leaving the main square the roads of the town are in a bad condition. Even worse is the road running southeast to **Ayrk** which has two small medieval churches. Ayrk itself is pleasantly set in rolling countryside but looks poor and even more rundown than Vardenis with many empty houses, probably deserted by fleeing Azeris and, with little potential employment to attract Armenians fleeing in the opposite direction, they have remained unoccupied. The two churches are about 150m apart. Both have barrel-vaulted roofs and good collections of khachkars. The northernmost church, dedicated to the Mother of God, dates from 1181 and the southernmost, St George's, is slightly later.

THE EASTERN SIDE OF LAKE SEVAN Although Vardenis is virtually a dead end so far as Armenians are concerned, this is not necessarily the case for tourists. They can either continue the circumnavigation of the lake or else continue across the difficult northern route to Nagorno Karabagh. Few tourists do either. The road on the easternside of the lake is mostly in good condition although there are some poor stretches, particularly in the south. The area at the extreme eastern end of the lake used to be an important wintering ground for wading birds but the reduction in lake level has destroyed the habitat (see page 173). In autumn, however, greater flamingos can still be seen around the southeastern part of the lake. The northern side of the lake has few specific tourist attractions although there are some pleasant beaches and attractive wild flowers. A railway parallels the road: it was built to serve the gold mines at Zod but there are no longer passenger services beyond Hrazdan except in summer when the service is extended to Shorzha. The embankment can be spectacular with poppies, catmint, vetches and hypericum. On the eastern shore of the lake salvias and iris can be found among the tamarisk trees. At the northern end, look out for the dark purple-pink mounds of *Onobrychis cornuta* and the pinkish-white carpets of rock jasmine (*Androsace* sp) in May/June.

The beautiful **Getik Valley**, quite different from the Sevan basin, can be reached by heading north from Shorzha over the **Chambarak (or Karmir) Pass** (2,176m) although the road may be closed in winter by snow. In early summer colourful wild flowers carpet the hillsides of the pass. The road over the pass itself is not too bad but once **Chambarak** is approached it deteriorates markedly then remains very poor for most of the way until just before crossing into Tavush province. Unfortunately the route cannot really be recommended at present but for anyone wishing to travel that way allow half an hour from Shorzha to Chambarak and then two hours' quite difficult driving from Chambarak to Dilijan. The valley of the Getik itself is very pleasant, particularly further west, although it lacks any specific sights of interest. Two which are sometimes mentioned are both near the village of **Martuni**, not to be confused with Martuni on the south shore of the lake. The so-called fortress of Aghjkaghala, built in the 10th century, can be seen on the top of a hill high above the north side of the road just west of Martuni. Those who make the climb, probably under an extremely hot sun from which there is no respite, will be rewarded with an unimpressive tiny rectangle of stone walls which might have been a signal station but could never have held a significant garrison. Inside the small rectangle formed by the walls are phenomenal numbers of flies which, given the unusual location, might prove to be an undescribed species of interest to *Diptera* enthusiasts though not to others. There are pleasant views from the site but nothing particularly special by Armenia's high standards.

The other site, also just to the west of Martuni but south of the road along a bad dirt track, comprises the remains of **Getik Monastery**: in reality there are just a couple of courses of stonework to be seen along with a few remains of walls and pillars and some fallen stones. The site is historically important since it was the destruction of this monastery in an earthquake in the late 12th century which led to Mkhitar Gosh leaving Getik to found Nor Getik ('New Getik'), now called Goshavank. (See the section on Tavush province on page 230 for more information.)

Travelling north from Sevan to Dilijan in Tavush province became easier in 2003 as a new road tunnel was opened avoiding the **Sevan Pass** (2,114m). Unfortunately some of the earthworks on the improved road seem to have been carried out with scant regard for the stability of the hillside, and landslips are predictable.

KOTAYK PROVINCE

A half-day excursion from Yerevan to **Garni Temple** and **Geghard Monastery** is probably Armenia's most popular trip for visitors and is well worth making. About halfway from Yerevan, near the village of Voghjaberd, it is worth also stopping at the memorial arch to the writer Eghishe Charents (see page 45) as it offers splendid views across the valley to Ararat. The provincial capital of Hrazdan is a rundown post-industrial town. Elsewhere in Kotayk the village of **Tsaghkadzor** is Armenia's principal ski resort and also offers pleasant walking in the surrounding wooded countryside.

To reach Tsaghkadzor by public transport take either the **train** (see page 73) or **minibus** (see pages 74–6) to Hrazden, then a local minibus or taxi. There are minibuses to Garni village but they do not go as far as Geghard; take a taxi from Garni.

WHERE TO STAY AND EAT Accommodation is available at Tsaghkadzor ('Valley of Flowers') in various guesthouses (some renovated), new hotels and bed and breakfasts. Below is a selection.

Kecharis Hotel (34 rooms) 15 Orbeli Brothers St; ☎ 223 60409/509/609; e info@kecharishotel.am; www.kecharishotel.am. A former department store, the space has been used imaginatively & attractively in this well-presented hotel. Many facilities including sauna & hire of ski equipment. Disco Fri, Sat & Sun. Cards accepted. There is a **Jazzve** coffee shop in the hotel. **$$$**

Bagart Hotel Bistro (6 rooms) Main Sq; ☎ 223 60295; m 093 594977, 091 439695. A new hotel with small but adequate rooms. Guests can eat in the restaurant or do their own cooking in the kitchen if they wish. **$$**

Jupiter Hotel (27 rooms) Main Sq; ☎ 223 60616/7; m 091 407394; e info@ jupiter-hotel.info; www.jupiter-hotel.info. A new build, 4 floors, no lift. Wi-Fi. Accepts Visa & MasterCard. **$$**

Tsaghkadzor General Sport Complex (150 rooms) Tsaghkadzor City; ☎ 223 60524; e sportcomplex_ts@yahoo.com. Built to train Soviet athletes for 1968 Mexico Olympics. Offers a range of sporting facilities both summer & winter. **$$**

Writers Hotel (77 rooms) Tsaghkadzor City; ☎ 223 60445/6; 10 281081 (Yerevan number); m 091 293331; e info@writershotel.am; www.writershotel.am. A pleasant option, once called the House of Creativity of Writers. The statue in front of the guesthouse is of the writer Eghishe Charents. Set in attractive grounds & very clean, this is possibly the most comfortable former guesthouse in Armenia. To stay here was until recently a pure Soviet experience but modernisation has destroyed some of its period charm. It is very popular with conferences, & visitors may well find themselves talking to cardiologists or language teachers or some other professional group. They may also encounter spontaneous traditional singing & dancing on the part of the delegates. The guesthouse can hire out equipment for skiing on the nearby slopes. Most rooms have been fully & colourfully renovated but there remain a few cheaper rooms (AMD13,000) which have not yet been upgraded & where visitors can still experience something of a Soviet-era bathroom. Wi-Fi. Cards accepted. **$$**

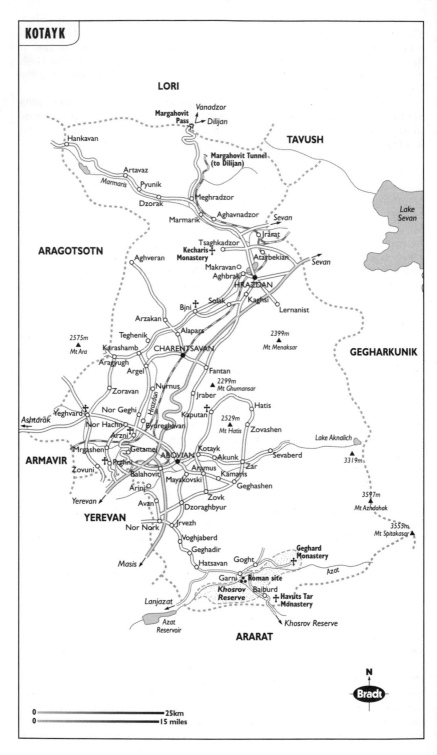

KOTAYK

LORI

Margahovit
Pass

Vanadzor
Dilijan

TAVUSH

Hankavan

Margahovit Tunnel
(to Dilijan)

Artavaz

Marmaris   Pyunik

Dzorak   Meghradzor

Marmarik   Aghavnadzor   Sevan

ARAGOTSOTN

Tsaghkadzor
Kecharis †
Monastery

Jrarat

Lake
Sevan

Aghveran

Makravan
Aghbrak

Atarbekian   Sevan

HRAZDAN

Bjni †   Solak   Kaghsi

Arzakan

Alapars

Lernanist

Teghenik

2575m
Mt Ara

2399m
Mt Menaksar

Karashamb   CHARENTSAVAN

GEGHARKUNIK

Aragyugh
Argel

Fantan

Zoravan   Nurnus

2299m
Mt Ghumansar

Nor Geghi   Jraber

Hatis

Yeghvard †

Kaputan   2529m
Mt Hatis

Zovashen

Ashtarak

Nor Hachn †
Arzni †

Byureghavan

Lake Aknalich

3319m

Mrgashen   Getamej

Kotayk   Akunk   Sevaberd

ARMAVIR

† Prghni

ABOVIAN

Zar

Zovuni   Balahovit   Aramus   Kamaris

3597m
Mt Azhdahak

Arinj   Mayakovski   Geghashen

Avan   Zovk

Yerevan

Dzoraghbyur

YEREVAN   Jrvezh

3555m
Mt Spitakasar

Nor Nork

Voghjaberd

Geghard
Monastery †

Geghadir

Goght

Masis   Hatsavan

Garni   Roman site

Azat

Khosrov
Reserve

Baiburd

Havuts Tar †
Monastery

Lanjazat

Azat
Reservoir

Khosrov Reserve

ARARAT

N

Bradt

0 ━━━━━━ 25km
0 ━━━━━━ 15 miles

182

YEGHVARD AND KAPUTAN These two villages in southern Kotayk have churches very similar in style although built of contrasting stone: warm pink in the case of Yeghvard but a rather forbidding grey at Kaputan. Both are dedicated to the Mother of God and are small in floor area but disproportionately tall, having two storeys and being topped not by a tambour with cupola but by a belfry supported by columns. The lower storey of each is more or less square and at Yeghvard the entrance is actually down steps from the present ground level. The upper storey is a cross-shaped church and is highly decorated externally at Yeghvard (as is also the interior of the church) but not at Kaputan, probably because of the use of basalt which is difficult to carve. Access to the upper storey was by an external cantilevered staircase of which the top steps were stone while the lower were wooden and have now vanished. The only way now into the upper storey is by ladder. The belfry at Yeghvard has 16 columns but there are only eight at Kaputan. Both belfries have a conical cupola. Yeghvard Church is in the middle of the village while Kaputan is on a hilltop above the village. At Yeghvard the bell has now been rehung in the upper church but there is no bell at Kaputan. Yeghvard is the earlier church and dates from 1301 while Kaputan was built in 1349.

Although Yeghvard is in Kotayk province it is probably more conveniently visited from Ashtarak to the west. Taking the main Ashtarak road, the turning to Yeghvard is signposted right just before Ashtarak is reached. It is about 10km from the junction to Yeghvard. Coming into Yeghvard a stretch of dual carriageway is reached. Keep on round the edge of the town until you see the church on the right above the houses. The upper church is particularly notable for its very fine carved animals: a lion and a bull on the west façade, an ibex on the north, a leopard killing an ibex on the east, and an eagle with a lamb in its talons on the south. Elsewhere in the village are the remains of a (harder-to-find) basilica church of the 5th or 6th century. Turn left, just after a large shop, near to where you turned right for the two-storey church; and/or ask the way.

To reach Kaputan, leave the main Yerevan to Sevan road at the Abovian turn-off and take the Kotayk road. At Kotayk take the left fork for Kaputan. The road goes on through this treeless upland to circumnavigate the eroded volcanic cone of **Mount Hatis** (2,529m).

NORTH FROM YEREVAN The main road from Yerevan to Sevan bisects the province from south to north. Leaving Yerevan it is notable for the number of casinos since they were banished from the city and also, in late summer, for the number of sheep herded into pens for sale. To the right of the road, on top of a hill, can be seen what looks like a Russian church. It is the mansion of the owner of the Kotayk brewery.

The first point of interest is the ruinous **Church of Ptghni** which can be seen from the road on the left-hand side in the middle of the village. To reach it take the exit for Ptghni shortly after crossing the railway: in practice this apparently requires doing a U-turn quite a distance beyond the exit and then turning right. The road skirts the outside of the village; keep going until you see the church through a gap in the houses. The church is a large basilica of the 6th century whose cupola and roof have collapsed. The north façade of the church and much of the west end are still standing and were stabilised in 1939–40. Further restoration was undertaken in 1964 which included demolishing a 19th-century church that had been built adjacent. The size of the building is impressive as is the massiveness of the one surviving arch of the four which once supported the cupola. Over the windows, most notably on the south façade, carvings depict angels, hunting scenes, saints, plants and fruits.

Continuing north on the main road the next turn-off to the left leads to **Arzni** which has a tiny 5th/6th-century octagonal church, the **St Kiraki Baptistry**. Octagonal on the outside, four-apsed inside with round windows in the thick walls, it is built on a stepped square base, which is probably older than the church, perhaps pagan. These features make it unique among similar contemporary Armenian buildings. It resembles early Christian baptistries and may be Armenia's only example of a separate baptistry building. Its red-painted metal roof is anachronistic. Arzni is a large village and apparently has seven churches. On a recent visit, after asking the way to 'the church' helpful locals directed me first to a newly built chapel, then a cyclist guided me to the renovated village *zham* before a third person recognised the description of the baptistry. To find it, take the left-hand road on entering Arzni (straight ahead leads to a sanatorium). Shortly afterwards turn right onto another surfaced road, then some way down that road turn right again. Arzni's main claim to fame is that it was developed from 1925 onwards as the Soviet Union's first purpose-built spa. Beyond the old village the road descends into the Hrazdan Gorge which is lined here with huge guesthouses, nowadays all apparently disused and spoiling what must once have been an attractive setting. The sheer number of people who could have been treated here simultaneously with water from the mineral springs is truly amazing.

The main road north now climbs steeply upwards to reach the plateau. Shortly before the summit, more conspicuous when travelling southbound, Lenin's name is clearly legible spelled out in trees on the hillside. Up on the plateau the industrial town of **Charentsavan** can be seen to the left. Most of the industry is now closed. Leave the road by the Charentsavan exit just north of the town, turn first right (not signposted) just before a gas station, and head west bypassing Charentsavan to **Arzakan**. At Arzakan turn right, immediately after crossing a bridge, for **Bjni** which has a fortress and two interesting churches. The dome of the **main church** in the village appears above trees on the left. It is dedicated to the Mother of God and dates from 1031. It has a disproportionately large circular tambour and umbrella cupola as well as some fine khachkars from the 13th to 15th centuries. The small belfry was added in 1275 and the fortified wall in the 17th century. Used as a byre in the Stalinist era, it was restored in 1956 with assistance from the Gulbenkian Foundation. Just below the church to the east is the 13th-century **St Gevorg Church** with older khachkars built into the walls. The **fortress**, up on the small plateau within the village, was built in the 9th or 10th century by the Pahlavuni family. Parts of the northern and western walls remain but there are only traces of other buildings in what is a fairly large area. The entrance to the secret passage down to the village can be seen but it is blocked after 40m. The best way up to the fortress is from the east. The **small church** at Bjni on top of a hill beyond the fortress is dedicated to St Sargis and dates from the 7th century. It has an octagonal tambour and retains a roof of tuff tiles. To reach it continue along the road then turn left just after crossing a tributary of the river. The track then winds up the right side of the hill to the church or you can park beside a byre at the bottom and walk up the path round the left of the hill.

It is possible to continue from Bjni direct to **Hrazdan** town along the scenic Hrazdan River. The number of often grandiose holiday homes shows that this is a place where the well-heeled of Yerevan come to get away from the city. Hrazdan itself has no appeal, although in the suburb of **Makravan** is the Monastery of Makravank whose 13th-century church dedicated to the Mother of God has a circular tambour and a conical cupola.

TSAGHKADZOR AND KECHARIS MONASTERY Tsaghkadzor (*telephone code 223*) is Armenia's principal ski resort and the number of guesthouses reflects this. It is also an excellent centre for walking and the scope for doing so is extended by using the chair lift, which operates all year. In summer thousands of anemones, *Pulsatilla armena,* can be seen in grassland a short distance above the chair-lift terminus. A useful brochure containing a map of the town, details of ski facilities and hotels is published by Collage Publishing House in Yerevan but I have only ever seen it in Tsaghkadzor. The ski resort, used for Olympic training in Soviet days, is located on the eastern slopes of Mount Tegenis. The main season is December to the end of February and the snow can be up to 1m deep. Instruction is available and equipment can be hired from a number of hotels in the town (see page 181), as can snowboards and sledges. In winter a **skating rink** is open in the town's main square. The **chair lift** (☉ *summer 09.45–17.45, shorter hours in winter*), opened in 1967 and rebuilt in 2004 by an Italian company, operates in three sections from the base of the ski slopes to the top at 1,966m. Each section costs AMD1,500, thus AMD4,500 the whole way. Two other chair lifts operate at different points on the slopes. There is a **rescue service** (✆ *223 60030*) and any injuries requiring hospital treatment go to the hospital in Hrazden. The Tsaghkadzor Sport Base, built to train Soviet athletes for the 1968 Mexico Summer Olympics is now a hotel offering its athletic facilities to a wider clientele (see *Where to stay and eat,* page 181).

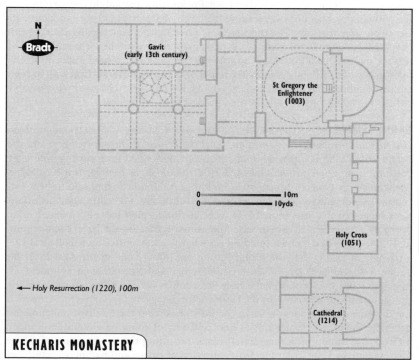

Gavit
(early 13th century)

St Gregory the
Enlightener
(1003)

0 ———— 10m
0 ———— 10yds

Holy Cross
(1051)

← Holy Resurrection (1220), 100m

Cathedral
(1214)

KECHARIS MONASTERY

The **Orbeli Brothers' House Museum** (✆ 223 60552; ⊕ 11.00–18.00 Tue–Sun; child/adult AMD200/500) is, appropriately, on Orbeli Brothers Street opposite Kecharis Hotel. Of the three brothers, Ruben (1880–1943) was a marine archaeologist, Levon (1882–1958) head of the Military Medical Academy and Joseph (1887–1961) an archaeologist who took part in the excavations of Ani as well as being director of the Hermitage Museum in Leningrad.

Kecharis Monastery is situated in the village of Tsaghkadzor, Kecharis being an earlier name for the village. The **main church**, dedicated to St Gregory the Illuminator, was erected in 1003 by Grigor Pahlavuni (990–1059). Given his age, his personal involvement must have been slight. Son of the Lord of Bjni, he was to become a distinguished theologian and writer acquiring the title Grigor Magistros from the Byzantine rulers after their takeover of the kingdom of Ani from Gagik II in 1045. The circular tambour and conical cupola were damaged by an earthquake in 1927 but were restored between 1997 and 2000. To the south of St Gregory's lies the small **Holy Cross Chapel** which dates from 1051. It too has a conical cupola but its circular tambour is decorated with six arcatures. After the construction of these buildings the Seljuk conquest put paid to any further work, the region remaining under their rule until their defeat by the Georgians with Armenian support in 1196. Work immediately restarted and by 1206 St Gregory's had acquired its large *gavit* whose roof is supported by four free-standing columns. The final church, the so-called **cathedral**, lies to the south of Holy Cross and was built immediately after the *gavit* by Prince Vasak Prosh, being completed in 1214. As in other churches of the period, the corner rooms at the west end have two storeys with the upper storey being accessed by cantilevered stairs. It too has a conical cupola, the circular tambour having 12 arcatures. The Mongol invasions in the late 1230s saw Kecharis badly damaged but it was restored by 1248. Presumably it was at this restoration that the tympanum of the doorway leading from the *gavit* into St Gregory's acquired its Georgian-style frescoes. The monastery is once more a functioning church with new furnishings and embroidered curtains in all three churches. The embroidered text on the north wall of Holy Cross is the Lord's Prayer. About 100m from the main group of buildings is the small **Chapel of the Holy Resurrection** with its high circular tambour and another conical cupola. It dates from 1220 and was probably used as the family burial vault for the founders of the cathedral.

GARNI TEMPLE (⊕ 10.00–17.30 Tue–Sun, often until 19.00–20.00 in summer; guided tours available in Armenian, English, French & Russian (the guides are volunteers so a tip is appreciated: about AMD1,000–1,500 from each person being guided is appropriate); child/adult AMD100/1,000) Garni Temple, as it is called, is Armenia's only Graeco-Roman-style building. Although usually said to be a 1st-century pagan temple, probably devoted to Mithra, more recently some historians have suggested that it is more likely to be the tomb built for a Romanised ruler, probably Sohaemus, in which case the construction would have been around AD175. It is the best-known building on what is an extensive archaeological site, a triangle of readily defensible land jutting out into a bend of the Azat River far below. Archaeologists have discovered the remains of a neolithic encampment; an inscription in cuneiform from the early 8th-century BC on a *vishap* stone recording the capture of Garni Fortress by the Urartian King Argishti I (*vishap* is the Armenian for 'dragon'; *vishap* stones are large carved stones from the first two millennia BC generally found near watercourses and probably of some religious significance); a Greek inscription on a huge basalt block recording the construction of a later fortress here by King Trdat I; a 3rd-century royal palace and bathhouse; churches from the 5th and 7th centuries; and the 9th-century palace of the Katholikos. Plainly the site has had a long and important history.

The 'temple' itself was destroyed in the great earthquake of 1679 but well restored between 1969 and 1975. It is easy to see which stones are the surviving originals and which are the modern replacements. It is one of the few historical monuments in Armenia for which an admission charge is made. The building looks rather like a miniature Parthenon and has 24 columns supporting the roof with Ionic capitals and Attic bases. The frieze depicts a variety of leaves and fruits while the cornice shows the heads of lions exhibiting a variety of expressions. Nine steep steps lead up to the interior in which are a reconstructed and probably inauthentic altar and sacrificial pit. The building differs from most other Graeco-Roman buildings in being constructed of basalt; the use of such a material probably required the employment of Armenian craftsmen skilled in the technique of carving so hard a rock.

Close to the temple are the remains of other buildings. The circular building next to the temple on the west side was a 7th-century church with four apses while northwest of the church was a palace and beyond it a bathhouse. The bathhouse has a mosaic floor which depicts sea gods framed by fish and nereids together with the ambiguous words: 'We worked but did not get anything'. If the door of the building protecting the bathhouse is locked the key can be obtained from the ticket kiosk. Some further reconstruction was started in the early years of this century and the walls of the church and palace were built up slightly. This does give an idea of the original layout but work on the church in particular was most insensitively carried out using black and bright-red stones which looked garish and out of place. There were understandable protests at the desecration and work was suspended.

OTHER SIGHTS AROUND GARNI The area has several other sights, notably the churches of the Mother of God and St Mashtots as well as the Monastery of Havuts Tar and the striking rock formations in Garni Gorge. Allow at least four hours to walk from Garni to Havuts Tar and back. The **Mother of God Church** in the centre of the town is a 12th-century basilica with a small porch incorporating a belfry. The more elaborate **Church of St Mashtots** is in the eastern part of the town. It is a small square single-aisle church with a 12-sided tambour. The pink cupola and roofs contrast attractively with the grey stonework of the walls and tambour. The tambour is surprisingly elaborate with much geometric carving and windows in four of the sides.

There are two main ways down into the **gorge**. The easiest way to follow is by taking the path which leaves from in front of the entrance to the temple and slopes down on the left-hand side as one faces the temple. The first part of the path is paved; when you come to a private gate take the path which goes right. Keep descending and, if in doubt at intersections, always keep going down. You eventually reach the dirt road along the bottom of the gorge. Turn left. The road passes astonishing **rock formations** – regular columns of basalt which are similar to those of the Giant's Causeway, County Antrim, Northern Ireland and Fingal's Cave, Staffa, Scotland. They are also similar to those further east in Armenia along the Arpa Gorge near Gndevaz. The gorge has a flora of drought-tolerant shrubs including *Spirea crenata,* willow-leaved pear (*Pyrus salicifolia*) and the rare yellow *Rosa hemisphaerica.* Herbaceous plants include *Campanula, Verbascum* and spiny *Astragalus* (goat's thorn).

Continuing upriver a medieval bridge is reached. Cross it and go uphill, following the occasional signs to the visitor centre of the **Khosrov Reserve** (entrance tickets to the reserve are available here; see page 158). If going to Havuts Tar turn left here onto

4

a path which follows the side of the gorge – the ranger from the reserve is happy to point it out. The path gives marvellous views both down into the gorge and also of Garni Temple on the opposite face. **Havuts Tar Monastery** is about 3km along this path and, at an altitude of 1,590m, is some 200m higher than Garni Temple. The extensive site comprises two main groups of ruins, eastern and western, though there is evidence that there were once structures, or possibly graves, between them. The path approaches the eastern group. Although dating from the 11th to 13th centuries the monastery was very badly damaged in the 1679 earthquake and much of what is now seen supposedly dates from its rebuilding in the early 18th century. It must be wondered how much rebuilding actually took place as the appearance of the site is such as to give the impression that Havuts Tar was effectively abandoned in 1679.

The eastern group of buildings was surrounded by a fortified wall which still stands to a considerable height on the north and east. The entrance is an arched doorway at the southeast corner. The main church is relatively well preserved. The western façade and the interior uses a mixture of red and black tuff to striking effect and the interior is notable for its carved niches with birds appearing in several. The church once had a *gavit* but few traces remain. On its north side work commenced in 1772 on the construction of a new church but it was never finished.

The west group is dominated by a cross-dome church whose walls are again constructed in a chessboard pattern using alternately red and black tuff blocks. This is probably the **Holy Saviour Church** founded in 1013 by Grigor Pahlavuni (c990–1058), founder also of Kecharis, although some sources state that Holy Saviour is the church in the east group. On the south side of this church is a small vaulted chapel built at a later date.

GEGHARD MONASTERY (⊕ *during usual church opening hours 09.00–18.00*) One of the great sites of Armenia and on the UNESCO World Heritage List since 2000, Geghard ('Spear') Monastery in its gorge setting should ideally be seen when several of the country's less extraordinary churches have been visited. It is then easier to appreciate what makes this one different. Its unusual feature is that it is partly an ordinary surface structure and partly cut into the cliff. The name dates from the 13th century and reflects the bringing here of a spear said to have been the one which pierced the side of Christ at Calvary. This spear, a shaft with a diamond-shaped head into which a cross has been cut, can now be seen in the treasury at Ejmiatsin. It is inside a gilded silver case made for it in 1687. Visiting Geghard on a Sunday morning is an enthralling experience with beautiful singing from the choir, and beautifully groomed animals brought for sacrifice after the service.

The first monastery at this site was called Ayrivank ('Cave monastery'). It was founded as early as the 4th century but was burned down and plundered in 923 by Nasr, a subordinate of Yusuf, the caliph's Governor of Azerbaijan. Yusuf had just spent five years in prison for rebellion against the caliph. Nasr continued the rebellion, seeking to extend his own power and to enforce conversion of the Christian population to Islam.

Thereafter the monastery declined until the revival of monastery building in the late 12th century. The earliest surviving part, the **Chapel of the Mother of God**, dates from before 1164 and is situated above the road just before the gateway to the main monastery complex. It is partly a surface structure and partly hewn into the rock, rectangular in plan but with a semicircular apse. Adjoining it are other passages and small rooms in the rock.

In total, surrounding the main site are more than 20 other rock-hewn chapels and service premises, many of which have carvings. Also outside the gate are small

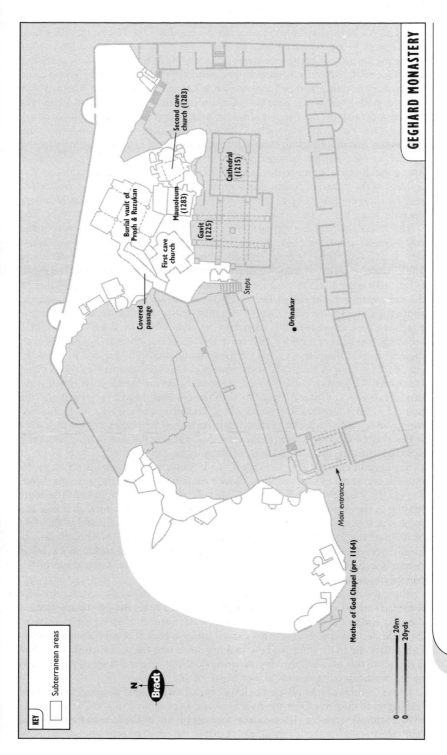

KEY

Subterranean areas

Second cave church (1283)

Cathedral (1215)

Burial vault of Prosh & Ruzukan

Mausoleum (1283)

Gavit (1225)

First cave church

Covered passage

Steps

• Orhnakar

Main entrance

Mother of God Chapel (pre 1164)

N

Bradt

0   20m
0   20yds

ledges onto which visitors try to throw stones. If a stone remains on the ledge then the thrower's wish is supposed to come true.

The main buildings of the monastery are surrounded by walls on three sides and a cliff face on the other. Construction was started by the Zakarian family who came into possession of it after they had commanded Armenian forces which joined with the Georgians to defeat the Seljuks. The main cathedral was built in 1215 and is of the cross-dome type, the circular tambour being decorated with graceful arcature and narrow windows and topped by a conical cupola. Between the spans of arcature and on the portals and cornices are depicted a variety of birds and animals as well as floral and geometrical patterns. The southern façade is particularly interesting. Above the doorway with two doves facing each other is a lion attacking an ox, the emblem of the Zakarian family. The *gavit* at the west side which is attached to the rock face was completed by 1225. It is much plainer than the main church though the tympanum has an attractive floral design within an ogee arch.

The Zakarians sold the monastery to the Prosh family who constructed the subterranean part carved out of rock. In the **first cave church**, on the northwest side, is a spring. It bears the architect's name, Galdzag, and incorporates some fine khachkars as well as stalactite decoration around the roof opening. The Prosh family **mausoleum** and the second cave church at the northeast were probably by the same architect and completed by 1283. On the north wall of the mausoleum above the archways is a relief carving of a goat with a ring in its mouth to which is attached a rope whose two ends are round the necks of two lions which are looking outwards. The ends of the lions' tails are dragons looking upwards. Below all this an eagle with spreading wings grasps a lamb in its talons. Both here and in the rock-cut churches there is much elaborate carving of crosses, geometrical shapes and khachkars. Rather surprisingly to the right of the entrance to the mausoleum are carved two sirens, mythical creatures with the crowned head of a woman and the body of a bird. These creatures who lived on rocky islets off the coast of Sicily lured men to their death, either by enchanting them with their singing so that they were shipwrecked on the rocks or, in some versions, by lulling the men to sleep with their singing so that the sirens could murder them while they slept.

The **second cave church**, dedicated to the Mother of God, leads off from the mausoleum. Some of the khachkars show human figures including one who holds a spear pointing down while he blows an uplifted horn. To the right at the stairs leading to the altar dais is the figure of a goat. At the left side on the altar dais is a stone seat with a lion's head forming the end of the top of the back and to the right of the dais is a khachkar of two doves each side of a cross. The church, despite being underground, retains the same cross shape with tambour and cupola as other Armenian churches. There is an opening to the outside world at the top of the cupola which admits light.

The *gavit* which formed the burial vault of Prince Papak Prosh and his wife Ruzukan was hewn in 1288. It is at a higher level and to reach it, go up the steps at the west end of the complex and then follow the narrow subterranean passage to the right decorated with khachkars carved into the rock. The roof is supported by four pillars and in the floor is a hole looking down into the mausoleum below. The acoustics in this *gavit* are amazing. Anyone standing here and singing, particularly by the northeast pillar, sounds like an entire choir.

Other features of interest are the small **rock-hewn chapel** adjacent to the steps leading up to the *gavit*. Over the door is a carving of a figure wearing what appears to be a Mithraic-style hat. The *orhnakar* is in the middle of the paved area within the monastery walls but the *mataghatun* is outside the small eastern gateway. Around the boundary wall are various service buildings; that at the northeast corner is a **bakery** complete with *tonir* (see page 83). Most date from the 17th century but those at the southwest corner only from 1968–71.

After so much culture it is worth, on leaving Geghard, buying some fruit *lavash* from the women who sell it near the entrance. The plum is particularly good.

Botanists may wish to explore the river valley with its wealth of herbaceous plants, including orchids, and trees. Oriental wild apple *Malus orientalis* and Caucasian pear *Pyrus caucasia* flourish on boulders in the middle of the fast-flowing river and wild grape vine *Vitis sylvestris* scrambles through trees, including *Euonymus, Cornus, Sorbus*, and *Acer ibericum*, on the riverbank.

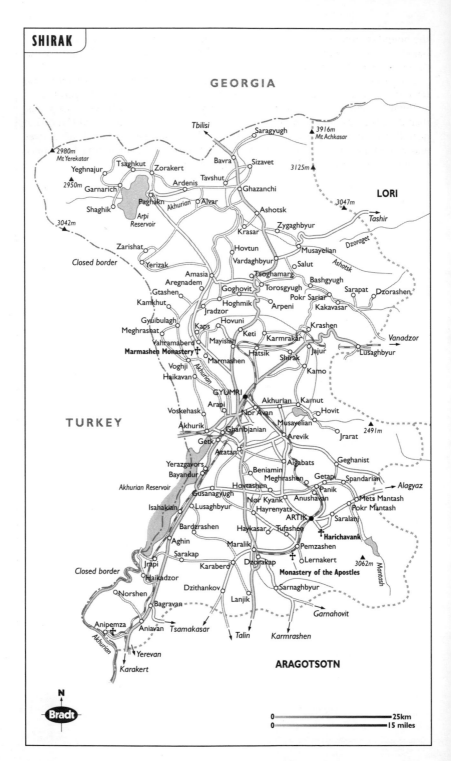

GEORGIA

Tbilisi

Saragyugh

3916m
Mt Achkasar

▲ 2980m
Mt Yerekatar

Yeghnajur   Tsaghkut   Zorakert

Bavra

Sizavet

3125m ▲

LORI

▲ 2950m
Garnarich

Ardenis   Tavshut

Ghazanchi

3047m ▲

Tashir

Shaghik   Paghakn   Akhurian   Alvar

Ashotsk

Zygaghbyur

Dzoroget

3042m ▲

Arpi
Reservoir

Krasar

Musayelian

Zarishat

Hovtun

Vardaghbyur

Salut

Ashotsk

Closed border   Yerizak

Amasia

Tsoghamarg

Bashgyugh

Sarapat   Dzorashen

Aregnadem

Goghovit   Torosgyugh

Gtashen

Pokr Sariar   Kakavasar

Kamkhut

Hoghmik   Arpeni

Jradzor

Hovuni

Krashen

Gyuibulagh

Kaps   Keti   Karmrakar

Vanadzor

Meghrashat

Vahramaberd   Mayisian

Marmashen Monastery ✝   Marmashen

Hatsik   Shirak   Jajur

Lusaghbyur

Voghji

Kamo

Haikavan

GYUMRI

Akhurlan   Karnut

Voskehask   Arapi   Nor Avan

Hovit

Akhurik

Ghatbjanian   Musayelian   Arevik   Jrarat   2491m ▲

Getk

Azatan

Aigabats   Geghanist

Yerazgavors   Beniamin

Bayandur   Meghrashen   Getap   Spandarian

Akhurian Reservoir   Hovtashen   Panik   Alagyaz

Gusanagyugh   Nor Kyank   Anushavan   Mets Mantash

Isahakian   Lusaghbyur   Hayrenyats   Pokr Mantash

ARTIK   Saralanj

Bardzrashen   Haykasar   Tufashen   Harichavank ✝

Aghin   Maralik   Pemzashen

Sarakap   Lernakert   3062m ▲

Jrapi   Karaberd   Dzorakap   Monastery of the Apostles   Mantash

Closed border   Haikadzor

Norshen   Dzithankov   Lanjik   Sarnaghbyur

Bagravan   Garnahovit

Anipemza ✝   Aniavan   Tsamakasar   Talin   Karmrashen

Akhurian   Yerevan

Karakert

ARAGOTSOTN

TURKEY

N

Bradt

0 ————— 25km
0 ————— 15 miles

5

The Northern Provinces

The three northern provinces of Shirak, Lori and Tavush are very different from each other. **Shirak** is mostly a high plateau while **Lori** is characterised by its deep gorges; **Tavush** retains extensive forest cover. Visitors who combine a visit to Armenia with one to Georgia cross Lori between Yerevan and the Georgian border, seeing some of the monasteries of the Debed Valley *en route*. Others go to the one-time resort town of Dilijan in Tavush with its attractive wooden buildings. The monasteries of Sanahin, Haghpat, Haghartsin and Goshavank are all much visited, and others such as Odzun receive a fair number of visitors, though such gems as Makaravank and Hnevank see only a few and the immensely worthwhile Khuchap and Khorakert see hardly any.

SHIRAK PROVINCE

Shirak province is bounded to the west by Turkey and to the north by Georgia. Mostly a high plateau, it becomes increasingly hilly nearer the Georgian border and to the east where it borders Lori province. Shirak is off the main tourist routes and even such fine monasteries as **Marmashen** and **Harichavank** are seen by few tourists. Those interested in churches should also visit **Anipemza** whose church, although roofless, is one of the oldest in Armenia and built in a quite different architectural style.

WHERE TO STAY The only hotels that can be recommended are in Gyumri. In Artik (see page 201) there is an unrenovated Soviet-era hotel, which could be used if all else fails. It is in the centre of the town; ask locally for directions.

Berlin Art Hotel (formerly Gästehaus Berlin) (13 rooms) 25 Haghtanak Av, Gyumri; 312 57659; e info@berlinhotel-gyumri.am; www.berlinhotel-gyumri.am. Opened by the German Red Cross after the earthquake – hence the former name. It is attached to a clinic although being ill is not a requisite of staying here. It is an attractive small hotel with helpful staff. There are displays of work by local artists & sculptors. Meals other than b/fast must be ordered in advance. Internet access available. Tours of the region can be organised for AMD9,000/pp. Cards accepted. Discounts for members of humanitarian organisations & long-term guests. **$$$**

Araks Hotel (17 rooms) 25 Gorki St, Gyumri; 312 51199, 32116; e araks95@web.am; www.arakshotel.am. This handsome black building with an impressive marble entrance hall is a former KGB office. It has been fully restored & has well-appointed rooms. Accepts Visa & MasterCard. **$$$**

Alhmas Hotel (20 rooms) 1 Garegin Nzhdeh St, Gyumri; 312 39444, 39445; m 093 416700; e info@hotelgyumri.com, alhmas-hotel@yandex.ru. Wi-Fi. B/fast extra, approx AMD1,500/pp. **$$**

Nane Hotel (formerly Hotel Isuz) 1/5 Garegin Nzhdeh St, Gyumri; 312 33369; e info@nanehotel.am. This relatively new hotel was closed for renovation at the time of writing but was previously a pleasant hotel with 12 comfortable rooms. The façade preserves that of a former factory which was destroyed during the earthquake.

✕ **WHERE TO EAT** Gyumri also has the pick of the province's eateries:

✕ **Phaeton Alek** 47 Haghtanak St, Gyumri; ☎ 312 57988; m 094 344369. On the ground floor of the local history museum where one can almost imagine oneself back in the days depicted upstairs. It is tastefully furnished with a mixture of old & reproduction furniture. Museum exhibits such as carpets & domestic utensils decorate the original stone walls. The eponymous horse-drawn carriage stands just inside the front door. Menu in English.

✕ **Café Verona** 4/3 Khaghaghutian Sq, Gyumri; ☎ 312 50088. Service a bit slow but the food is freshly prepared & worth the wait.

✕ **Vanatour** At the junction of Rizhkov & Gorki sts, Gyumri; ☎ 312 30192. Popular with locals. Serves Georgian dishes as well as Armenian; the cheese ones are tasty.

✕ **Café Kalinka** Halfway up Rizhkov St, Gyumri; ☎ 312 61116. Cheerful café serving kebabs, pizzas & omelettes.

OTHER PRACTICALITIES The only sizeable town in the province is **Gyumri**. It has all major facilities such as banks, post office, shops, market, internet cafés, etc. Most are on the main square or Khaghaghutian and Ankakhutian squares. There is no tourist information office. Numerous USAID information boards give details about what there is to see in the centre of Gyumri. A map of Gyumri (Armenian script only) exists but it is not easily obtainable. Even likely shops will tell you that there is no map. I obtained mine by rummaging in the wall-map section in Norma-Terzian on the main square. For train and minibuses to Gyumri see *Chapter 2*, pages 73–6.

Shirak Tours, run by the proprietor of Berlin Art Hotel (see page 193) can arrange tours of the region.

GYUMRI (*Telephone code 312*) Gyumri is the principal city of northwest Armenia and the administrative centre of Shirak. At 11.41 on Wednesday 7 December 1988 – when most adults were at work and most children at school – around 60% of the buildings were destroyed by an earthquake. The epicentre of the earthquake, which measured 6.9 on the Richter scale, was 30km east of Gyumri in Lori province near the small town of Spitak (population then about 25,000) where every building was destroyed. In all, at least 25,000 people were killed and 500,000 made homeless in Gyumri and the surrounding region. (See box, page 198, for more information.) The problems Armenia has had in dealing with the aftermath of the earthquake have long made any visit to Gyumri a salutary experience. However, not to go there means missing an important aspect of modern Armenian history. Apart from the direct impact of the earthquake, an indirect consequence was the shutting of Metsamor nuclear power station because of its vulnerability to any further earthquakes. It was the closure of Metsamor, by far Armenia's biggest source of electricity, coupled with the blockade by Azerbaijan and Turkey as a result of the war over Nagorno Karabagh, which led to most Armenians having no electricity and hence no heat during the winters of 1992/93, 1993/94 and 1994/95 (see page 168).

Gyumri was called Leninakan at the time of the earthquake and there is a certain irony in that Lenin's entire system of government was to collapse so soon after a city which had been named in his honour. Immediately after the earthquake, the Soviet prime minister Nikolai Ryzhkov promised the inhabitants that the city would be rebuilt within two years. That timetable was unachievable in the last days of the Soviet Union and, after the Armenian vote for independence in 1991, the

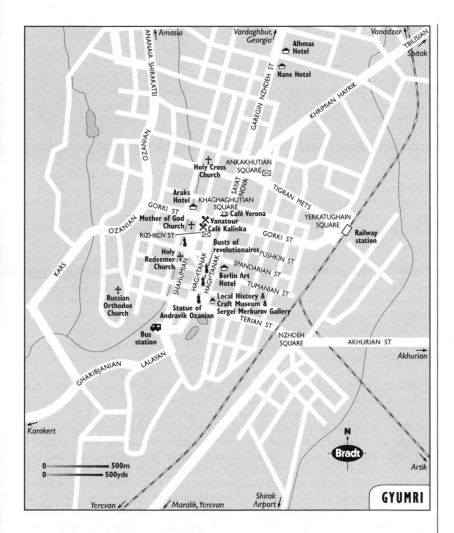

Inside the map:

Amasia ↑
Vardaghbur, Georgia ↗
Vanadzor ↑
TBILISIAN
Spitak ↘

Alhmas Hotel
Nane Hotel

ANANAIA
SHIRAKATSI
GAREGIN NZHDEH ST
KHRIMIAN HAYRIK

OZANIAN

Holy Cross Church
ANKAKHUTIAN SQUARE
SAYAT NOVA
TIGRAN METS

Araks Hotel
KHAGHAGHUTIAN SQUARE
Café Verona
YERKATUGHAIN SQUARE

GORKI ST
Mother of God Church
Vanatour
Café Kalinka
GORKI ST

RIZHKOV ST
Busts of revolutionaires
Railway station

Holy Redeemer Church
PUSHKIN ST
SHAHUMIAN
HAGHTANAK
HAGHTANAK
SPANDARIAN ST
Berlin Art Hotel
TUMANIAN ST

Russian Orthodox Church
Local History & Craft Museum & Sergei Merkurov Gallery
Statue of Andravik Ozanian
TERIAN ST

NZHDEH SQUARE
AKHURIAN ST
Akhurian

Bus station

GHARIBJANIAN
LALAYAN

KARS

Karakert

0 ___ 500m
0 ___ 500yds

N
Bradt

Artik

Yerevan
Maralik, Yerevan
Shirak Airport

GYUMRI

Armenians ceased work on the partly completed buildings since they had not been designed with adequate earthquake protection. Nowadays, approaching the city from some directions (notably the northwest), visitors still see unfinished blocks of flats (known locally as the carcasses). Some of the blocks were almost finished. In others merely the foundations had been dug. They were being built on good agricultural land and farming continues between the buildings. In places, the rubble dumped from the many buildings which collapsed is still evident but nature is gradually taking over.

In 2001 around 40% of the population was still living in old railway containers into which windows had been cut. However, following substantial gifts from the American–Armenian Kirk Kerkorian from 1998 and USAID from 2000, progress was made and by 2002 it was possible to imagine that the air of depression was starting to lift and that eventually sufficient new housing might be built for those who had by then spent almost 15 years in those metal boxes. By autumn 2005 the number living in containers had fallen to 3,500, but an air of depression remained. Since then the rate of improvement has increased with rebuilding of much of the town centre either completed or in progress. However, there still remains much to be done. Behind the new buildings some of the old railway containers are still inhabited and there are historic buildings awaiting attention. (According to Armenian government data 7,000 families in northern Armenia who lost their homes in the earthquake still lived in shacks or other temporary accommodation in 2008. Some 5,300 of them are due to receive new accommodation by 2013.) On the whole, Gyumri is now a bustling city like any other although the scars are evident in the populace as well as in the buildings. Gyumri is the only town in Armenia where I have encountered begging (outside Mother of God Church), no doubt due to the long-term effects of the earthquake. One can only wonder at the psychological damage to the inhabitants. There was not a single Gyumri resident who did not lose a family member in 1988.

The city itself is an ancient settlement, and was caught up in the long struggles for supremacy between the Persian and Ottoman empires. However, the older surviving buildings, mostly in the centre, date from the period after Russia gained control of the region following the Russo-Turkish war of 1828–29. A fortress was quickly built to defend the new border and in 1837, when Tsar Nicholas I visited Gyumri, the town was renamed Alexandropol after Nicholas's wife, Tsaritsa Alexandra Fedorovna. That name lasted until 1924 when it was again renamed, this time in honour of the recently deceased Lenin. The survival of the older buildings indicates that under Tsarist rule construction was to higher standards than in the Soviet era.

It is possible to imagine a time when Gyumri, with its mix of smart new buildings and renovated attractive old buildings, the shoddy Soviet-era constructions having been swept away by the earthquake, will once again be a pleasant place to live.

What to see Many USAID information boards have been placed around the centre of Gyumri with much useful, interesting detailed information. While the boards are helpful visitors may wish, as I did, that the information had also been produced in booklet form which could be carried around while exploring the town.

There are more surviving Tsarist-era buildings here than in any other Armenian city and the older central streets offer an insight into 19th-century Russian provincial architecture. These buildings are concentrated in an area to the west of the main square. On the main square, two 19th-century churches face each other, **Mother of God** on the north side and **Holy Redeemer** on the south. Both were damaged by the earthquake, the latter suffering considerably when its large central cupola collapsed. Mother of God is functioning again and is busy with many people coming and going. While the church is definitely Armenian the blue altar screen with its painted pictures lends something of an Orthodox feel, perhaps not surprising given its date. Holy Redeemer is still under restoration. The new red-and-grey stone is being carefully matched to the colours of the old but is being left plain to distinguish it from the older decorated stonework. The inscription on the monument to the south of Holy Redeemer church reads 'To the innocent victims, to the merciful hearts', namely the victims of the earthquake and those who came to help. By contrast, Gyumri's largest and most impressive 19th-century church, **Holy Cross**, which is situated to the north of the centre on Shahumian Street, escaped lightly. For many years following the earthquake it housed families who had lost their homes but it too is now a functioning church again. The small **Russian Orthodox Church**, in typical Orthodox style with a silver-coloured onion dome, appears to have suffered little damage but is now closed. None of these churches need detain the visitor long but they do combine with the older residential streets to provide one of the few extant pictures of the Tsarist era in Armenia.

The new pale tuff building occupying the whole of the east side of the main square is to be the **town hall**. Facing it, on the west side of the square, is a monument to those who fought Persian troops in AD451 at the Battle of Avarayr (see *Chapter 1, History*, page 16). Their leader, Mamikonian, is mounted and below him are four figures representing all ranks of society. Although the Armenians were defeated, subsequent events allowed the battle to be seen as a moral victory and one which preserved the Armenian language, hence the names of the first four letters of the Armenian alphabet carved on the tablet. From the southeast corner of the main square the colourful market stretches south and from the northeast corner the popular pedestrianised Rizhkov Street (named after the person in charge of organising aid after the earthquake) with many small shops leads to Khaghaghutian Square with its several cafés.

The **local history and craft museum** (*47 Haghtanak St; ⊕ 11.00–17.00 Tue–Sun; adult AMD500*) merits a visit. It is located in a restored 1872 town house, the façade of which comprises black and orange-red tuff blocks together with a wrought-iron balcony. Inside are paintings by local artists and rooms furnished as they would have been in Tsarist days. It is particularly conspicuous that virtually all items in the rooms for the wealthier inhabitants came from western Europe and little from Russia, eastern Europe or Asia. This presumably reflects the aspirations of prosperous Armenians under Tsarist rule. The museum is on the upper floor and in the basement is an attractive restaurant (see page 194).

The adjacent gallery, the **Sergei Merkurov Gallery** (*closed for renovation at the time of writing*), was the home of Sergei Merkurov, a prominent Soviet sculptor-monumentalist and native of Gyumri. He was considered to be the greatest Soviet master of post-mortem masks, making death masks of Lenin, Tolstoy and Gorky among many others. The statue of Lenin which stood in Yerevan's Republic Square during Soviet times was his work (see *Chapter 3, Yerevan*, pages 117–20). The gallery houses his work.

At the bottom of Haghtanak Street, opposite the Sergei Merkurov Gallery, is a statue of Andranik Ozanian (see *Chapter 3, Yerevan*, page 121). Behind him, in the central reservation of the dual carriageway, are busts of Armenian revolutionaries. They include Gevorg V (1847–1930), Katholikos during the Armenian genocide and early Soviet period; Garegin Nzhdeh (1886–1955), statesman and Armenian commander; and Nikol Duman (1867–1914), freedom fighter in Baku and Yerevan.

Gyumri **railway station** is a vast edifice which looks typically Soviet from the outside but whose entrance hall is reminiscent of the *gavit* of a church with its central dome, from which hangs an enormous chandelier, and a mosaic of the Armenian symbol of eternity on the floor under the dome.

Southeast of the city is **Shirak Airport** which still has a few flights including a weekly one from Moscow. The airport looks deserted between flights but the sole policeman and solitary military person on duty when I visited did not seem to object to a foreigner wandering around. Fortunately the runway looks in better condition than the extremely pot-holed road which leads to the airport. (The wrought-iron sign indicating the principal road to the airport is easy to miss; a little further south is a much more obvious sign but following this second sign will take you via an even worse 'road'.) Taxis are said to meet the three flights a week. The airport was reportedly designed to look like an airport in provincial Turkey so that, in the event of a hijacking, a plane could be diverted here and the hijackers then deceived into thinking that they had made it to the West. Apparently the normal airport signs could be rapidly changed to (apparently) Turkish ones, there were stocks of Turkish uniforms for the staff, and suitable photographs of such people as the Turkish president.

MARMASHEN MONASTERY (☉ *in good weather, the main church is open 09.00–20.00, but if the door is locked when you arrive it is likely that the caretaker will soon appear, having seen visitors arriving. If not he can be contacted on* m *091 577696; his name is Samvel. The notice on the door, in Armenian, simply asks visitors not to bring candles from elsewhere*) The Monastery of Marmashen is one of Armenia's most interesting and is beautifully situated. That said, it is not on a main tourist route and is consequently little visited. To reach it take the main north road out of Gyumri and then fork left on the road to Vahramaberd just after a Russian military

THE 1988 EARTHQUAKE

The first shock, of magnitude 6.9, was at 11.41 on Wednesday 7 December 1988. It lasted for 47 seconds. Four minutes later there was a second shock of magnitude 5.4 and within the first fortnight there were 1,500 tremors. Unfortunately most of the hospitals and schools were of modern Soviet construction and so collapsed immediately: urgent medical care for the survivors was difficult, not just because of the collapse of the hospitals but because over half of Gyumri's doctors died in their ruins. All 60 expectant mothers in the maternity hospital died, along with the newborn and their mothers. In one area of nine-storey flats only five or six of the original 49 blocks remained. (Flats similar in design to these are common even today throughout earthquake-prone Armenia.) Out in the villages the older peasant houses sometimes survived but the children had usually been in modern schools and hence died.

The wounded had to be evacuated by helicopter to hospitals in Yerevan and emergency supplies (including large numbers of coffins) had to be flown in. As well as useful items, numerous bureaucrats also arrived with no ability to organise anything but who, imagining themselves to be important people, decided they should be there. Gorbachev himself cut short a visit to the USA to visit the scene, though earned the contempt of the survivors and rescuers by having his Zil limousine brought in by transport plane so that he could inspect the ruins in comfort. Help came from abroad as well as other parts of the Soviet Union – even from Azerbaijan despite the growing tension over Nagorno Karabagh. However, Armenian television was able to show Muslim demonstrators on the streets of Baku with placards: 'Allah be praised, He has punished the infidel'; 'Hurrah for the earthquake'; 'God is just, He knows whom to punish'.

Electricity, telephone and water supplies all failed. The absence of electricity and telephones, coupled with the perpetual shortage of batteries (to power radios) in the Soviet Union, meant that people, especially in the villages, had no sources of information and there were many who believed for days that the entire world had been affected. As well as being bereaved, many survivors had lost most of their possessions and were financially ruined. Looting and pillage soon broke out and as a result cars leaving the region were searched by soldiers and the forces of the Ministry of the Interior.

Could the earthquake have been predicted? Probably not, at least so far as the exact date and location were concerned, although after the event some shepherds said that they had noticed changes in the preceding days: specifically that the water in the artesian wells had become several degrees warmer.

base on the left. There is an inconspicuous wrought-iron signpost to Marmashen but it is very easy to miss, especially when driving. The road from the town centre to the turn-off has bad pot-holes but that to Vahramaberd is a good tarmac road. In **Vahramaberd** (about 8km from the left fork) turn sharp left between fields where rubble and more recent rubbish has been dumped. After about 2km the road starts to descend into the valley of the Akhurian River. The monastery can be seen below the road, picturesquely situated by the river and surrounded by fruit trees. The road eventually zigzags down to it. This road is in poor condition but may be rebuilt once the small hydro-electric plant which is being constructed down-stream from the monastery is finished.

There are three separate surviving buildings although the remains of many more can be seen, as can parts of the surrounding wall, particularly on the northwest side. The **main church** was built between 986 and 1029 in red tuff and is in the style of those at Ani, the former capital. It is particularly elegant with decorative arcatures on each façade and columns supporting the corners of the umbrella cupola. Inside, the front of the altar has been restored using the original carved stones where possible but supplemented where necessary with other stones found on the site. Much restoration has been expertly carried out, funded by an Italian-Armenian couple who went to the length of having experiments carried out in Italy to find an ideal mortar to repair the stonework. The **10th-century church** to the north of the main church is now roofless. The church on the south side is rather like a smaller version of the main one. Archaeologists have uncovered the foundations of a fourth, circular, much earlier, church which lies to the west. There is also a good array of khachkars, those marking the graves of men in front of the church with those of women to the sides and back. Close by the monastery complex there are several waterfalls on minor tributaries of the Akhurian.

JRAPI AND ANIPEMZA Heading southwest from Gyumri and parallel to the Turkish border, the road crosses the only rail link between Armenia and Turkey at a level crossing. This rail link was opened in 1898 to provide a connection between Tiflis (present-day Tbilisi, Georgia) and Kars (in present-day Turkey) at a time when both cities were in the Russian Empire. By the latter days of the Soviet Union there was only one train each week across the border but even this has been suspended since 1992 because the border is officially closed. Continuing southwest and very close to the border the nests of white storks can be seen on top of telegraph poles: the storks have only a limited distribution in Armenia but there are several pairs here. The military significance of the area, the frontier between the former Warsaw Pact and NATO, can be judged from the continued presence of Russian soldiers. Until a few years ago the markings on one stretch of road which enabled it to be used as an emergency runway could still be seen but much needed resurfacing has eliminated the markings along with the pot-holes.

After about 25km the ruins of 10th–11th-century **Jrapi caravanserai** can be seen on the left. There is also a small 7th-century church and the ruins of another 7th-century church, rebuilt as a castle in the 11th century. The road continues through pleasant hilly country and as it starts to descend again to the plain there is a small picnic spot with a natural spring on the east side. An early summer lunch break here might be enlivened by nesting crag martins, Isabelline wheatears and black-headed buntings.

Continuing south past the village of **Aniavan** a road branches off right (look out for rose-coloured starlings) to **Anipemza** whose Yereruyk Church, though roofless, is one of the most architecturally important in Armenia and often features in collections of photographs of the country. Its significance rests with its early date (5th–6th century) and the idea it gives of early Armenian church architecture which was modelled on the style of churches in the eastern provinces of the Roman Empire. The basilica-style building is erected on a large plinth approached by steps. The porches are framed by elaborately carved pediments of Graeco-Roman style, contrasting with the different style of the carved window arches and the plain pilasters. There were galleries on three sides, north, south and west, constructed between the eastern and western corner rooms which project beyond the nave. Unusually, the eastern corner rooms are elongated along a north–south axis. The whole site covers an enormous area. To the north are natural caves and pits carved into the rock, some of which may have been for storage: others are coffin-like. Even the name 'Anipemza' has particular significance for Armenians since it reminds them of their inaccessible capital Ani; the 'pemza' part of the name refers to pumice which is mined locally.

The Turkish border is only a few hundred metres from the church and, on a clear day, both Mount Aragats, the highest peak in present-day Armenia, and Mount Ararat, the highest peak in historic Armenia, can be seen. From Aniavan a road goes west to Norshen (Karkov) near to which is a specially constructed viewpoint over the abandoned capital of Ani which is immediately over the border in Turkey. However, advance permission to go into this sensitive area has to be obtained from the Foreign Ministry in Yerevan and a small fee paid. It is quite easy to secure the permission but several days' notice is required. For Western visitors it may be more satisfactory to visit Ani itself via the Turkish city of Kars. Even then it is necessary to seek police permission in Kars. That the Armenians are cut off from their historic capital is a consequence of the Soviet–Turkish treaty of 1921 which ceded to Turkey areas including Kars and Ani even though they had been under Russian control since 1877 and had even been awarded to Armenia under the Treaty of Sèvres in 1920. (See the *History* section in *Chapter 1* for a discussion of this issue.) The possible return of Ani to Armenia in exchange for two Kurdish villages further north was raised in intergovernmental talks in 1968 but nothing resulted.

To reach Anipemza from Yerevan the quickest way is probably via Armavir and then continue on the H17 which follows the railway from Armavir to Gyumri. The road mostly has a good surface. The alternative route via Ashtarak, Talin, Tatul, Hatsashen, Tsamakasar, Suser and Bagravan, where one turns left onto the road from Gyumri, is good until Tsamakasar. From there to Bagravan it is decidedly not good; in particular, Nor Artik to Bagravan would be difficult in a car without high clearance. However, it is a scenic route which passes through several very rural villages with village ponds, donkey carts and an interesting cemetery at Bagravan.

TO THE ARTIK DISTRICT The easiest way to get there (in that the road has the best surface) is to head south on the main road from Gyumri towards Yerevan. Some 15km south from Gyumri there is a crossroads. Anyone wishing to see an 11th-century church, disused since Soviet days (and guarded by hostile geese on the occasion of the author's visit), plus two surviving fragments of wall from a medieval castle at the heart of a (decidedly) unspoilt village, should turn right for **Gusanagyugh**. However, the detour does not really justify the time spent.

Around 25km south of Gyumri the road reaches **Maralik**. Turn left towards Artik just before the railway bridge. On the right, opposite the road junction, there is a gigantic example of Soviet central planning: an enormous cotton-spinning factory, now operating at a fraction of its original capacity. It was typical of Soviet economic policy to site a large cotton-spinning factory far from the sources of cotton (in Uzbekistan and Tajikistan), far from the markets for cloth (mostly in the western USSR), requiring a dedicated railway line to be built to transport materials in and out, and not even near significant sources of power.

Several interesting monasteries lie close to this road. The first, which can be seen across the fields to the right, is the **Monastery of the Apostles**. Built of red tuff it can be approached to within a few hundred metres by dirt road and a quiet walk after leaving the vehicle might be rewarded by the sight of European sousliks (a burrow-dwelling member of the squirrel family) between the road and the monastery. The dome of the 11th-century monastery has long since collapsed and there was considerable further earthquake damage in 2009 but it is still possible to get an idea of how the building must have looked. Notwithstanding its damaged state, the building is still used and there are the remains of recently burnt candles and of the cloths and handkerchiefs which believers leave when a special wish is expressed.

Turning right about 7km from Maralik a road leads to Pemzashen and Lernakert. **Pemzashen** has a complex of three medieval churches at a lower ground level than the present village. The now domeless 6th-century **St Gevorg Church** has three apses within its rectangular walls and an octagonal tambour. The tambour is notable with its four windows alternating with niches and shell-like fan vaults allowing the transition from octagonal tambour to dome. The tympanum over the entrance shows the Virgin Mary holding Jesus with, on the right, an angel and another figure. There was a similar composition on the left, now defaced. The small chapel to the south, reconsecrated in 2010 to act as the village church, is also 6th century. To the north of St Gevorg are the foundations of a 5th-century basilica. Continuing on to **Lernakert** you pass the ruins of a 9th-century domed basilica and a new church (2005) before turning left from the asphalt road onto a good cobbled road which winds up through the village to the 4th-century church of St John the Baptist. This large barrel-vaulted basilica has a new roof courtesy of the Women's Association of Lebanon. The trim village is said to be one of the oldest in Armenia. It has a khachkar-carver's workshop, on the right as you descend from the church.

Returning to the Artik road, turn right in Artik to cross the railway line by an improbably large flyover and then turn right and right again. Partway up the hill southwest of the town is **Lmbatavank**. This small 7th-century monastery whose single-aisle church is dedicated to St Stephen, is also built of red tuff and, with its high dome, is very well preserved being particularly notable for its frescoes. There are good views to the north from the hillside location. Scattered around the church are old hollowed-out coffins, also made of tuff.

Artik has a few older buildings but most of the town obviously dates from the post-1945 Soviet period. It was developed as a centre of tuff mining and the recent upsurge in construction work means that unemployment has fallen slightly from its very high level after the collapse of the Soviet Union.

HARICHAVANK (MONASTERY) To reach the large and important Monastery of Harichavank turn left in Artik after crossing the railway and then turn right up the hill. Just before the prison turn right for the village of **Harich**: the monastery is at the far end of the main street. It is situated on the edge of a small ravine.

The monastery was founded by the 7th century and expanded during the 13th. Most of the ancillary buildings were added after 1850 when the Katholikos moved his summer residence here. The original 7th-century church, St Gregory's, has a round dome. From the southwest corner room a secret passage leads down into the gorge and a secret room is concealed above the roof of the same room. Its bell tower, resting on large columns, is a 19th-century addition as are the small chapels which adjoin it. The much larger Mother of God Church of 1201 has an unusual 16-sided umbrella dome and much elaborate decoration around the tambour. Inside, cantilevered steps lead to the upper storeys of the western corner rooms which are unusual in having arcaded windows looking onto the nave. In between the two churches is a very large *gavit* whose porch is particularly finely decorated with small twisted columns and inlaid carved red and black stones which show a striking oriental influence. On the east façade of the Mother of God Church is a relief showing the founders of the church and also one of a lion. An unusual feature is the small chapel perched on top of a high pillar of rock in the gorge; it owes its present inaccessible location to an earthquake.

LORI PROVINCE

Lori, Armenia's largest province in terms of land area, is very beautiful. Largely a high plateau with small mountain ranges, its outstanding features are the deep gorges which fissure the landscape. Apart from these river valleys, Lori is sparsely populated. The principal rivers are the Debed and the Dzoraget. The Debed rises in the southwest of the province where it is called the Pambak, flows east and then turns north towards the Georgian border. It ultimately joins the Kura whose delta is on the Caspian Sea south of Baku, Azerbaijan. The Debed Valley on the Georgian border is the lowest-lying part of Armenia with an altitude of 400m above sea level. The Dzoraget rises to the west in Shirak province and then flows east past Stepanavan to join the Debed halfway between Vanadzor and Alaverdi. The spectacular gorges of these rivers are excellent places to find eagles, vultures and also interesting smaller birds such as rock nuthatches. In addition, they are where Lori's most appealing sights, its ancient monasteries and fortresses, are to be found.

WHERE TO STAY AND EAT Lori is a relatively cheap area of Armenia and very acceptable accommodation can be had for 'shoestring' or 'budget' prices. Because of the terrain there is no one place from which it is easy to visit all there is to see. Stepanavan is the best place to stay if wishing to visit Lori Berd or any of the remoter areas north of Stepanavan. For the monasteries of the Debed Gorge, the most popular sites, the Tufenkian at Dzoraget is currently the only good, convenient hotel. A cheaper option, of course, would be a homestay in any of the towns or villages. Allow at least a full day to visit all the monasteries in the Debed Gorge. Vanadzor is a useful overnight stop when moving from one area to another.

Stepanavan

MM Hotel (5 rooms) 9 Nzhdeh St; ☎256 24050; m 099 072414. A pleasant small hotel on the site of the pre-earthquake bus station, attached to a café. Café ⊕ from b/fast to 23.00. Cheaper rate in winter. **$**

Anahit Holiday Hotel (8 cottages each with 2 dbl, sitting room & shower room) 1 Antarayan St; ☎256 22578; m 093 072689 (Galina). A former Soviet holiday complex in enormous grounds on the west of the town. The approach up a long drive is dismal but the renovated cottages are satisfactory, if basic. Swimming pool. Restaurant (⊕ 08.00–midnight

in summer, otherwise 10.00 until the last customer goes) is a popular venue for celebratory parties. No cards. Price includes FB. **$**

Lori Hotel (12 rooms) 11 Nzhdeh St; ☎256 22323. B/fast not served until 09.00. Evening meal AMD2,500/pp. No cards. **$**

Stepanavan Information Centre Guest House (2 rooms) See page 205 for contact details or contact Armine directly, m 093 196096; e armine5@yahoo.com. Shared shower room. Wi-Fi. Dinner upon request. Good reports from those who have stayed there. B/fast included. AMD5,000/pp. **$**

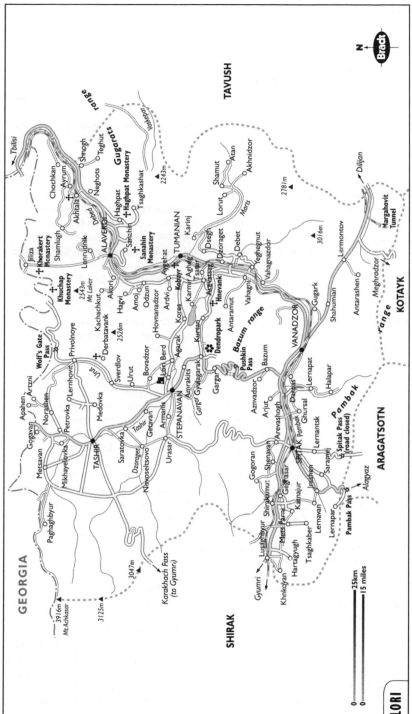

LORI

GEORGIA

TAVUSH

KOTAYK

ARAGATSOTN

SHIRAK

N

Tbilisi

Gugarats range

Chochkan
Ayrum
Smogh
Teghut
Neghots
Tsaghkashat
Yostepor

Akhtala
Haghpat
Haghpat Monastery
Shamlugh
2243m

Jiliza
Khorakert Monastery
Lernrubihk
Sanahin
Sanahin Monastery

Khuchap Monastery
2543m
Mt Lalver
Akori
Hagvi
Amol
Odzun
Karni
Aghte
Tsater
Sahinh
ALAVERDI
TUMANIAN
Avetran
Karinj
Lorut
Shamut
Atan
Akhnidzor

Debed
Kachachkut
Hovnanadzor
Kores
Ardvi
Kurtan
Hnevank
Vahagni
Vahagnazdor
Dsegh
Dzoraget
Debet
Yeghegnut

Wolf's Gate Pass
Privolnoye
Derbatavank
2526m
Bovadzor
Agarak
Antaramut
Bazum range
Pushkin Pass
Bazum
3016m
Lermontov

Urut
Sverdlov
Lori Berd
Gyulagarak
Dendropark
Gargar
Aznvadzor
VANADZOR
Gugark
Shahumian
Antarashen
Meghradzor range
Dilijan
Margahovit Tunnel

Apahen
Artzni
Lernhovit
Gargar
Arjut
Lernapat
Halapar

Gogavan
Noralshen
Petrovka
Medovka
Amrakts
Arevashogh
Dpitps
Ghursal
Pambak range

Metsavan
Mikhayelovka
Saratovka
Getavan
STEPANAVAN
Lernantsk

Paghaghbyur
TASHIR
Dzoraget
Novoseltsovo
Tashir
Urasar
Armanis
Gogoran
Shenavan
Arevashogh
SPITAK
Pambak
Sarapsi

3047m
Karakhach Pass (to Gyumri)
Lusaghbyur
Shirakamut
Gegharar
Jrashen
Spitak Pass (road closed)

Gyumri
Khnkoyan
Meta Parni
Katnajur
Lernavan
Lernapar
Pambak Pass
Alogyaz

3916m
Mt Achkasar
3125m
Hartagyugh
Tsaghkaber

25km
15 miles

0
0

203

Vanadzor

🏠 **Argishti** (22 rooms) 1 Batoumi St; ☎322 42556/7. A good hotel in the centre of town with attractive marble floors & stairs. No cards. **$$**

🏠 **Green House** (16 rooms) 8d Banaki St; ☎322 40015; m 091 310070 (Anahit); e greenhousehotel@yahoo.com. Banaki St is parallel to & 4 streets south of main Tigran Mets Av, between Miasnikian & Nzhdeh sts. A comfortable hotel but the soundproofing is poor. Evening meal can be ordered in advance. Internet available. Pay on arrival. **$$**

🏠 **Metropolina Hotel** (formerly Gugark Hotel) (17 rooms) 20 Tigran Mets Av; ☎322 41519. Very central. Occupies 3rd & 4th floors of the building; reception on 4th. A cheap, no frills option. No restaurant. B/fast not available but plenty of nearby places to eat. No cards. Some rooms have no hot water. Room with no hot water & no TV AMD9,000 (sgl occupancy AMD4,500). With hot water & TV AMD11,000–15,000. **$**

Elsewhere in the province

🏠 **Tufenkian Avan Dzoraget** (34 rooms) Debed Gorge at Dzoraget. Bookings through the Tufenkian office in Yerevan; ☎10 655877; e hotels@tufenkian.am; www.tufenkian.am. Still the best in the area but the standard of food & service in the restaurant had slipped a little when I was there in 2010. Hotel is about halfway between Vanadzor, the provincial capital, & Alaverdi. Wi-Fi. Cards accepted. Stiff supplement for a view of the river. Without/with a view **$$$$/$$$$$**

🏠 **Hekyat Restaurant/Hotel** (3 rooms & 2 cottages) Gyulagarak, near Dendropark; m 093 303100 (Hrair). There is no sign outside this excellent restaurant whose name means 'fairy tale' but it is the collection of buildings on the left just before entering the wooded hillside at Dendropark. Restaurant highly recommended. A very generous collection of salads, cheeses, beer, jug of fresh homemade lemonade & tea/coffee for 2 cost AMD8,500. Well-presented cottages, 3 floors, sleep up to 8 persons. AMD40,000/cottage. B/fast extra approx AMD3,000/pp. **$**

🏠 **Spitak YMCA** (3 rooms, 2–3 beds each; 1 family room, up to 6 persons) 4a Aygestan, Spitak; ☎255 62901; e spitak@ymca.am; www.ymca.am. It was due to open late 2010. B/fast included. AMD5,000/pp. **$**

✗ **Armen's** Alaverdi; ☎0374 22474; m 0912 10624. One of Armenia's pleasantest restaurants & very highly recommended. It is reached by crossing the main bridge at Alaverdi (the one which is actually 2 separate bridges – one for each direction) & then turning immediately left. The restaurant is 1km along this road on the right. The fare is the ubiquitous Armenian barbecued food, *khorovats*, but it is easily among the best. Armen, the proprietor, won first prize in a local BBQ competition to celebrate the removal of the wooden scaffolding from Akhtala Monastery (see page 217) & was then invited to appear in a cookery programme on one of the major national TV channels. He now judges in what has become an annual BBQ competition. Vegetarians can eat well here. Armen can also arrange local homestays.

New accommodation near **Akhtala** may become available during the lifetime of this book; be sure to check updates.bradtguides.com for the latest developments. What promises to be to be an attractive complex is being developed north of Akhtala. The estate originally belonged to a noble family and was a military establishment in Soviet days. One house, having been extensively rebuilt (including seismic protection), is nearing completion and what was the laundry block in Soviet days is fast becoming holiday rooms. The first guests were planned to be accommodated in late 2010. The hotel will be an excellent centre for walking, wildlife and exploring the Debed region. From the balcony of the still-to-be-restored Swiss-style mansion I looked down on three golden eagles soaring high above the valley. The estate is reached by going straight ahead at the junction where the road to Akhtala Monastery turns left round a hairpin bend towards Shamlugh (see page 217).

OTHER PRACTICALITIES For **train and bus services** to the province see *Chapter 2*, pages 73–6. **Minibuses** ply frequently between towns and from Vanadzor run almost everywhere, both locally and long distance, for example, hourly to Yerevan from 07.00 to 19.30 at a cost of about AMD1,500. The 120km journey takes 1½ hours. Buses run to Tbilisi every day, with the route shared between Armenian and Georgian operators on alternate days; expect to pay AMD3,500. On Friday mornings a 15-seat minibus runs to Stepanakert for AMD6,000. A good view of the Debed Gorge is obtained from the minibus between Alaverdi and Vanadzor. **Taxis** are often a convenient way to travel between historic sites; a round trip to Sanahin, Haghpat, Akhtala and Odzun, for example, costs around AMD6,000.

Vanadzor, the largest town, has all facilities, with Stepanavan and Spitak being reasonably provided. Stepanavan is the only place which has a **tourist information centre** (*11 Milion St;* ✆ *256 22158;* e *stepanavaninfo@gmail.com; www.stepanavaninfo.am;* ⊕ *10.00–19.00 Mon–Sat*). This is an excellent information centre, with a good website, which offers information on local minibus routes, places of interest and accommodation. They can provide a map of Stepanavan. There is also some accommodation within the centre (see page 202).

There are a number of **tour operators** in Vanadzor but they deal mainly with out-going tourism for Armenians, not in-coming tourism for visitors. Aerostar Ltd (*71/2 Tigran Mets Av;* ✆ *322 22790*) is one such operator but staff were helpful in finding out local addresses and telephone numbers. Only Armenian spoken.

VANADZOR (*Telephone code 322*) Vanadzor, the provincial capital, is situated on the River Debed at 1,350m above sea level between the Pambak mountain range to the south and the Bazum range to the north; both ranges exceed 3,000m in height. Prior to 1935 Vanadzor was called Kharaklisa. In 1935, it was renamed Kirovakan after Sergei Kirov (1886–1934), the head of the Communist Party in Leningrad, whom Stalin arranged to have assassinated because his popularity in the party made him a potential rival. In 1993, the city acquired its present name from the local Vanadzor River. Formerly the third-largest city in Armenia it was damaged by the 1988 earthquake but not to anything like the same extent as Gyumri and Spitak and its central square with buildings of pink tuff and its main shopping street survived more or less intact. Since then Gyumri's falling population means that Vanadzor is now Armenia's second city. An important industrial centre in Soviet times, most of the former chemical plants making products as diverse as glue and nail polish remover are now closed. The continued closure of most of the huge factories means that the city no longer lives under a dense pall of acrid smoke and the atmosphere is now clean and pleasant. Although there is little to tempt visitors to stay except as a transit stop on the way to Georgia or the monasteries further north, Vanadzor could also provide a suitable base for hiking in the surrounding hills. Banks, currency exchanges, tour operators, eateries, shops and most other facilities can be found on Tigran Mets Avenue, the main street. Parallel Lusavorich Street has the main markets while Miasnikian Street running between the two has clothes shops. From the main square, Lori Square, a short dual carriageway leads to the **bus and train stations**. **Taxis** are also stationed here.

What to see and do If you are staying in Vanadzor or find you have a couple of hours to spare in the town then there are a number of places of minor interest to visit. The **Stepan Zorian House Museum** (*24 Stepan Zorian St;* ✆ *43093;* ⊕ *10.00–17.00 Tue–Sat, 10.00–15.00 Sun; AMD100*) is bright and well presented with enough English to make it accessible. The writer Stepan Zorian (1889–1967) is best known for his novels and short stories based on Armenian village life. The small **Local History Museum** (*1/1 Tigran Mets Av;* \ *41751;* ☉ *10.30–17.30 Mon–Fri, 10.30–16.30 Sat; closed for lunch 12.00–12.30; guided tour in English inc AMD1,000*) displays local artefacts including a good collection of decorative metalwork. **Vanadzor Museum of Fine Art** (*52 Tigran Mets Av;* \ *43938;* e *info@vanart.org; www.vanart.com;* ☉ *10.00–17.00 Tue–Sat, 10.00–16.00 Sun; for guided tour in English contact 1 day in advance; AMD500*) was founded as a branch of the national gallery; it concentrates on artists of Lori region.

There are three **churches** in the town centre, a small Russian one near the train station, a large new one at the junction of Miasnikian and Stepan Zorian streets and a third, built in 1831 on the site of an earlier church, where the road to Alaverdi crosses the river.

SPITAK West from Vanadzor, the main road and rail lines to Gyumri follow the Debed to pass by the town of Spitak, in the district where many of Armenia's cabbages and carrots are grown. Spitak was close to the epicentre of the 1988 earthquake and was completely destroyed by it. Much rebuilding, including a new church, has been funded by the international community but the former factories still lie ruined and derelict. On a hill overlooking the town is the official **memorial to the victims of the earthquake**. Visiting it is thought-provoking. Firstly it is reached by a long flight of concrete steps, over half of which have disintegrated and all of which are overgrown by tall thistles as well as a colourful range of weeds. At the top of the steps one reaches the rather grandiose memorial, now equally neglected with much of its marble cladding having fallen off and giving the appearance that total collapse may not be long delayed. Possibly the memorial's neglect reflects the residents' wish not to remember: to look, as far as possible, forward rather than back. Or is there an implied criticism of the shoddy Soviet building standards which contributed so much to increasing the death toll? It is readily apparent that local residents never go there and perhaps they even wish it to be removed. There is no inscription in any language.

Opposite the hill with the memorial is the town **graveyard**. Many of the victims are buried here. Some graves show not only a picture of the deceased but also a clock face with the hands pointing to 11.41, the time the earthquake struck. Those of younger people often show a flower with a broken stalk symbolising a life broken while in full bloom. The graveyard is less neglected than the monument but is clearly little frequented. Though the survivors can never forget, would they really want to remind themselves by coming here? And perhaps many of the deceased have no surviving relatives. Certainly some of the graves show three generations of victims from the baby a few weeks old to the grandparents. Still remaining in the graveyard is the prefabricated metal church which served in the immediate aftermath of the earthquake and which was erected within 40 days of the disaster.

There is another graveyard in Spitak round the other side of the hill. It is a **war cemetery** where German prisoners of war lie buried. It's a tranquil place – a flowery meadow with rows of metal crosses. Although the identity of each person is known, this is not marked on the grave with the sole exception of one grave where a relative has provided a normal tombstone. There is also a large cross bearing the words *Hier ruhen Kriegesgefangene – Opfer des zweites Weltkrieges* ('Here rest prisoners of war – victims of World War II'). The prisoners worked on the construction of a nearby sugar factory but that was destroyed in the earthquake. The German government pays a local man to look after the graves and to preserve the meadow by cutting the vegetation annually. This is the largest of the German war cemeteries in Armenia. The second largest is at Sevan and others are at Artashat and Abovian.

THE PUSHKIN PASS There are two main roads north from Vanadzor, both of which continue to Georgia. The more westerly can be reached by heading west out of the city for about 6km along the main Gyumri road and then turning right. The present-day road avoids the Pushkin Pass (2,037m) by a 2km-long tunnel which has now been renovated and (dimly) lit. If driving, keep to the 40km/h speed limit in the tunnel: on two occasions when the author used it there were unlit obstructions blocking half the road. On one occasion a driver was changing a tyre on his lorry and the next time workmen were carrying out repairs.

The pass gets its name from Pushkin who, on a visit to the Caucasus, met there in 1829 a cart carrying the body of Alexander Griboyedov (1795–1829) who had been killed in Persia, an incident described in Pushkin's *Journey to Erzrurum*. Griboyedov, whom Pushkin knew well, was a satirical playwright whose best-known play, *Woe from Wit* (1824), was only performed and published posthumously – its hero is branded a lunatic when he arrives in Moscow full of liberal and progressive ideas, a dangerous practice there in either the Tsarist or the communist era. Griboyedov was also a diplomat and instrumental in Russia's peace negotiations with Turkey following the war of 1828–29 when Russia gained control of much of Armenia. After that he was appointed Russia's ambassador to Persia. Russia's defeats of Turkey and Persia and its consequent territorial expansion were followed by a change of tack in Russia's foreign policy as it was now considered important to ensure that both Turkey and Persia nevertheless survived as significant powers. Russia feared that dissolution of either might lead to the possible appearance of other, stronger powers on its borders. Both states accepted Russian control of the Caucasus but while Griboyedov was in Teheran negotiating with Persia an angry mob stormed the Russian embassy. His mangled body, barely recognisable, was being returned on the cart which Pushkin encountered.

STEPANAVAN AND LORI BERD (FORTRESS) (*Stepanavan telephone code 256*) After the tunnel the road descends in a long series of zigzags to reach the town of **Stepanavan**. There is a dramatic change of scenery as one emerges from the tunnel: gone are the bare stony hillsides and in their place are lush wooded ones. In early summer the fields as one descends are an amazing sight of yellows and reds with masses of buttercups and poppies. Stepanavan suffered damage in 1988 but received little outside help and it has only relatively recently started to recover. Stepanavan is named in honour of Stepan Shahumian (1878–1918), an Armenian who was instrumental in imposing Bolshevik rule in Baku, Azerbaijan. Faced with an uprising he fled but was captured and executed by local anti-Bolsheviks, with some British involvement. The town is centred on the statue of Shahumian, near which can be found small shops, cafés, the museum, information centre (see page 205) and the bus station.

Stepanavan itself has a few places of minor interest. The **Stepan Shahumian Museum** (*housed in the square orange tuff building on Nzhdeh St;* ⊕ *09.00–17.00 Mon–Fri; AMD100*) is actually built around the Shahumian homestead, an intriguing concept. The museum is labelled only in Armenian and no English is spoken. The house itself is of some interest, as is the model of the secret passage to the underground printing press where Shahumian printed communist leaflets. The **Communist Caves** (signposted on the left on the road south), where Shahumian and fellow revolutionaries met, can be visited. There is not much to see but the views of the Dzoraget Gorge are good. **St Sargis Church** is reached by turning left down one of the small side streets on the main road south shortly after leaving the town centre. Renovated in 2009, it dates from the 13th century. A khachkar, now on the east façade, gives the foundation date in Armenian letters (see *Chapter 1, Sundials*, page 36) as 666. Adding the 551 years needed for calendrical adjustment, this equates to AD1217.

However, the main reason for visiting Stepanavan is **Lori Berd** ('Lori Fortress') (⊕ *always*) just outside the town. It is one of Armenia's most impressive medieval fortress sites. To reach it cross the large viaduct over the gorge of the Dzoraget ('Gorge River') at the north end of the town. At the far end of the viaduct, turn right and continue for about 2km, then turn right again onto an unmade road through the village of Lori Berd and continue for another 2km. (A taxi from Stepanavan costs AMD1,000 one-way, plus waiting time.) There is a small car park just before the fortress where substantial remains of the defensive wall and towers survive, as well as other buildings. A locked gate formerly prevented direct entry and it was necessary to climb over the ruined wall. However, the gate is now usually left open. The triangular site is spectacularly situated between two gorges: that of the Dzoraget and that of the Urut. The only side of the site not protected by these gorges, which are too steep-sided easily to scale, is the northern one and this was protected by a high stone wall with towers, at the foot of which there was a moat. As well as the area within the fortifications the town spread outside them and outlying districts also developed across the two gorges. Bridges were constructed to provide access from these outlying districts: that over the Urut survives and can be seen from the eastern part of the site. It can be reached by a steep path which winds down from just inside the gate and which is very slippery in wet weather.

The fortress was built by David Anghonin (ruled 989–1049), member of a junior branch of Ani's Bagratid dynasty, to be the new capital of the Tashir-Dzoraget kingdom: there were five Armenian kingdoms at the time. Though suffering heavy casualties, the Seljuk Emir Kizil managed to capture Lori Berd in 1105 and it subsequently came under Georgian rule following the Seljuk defeat by Davit IV Agmashenebelis (David the Builder) (ruled 1089–1121). Davit's great-granddaughter Queen Tamar transferred Lori to the ownership of the Armenian Prince Sargis Zakarian for his assistance in inflicting further defeats on the Seljuks between 1195 and 1204. The town subsequently flourished under his rule and that of his son, but in 1228 Shah Jala-Edin of Khoremsk captured the outlying districts and in 1238 the fortress itself fell to the Mongol Khan Jagat, allegedly because the captains charged with organising the defence spent too much time drinking and too little praying, or so their brother-in-law wrote. The town was ransacked and for over 200 years it passed through various hands only to fall to invaders again in 1430. Decline, however, continued and the last inhabitants left as recently as 1931, largely because of problems with the water supply.

The first building encountered is a **bathhouse** with two baths and evidence of pipes running in the walls. In the centre of the fortress can be seen a rectangular-roofed building comprising six square-domed bays with pillars supporting the arches dividing the bays. The building incorporates medieval tombstones and the doorway is flanked by two khachkars. The exterior walls show evidence of several phases of building. The fortress remained under Muslim occupation until the 18th century and this building has a niche in the south wall facing Mecca, indicating that it dates from that period, although there may have been an earlier church on the site. Built onto north side is what looks like a **dwelling house** with fireplace and chimney. It is home to a family of redstarts in the breeding season. In buildings on the side of the Dzoraget Gorge there is more evidence of pipes suggesting a washroom or latrine.

NORTHWEST FROM STEPANAVAN To head north from Stepanavan one should turn left after crossing the viaduct. For some length the road keeps east of the river at a distance of a few hundred metres. It is well worth stopping and walking across to look down into the immensely impressive gorge. The road passes through a series of Russian villages built by refugees who fled here to avoid religious persecution during the time of Catherine the Great. The houses typically have two storeys with living accommodation for the family being on the upper storey with its balcony and the lower storey being used for storage. About 15km from Stepanavan the road reaches the small town now called **Tashir**. Founded in 1844, it was originally named Vorontsovka after Prince Mikhail Vorontsov (1785–1856), viceroy to Tsar Nicholas I, who had been brought up in Britain where his father was Russian ambassador. Vorontsov's role in the Caucasus was considerable. Appointed Governor General of New Russia with 'unlimited powers' during the reign of Tsar Alexander I he was so successful in integrating southern Ukraine into Russia that he was promoted to viceroy in 1845 and his mandate was extended to the newly acquired territories in the Caucasus. In 1935, Vorontsovka was renamed Kalinino after Mikhail Kalinin (1875–1946), the communist functionary who became titular head of the Soviet state.

At the far end of Tashir a road branches left from the main road to Tbilisi and heads northwest across marshy ground to the village of **Metsavan**. On the hillside at the far end of Metsavan is the small 10th-century **Monastery of St John**. Church and graveyard are themselves surrounded by a wall made of gravestones. Retracing one's steps and then bearing left through the village, the bad road becomes a worse track across grasslands before reaching, in about 4km, the exceptionally ruined **Church of St George**. In no way does the surviving fragment of a wall justify the visit but the whole area on a fine sunny evening is magical. The lower grassy slopes give way to a stupendous natural rock garden on the higher ground with its wonderful carpets of alpine plants. There are views across the plain to the distant eastern mountains and a small river tumbles down from the Georgian border. However, it wouldn't be worth going in the rain!

NORTHEAST FROM STEPANAVAN The road northeast from Stepanavan is in poor condition for the first part where it follows the fertile valley of the Urut and in dire condition later on when it crosses the pass. It should be attempted only in dry weather and preferably on a lorry.

Ten kilometres from Stepanavan, the Urut is crossed at the village of **Sverdlov**, named after Yakov Sverdlov (1885–1919), a Bolshevik who was instrumental in overthrowing the elected Russian constitutional assembly in January 1918. He died from influenza the following year. Beyond Sverdlov the **Monastery of Derbatavank** can be seen across fields to the right. Dating from the 11th century it is a single-nave structure with barrel vaulting and rather tall for its size. Although attractively situated it was insensitively restored using concrete blocks during the Soviet era.

Continuing up the narrowing valley the road passes **Privolnoye**, a village with a Russian church and Russian-style houses and the last point where food and drink can be bought. Turn right and then second left in the village. Four kilometres beyond the village a customs post can be seen straight ahead. Turn right before reaching it to climb up to the **Wolf's Gate Pass** (1,787m). The road is closed in winter and absolutely dreadful in summer with sections which resemble the bed of a river: deep pot-holes, deep mud and huge puddles. Eventually, 33km from Stepanavan one reaches the border post. At one time it was possible to negotiate with the border guards to continue to **Khuchap Monastery** (see page 219), negotiation being necessary because of the need to cross a sliver of Georgian territory. This is said to have become more difficult recently. However, it is actually better to visit Khuchap via the village of **Jiliza** as Khuchap can then be combined with equally worthwhile Khorakert (but see note on page 218). If the visit *is* possible, the border guards are likely to press the usual Armenian hospitality on visitors and will almost certainly send someone to act as a guide for anyone going to the monastery, partly because it is hard to find, partly for something different to do, and partly because they will have cleared with their Georgian opposite numbers permission to cross the bit of Georgia. It takes about an hour to walk to it in a side valley south of the river: it takes longer to return because visitors will have been spotted as they walk past a small isolated house on the way out and will be unable to refuse coffee and refreshments on the way back. The walk is very beautiful along the river and then through orchards into the forest. It involves crossing the river, and wading may be required.

THE DEBED GORGE The other road north from Vanadzor, as well as the railway to Tbilisi, follows the scenic gorge of the Debed. The gorge is noteworthy for having five of Armenia's finest churches/monasteries, all of them worth visiting. Of the churches two are very touristy, two see fewer tourists and the other is somewhere in between. Leave Vanadzor by Tumanian Street, cross the river and continue straight on. (Note: for anyone who is coming from Stepanavan and has 4x4 transport available it is much better to head east from there and visit Hnevank as well. See page 220.) There are several short tunnels on this road, some of them curving and all unlit. Drive very carefully indeed through these tunnels – the official speed limit is 35km/h – as they are used by pedestrians and can have memorable pot-holes.

After 20km a road goes off right across the river to follow the valley of a tributary for a few kilometres before turning abruptly left to wind up the side of the valley to the plateau. It reaches the village of **Dsegh** where the house museum of the poet Hovhannes Tumanian (1869–1923) is situated (see page 44). Although tourists who do not speak Armenian are unlikely to have encountered his works, the museum itself gives an interesting insight into living conditions in Tsarist days, notably the two older rooms with their rock floors and chest-like bed. The monument outside the museum was erected after the collapse of the Soviet Union when Vano Siradeghian, Minister of Internal Affairs, decided that the poet's heart should be buried here rather than kept in a jar in the anatomical museum of the medical university in Yerevan. Opposite the museum is a church, built in the 7th century and quite unlike most Armenian churches; it resembles a large village hall, very plain and with a flat wooden ceiling. Retracing one's steps to the main road it is worth stopping to admire the view over the valley. Golden eagles and lammergeyers, Europe's largest vultures, are quite common here and alpine swifts nest in crevices in the valley side.

KOBAYR MONASTERY (⊕ *always*) Back at the main road turn right to head north again. At the village of **Dzoraget** the road from Stepanavan via Hnevank comes in on the left shortly before the site of the new Tufenkian hotel. In about 5km the road passes the small industrial town of **Tumanian**, named after the poet and seriously marred by a huge abandoned brick factory. About 2km further north look out for a small railway station up above the road on the left. This is **Kobayr**, site of one of Armenia's most impressive ruins. About 400m south of the station a track goes off left, passing underneath the railway by a low bridge. Park here and walk up to the monastery. Take the path to the right as you face the bridge for a short distance then cross the railway line (beware of trains: this line is used) opposite some steps. Go up the steps then follow the path, which becomes steps, as it winds back and forth between small houses with their gardens. Keep making for the monastic-looking building straight ahead, bearing right at the spring and then left. The ten-minute climb is well worth it. The track underneath the bridge also leads to the monastery but it is steeper and can be muddy.

According to an inscription, the **main church** was built in 1171 by Mariam, daughter of Kyurik II. At this time the Turkish Seljuks ruled Armenia but delegated control to local princes. Following Georgian victories over the Seljuk Turks in 1195 and 1202 the monastery came under Georgian rule, passing into the control of the Zakarian family who adhered to the Georgian Orthodox Church rather than the Armenian Church. (The Georgian Church differed in having accepted the views of the Council of Chalcedon, which took place in 451, over the duality of Christ's nature.) This explains the occurrence of Georgian features, notably the Georgian-style frescoes and carved inscriptions. One of these inscriptions records the building of the bell tower and mausoleum in the centre of the monastery in 1279, the mausoleum housing the tombs of Shahnshah Mkhargryel and his wife Vaneni. Much of the south side of the complex has descended into the gorge below but the roofless apse and parts of the other walls survive with Georgian-style frescoes in the apse and chapel. The frescoes were well restored in 1971 but those in the apse have been exposed to the elements for years. Restoration of the church is now underway. While it will no doubt better protect the frescoes it is making the church darker and the dramatic view from inside the church down to the river in its gorge may well soon be blocked. In the apse the frescoes comprise three rows: in the top row the Virgin Mary and archangels; in the middle row Jesus and the Last Supper; in the bottom row figures of saints. The frescoes in the chapel are in a similar style with vivid portrayals of Jesus and the disciples. At the time of writing the chapel was locked and even on peeping through the door the frescoes were not visible because the chapel was full of building material. Presumably at some time in the future it will be possible to admire them again. Note that a torch is needed to see them. The bell tower has also collapsed and only the foundations and the bases of pillars can be seen. The **13th-century refectory** is on the northwestern side of the main church slightly up the hill. Surrounding the whole complex was a fortified wall, and the well-preserved gateway together with a further small church dated 1223 lie to the north of the main group of buildings. It is possible for those suitably shod to climb further up the hillside and look down on the site. The views from there are even more impressive and there is another excellent chance of seeing lammergeyers.

ODZUN AND ARDVI Continuing north along the main road one reaches the left turn for Odzun in about 7km. **Odzun** itself is on the plateau and the road winds up the valley side to reach it. It is worth visiting for its **church** constructed of pink felsite (☉ *usually in the tourist season from 10.00 to 19.00. If shut the caretaker can often be found & the priest lives nearby*). It is a large building, dating from the 6th century, reconstructed in the 8th, and one of Armenia's finest basilicas with a cupola. It stands on the site of an early 4th-century church (303–13) which was destroyed by an earthquake in the 5th century. Tradition holds that the apostle Thomas ordained priests at Odzun on his way to India and that before he left he buried Christ's swaddling clothes where the present altar stands. A 6th-century inscription above the southern door of the church records this tradition. The two small bell towers at the east end were a much later addition in the late 19th century. On the north and south sides of the church were unusual arcaded cloisters, though those on the north no longer exist. The west cloister has a blind wall with an arched entrance in the middle. Inside there are three naves, the two side naves very narrow. The roof is barrel vaulted and the rib-vaulted octagonal tambour is supported by four free-standing columns. There are two additional supporting columns at the west end of the church. Carved stones from the 4th-century church were built into the wall of the church, most notably a carving of the Virgin Mary and Christ Child above the font in the north wall. The 2009 fresco in the apse depicts the Virgin and Child in the same postures. The most notable feature of the exterior carving is on the east façade above the central window where Christ can be seen holding open the Gospel of St John with angels below. At each side of the central window on the south side stands an angel with traces of another figure, probably Christ.

In the surrounding graveyard the clergy were buried near the church and were depicted on the gravestones holding staffs. Beside the church is a most unusual **funerary monument**, one of only two in this style in Armenia – the other is at Aghudi in Syunik province. It comprises a stepped platform supporting two slender obelisk-shaped carved stelae set between double arches. The carvings on the stelae are divided into panels depicting, on the east and west sides, biblical scenes together with the coming of Christianity to Armenia, and on the north and south sides, geometrical motifs and floral shapes. It has been suggested that the monument might commemorate Hovhannes Odznetsi who was Katholikos from 717 until 728 and undertook rebuilding work at Odzun but its style suggests an earlier date and erection in the 6th century seems more likely.

Continuing through Odzun across the plateau the road heads south and then west towards Ardvi. It is worth stopping on a fine day and going across to the ruined **Horomigh Church** which is right on the edge of the gorge. It was built in the 7th century and rebuilt in the 13th using a darker stone which contrasts considerably and, having scarcely weathered, almost has the appearance of concrete. The view down into the gorge of the Debed is impressive. The tiny **Holy Cross Chapel** can be seen below and in spring the plateau is covered by an amazing carpet of flowers. Continuing to **Ardvi**, the 10th-century Holy Resurrection Church is on the left as you enter the village, a small rectangular structure on a knoll. The roof of the barrel-vaulted nave has collapsed but that of the apse still stands. Two of the gravestones here depict a figure with a smaller figure within it, indicating the grave of a woman who had been pregnant when she died. Beyond the village is the small Monastery of St John on a hillside. The 17th-century church and its separate bell tower have very low doors, only a little over 1m high. The bell tower incorporates an unusual khachkar of a person wearing a hat and shoes and carrying a round object and a square one. The cemetery, on an adjoining hillock, has a very fine collection of khachkars; graves here span the centuries from the 6th to the 19th.

ALAVERDI AND SANAHIN MONASTERY (*Alaverdi telephone code 253*) The two monasteries of Sanahin and Haghpat were, in 1996, Armenia's first sites to be added to UNESCO's World Heritage List.

Returning through Odzun to the main road it is a short distance to the important copper-mining centre of **Alaverdi** ('Allah gave' in Turkish). This industrial city clings to the side of the gorge and is the commercial centre of the district. The copper-smelting plant still functions and casts a pall of smoke over the town but at least provides some desperately needed employment. The famous **monastery complex of Sanahin** (⊕ *all day*) is just outside the city limits of Alaverdi. To reach it on foot continue up the river to the medieval bridge built in 1192: note the carved animals on top of the parapet. Cross this bridge and walk up the hill for about 500m. Another possibility is to go by cable car from

It is possible to walk from Odzun to Kobayr, though make an early start, or else choose an overcast day as there is no shade. Allow a long half day, with extra time to explore Kobayr. Continue for about 100m beyond the Odzun bus terminus and then turn left down a track to reach the gorge in less than 100m. The track descends slightly and then turns right. In reality it divides and redivides but keep going on a fairly level route never more than 50–70m from the cliff face on your right. If you descend more than this, you have gone too low. The path passes the Holy Cross Chapel (see opposite) and there are wonderful views down into the gorge. When you eventually come round a large outcrop and see an A-shaped electricity pole on the horizon ahead of you, then and only then is it time to descend. In theory it is possible to descend part way and then continue straight to Kobayr on the level, but the way is hard to find. It is much easier to walk down to the road, along it and back up as detailed on pages 210–11.

close to the copper factory 500m north of the centre up to the plateau close to the Debed Hotel: the cable car had the steepest climb of any in the former Soviet Union. Alternatively, to get there by road cross the newer bridge further south and continue up the hill past the Debed Hotel before bearing right to reach the monastery. Nowadays one of Armenia's most frequently visited sights, it was established in 966 by Queen Khosrovanush, wife of King Ashot III Bagratuni, on the site of two existing churches, St Jacob which dates from the 9th century and the Mother of God which was built sometime between 928 and 944. Sanahin became a centre of considerable cultural influence during the 10th and 11th centuries with its monastic school and important library where copyists worked to produce illuminated manuscripts. Sanahin's role declined as Armenia suffered waves of invaders although the local Argoutian family was exceptional in managing to retain its estates through to the 20th century.

The ensemble is very picturesque but does rather give the impression of having grown piecemeal. It is dominated by the **Church of the Holy Redeemer** with its conical dome; construction probably began in 966. This church, built of basalt, has its eastern façade decorated with arcature and the main window is similarly decorated. The gable of this façade has a sculptural relief depicting Smbat and Gurgen Bagratuni, two of the three sons of the founder, with a model of a church, the first appearance of such a scene in Armenia. Smbat became King Smbat II of the Bagratid dynasty, rulers of Ani, and Gurgen was the father of David Anghonin who constructed Lori Berd. The Church of the Holy Redeemer is separated from the smaller Mother of God Church by a gallery covered by a barrel vault, the **Academy of Gregory Magistros**, which is believed to have been used for teaching. Possibly the students sat in the niches between the monumental pillars.

On the west side of the churches are large *gavits* constructed in 1181 and 1211 and somewhat different from each other in style. The *gavit* of the Church of the Holy Redeemer is the earlier. It has four tall free-standing internal pillars supporting arches. The bases and capitals of the columns are decorated with carvings and reliefs depicting the heads of animals, fruits and geometric patterns. The *gavit* of the Mother of God Church is a three-nave hall with much lower arches than the earlier *gavit* and with less elaborate bases and capitals for the columns. Externally the western façade of this *gavit* has six arches, two to each gable. Abutting the *gavit*

The Northern Provinces   LORI PROVINCE

5

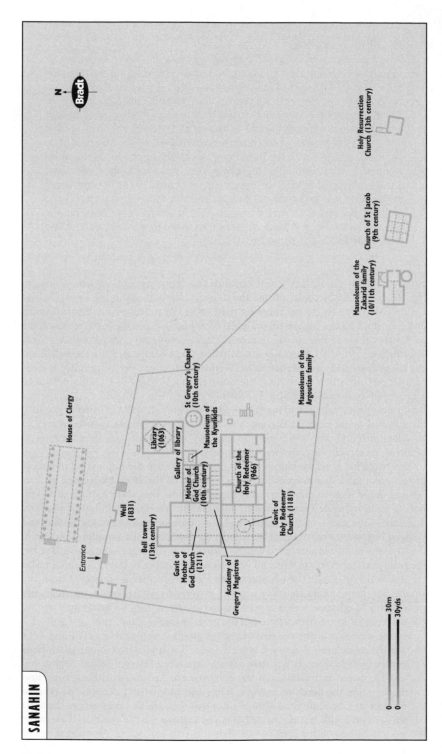

SANAHIN

N ← Bradt

House of Clergy

Well (1831)

Entrance

Bell tower (13th century)

Library (1063)

Gallery of library

Mother of God Church (10th century)

St Gregory's Chapel (10th century)

Mausoleum of the Kyurikids

Gavit of Mother of God Church (1211)

Academy of Gregory Magistros

Church of the Holy Redeemer (966)

Gavit of Holy Redeemer Church (1181)

Mausoleum of the Argoutian family

Mausoleum of the Zakarid family (10/11th century)

Church of St Jacob (9th century)

Holy Resurrection Church (13th century)

0 ⊢━━━┫ 30m
0 ⊢━━━┫ 30yds

at its western end is the **bell tower**, crowned by a small rotunda, which is also early 13th century and thought to be Armenia's earliest.

On the complex's north side is the **library** of 1063 which has an octagonal tent roof resting on diagonally arranged arches. At the eastern end of the library is the small domed round **Chapel of St Gregory the Illuminator** built in the late 10th century. It is a two-storey structure with a pointed roof. To the northeast of the main complex are two **mausoleums** which date from the 10th and 11th centuries and beyond them are the 9th-century **Church of St Jacob** (the nearer one) and the early 13th-century **Holy Resurrection Church** which has two identical apses. Much of the floor of the *gavit* is covered by gravestones and there is also a wealth of khachkars, not all of them religious: one commemorates the building of the bridge at Alaverdi in 1192 and another the construction of an inn in 1205. By the boundary wall on the north side is the monastery's **spring**. It is covered by a structure which dates to 1831.

HAGHPAT MONASTERY Haghpat Monastery (⊕ *all day*) is contemporaneous with Sanahin and very similar in style. Pilgrims in the monasteries' heyday were inevitably driven to compare the two and from this comparison derive the present names: Haghpat means 'huge wall' because that was one of its striking features, whereas Sanahin means 'older than the other'. Although Haghpat can be seen from Sanahin, to reach it requires a return to Alaverdi. Then head east along the main road for about 5km and turn right up the hill. A left fork leads to the monastery which can be seen high on the hillside. It is nowadays much more attractively sited than Sanahin, and consequently more pleasant to visit, as the approach is not through an area of rundown Soviet-era buildings. It is, however, also touristy. The **main church**

ANASTAS MIKOYAN AND ARTEM MIKOYAN

Sanahin's other claim to fame is as the birthplace of the brothers Anastas Mikoyan (1895–1978) and Artem Mikoyan (1905–70). A **museum** about them is located in a former school down the hill from the monastery (⊕ *11.00–17.00 daily, closed Mon; AMD500*). Anastas achieved the distinction of being the longest-serving member of the Soviet Politburo. He survived a series of political upheavals to remain a member from 1935 to 1966 and was involved in many important events. In 1939, he was responsible for the discussions with Germany on trade prior to the signing of the Nazi–Soviet pact; in 1955 he was part of the delegation which sought to heal the rift with Tito in Yugoslavia; in 1962 he dealt with Cuba during the missile crisis (he spoke Spanish); in 1964 he was instrumental in ousting Khrushchev. Artem Mikoyan, by contrast, played a leading role in the development of Soviet fighter aircraft. He was named head of a new design bureau in 1939. His bureau collaborated with that headed by Mikhail Gurevich and at first produced a number of relatively unsuccessful planes. Then the turbojet-powered MiG-15, which first flew in 1947, proved a world-beating design and was the forerunner of a series of light fighter aircraft which saw extensive deployment during the Cold War era. MiG is actually an acronym for Mikoyan and Gurevich. In the museum itself, downstairs are everyday artefacts belonging to the family including furniture made by the illiterate father of the brothers. Upstairs is an exposition of their careers. In the forecourt is a MiG-21 fighter plane and a car belonging to Anastas.

with its huge dome is dedicated to the Holy Cross and was built between 976 and 991 at the behest of Queen Khosrovanush, also the founder of Sanahin. From the exterior it appears rectangular but internally is cross-shaped and, as at Sanahin, there is a relief of Smbat and Gurgen holding a model of a church on the east façade. Unlike Sanahin the buildings, which were gradually added, do not lead directly off each other. A smaller church, dedicated to **St Gregory the Illuminator**, was added in 1005 at the southwest side of the site and a domed **Mother of God Church** was added on the northwest side in 1025. The St Gregory Church lost its dome during rebuilding in 1211. A *gavit* was built in 1185 to the west of the cathedral and the cathedral itself gained a magnificent porch in 1201.

The three-storey **bell tower** was built in 1245, a much more substantial structure than at Sanahin. Its ground floor has the plan of a cross-dome church and serves as a chapel. The second storey by contrast is rectangular with the corners cut off thus turning into an octagonal shape. The transition between the two shapes is ingenious. The third storey, the belfry, is unusually seven sided and supported by seven columns. Another *gavit*, called the **Hamazasp building** after its donor, was built to the north of the cathedral in 1257 and is unusual for a *gavit* in being free-standing. The **library**, originally built with a wooden roof in the 10th century, was rebuilt with a stone roof in 1262. One of Armenia's most famous and beautiful khachkars, the **Holy Redeemer khachkar** of 1273, is in the passage leading to the library. This amazing work shows Christ crucified surrounded by saints and Apostles with angels looking down and God the Father raising his hand in blessing. Haghpat's library became a store room after invaders had taken the manuscripts and the floor now has many storage jars sunk into it. The 13th-century **refectory** is an isolated building on the north side of the site. There is a separate entrance from

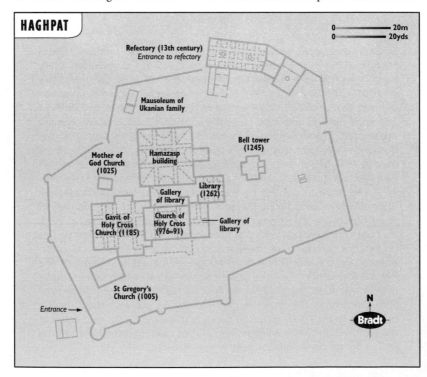

HAGHPAT

0 —— 20m
0 —— 20yds

Refectory (13th century)
Entrance to refectory

Mausoleum of Ukanian family

Bell tower (1245)

Mother of God Church (1025)

Hamazasp building

Library (1262)

Gallery of library

Gavit of Holy Cross Church (1185)

Church of Holy Cross (976–91)

Gallery of library

St Gregory's Church (1005)

Entrance →

N

Bradt

outside the perimeter wall. It is therefore normally locked but the caretaker's wife will happily open it up when she is around – the caretaker himself has to stay at the main part of the site. The refectory is a long building whose tall roof is borne by intersecting arches supported by pairs of free-standing columns. The central section is crowned by octagonal domed vaults which admit light. This unusual structure adjoins the defensive wall of the monastery. Also notable to the west of the refectory is the spring. It is in a three-arched structure built in 1258. There are stone troughs along the back wall for watering cattle and a reservoir for general use.

AKHTALA MONASTERY (☼ *in summer the caretaker usually arrives about 11.00, tourists rarely arriving before then, & stays until about 19.30. There are phone numbers on the door of the church to contact her if she is not there & holes in the door through which one can peep if the door is locked*) Akhtala is further north towards the Georgian border and receives only a tiny fraction of the visitors who go to Sanahin and Haghpat. It is built in a quite different style but its setting is equally dramatic, perched up on a cliff. Unfortunately the view is now marred by copper mining taking place on the opposite side of the valley, but the wooden scaffolding, which for decades obscured the view of Armenia's finest frescoes, has now been removed making a visit to Akhtala even more worthwhile. To reach it take the main road east from Alaverdi for about 15km until there is a bridge left over the Debed close to a derelict cable car and leading into an industrial area. Cross the bridge and turn right, crossing the railway at a level crossing. Follow the road, bearing right over a bridge going uphill. At the next junction, go left round a hairpin bend, signposted to Shamlugh. Continue on this road along a tributary gorge. When you come to a fork next to a bridge you can see the monastery high up on a promontory in front of you. Keep right. The steadily deteriorating road goes past the monastery but then bears left to approach it from the north side.

Akhtala is surrounded either by precipitous drops or by defensive walls. Entry is through the main gate in the defensive fortifications. Although this may be locked, entry can be achieved easily as there is an inconspicuous wicket gate within the main gate. Take very great care on the site as the long grass conceals drops into subterranean rooms of the original fortress whose roofs have collapsed. The 10th-century fortifications, constructed of basalt, were built by the Kurikian branch of the Bagratid dynasty: Kurikian was a vassal state of the king at Ani. The fortress is contemporary with that at Lori (see page 208): Akhtala, like Lori, was a highly defensible site and one of the main strongholds of northern Armenia. Within the fortress stands the monastery, and the remains of other buildings can be seen. The **main existing church**, dedicated to the Mother of God, was built between 1212 and 1250 at the behest of Prince Ivan Zakarian who belonged to the same dynasty that obtained control of Lori Berd and Kobayr Monastery. It was therefore built as a Georgian Orthodox church but is on the site of an earlier Armenian one. It is of the domed basilica type with four massive pillars, two of which are free-standing. The dome collapsed in the 18th century and the existing small pyramidal roof was itself replaced in 1978. Built, like the fortress, of basalt, the monastery is quite different in appearance from those at Sanahin and Haghpat, reflecting the Georgian influence on its design. The interior frescoes are absolutely magnificent. Especially notable is the Virgin Mary enthroned in the apse. Her face has been defaced by artillery; the hole in the wall can be seen in the centre of the cross high up on the exterior of the east façade. Beneath the Virgin Mary is a depiction of the Last Supper with Christ giving the bread to St Peter on the left and the wine to St Paul on the right. Two ranks of saints stand below. Other scenes include the Last Judgement over the west door, the trial and Crucifixion of Jesus and the Resurrection. Figures of saints adorn the pillars which divide the building into three naves.

Large relief crosses on each façade together with smaller more intricate crosses on the elaborate arcaded porch also show Georgian influence

TO JILIZA, KHUCHAP AND KHORAKERT MONASTERIES A visit to this remote corner of Armenia is very worthwhile. The village of Jiliza is only 1km from the Georgian border and is ideally situated in beautiful countryside for visiting the fascinating but rarely seen monasteries of Khuchap and Khorakert. Note that reaching these two monasteries may now be more complicated than it was because of a rumoured change in the exact position of the border. However, in 2010 the usually well-informed tourist information office in Yerevan knew of no such proposed changes. Check at the tourist office in Yerevan or ask in Alaverdi – Armen at his restaurant (see page 204) in Alaverdi can help by phoning Jiliza and can also advise on current times of departure of *marshrutka*. Until 1992 no road linked Jiliza district with the rest of Armenia but following independence a new dirt road was constructed direct from Alaverdi. This road has now been upgraded and surfaced allowing *marshrutka* (fare approximately AMD300) to travel between Alaverdi and Jiliza. Bus aficionados can no longer experience the previous mode of transport, a six-wheel-drive (!) lorry chassis with a bus body mounted on top, which was necessary to negotiate the seas of mud and water-filled deep pot-holes. From Jiliza it is a 7km walk to Khuchap, 4km to Khorakert and the monasteries are 5km from each other. The very helpful mayor of this isolated village can help with homestay accommodation

To get to Jiliza, leave Alaverdi by the Madan road which climbs out of the valley behind the copper plant. At the far end of Madan there is a customs post as the whole of this northern area has numerous minor crossing points to Georgia. However, the customs point does not always function. The road winds through increasingly forested country for 30km with many beautiful views. Jiliza itself has a post of border guards who are very helpful and probably glad of having someone different to talk to.

Khuchap Monastery (☉ *always*), at the foot of Mount Lalvar, is well worth the trouble of reaching. It is a beautiful building, delightfully situated and hidden away in its small wooded valley. It was abandoned in the 1940s when the last nuns left but the main church, which dates from the 13th century, is intact. Red felsite was used for construction of the outer walls and forms an unusual and pleasing contrast with the yellow felsite used for the window surrounds, large crosses on two of the gable ends, and to produce a banded effect on the tall tambour. The church is entered through the door in the west façade (close it again on leaving to keep out the cattle) which, like the south façade, sports a large carved cross as part of its decoration. Inside, the church is rectangular with a very high cupola and two supporting octagonal pillars. There are separate naves at the west end of the church and vestibules were added at the east end sometime after the construction. Outside, the decoration is amazingly varied with door and window surrounds being carved with a whole range of geometric patterns while carved figures of animals and projecting carved animal heads can be seen high up on the tambour. Every one of the 12 carved windows around the tambour has a different geometric pattern. On the west façade the remains of a cloister-like addition with four arches make a picturesque addition. North of the main church are the remains of other monastic buildings, much plainer and built of grey andesite.

To reach Khorakert Monastery (☉ *always*), slightly nearer the village on the west side, involves fording the river and can be difficult at times of flood. Built in the late 12th and early 13th centuries, the really striking feature, unique in Armenia, is that the tambour (which has ten sides – very rare in Armenia) is not a solid construction but comprises in the upper part 30 separate six-sided columns. The effect of this open-sided tambour is to admit light into the church. The interior of the cupola is also most unusual: six intersecting arches form a six-pointed star in the centre of which is a hexagon which itself encloses another six-pointed star. The *gavit* of 1257 was also highly distinctive in that it was roofed by another set of intersecting arches but unfortunately this collapsed in an earthquake in 1965. The whole ensemble gives the impression that it would not survive another. Outside the church on the south side is a stone frog which has been placed on a plinth, another unexpected sight. It looks as if the frog could originally have been mounted on a roof and there is certainly an unidentified animal on top of the cupola of the church. Traces of the main gateway, chapels and various other buildings also survive as does the well with its secret passage down to the river.

FROM STEPANAVAN TO THE DEBED Rather than travelling via Vanadzor it is possible to travel via **Hnevank Monastery**, a very worthwhile route but lacking public transport and unsuitable for larger vehicles at the eastern end. The road deteriorates east of Kurtan but is manageable by car as far as Hnevank. For the descent from Hnevank into the Debed Gorge a 4x4 is advisable. *En route* it is also possible to visit **DendroPark** (☉ *10.00–19.00 daily, a notice says 'after 19.00 beware of loosed guard dogs'; free*), an arboretum covering 35ha which was founded by a Pole in 1931 for the cultivation and acclimatisation of trees. The arboretum is well maintained; specimen trees are labelled. It is one of the pleasantest places in Armenia for a stroll. Adjoining the arboretum is a sanatorium used by invalids with lung diseases. Apparently the clouds of pollen blowing from the conifers are regarded as therapeutic. From Stepanavan head back towards Vanadzor for 10km as far as the village of **Gyulagarak**. In the village turn left. The road then passes the derelict village church of 1874 on the left. If you wish to visit DendroPark turn right onto an unmade road (poor condition in places) signposted to the arboretum and bear left at the fork. The extremely ruinous 6th-century **Toromavank** (monastery) is then passed on the right; continue straight ahead for DendroPark.

If you do not wish to visit DendroPark then keep left after the 1874 church. The road runs east through an area of strip farming with the Dzoraget River in its increasingly deep gorge on the right and (often snow-capped) peaks in the distance. Just before **Kurtan** village the road bears right to cross the river and shortly after this there are some immensely impressive views down into the gorge on the left. It is worth stopping and walking not just because of the views but because this is an excellent area for eagles. Both booted eagles and golden eagles can be seen along the gorge. The highlight comes in a few minutes when, during the descent of some hairpin bends the extensive ruins of **Hnevank Monastery** (⊕ *always*) can be seen down in the gorge on a small hill close to the confluence of the Dzoraget and Gargar rivers. This spectacularly beautiful site can be reached by a short track, which should only be driven in a 4x4, going off left just as the monastery comes into view. It is not far and it is pleasant to walk, the better to admire the wild flowers; in early summer the sheer brilliance of colour is stunning. The monastery was founded in the 7th century but rebuilt with a much higher tambour in 1144. The *gavit* dates from the late 12th century and leads to both the small cross-dome main church on the east and a chapel to the west. Restoration is underway. While some of the charm of undisturbed ruins is being lost, the restoration does enable the visitor to make more sense of the layout. A barrel-vaulted building lies to the west and what was thought to be the refectory a short distance to the east. To the south of the *gavit* are the low remains of other monastic buildings, all but hidden when the vegetation grows waist-high. Eagles can again be seen in this magical spot.

Continuing east the unsurfaced road eventually leaves the plateau and descends countless zigzags to reach the Debed River at **Dzoraget** village, a short distance south of the confluence of the Dzoraget and the Debed.

TAVUSH PROVINCE

Armenia's heavily wooded and most northeasterly province is bounded to the north by Georgia and to the east by Azerbaijan. Land captured from Azerbaijan in 1994 has since been incorporated into Tavush: in particular the road from the provincial capital of Ijevan north to Noyemberian and on to Lori and the Georgian border crosses an area of Azerbaijan which, since 1994, has in practice been Armenian. It is most important here to use the new road which keeps a safe distance from the border: the old road passes dangerously close to the ceasefire line and is subject to attack by Azeri snipers.

The aftermath of the war is evident in other ways in Tavush: some sites close to the border, notably Khoranashat Monastery, are also inaccessible because of the risk from Azeri snipers and the former main road and rail routes from Yerevan to Georgia and the rest of the former Soviet Union are closed at the border with Azerbaijan since they crossed Azeri territory to reach Tbilisi. The rail route is actually completely closed north of Haghartsin station (just north of Dilijan) and the overhead catenary has been dismantled. Freight trains do still operate from Yerevan as far as Haghartsin, passing under the Arjanots range by the 8,311m-long Margahovit Tunnel, but passenger services have been withdrawn. Tavush's two largest towns, Ijevan and Dilijan, are sited on the Aghtsev River whose valley broadens out as it flows northwards towards Azerbaijan. It rises in the southeast of Lori province in the Gugarats range and, as is the case with other north-flowing

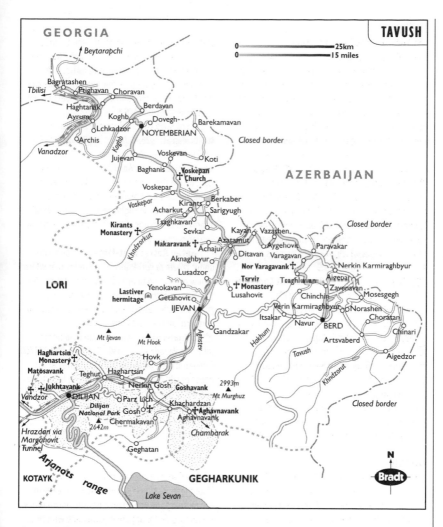

GEORGIA

↑ Beytarapchi

Bagratashen
Tbilisi
Ptighavan Choravan
Haghtanak Berdavan
Ayrum Koghb Dovegh
Lchkadzor Barekamavan
Archis NOYEMBERIAN
Koghb
Vanadzor Voskevan
Jujevan Koti

Closed border

AZERBAIJAN

Baghanis Voskepan
Church
Voskepar

Voskepar Berkaber
Kirants
Acharkut Sarigyugh
Kirants Tsaghkavan
Monastery Sevkar Kayan Vazashen
Makaravank Azatamut Aygehovit Paravakar
Achajur
Aknaghbyur Ditavan Varagavan
Lusadzor Nor Varagavank Nerkin Karmiraghbyur
Yenokavan Tsrviz Toaghlavan Aigepar
Lastiver Monastery Zavenavan
hermitage Getahovit Lusahovit Chinchin Mosesgegh
IJEVAN Verin Karmiraghbyur Norashen
Itsakar Choratan
Gandzakar Navur BERD
Mt Ijevan Mt Hook Chinari
Artsvaberd
Tavush Aigedzor

LORI

Khndzorkut

Aghstev

Hokhum

Khndzorut

Haghartsin
Monastery
Matosavank Hovk
Teghut Haghartsin
Jukhtavank Nerkin Gosh Goshavank 2993m
Vandzor DILIJAN Parz Lich Mt Murghuz
Dilijan Gosh Khachardzan
National Park Aghavnavank
Chermakavan Aghavnavank Closed border
2642m
Hrazdan via Chambarak
Margahovit
Tunnel Geghatan

Arjanots range
KOTAYK GEGHARKUNIK
Lake Sevan

N
Bradt

0 ——— 25km
0 ——— 15 miles

Armenian rivers, its waters join the Kura River ultimately to reach the Caspian Sea south of Baku.

Travelling south from Dilijan to Sevan in Gegharkunik province became easier in 2003 as a new road tunnel was opened avoiding the **Sevan Pass** (2,114m). Unfortunately some of the earthworks on the improved road seem to have been carried out with scant regard for the stability of the hillside, and continuing landslips are predictable.

Hotel accommodation in the province is now readily available as are homestays, some of which are really good.

WHERE TO STAY The region can be explored from either Dilijan or Ijevan, the latter obviously being more suitable for northern Tavush. Dilijan is nearer the more popular monastic sites and is convenient for those wishing to travel south to Lake Sevan. There is plentiful accommodation in the region, from the upper end of the hotel range to a riverside campsite.

Dilijan

🏠 **Tufenkian Old Dilijan** (2 apts)
Sharambeyan St; book through the Tufenkian office
in Yerevan, 🔌 10 655877; e hotels@tufenkian.am;
www.tufenkian.am. A restored 19th-century town
house in the centre of the town with 2 floors, each
forming an apt, with balcony, accommodating 2
persons. B/fast taken in Tufenkian restaurant a
short distance along the street. No room service.
Cards only accepted if paying in advance in
Yerevan. Lower floor/upper floor **$$$/$$$$**

🏠 **Hotel Dilijan Resort** (71 rooms) 66
Getapnya St; 🔌 2680 26219, 24303; e info@
hoteldilijan.am; www.hoteldilijan.am.
Comfortable, fully restored & equipped Soviet
hotel. Wi-Fi. Cards accepted. Lunch included.
Also has cottages which sleep 4–8 persons at
AMD120,000–180,000. **$$$**

🏠 **Haghhartsin Hotel-Restaurant Complex**
(22 rooms) 121 Kamo St; 🔌 2680 27770;
m 093 044700; e info@haghartsin.com;
www.haghartsin.com. A very pleasant stylish new
(2008) hotel with helpful staff just outside the
town on the Sevan–Yerevan road. **$$**

🏠 **Lernayin Hayastan Sanatorium/Spa**
(76 rooms) Kamo St; 🔌 2680 25940, 10 283480
(Yerevan office). An enormous edifice with an
impressive façade on the Sevan–Yerevan road.
A previous Soviet government building, taken
over by the Ministry of Defence after the collapse
of the Soviet Union & used for the treatment &
rehabilitation of soldiers involved in the Nagorno
Karabagh war. Now a private enterprise. Still
functions as a sanatorium but healthy people can
stay there. Has something of a Soviet feel to it. FB
& treatment included. **$$**

🏠 **Daravand Guest House** (7 rooms)
46 Abovian St; 🔌 2680 7857; m 094 420965, 091
411766; e info@daravand.com;
www.daravand.com. An attractive 3-storey house
just outside the town on the way to Jukhtavank
Monastery. All food prepared from fresh local
produce. Restaurant highly recommended. Meals
approx AMD4,000/pp. English, Russian, German &
Persian spoken. **$$**

🏠 **Getap Restaurant-Motel** (see opposite
under *Where to eat*) Principally a restaurant which
is now expanding to include accommodation. **$$**

🏠 **Soonk Motel** (10 rooms) Parz Lich St;
m 093 414255. 5km from town centre on road to
Pars Lich, off the road to Ijevan. **$$**

🏠 **Dilijans** 64a Kalinin St (main road from
Dilijan to Vanadzor); 🔌 2680 23147; m 093 044700
(preferred method of contact). Homestay at the
house of Lilit Muradlian. Lilit's cooking is such that
it is worth going there just to eat – groups are also
welcome for meals. Like most homestays, give
24hrs notice for food to be prepared. Dinner, B&B
10,000AMD/pp. **$**

Ijevan

🏠 **Hotel Mosh** (8 rooms) 3 Yerevanian St;
🔌 263 35611; f 36471; www.moshhotel.nxt.ru.
Central, near main market. A very acceptable
basic hotel. Rooms without bathroom are
even cheaper. Wi-Fi. No cards. B/fast extra at
AMD1,000/pp. **$**

🏠 **Motel Elite** (5 rooms) Yerevanian St;
m 091 111300. A short distance outside the town
near the wine factory on the road south. Set in a
well-tended garden. The proprietors are on site
between 10.30 & 22.30; outside of these hours the
staff comprises a chap manning the security gate.
Note therefore that if you want to leave early in
the morning you will have to pay the previous day.
No cards. B/fast is apparently available with prior
notice. B/fast extra AMD1,000/pp. FB AMD5,000/
pp. **$**

🏠 **Hotel Elina** (6 rooms) 16 Yeritasardakan;
m 099 263449 (Edik). A short walk from the main
street, across the river off Ankakhutian St. Simple,
clean, well-finished hotel. No cards. B/fast extra
AMD1,000/pp. **$**

Elsewhere

🏠 **Apaga Tour** (see page 227) Not a tour
operator but an enterprise near Yenokavan offering
complete packages which include horseriding,
trekking & accommodation. Does not offer
accommodation alone.

🏠 **Mkhitar Gosh Hotel** (10 rooms) Gosh
village; m 093 758595, 098 441019. This
delightful small hotel at the head of the village
square opened in 2010. En-suite shower rooms
are small but smart. Superb views of the
monastery from front bedrooms. At time of

research internet access only just acquired, but a website is planned through which bookings can be made. **$$**

⚑ Peace in the world campsite Ichachaghbyur River, near Yenokavan. For further details, see page 227.

✗ WHERE TO EAT Dilijan has better eating places than Ijevan but Ijevan is better provided with cafés for a snack late at night. In my experience, the best food in the province is at Daravand Guest House (see opposite) just outside Dilijan. On the main roads there are numbers of barbecue and motel-style eateries, apart from those listed below. Some of the hotels listed above also function as restaurants.

✗ Artbridge Café 1 Sharambeyan St, Dilijan; m 093 581284; ⏲ during the tourist season, approx Apr–Oct but may stay open longer if business is good. A branch of the well-known bookshop/café of the same name in Yerevan (see page 111). The bookshop element in Dilijan is in the upper part of the Old Dilijan Complex, entered from Miasnikian St. A good place for coffee & pastries. Serves light meals, including omelettes, salads & *dolma*.

✗ Getap Restaurant-Motel Tbilisi Highway; ☎ 2680 25614; m 093 808642, 094 944303. Outside Dilijan on the road to Ijevan. Built in 2000

& continuing to expand it consists of a number of chalets beside the river in restful gardens. Perhaps the most pleasant of several such complexes. The food here is good. Also has accommodation.

✗ Haykanoush Restaurant Sharambeyan St, Dilijan. Contact through Tufenkian office in Yerevan; see Tufenkian Old Dilijan Hotel, opposite; ⏲ 10.00–22.00 daily. Part of the restored Old Dilijan Complex. In the style of a late 19th- early 20th-century Dilijan dining room. Wooden floors covered with handmade Tufenkian carpets. Typical Armenian dishes.

Ijevan has a number of **cafés** with canopied open-air tables, on both sides of the river, at the southern end of the town centre. The one on the east bank has quieter music.

OTHER PRACTICALITIES For **minibuses** from Yerevan see *Chapter 2*, pages 74–6. Ijevan and Dilijan both have **tourist information centres** (see pages 224 and 228) which can provide maps of their respective towns and help to arrange accommodation. Ijevan has a large market as well as smaller shops and is better for shopping than Dilijan. It also has more cafés which stay open until late.

As elsewhere, **taxis** can be a convenient and relatively cheap way of reaching places of interest. For example, a round trip from Dilijan to Haghartsin and Goshavank monasteries costs about AMD8,000.

IJEVAN (*Telephone code 263*) The name of Ijevan, meaning 'inn' recalls the scarcely imaginable days when silk route traders passed through these forests. Ijevan is nowadays a pleasant though unremarkable town with good accommodation and there are many excellent walking possibilities in the hilly forests. Its appearance is enhanced by the extensive use of white felsite for building. The local dry red and white wines, made from grapes more usually associated with Georgia, are among Armenia's best. The province's more improbable visitors have included the English composer Benjamin Britten (1913–76) and his friend the tenor Peter Pears (1910–86) who spent their summer holiday in Dilijan in August 1965 as guests of the Armenian Composers' Union along with the cellist Mstislav Rostropovich and his wife, the soprano Galina Vishnevskaya. Both Peter Pears and Galina Vishnevskaya have left accounts of the experience: while everybody seems to have enjoyed their visit, the English visitors had to listen to performances of the latest compositions of the Armenian composers, while headaches for the hosts included having to deal with Benjamin Britten wanting to buy a pair of shoes when his existing ones gave out – shoes were virtually unobtainable in the Soviet Union at the time.

The main street of Ijevan follows the west bank of the Aghstev River and the market, **post office** and **bus station** are all within a short distance of each other. The park along the east bank is a favourite place for locals to stroll. Also on the east side are **banks** and the **tourist information centre** (*5 Melikbekian St;* ☎ *263 33301;* ⏰ *19.00–18.00 Mon–Sat, 09.00–16.00 Sun*). This helpful information centre has leaflets about the town, can arrange homestays, monastery tours and (free) visits to the wine factory. Only Armenian is spoken in the centre but a translator can be obtained if necessary. You may also be able to buy a copy of the catalogue to the sculptures in the **sculpture park**. A relaxing hour or two can be had wandering around this park on the river's east bank. The thought-provoking sculptures are not labelled so the catalogue enhances any visit. Several of the sculptures listed in the catalogue are actually in the grounds of the local **historical-ethnographical museum** (⏰ *09.00–18.00 Tue–Sun, but often shut when it should be open*) about 1km south of the town. Even when the museum building itself is shut the statues in front of it are accessible.

NORTHEAST FROM IJEVAN The former main rail and road routes to Azerbaijan follow the gradually broadening valley of the Aghtsev. The first turn right after leaving Ijevan leads to the village of **Lusahovit** where the **Tsrviz or Moro-Dzor Monastery** is located. (The right turn is signposted for Khashtarak. In Khashtarak turn right 2km from the main road, almost a U-turn, and then continue straight ahead until Lusahovit is reached and you see the church below the village.) Established in the 5th century, the main **Mother of God Church** was rebuilt in the 12th and 13th centuries and has been restored fairly recently. It is a four-apse church, one of only nine such early medieval churches in Armenia. It has a curious appearance, rather like a small dome surrounded by even smaller ones. The lower courses are of rough-hewn basalt, the upper of dressed stone. After 32km the main road now bears right at Kayan before reaching the border: even newer maps still show it going straight ahead into Azerbaijan. At the village of **Aygehovit**, is a church called **Srvegh** or (by locals) Srvis, high up on the hillside to the south. Its name, which means 'long pointed neck', is very apt. The ruined church, with its tall tambour and pointed dome, is very similar to Kirants Monastery (see opposite) both in style and the use of bricks for construction. To reach it, turn right in Aygehovit onto an unmade road. Eventually it turns into a track going uphill through a field. Park here and walk the rest of the way, about 30 minutes up a steep rutted track. Or park in the village, in which case it would take about an hour to walk. The entrance to the monastery is through a gate on the left where there is a welcome spring. The path to the church goes from the far end of the barbecue shelter; after a short distance the church appears through the trees.

After Aygehovit the main road winds up and over a pass with numerous hairpin bends as far as the village of **Varagavan**. Turn right onto the main street of the village (Nor Varagavank is signposted 4.5km) and continue through it. A good road to the monastery winds up through attractive forest where both green and black woodpeckers can be found. The **Monastery of Nor Varagavank** is very important historically but in a sadly ruined state. It was founded, as Anapat, by David Bagratuni, son of King Vasak I. The oldest part of the complex is the small Church of the Holy Cross built in 1198 at the southeast side. A two-storey burial vault was added at its north side in 1200. The monastery's importance, however, increased considerably in 1213 when it was chosen as the site for a relic, a piece of the True Cross brought to Armenia by Sts Hripsime and Gayane, which had been removed from the Monastery of Varagavank, near Van in present-day Turkey, when that monastery was threatened by Mongol invaders. Hence the name Anapat was changed to Nor ('New') Varagavank. (The relic, back by then at the original Varagavank, was destroyed along with the monastery during fighting in 1915.) The larger Mother of God Church was built between 1224 and 1237 by David Bagratuni's son King Vasak II. A massive *gavit* adjoins the west wall of this church and another, now very ruined, gives entry to Holy Cross Church and its flanking chapels. There are unusual door portals, fine carving and interesting khachkars at this attractive site overlooking the forest.

MAKARAVANK (MONASTERY) (⊕ *summer (Apr–late Oct); the keyholder comes every day & opens the church from about 08.30 to 21.30. He lives in Achajur & walks up; if you arrive early he may hitch a lift. He offers a wealth of information*) Makaravank, on the slopes of Mount Paytatar, is beautifully situated with fine views over the Aghtsev Valley and into Azerbaijan. It is well restored and has probably Armenia's finest carvings. Road improvements have made this splendid monastery more accessible. To reach Makaravank from Ijevan take the main road towards the Azeri border as far as the junction with the road to **Noyemberian**. At this junction, just after a barracks on the left, turn left onto a dirt road heading for the village of **Achajur**. In the village centre a sign points right to Makaravank. Continue for 6km keeping a lookout on the right for the domes of the monastery peeping out of a clump of trees. From the main road to Achajur the road is unsurfaced (it was hoped it would be surfaced in late 2010) but from Achajur to within about a kilometre of the monastery the road is surfaced; the intention is to renovate the final stretch.

The monastery is approached through a gate in the wall. If the gate happens to be locked, simply walk along the path to the right, past domestic monastic buildings, to gain access. The **oldest church**, whose dedicatee is unknown, was probably built in the 10th century. Inside it has beautifully carved window surrounds and an equally beautiful front to the altar dais with floral and linear designs. However, even this fine carving is wholly overshadowed by the amazing carving of the **main church**, built in 1204 by Vardan, son of Prince Bazaz. It is dedicated to the Mother of God. The carving here is wonderful. In particular the front of this altar dais is covered with eight-pointed stars separated by octagons in each of which is a different elaborate design: a man in a boat, sphinxes, sirens, birds, floral arrangements and other unusual designs. Outside there is more fine carving; the south façade has a sundial above the main window and a bird below it, while the smaller round windows each have a different intricate design. The *gavit* was added by Prince Vache Vachutian early in the 13th century. Plain outside except for a bull and lion fighting to the left of the door and a winged sphinx with a crown on its head to the right, it is a riot of carving inside. Adjoining the north side of the original church is a **bakery** for the making of communion loaves. Behind the complex is an **unusual church** built in 1198 and dedicated to the Mother of God. It has an octagonal base but a round tambour.

NORTHWARD TOWARDS LORI Taking the Noyemberian road from the barracks, the village of Kirants is reached after 10km. To go to **Kirants Monastery** (⊕ *always*) turn left here and continue through the village of Acharkut for about 4km until the road ends at a barrier erected to stop illegal logging. It is possible to get the barrier opened but the track is so bad beyond here that walking is preferable, at least after the next kilometre or so. To reach the monastery it is necessary always to keep close to the Khndzorkut River and to remain on the north side without crossing it. From the barrier to Kirants Monastery is about 10km. About halfway there a track goes

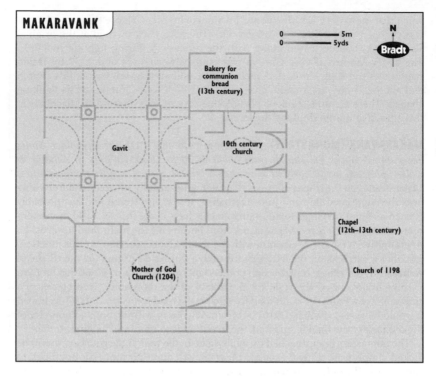

off left bridging the river. Do not take it. The walk through the forest with the river close by is extremely pleasant with myriads of beautiful flowers in early summer. A family from one of the local villages have their summer house here where they bring their cattle and beehives and tend their fruit. Granny and her son gave us home-baked bread with their own delicious honey with its flavours of lime and thyme. The son's wife was to join them with their children once the school term had finished.

Beyond the turn-off over the bridge, the track is in an even worse state with 30cm-deep ruts made by lorries involved in forestry operations. The track fords the river twice and wading is required which might be difficult after heavy rain. The monastery is not far beyond the second ford. Bear right on a less-used track uphill through the forest away from the main track. This leads to the monastery which can be seen surrounded by dense thickets of giant hogweed *Hieracium mantegazzianum*. Avoid touching the plant as it causes painful weals on the skin. Unless someone has been here recently, you will need sticks, or preferably a machete, to batter it down.

The monastery is very unusual in that it is constructed of fired tuff bricks decorated with glazed tiles. The main church dates from the 13th century and has a tall octagonal tambour with an octagonal dome. The monastery was built as a Georgian Orthodox foundation and Georgian influence can be seen in the interior frescoes. Unfortunately these are covered in graffiti, some written in Russian and some in Armenian. It seemed a sad place: derelict, overgrown and defaced.

TO THE GEORGIAN BORDER Immediately after the Kirants turn-off the Noyemberian road crosses Azeri territory which since 1994 has been occupied by

Armenia. The road passes through several ruined villages in some of which just one wall of each building has been left standing. A weird sight on a hillside right of the road is the completely restored 7th-century **Voskepan Church** surrounded by ruined and abandoned houses. The road re-enters Armenia proper and 41km from the junction with the former main road to Azerbaijan it reaches the town of Noyemberian, damaged by an earthquake in July 1997. Beyond the town it crosses the Koghb River before reaching Lori province and joining the main road north from Alaverdi south of the Georgian border.

LASTIVER AND THE RIVER ICHACHAGHBYUR Two very appealing holiday enterprises have been developed near the village of Yenokavan just north of Ijevan. The owners of Yerevan riding school (see page 114) have a horseriding and trekking centre called Apaga Tour, and a local family has established a campsite with accommodation (in tents) and meals available in an exceptionally beautiful spot by the tumbling waters of the Ichachaghbyur ('Cross-spring') River. From Ijevan take the main road north for about 5km and, after crossing the Ichachaghbyur, turn left for **Yenokavan** which lies about 8km further on. The riding school only allows parking for its residents, so if making for the campsite leave vehicles in Yenokavan. There are about three *marshrutkas* a day from Ijevan, or take a taxi. **Apaga Tour** (263 60702; m 091 290700; e info@apaga.info; www.apaga.info, www.apaga-tour.com) offers packages (only) which include full board, accommodation (in very attractive chalets) and riding or trekking with guides. They offer day excursions from the centre (AMD30,000/day/pp) and longer camping trips (AMD35,000/day/pp).

It's a little over an hour's uphill walk from Yenokavan village to the school although anyone booked can be met with horses. The whole area on the slopes of the Mtnasar range is ideal for riding.

The **riverside campsite**, called 'Peace in the world', is approached from the riding school along paths (3km) which ultimately give access to the high summer pastures and are ideal for walking. The flowers in the forest here are among the most attractive in Armenia and the paths winding along the steep sides of the gorge offer fantastic views. The final scramble down to the campsite is steep. The camp with the waters cascading by has been developed by three brothers, Vahagn, Tatoul and Hovhannes Tananian (263 31465; m 091 365437) because they have such fond memories of coming to this place in their childhood. Rock climbing, hiking and fishing are also available. They have tents for up to 35 people (AMD10,000/pp inc b/fast) and a tree house for two. Sleeping bags can be hired. The brothers will collect guests from Ijevan or Yenokavan. Bookings can also be made via the tourist information office in Ijevan.

Not far from the campsite is **Lastiver hermitage**. It comprises several rooms carved out of the rock on different levels, some of which are reached by ladder. As well as carved crosses, there are also carved faces and animals, strange enough that we wondered if they were modern but apparently they are very old. If going there, take a torch.

DILIJAN (*Telephone code 2680*) Dilijan, a major holiday and health resort in Soviet days, lies 36km southwest of Ijevan and is one of the country's most attractive towns. Considerable renovation is in progress and hotel accommodation is now plentiful. Many of the surviving 19th-century buildings are built in a distinctive style, unique in Armenia: they have wooden balconies with carved handrails which are often supported by wooden struts. In the centre of the town the finely restored short **Sharambeyan Street** is home to a number of places which may interest the visitor in addition to the Tufenkian hotel and restaurant. The **visitor information centre** (✆ *2680 22050;* e *dilijan@armeniainfo.am;* ◷ *10.00–19.00 daily*) has a map of the town, hires out bicycles and provides internet access and help with accommodation. The **History of Dilijan Museum** (◷ *10.00–16.00; AMD1,000. Tickets are obtained from the receptionist in the Tufenkian office about half way along the street; she will also show you round the museum, in excellent English, between 16.00 & 19.00*) is at the bottom of Sharambeyan Street, near the restaurant. It contains collections of domestic and farming implements and carpets. A number of craft shops are in the restored complex; particularly appealing is that of the wood carver, who carves his wares on site. The **commercial centre** of Dilijan (banks etc) is Miasnikian Street, above Sharambeyan Street. Across the river is the **Folk Art Museum** (*1 Getapnya St;* m *094 433293;* ◷ *10.00–16.00 Tue–Sun; guided tour in English AMD1,000; AMD500*) in a late 19th-century house, originally the summer house of Mariam Tamanian and latterly the home of the painter Hovhannes Sharambeyan (1926– 1986), whose *Early Spring* is in the National Gallery, Yerevan. Items from the 19th century to the present day are on display. It is a surprisingly interesting display; however, one may have to curtail slightly the enthusiastic guide's Intourist-style presentation. It is sometimes possible to buy locally made handicrafts there.

Some 23,400ha of the surrounding forest were designated as a nature reserve in 1958 and then as **Dilijan National Park** from 2002, the change in designation being to take account of commercial activity in the area. The park stretches over the forested slopes of the Pambak, Areguni, Miapor, Ijevan and Halab mountain ranges, from 1,070–2,300m above sea level, the mountain meadows above this altitude being excluded.

As at Ijevan, there is considerable scope for walking over the forested hills or in the valley of the Aghstev River on which Dilijan lies. There are also **five monasteries** nearby each of which is in good walking country. Close to the main road in Dilijan is a striking Soviet-era **monument** erected to mark the 50th anniversary of Soviet power in the Caucasus: its design was intended symbolically to represent the eternal union of Armenia, Georgia and Azerbaijan under Soviet rule. That it is still standing perhaps shows that the Armenians have a well-developed sense of irony. Dilijan also has a well-known spring to the west of the town and the mineral water bottled there is a familiar sight.

Haghartsin Monastery (◷ *always*) Haghartsin lies in forest and was always one of Armenia's most-visited monasteries. To reach it head east towards Ijevan for 7km and then turn left under a railway bridge and continue up the winding road for 9km.

In 2005 we wrote that the well-preserved monastery was both evocative in itself and beautifully situated. Unfortunately, at the time of research for this edition Haghartsin could only be described as a building site. The ecclesiastical authorities have decided that the monastery is to be the site of a new seminary and extensive renovation is underway, although rebuilding would be a more accurate term. Over the centuries Haghartsin has seen many such changes but for those who prefer historic medieval buildings to look their age, the reconstruction of Haghartsin is a disappointment. It was not only a shock to me; my experienced Armenian guide was very upset. The restoration was due to be completed at the end of 2010, after finalisation of this text. While the essential layout is unlikely to change significantly there may well be changes to the following description.

As at so many monasteries the original small church had buildings added over the centuries and is now rather dwarfed by its less ancient neighbours. The oldest part is the **St Gregory Church**, probably dating from the 10th century, and with octagonal tambour although the original building was damaged by Seljuk invaders and had to be reconstructed after the Georgian victories over them. This reconstruction was followed by a large increase in the monastery's size and an important school of church music became established here which developed a new system of notation for the Armenian liturgy. The original church acquired a *gavit* at a lower level reached by steps; it is unusual in that part of the pillar in the south wall to the east of the central arch rotates to provide a secret hiding place for use when the monastery was threatened. **St Stephen's Church** was built in 1244, the large **refectory** in 1248 and the bigger **Mother of God Church** with a high 16-sided tambour, and also with *gavit*, was added in 1281. A relief of the donors with a dove (symbolising the Holy Spirit) above them can be seen on the east façade pointing to a model of the church. Among the other buildings which can be seen are the monastic **bakery** complete with oven.

Contemporaneous with this spate of building is the large walnut tree at the southeast corner of the Mother of God Church: it is estimated to be around 700 years old and was probably planted as a source of food. Walnut trees are often found at the sites of monasteries. To the south of the *gavit* of St Gregory's are the remains of royal tombs of the Bagratid dynasty. At the final bend in the road as one approaches the monastery, a group of khachkars has been marooned on a small roundabout contained by an ugly concrete wall. Nearby, on the roadside east of the site (a good photographic vantage point) are some small chapels and both here and at the monastery are particularly fine khachkars. Finest of all is the **khachkar** carved by Poghos in the 13th century which is outside the south door of the Mother of God Church. The interesting refectory, divided into two parts by arches, has stone benches along the sides. In recent years a rather incongruous modern floor was installed. Perhaps the 2010 restoration will provide an opportunity to replace it.

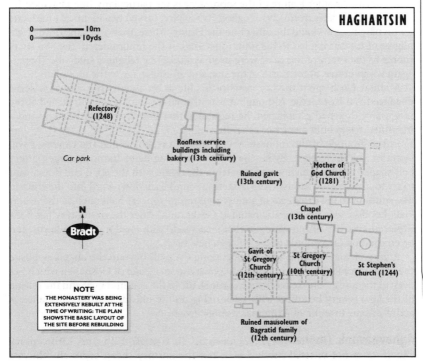

HAGHARTSIN

0 ———— 10m
0 ———— 10yds

Refectory
(1248)

Car park

Roofless service
buildings including
bakery (13th century)

Ruined gavit
(13th century)

Mother of
God Church
(1281)

N

Bradt

Chapel
(13th century)

Gavit of
St Gregory
Church
(12th century)

St Gregory
Church
(10th century)

St Stephen's
Church (1244)

NOTE
THE MONASTERY WAS BEING
EXTENSIVELY REBUILT AT THE
TIME OF WRITING: THE PLAN
SHOWS THE BASIC LAYOUT OF
THE SITE BEFORE REBUILDING

Ruined mausoleum of
Bagratid family
(12th century)

Visiting was still possible in the midst of the building work: no-one objected to visitors clambering around the site. The new seminary is being erected on the hillside to the west of the complex. Time will tell whether Haghartsin will retain its former popularity with visitors.

Goshavank (monastery) (☉ *always*) To reach the village of **Gosh** it is necessary to continue along the Ijevan road for another 8km beyond the turn-off for Haghartsin and then turn right towards **Chambarak**. The road to Gosh branches right off this road after about 2km. To reach Goshavank continue uphill into the centre of the village.

Goshavank was established in the late 12th century by the cleric Mkhitar Gosh (1130–1213) with the support of Prince Ivan Zakarian to replace the Monastery of Getik, about 20km further east, where he had previously worked but which had been destroyed in an earthquake. Originally called Nor ('New') Getik, it was renamed in honour of its founder immediately after his death. The earliest part of the complex, the **Mother of God Church**, dates from 1191; its *gavit* was completed in 1197 followed by the two **St Gregory chapels**, the free-standing one with its particularly fine carving in 1208 and the one attached to the *gavit* in 1237. The **library** and the adjacent school buildings were built in 1241 of large rough-hewn stones. In 1291 the **Holy Archangels Church** with bell tower was added on top of the library, access to the church being via the external cantilevered steps. The belfry later collapsed and the building is now protected by a conical transparent dome. At its peak the library held 1,600 volumes until Mongol invaders set fire to it in 1375. It was at Nor Getik that Mkhitar Gosh first formally codified Armenian law (partly as a defence against the imposition of Islamic sharia law) and also wrote his fables which make moral points using birds as the protagonists. Another feature of the monastery is the particularly fine **khachkar** by the door which dates from 1291. Poghos, its sculptor, carved two identical khachkars for his parents' graves and the other is in the History Museum in Yerevan. The delicate filigree of his carving led to his soubriquet Poghos the Embroiderer. The two small rooms to the south of the *gavit* were used as studies by religious students. There is again a walnut tree, at the north of the site, and of similar age to the monastery.

Mkhitar Gosh spent the last years of his life as an ascetic in a retreat at some distance from Nor Getik. Although it was normal for founders to be buried at the monastery they had established, he requested that this should not be done and a mausoleum was built away from the site.

In the grounds of the monastery is a **small museum** which the caretaker will open for you on request. By far the most interesting items there are large pottery bell-shaped objects which were hung from the dome with the open end downward to try to improve the acoustics by reflecting sound back downward into the church. The solution to the problems of some more recent concert halls such as the Albert Hall, London, was clearly anticipated at Goshavank! After the monastery has been explored a variety of refreshing herbal teas, made with local mountain herbs, can be enjoyed on the veranda of the village's new hotel.

A very pleasant walk is to continue along the path beyond the chapel opposite the monastery for about 45 minutes to reach the small lake of Goshalich which lies deep in the forest. The trees offer welcome shade in the summer heat and the setting of the lake is very beautiful with trees rising on the hillside behind. Goshalich is audibly home to some of Armenia's noisiest frogs.

Aghavnavank (monastery) (☉ *always*) This small 12th- or 13th-century church does not of itself merit a visit but the journey there, especially the last

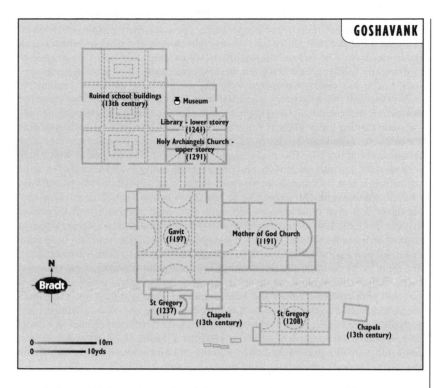

Ruined school buildings
(13th century)

♨ Museum

Library - lower storey
(1241)

Holy Archangels Church -
upper storey
(1291)

Gavit
(1197)

Mother of God Church
(1191)

N

Bradt

St Gregory
(1237)

Chapels
(13th century)

St Gregory
(1208)

Chapels
(13th century)

0 ——————— 10m
0 ——————— 10yds

stretch through Dilijan National Park (see page 228), is very enjoyable. It can easily be combined with a visit to Goshavank. Instead of turning right for Gosh village carry on towards Chambarak for another 8km. The village of Aghavnavank is signposted left. Cross the River Getik and turn left up a dirt road until the centre of the small village is reached. A sharp right hairpin bend takes you onto another dirt track which goes to the monastery. (One of the white-on-green Armenian signs for Dilijan National Park points the way.) You will need a 4x4 to drive up to the church as a stream has to be driven along for a short distance. Also the key to open the barrier into the national park has to be obtained but this is not usually a problem; ask one of the villagers. It is probably easier to walk; it is a very lovely walk through the woods beside the stream. It takes about ten minutes from the village to the park barrier and another 20 minutes to the church. Situated on the wooded slopes of Mount Tsaghkot in the Miapor mountain range the Mother of God Hermitage Church is of the cross-dome type with a relatively tall tambour. It abuts a rocky outcrop suggesting that it may have been built on the site of a pagan spring shrine. In the vicinity are virgin yew *Taxus baccata* groves, some of the trees estimated to be 300–400 years old. Both bears and wolves inhabit the national park but I did not encounter either on my walk.

Jukhtakvank and Matosavank monasteries (⊕ *always*) Visits to these two small monasteries can easily be combined, as you park at the same place for both. Head west from Dilijan for 3km along the main Vanadzor road and then turn right to pass under a high railway viaduct whose girders are painted in red ochre. If walking from Dilijan, take the road on the south side of the river to start with, rather than the main road, and cross the river at one of the footbridges before reaching

Hotel Dilijan Resort, thereby avoiding much of the noisy, dirty main road. Drive up this road for about 2km until a sign points right along a dirt track to **Jukhtakvank** (*jukht* means 'pair' or 'couple'; the site has two remaining churches). Do not attempt to drive any further as the track has been washed away. It is about ten minutes' walk to the monastery. Compared with the architectural glories of Haghartsin and Goshavank this monastery is modest indeed with its two small churches. The nearer one, dedicated to St Gregory, has lost its dome although it retains some very elaborate carving inside and a frieze round the walls. The further church, probably the older one, is dedicated to the Mother of God and bears an inscription indicating that it was built in 1201. This peaceful site in the wooded valley makes a visit here very pleasant, the only other visitor on one occasion being a calf which had escaped the summer heat by lying down in front of the altar inside the Mother of God Church. **Matosavank** (Monastery of St Matthew) is less visited than Jukhtavank but the walk is even more pleasant, although somewhat steep at first. A very short distance from the sign to Jukhtavank a path goes off left down to a stream which is crossed on a low footbridge. There is a sign pointing to Matosavank but unlike the one to Jukhtavank, which is in both Armenian and English, it is in Armenian only. The route to the monastery is clearly marked by red-paint waymarkers on trees and rocks. Follow them uphill and then left across open woodland which in spring is carpeted with cowslips, violets and blue anemones. One is almost upon the small monastery before seeing it, built as it is into the hillside and with its ruined roofs partially covered in vegetation. The undistinguished external appearance in no way prepares one for the wealth of attractive khachkars inside. The barrel-vaulted *gavit* leads into a small barrel-vaulted chapel to the east and into a domed chamber on the south. The walk takes about 25 minutes each way.

6

The Southern Provinces

Southern Armenia is the least-visited part of the country. That is a pity and is largely the consequence of visitors giving themselves inadequate time. There is spectacular scenery with roads zigzagging up and down over mountain passes. Two of Armenia's best-known monasteries are here, one visited by almost every tourist on a day trip from Yerevan, one requiring an overnight stay in the province. Other monasteries are to be found in remote settings allowing the possibility of walks through wonderful countryside to reach them. Petroglyphs, cave villages, Armenia's best-known megalithic site and one of the world's best-preserved caravanserais are other gems.

VAYOTS DZOR PROVINCE

Many visitors come to Vayots Dzor ('Gorge of Woes') on a day trip from Yerevan – principally to see the Monastery of Noravank – but it is not really possible to see much else in this province unless you are prepared to stay for a few days. Vayots Dzor is crowded with interesting historic sites, all attractively situated, and a few days here are well justified.

For the most part, Vayots Dzor certainly lives up to the *dzor* ('gorge') part of its name. Visitors travelling from Yerevan cross the Tukh Manuk Pass and then descend to the Arpa River. The gorge here is at times narrow and spectacular, notably between Areni and Arpi and even more so beyond Gndevank. Even in autumn, after a long dry summer, the river is surprisingly full. Presumably this is because of water management at the hydro-electric power station, and despite the abstraction of the water which is being diverted in an attempt to raise the level of Lake Sevan (see pages 173–5). The Arpa rises in the northeast of the province between **Mount Sartsali** (3,433m) and **Mount Chaghat** (3,333m), flows south through Jermuk before assuming a more westerly course until it enters Nakhichevan after which it joins the Arax. There are many other gorges in the province, the more wooded ones being good places to see golden orioles in the breeding season, flocks of rose-coloured starlings, and also offering the occasional view of a Levant sparrowhawk.

WHERE TO STAY The sights of Vayots Dzor itself can be seen during a stay of about four nights, although of course many visitors will combine it with either a visit to the Lake Sevan area, visiting Selim caravanserai *en route*, or to Syunik province, thus taking in some of the sights on the way south. Yeghegnadzor is central although the best hotel accommodation is in Jermuk.

Homestays are easy to find, there is a pleasant hotel at Vaik, acceptable hotel accommodation in Yeghegnadzor and plentiful accommodation in the spa town of

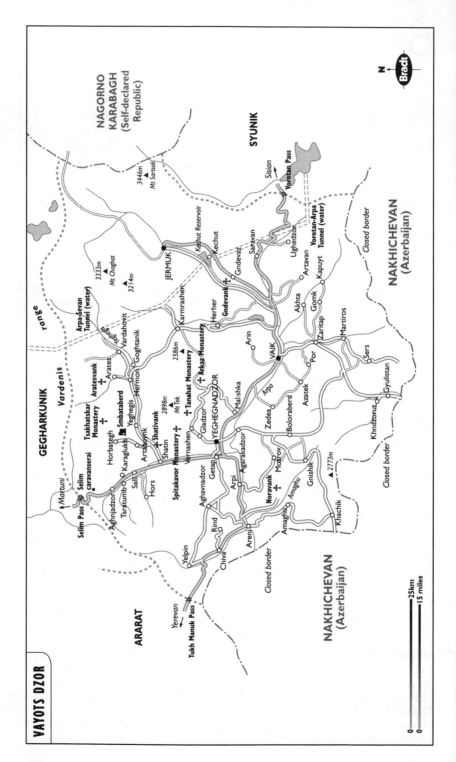

NAGORNO
KARABAGH
(Self-declared
Republic)

SYUNIK

3446m
Mt Sortsali

Yorotan Pass

GEGHARKUNIK

Vardenis

range

Kechut Reservoir

Kechut

Arpa-Sevan
Tunnel (water)

Saravan

Gndevaz

Ughedzor

Vorotan-Arpa
Tunnel (water)

Sisian

Vorotan Pass

Closed border

NAKHICHEVAN
(Azerbaijan)

3333m
Mt Choghat

3214m

JERMUK

Karmrashen

Herher

Gndevank ✝

Akhta

Gomk

Martiros

Sers

Gyulistan

Selim
caravanserai

Matrruni

Selim Pass

Tsakhatskar
Monastery ✝

Arates

Aratesvank ✝

Vardahovit

Goghtanik

Hermon

Yeghegis

Smbataberd ▲

Artabuynk

Shativank ✝

2586m

Mt Tek

2898m

Tanahat Monastery ✝

Akaz Monastery ✝

Arin

VAIK

Por

Azatek

Zaritap

Gnshik

2773m ▲

Khndzorut

Closed border

Horbategh

Karaglukh

Shatin

Spitakavor Monastery ✝

Vernashen

Gladzor

YEGHEGNADZOR

Malishka

Arpa

Zedea

Boloraberd

Motrov

Amaghu

Khachik

Tartumb

Salli

Hors

Aghnjadzor

Rind

Aghavnadzor

Getap

Arpi

Agarakadzor

Norvank ✝

Amaghu

NAKHICHEVAN
(Azerbaijan)

Yelpin

Chiva

Areni

Closed border

ARARAT

Yerevan

Tukh Manuk Pass

Kapuyt

Artavan

0 — 25km
0 — 15 miles

N

Bradt

Jermuk (in homestays, hotels and sanatoria). It is possible for anyone to stay at the sanatoria but prices are usually inclusive of treatments regardless of whether you take them or not. The promised Tufenkian hotel at Areni is sorely needed; let's hope that it is eventually constructed.

Arpi

🏠 **Ijevanatoun** (10 rooms) ☎ 281 63785; 📱 093 952550. The rooms in the main building have not changed in 10 years. 2 of them are adequate, if basic & rundown. The others have only a tiny toilet/sink/shower room where there is barely space to take a shower. However, there are 2 new cottages right beside the river which are much better. The motel is situated about 300m north of the cluster of roadside stalls next to the Hotel Noy. If you do choose to stay here, then try to get a room at the back to minimise the noise from the Iranian lorries which come & go 24hrs a day & to enjoy the view of the river. Cash only. Restaurant ⊕ 08.00–midnight. B/fast extra, AMD1,000/pp. **$**

Jermuk

🏠 **Jermuk Armenia** (60 rooms) 2 Miasnikyan St; ☎ 287 21290, 10 281224 (Yerevan number); 📧 contact@jermukarmenia.com, jermukarmenia@yahoo.com; www.jermukarmenia.com. Until recently this was the most comfortable establishment in Jermuk, but other hotels have now caught up with & even overtaken it. Splendidly refurbished to its former glory in the hope that patients will return, meals are still served in an unsigned room hidden in the basement called the canteen. By contrast, the large & prominent bar serves many non-residents whose tastes it presumably reflects by not selling beer that has been brewed in Armenia. Signage – except on a long corridor whose doors are marked 'gastroenterologist', 'proctologist', 'chief doctor', 'deputy chief doctor', etc – is non-existent. In this vast building there are no evacuation diagrams either in the rooms or corridors & the only exits apart from the front door are a back door from the kitchen & an exit via the splendid new swimming pool. Price includes all meals & medical treatment, whether taken or not. Cards accepted. Wi-Fi. **$$$$$**

🏠 **Jermuk Olympia** (52 rooms) 16 Shahumyan St; ☎ 287 22366; 📱 094 444904; 📧 info@jermukolympia.am; www.jermukolympia.am. This recently renovated sanatorium looks light & airy with carefully thought-out décor. Wheelchair access to hotel, but not to the pleasant dining room overlooking the grounds. Evacuation plans present. FB & medical treatment included. Cards accepted. Wi-Fi. **$$$$**

🏠 **Ani Hotel** (9 rooms) 26 Shahumyan St; 📱 097 211727; 📧 robnan@jermukani.am; www.jermukani.am. Small, newly built hotel with good-quality interestingly shaped rooms. FB. B/fast in hotel, other meals in hotel's restaurant next door. **$$$**

🏠 **Evmari** (pronounced Yevmarie) (1 dbl, 5 suites with 2 dbl rooms, 1 suite with 3 dbl rooms) 3 Shahumyan St; ☎ 287 21814; 📱 099 011814; 📧 hayro@inbox.ru. Internet access included in price. B/fast extra, approx AMD750/pp. **$**

Vaik

🏠 **Vayots Dzor Tourism Centre & Hotel** 10a Jermuk Rd, 3801; ☎ 282 21170; 📱 093 021170; 📧 vaykshirak@rambler.ru. This recently opened hotel cum private-initiative information centre has nice rooms with photographs of the region, taken by the owner. Very helpful staff. Information desk ⊕ 10.00–19.00 Mon–Fri, 10.00–16.00 Sat. Owner can arrange cultural, wine, camping tours & leads caving expeditions himself. Wi-Fi use AMD1,000. B/fast extra, approx AMD1,000/pp. **$**

Yeghegnadzor

🏠 **Hotel Vayots Dzor** (4 rooms) Yerevan highway; ☎ 281 62051; 📱 0777 24999. A restaurant with a few rooms which are satisfactory, provided you're happy with pink or blue satin. **$**

🏠 **Gohar Gevorgyan** (7 rooms) 44 Spendaryan St; ☎ 281 23324, 23373; 📱 093 826477 or English-speaker: 094 332993; 📧 arminw7@yahoo.com. I can personally recommend this deservedly popular homestay. B/fast (a good one) included, evening meal available if notice given. AMD10,000 pp. **$**

OTHER PRACTICALITIES Most visitors coming to Vayots Dzor travel down the main road from Yerevan, entering the province at the **Tukh Manuk Pass** (1,795m). This route has been completely rebuilt and is in good condition throughout. It carries heavy lorry traffic, mainly Iranian vehicles travelling between Teheran and Yerevan. The other road from the north crosses the **Selim Pass** (2,410m) and is open only in summer. Recent reconstruction means that it is accessible to all vehicles. **Minibuses** travel from Yerevan to Yeghegnadzor, Vaik and Jermuk (see *Chapter 2*, pages 74–6). The minibus from Yerevan to Yeghegnadzor takes about two hours for the 120km trip but a sensible driver might take somewhat longer. From these centres minibuses go to local villages but to reach many of the sites mentioned, either a car or taxi is needed.

The towns in the province are small but have basic facilities such as shops, post offices, banks, cafés and taxis. Any special requirements should be brought from Yerevan. Vaik has a private **tourist information centre** within a hotel (*Vayots Dzor Tourism Centre & Hotel; 10a Jermuk Rd, 3801;* ☎ *282 21170;* 📱 *093 021170; information desk* ⊕ *10.00–19.00 Mon–Fri, 10.00–16.00 Sat*) (see page 235) and the proprietor can help with arranging almost anything.

ARENI Heading south from the provincial border the main road from Yerevan descends a side valley to join the gorge of the Arpa at the village of Areni, a centre of Armenia's wine industry. It is possible to visit the **winery** (*Areni Wine;* ☎ *281 20744; www.areni.am*) on the east side of the main road in the village. Visits can be arranged through tour operators in Yerevan (see pages 55–6) or by just calling into the winery – you rarely have to wait more than 30 minutes for a tour. Tours are free but of course there is an opportunity to buy at the end. Areni gives its name to an indigenous grape variety mainly used for making dry red table wines. Roadside stalls in the Areni area prominently display for sale large bottles labelled Coca-Cola. Should you be feeling thirsty and tempted to buy one, then prepare for a shock. The usual purchasers are Iranian truck drivers and they are taking home to alcohol-free Iran a beverage with considerably more body and flavour than Coca-Cola.

In Areni village, but on the opposite bank of the Arpa, can be seen in the distance from the main road a **red cross-dome church** dedicated to the Mother of God and built in 1321. It was restored in 1997. The church's most remarkable feature is the tympanum of the west door which is a wonderfully carved effigy of the Virgin Mary created by Momik, one of Armenia's greatest stone carvers and also a great illustrator of manuscripts; he worked in this region in the late 13th and early 14th centuries. High on the west façade, the representation of a head gazing down is said to be that of a Mongolian, a reminder that at the time the church was constructed Armenia was under Mongol rule and that persecution of non-Muslims was increasing. Inside the church in the pendentives below the tambour are more fine carvings, again by Momik, of the symbols of the four evangelists. The graveyard too has some exceptional carving with tombstones apparently demonstrating Areni's long wine-making history as they show a figure with a wine flask or wine glass. Another tombstone shows a horse and also a person playing a *saz*, a musical instrument rather like a lute and the ancestor of the Greek *bouzouki*. Close by there is a row of five modern graves belonging to young men killed in 1992 in the war with Azerbaijan, a reminder that the frontier is only 5km away.

NORAVANK (MONASTERY) (⊕ *always although it may not be possible to reach it in winter*) Just south of Areni a road goes off west across a bridge and enters the narrow gorge of the Gnishik. It leads after 6km to one of Armenia's best-known and most worthwhile tourist sights: Noravank ('New Monastery'). About 1km from the junction a gigantic boulder, which has fallen from the cliff, bridges the Gnishik and now forms the backdrop to many a photograph. Another 2km further on, carpets can be seen hanging across the entrance to a cavern. There is no sign and, while it would be reasonable to suppose that the cavern is the premises of a carpet vendor, that would be wholly incorrect as it is actually a pleasantly situated **café**, which will be open whenever there is a chance of visitors passing. There is no sign indicating that it is a café since the proprietor believes one to be unnecessary: 'everyone knows it is a café'. Shortly beyond the café, Noravank can be seen high on the cliff face to the left. Its construction in red stone set against the similarly coloured rock of the mountainside is particularly evocative in the early morning or late evening light. If at all possible avoid coming here in the middle of the day as that is when the place is thronged with tourist buses from Yerevan and it is also stiflingly hot in the valley in summer. Nowadays, however, the monastery does boast a **café** (⊕ *09.30–21.30 during the tourist season, approx May–Oct, depending on the weather*) where it is possible to recover from the heat if one is obliged to visit in the middle of the day. There are also **toilets** on the approach to the monastery. The toilets are under the same management as the café and consequently are only open at the same times.

Approaching the monastery today the striking two-storey building that one reaches first is actually a mausoleum with another church on top of it and is the newest part of the establishment. The larger complex of buildings beyond is older; the oldest part of all, the 9th- or 10th-century **Church of John the Baptist** is the ruin at the southeast corner.

The site was developed mainly in the 13th century by the Orbelian princes. They were a branch of the Mamikonian family, which had settled in Georgia in the 9th century and members of which had held the position of commander-in-chief of the Georgian forces in the 10th and 11th centuries. The Georgian army, which included many Armenians, defeated the sultan in 1204 and many families from

---

THE FOUNDING OF NORAVANK

According to Bishop Stepanos Orbelian, who was writing almost 200 years after the events he described, Noravank was founded by Hovhannes, Bishop of Vahanavank (in Syunik province). Hovhannes reportedly went to the Seljuk sultan Mahmud and came back with a *firman* giving him possession. He then moved here in 1105 and built the original church dedicated to John the Baptist (though present-day historians date this now-ruined church rather earlier), establishing a firm rule which barred all women and lewd persons. Meanwhile, however, the emir of nearby Hrashkaberd plotted to kill him and destroy the monastery. Hovhannes then went to Isfahan (in present-day Iran) where he cured the sultan's sick son and was rewarded with the title deeds to Hrashkaberd as well as other nearby estates. In consequence of this Hovhannes took a band of armed followers who captured the emir and his family and pushed them off a cliff. Bishop Hovhannes thereafter reportedly led a holy life and worked numerous miracles, such as catching in his hands unharmed a woman and infant who fell off a cliff, though presumably not near the monastery from which the mother would, of course, have been barred.

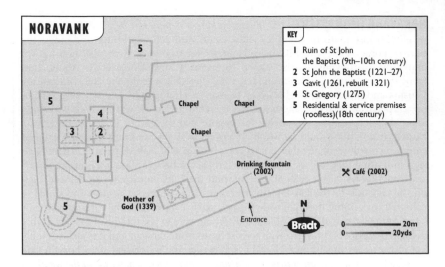

NORAVANK

KEY

1 Ruin of St John
the Baptist (9th–10th century)
2 St John the Baptist (1221–27)
3 Gavit (1261, rebuilt 1321)
4 St Gregory (1275)
5 Residential & service premises
(roofless)(18th century)

Chapel   Chapel

Chapel

Drinking fountain
(2002)   ✗ Café (2002)

Mother of
God (1339)

N

Entrance   **Bradt**   0 ━━━━━ 20m
                                    0 ━━━━━ 20yds

Georgia moved into Armenia including the Orbelians who settled in Syunik. The Orbelians built several churches to act as burial places for the family and the see of the bishopric of Syunik was moved here to Noravank. The **oldest surviving church** is the one in the centre of the further complex of buildings. Erected in 1221–27, it is also dedicated to John the Baptist and is of the cross-dome type with two-storey corner rooms. To judge from a fragment of the church model which has survived, it originally had an octagonal tambour with an umbrella cupola but this collapsed during an earthquake in 1840 and has been replaced by a circular tambour and conical cupola. The more modest **Church of St Gregory** was added on the north side in 1275 as the burial place of the Orbelians. In the floor are gravestones including one dated 1300 for Elikum, son of Prince Tarsayich Orbelian, who is represented by a lion figure resting its head on one paw. There are two carved doves by the altar dais, which is flanked by khachkars, and the remains of frescoes can be seen. The window is set slanting in the east wall, probably so that on some particular day of the year the rays of the dawning sun will illuminate the grave of Prince Smbat who is also buried here.

The original *gavit* of the John the Baptist Church was built on the west side in 1261 by Prince Smbat Orbelian but it was completely rebuilt in 1321 following earthquake damage. Both the *gavit* and the Mother of God Church nearer the car park are the work of Momik who was also responsible for the fine carving at Areni (see page 236). The two tympana (one above the other, separated by a window opening) of the doorway are in every way remarkable. The carved relief of the upper, pointed one shows God, with his almond-shaped eyes looking straight ahead while a dove is entangled in his beard. He is raising his right hand in blessing while holding a head in his left. Whose head must remain a matter of speculation: possibly that of John the Baptist to whom the church is dedicated and who was decapitated, or perhaps it is the head of the Son or perhaps that of Adam. Above the head is a dove symbolising the Holy Spirit. To the right there is the winged head of a child, the medieval symbol of a seraph, while to the left the scene of Crucifixion. The lower tympanum is semicircular and depicts Mary, wearing a dress whose folds are accurately depicted, sitting with Jesus in her arms, on a patterned rug that is adorned with tassels. On the right is the Prophet Isaiah together with a banner that reads 'Holy Virgin Isaiah'. On the left is St John the Baptist with further words visible in the tracery. The whole is surrounded by an inscription which, according to a recent Armenian booklet describing Noravank, reads: 'Here is the blessed and awful name of my God from the beginnings to the verge of edges that is out of ends and ruptures.' Unfortunately the rest of the booklet achieves a similar level of obscurity. Inside the *gavit* there is further carving but nothing to rival the tympana.

The **two-storey church** nearer the entrance also has very fine carving. Built by Prince Burtel Orbelian, it is dedicated to the Mother of God and was completed in 1339, proving to be Momik's last work. Considerable damage was caused by the 1840 earthquake, and the church lost its tambour and cupola which were not restored until 1997, using fallen fragments as a pattern. The appearance of this church is very unusual: the lower storey is rectangular but the upper is of cross-dome form. The lower storey can be accessed by descending six steps at the west end and comprises the burial vault of the donor and his family. Over the doorway the tympanum depicts Mary with Jesus in her arms, but sitting on a throne this time, flanked by the archangels Gabriel and Michael. Inside the vault can be seen the figures of the evangelists. The church, in the upper storey, is accessed by narrow steps cantilevered up the outside face of the lower façade. Only those who are happy on narrow ledges should climb them. The tympanum over the upper doorway depicts a half-length Christ flanked by the apostles Peter and Paul. From the ceiling of the corner room to the right of the altar the head of a lion looks down.

The reinstated conical cupola is, unusually, not supported by a tambour but by 12 columns. On three of the columns at the western end can just be seen (binoculars help) carved figures of Mary with Jesus and of two donors of the church, one of whom is holding a model of it. There are still some very fine khachkars here although the finest of all have been moved to Ejmiatsin. One good and very intricate one which remains was carved by Momik in 1308.

From a gateway behind the Church of St Gregory (see above) a path goes up the hillside to a good viewpoint.

Descending into the gorge again, but then turning to the left by the river, a track leads to the small **Chapel of St Pokas**, in which is a 4th-century khachkar, oval with a simple cross, and a spring whose water is covered by a film of oil, supposedly oil from the saint's burial ground. According to Stepanos Orbelian writing in the late 13th century, surprising miracles formerly occurred here: all manner of pains, whose cure by men was impossible, such as leprosy and long-infected and gangrenous wounds, were cured when people came here, bathed in the water and were anointed with the oil. However, in cases where the diseases were incurable, the people died immediately upon drinking the water!

THE YEGHEGIS VALLEY After Areni the main road turns east to follow the Arpa and in about 15km it crosses the Yeghegis River. Turn left immediately after the bridge to see a number of interesting and attractively located sights – some walking is required to reach most of them, though Selim caravanserai is close to the road. The sights, from the village of Shatin eastwards are the monastery of Shativank; Tsakhatskar Monastery and the fortress of Smbataberd; Yeghegis village (Zorats Church and the Jewish cemetery); and Arates Monastery.

Shativank (monastery) (⊕ *always*) For 10km from its junction with the main road, the Selim road follows the Yeghegis River north but the river then turns east into the village of **Shatin**. Go into Shatin and near the far end of the village fork right down to the river which you cross on a bridge. About 150m beyond the bridge, fork right and then 500m beyond that left up a hill to the village cemetery. In a 4x4 it is just about possible to drive beyond here to the **Monastery of Shativank**, but it is a pleasant 7km walk along the track with fine views down into the valley on each side from the crest of the ridge. (Note that there is an alternative path direct up from the gorge. It is shorter but much steeper, frequently muddy, and there are no views.) From the village cemetery the track to the monastery goes up between the graves and then bears left. After a few kilometres it is possible to see Shativank in the distance and the track winds down to it. Shativank was founded in 929 but was destroyed in the 14th century and then rebuilt. Like other Armenian churches in the late medieval period it was provided with massive fortified walls which are here well preserved, and the substantial remains of three round defensive towers can also be seen on the south side. The **Zion church** itself, rebuilt again in 1665, is a three-aisle basilica built of basalt and of limited interest apart from its evocative site. The remains of other monastic buildings and khachkars can be seen.

Tsakhatskar Monastery and Smbataberd (fortress) (⏱ *always*) The next two sights along the Yeghegis, the Monastery of Tsakhatskar and the fortress of Smabataberd, can be combined to give a pleasant walk. Continuing east from Shatin village, take the left fork towards **Artabuynk**. About 1km beyond Artabuynk a track angles steeply down on the right-hand side, fording an irrigation channel as it descends. At the bottom of the hill the track formerly crossed the Yeghegis by a bridge but this is no longer safe for vehicles, although it can be used by pedestrians. Vehicles must now ford the river and, while this is possible for a lorry with high ground clearance, it is risky for others unless the river is exceptionally low. It is therefore better to park here and walk. **Tsakhatskar Monastery** should be visited first as this makes the navigation easier and gets the greater part of the climbing accomplished earlier in the day. A moderately fit person should allow 90 minutes to walk from the river up to Tsakhatskar, then 45 minutes from Tsakhatskar to Smbataberd, and 30 minutes back from Smbataberd to the river plus some time at each site and to admire the views. Follow the main track up from the far side of the ford or bridge. In about 500m there is a spring on the right where water bottles can be filled; there is another spring at Tsakhatskar itself.

Continue up the main track always keeping left if in doubt. One junction in the track is signposted, left 2km to Tsakhatskar and right 1km to Smbataberd. The monastery can be seen high up on the mountainside to the left long before reaching it, but in practice it is hard to detect, so similar is the colour of its basalt stone to the colour of the mountainside. The ruined monastery is reached after about 5km of continuous ascent and is astonishingly large for so isolated a place. The easternmost of the two churches, Holy Cross, dates from the 11th century and appears to have been a mausoleum. A square entrance area, above which is what looks as if it could have been a second storey, leads through to a lower chapel. A large stone structure has been built across the original entrance for the full width of the building and on it stand large khachkars.

The more western of the two churches, St John the Baptist, was built in 1041 but it is less ruinous and the circular tambour and cupola are fairly intact. Outside on the north wall can be seen a carving of a lion tearing a lamb, possibly the coat of arms of the Orbelian family who built the church. The doorway is elaborately decorated with geometric designs and inscriptions and the remaining slabs of the altar dais show carved jugs, which may once have formed a design across the whole. Outside there are many khachkars, including two very large ones near the entrance, as well as a stone depicting an eagle clutching a lamb in its talons. Both churches were being renovated in 2010.

The main part of the monastery was at a distance from these churches on the west side. Extensive remains of buildings can be seen, most of them presumably the service buildings of the monastery, although including further churches dedicated to the Mother of God and, at the southern end, to St John. The latter bears an inscription dated to 999. There are what appear to be the remains of cloisters and all of these buildings on the western side were once surrounded by a defensive wall, of which only the eastern part with its gateway survives. An inscription at the gateway records its restoration in 1221. The sheer scale of these remains, which stretch for over 200m, indicates clearly the former importance of this now forgotten place. From the site the view is over alpine meadows and apple trees down into the valley below but a mountain ridge stretches away to the south, on the furthest summit of which can be seen with binoculars the **fortress of Smbataberd**. It is fairly easy to work out a route, the key point being to determine how far to retrace the route up from the river before branching off left along the side of the ridge. The walk again provides magnificent views down into the valley on each side and is mostly downhill apart from the final slope up into the fortress. If visibility is poor it is safer to retrace your steps to the signposted junction and follow that track up to the fortress.

Stabilisation work has been carried out on the walls of the fortress and a paved path leads to one of the postern gates outside of which a small viewing platform has been built. Unfortunately the sensitivity evident in the work inside the fortress has not been shown in the prominent placing of a toilet block on one of the ridges looking down into the valleys. When I visited the state of the toilets could only be described as disgusting.

Smbataberd (fortress of Smbat, Prince of Syunik) was probably founded in the 5th century but considerably strengthened in the 10th and is perhaps Armenia's most impressive fortress. Few visitors can fail to be impressed by the gigantic ramparts built on the precipitous cliff face, especially those on the eastern side. (Those without a head for heights should avoid climbing onto the walls.) Smbataberd is in a magnificent defensive position, crowning the southern end of the ridge and guarded by steep cliffs on three sides. Even on those sides, walls with frequent towers were built wherever the drop was less than precipitous and much of this survives. Inside the walls relatively little remains, although the outline of buildings can be discerned around the walls as well as the fortress's keep at the highest point of the site. According to local legend, Smbataberd fell to the Seljuk Turks when they employed a thirsty horse to sniff out the water supply: it came in an underground pipe from Tsakhatskar. This would indicate an 11th century date. However, other reports suggest that the castle was defended until the 13th century, which would imply that it was eventually captured by the Mongols rather than the Seljuks. See page 242, for a route from Yeghegis to the fortress.

Yeghegis Looking far down into the valley from the eastern rampart of Smbataberd you can see the ruins of the town of Yeghegis by the Yeghegis River. The town had two separate periods of prosperity: firstly during the Syunik princedom (10th–11th century) at the end of which it was destroyed, possibly by an earthquake; and then under the Orbelians from the 13th century to the 15th. Yeghegis is at present no more than a village and can be seen to the northeast. A visit there is worthwhile but can seem rather a let-down after a morning spent up on the ridge. A track leads down from Smbataberd to Yeghegis but it is very muddy after rain and it becomes less obvious nearer to the village. It may be easier simply to walk back to the car, retrace the route as far as the junction with the Yeghegis road, and then return up the parallel valley. Should one wish to walk up to **Smbataberd from the Yeghegis side** (the view of the fortress is actually better from this approach) the track goes off left just after the village sign when driving from Shatin. Walk up this track until it turns sharply right at some low cliffs and look for a metal pipe crossing a gully. The path to Smbataberd goes across the hillside just to the left of this pipe.

Yeghegis is a pleasant, unspoiled village with three churches and an old Jewish cemetery. The three-aisle **basilica church** with a grass-covered roof in the centre of the village was built in 1708 and is dedicated to the Mother of God. Four massive pillars support the roof of this basalt structure. A curious feature, apart from the absence of a cupola, is that it is built into the hillside so that the roof at the back is almost at ground level. At the east end of the village the 13th-century **Church of John the Baptist** does have a cupola and has a surprisingly small interior for its height. However, the village's most notable church is the **Zorats (Army) Church** dedicated to St Stephen. It is highly unusual, not only by Armenian standards, in that the congregation stood in the open air facing the altar. The roof was built to only cover the east end of the church and covers just the altar in the centre with a sacristy on each side. The name Zorats, and possibly the reason why it was an open-air structure, came from its use as the place where arms and horses were consecrated before battle. Obviously it would have been more convenient not to have the horses inside a building! The church was constructed in 1303 by a grandson of Prince Tarsayich Orbelian, governor of the province of Syunik. Excavations have uncovered medieval foundations on the north side of the church and to the east are many tombstones and an extensive area with large boulders forming walls and pathways around a plateau overlooking the valley. In season the walnut tree planted below the church still yields excellent fruit!

The **Jewish cemetery** here was rediscovered in 1996 by the Bishop of Syunik. It is one of the oldest known in the world and has been excavated since 2000 by a team from the Jewish University of Jerusalem under Professor Michael Stone. It is reached by a rickety footbridge over the Yeghegis River. So far more than 60 gravestones have been identified including those used for the foundations of the footbridge and others used in the foundations of a mill. At the cemetery, some of the stones are positioned on open graves while others are on sealed graves. A number of the stones have magnificent ornamentation. Some of the symbols on the Jewish gravestones – like a spiral wheel – were also in use on Armenian Christian stonecrafts around the same time. It is most interesting that the same decorative motifs were shared by Jews and Christians. While some of the inscriptions were worn down over the centuries, a lot of them are decipherable. One stone dated the 18th of Tishrei of AD1266 is of 'the virgin maiden, the affianced Esther, daughter of Michael. May her portion be with our matriarch Sarah.' The opposite side quotes 'Grace is a lie and beauty is vanity' (Proverbs 31:20) and continues with a statement that Esther was 'God-fearing'. Another gravestone contains an emotional statement from a father mourning his son's passing in which the father claims that the soul is eternal and cites passages from the book of Isaiah that relate to the resurrection of the dead.

Comparing the style of the Jewish stones with those in Christian cemeteries of the period it seems likely that they were carved by the same craftsmen who served both communities. The evidence suggests that Jews were important members of the society at Yeghegis, probably engaged in flour milling, since the remains of three watermills have been uncovered in the Jewish district. On the evidence of the graves discovered, Jews probably arrived here in the 13th century during the period of Mongol rule, remained throughout the era of Turkmen control but left in the 15th, possibly around the time of Ottoman takeover.

Opposite the Jewish cemetery on the same side of the river as the road, there is a field where gravestones have been pushed over. I was told that this used to be an Azeri village.

Aratesvank (monastery) Some kilometres east of Yeghegis are the ruins of Arates Monastery. Few visitors reach it, apart from those with a particular penchant for monasteries. Beyond Yeghegis the road deteriorates a little but 4x4 is not required. Fork left in the centre of Hermon and then left again at the next fork, where there is a decrepit sign to Aratesvank in Armenian and Russian. The road climbs uphill and reaches a disused military checkpoint. Continue on the asphalt road which bears right past the checkpoint until the village of Arates is reached. The monastery is obvious, up on a knoll to your left. It is ruinous but I found it interesting to try to work out the plan of the monastery. There are three small churches side by side – the 7th-century **St Sion Church** (probably the middle of the three), the 10th-century **Mother of God Church** and the 13th-century **St John the Baptist Church** – and a *gavit*, flagged with gravestones, built in 1265–70 by order of Prince Smbat Orbelian. Multiple small chapels lead off the churches. The village itself, having been an Azeri village, is deserted with just one person living here to look after the sheep and the well-tended orchards. The steeply sided river gorge between Yeghegis and Hermon, the hills surrounding Arates and the wild flowers *en route* all make this an attractive extension to the visit of the Yeghegis Valley.

SELIM CARAVANSERAI Selim caravanserai is the best-preserved caravanserai in Armenia and one of the best preserved in the world; its formerly remote site high on the Selim Pass prevented its being quarried for building materials. To reach it, retrace the route as far as Shatin and then turn right onto the main road. There is now a good surface the whole way over the pass (2,410m). The caravanserai is situated just below the summit of the pass and affords wonderful views down along the valley. Nowadays it has become a favoured picnic spot.

Constructed of basalt and with a roof of flat tiles, it is a long building with a single entrance at one end: having only one entrance made the building more readily defensible against thieves. To the left of the doorway of the entrance vestibule is a griffin while to the right there is a lion. Above it is an inscription written in Persian using Arabic letters, while inside the vestibule to the right there is one in Armenian, recording that the caravanserai was built in 1332 by Chesar Orbelian during the reign of Khan Abu Said II. The main hall of the caravanserai is divided into three naves by means of seven pairs of pillars. The two narrower side naves were used for the merchants and their wares while the animals were kept in the central one. Stone troughs were provided for feedstuffs for the animals and there is a basalt trough in one corner to supply them with water. Light and ventilation were provided by small openings in the roof but the interior is dark and a torch is useful although not essential. Looking at all these arrangements it is possible to capture an image of the life of the 14th-century merchants who passed this way, to an extent which can rarely be experienced anywhere in Europe. The restoration carried out in 1956–59 did nothing to mar the atmosphere and it is only to be hoped that the greatly increased numbers of visitors will leave it similarly unscathed.

YEGHEGNADZOR (*Telephone code 281*) The centre of the provincial capital lies to the north of the main road. Yeghegnadzor ('Valley of the reeds') has a couple of museums but is not in itself otherwise of any interest except as a place to shop or change money. There are, however, a number of interesting sights outside the town, in particular Spitakavor Monastery and Tanahat Monastery (with the related, but separately housed, Museum of Gladzor University). Just visible in the distance from the main road immediately east of its junction with the Selim road is a **13th-century bridge over the Arpa**. The bridge can be reached by taking the track which heads across the fields towards the river from just north of the main road's junction with the Selim road. The bridge, once upon a time on the main road to Julfa, consists of a single arch of 16m span. The bridge is unlike other medieval Armenian bridges in being a lancet arch: in other words it is an acutely pointed arch having two separate centres of equal radii. This gives it a pointed appearance with a high clearance over the river in the centre. The bridge is very picturesquely situated away from any main road and makes an ideal place for a picnic.

The Museum of Gladzor University ($\oplus$ 09.00–17.30 Tue–Sun; AMD500) From the centre of Yeghegnadzor a road leads northeast up the hill through residential areas. The Museum of Gladzor University is just beyond the town on the left, housed in a former basilica church. This museum does not rank among Armenia's must-sees but it does explain why visitors may hear of Gladzor University at a number of sites they visit (it moved from place to place according to the wishes of the principal of the day). The former church in which it is housed has been well restored (there are some interesting carvings on stones incorporated into the walls) apart from the incongruous shiny reddish floor tiles and the seven unattractive modern khachkars outside representing the seven subjects of medieval learning: the trivium or lower part comprised grammar, rhetoric and logic while the quadrivium or higher part comprised arithmetic, geometry, astronomy and music. The museum has photographs of the various monasteries to which the university moved, illustrations of illuminated manuscripts produced at the university, and places where former students went to establish schools. In all, 350 *vardapets* graduated between 1282 when the university was established by Momik (see *Noravank*, pages 237–9) and 1338 when it ceased to function. Throughout its working life the university was concerned with maintaining the independence of the Armenian Church and the rejection of papal authority.

Spitakavor Monastery The Monastery of Spitakavor ('White-ish') can be reached from Gladzor University Museum (see above) either by car or on foot. Driving definitely needs a 4x4, good weather and a driver experienced in this sort of terrain. Even then it is a difficult 8.4km drive. The track to the monastery goes off left a few metres beyond the museum. The determined can also visit the fortress of Proshaberd although there isn't much to see. If walking, park by the museum. The walk of about 6km is very pleasant, if rather steep at times. The first short section is through the village, after which the stream is crossed. The main track turns left but walkers should ignore the sign in Armenian instructing vehicular traffic for Spitakavor to turn left and should carry straight on while keeping the stream and a small dam on the right. The rocky path then ascends up the side of the ever-narrowing and dramatic gorge until it angles left and emerges into an alpine meadow as the gorge widens out. There are caves on the hillside in which presumably live the bears whose droppings can be seen along the path. The next section of the path is through a summer village where farmers from the villages below come to pasture their stock during the warmer months. The only way any visitor will ever be allowed to pass through here without accepting hospitality is by

Born Garegin Ter-Harutyunian in 1886, Garegin Nzhdeh was the son of a village priest in Nakhichevan. Later he led an Armenian band fighting alongside the Bulgarians in 1912 as Bulgaria battled for independence from the Ottoman Empire. During World War I he fought alongside the Russian troops against Turkey. By 1921, his guerrilla band was holding off both Bolshevik and Turkish forces in Syunik and Zangezur (southern Armenia) and he declared an independent Republic of Mountainous Armenia at Tatev Monastery in May 1921. This he used as a bargaining tool with Lenin to ensure that both Syunik and Zangezur were incorporated into Armenia, rather than into Azerbaijan as the Bolshevik government had at first agreed in its bid to achieve good relations with Turkey. After agreement with Lenin was reached, the tiny state capitulated in July 1921 and Nzhdeh went into exile via Persia. He later negotiated fruitlessly with Nazi Germany in a bid to recover the lost territories of western Armenia and in 1945 he was arrested in Bulgaria by Soviet troops. He was executed in 1955 for 'anti-Soviet activities'. He is regarded as the person who saved southern Armenia for the nation and, in the light of more recent events, he may almost be regarded as the saviour of Armenia since it is doubtful whether Armenia could have survived the early 1990s without the lifeline to Iran which those territories provided. His remains were secretly brought to Armenia in 1983 and reburied at Spitakavor after independence.

promising to stop on the way back. Beyond the summer village keep right and you will soon see Spitakavor high above you. In places the path has been washed away but it is fairly easy to follow the stream, which flows down the steep mountainside from the monastery. There is a very welcome spring at the top. Watch out for interesting reptiles on the way such as the nose-horned viper and Caucasian green lizard. Drivers will follow the main track left at the sign mentioned above. The track winds up round the hillside, giving magnificent views over the mountains and the valley in which Yeghegnadzor lies. It appears to go past the monastery but then doubles back to a small car park.

The **church**, dedicated to the Mother of God, dates from 1321 and was built by Prince Prosh of the Proshian family on the site of a 5th-century basilica. The bell tower was added in 1330. The *gavit* has seen some restoration with the result that it now has only three doors rather than the unusual four it had previously. The church itself is a cross-dome church with cylindrical tambour and conical cupola. It has apses on the north and south sides but just arches on the east and west. There are carvings in the apse and high up in the apex of the dome. The tympanum is richly carved in a style similar to Areni and Noravank: stalactite decoration arches over a beautiful Madonna and Child. On the east façade is a curious irregular and asymmetrical cross.

Outside the church the **modern grave** is that of Garegin Nzhdeh (see box, above).

The track behind the monastery continues uphill. Passing another summer village on the right-hand side, it bears left and on the hilltop to the right can be seen the remains of the small **fortress of Proshaberd**, also built by Prince Prosh. A rectangle of walls survives with a tower at each corner and a deep pit inside. Only the very determined should bother making the ascent.

Tanahat Monastery Tanahat Monastery, where Gladzor University was probably first established, is 5km beyond the museum on the same road. A monastery was first established here in 753 but the present buildings date from 1273–79. Approaching it on a late summer day, its dark basalt is a striking and beautiful contrast to the arid hills with only the odd tree presenting any contrasting green colour. The lavishly laid-out car parks and remains of other facilities were provided for celebrations which marked the 700th anniversary of the university's founding in 1982. The **main church**, St Stephen's, is a cross-dome structure with a 12-sided tambour and umbrella cupola. Rather plain inside, there is much elaborate carving outside with a heavy preponderance of ones depicting animals and birds. Above the sundial on the south façade, two doves drink from a common cup. The crest of the Orbelian family (a lion and a bull) is high on the tambour; that of the Proshians (an eagle holding a lamb in its talons) is on the side over the door. Another eagle has a smaller bird in its claws and round the top of the tambour can be seen a whole range of animal heads. To the north of St Stephen's Church is the small 14th-century **Church of the Holy Cross**. There are more animals here – the tympanum depicts a mounted horseman attacking a lion. The reason for so much animal carving is not clear – it is certainly atypical – and the suggestion has been made that it was wishful thinking on the monks' part since the monastic diet at Tanahat Monastery largely comprised soup. The foundations of numerous other buildings can be clearly seen, indicating that the monastery was once large and important.

Arkaz Monastery (⊕ *if you want to go inside when the door is closed, ring the bell hanging from the wall*) About 3km beyond Tanahat Monastery along the same road is the church of the Monastery of Arkaz dedicated to the Holy Cross. Rebuilding in 1870–71 has deprived it of interest, although it is a significant pilgrimage site in early October, as under the walls is said to be a piece of the True Cross (see box above).

From the church there are some fine views of **Mount Ararat** towering high over Tanahat. Bears' droppings can be seen in the vicinity; the bears are partial to the bunches of ripe grapes in the autumn vineyards.

AROUND VAIK AND MARTIROS The main road south passes through **Vaik** (*telephone code 282*), at the north end of which is the new **St Trdat III Church**, consecrated in 2000 and very much in the American–Armenian style with pews, and a balcony for the choir as well as several modern paintings and a chandelier. The floor is of marble and the whole is lit by far more windows than are normal in Armenia. Despite all this modernity and obvious diaspora influence, it manages much more successfully than the cathedral at Yerevan to embody the spirit of Armenian tradition.

There is a **tourist information centre** in Vaik at the Vayots Dzor Tourism Centre and Hotel (see page 235) which has useful information, including a booklet about the region.

Shortly beyond Vaik a road goes off right across a bridge over the river. It leads to **Martiros** whose church, if not especially beautiful, is at least decidedly curious. In the first village, **Zaritap** – a centre of tobacco growing – keep right at the fork and continue with the river on the left. On reaching Martiros keep left until the military barracks is in front of you. Turn left in front of it and then left again. After 2km the road turns sharp left but instead take the rough track which turns right, runs along the base of a hill and then goes left towards a lone khachkar. Keep on the track as it winds around until you reach a picnic table. Park here, descend the steps to the river, cross the river, and scramble a few metres up the other bank until you reach a faint path parallel to the river. Turn left and walk down the path keeping at roughly the same height. In a couple of hundred metres there is a door in the hillside on your right, outside which is a picnic table, a tree with handkerchiefs tied to it and a few broken khachkars. The door belongs to an entirely **subterranean church**, dedicated to the Mother of God, and built here by the Proshian family in 1286. It comprises the main church together with a small separate chapel. There is a little light inside from windows high up in the hillside but a torch is useful. The most bizarre feature of this extraordinary excavation is that the form of the church is exactly that of a typical cross-dome church. Standing inside, the shape one sees is the same as if one were in the interior of any normal Armenian church.

NORTHEASTERN VAYOTS DZOR About 6.5km beyond Vaik there is a left turn for **Herher**. The road skirts a hydro-electric dam before reaching the village which has a tiny 7th-century Zion monastery, which is more like a hermitage and to which it is necessary to walk, as well as a more modern basilica-type church.

On the main road slightly beyond the Herher junction the Arpa River changes direction. It is well worth leaving the main road to explore its valley between here and Jermuk. There is a road each side of the river. The new road is up on the plateau on the east side of the river; it offers some splendid views down into the gorge, and is accessible to tourist buses. The old road follows the west bank of the river down in the gorge and is far more spectacular than the new road, but beyond the **Monastery of Gndevank** it is accessible only to a 4x4 and even then only in good weather when there have been no recent rock falls. Gndevank is just off this old road across a bridge about 15km from the junction with the main road south.

To reach Gndevank from the new road, leave it at Gndevaz village (from which splendid views of Gndevank can be obtained by looking down on it in the ravine) and then walk down the path from the end of the village: it takes about 45 minutes though the walk back may take longer depending on your degree of fitness.

Gndevank was founded in 936 by Princess Sophia of Syunik who claimed that 'Vayots Dzor was a ring without a jewel; but I built this monastery as the jewel for the ring'. The main church, dedicated to St Stephen, is of the cross-dome type with circular tambour and conical cupola. A large *gavit* was added in 999 and encircling fortified walls were added later. On the southern and western parts of the site are other buildings that were formerly used by the monks. The complex was restored between 1965 and 1969 following earthquake damage. There are some particularly fine gravestones here: one shows ibex being hunted alongside falconry while another depicts a boar hunt. There are picnic tables at the monastery, which is an exceedingly pleasant place to visit.

The real gem of the district is the **old road on from here to Kechut Reservoir** on the Arpa. It hugs the side of the narrow gorge underneath beetling cliffs with breathtaking views of the river and the ravine. However, there is ample evidence of numerous rockfalls and it would be unwise to use the road at times of high avalanche risk. The route is strongly recommended and even those without a 4x4 should consider walking down the valley; there is hardly any traffic to mar the experience although a passing vehicle did stop to warn us of a she-bear with her cubs in the vicinity. Also often in evidence in the gorge are European glass lizards *Ophisaurus apodus* which are legless, thus looking like snakes, and often quite sizeable at up to 1.2m long. They are harmless to human beings, eating nothing larger than mice. Those wishing to access the road from the north end can do so by crossing the Kechut dam over which a road has been built. This dam, although originally constructed for hydro-electric purposes, is now also the starting point for the tunnel which carries water from the Arpa River under the Vardenis range to help maintain the level of Lake Sevan (see pages 173–5). At Kechut, a new church, on the right as one drives to Jermuk on the new road, is attractively situated against a backdrop of hills, while in spring the land overlooking the reservoir is covered with fritillaries.

Beyond the reservoir the roads continue to **Jermuk** (*telephone code 287*), whose name is one which every visitor to Armenia is likely to learn since it is the source of much of the country's mineral water. The town was a very large and popular Soviet spa resort and once more is attracting visitors. Some of the sanatoria have been renovated and are combining this role with that of a modern hotel. The town is gradually losing its previously rundown air although some unattractive concrete buildings remain. In the centre of the town is a row of urns, each of which has water of a different specified temperature pouring from a tap. Visitors bring their mugs, jugs and vacuum flasks to fill them at the taps and in high season, late July to mid September, queues build up. Down by the river is a waterfall near a café which has been built under a natural land bridge. The **statue**, as one approaches the town just before the main bridge, is of Israel Ori (1659–1711), Armenia's first diplomat. From 1678 onwards, he travelled throughout Europe and Russia trying to establish contacts with the leaders of the Christian powers. Seeking protection for Armenia against the Persians and Turks, he met with Leopold I, Holy Roman Emperor, in 1700; Peter the Great, Tsar of Russia, in 1701; and Pope Clement XI in 1704. In 1709, he headed the Armenian delegation to the Persian shah.

Jermuk would be a good centre for walking but there are no detailed maps or marked trails. Vaik tourist information centre might be able to help with guides (see page 235). A ski lift was built at the entry to the town in 2007. It goes from an altitude of 2,100m to 2,500m and the total length of ski slopes is 2.6km. The resort is low key and very much in its infancy although skis and accessories can apparently be hired in some of the larger hotels and there is a café at the chair-lift terminal.

Armenia's southernmost province has two well-known sites and one which, although much less well known, ranks as one of the most interesting in the country. The far south along the Iranian border is, not surprisingly, the warmest part of Armenia and a centre of fruit growing. The original road to the far south crossed Nakhichevan and the closure of the border required a difficult hill road to be considerably upgraded to take the heavy lorry traffic to and from Iran. An alternative road has now been built from Kapan to Meghri running through the Shikahogh Reserve in the east of the province. The routing of this road caused controversy because of fears about the impact on wildlife and also because it could open the area to illegal logging. Both roads traverse spectacular scenery and you may wish to do a loop, travelling south via one road and north via the other.

WHERE TO STAY AND EAT Apart from the accommodation listed below, **homestays** can be arranged and are the only option for the far south. They can be arranged through tour operators in Yerevan (see pages 55–6) or Armenia Information (see page 107). The tourist information centre at Tatev Monastery (see page 255) can arrange homestays in Tatev village. If really stuck for accommodation, asking around almost anywhere will probably produce someone who is willing to provide accommodation for the night but this is very much pot luck.

Goris

Mirhav Hotel (19 rooms) 100 Mashtots St; 284 24612, 24632, 10 284 402 (Yerevan number); e hotelmirhav@yahoo.com. This delightful hotel, run by an Iranian Armenian retired neurosurgeon who speaks several languages, including German & English, is tastefully decorated in natural materials. The restaurant serves excellent meals (the apricot pilaff is wonderful) – notice of 1–2hrs is required. The hotel stocks a good range of postcards & maps. Wi-Fi included. Cards accepted, 3% charge. Discounts for groups & children. **$$**

Hotel Olympia (20 rooms) 53 Khorenatsi St; 284 30003; e olympia.goris@rambler.ru. The approach to this Soviet building is not encouraging but once inside one finds a warm, well-renovated hotel & helpful staff. The director of the Mirhav Hotel suggests this hotel to visitors when his own is full. Internet available. **$$**

Hostel Goris (2 rooms) 55 Khorenatsi St; 284 21886; e jirmar28@freenet.am. Currently there is 1 bathroom for the 2 rooms (which can accommodate 6 people) but a 2nd is being built. Extra guests can be accommodated in the owners' house next door. The host, J Martirosyan, is an artist & member of the Armenian Painters Union. His gallery is in a rock cave & visitors are welcome. Guided tours to Goris, including the Aksel Bakunts House Museum, can be arranged (AMD15,000 inc lunch). Members of the family speak English, French, Russian & Turkish. **$**

Kajaran

Hotel Kajaran (48 rooms) 3 Abovyan St; 285 32055; m 098 575820, 077 180577. This satisfactorily renovated hotel is owned by the Zangezur Copper Molybdenum Combine & at present is the nearest good accommodation to Meghri. They coped well with unexpected guests arriving late at night. B/fast extra, approx AMD1,000/pp. **$**

Kapan

Hotel Darist (40 rooms) 1a Aram Manukian St; 285 28262; e hotel_darist@ yahoo.com. This hotel has now been fully refurbished & is probably still the best place to stay in Kapan. The restaurant serves tasty meals although the occasional live music is too loud for some tastes. Reception is on the 4th floor. Wi-Fi. **$$**

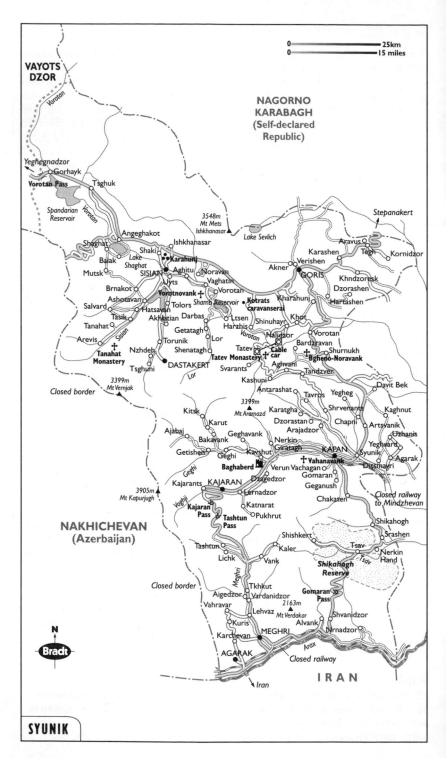

SYUNIK

VAYOTS DZOR

Vorotan

NAGORNO KARABAGH (Self-declared Republic)

Yeghegnadzor
Gorhayk
Vorotan Pass
Tsghuk

Spandarian Reservoir

Vorotan

Angeghakot

Stepanakert

3548m
Mt Mets
Ishkhanasar

Ishkhanasar

Lake Sevlich

Shaghat

Shaki
Lake Shaghat
Aravus
Balak
Mutsk
Karahunj
Karashen
Verishen
Tegh
Kornidzor

SISIAN
Aghitu
Noravan
Akner
GORIS

Uyts
Vaghatin
Khndzoresk

Brnakot
Vorotnovank ✝
Vorotan
Dzorashen

Ashotavan
Tolors
Shamb Reservoir
Kotrats caravanserai
Kharahunj
Hartashen

Salvard
Hatsavan
Akhlatian
Darbas
Ltsen
Shinuhayr
Khot

Tanahat
Tasik
Getatagh
Lor
Harzhis
Tatev
Halidzor
Vorotan

Arevis
Nzhdeh
Torunik
Shenatagh
Vorotan
Tatev Monastery
Cable car
Bardzravan
Shurnukh

Sisian
Tanahat Monastery ✝
Tsghuni
DASTAKERT
Svarants
Aghvani
✝ **Bgheno-Noravank**

Lor
Kashuni
Tandzver

3399m
Mt Vernjak
Antarashat
Tavras
Yegheg
Davit Bek

Closed border
3399m
Mt Aramazd
Karatgha
Shrvenants
Kaghnut

Kitsk
Karut
Dzorastan
Arajadzor
Chapni
Artsvanik

Ajabaj
Geghavank
Nerkin Giratagh
Yeghvard

Bakavank
Uzhanis

Getishen
Kavshut
KAPAN
Syunik
Agarak

Geghi
✝ **Vahanavank**
Ditsmayri

Verun Vachagan

Baghaberd
Dzagedzor
Gomaran

Geghi
Verun Vachagan
Geganush

Kajarants
KAJARAN
Lernadzor
Chakaten
Closed railway to Mindzhevan

3905m
Mt Kapurjugh
Katnarat
Pukhrut

Voghji
Kajaran Pass
Tashtun Pass
Shishkert
Shikahogh
Srashen

NAKHICHEVAN (Azerbaijan)

Tashtun
Kaler
Tsav
Nerkin Hand

Lichk
Vank
Shikahogh Reserve

Meghri

Closed border
Tkhkut
Vardanidzor
Gomaran Pass

Aigedzor
2163m
Mt Verdakar
Shvanidzor

Vahravar
Lehvaz

Kuris
Alvank
Nrnadzor

Karchevan
MEGHRI

N
Bradt

AGARAK
Arax
Closed railway

I R A N

Iran

0 — 25km
0 — 15 miles

🏠 **Hotel Lernagorts** (48 rooms) 2 Karen Demirchyan St; ☏ 285 28039. Has both renovated rooms which are satisfactory & unrenovated rooms which are not advised. B/fast included in the cost of renovated rooms only. **$**

Sisian

🏠 **Lalaner Hotel** (16 rooms) 29 Sisakan St, Sisian; ☏ 2830 6600, 5600; e info@lalahotel.am; www.lalahotel.am. A refurbished comfortable hotel, if a little pretentious at times. The deluxe room had a jacuzzi in the bedroom but the only way to switch off the bedside lamp was to unplug it. Had it not been for the street lights it might have been difficult to find the socket again in the dark! The staff are helpful & were not at all put out by a late arrival. **$$**

🏠 **Dina Hotel** (16 rooms) 35 Sisakan St; ☏ 2830 3333; e sisiano@mail.ru; www.dinahotel.am. This remains my favourite hotel in Sisian. All rooms have now been renovated & the staff are as cheerful & friendly as ever. There is information about local sites of interest & staff can arrange transport to them, including to the petroglyphs on Mount Ughtasar (see below). The small bright restaurant can provide meals, but larger groups need to give notice. **$**

🏠 **Oasis Hotel** (5 rooms) Shaki Community, Yerevan Highway; m 09322 6677. On the Yerevan–Stepanakert highway at the Sisian turn-off. A new restaurant with decent rooms. The 2 rooms upstairs can be joined to form a suite. **$**

OTHER PRACTICALITIES Most visitors enter Syunik along the main road from Yerevan. The border with Vayots Dzor at the **Vorotan Pass** (2,344m) is marked by a large concrete structure on each side of the road: the symbolic Gates of Syunik. There is a good spring here at which water bottles can be filled. The road then descends past Spandarian and Shaghat reservoirs running parallel to the Vorotan River which lies some distance to the south. After winter pot-holes can be a significant problem on this stretch of road. **Minibuses** run from Yerevan to Sisian, Goris and Kapan (see *Chapter 2*, pages 75–6).

Sissian and Goris both have good **accommodation** and can act as a base from which to visit most of the province, with further overnight stays in Kapan and/or Kajaran if travelling to the far south. Unless you want to spend time walking in the Meghri area or visiting the Shikahogh reserve, the sights of Meghri can be covered in a day trip from Kapan or Kajaran.

There is no hotel in Meghri, work having ceased on the one which was being built, but homestays can be arranged. With the closure of the information centre in Goris, the only one in the province is at Tatev Monastery (see page 255) run by the Tatev Foundation (*www.tatev.org*). The centre can arrange homestays and hikes and it runs the small café in the centre. A **cable car** to Tatev Monastery opened in 2010 cutting travelling time considerably. Also in 2010 the road to Tatev was improved although it still awaits an asphalt surface. Even with the better surface, allow the best part of a day if travelling all the way by road; it is not a fast road and there is much to see at Tatev.

Sisian, Goris and Kapan are the larger towns and have most facilities but bring any special requirements with you.

MOUNT METS ISHKHANASAR Mount Mets Ishkhanasar (3,548m), an extinct volcano, is the tallest peak of the Ishkhanasar range which lies to the northwest of Goris on what was the border with Azerbaijan and is now the de facto border with the self-declared Republic of Nagorno Karabagh. It lies to the left of the road but visitors wishing to see the immensely worthwhile and fascinating **petroglyphs at Ughtasar** will need a local guide and probably transport, since the track is too rough for even a Niva 4x4. The very helpful manager of the Hotel Dina (see page

251) in the centre of Sisian can organise a guide and transport but she doesn't speak any English so it might be better to fix something up in advance through a Yerevan agent; see pages 55–6. A guide and vehicle seating up to seven persons costs AMD30,000. It takes about 90 minutes to drive to the site from Sisian although the last 500m has to be walked as the vehicle cannot make the steep ascent when fully laden. The petroglyphs are accessible only from mid July to late September because of snow and it can be bitterly cold at the high site even in summer. To anyone who has seen supposed rock carvings in museums the petroglyphs here are an absolute revelation with numerous designs scattered on boulders over a large area. The site is beautiful in itself with the volcano towering above and a small lake. It is also the haunt of bears and wolves, as is attested by the droppings and footprints.

Petroglyphs, called 'goat letters' in Armenian, are found in several parts of Armenia but these at Ughtasar are the most accessible. The site itself is at 3,300m altitude and over 2,000 individual petroglyphs have been found here scattered over tens of square kilometres. Some of the carvings depict animals, mostly the wild animals of the region but also domestic ones. Deer and wild goats are especially common as are aurochs, ancestors of domestic cattle. There are carvings of hunting scenes and ones showing the impedimenta of hunting. Birds are rarely depicted, while snakes feature frequently. People also feature in scenes depicting dancers, either two dancers together or communal dancing. Some rocks have just a single design but others have a whole collection of carvings, as many as 50 in extreme cases. The preponderance of hunting scenes and cattle has led to speculation that the people who carved the stones lived partly by cattle breeding, presumably pasturing their cattle here in summer, and partly by hunting. They must have been at least semi-nomadic since it would not be possible to survive here in winter. The age of the carvings is difficult to ascertain but estimates have varied between 10000BC and 2000BC.

SISIAN AND KARAHUNJ (*Sisian telephone code 2830*) Much better known than the petroglyphs is another, slightly more recent site. **Karahunj** (also known as Zorats Kar), sometimes called Armenia's Stonehenge although the appellation is misleading since the two look very different, comprises 204 rough-hewn stones. They are arranged in an elaborate layout and almost certainly formed an ancient astronomical observatory dating from some time prior to 2000BC. The stones are basalt and the largest, 3m tall, weighs 10 tonnes. Of the stones, 76 have apertures near the top. The configuration is of 39 stones laid in an oval formation with its main axis running east–west for a distance of 43m. Within this oval are some contemporary graves. Bisecting the oval is an arc comprising a further 20 stones. Three arms of stones lie off this central shape running to the north, south and southeast. The north and south arms are much longer than the southeast arm and bend west towards their tips. Stones with apertures occur only in the arms but not all stones in the arms have apertures.

There has been much theorising on how the monument was used. It certainly seems clear that the apertures must be significant but they are too large (at least 5cm diameter) to look through a single one in a precise direction and they don't seem to be lined up with each other for looking through pairs of apertures. Had this been possible it would have facilitated more precise observation. Conceivably the stones could have been used for observing the moon, but observation of stars seems difficult to imagine. Anyone looking at the sun would have suffered severe damage to their central vision. Karahunj, on its rock-strewn site, is impressive but the lack of any convincing explanation makes a visit somewhat frustrating.

Some sizeable lizards (40cm in length) of rather prehistoric appearance clamber about on the stones. They are Caucasian agama (*Laudakia caucasius*), a species, despite its name, with a range from northeast Turkey to Pakistan. Note that Karahunj is off the main Sisian to Goris road, just east of Sisian, and is not near the village of Karahunj to the south of Goris.

Some material excavated from Karahunj is now in the **historical museum** in the centre of Sisian (*Adonts National Historical Museum; 1 Adonts St; ⟍ 2830 33 31; ⊕ 09.00–18.00 Tue–Sat; guided tour in English AMD2,000; photographic fee AMD1,000; adult AMD400*). The museum itself does not actually have the opening times on its door and it is uncertain whether the photographic fee relates to items inside the museum or to those outside. In front of the museum, readily visible from the street, is a collection of gravestones in the form of sheep brought from various churches in the province. On a previous visit museum staff demanded a fee of US$50 per photograph even though they are totally visible to passers-by. They then said that photography was forbidden because tourists might claim that they found the stones themselves in some country other than Armenia! When I was last there it did not matter anyway because the museum was shut, even though it should have been open, and I could photograph the outside exhibits freely.

Visitors will be much more welcome at **Sisavank**, the fine early church dedicated to St John which overlooks the town. Similar in style to the Church of St Hripsime at Ejmiatsin, this was built of basalt by Prince Kohazat and Bishop Hovsep I between 670 and 689. Of cross-dome style, it has a conical cupola supported by a circular tambour decorated with 12 graceful arcatures: there is a window in the arcature positioned directly over each of the four apses. The interior of the church is decorated by a sort of frieze depicting vine leaves and grapes which runs round most of it, presumably a reference to Jesus being the true vine since this is not a district traditionally associated with winemaking. The altar table with a carved eagle on its front is new (2001) and was carved by the son of the present caretaker. The font, to the left of the *bema*, is also new (2008) and was carved by the caretaker's grandson. The old font, which is now in the southeast corner room, was unsatisfactory on two counts. The water did not drain away properly, so making the church damp, and the basin was in the form of a cross with sharp corners making it dangerous for the baby, given the baptismal practice of immersion. The church has a small collection of old books, the oldest dating from 1686, and also some miniatures by Eduard Ghazarian carved on items such as rice grains, which can be viewed through a microscope.

AROUND SISIAN
Southeast from Sisian To the southeast there are two worthwhile sights, Aghitu funerary monument and Vorotnavank (monastery). Stay on the north side of the river and take Sisakan Street, which runs in front of the Dina Hotel, making for the village of **Vorotan**. If asking for directions (the road out of Sisian is confusing at times) note that locals still refer to Vorotan by its old name, Urut. After about 5km the first village is **Aghitu** where there is an unusual 6th- or 7th-century **funerary monument**, unlike anything else in the country apart from the monument at Odzun Church in Lori province. It is mounted on an arched base. Above that two rectangular columns support a two-tier structure. The lower tier has a circular central column with decorated capitals while the smaller upper tier has two carved round columns, again with decorated capitals. For whom such an elaborate monument was created is unknown and it is paradoxical that the efforts to ensure that he would be remembered have come to naught. Low ruins and tombstones show this was once an extensive site.

The road continues beyond Aghitu. Keep the Vorotan River on your right until, about 9km from Sisian, you encounter the **Monastery of Vorotnavank** above the river. The oldest church, dedicated to St Stephen, was built in 1000 by Queen Shahandukht. It is barrel vaulted and has a much lower *gavit* on the west side. (Beware the extremely deep hole at the west end of the *gavit*.) In 1007, the queen's son Sevada built a second church dedicated to John the Baptist. It is a cross-dome construction and lies to the southeast of the first church. Both churches have arcaded cloisters, uncommon in Armenia, but of different styles and presumably of different dates. A further smaller church, various service buildings and a fortified wall complete the complex. There was severe damage here in the 1931 earthquake but it has mostly been repaired. What makes a visit so worthwhile is the plethora of gravestones which have rich figure carving. Some of them have at sometime (since restoration after the earthquake?) been incorporated into the buildings. The carvings depict both human beings, often in domestic scenes, and domesticated animals such as horses and cattle. Just why such decoration was considered appropriate for gravestones is not apparent.

Southwest from Sisian Heading southwest, a road follows the Sisian River. To reach it cross the bridge in the town and turn left at the T-junction, then right at traffic lights, then left and finally right again just after the large electricity substation. The ride along the valley is extremely beautiful and worth experiencing for its own sake. Just after a road branches off right for Tanahat village the remains of **Tanahat Monastery** can be seen on an outcrop on the valley side across the river. Unlike its namesake, Tanahat Monastery in Vayots Dzor, this monastery is very ruinous, but reaching it involves a pleasant walk with many flowers in early summer. The midsummer vegetation is just as colourful, although taller, and attracts many butterflies. There is a footbridge across the river some way past the monastery. It has partly collapsed but it is still possible to cross. A footpath leads across the hill to the monastery. (Wear sturdy footwear: in summer I saw several snakes in the area.) At times it may be possible to wade across or ford the river in a vehicle just after the road branches off to Tanahat village, but this is impossible when the river is in spate. Some work was evidently planned at the site but no restoration of the pink 5th-century single-nave church has been undertaken. There is some surviving decoration which looks rather like tulips – highly appropriate since wild white tulips are one of the earliest flowers to appear here after the snow has melted. An unusual feature of the cemetery at the west side is that some of the graves look very like the chambered tombs of northwest Europe, the burial vault being covered by up to three large slabs. One 11th-century khachkar found here re-used a stone with an earlier cuneiform inscription and is now in the museum at Erebuni.

East from Sisian The main road to the south actually heads east as far as **Goris**. About 20km after the Sisian turn-off a road branches right for the village of **Harzhis**. About 2.5km along this road a track branches off right and after 500m reaches the remains of the smallish **Kotrats caravanserai** built in 1319 by the Orbelian family. It is still possible to see the interior layout although most of the roof has collapsed. There is an inscription in Persian and Armenian over the doorway. In the area are several standing stones with a hole (sometimes broken) near the top. According to local people there used to be many more of them and they were signposts indicating the location of the caravanserai; the hole was to enable the stones to be hauled into position using animals. It does not at any rate seem likely that their function was really as signposts since there is one right next to the caravanserai.

Tatev Syunik's best-known site, **Tatev Monastery**, is reached by continuing down the main road beyond the Sisian turn-off for a further 25km and then turning right. The road to Tatev (29km), having been in very poor condition for years, has now been improved although it still lacks an asphalt surface. The journey time to Tatev, for those with a head for heights, has been still further shortened by a **cable car** (⊕ *09.30–17.30 in winter, 09.30–19.00 in summer, both daily*) which transports passengers from a terminal near Halidzor village to Tatev village. The longest cable car ride in the world, it spans the 5.7km between the two villages and was built by an Italian company. It opened in October 2010. Each cabin carries 25 passengers for the 12-minute ride high above the valley of the Vorotan River. A return ticket costs AMD3,000 per passenger; a one-way ticket AMD2,000. It is hoped that the 'aerial tramway', as the Armenians like to call it, will make Tatev village and monastery accessible even in winter, something which will certainly benefit the villagers who travel free. For those who prefer a less exalted form of transport there is a daily, excluding Sundays, minibus from Goris to Tatev at 15.00, taking 1½ hours and costing AMD700. The bus returns to Goris at 09.00 the next day. A taxi from Goris costs about AMD8,000.

Before reaching Halidzor the road passes **Shinuhayr**, whose 17th-century church dedicated to St Stephen is on the valley side a long way below the village. The first part of the path to the church offers good views into the broad valley of the Vorotan with its striking rock formations but it then winds down through orchards and after one zigzag becomes the bed of a stream in which it is difficult to find a dry route. The three-aisle basilica church is ruinous as are the ancillary buildings formerly used by the monks. Many of these ancillary buildings have been adapted by the local residents for growing vegetables: one monk's cell now supports a good crop of runner beans while another houses potatoes. The climb back up to the village is long and hot.

There is a legend about Tatev Monastery. It is said that the architect couldn't get down when he finished the cupola of the main church. He cried out: '*Togh astvats indz ta-tev*', which means 'May God give me wings'. And so the monastery got its name. The first sight is in some ways more impressive than seeing it close up. An excellent distant view can be had from the left of the road where there is a small gazebo-type structure. The short path to the gazebo starts from the lay-by at the top of the climb from Halidzor. The gazebo is variously stated to mark the signalling point from which the monastery could be warned of the approach of possibly unwelcome visitors, or alternatively the spot from which a young lady threw herself into the gorge rather than submit to an unwelcome marriage with a local Muslim ruler. After the gazebo the road winds down to the Vorotan and crosses it adjacent to the so-called **Satan's bridge**, a natural bridge over the swift-flowing river: a path leads down through eroded rock formations to a popular swimming pool. The road then winds up the far side of the valley to the monastery. Adjacent to the monastery is an **information centre** (⊕ *Apr–Oct 09.00–21.00 although this may change now the cable car is up & running;* m *093 943996, 095 880102;* e *annshik14@yahoo.com*) run by the Tatev Foundation (*www.tatev.org*). The centre can arrange homestays and hikes and it runs the small café in the centre. There are ambitious plans for the Tatev region now the cable car is completed, including a hotel at Halidzor and extensive development of Tatev Monastery, which is detailed on the Foundation's website. Some plans have stalled for lack of finance but there has been some recent restoration plus excavation of the oil press.

The date of the now-vanished first church at the **monastery** is unknown, but in 844 Bishop Davit persuaded the Princes of Syunik to grant lands which would support the founding of a monastery worthy to house the relics which the church in Syunik possessed. It was his successor, Bishop Ter-Hovhannes, who built the **main church**, dedicated to Sts Paul and Peter between 895 and 906. It was badly damaged by the earthquake in 1931 during which the cupola collapsed, but the whole has now been restored except for the bell tower which formerly had three storeys. It is planned to complete the restoration of the bell tower in due course which is why the large crane has been left *in situ* for several years disfiguring many visitors' photographs. Tatev's reconstruction has not always been sensitively carried out: installing a marble floor rather than stone flags in the church and library rather jars for example, although its removal is now promised. However, the restoration does give an excellent idea of how the monastery must have looked when it was a thriving centre of learning and 1,000 people lived here; its greatest importance was in the 14th and 15th centuries under Hovnan Vorotnetsi (1315–88) and Grigor Tatevatsi (1346–1411). Tatevatsi was both a philosopher and a painter and is portrayed surrounded by his students in one of the few portraits in Armenian manuscript illustration. This is in the 1449 *Interpretation of the Psalms of David* and is presumably the work of one of his former pupils.

The complex is surrounded by a large fortified wall on which it is possible to walk. The church is somewhat intermediate in style between the earlier domed basilica churches and the later cross-dome churches. The umbrella cupola is supported by an unusually tall decorated circular tambour. On the east façade, above the triangular niches, long snakes are looking at two heads while on the north façade, above a window, two shorter snakes are looking at a person: Armenians supposedly regarded snakes as protectors of their homes. On the north façade are also representations of the founders of the church – Prince Ashot, his wife Shushan, Grigor Supan, the ruler of Gegharkunik, and Prince Dzagik. In 930, the walls of the church were decorated with frescoes but these have almost totally vanished except for some scant remnants in the apse and the interior is now rather plain. Grigor Tatevatsi is buried inside the small chapel on the south side of the main church. His tomb is the highly decorated structure which abuts the church.

Outside the church on the south side is a monument erected in 904 called the *gavazan* (meaning a priest's or clergyman's pastoral staff or stick). It is an octagonal pillar built of small stones with an elaborate cornice and a small khachkar on top. The pillar formerly detected earth tremors by rocking on the horizontal course of masonry on which it is constructed. It does not appear to have worked, however, for some years and the lower part is bound up by iron bands.

The modest **St Gregory Church** adjoins the main church also on the south side. Dating from 1295, it replaced an earlier 9th-century building. To the west of the St Gregory Church there was a vaulted gallery with arched openings on the southern side, and to the west of Paul and Peter church, the **bell tower** built in the 17th century on the site of a *gavit* which had been destroyed in an earlier earthquake. Built over the main entrance to the complex and the adjoining chapel is the unusual 11th-century **Mother of God Church**. It is a small cross-dome church with an octagonal tambour and umbrella cupola. The chambers of the clergy, the refectory with a kitchen and storerooms, and the dwelling and service premises form a rectangle around these structures within the fortified wall. They date from the 17th and 18th centuries. Outside the walls can be seen the ruins of various buildings including an **oil press** and the **school**. Wild red tulips *Tulipa julia* grow behind the monastery; unfortunately they often end up as cut flowers.

Goris *(Telephone code 284)* Goris, situated on the Goris River, is the most attractive town in southern Armenia with many two-storey houses built of grey stone and an

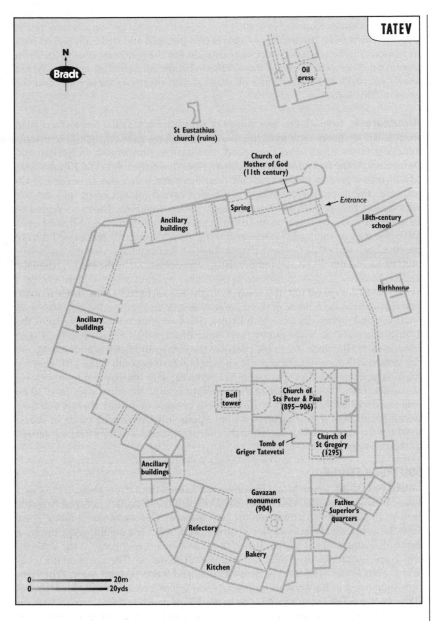

N

Bradt

Oil
press

St Eustathius
church (ruins)

Church of
Mother of God
(11th century)

Spring

← *Entrance*

Ancillary
buildings

18th-century
school

Bathhouse

Ancillary
buildings

Bell
tower

Church of
Sts Peter & Paul
(895–906)

Tomb of
Grigor Tatevetsi

Church of
St Gregory
(1295)

Ancillary
buildings

Gavazan
monument
(904)

Father
Superior's
quarters

Refectory

Bakery

Kitchen

0 ————— 20m
0 ————— 20yds

absence of tall blocks of flats. The houses, whose design was apparently influenced by a German architect who came to live here, have doors opening directly onto the street and some have balconies. The 17th- or 18th-century church has sheep gravestones outside which, unlike those at Sisian, can be freely photographed. On the south façade can be seen the trajectory of an artillery shell, which narrowly missed the building while the town was being bombarded during the conflict with Azerbaijan. The **house museum of Axel Bakunts** (*41 Mesrop Mashtots St;* ☎ *284 22966;* ⏰ *10.00–17.00 Tue–Sun; guide (English, French, Russian) AMD1,000;*

AMD200), a writer who died in Stalin's purges, contains his personal belongings in a typical Goris villa. The setting of Goris is very pleasant and strikingly jagged rock formations can be seen on the opposite hillside. On the southeast edge of the town a good open-air **café** (⊕ *when the weather is warm enough to sit outside, approx May–Oct, 10.00–late evening*) in a pleasant garden overlooks these rocks and the caves of Old Goris.

Khndzoresk To reach the cave village of Khndzoresk take the Stepanakert road from Goris for about 6km until the road to the village goes off right, underneath a metal gateway which bears the legend 'Welcome to Khndzoresk' in Russian and Armenian. At the far end of the village turn right down the hill to Old Khndzoresk. Most visitors give themselves half an hour here but half a day is needed to do justice to the place. The old village comprised cave dwellings hewn into the soft rock amidst the spectacular limestone karst rock formations. The caves ceased to be used for housing people in the 19th century though some are still used even today for storage and for livestock (and some were temporarily reoccupied during the Karabagh war while Goris was being shelled). As the villagers left the caves they built surface buildings nearby, but the village was devastated by the 1931 earthquake and a decision was made to relocate to the higher position of the modern village.

The caves are spread out over a surprisingly large area indicating that a sizeable population lived here. Some of them are very simple and some quite elaborate with windows and niches cut into the hillsides. The two churches both date from the 17th century and survived better than most of the other surface buildings. The lower one, St Hripsime, was in the centre of the village and dates from 1663. Across the stream at the bottom of the gorge and slightly further south is the 17th-century hermitage where Mkhitar Sparapet is buried along with his wife and followers. He succeeded David Bek as leader of the rebellion against Ottoman rule. In 1730 he was murdered by the villagers of Khndzoresk because of Turkish threats that they would be attacked if they harboured him. Apparently the Turkish pasha in Tabriz to whom they presented his head had the murderers beheaded for what he regarded as their treachery.

SOUTHERN SYUNIK
South to Kapan South from Goris the road follows the narrow gorge of the Goris River. In Soviet days the road more or less marked the boundary between Armenia and Azerbaijan and was actually on the Azerbaijan side of the border at times. Since 1994, however, the de facto border is further east. After leaving the gorge the road descends a long series of hairpin bends in to the much deeper gorge of the Vorotan, which is eventually bridged close to a hydro-electric station. The ascent up the other side is even longer with innumerable hairpins and some fantastic views. The right turn signposted to **Bardzravan** leads after 3km to the remains of the **Monastery of Bgheno-Noravank** in thick forest. The monastery is invisible from the road: look for a small turning on the right. The only surviving part is a small, reconstructed basalt church of 1062 which incorporates several stones carved with human figures. There is also much geometric carving including swastika designs around the doorway and on the pillars. The monastery is evidently popular for picnics.

Kapan Yet another watershed is crossed before the descent into the gorge of the Voghji. Kapan is a complete contrast to Goris. Formerly an industrial city whose workers lived in high-rise flats, the industry has now closed and the flats look as if they won't survive the next earth tremor. Although there is some new building, including a new church, cafés and shops, Kapan has not changed as much as many towns in Armenia. The church, built in 2002 and dedicated to Mesrop Mashtots, is a large cross-dome church with a balcony at the west end for the choir.

Kapan is bisected by the Voghji River. Most facilities are within a short distance of each other in the centre of the town on the south bank of the river. The market is on the north bank. The **statue** of a horseman by the bridge in the centre is of David Bek. Otherwise Kapan has little to attract the visitor, but a visit to the **railway station** offers an unusual experience. In 1932, a branch line was opened to Kapan from Mindzhevan in Azerbaijan and it was operated by the Azerbaijan division of Soviet railways. The Nagorno Karabagh war meant that the line became isolated from both the Armenian and Azeri rail networks. As a consequence, a dozen Azeri diesel locomotives were marooned here along with an assortment of goods wagons and passenger coaches. They were still in place in 2005 but since then the rolling stock has gradually been removed and all that now remains are two coaches, stripped of everything including their wheels. The rails remain, as does the derelict station building, and livestock browse along the grass-grown tracks. Anyone attempting to walk across the footbridge over the rails should beware – it is wobbly and also very slippery when wet.

Shikahogh Reserve (*To visit the reserve it is necessary to obtain a permit by contacting the director of the park in Kapan:* \ *285 20064, 60655; at present entry is free but a fee may be introduced in future*) The reserve lies some 40km south of Kapan. It is reached via the new road south which leaves the main road from the north immediately before the road-tunnel as you enter Kapan. It is signposted to the reserve. The forest-clad mountains on both sides of the Tsav and Shikahogh rivers are included in the 100km^2 reserve. Of particular importance is the Mtnadzor Canyon, near Tsav, where there is perpetual twilight because of the north–south orientation of the high canyon sides and the thick virgin forest. Bears are found in the forest although they are difficult to see without guidance. The rivers have some large freshwater crabs. The most unusual feature is an avenue of oriental plane trees (*Platanus orientalis*) along the banks of the Tsav River. Thought to have an average age of almost 500 years (some are very ancient and hollow), it is extraordinary to see them growing with their roots in the river. Some of the bases of the trees are as much as 5m in circumference. Oriental plane is doubtfully native to Armenia and it is speculated that merchants on the silk route stuck their staffs into the ground and then forgot them.

South to Meghri There is now a choice of roads from Kapan to Meghri, the older road via Kajaran and the newer one in the east of the province through the Shikahogh Reserve. Both traverse spectacular scenery and both have good surfaces although they are subject to rockfalls, the new road perhaps more so because the steeply cut-away hillsides have had less time to stabilise. The new road was built ostensibly to bypass the most mountainous section of the old road, thus being less prone to closure in winter. Whether or not this turns out to be correct, the new road does provide an alternative to a vital supply route for Armenia. Most local drivers seem still to prefer to use the older road, as do the truck drivers from Iran. The road signs in Kapan direct drivers to the older road. The new road leaves the main road from the north immediately before the road tunnel on entering Kapan. The only sign is to the Shikahogh Reserve. Going south via the old road and north via the new road provides a good contrast. The following description assumes this route, although of course both roads can be travelled in either direction.

On the older road south, about 6km from Kapan, a road goes off left to the **Monastery of Vahanavank**. It was founded in 911 by Vahan, son of Prince Gagik of Kapan, who sought to become a monk in order to rid himself of the demons which possessed him. He is buried at the site and in the 11th century Queen Shahandukht of Syunik built the Mother of God Church here. The site, in woodland, is pleasant but the monastery itself has been ruined by the grossly insensitive restoration which began in 1978. It has now evidently ceased. All the surviving material from the old buildings has been piled up and completely new stones of a garish pale colour have been used for the reconstruction. Building a new monastery in medieval style might have some merit, but it did not need to have been done here, thereby destroying the integrity of what remained. Considering just how much appropriate and sympathetic reconstruction has been carried out in Armenia it is sad to see such philistinism at Vahanavank. The monastery is famous for the large arches on one of its buildings. These can still be seen.

After the turn to Vahanavank there is a **statue of a bear** with a ring in its mouth by the river. There should be a key hanging from the ring as that is the arms of Syunik, but it has disappeared. About 15km from Kapan the Geghi River flows south into the Voghji and just beyond is the **fortress of Baghaberd.** It is difficult to see the main part of the fortress when heading south (although much easier heading north) but a small fortification adjacent to the road on the right is conspicuous. A path leads up from the village just beyond the site. It is extremely steep and also difficult because of the loose scree. Baghaberd was briefly capital of the Syunik kingdom in the 12th century before it was sacked by the Seljuks in 1170. It was reoccupied by David Bek in the 18th century and has significant remains of the boundary wall but little else.

Continuing south, the road follows the river as far as the molybdenum-mining town of **Kajaran** which was relocated here in the 1960s after earthquake damage on its former site further up the hill. In the town turn left over the bridge and then head up the hill. The road climbs up over the **Kajaran** and **Tashtun Passes** (2,489m and 2,359m respectively according to the map) and then descends to the Iranian border.

Meghri (*Telephone code 2860*) The principal town in the most southerly region of the country, Meghri has some attractive houses of the 18th and 19th centuries and is pleasantly situated amidst an arid mountainous landscape, the well-tended and watered gardens making a stark contrast with the surrounding barrenness. Walking around the narrow, cobbled alleys with their canopy of vines gives an insight into life in old Meghri. The wooden beams which were incorporated into the walls to give some protection against earthquakes can be seen in places, as can the cement of mud, straw and egg which was used. The houses were built in a terraced fashion on the hillside, the roofs of houses on a lower level forming the gardens of those on the level above. Apparently large slabs of stone were used in the roofs to keep the house below dry, but one wonders how successful this was. The **Mother of God Church** in the centre of the town was built in the 15th century and rebuilt in the 17th. It had the singular distinction of housing the first piano brought to Armenia, brought from Berlin to form part of the dowry of the daughter of a local family. The piano, in a somewhat sorry state, currently sits on a veranda of the house of the hospitable local priest. The pale-coloured stonework of the church contrasts with the 12-sided pink tambour and cupola. The plain exterior in no way prepares visitors for the interior, which is covered with 19th-century murals. Those on the arches and cupola are mainly abstract or floral in design but the walls and pillars depict saints or Bible stories. In the Baptism of Jesus he is shown standing on a snake, and Hell looks suitably Brueghelish in the Last Judgement. The church was used as a store in the Soviet era and the murals were apparently painted over so it is pleasing to see how well they have survived.

There are two other churches in Meghri. **St Karapet Church** is reached by taking the street which leads north from the town square, from the right-hand side of the town hall as one faces it. The church is tucked away behind a storage barn, built deliberately to obscure the church in Stalin's era. Keep to the path when walking on the south side of the church: straying off it could mean a fall through the roof of the adjacent property. The seriously ruined church is a domed basilica with three aisles and there are the remains of frescoes on the columns. The arches are all slightly pointed. Like the houses wooden beams were incorporated into the structure as seismic protection, but the church was damaged in the 1960s by the earthquake which led to the relocation of Kajaran and the huge cracks in the masonry do not bode well for the future. **St Sargis Church**, on the other side of the town, was restored in the 1990s and is in good condition, the frescoes inside having been renovated in a sensitive way. Attached to the outside of the church is a small building, the morgue, in which the bodies of the dead were washed before being taken into the church. Such a building is unusual in Armenia, the ablution normally being performed at home. The church is perched on a hill overlooking the town and is reached by a tortuous narrow road in poor condition. A 4x4 can just about negotiate it. The way to the church is complicated – probably best to ask a local person.

Overlooking the narrow lanes of the town are the remains of a **small fortress**, originally built in the 10th century but rebuilt in the 18th by David Bek. It is an excellent viewpoint although not particularly interesting in itself. The remains of three other small fortifications can be seen on the horseshoe-shaped ridge around the town.

Meghri to Kapan South from Meghri the road continues another 5km to the Iranian border. The new road to Kapan follows the border eastwards before turning north at the village of Andadzor. Even if the new road north is not being taken, it is worth driving east to Andadzor and then west to the border crossing at Agarak to see the magnificent landscape along the River Arax, which forms the actual border. There is an alarmed fence on the Armenian side of the river, photography is forbidden and one is advised not to stop, although driving moderately slowly seems to be tolerated. Another abandoned railway follows the border: the former main line from Yerevan to Baku.

Shortly after the main road to Kapan turns north is the village of **Shvanidzor** where there is 17th-century aqueduct which is still in use for irrigation. To reach it, take the Shvanidzor turn-off from the main road and then the first left turn, just before entering the village itself. There is a church in the village where, in Stalinist times, a cultural civic centre was built onto the west end thus blocking the main entrance and, as with St Karapet in Meghri, disguising the fact that it was a church.

From Shvanidzor the road climbs to the **Gomaran Pass** (2,362m) then enters the wooded Shikahogh Reserve. Near the village of Nerkin Hand is a remarkable relict **grove of oriental plane trees** (*Platanus orientalis*) (see page 259), along the Tsav River. This road feels much more remote than the older road through Kajaran, perhaps because of the absence of human habitation for much of the way and the lack of traffic. Descending into Kapan one of the blue waste-chemical collecting reservoirs is visible, another being seen as one arrives in Kapan from the north.

7

Nagorno Karabagh

Known by the name Artsakh to its present inhabitants and to Armenians, the alternative name Nagorno Karabagh dates from the Khanate of Karabagh's formal entry to the Russian Empire in 1813, *nagorno* being Russian for 'mountainous'. (*karabagh* is Turkish for 'black garden'.) Today Nagorno Karabagh is very predominantly inhabited by ethnic Armenians – they make up around 95% of the population. The language in the streets of its towns is Armenian – albeit with a strikingly different accent – and the banknotes are Armenian. However, it is not part of Armenia: it has its own government with its own foreign ministry, its own flag, its own stamps and its own national anthem. Despite all this, its existence as a state is unrecognised by any other state and no Western government can provide consular services there. It can only be entered from Armenia. Why go? One answer is that it has some magnificent scenery. It isn't called Nagorno for nothing: even within the pre-1994 boundaries the land rose to 2,725m at Mount Kirs but the incorporation of the territory which formerly separated Nagorno Karabagh from Armenia means that the highest point is now the 3,584m summit of Mount Tsghuk. Other reasons for going are that it has some very fine monasteries, and some thought-provoking damaged streets from which the ethnic Azeri population has fled. There are differences from Armenia. Inevitably, the military presence is more conspicuous. Additionally, Christian repression was greater here in Soviet days and all 220 churches which existed in Nagorno Karabagh during the Tsarist era had closed by the 1930s. Since 1989 there has been a steady reopening programme. A more mundane difference from Armenia is that the groups of men in the street are often playing cards rather than backgammon, which is the norm in Armenia.

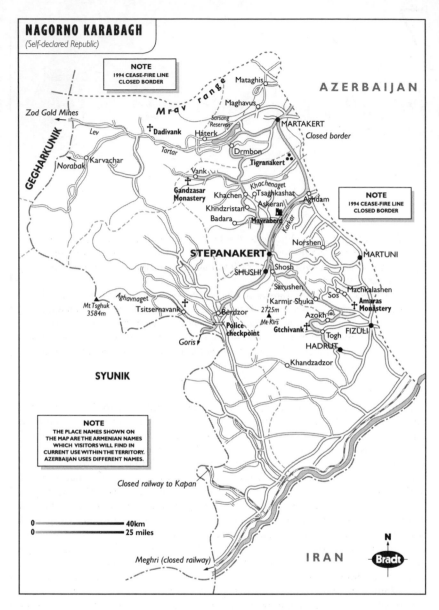

NAGORNO KARABAGH
(Self-declared Republic)

NOTE
1994 CEASE-FIRE LINE
CLOSED BORDER

NOTE
1994 CEASE-FIRE LINE
CLOSED BORDER

NOTE
THE PLACE NAMES SHOWN ON
THE MAP ARE THE ARMENIAN NAMES
WHICH VISITORS WILL FIND IN
CURRENT USE WITHIN THE TERRITORY.
AZERBAIJAN USES DIFFERENT NAMES.

A Z E R B A I J A N

M r a v   r a n g e

Mataghis

Maghavus

MARTAKERT

Closed border

Zod Gold Mines

Sarsang
Reservoir

† **Dadivank**

Haterk

Drmbon

Tigranakert

Lev

Tartar

Karvachar

Norabak

Vank †

**Gandzasar
Monastery**

Khachen

Khachenaget

Tsaghkashat

Askeran

Agdam

GEGHARKUNIK

Khndzristan

Badara

Mayraberd

Karkar

Norshen

STEPANAKERT

MARTUNI

SHUSHI

Shosh

Sarushen

Machkalashen

Karmir Shuka

Sos

**Amaras
Monastery** †

Mt Tsghuk
3584m

Aghavnaget

Tsitsernavank †

Berdzor

2725m
Mt Kirs

Azokh

SYUNIK

**Police
checkpoint**

Gtchivank †

Togh

FIZULI

Goris

HADRUT

Khandzadzor

Closed railway to Kapan

0 ———— 40km
0 ———— 25 miles

Meghri (closed railway)

I R A N

N

Bradt

Nagorno Karabagh has some interesting sights although they do tend to be rather spread out. Certain of the best sights are inaccessible because of their proximity to the ceasefire line and the risk from snipers. Hiking would be superb but should not be attempted without a local guide because of the continued existence of minefields (see box text opposite and on page 268). Some of these have been cleared but local knowledge is vital before leaving obviously used routes. Some visitors consider the abandoned Azeri villages with their ruined houses to be of interest though they are hardly very appealing. Burnt-out military hardware can still be seen in places. The territory is under martial law: problems can arise with roads being closed for military manoeuvres.

Nagorno Karabagh was under Persian rule in 1805 when, along with other areas in eastern Transcaucasia, it was annexed to the 'everlasting rule' of the Russian Empire. The Gulistan Treaty of 1813 signed by Russia and Persia ratified this. The collapse of the Russian Empire in 1917 resulted in a changed arrangement of states in the Caucasus. The newly formed Republic of Armenia and the equally new Azerbaijan Democratic Republic both sought control over Nagorno Karabagh between 1918 and 1920. From the outset the Azerbaijan Democratic Republic made territorial demands for large areas of historic Armenia, even though the Tsarist census of the whole Karabagh region showed in 1917 a population which was 72% Armenian. (These figures are disputed by the Azeris who consider the Russian Imperial Census of 1897, showing an Armenian population of about 40%, to be more reliable.) Taking advantage of the confused state of affairs resulting from World War I, the collapse of the Russian Empire and continuing persecution of Armenians by Turks, Turkish forces along with Azeri military units destroyed hundreds of ethnically Armenian villages. (It was a feature of the whole region that all villages were dominated by one ethnic group, some Armenian, some Azeri, and elsewhere some Georgian and some Turkish.) Only in Nagorno Karabagh did the Armenian population succeed in repelling the attacks. In July 1918, the First Armenian Assembly of Nagorno Karabagh declared the region to be self-governing and created the Karabagh National Council. In August 1919, this National Council entered into a provisional treaty arrangement with the Azerbaijan government to try to halt the military conflict. This, however, did not prevent Azerbaijan's violation of the treaty, culminating on 28 March 1920 with the massacre of Armenians, accompanied by burning and plundering, in Shushi, the then capital. As a result the Karabagh Assembly nullified the treaty and declared union with Armenia.

The First League of Nations had its inaugural meeting in late 1920. Applications for membership were considered by the 5th committee, chaired by Chile, which recommended that Azerbaijan should not be admitted (mainly because of its Bolshevik government) while consideration of Armenia's admission should be postponed (because it was occupied). However, the League of Nations, before final resolution of the issue, recognised Nagorno Karabagh as a disputed territory since it had not in practice been ruled by any outside power since the Russian collapse

SAFETY – ADVICE ON AVOIDING MINES

The following list of points for travellers is provided by the HALO Trust (see box, page 268) which carries out mine clearance in Nagorno Karabagh:

- Mines and unexploded ordnance (UXO), including cluster munitions, litter the region and can be found in both remote areas and close to towns and villages
- Always speak to the local people before entering an area
- Keep to well-used tracks and paths
- If a track does not look used then avoid it
- Be aware that although a track may be used it could pass through a minefield or area contaminated with UXO
- Do not touch anything which looks like a mine or ordnance
- If you don't know what something is then don't touch it

in 1917. That only changed when Bolshevik forces occupied Nagorno Karabagh in 1920. Immediately following the establishment of the Soviet regime in Armenia, the Azerbaijan Revolutionary Committee on 30 November 1920 formally recognised Nagorno Karabagh, as well as Zangezur (southern Armenia) and Nakhichevan, to be parts of Armenia and in June 1921, Armenia itself declared Nagorno Karabagh to be part of Armenia.

Meanwhile the Bolshevik leaders in Russia were having visions of an imminent international communist revolution and believed that the new Turkish government under Ataturk was a believer in their cause. This resulted in a change of attitude regarding Turkey's ethnically close relations with Azerbaijan and the question of the disputed territories including Nagorno Karabagh. Stalin, Commissar of Nationalities in the Council of People's Commissars in Moscow, therefore persuaded the Caucasian Bureau of the Russian Communist Party to adopt on 5 July 1921 a policy of annexing Nagorno Karabagh to Azerbaijan rather than Armenia. This was despite the fact that both Armenia and Azerbaijan were still independent, albeit communist controlled, countries: the Soviet Union into which they would be incorporated along with Russia was not formed until December 1922 and it was no business of the Russian Communist Party to decide on the wishes of the Karabagh population. This Russian decision was put into effect but with the proviso that Nagorno Karabagh would be granted the status of an autonomous region.

On 7 July 1923, the Soviet Azerbaijan Revolutionary Committee resolved to dismember Nagorno Karabagh and to create – on only part of its territory amounting to 4,400km^2 – the promised autonomous region. A large part of the remainder, comprising the present-day districts of Lachin and Kelbajar, became the Kurdistan Autonomous Soviet Socialist Republic. Thus Armenia and Nagorno Karabagh were now separated by the territory of Kurdistan. In 1929, Kurdistan was abolished and the territory fully incorporated into Azerbaijan, so that from 1929 onwards, Armenia was separated from Nagorno Karabagh by Azerbaijan proper.

In 1935, there were protests in the region against Nagorno Karabagh remaining within Azerbaijan and these became an almost annual feature after 1960 following the Khrushchev thaw. Gorbachev's policy of openness, established after he came to power in 1985, merely served to bring matters further into the open. The year 1988 became a turning point in the history of Nagorno Karabagh. Mass demonstrations started there on 11 February 1988 demanding union with Armenia. On 20 February in an extraordinary session of the Nagorno Karabagh Autonomous Republic Council, the People's Deputies voted to secede from Azerbaijan and join Armenia and appealed to the Supreme Soviet of the USSR to recognise this decision. This was matched by massive demonstrations in Yerevan, accompanied by a petition signed by 75,000 Armenians, demanding the annexation of Nagorno Karabagh. A pogrom on 28 February at Sumgait, Azerbaijan, which was directed against ethnic Armenians, resulted in around 30 deaths (or some estimates claim up to 120) of Armenians by their Azeri neighbours. This unprecedented killing shocked the Soviet Union and the Soviet authorities arrested 400 rioters. Some 84 perpetrators were tried and sentenced in Moscow. (The incident which purportedly led directly to the Sumgait massacre was the death five days earlier of two Azeri young men, by youths reported by the press to be Armenians, in a skirmish between the two ethnic groups in the Aghdam region of Karabagh.) Thereafter ethnic tensions continued to rise and during the fighting over Nagorno Karabagh there were civilian deaths on both sides. (Perhaps the incident which gained most international notice and condemnation was the deaths of 161–613 (numbers are disputed) Azeri civilians, fired on by Armenian forces in February 1992, as they tried to leave Khojaly, near

Aghdam, as it was about to be occupied by Armenian forces. Khojaly was used as a military base by the Azeris to shell Stepanakert, or Khankendi as it is known by the Azeris. The Sumgait massacre was followed by even bigger mass protests in Armenia itself when almost a million people were estimated to have participated. The inaction by Moscow produced massive unrest with an estimated 200,000 Azeris fleeing Armenia and 260,000 Armenians fleeing Azerbaijan. In July the Nagorno Karabagh Supreme Soviet, Nagorno Karabagh's supreme governing body, took the decision to secede from Azerbaijan and adopted measures to become part of Armenia.

The members of the Karabagh Committee, a group leading the fight for union with Armenia, were arrested in December 1988 and held in Moscow without trial whilst on 12 January 1989 direct rule of Nagorno Karabagh from Moscow was imposed. International protests eventually led to the Karabagh Committee members being freed on 31 May. Showing how little control of events Moscow had by now (the Soviet Empire in central and eastern Europe was fast disintegrating at the time) Azerbaijan started partially blockading Armenia in September. With a breathtaking disregard for the likely consequences, Moscow abandoned direct rule of Nagorno Karabagh on 28 November and handed control to Azerbaijan.

Armenia's response was swift and on 1 December the Armenian Supreme Soviet voted for unification with Nagorno Karabagh. The vote was declared illegal by the Supreme Soviet of the USSR to which Yerevan's response was to pass a new law giving it the right of veto over laws passed in Moscow. As of 10 January 1990 residents of Nagorno Karabagh were allowed to vote in Armenian elections. The year 1990 was to be a year of conflict between Armenians and central Soviet forces with massive protests over the Karabagh issue and often brutal police and military repression: six Armenians were killed in Yerevan by Soviet troops in a confrontation on 24 May. Eventually, after two changes of leadership, the appointment of Levon Ter-Petrossian as Chairman of the Supreme Soviet of Armenia on 4 August led to Armenia declaring independence within the USSR on 23 August.

The next year was to see momentous change. The failed coup against Gorbachev on 19 August 1991 led to the inevitable break-up of the Soviet Union at the end of the year. More immediately Azerbaijan's response on 27 August was to annul Nagorno Karabagh's status as an Autonomous Region which then led, on 2 September to the declaration of the independent Republic of Nagorno Karabagh – the goal had changed and union with Armenia had ceased to be the objective. A plebiscite in Nagorno Karabagh on 10 December resulted in an overwhelming vote for independence. Azerbaijan began a blockade of the territory (which of course it completely encircled) and launched military attacks using the equipment of the USSR 4th army stationed in Azerbaijan. Meanwhile newly emergent Russia saw Armenia as a key ally – notably because of its long border with Turkey, a member of NATO. Accordingly Russia signed a treaty of friendship and co-operation with Armenia on 29 December, two days before the demise of the USSR. This was to be followed, much more crucially for Nagorno Karabagh, by a collective security pact signed by Russia and Armenia along with Kazakhstan, Kyrgyzstan, Tajikistan and Uzbekistan on 15 May 1992.

Azeri military attacks made initial territorial gains but by 8 May 1992 they had been driven back from Martakert and Shushi while on 18 May the Armenian army was able to force a corridor through the Azeri lines at Lachin and break the blockade of Nagorno Karabagh. This, however, was to be followed by a renewed Azeri offensive which resulted in considerable further Azeri gains so that by the end of July they had taken the whole of the Shahumian region, a great portion of the Martakert region, and portions of Martuni, Askeran and Hadrut controlling about 60% of the entire territory. These Azeri victories had several effects: there were demonstrations against Ter-Petrossian, by now the Armenian president, and he survived an assassination attempt on 17 August; the US Congress adopted a resolution condemning the actions of Azerbaijan and prohibited US government economic assistance; and Ter-Petrossian on 9 August invoked the less than three-month-old security pact asking for Russian help.

Russian support arrived in the form of supplies and equipment. By March 1993 the Armenian army was able once more to go on the offensive and it not only over the next few months recouped its losses but also gained almost all of Nagorno Karabagh, together with the former Kurdistan and a considerable swathe of Azeri territory bordering Iran. Finally on 5 May 1994, a ceasefire brokered by Russia, Kyrgyzstan and the CIS Interparliamentary Council, was signed which took effect on 12 May. By this time Azerbaijan had lost control of a substantial area of its territory. Since then the self-declared Republic of Nagorno Karabagh has incorporated into its administrative districts even the occupied areas of Azerbaijan which were not in the former autonomous region, considerably increasing its size in the process.

The job of finding a solution to the conflict is in the hands of the Minsk group of the Organisation for Security and Co-operation in Europe which was set up in 1992. It looks as far away as ever. Azerbaijan might be willing to hand over Nagorno Karabagh to Armenia in exchange for southern Armenia but that is unacceptable to Armenia since Armenia would lose its important direct link to Iran. Armenia wants a resolution of the problem which it believes would help economic growth but Armenians feel that they cannot desert their kith and kin. Nagorno Karabagh is a key factor in the unwillingness of certain factions in Turkey to ratify the protocol, signed by the foreign ministers of Armenia and Turkey in October 2009 (see *Chapter 1, History,* page 27), aimed at normalising

MINE CLEARING

Landmines were used extensively (by both sides) during the war in Nagorno Karabagh, as were large amounts of cluster munitions and other explosive ordnance. Since the ceasefire in 1994, 328 people have been killed or maimed by landmines and unexploded ordnance (UXO). The presence of minefields leaves farmers unable to cultivate vast swathes of fertile agricultural land and also inhibits development and infrastructure projects. Towns and villages are alike affected.

The HALO Trust (see *Chapter 2, Travelling postively,* page 97), the largest humanitarian mine-clearance organisation in the world, has been active in Nagorno Karabagh since 2000, where it provides the only large-scale mine-clearance capacity. By 2010 it had cleared 10,000 mines, 10,000 cluster bombs and 45,000 other items of UXO from 3,700ha (9,140 acres) of minefield and over 20,000ha (49,400 acres) of battlefield. Almost 80% of known minefields and about 70% of the area contaminated by cluster munitions have been cleared and most of this land has been returned to cultivation – mainly of wheat. At 2010 funding levels, HALO believes that the remaining areas within the pre-1991 boundaries of Nagorno Karabagh could be cleared by 2016 but if donors reduce funding, as is already happening, this timescale will inevitably stretch.

relationships between the two countries. Turkey's prime minister has promised its ally, Azerbaijan, that it will not open its border with Armenia until the Nagorno Karabagh dispute is resolved and Armenian forces are withdrawn from what Azerbaijan regards as Azeri territory. This Armenia is not prepared to do. Meanwhile the ceasefire holds, despite occasional sniper fire across the ceasefire line with no war and no peace either.

GOVERNMENT

Although still part of Azerbaijan under international law, the self-declared Republic of Nagorno Karabagh is a de facto independent state with the necessary organs of government. The president, who is eligible to stand for not more than two five-year terms, and the 33 members of the chamber of deputies are directly elected by the population of around 150,000. Nagorno Karabagh has its own police, court system, education system and so on. The national flag of Nagorno Karabagh is basically the Armenian one but with a white five-toothed stepped arrow pattern on the right-hand side. In September 2005, the government announced that it would shortly start putting into circulation its own currency – the Nagorno Karabagh dram (NKD). Notes and coins have been produced and some are already available from specialist numismatic dealers, but the currency in circulation continues to be that of Armenia.

The government has given assistance to the estimated 40,000 people who have settled in Nagorno Karabagh since 1991 (mostly ethnic Armenian refugees fleeing Azerbaijan) in the form of allocating housing, providing livestock and charging half the Armenian price for electricity. There are also incentives in place for couples to have larger families.

RED TAPE

Visitors require **visas**. Visas can be obtained from the Republic of Nagorno Karabagh permanent representation in Yerevan. Unfortunately this is in the inconvenient suburb of Arabkir to the north of the centre (*17a Nairi Zarian St;* \ *10 249705;* e *nkr@arminco.com;* ⊕ *09.00–13.00 & 14.00–17.00 Mon–Fri*). It is advised that visa applications are made in the morning, especially if same-day visa service is requested. A photograph must accompany the application. A 21-day tourist visa costs AMD3,000 if collected the following day. Same-day service costs AMD6,000. There are also permanent representations in Paris, Berlin, Moscow, Sydney (Australia) and Washington DC but they cannot issue visas. If there is any possibility of travelling in future to Azerbaijan then it is essential to obtain the visa on a separate piece of paper. A Nagorno Karabagh visa entered in a passport means that entry to Azerbaijan will be refused. It is also possible to obtain visas from the Foreign Ministry after arrival in Stepanakert, provided visitors show the required identification documents at the border. Occasionally, however, travellers without visas have had trouble at the border and the Foreign Ministry staff advise that it is best to obtain visas before leaving Yerevan.

At present, after arrival in Stepanakert all passports must be taken to register with the consular department of the Foreign Ministry at 28 Azatamartikneri Street. It is necessary to state where you want to go and, provided the places are in safe areas, the names are written on a form which is handed to you and serves as a travel permit. Nobody, however, usually asks to see it. The staff speak only Armenian and Russian and, if you want to go somewhere off the beaten track, you will have to show them on the map where it is. This cumbersome procedure is in the process of being changed. In future the form which is currently issued in Stepanakert will be issued in Yerevan with the visa. Both visa and travel permit should be shown at the border checkpoint. There will then be no need to register in Stepanakert. If, for any reason, the form has not been obtained in Yerevan it will still be necessary to register in Stepanakert. Note that the travel permit must be presented to border officials on leaving Nagorno Karabagh. Visitors who have arrived in Stepanakert without accommodation booked, report that the staff in the Foreign Ministry were extremely helpful and found them somewhere to stay. Probably this is unique among the world's foreign ministries.

GETTING THERE

There are several **minibuses** daily from Yerevan to Stepanakert, the capital, which leave hourly from 07.00 to 10.00 from Yerevan's central bus station, taking around eight hours for a fare of AMD5,000. For those travelling by **car** it is possible to use the good main road from Goris to Stepanakert in which case the driver must stop at the **checkpoint at Lachin** on entering and leaving so as to register the vehicle. Visitors are usually asked for their passports and visas at the checkpoint. There are also more northerly routes from the east side of Lake Sevan, for which a 4x4 is strongly recommended.

The main road from Goris has been largely reconstructed. It crosses the so-called Lachin corridor through what had been, since 1929, part of Azerbaijan proper. (Somewhat confusingly the town of Lachin has now been renamed Berdzor and the district is now called Kashatagh.) After an impressive climb the road descends to the valley of the Aghavnaget where there is a new chapel up on the left dedicated to soldiers who died in battle in Karabagh. (The police checkpoint is immediately after the river crossing.) The road continues and enters Nagorno Karabagh's pre-1994 boundaries just before the town of Berdzor. This is the last sizeable place before Shushi 43km further on. Although over 50% of its houses were damaged in the war many, but not all, have been rebuilt. The houses not destroyed were largely occupied by refugees who chose to settle here. The road then climbs up and after the summit runs through sparsely populated country to bypass Shushi and descend rapidly into Stepanakert.

There are **two other roads** into Nagorno Karabagh from Armenia. That from Norabak (Armenia) to Karvachar (Nagorno Karabagh) is in dire condition and should not be attempted in any normal vehicle. That from Zod (Armenia) over the Zod Pass (2,400m) is passable in summer, though a 4x4 is recommended. After the pass the road follows the beautiful valley of the Lev, at times with toweringly high cliffs on each side until its confluence with the Tartar where the road meets another coming along the Tartar Valley. Turn left at the junction and follow the Tartar until Nagorno Karabagh's pre-1994 borders are entered just past the monastery of Dadivank on the left. The road is extremely scenic all the way along the valley to Sarsang reservoir.

GETTING AROUND

The new **north–south highway** built with funds from the charitable Hayastan All-Armenian Fund (see *Chapter 2, Travelling postively,* page 97) has made travelling in Karabagh much easier than it was. As in Armenia it is possible to travel between most towns and villages by **minibus** (*marshrutka*). The best way to find out current times of departure is by asking at either the tourist office in Shushi (see page 279) or that in Stepanakert, which should be open by 2011 (see below) or at your hotel or homestay. The bus station in Stepanakert is at the northern end of Azatamartikneri Avenue. **Taxis** are plentiful and cheap and are a reasonable and convenient alternative to the *marshrutkas*. **Car hire** can be arranged through Asbar Travel Agency (see below) in Stepanakert.

TOURIST INFORMATION

The **Karabakh Tourism Development Agency** (also known as the Government Tourism Department) website (*www.karabakh.travel*) has much useful background information, in the midst of its flowery language, including details of the regions of Karabagh, accommodation, transport, museums and cuisine. It also publishes a guidebook, *Discovered Paradise*, which contains similar information and a series of free booklets which contain background information and good photographs, but few practical details. Titles include *Karabakh, Stepanakert, Gandzasar, Carpets* and *Nicol Duman*. I obtained mine from the tourist information office in Shushi. Some can be downloaded from the agency's website. Another good internet source is www.armeniapedia.org which has information on Nagorno Karabagh

A useful, although old, **map** of Nagorno Karabagh, with street plans of Stepanakert and Shushi and notes on sites of interest, is published by Asbar Tourism Agency (see below). I found it at the stationery shop Kanzler (*26 Vazgen Sargsian St, Stepanakert*). The Collage maps of Armenia (see *Chapter 2,* page 53) also cover Nagorno Karabagh.

There is a good tourist information office in Shushi (see page 279) and another is due to open in Stepanakert in 2011. It is, according to the Department of Tourism, likely to be at 2 Knunyants Street, off Veratsnound (Renaissance) Square.

Asbar Travel Agency (*16a Vazgen Sargsian St, Stepanakert;* ⟍ *47 944758;* e *travel@asbar.nk.am; www.asbar.nk.am*) can arrange all that a visitor may need – accommodation (hotels, homestays and apartment rental), car hire (with or without driver), tours within Karabagh including special-interest tours (such as hiking), restaurant bookings and guides.

JANAPAR TRAIL For experienced walkers there is now a long-distance marked footpath from Hadrut in the south to Dadivank in the north. Markers are blue with a yellow footprint and it is said to take two weeks to walk the entire route. Detailed information, including maps, can be found at www.janapar.org. Anyone intending to walk the trail should also bear in mind the warnings given earlier in this chapter about mines and other unexploded ordnance.

It is best either to book into one of the modern hotels, concentrated in Stepanakert and nearby Shushi, or else to opt for a homestay. The older rundown Soviet-era hotels which have not been refurbished can rarely be recommended. **Homestays** in different parts of Nagorno Karabagh can be booked via a Yerevan travel agent before leaving, through the tourist information offices in Shushi (see page 279) or Stepanakert (see page 271) or via Asbar Travel Agency (see page 271), as can the hotels (see below). The website of the Karabakh Tourism Development Agency (see page 271) lists possible homestays as well as details of hotels in Karabagh.

At present Stepanakert has far more facilities than Shushi. Most places of interest to tourists can be visited as day trips from Stepanakert. The two most popular, Dadivank and Gandzasar, can be visited on the same day if travelling by car.

HOTELS
Stepanakert

🏠 **Armenia Hotel** (55 rooms) Veratsnound Sq; ☎ 47 949400; e info@armeniahotel.am; www.armeniahotel.am. A hotel of international standard next door to the parliament building. Cards accepted. **$$$**

🏠 **Hotel Nairi** (46 rooms) 14a Hekimian St; ☎ 47 947802, 971502, 971503; e nairi@ktsurf.net; www.hotelnairi.com. Modern hotel north of the centre run by an Australian Armenian. Internet available. **$$**

🏠 **Hotel Heghnar** (28 rooms) 39–41 Abovian St; ☎ 47 948677, 971221, 946626; e heghnar@

ktsurf.net; www.heghnarhotel.com. A fully renovated hotel tastefully decorated in natural materials, with healthy plants gracing lobby & landings. Attractive original modern paintings, many for sale, adorn the walls. B/fast included, other meals can be provided if notice given. Internet available. **$$**

🏠 **Hotel Lotus** (25 rooms) 81 Vagharshian St; ☎ 47 950094; e lotus-hotel@mail.ru. This hotel opened in 1998 & is 15 mins' walk from the centre. It is popular with groups. Note that there are a lot of stairs & there is no lift. **$$**

Shushi

🏠 **Hotel Shoushi** (12 rooms) 3 Amirian St; ☎ 47 731357; e shoushihotel@yahoo.com. The only hotel in Shushi. In the centre of the town, close to the cathedral. About 15mins' drive down

the hill into Stepanakert. Staircases a bit bleak but rooms warm & comfortable. Good reports from guests. **$$**

Elsewhere in Karabagh

🏠 **Sea Stone Hotel** (18 rooms) Vank village, Martakert region; m 097 286285, 097 235072, 10 500168 (Yerevan number). This hotel is 3km outside Vank village & is run by the same people as the Eclectica (see below). It is a more luxurious hotel, with comfortable rooms, but is just as extraordinary. The large plaster casts of eyes, lips & mouths which decorate the outside of the hotel & are repeated inside, the statues of lions & nymphs guarding the front door & the huge representation of a lion's mouth, which roars as one passes, all seem out of place in the attractive riverside setting. **$$**

🏠 **Ani Paradise Hotel Resort** (8 rooms) Khndzristan village, Askeran region; m 097

282000; e aniparadise@ktsurf.net. On the Stepanakert–Gandzasar highway 20km from Stepanakert. This pleasant small hotel in a country house has a swimming pool & can arrange horseriding, fishing & hiking. B/fast included, other meals can be provided with notice. **$$**

🏠 **Hotel Eclectica** (19 rooms) Vank village, Martakert region; m 097 286285, 10 500168 (Yerevan number). In Vank village just below Gandzasar Monastery. Rooms basic. The 6 rooms on the ground floor (1 dbl, 2 twin, 1 trpl, 1 quad, 1 for 5 persons) share 2 bathrooms. 13 rooms upstairs (9 dbl, 4 sgl) similarly. This hotel lives up to its name: the extraordinary entrance hall is decorated as an undersea world with perspex cases, containing models depicting Armenian life, set into the floor. The restaurant ceiling is held up by half a dozen Atlas-like figures & Corinthian columns, between which is a frieze embellished with casts of Armenian coins. The pictures on the wall are reproductions of Van Gogh. Outside, an open-air stage has tiered green & yellow plastic seats. **$$**

WHERE TO EAT The above hotels can provide meals although some of the smaller ones need notice. Eating places in Stepanakert serve mainly the standard fare of *khorovats* (barbecued food) or pizzas.

✖ **Asbar Summer Café** 16a Vazgen Sargsian St, Stepanakert; ☎ 47 944758
✖ **Niko** 25 Vazgen Sargsian St, Stepanakert; ☎ 47 952489

✖ **Ureni** 66 Tumanian St, Stepanakert; ☎ 47 944544

The gas station on the edge of Stepanakert on the road north has a well-provisioned, clean, bright café. When spending a day away from the main towns, as when visiting Dadivank, a picnic is possibly the best option.

SHOPPING

Most **shops, banks, post office, internet cafés, currency exchanges,** etc are to be found on or near Vazgen Sargsian Street (formerly, and sometimes still, called Yerevanian Avenue) or Azatamartikneri Street in Stepanakert.

English-language books are rare. Maps can be bought at Kanzler, a **stationery shop** (*26 Vazgen Sargsian St, Stepanakert*). The **market** on Sasountsi Davit Street sells household items and clothes as well as food.

For souvenirs try **Nereni Arts and Crafts** (*10 Grigor Lusavorich St*), which has handmade local crafts. Handmade **carpets** can be found at 31 Azatamartikneri Street in Stepanakert.

OTHER PRACTICALITIES

Telephone and **internet** services are provided by Karabagh Telecom (*14 Nelson Stepanian St, Stepanakert;* ☎ *47 979702;* e *info@karabakhtelecom.com; www.karabakhtelecom.com*). **Emergency phone numbers** are the same as in Armenia: fire ☎ 101, police ☎ 102, ambulance ☎ 103. Anyone wishing to use a

Nagorno Karabagh OTHER PRACTICALITIES

7

mobile phone in Nagorno Karabagh should note that Armenian SIM cards work as roaming cards and are thus relatively expensive. It may be cheaper to buy a Karabagh SIM card. Options available include pre-paid and post-paid cards with tariffs dependent on whether NKR, Armenian or international access is desired. Information on cards and tariffs is available from Karabakh Telecom's website.

WHAT TO SEE AND DO

Entrance to museums in Nagorno Karabagh is generally free. A contribution, and perhaps a tip to the guide, is always welcome. Historic sites which are ruinous are always open. Where there is a church which is now active it will be open every day, at least 09.00–18.00 and often longer. The rest of a monastery site is usually accessible at all times.

STEPANAKERT (*Telephone code 47*) Formerly Khankendi, the capital of Nagorno Karabagh (population 40,000) was renamed Stepanakert in 1923 in honour of the Armenian Bolshevik Stepan Shahumian (1878–1918) after whom Stepanavan is also named. His statue stands in Shahumian Square at the northern end of Vazgen Sargsian Street, one of the main shopping streets. Newly independent Azerbaijan renamed it back to Khankendi in 1992, but the name in use within Nagorno Karabagh today remains Stepanakert. The town suffered considerable damage in the war but this has now been repaired and the town centre begins to have the feel and appearance of a capital city, albeit a small one. The town is clean and there are many notices saying 'Do not litter'. The new **parliament building** on Veratsnound (Renaissance) Square is topped by a transparent cupola reminiscent of Armenian church architecture. Until recently Stepanakert had no churches but a new **cathedral**

PUBLIC HOLIDAYS

1 January	New Year
6 January	Christmas
8 March	International Women's Day
March/April	Good Friday
March/April	Easter Monday
7 April	Day of Motherhood and Beauty
24 April	Genocide Memorial Day
1 May	May Day
9 May	Victory and Peace day
28 May	First Republic Day
2 September	Independence Day
10 December	Constitution Day
31 December	New Year's Eve

NOTE
THE PLACE NAMES SHOWN ON THE MAP ARE THE ARMENIAN NAMES WHICH VISITORS WILL FIND IN CURRENT USE WITHIN THE TOWN. AZERBAIJAN USES DIFFERENT NAMES.

0 ———— 500m
0 ———— 500yds

↑ Askeran,
Mamik yel Babik

MESROP MASHTOTS STREET

Hotel Nairi

HEKIMIAN
STREET

TIGRAN METS STREET

VICTORY SQUARE

South–north highway

ALEK MANOOGIAN ST

Hotel Heghnar

ABOVIAN STREET

MKHITAR GOSH ST

SAROYAN -T

TOUMANIAN STREET

AZATAMARTIKNERJ AVENUE

DAVIT BEK STREET

PARUYR SEVAK STREET

SASOUNTSI DAVIT STREET

Nairi Supermarket

Ministry of Foreign Affairs

Stadium

Market

Stepan Shahumian Monument

Artsakh State Museum

Parliament building

Armenia Hotel

VERATSNOUND SQ

HISTORICAL QUARTERS

GAREGIN NZHDEH ST

South–north highway

STEPANIAN ST

Karabagh War Museum

Victory Monument

HAKOBIAN ST

K NUNIANTS ST

NELSON STEPANIAN AVE

Republic Hospital

BAGHRAMIAN STREET

Vahram Papazian Armenian Theatre

Karabagh Telecom

LUSAVORICH ST

Cemetery

MARTOUNI ST

Nereni arts & crafts

SARGSIAN (YEREVANIAN) AVE

VARDAN MAMIKONIAN ST

Asbar Travel Agency

GENERAL ANDRANIK ST

Cathedral †

Children's Hospital

VAGHARSHIAN ST

N

Bradt

STEPANAKERT

Lotus Hotel ↓

is under construction south of the historical quarters. The Astvatsatsin (Mother of God) Church will be of the hanging-dome type and it is hoped to complete it sometime in 2011. I was privileged to be given, by the builders, a guided tour of the partially built cathedral, including the crypt with all its wooden scaffolding, an experience which certainly would not have been vouchsafed under Western safety regulations! In the **market** it is possible to see the herb bread being made (see box text, page 273) and it is a good place to buy food for picnics and self-catering. **Artsakh State Museum** (*1 Sasounti Davit St;* ✆ *47 941042;* e *tangaran@ktsurf.net; www.karabakh.travel;* ⊕ *09.00–17.00 Mon–Sat*), is just up the hill from the market. It gives an interesting portrayal of Nagorno Karabagh from prehistoric times to the present day. The Soviet era is not totally ducked as sometimes happens but, World War II apart, the focus was on the positive side (industrialisation) rather than the negative (the purges). The two sides in the days of the First Armenian Republic, the Bolsheviks and the Dashnaks, are given complementary displays opposite each other. The **Karabagh War Museum**, or Museum of Fallen Soldiers (*25 Vazgen Sargsian St;* ✆ *47 950738*), depicts the 1990–94 war with displays of weaponry and portraits of soldiers killed during the war.

On the north side of Stepanakert is a **statue** reproduced in a thousand Karabagh souvenirs. The creation of the sculptor Sargis Baghdasarian in Soviet times, it is called *We Are Our Mountains*. Looking like an elderly couple with peaked skulls, the statue is intended to symbolise the unity of the Karabagh people with their mountains. It is universally referred to as *Mamik yel Babik* (*Granny and Grandad*).

NORTHEAST FROM STEPANAKERT Some 15km from Stepanakert just before the town of **Askeran** the main road passes right through the fortress known variously as **Mayraberd** ('Head Fortress') or Zoraberd ('Powerful Fortress'). It was reinforced in 1788–89 by the Persians because of the increasing Russian threat and most of what can be seen today dates from then. The fortress is on both sides of the Karkar River and locals say that originally the two parts were connected by a continuous rampart 1.5km long. That seems improbable given the difficulty of constructing adequate foundations in the boggy land by the river and in the absence of any obvious traces of this central section today. What survives is a triangle of walls breached by the road on the northern side plus a smaller fortification together with several towers and a length of wall with the remains of a walkway on top on the southern side.

Beyond Askeran the road continues another 5km to the ruins of **Aghdam**. Aghdam was a sizeable town, formerly inhabited by Azeris, but it was destroyed by the Karabagh army after they captured it to prevent it falling back into Azeri hands. To go there is either weird or depressing depending on perspective but many visitors do so. Beyond Aghdam, on the Martakert road, is the **fortress and State Archaeological Museum of Tigranakert** (*about 36km north of Stepanakert, halfway between Askeran & Martakert; www.tigrankert.am;* ⊕ *daily 09.00–19.00*). A medieval fortress sits at the foot of the dramatic site of the ancient city of Tigranakert, founded by Tigran the Great (95–55BC). The site covers some 50ha and excavations, started in 2005, are continuing. Already two of the main walls of the city and a 5th–7th-century church have been uncovered. The many finds, dating from the 5th century BC to the 17th century AD, are now displayed in the museum which opened in the medieval fortress in June 2010. Information is in Armenian, English and Russian. The website's English pages were not active at the time of writing but photographs of this fascinating and impressive site can be viewed on the Armenian and Russian pages.

NORTH FROM STEPANAKERT After passing *Mamik yel Babik* turn left and then right at the roundabout at Aygestan. About 40km from Stepanakert the road descends a hill into the valley of the Khachenaget River which it bridges. After the bridge the road to Gandzasar goes off left, the main road continuing to Drmbon, where the road for Dadivank goes off, and then to Martakert.

Some 22km north of Stepanakert, in the village of **Tsaghkashat** (Ghshlag), is the **house museum of freedom fighter Nikol Duman** (✆ 47 944758; ☼ 10.00–19.00 *daily*). The lower floor of the restored 19th-century house is dedicated to the life and work of Nikol Duman (1867–1914) and includes a collection of military items. The upper floor shows a typical living room of the era. Other ethnographical displays are nearby. Within the complex is a souvenir shop with local handicrafts and produce, snacks are available and traditional meals can be organised.

Gandzasar Monastery Gandzasar is once more a working monastery and seminary and is open daily (see note on page 274). Gandzasar ('Treasure Mountain') Monastery, dedicated to John the Baptist, is on a hilltop outside **Vank** ('Monastery') village, Martakert district. The name derives from the presence of silver deposits in the district. To reach it, turn left after crossing the bridge over the Khachenaget and continue a further 14km to Vank, following the river valley. Gandzasar has been fully restored since 1991. It is particularly notable for its exquisite carved detail. Surrounded by walls, outside which are graves, it is a cross-dome church with its 16-sided tambour topped by an umbrella cupola. Owing to its inaccessibility, Nagorno Karabagh partly avoided the large-scale Seljuk invasion in the 11th and 12th centuries, as well as the Mongolian invasions in the 13th century. Consequently some of the finest church architecture of the period is found here. The monastery was founded in 1216, the church being built between 1232 and 1238, while the *gavit* was added in 1261. The founders were Melik Jalal-Dolan, ruler of Khachen, the most important of the principalities of the region, together with his wife Mamkan and son Atabeg. The monastery was to serve as the burial place of the Khachen rulers, and until the 19th century as the seat of the Katholikos of Agvank.

The tambour is an outstanding work of art, decorated with numerous sculptured images. On the western side two bearded figures with long moustaches are sitting in an oriental posture with their feet tucked under them. On the south side are kneeling figures facing each other with arms outstretched and haloes round their heads while angels spread their wings over them in blessing. One side shows the Virgin and Child, there are two bulls' heads and an eagle with spreading wings. The *gavit* obscures another sculptural composition – a crucifix under the gable of the west façade with seraphs hovering over Jesus and Mary, and John the Baptist kneeling in prayer with outstretched hands. The north façade shows a bird in the west and the south façade shows galloping horses. The west and east façades have large relief crosses. The *gavit* has an immense door portal which shows two birds as well as much varied abstract design. It is surmounted by a belfry supported by six columns. The interior is also pleasing with the finely carved front of the altar dais, the pattern of each triangle or square being different. There are further carvings of bulls as well as abstract designs.

Compared with the tranquil traditional appearance of the monastery, Vank village is certainly a contrast. Someone with a fondness for yellow and green has painted all the gas pipes to match the tiered plastic seats of the outdoor theatre attached to one of the hotels, part of which is in the form of a ship.

Dadivank (monastery) Dadivank, one of the largest medieval monastery complexes, is on the northern route to Armenia from Nagorno Karabagh. Take a

7

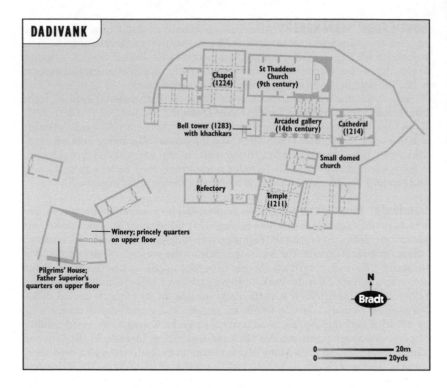

DADIVANK

Chapel (1224)

St Thaddeus Church (9th century)

Bell tower (1283) with khachkars

Arcaded gallery (14th century)

Cathedral (1214)

Small domed church

Refectory

Temple (1211)

Winery; princely quarters on upper floor

Pilgrims' House; Father Superior's quarters on upper floor

N

Bradt

0 —————— 20m
0 —————— 20yds

picnic and if your car is dual-fuel, fill up with gas before leaving Stepanakert: the last gas station at the time of writing was just beyond *Mamik yel Babik,* although it looked as if one might be being built at Drmbon. The road to Dadivank bears right after the junction with the Gandzasar road just after the Khachenaget bridge. The main road continues north through the hills until eventually Sarsang Reservoir can be seen with the village of **Drmbon** in the foreground and the Mrav range forming a backdrop. Until Drmbon the road is mostly in good condition. Drmbon is an important mining area and the signposted road to Dadivank goes off left beside the large white-and-green building of the Base Metals Mining Company. The road deteriorates rapidly from here. Initially mining activities are evident along the Sarsang Reservoir but eventually these are left behind and then the rest of the journey is extremely beautiful along the gorge of the fast-flowing Tartar River as far as the monastery.

It is possible to drive up to the monastery in a 4x4, the road winding round what look like two slag heaps. (Take the track to the right just *after* the yellow sign to Dadivank.)

Dadivank is traditionally believed to be on the site of the grave of St Thaddeus who was martyred in the 1st century for preaching Christianity, 'Dadi' being a phonetic transposition of his name. Although there was probably a church here by the 4th century, the oldest surviving remains date from the 9th century. The church was pillaged in 1145–46 by the Persians but reconstruction started in the 1170s. The monastery went into decline in the 18th century and the monastery estates were only half occupied when the Khan of Shushi invited the Kurds to move on to them from Yerevan. The late 18th century saw further Persian military action, and plague and famine in 1798 saw the final abandonment of the site. Restoration is underway.

The layout is exceedingly complex and there are buildings on two levels. The 9th-century **Church of St Thaddeus**, built over his grave, is at the north side of the complex. Less than ideal restoration work following excavations has resulted in some loss of atmosphere from this ancient church. To its west lies a **chapel** built in 1224 and there are further contemporary buildings to the west of that within the wall. Southeast of St Thaddeus is the main **cathedral** which dates from 1214. The 16-sided tambour has graceful arcatures and the cupola is conical. On both the south and east façades are two figures holding a model of the church. In front of it is a 14th-century **arcaded gallery** which extends as far as the **bell tower** of 1283. New steps at the bell tower enable the two intricately carved khachkars to be fully appreciated. To the south there is a **small-domed church** with circular tambour and a tiled dome; its date is uncertain. The restoration of this church is also somewhat insensitive but the remains of frescoes can still be seen high on the north wall. On the lower level are the **kitchen**, **refectory** and **wine press**, as well as various accommodation quarters. The building with four round pillars on square bases is, according to an inscription of 1211, the **temple**.

There is a spring at Dadivank and the monastery is a pleasant place to have a picnic.

SOUTH FROM STEPANAKERT

Shushi (*Telephone code 477*) The former capital of Shushi is about 15 minutes up the hill from Stepanakert and lies to the left just off the main Goris road. Unlike Stepanakert the scars of ethnic conflict are still very evident in Shushi with its many ruined buildings. There are signs of some recovery and Shushi now has a handsome **tourist office** in the former bus station, off the north end of Nzhdeh Street (*3 Garegin Nzhdeh St;* \ *47 733296;* ☉ *daily, 09.30–17.30 in winter, 09.30– 18.30 in summer*). When I visited it had only just opened, in fact I was their first visitor, and it was not fully up and running. However, it promises to be an excellent source of information with helpful staff. Prior to 1988 the town had a mixed Armenian and Azeri population, notwithstanding the destruction of many Armenian homes during fighting in 1920. Now the Azeri population has gone while the Armenians remain. Half the blocks of flats are occupied, the other half are burnt-out shells. There is simply insufficient money to demolish these scorched roofless reminders and what the town's (mostly unemployed) inhabitants think as they walk past each day is difficult to say. In one way the place is more striking than the completely abandoned towns and villages because here life goes on around the destruction. The encroaching vegetation shows how long places have lain empty and unused.

The town itself, set on a precipice overlooking the impressive gorge of the Karkar has several points of interest. Part of the medieval town wall remains and two 19th-century churches have been restored, both striking with their very pale stone. The massive, almost white **Ghazanchetsots Cathedral** (Ghazan refers to some very large vessels which were gifted to the church) was built between 1868 and 1887. Like all Karabagh churches it was closed during the Soviet period and saw service variously as a granary, a garage and a munitions store. Inside it is plain apart from some modern paintings. Oddly enough the bell tower, decorated with figures of angels playing musical instruments which stands beside it, was built earlier, in 1858. All but one of the angels decorating the bell tower were destroyed in the war, the remaining one being christened the 'guardian angel of Artsakh'. After renovation the church and bell tower, with new angels, were re-consecrated in 1998. The other church is the so-called **green church** (*kanach zham*), in the northwestern part of the town. It has a silver metallic cupola and was completed in 1847. Elsewhere in the town **mosques** survive: religious buildings were not destroyed after the war. The Church in 2005 took the most interesting one, the **Mets Meched Mosque** of 1883, under its protection and invited the Shiite authorities in Teheran to send specialists to restore it. In Soviet days it served as the town's historical museum. Across the square from the mosque the **bazaar**, soon to become a functioning market again, is being rebuilt to its original design. Down the road opposite the bazaar is an overgrown second mosque of 1875. **Shushi Museum** (*17 Mesrop Mashtots St;* ⟍ *47 731948;* ⊕ *09.00–17.00 Mon–Sat*) displays the history of Shushi in a mid-19th-century house.

SOUTHEAST FROM STEPANAKERT Take the main Goris road as far as the city boundary but then turn left down the hill. The road heads out through **Shosh** where there are many plantations of mulberry trees, as silk was made here in Soviet days. There is a possibility that the industry might be revived but meanwhile the mulberries are used for producing mulberry vodka. The ruined 12th–13th-century **Pirumashen Church**, a single-aisle basilica, is passed before the village of **Sarushen** and the road continues to the large village of **Karmir Shuka**. From Karmir Shuka it is possible to turn off the main road and travel eastwards along a poor road to the **Monastery of Amaras**, near the village of Machkalashen. Amaras was founded by St Gregory the Illuminator in the early 4th century and Mesrop Mashtots is said to have taught there. The complex comprises a fortified wall within which is the relatively recent church of St Gregory built in the 19th century and restored in 1996. South from Karmir Shuka and near the village of Azokh is **Azokh Cave**, reached by a scramble up the hillside. The eight linked caves have a total length of 600m and an area of 8,000m² with the largest chamber being 3,000m². The caves are equally famous for their stalactites and stalagmites and for the prehistoric finds which have been made there. These include the 1–1.5 million-year-old remains of Palaeolithic and Mesolithic man together with more than 2,000 bones from 45 species of animal, some of them now extinct.

About 3km south of Azokh is the village of **Togh**. At the far end of the village bear right on a dirt road and continue until another dirt road goes off right in about 2km. Take this right turn and continue until the summit is reached and there is a small parking place on the right. Unless the cloud is low it is possible to see the tambour and cupola of the ruined **Monastery of Gtchivank** breaking the skyline on the hill to the right. From the top of the parking area a (faint in places) path leads up the hillside and then across left to the monastery. (There is also a track up from the other side, possibly accessible by a 4x4 in good weather but impossibly muddy when I was there.) It is a very beautiful walk up the flower-covered hillside with wonderful views over the hilly countryside of southern Karabagh. The approach to the monastery is one of the finest imaginable but the monastery itself is an incredibly sad place. Where so many lived and worked to the glory of God vandals have spray-painted with graffiti every square inch inside and out, even climbing up to the most inaccessible parts of the cupola to cause as much desecration as possible. The graffiti comprise mostly people's names, written in Russian letters and often dated. The monastery was the seat of the archbishopric as early as the 5th century. The inscription records that the existing main cross-dome church was built between 1241 and 1248 by the brothers Sargis and Vrtanes, bishops at Amaras. The *gavit* survives together with another very ruinous building and some fine khachkars. All are covered in graffiti. This is not a place where one wishes to linger.

SOUTHWEST FROM STEPANAKERT

Tsitsernavank (monastery) This monastery is very close to the Armenian border. From Stepanakert take the main Goris road to the border post in the Lachin corridor. Go through the border post and then turn immediately right along the signposted road. Keeping the Aghavnaget River on your left, continue for 15km (4x4 essential) until the monastery can be seen on an outcrop between the Aghnavnaget and its tributary the Khovnavar. At the fork take the lower track which crosses a bridge. It is better to park at the bottom of the steep final slope up to the monastery and walk the last few metres. The narrow, tall three-aisle **basilica** was built in the 4th century but renovated in the 5th and again in the 7th. Unusually, there are three arches above the apse. There is some decoration on the square pillars and on the front of the *bema*. Near the *bema* some of the 13th-century floor stones have been exposed to view. Outside, one of the gravestones in particular shows very fine figure carving. The 16th-century refectory is now a small **museum** which the priest will open and show you if he is around. Items on display include clay communion vessels dating from the 5th or 6th century, carpets and khachkars. One early khachkar originally bore two carved doves but one has been defaced, possibly by order of a cleric who believed that Christ had one nature, not two (see *Chapter 1, Religion*, page 31). Both the church and the later fortified wall have recently been restored. The name Tsitsernavank derives either from the Armenian for 'swallow' (the bird) or from the word for the tip of the little finger; St Peter's was reputed to have been brought to the monastery.

Appendix 1

LANGUAGE

Armenian is an Indo-European language but a significant number of words have been borrowed from the country's various occupiers, mostly Persian and Turkish. There are differences in grammar, vocabulary and pronunciation between eastern Armenian (as spoken in Armenia) and western Armenian (as formerly spoken in Anatolia and still spoken by the diaspora) although the two are mutually intelligible. An older form of the language called Grabar is still used by the Church.

SOME OF THE GRAMMATICAL RULES OF EASTERN ARMENIAN

- There is no gender and the same word is used for he, she and it. There are, however, separate masculine and feminine nouns where there is a clear difference, eg: man/woman; ram/ewe; male saint/female saint.
- The definite article appears as a suffix to the noun (as in a few other Indo-European languages such as Swedish and Norwegian). There is no indefinite article: a noun without the definite article suffix is assumed to be indefinite. (This is different in western Armenian where the indefinite article appears as a separate word after the noun.) If the following word starts with a vowel, then the definite article suffix is spoken as if it were the first syllable of the following word rather than the last syllable of the noun of which it is a suffix.
- The stress is on the last syllable of a word but the definite article suffix is not regarded as a syllable for this purpose and is never stressed.
- There is no interrogative form. Questions are indicated only by tone of voice in speech, and in writing by a special mark (˚) over the stressed vowel of the word about which the question is being asked. For example, in the question 'You have an apple?' the question mark in Armenian would be placed either over the word 'you' or over the stressed vowel of 'apple' depending on precisely what the questioner wanted to know.
- Nouns decline (as in Latin, Russian, German). There are seven cases.
- Pronouns also decline. Infinitives can act as nouns and then they similarly decline.
- Adjectives are placed before the noun; they do not change to agree with the noun.
- Most prepositions follow the noun rather than precede it (and are therefore sometimes called postpositions) and they govern the case which the noun takes.
- There are two main conjugations of verbs plus irregular verbs.
- Some Armenian words are never heard in spoken Armenian, the Russian equivalent being used instead.
- The second person singular is used when addressing close family members, close friends and also God in prayer.

THE ARMENIAN ALPHABET: PRONUNCIATION

(Note: letters may be pronounced slightly differently in spoken east Armenian in accordance with their position in the word.)

Ա ա	As the a in father
Բ բ	As the b in book
Գ գ	As the g in go
Դ դ	As the d in dog
Ե ե	As the ye in yes at the beginning of a word; like the e in pen within a word
Զ զ	As the z in zoo
Է է	As the e in elf
Ը ը	As the u in but
Թ թ	As the t in today
Ժ ժ	As the s in treasure
Ի ի	As the ea in meat
Լ լ	As the l in lip
Խ խ	As the ch in Scottish loch
Ծ ծ	As the tz in Ritz
Կ կ	As the ck in tricky
Հ հ	As the h in healthy
Ձ ձ	As the ds in lids
Ղ ղ	As a French r
Ճ ճ	As the j in job
Մ մ	As the m in moon
Յ յ	As the y in year

Ն ն	As the n in nought
Շ շ	As the sh in shoe
Ո ո	As the vo in vocal at the beginning of a word; like the o in no within a word
Չ չ	As the ch in children
Պ պ	As the p in piece
Ջ ջ	As the j in juice
Ռ ռ	As the rolled Scottish r
Ս ս	As the s in soft
Վ վ	As the v in voice
Տ տ	As the clipped t in but
Ր ր	As an English r
Ց ց	As the ts in lots
Ու ու	As the oo in fool
Փ փ	As the p in pink
Ք ք	As the k in key
Օ օ	As the o in stone
Ֆ ֆ	As the f in fool
և	(Lower case only) Pronounced yev at the beginning of a word but otherwise ev; it also has the meaning and.

TRANSLITERATION OF FOREIGN WORDS As mentioned, extensive use is made of certain Russian words in preference to the Armenian. In this appendix Russian words have been given as transliterations direct from Russian into English although in some cases the transliteration into Armenian is also given, depending on how useful I thought it was likely to be. For simplicity, the Cyrillic alphabet, in which Russian is written, has not been used.

One hybrid expression you must not fail to understand
If you ask an Armenian if he or she can do something for you, the usual answer is *Problem chka*. This is a Russo-Armenian hybrid expression which means 'NO problem'. It does NOT mean that there is any difficulty!

WORDS AND PHRASES
Essentials

Good morning	Բարի լույս	*Bari luys*
Good afternoon	Բարի օր	*Bari or* (Not much used in spoken Armenian)
Good evening	Բարի երեկո	*Bari yereko*
Goodnight	Բարի գիշեր	*Bari gisher*
Hello (formal)	Բարև	*Barev*
Hello (informal)	Բարև ձեզ	*Barev dzez*
Goodbye	Ցտեսություն	*Tstesootyoon*
My name is ...	Իմ անունը ... է	*Eem anoonu ... e*
What is your name? (formal)	Ի՞նչ է ձեր անունը	*Inch e dser anoonu?*

What is your name? (informal)	Ի՞նչ է անունդ	Inch e anoonut?
Where are you from?	Որտեղի՞ց եք	Vortereets ek?
Australia	Ավստրալիա	Avstralia
Britain	Բրիտանիա	Breetania
Canada	Կանադա	Canada
Ireland	Իռլանդիա	Eerlandia
New Zealand	Նոր Զելանդիա	Nor Zeelandia
USA	Ամերիկա	America
I am from ...	Expressed by saying Ես (pronounced *Yes*) followed by the name of the country in the ablative case, followed by եմ (pronounced *em*). The ablative case is formed from the nominative case listed above by adding the suffix յից (pronounced *yeets*) if the name of the country ends in a vowel; or the suffix ից (pronounced *eets*) if the name of the country ends in a consonant. For example:	
I am from Scotland.	Ես Շոտլանդիայից եմ	Yes Shotlandiayeets em
How are you?	Ինչպե՞ս եք	Inchpes ek?
I'm fine	Լավ եմ	Lav em
Please	Խնդրում եմ	Khndroom em
Thank you	Շնորհակալություն	Shnorhakalatyoon
	(most people use the French *Merci* for the sake of brevity)	
Excuse me/Sorry	Ներողություն	Nerorootyoon
Pleased to meet you	Շատ ուրախ եմ	Shat oorakh em
Yes	Այո	Ayo
No	Ոչ	Votsh
I don't understand	Ես չեմ հասկանում	Yes chem haskanoom
Please speak more slowly	Խնդրում եմ ավելի դանդաղ խոսեք	Khntroom em avelee dandagh khosek
Do you understand?	This would be considered impolite in Armenian. Say instead:	
I hope it is clear	Հուսով եմ, որ պարզ է	Hoosov em, vor parz e

Questions

How?	Ինչպե՞ս	Inchpes?
What?	Ի՞նչ	Inch?
	(This is frequently used when you don't understand, haven't heard, or are surprised.)	
Where is ... ?	Որտե՞ղ է ...	Vorterr e ... ?
What is it?	Ի՞նչ է սա	Inch e sa?
Which?	Ո՞ր	Vor?
	(Used when, for example, you've been shown several rooms in a hotel, to ascertain which of them you would prefer.)	
When?	Ե՞րբ	Yerp?
Why?	Ինչու՞	Inchoo?
Who?	Ո՞վ	Ov?
How much does it cost?	Ի՞նչ արժե	Inch arzhe?

Numbers

1	mek	4	chors	7	yot
2	yerkoo	5	hing	8	oot
3	yerek	6	vets	9	innu

10	*tas*	17	*tasnyot*	50	*hisoon*
11	*tasnmek*	18	*tasnoot*	60	*vatsun*
12	*tasnerkoo*	19	*tasninnu*	70	*yotanasoon*
13	*tasnerek*	20	*ksan*	80	*ootsun*
14	*tasnchors*	21	*ksan mek*	90	*innusoon*
15	*tasnhing*	30	*yeresoon*	100	*haryoor*
16	*tasnvets*	40	*karasoon*	1,000	*hazar*

Time

What time is it?	ժամը քանի՞ն է	*Zhamu kanees ne?*
It's … am/pm	(The expressions am and pm are not used in Armenian. Say instead '… hours in the morning/in the afternoon/in the evening/in the night.')	
in the morning	առավոտյան	*aravotyan*
in the afternoon	ցերեկվա	*tserekva*
in the evening	երեկոյան	*yerekoyan*
in the night	գիշերվա	*geesherva*
	(Thus, 'It is 7.00am' becomes 'առավոտյան ժամը յոթն է' – pronounced '*aravotyan zhamu yot ne*', literally meaning 'in the morning the hour seven is'. The suffix *n* on the word seven is the definite article, which is the letter *n* for all hours except two o'clock for which it is *sn*.)	
today	Այսօր	*Ice-or*
this morning	Այս առավոտ	*Ice aravot*
this afternoon	Այս ցերեկ	*Ice tserek*
this evening	Այս երեկո	*Ice yereko*
this night/tonight	Այս գիշեր	*Ice geesher*
tomorrow	Վաղը	*Varu*
yesterday	Երեկ	*Yerek*
Monday	Երկուշաբթի	*Yerkooshabtee*
Tuesday	Երեքշաբթի	*Yerekshabtee*
Wednesday	Չորեքշաբթի	*Chorekshabtee*
Thursday	Հինգշաբթի	*Heengshabtee*
Friday	Ուրբաթ	*Yoorbat*
Saturday	Շաբաթ	*Shabat*
Sunday	Կիրակի	*Kiraki*

(The names of months do not require initial capital letters in Armenian.)

January	հունվար	*hoonvar*
February	փետրվար	*petrvar*
March	մարտ	*mart*
April	ապրիլ	*apreel*
May	մայիս	*mayees*
June	հունիս	*hoonees*
July	հուլիս	*hoolees*
August	օգոստոս	*ogostos*
September	սեպտեմբեր	*september*
October	հոկտեմբեր	*hoktember*
November	նոյեմբեր	*noyember*
December	դեկտեմբեր	*dektember*

Getting around

English	Armenian	Transliteration
I'd like ...	Ես կցանկանայի ...	Yes ktsankanayee ...
... a one-way ticket	... տոմս մեկ ուղղությամբ	...toms mek oorrootyamp

(Return tickets are not issued for journeys within Armenia. Also trains and buses within Armenia are one class only. There are various categories of ticket on the overnight train to Tbilisi, Georgia. See page 61.)

| I want to go to ... | Ես ցանկանում եմ մեկնել ... | Yes tsankanoom em meknel ... |
| How much is it? | Ի՞նչ արժե | Inch arzhe? |

(In the following three sentences insert the word for bus, minibus, train or plane – given below – but with the suffix ը (pronounced like an unstressed *u*) to indicate the definite article.)

What time does the ... depart?	ժամը քանիսի՞ն է ... մեկնում	Zhamu kaneeseen e ... meknoom?
The ... has been delayed	... ուշանում է	...ooshanoom e
The ... has been cancelled	... չի մեքնելու	...chee mekneloo
bus	Ավտոբուս	Avtoboos
train	Գնացք	Gnatsk
plane	Ոռանավ	Otanav
minibus	(Use the Russian word pronounced *marshrootka*)	
boat	Նավակ	Navak
platform	(Use the Russian word pronounced *platform*.)	
ticket office	Դրամարկղ	Dramakurr

(Also used for the box office at a theatre.)

timetable	Չվացուցակ	Chvatsootsak
bus station	Ավտոկայան	Avtokayan
railway station	Կայարան	Kayaran
airport	Օդանավակայան	Otanavakayan
car	(Ավտո)մեքենա	(Avto)mekeena
4x4		

(Although 4x4 drive vehicles are common and useful in Armenia, there is no proper word for them. Use the word *Neeva* which is the commonest Russian make; or the word *Jeep* which is the commonest American make; or the Persian expression *Dord jhar* which is the term used when two fours are thrown with the dice while playing backgammon.)

taxi	Տաքսի	Taksee
motorbike	Մոտոցիկլ	Mototseekl
moped	Մոպեդ	Moped
bicycle	Հեծանիվ	Hetsaneev
arrival/departure	ժամանում/Մեկնում	Zhamanoom/Meknoom
here/there	Այստեղ/Այնտեղ	Ice-terr/Ine-terr
Is this the road to ... ?	Սա ... տանող ճանապա՞րհն է	Sa ...tanorr janapar ne?
Where can I buy petrol?	Որտե՞ղ կարող եմ գնել բենզին	Vorterh karorh em gnel benzeen?

(When buying petrol in Armenia, one does not usually say 'Please fill it up'. One always asks for a specific number of litres or else specifies how much one wishes to pay. Occasionally, in remote areas, petrol is still bought from parked roadside tankers.)

Appendix 1 LANGUAGE

A1

... litres, please	... լիտր, խնդրում եմ	*... leetr, khntroom em*
... drams worth, please	... դրամի, խնդրում եմ	*... dramee, khntroom em*
diesel	(Use the Russian word pronounced *salyarka*)	
petrol	Բենզին	*Benzeen*
	(Unleaded petrol is not available in Armenia. So far as leaded petrol is concerned, regular – 93 octane – is available everywhere. Premium – 95 octane – is available at some petrol stations.)	
My car has broken down	Մեքենաս փչացել է	*Mekenas pchatsel e*
danger	Վտանգ	*Vtang*
Go straight ahead	Ուղիղ գնաց եք	*Oorreer gnats ek*
left	Ձախ	*Dsakh*
right	Աջ	*Atch*
traffic lights	(Use the Russian word pronounced *svetafor*)	
north	Հյուսիս	*Hyoosees*
south	Հարավ	*Haraf*
east	Արևելք	*Aravelk*
west	Արևմուտք	*Aravmootk*
behind	Ետև	*Yetev*
in front of	Առջև	*Archev*
near	Մոտ	*Mot*
opposite	Դիմաց	*Deemats*

Street signs

entry	Մուտք	*Mootk*
no entry	Մուտքը արգելված է	*Mootku argelvats e*
exit	Ելք	*Yelk*
no parking	Կանգառն արգելված է	*Kangarn argelvats e*
open	Բաց է	*Bats e*
closed	Փակ է	*Pak e*
toilets	Զուգարան	*Zookaran*
information	Տեղեկատու	*Terrekatoo*

Accommodation

hotel	Հյուրանոց	*Hyooranots*
Where is there a cheap/good hotel?	Որտե՞ղ կա էժան/լավ հյուրանոց	*Vorterr ka ezhan/lav hyooranots*
Could you please write the address?	Խնդրում եմ հասցեն գրեք	*Khndroom em hastsen gurek*
Is there a vacant room?	Ազատ սենյակ կ՞ա	*Azat senyak ka*
I'd like ...	Ես կցանկանայի ...	*Yes ktsankanayee ...*
... a single room	... մեկտեղանոց սենյակ	*... mekterranots senyak*
... a double toom	... երկտեղանոց սենյակ	*... yerkterranots senyak*
... a room with two beds	... սենյակ երկու մահճակալով	*... senyak yerkoo mahjakalov*
... a room with a toilet and shower	... սենյակ զուգարանով և լոգարանով	*... senyak zookaranov yev logaranov*
How much is it per night?	Գիշերը ի՞նչ արժե	*Geesheru inch arzhe?*
How much is it per person?	Անձը ի՞նչ արժե	*Andsu inch arzhe?*
Where is the toilet?	Զուգարանը որտե՞ղ է	*Zookaranu vorterr e?*
Is there water?	Ջուր կ՞ա	*Joor ka?*
Is there hot water?	Տաք ջուր կ՞ա	*Tak joor ka?*

| Is breakfast included in the price? | Նախաճաշը մտնու՞մ է գնի մեջ | *Nakhajashu mtnoom e gnee metch?* |
| I am leaving today | Ես մեկնում եմ այսօր | *Yes meknoom em ice-ore* |

Eating and drinking

restaurant	Ռեստորան	*Restoran*
breakfast	Նախաճաշ	*Nakhajash*
lunch	Ճաշ	*Jash*
dinner	Ընթրիք	*Untreek*

(On entering a restaurant one is usually asked: Քանի՞ հոգի եք (pronounced *Kanee hokee ek?*). It means 'How many of you are there?')

Is there a table for ... people?	... հոգու համար սեղան կա՞	*... hokoo hamar serran ka?*
Are there any vegetarian dishes?	Բուսական ուտեստներ կա՞ն	*Boosakan ootestner kan?*
Please bring me ...	Խնդրում եմ ... բերեք	*Khntroom em ... berek*
... a fork/knife/spoon	... պատարաքաղ/դանակ/գդալ	*... patarakarr/danak/gtal*
The bill, please	Հաշիվը բերեք, խնդրում եմ	*Hasheevu berek, khntroom em*
soup	Ապուր	*Apoor*
bread	Հաց	*Hats*
butter	Կարագ	*Karag*
lavash (Armenian flatbread)	Լավաշ	*Lavash*
cheese	Պանիր	*Paneer*
honey	Մեղր	*Merr*
oil	Ձեթ	*Dset*
vinegar	Քացախ	*Katsakh*
pepper	պիպար/պղպեղ	*Beebar/peperr*
salt	Աղ	*Arr*
sugar	Շաքարավազ	*Shakaravaz*
apple	Խնձոր	*Khndsor*
banana	(The correct word is Ադամաթուզ – pronounced *adamatooz*, but the word generally used is Բանան – pronounced *banan*)	
grapes	Խաղող	*Kharrorr*
orange	Նարինջ	*Nareenj*
peach	Դեղձ	*Derrds*
pear	Տանձ	*Tands*
watermelon	Ձմերուկ	*Dsmerook*
apricot	Ծիրան	*Tseeran*
cherries	Կեռաս	*Keras*
strawberries	Ելակ	*Yelak*
plum	Սալոր	*Salor*
carrot	Գազար	*Gazar*
garlic	Սխտոր	*Skhtor*
onion	Սոխ	*Sokh*
sweet pepper	Պիպար	*Beebar*
potato	Կարտոֆիլ	*Kartofeel*
rice	Բրինձ	*Brindz*
tomato	Լոլիկ	*Loleek*
cucumber	Վարունգ	*Varoong*
salad	Սալաթ	*Salat*
salmon	Սաղմոն	*Sarrmon*

tuna	Թյուննա	*Tyoonos*
whitefish	Սիգ	*Sig*
smoked whitefish	Ծխացրած սիգ	*Tskhatsrats sig*
beef	Տավարի միս	*Tavaree mees*
lamb	Ոչխարի միս	*Vochkhari mees*
pork	Խոզի միս	*Khozee mees*
goat	Այծի միս	*Aytsee mees*
chicken	Հավ	*Hav*
barbecued	Խորոված	*Khorovats*
sausage	Նրբերշիկ	*Nrpersheek*
(white) ice cream	(Սպիտակ) պաղպաղակ	*(Spitak) parrparrak*
chocolate	Շոկոլադ	*Shocolad*
tea	Թեյ	*Tay*
coffee	Սուրճ	*Soorj*
juice	Հյութ	*Hyoot*
milk	Կաթ	*Kat*
water	Ջուր	*Joor*
mineral water	Հանքային ջուր	*Hankayeen joor*
wine	Գինի	*Ginee*
beer	Գարեջուր	*Garejoor*
brandy	Կոնյակ	*Konyak*

Shopping

I'd like to buy ...	Ես կցանկանայի գնել ...	*Yes ktsankanayee gnel ...*
How much is it?	Ի՞նչ արժե?	*Inch arzhe?*
It's too expensive	Չափազանց թանկ է	*Chapazants tank e*
I'll take it	Ես սա կվերցնեմ	*Yes sa kvertsnem*
Do you accept credit cards?	Կրեդիտ քարտ ընդունու՞մ եք	*Kredeet kart untoonoom ek?*
A little more	Մի քիչ ավել	*Mee keech avel*
A little less	Ավելի քիչ	*Avelee keech*

Communications

| Where is ... ? | Որտե՞ղ է ... | *Vorterr e ... ?* |

(If any of the following nouns were used after *Vorterr e....?*, it would indicate the indefinite article: for example, 'where is there a church?'; 'where is there a museum?' etc. If the definite article is required, then add the unstressed suffix ը – pronounced *u* – when the noun ends with a consonant or the suffix ն – pronounced *n* – when the noun ends with a vowel. This results in the meanings: 'where is the church?'; 'where is the museum?' etc.

church	Եկեղեցի	*Yekeretsee*
monastery	Վանք	*Vank*
castle	Բերդ, Ամրոց	*Berd, Amrots*
museum	Թանգարան	*Tangaran*
post office	Փոստ	*Post*
bank	Բանկ	*Bank*
market	Շուկա	*Shooka*
embassy	Դեսպանատուն	*Despanatoon*
exchange office	(Use the English word *change*)	

Emergency

Help!	Օգնություն	Oknootyoon
Call a doctor!	Բժիշկ կանչեցեք	Bzheeshk kanchetsek
There's been a road accident	Ավտովթար է տեղի ունեցել	Avtovtar e terree oonetsel
There's been an accident (non-road)	Դժբախտ պատահար է	Dzhbakht patahar e
I'm lost	Ես մոլորվել եմ	Yes molorvel em
Go away!	Հեռու գնա	Heroo gna
police	Ոստիկանություն	Vosteekarnootyoon
fire service	Հրշեջ ծառայություն	Hrshetch tsarayootyoon
ambulance	Շտապ օգնություն	Shtap oknotyoon
thief	Կողոպուտ	Korropoot

Health

hospital	Հիվանդանոց	Heevandanots
I am ill	Ես հիվանդ եմ	Yes heevand em
diarrhoea	Լուծ	Loots
nausea	Սրխսառնոց	Srtkharnots
doctor	Բժիշկ	Bzheeshk
prescription	Դեղատոմս	Derratoms
pharmacy	Դեղատուն	Derratoon
paracetamol	Պարացետամոլ	Paratsetamol
antibiotic	Հակաբիոտիկ	Hakabeeoteek
antiseptic	Հականեխիչ	Hakanekheech
tampon	Վիրախծուծ	Veerakhtsoots
condom	Պահպանակ	Pahpanak
sunblock	Հակաարևահարման քսուկ	Haka-arevaharman ksook
I have ...	Ես ... ունեմ	Yes ... oonem
... asthma	... աստմա ...	... astma
... epilepsy	... էպիլեպսիա ...	... epilepsia
... diabetes	... շաքարախտ ...	... shakarakht
I'm allergic to ...	Ես ալերգիկ եմ ...	Yes alergeek em ...
... penicillin	... պենիցիլինի	... peneetseeleenee
... bee stings	... մեղվի խայթոցի	... merrvee khaytotsee
... all kinds of nuts	... բոլոր տեսակի ընկույզների	... bolor tesakee unkonyzneree

Other

my/ours/yours	իմ/մեր/ձեր	eem/mer/dser
and	և (or) ու	yev (or) oo
some	մի քիչ	mee keech
this/that	այս/այն	ice/ine (as in nine)
expensive/cheap	թանկ/էժան	tank/ezhan
beautiful/ugly	գեղեցիկ/տգեղ	gerretseek/tgerr
old/new	հին/նոր	heen/nor
good/bad	լավ/վատ	lav/vat
early/late	շուտ/ուշ	shoot/oosh
hot/cold	տաք/սառը	tak/saaru
difficult/easy	բարդ/հեշտ	bart/hesht
boring/interesting	ձանձրալի/հետաքրքիր	dsandsralee/hetakrkeer

PLACE NAMES

Երևան	YEREVAN	Էջմիածին	EJMIATSIN
Գյումրի	GYUMRI	Եղեգնաձոր	YEGHEGNADZOR
Վանաձոր	VANADZOR	Ջերմուկ	JERMUK
Ստեփանավան	STEPANAVAN	Սիսիան	SISIAN
Ալավերդի	ALAVERDI	Գորիս	GORIS
Դիլիջան	DILIJAN	Կապան	KAPAN
Իջևան	IJEVAN	Մեղրի	MEGHRI
Սևան	SEVAN	Ստեփանակերտ	STEPANAKERT
Ծաղկաձոր	TSAGHKADZOR		

Appendix 2

FURTHER INFORMATION

Thanks largely to the diaspora, the current literature on Armenia is vast. There are also numerous out-of-print titles, many from Soviet days. It is clear that nobody could read more than a small fraction of the total. The following represents no more than some of the books which the authors have found interesting or useful.

NHBS (*www.nhbs.co.uk*) is a good source for books on natural history. Out-of-print books can often be found via AbeBooks (*www.abebooks.co.uk*).

HISTORY

Armenian Churches – Holy See of Echmiadzin Calouste Gulbenkian Foundation, 1970. Largely a book of black and white photographs with limited text, it is interesting to compare some of the 1960s photographs with the same church today and see the extent of reconstruction. Also covers a few churches in present-day Turkey.

Hasratian, Murad *Early Christian Architecture of Armenia* Inkombook, Moscow, 2000. Covers churches intact and ruined, large and small, well known and desperately obscure. Does not include churches from the later medieval period so some of the most famous are excluded.

Hovannisian, Richard G *The Republic of Armenia* (4 volumes) University of California Press, 1996. An exhaustive and scholarly but readable account of Armenia in the crucial years from 1918 to 1921.

Karapetian, Samvel *Armenian Cultural Monuments in the Region of Karabakh* Gitutian Publishing House of NAS RAA, Yerevan, 2001. An interesting up-to-date account of what is to be found there. It includes territories occupied since 1994 but regrettably does not include all districts so that Nagorno Karabagh's best-known sight – Gandzasar Monastery – is omitted.

Khalpakhchian, O *Architectural Ensembles of Armenia* Iskusstvo, Moscow, 1980. This thorough survey would have been more useful if only it had been better translated. It desperately needed review by a native English speaker. Standing with it in hand at the place being described it is, however, usually possible to work out what the author probably means. Covers only 19 sites but quite thorough.

Masih, Joseph and Krikorian, Robert *Armenia: At the Crossroads* Routledge, 1999. Although the English is occasionally curious the book does give a feel for Armenia's crossroad position – historically, geographically, politically and economically.

Nassibian, Akaby *Britain and the Armenian Question 1915–1923* Croom Helm, 1984. A good account of the British government's failure to help the Armenian people. Despite the title it includes the background to the events from the 1870s onwards.

Nersessian, Vrej *Treasures from the Ark* The British Library, 2001. The catalogue of the wonderful exhibition of Armenian art held in London that year. It is the best illustrated book of Armenian art treasures available.

Piotrovsky, Boris *Urartu* Nagel, 1969. Translated from the Russian by James Hogarth. Written by the director of Leningrad's Hermitage Museum and director of excavations at the Uratian site of Karmir Blur near Yerevan for over 20 years, this book brings to life the dry, both literally and metaphorically, remains of the kingdom of Urartu. Photographs of unearthed treasures, many of which are on display in the State History Museum, Yerevan.

Redgate, Anne E *The Armenians* Blackwell, 1998. A strongly recommended history of the Armenian people although rather sketchy on the period after 1100.

Rost, Yuri *Armenian Tragedy* Weidenfeld and Nicolson, 1990. A journalist's eyewitness accounts of the early stages of the conflict between Armenia and Azerbaijan and the devastating earthquake of 1988.

NATURAL HISTORY

Adamian, Martin S and Klem Jr, Daniel *A Field Guide to the Birds of Armenia* American University of Armenia, 1997. An invaluable well-illustrated field guide.

Baytaş Ahmet *A Field Guide to the Butterflies of Turkey* Ntv, 2007. Although it doesn't specifically cover the area of Armenia it would be generally useful and certainly more portable than Tuzov's *Guide to the Butterflies of Russia & Adjacent Territories* – see below.

Gabrielian, Eleonora and Fragman-Sapir, Ori *Flowers of the Transcaucasus and Adjacent Areas* Gantner Verlag, 2008. Available from NHBS. Expensive.

Greenhalgh, Malcolm *A Pocket Guide to the Freshwater Fish of Britain and Europe* Mitchell Beazley, 2001. Does not include all Armenian species but quite useful.

Holubec, Vojtech and Krivka, Pavel *The Caucasus and its Flowers* LOXIA, 2006. Available from NHBS. Expensive

MacDonald, David *Collins Field Guide to the Mammals of Britain and Europe* HarperCollins, 2005. Omits a few species such as leopard, but useful.

Pils, Gerhard *Flowers of Turkey* published by the author, 2006. The most useful field guide for the average botanical traveller, but expensive. No text but lots of photographs, arranged by plant families. Available from NHBS.

Shetekauri, Shamil and Jacoby, Martin *Mountain Flowers and Trees of Caucasia* Martin Jacoby, 2009. Available from NHBS. Paperback and the cheapest of the botanical guides.

Szczerbak, N N *Guide to the Reptiles of the Eastern Palearctic* Krieger, 2003. One sees lots of reptiles in Armenia and this guide is useful although it does not always make it clear how to distinguish between related species.

Tuzov V K (ed) *Guide to the Butterflies of Russia and Adjacent Territories* (2 volumes) Pensoft, Sofia, 2000. A thorough guide illustrated with photographs of specimens and covering the whole of the former USSR but unfortunately not very portable.

GENERAL

Petrosian, Irina and Underwood, David *Armenian Food: Fact, Fiction and Folklore* Yerkir Publishing, 2006. This is not a cookery book! Written by an Armenian wife and American husband, it's a fascinating and revealing insight into Armenia as seen through the country's food. Entertainingly written and very informative. Highly recommended.

Solomon, Susan *Culture Smart! Armenia* Kuperard 2010. A guide to the customs and culture of Armenia. Helpful tips on social etiquette, dos and don'ts.

TRAVEL

Bachmann, Carine and Tufenkian, Jeffrey *Adventure Armenia – Hiking and Rock Climbing* Kanach, 2004. Describes 20 walks and five climbs. The first attempt to publish practical information about the country's potential though it only scratches the surface.

Hepworth, Revd George H *Through Armenia on Horseback* Isbister, 1898. One of the best accounts of life among the Armenians of Anatolia shortly before the genocide, the evidently unbiased author gives an account of their hardships and oppression.

Kiesling, Brady and Kojian, Raffi *Rediscovering Armenia* Tigran Mets, 2001. A gazetteer which lists most of Armenia's villages and monuments and tells you how to find them. Not really a guidebook itself but it was often useful to the authors of this one in indicating what exists.

Nansen, Fridtjof *Armenia and the Near East* George Allen & Unwin, 1928. The great Polar explorer was appointed League of Nations Commissioner for Refugees and in that capacity visited Soviet Armenia in its early days accompanied by Vidkun Quisling (later to become Norway's prime minister during the Nazi occupation and consequently executed for treason in 1945) who acted as his secretary. He was favourably impressed by the plans to use the water from Lake Sevan to irrigate the Ararat Valley.

PP (ie: Peter Pears) *Armenian Holiday August 1965* Privately published, 1965. The English tenor's account of his visit with Britten, Rostropovich and Galina Vishnevskaya. The Russian soprano, Rostropovich's wife, also gives an account in her autobiography *Galina – A Russian Story* (Hodder & Stoughton, 1985).

Shaginyan, Marietta *Journey through Soviet Armenia* Foreign Languages Publishing House, Moscow, 1954. A wonderful period piece of Stalin-era writing – the Russian original was published in 1952 before his death. Unfortunately out of print but eminently worth seeking a copy for anyone with a taste for the bizarre.

LITERATURE

Pushkin, Alexander *A Journey to Arzrum* (ie: Erzurum) 1835, English translation by Birgitta Ingemanson published by Ardis, 1974. An excellent translation with extremely useful notes explaining matters unlikely to be familiar to modern Western readers.

Saroyan, William *The Human Comedy* 1943 and *Boys and Girls Together* 1963. Two works suggested as an introduction to the Armenian-American author.

LANGUAGE A variety of teaching material is now offered on the internet although much is for western rather than eastern Armenian. Try www.armeniapedia.org or search via Google for Eastern Armenian courses.

Avetisyan, Anahit *Eastern Armenian* Comprehensive self-study language course published by the author, Yerevan 2008. The most accessible Eastern Armenian course I have found. Everything is provided in three forms: Armenian, Armenian transliteration and English translation. It also introduces the learner to cursive handwritten Armenian. The sort of teach yourself book now available in most languages but which has been lacking for Armenian until now. Far better than the books previously available. Apparently unavailable outside Armenia.

Eurotalk *Learn Armenian* CD-ROM (*www.eurotalk.com*) Introduces the reader to basic words and phrases in what it describes as a fun way. It has the advantage that one can hear as well as see the language and it provides an element of feedback.

Grigorian, Kh *English–Armenian/Armenian–English Dictionary* Published in Armenia 2005. Compiled for English speakers. The best small dictionary I have found. Apparently unavailable outside Armenia.

USEFUL WEBSITES

www.armeniaforeignministry.com The official website of the Armenian Foreign Ministry. Gives information on visa requirements and other official government announcements. Has a link to the website of the Nagorno Karabagh Foreign Ministry (*www.nkr.am*) which has information on visas, geography, flora, etc.

www.armeniainfo.am Official website of Armenia Information, a service provided by the Armenian Tourism Development Agency. Features much useful practical information and attractive pictures to tempt you to the country.

www.armenianembassy.org.uk The website of the Armenian embassy in London. Has much useful information and links to other websites.

www.ArmenianMonuments.org An evolving website. Has a useful guide to Noratus field of khachkars.

www.armenianow.com The weekly English-language web magazine, *Armenia Now*, gives a flavour of contemporary events.

www.armeniapedia.org The best internet source of information on Armenia's top sights but it is patchy on practical information. This website also covers Nagorno Karabagh.

www.fco.gov.uk UK Foreign Office website. Has advice for travellers to Armenia.

www.gallery.am Website of the National Gallery of Armenia with information on the collections. Has pictures of many of the paintings

www.nt.am The website of Noyan Tapan, the English-language newspaper.

www.spyur.am Armenia's Yellow Pages.

www.tacentral.com Useful practical information although much of the country is not covered and a bit out of date at times. Interesting articles on topics such as Armenian carpets, flowers, language and archaeology. Useful guides (the only ones) to the State History Museum (a little out of date after recent redevelopment) and to Metsamor Museum.

WIN A FREE BRADT GUIDE
READER QUESTIONNAIRE

**Send in your completed questionnaire and enter our monthly draw
for the chance to win a Bradt guide of your choice.**

To take up our special reader offer of 40% off, please visit our website at
www.bradtguides.com/freeguide or answer the questions below and return to us
with the order form overleaf.

(Forms may be posted or faxed to us.)

Have you used any other Bradt guides? If so, which titles? . . . .
. . . .

What other publishers' travel guides do you use regularly? . . . .
. . . .

Where did you buy this guidebook? . . . .

What was the main purpose of your trip to Armenia (or for what other reason did
you read our guide)? eg: holiday/business/charity . . . .
. . . .

How long did you travel for? (circle one)

weekend/long weekend   1–2 weeks   3–4 weeks   4 weeks plus

Which countries did you visit in connection with this trip? . . . .
. . . .

Did you travel with a tour operator?' If so, which one? . . . .
. . . .

What other destinations would you like to see covered by a Bradt guide?
. . . .

If you could make one improvement to this guide, what would it be?
. . . .

Age (circle relevant category) 16–25   26–45   46–60   60+

Male/Female (delete as appropriate)

Home country . . . .

Please send us any comments about this guide (or others on our list).
. . . .
. . . .
. . . .

Bradt Travel Guides
IDC House, The Vale, Chalfont St Peter, Bucks SL9 9RZ, UK
☏ +44 (0)1753 893444 f +44 (0)1753 892333
e info@bradtguides.com
www.bradtguides.com

TAKE 40% OFF YOUR NEXT BRADT GUIDE!
Order Form

To take advantage of this special offer visit www.bradtguides.com/freeguide and enter our monthly giveaway, or fill in the order form below, complete the questionnaire overleaf and send it to Bradt Travel Guides by post or fax.

Please send me one copy of the following guide at 40% off the UK retail price

No	Title	Retail price	40% price
1	. . . .	. . . .	. . . .

Please send the following additional guides at full UK retail price

No	Title	Retail price	Total
. . .	. . . .	. . . .	. . . .
. . .	. . . .	. . . .	. . . .
. . .	. . . .	. . . .	. . . .

Sub total . . . .
Post & packing . . . .
(Free shipping UK, £1 per book Europe, £3 per book rest of world)
Total . . . .

Name . . . .

Address . . . .

Tel . . . .   Email . . . .

☐ I enclose a cheque for £. . . . . made payable to Bradt Travel Guides Ltd

☐ I would like to pay by credit card. Number: . . . .

   Expiry date: . . . / . . . . 3-digit security code (on reverse of card) . . . . .

   Issue no (debit cards only) . . . . .

☐ Please sign me up to Bradt's monthly enewsletter, Bradtpackers' News.

☐ I would be happy for you to use my name and comments in Bradt marketing material.

Send your order on this form, with the completed questionnaire, to:

Bradt Travel Guides
IDC House, The Vale, Chalfont St Peter, Bucks SL9 9RZ, UK
☎ +44 (0)1753 893444   f +44 (0)1753 892333
e info@bradtguides.com   www.bradtguides.com

Bradt Travel Guides

www.bradtguides.com

Africa

Access Africa: Safaris for People	
with Limited Mobility	£16.99
Africa Overland	£16.99
Algeria	£15.99
Angola	£17.99
Botswana	£16.99
Cameroon	£15.99
Cape Verde Islands	£14.99
Congo	£15.99
Eritrea	£15.99
Ethiopia	£16.99
Ghana	£15.99
Kenya Highlights	£15.99
Madagascar	£16.99
Malawi	£15.99
Mali	£14.99
Mauritius, Rodrigues &	
Réunion	£15.99
Mozambique	£15.99
Namibia	£15.99
Niger	£14.99
Nigeria	£17.99
North Africa: Roman Coast	£15.99
Rwanda	£15.99
São Tomé & Príncipe	£14.99
Seychelles	£14.99
Sierra Leone	£16.99
Sudan	£15.99
Tanzania, Northern	£14.99
Tanzania	£17.99
Uganda	£16.99
Zambia	£17.99
Zanzibar	£14.99
Zimbabwe	£15.99

The Americas and the Caribbean

Alaska	£15.99
Amazon, The	£14.99
Argentina	£15.99
Bahia	£14.99
Cayman Islands	£14.99
Colombia	£16.99
Dominica	£14.99
Grenada, Carriacou &	
Petite Martinique	£14.99
Guyana	£14.99
Nova Scotia	£14.99
Panama	£14.99
Paraguay	£14.99
Turks & Caicos Islands	£14.99
Uruguay	£14.99
USA by Rail	£14.99
Venezuela	£16.99
Yukon	£14.99

British Isles

Britain from the Rails	£14.99
Eccentric Britain	£13.99
Eccentric London	£13.99
Slow: Cotswolds	£14.99
Slow: Devon & Exmoor	£14.99
Slow: Norfolk & Suffolk	£14.99
Slow: North Yorkshire	£14.99
Slow: Sussex & South	
Downs National Park	£14.99

Europe

Abruzzo	£14.99
Albania	£15.99
Armenia	£15.99
Azores	£14.99
Baltic Cities	£14.99
Belarus	£15.99
Bosnia & Herzegovina	£14.99
Bratislava	£9.99
Budapest	£9.99
Bulgaria	£13.99
Cork	£6.99
Croatia	£13.99
Cross-Channel France:	
Nord-Pas de Calais	£13.99
Cyprus see North Cyprus	
Dresden	£7.99
Estonia	£14.99
Faroe Islands	£15.99
Georgia	£15.99
Greece: The Peloponnese	£14.99
Helsinki	£7.99
Hungary	£15.99
Iceland	£14.99
Kosovo	£15.99
Lapland	£13.99
Latvia	£13.99
Lille	£9.99
Lithuania	£14.99
Luxembourg	£13.99
Macedonia	£15.99
Malta & Gozo	£12.99
Montenegro	£14.99
North Cyprus	£12.99
Riga	£6.99
Serbia	£15.99
Slovakia	£14.99
Slovenia	£13.99
Spitsbergen	£16.99
Switzerland Without	
a Car	£14.99
Transylvania	£14.99
Ukraine	£15.99
Zagreb	£6.99

Middle East, Asia and Australasia

Bangladesh	£15.99
Borneo	£17.99
Eastern Turkey	£16.99
Iran	£15.99
Iraq: Then & Now	£15.99
Israel	£15.99
Kazakhstan	£15.99
Kyrgyzstan	£15.99
Lake Baikal	£15.99
Maldives	£15.99
Mongolia	£16.99
North Korea	£14.99
Oman	£15.99
Shangri-La:	
A Travel Guide to the	
Himalayan Dream	£14.99
Sri Lanka	£15.99
Syria	£15.99
Taiwan	£16.99
Tibet	£13.99
Yemen	£14.99

Wildlife

Antarctica: Guide to the	
Wildlife	£15.99
Arctic: Guide to Coastal	
Wildlife	£15.99
Australian Wildlife	£14.99
Central & Eastern	
European Wildlife	£15.99
Chinese Wildlife	£16.99
East African Wildlife	£19.99
Galápagos Wildlife	£15.99
Madagascar Wildlife	£16.99
New Zealand Wildlife	£14.99
North Atlantic Wildlife	£16.99
Pantanal Wildlife	£16.99
Peruvian Wildlife	£15.99
Southern African	
Wildlife	£18.95
Sri Lankan Wildlife	£15.99

Pictorials and other guides

100 Animals to See	
Before They Die	£16.99
100 Bizarre Animals	£16.99
Eccentric Australia	£12.99
Northern Lights	£6.99
Wildlife and Conservation	
Volunteering: The	
Complete Guide	£13.99

NOTES

NOTES

Index